COLLISION OF EMPIRES

THE WAR ON THE EASTERN FRONT IN 1914

PRIT BUTTAR

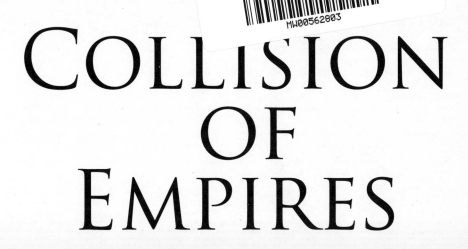

First published in Great Britain in 2014 by Osprey Publishing,
PO Box 883, Oxford, OX1 9PL, UK
PO Box 3985, New York, NY 10185-3985, USA
E-mail: info@ospreypublishing.com

OSPREY PUBLISHING IS PART OF BLOOMSBURY PUBLISHING PLC

ISBN: 978 1 4728 1318 3
ePub ISBN: 978 1 78200 972 6
PDF ISBN: 978 1 78200 971 9

Index by Mark Swift
Typeset in Adobe Garamond Pro, Garamond Premier Pro and Trajan
Originated by PDQ Digital Media Solutions, Suffolk
Printed in China through World Print Ltd.

16 17 18 19 20   10 9 8 7 6 5 4 3 2 1

Front cover: The trumpet corps of a Saxon unit 1914. Musicians' wings can be seen on their shoulders. Nik Cornish at www.Stavka.org.uk

All the images in this book are reproduced courtesy of TopFoto. www.topfoto.co.uk

Osprey Publishing supports the Woodland Trust, the UK's leading woodland conservation charity. Between 2014 and 2018 our donations will be spent on their Centenary Woods project in the UK.

www.ospreypublishing.com

CONTENTS

LIST OF ILLUSTRATIONS

Russian soldiers in a defence, Galicia.
Fallen Russians at Tannenberg.
Austro-Hungarian wounded, Galicia.
German infantry at Tannenberg.
Mobile communications, Tannenberg.
German defence lines, Johannisburg.

LIST OF MAPS

AUTHOR'S NOTE

As ever, more people than I can mention have played a part in the creation of this book. In particular, I am grateful to David 'Klaus' Shore for his encouragement in the early stages, and Amit Sumal, whose willingness to track down rare documents for me was of incalculable value.

As always, the lovely people at Osprey, particularly Kate Moore and Emily Holmes, were hugely supportive, as was my agent Robert Dudley. And none of this would have been possible without the patience and forbearance of my family.

DRAMATIS PERSONAE

AUSTRIA-HUNGARY

Ährenthal, Alois Lexa von – Foreign Minister 1906–08
Auffenberg, Moritz von – commander of Fourth Army
Berchtold, Leopold von – Foreign Minister in 1914
Bilinsky, Leon – Austro-Hungarian Finance Minister 1912–15 and simultaneously head of civil administration in Bosnia-Herzegovina
Böhm-Ermolli, Eduard von – commander of Second Army
Boroević, Svetozar – commander of VI Corps, then commander of Third Army (replaced Brudermann)
Brudermann, Rudolf Ritter von – commander of Third Army
Conrad von Hötzendorf, Franz Xaver Josef – Chief of the General Staff in 1914
Czernin, Ottokar Graf – ambassador to Romania
Dankl, Viktor – commander of First Army
Falkenfeld, Heinrich Rittmeister Kummer von – commander of eponymous force in 1914
Frank, Liborius Ritter von – commander of Fifth Army
Hoyos, Alexander von – *chef de cabinet* in the Foreign Office, 1914
Joseph Ferdinand (Archduke) – commander of XIV Corps, then commander of Fourth Army (replaced Auffenberg)
Kirchbach, Karl Freiherr von – commander of I Corps
Kolossváry, Dezső – commander of XI Corps
Kövesz, Hermann von – commander of XII Corps
Křitek, Karl – commander of XVII Corps
Kusmanek, Hermann von – commander of the garrison of Przemyśl
Potiorek, Oskar – military governor of Bosnia-Herzegovina 1911–14, commander of Sixth Army, then of all *k.u.k.* forces on the Serbian front

Puhallo, Puławy – commander of V Corps
Redl, Alfred – head of counter-intelligence 1907–13; spy for Russia (and other foreign powers)
Schemua, Blasius – Chief of the General Staff 1911–12, commander of II Corps in 1914
Schönaich, Franz von – Minister for War 1906–11
Tersztyánszky, Karl – commander of IV Corps, later commander of Fifth Army (replaced Frank)
Tisza, István – Hungarian Prime Minister 1913–17

FRANCE

Paléologue, Maurice – French Ambassador to Russia

GERMANY

Below, Otto von – commander of I Reserve Corps in 1914
Bernhardi, Friedrich Adolf Julius von – cavalry officer, influential in developing tactical doctrine in late 19th century
Bethmann-Hollweg, Theobald von – Chancellor 1909–17
Brodrück, Georg – commander of Königsberg Garrison Division in 1914
Conta, Richard von – commander of 1st Infantry Division
Falk, Adalbert von – commander of 2nd Infantry Division
Falkenhayn, Erich von – Minister for War 1913–15, Chief of the General Staff 1914–16
François, Hermann von – commander of I Corps in 1914, later commander of Eighth Army
Gallwitz, Max von – commander of Guard Reserve Corps
Heineccius, Konstanz von – commander of 36th Infantry Division
Hell, Emil – chief of staff of XX Corps
Hindenburg, Paul Ludwig Hans Anton von Beneckendorff und von – appointed commander of Eighth Army in 1914, then Ninth Army, then commander of all German forces on the Eastern Front
Hoffmann, Max – deputy chief of staff of Eighth Army
Ludendorff, Erich – appointed chief of staff of Eighth Army in 1914
Mackensen, August von – commander of XVII Corps in 1914, later

commander of Ninth Army

Moltke, Helmuth von ('the elder') – Chief of the Prussian General Staff during the German wars of unification, founder of the German General Staff

Moltke, Helmuth von ('the younger') – nephew of the elder Moltke, Chief of the General Staff 1906–14

Morgen, Curt von – commander of Third Reserve Infantry Division in 1914, later commander of I Reserve Corps

Pourtalès, Friedrich von – ambassador to Russia in 1914

Prittwitz, Maximilian von – commander of Eighth Army in 1914

Schlichting, Sigismund von – infantry officer, influential in developing tactical doctrine in late 19th century

Schlieffen, Alfred von – Chief of the German General Staff 1891–1906, author of what became known as the Schlieffen Plan

Schmidtseck, Walter Schmidt von – chief of staff of I Corps in 1914

Scholtz, Friedrich von – commander of XX Corps in 1914

Schubert, Richard von – commander of Eighth Army, replaced Hindenburg

Stein, Hermann von – Quartermaster-General in 1914

Waldersee, Georg von – chief of staff, Eighth Army in 1914

Woyrsch, Remus von – commander of Silesian *Landwehr*, and of eponymous corps

RUSSIA

Alexeyev, Mikhail Vasileyevich – Chief of Staff of Southwest Front in 1914

Aliev, Eris Khan Sultan Giryei – commander of IV Corps

Artamonov, Leonid – commander of I Corps

Blagoveschensky, Alexander Alexandrovich – commander of VI Corps

Brusilov, Alexei Alexeevich – commander of Eighth Army in 1914

Danilov, Yuri Nikoforovich – Quartermaster-General in 1914

Dimitriev, Radko – commander of VIII Corps, then commander of Third Army (replaced Ruzsky)

Dobrorolsky, Sergei – head of Russian General Staff's mobilisation section

Dushkevich, Alexander – commander of 2nd Infantry Division, then commander of I Corps

Evert, Alexei – commander of Fourth Army, replaced Saltza

Geysmans, Platon Alexandrovich – commander of XVI Corps

Golovine, Nikolai – commander of Grodno Hussars, 1914

Ivanov, Nikolai – commander Southwest Front in 1914

Klyuev, Nikolai – Chief of Staff, Warsaw District, then commander of XIII Corps

Martos, Nikolai Nikolaevich – commander of XV Corps

Mileant, Georgi – Chief of Staff, First Army in 1914

Nahitchevanski, Huseyn Khan – commander of cavalry, First Army in 1914

Nikolayevich, Nikolai – Grand Duke, cousin of Tsar Nicholas II, Commander-in-Chief in 1914

Palitsyn, Fedor Fedorovich – Chief of the General Staff 1905–08

Pflug, Vasili – commander of Tenth Army

Plehve, Wenzel von – commander of Fifth Army in 1914

Postovsky, Pyotr Ivanovich – chief of staff of Second Army

Rennenkampf, Pavel Karlovich – commander of First Army in 1914

Ruzsky, Nikolai Vladimirovich – commander of Third Army in 1914, later commander of Northwest Front

Saltza, Anton Jegorowich von – commander of Fourth Army in 1914

Samsonov, Alexander Vassilievich – commander of Second Army in 1914

Sazonov, Sergei – Foreign Minister 1909–17

Selivanov, Andrei Nikolaevich – commander of Eleventh Army

Sievers, Faddei (Thadeus) von – commander X Corps, then commander of Tenth Army (replaced Pflug)

Sukhomlinov, Vladimir Alexandrovich – Chief of the General Staff 1908–09, Minister for War 1909–16

Tumanov, Georgi Evseevich – commander of Fourth Army's cavalry

Voyshin Murdas-Zhilinski, Hippolyte Paulinovich – commander of XIV Corps

Yanushkevich, Nikolai Nikolaevich – Chief of the General Staff 1914–15

Zhilinski, Yakov – Commander Northwest Front, 1914

Zhuyev, Dmitri Petrovich – commander of XXV Corps

SERBIA

Bojović, Petar – commander of First Army

Božanović, Miloš – commander of Army Group Užice

Cabrinovic, Nedeljko – member of the Black Hand organisation, one of the assassins of Sarajevo

Mišić, Živojin – commander of First Army, replaced Bojović

Pašić, Nikola – Prime Minister 1912–18
Princip, Gavrilo – member of the Black Hand organisation, fired the shots
that killed Franz Ferdinand
Putnik, Radomir – Chief of the General Staff
Stepanović, Stepa – commander of Second Army
Šturm, Pavle Jurišić – commander of Third Army

INTRODUCTION

Most English-language accounts of the First World War have left a strong image in the public mind. Europe is seen as a continent of rich, opulent aristocrats, enjoying the fruits of empires and successful industrialisation, with 'common people' living modestly, but in far greater comfort than in the preceding century. This vision of Europe's 'eternal summer' is then swept away in a sudden convulsion, and transformed into a landscape of muddy trenches, where hundreds of thousands of men live, struggle and kill each other. Constantly bombarded by artillery and subjected to gas attacks, the soldiers occasionally attempt to push forward across an alien landscape of craters and barbed wire, perishing in huge numbers as their attacks falter and fade, for little or no gain.

Like all such images, these contain a great deal that is true, but also fail to capture the entire picture. Even before the fatal shots fired in Sarajevo started the avalanche that led to war, tensions threatened the entire continent. Workers in Russia remained restless, frequently clashing with the police and troops; Italy and the Austro-Hungarian Empire eyed each other warily over their common border; and even in Britain, it was clear that the crisis in Ireland had the potential to erupt into serious violence.

Similarly the picture of trench warfare as a motif for the First World War is misleading. During the years that British, French, German, Belgian and American soldiers fought and died in northern France and western Belgium, another war raged in Eastern Europe, consuming soldiers on a scale to match the bloody battles of the Western Front. Yet although this war, too, had long periods of static warfare, it was dominated by huge movements, as the armies advanced and retreated hundreds of miles. Major cities changed hands, the initiative swung back and forth between the nations involved, and by the end of the war, the conflict had consumed the empires of Germany, Russia and Austria-Hungary, as well as devastating Serbia and Romania. The splintering of these empires created a patchwork of nations, from Finland and Estonia in the north to the new Yugoslavia in the south, sowing the seeds for conflicts that continued for the rest of the century. Yet this war in the East has received scant attention in accounts written in the West.

Despite the many differences between the two theatres, the Eastern Front and Western Front also had their similarities. Forcing a decisive result proved to be equally difficult in the East as in the West, and troops positioned in prepared defences were able to repulse almost any attack. But the density of troops in the East was far less than in the West, meaning that there was always the possibility of finding a vulnerable flank, or exploiting a local weakness. The inability to win a clear-cut victory was due more to the combination of the scale of the landscape, and the enormous military advantage gained by Germany from her railway system, allowing the German Army to shuttle troops back and forth in order to defeat the initial Russian thrusts. Thereafter, although the Russians did launch major offensives, these never threatened Germany again. Conversely, the Germans were acutely aware of the fate of Napoléon's army a century before, and were reluctant to venture into the vast spaces of Western Russia; there were no obvious objectives within reach that might allow them to knock Russia out of the war. The war in the East was fought in ways that officers on the Western Front in 1914 would have found familiar; thereafter, the experience of static warfare changed the Western mindset radically.

The terrain in the East was also vastly different from the West. British accounts of the battlefields of Flanders are coloured by the flat landscape, in which even gentle hills assumed huge importance. Any woodland near the front line was rapidly reduced to stumps in the fighting, and the few villages close to the trenches became little more than clusters of ruins. Although the landscape varied further south, with more substantial hills and rivers, these features played little part in shaping the fighting. By contrast, the Eastern Front was fought over a hugely varied region. Some areas, such as central Poland, were relatively flat and open, while dense forests and swamps dominated others, for example on the borders of East Prussia. The great Pripet Marshes forced the Russian Army to operate as two almost independent commands, and at the southern end of the long front was the line of the Carpathian Mountains, a natural barrier that protected the Hungarian plain. All of these landscapes had a major influence on the fighting, and helped to shape the campaigns.

The armies of the three Great Powers on the Western Front – Britain, France and Germany – operated in ways that were broadly similar. By contrast, the armies on the Eastern Front were radically different. The German Army was perhaps the most 'professional' of the three, with an experienced body of skilled senior officers, bound together by a camaraderie that gave them additional resilience. The army of the Austro-Hungarian Empire was to a very large extent the creation of a single man's vision of war, and its success of failure would depend upon how good this vision was. The tsar's army was a political battlefield, with different factions fighting for supremacy and regarding their own conflicts as being of paramount importance. All of the armies of the First World War had to adapt rapidly to the reality of war, and their ability to do so would have huge implications for the outcome of the conflict.

Just as in the West, the nations fighting on the Eastern Front attempted to learn and apply the lessons of previous conflicts, much as they had analysed these earlier wars in order to prepare for future wars. One of the consistent features of the way that lessons from the past are learned by armies and nations has been that such lessons are usually only learned imperfectly, if at all. The failure to learn from previous wars, or even from the initial experiences of the fighting once it began, had catastrophic consequences. Millions were slaughtered on the battlefields of Europe, both East and West, on a scale that had previously been unimaginable.

There had been plenty of indicators in the later part of the 19th century that future wars would be very different. Despite this, there was a strong desire by all of the nations involved in the First World War to attempt to apply what had been learned to existing doctrine, rather than face the task of creating an entirely new doctrine. This, too, has been a common feature throughout history, with few nations or armies prepared to take the risk of abandoning familiar and widely established policies in favour of new ways of fighting. In the conflict between the Central Powers and Russia the casualties suffered by both sides were as great as those in the West, but the battlefront moved back and forth over large areas. These movements offered the combatants the tantalising prospect of a decisive victory. The fact that the three major antagonists in the East – the Germans, the Austro-Hungarians, and the Russians – had all, in their own ways, anticipated the difficulties of imposing their will upon the battlefield appeared to do little to stop them from pressing on regardless.

Perhaps the most important war that influenced military thinking during the build-up to the First World War was the conflict between France and Prussia in 1870–71. The stark fact resulting from this was that the North German Confederation, which would combine to form Germany before its end, inflicted a decisive defeat upon France. The conflict was effectively decided on 2 September 1870, when Napoléon III and over 100,000 French soldiers surrendered at Sedan, only forty-five days after the start of hostilities, though the Siege of Paris

Northeast Europe, 1914

50 miles
80 km

N

Germany

Russian Empire

Austro-Hungarian Empire

Carpathian Mountains

Tilsit
Königsberg
Gumbinnen
Insterburg
Kovno
Vilna
Olita
Danzig
Goldap
Angerburg
Suvalki
Seeburg
Lötzen
Marienburg
Rastenburg
Lyck
Augustovo
Allenstein
Grodno
Deutsch Hohenstein
Rudczanny
Eylau
Graudenz
Ortelsburg
Neidenburg
Osowiec
Soldau
Lomza
Bialystok
Thorn
Mlawa
Narew
Wloclawek
Posen
Novogeorgievsk
Plock
Warsaw
Kutno
Siedlce
Bug
Lowicz
Brest-Litovsk
Kalisz
Łódź
Grójek
Góra Kalwaria
Pilica
Ivangorod
Radom
Nowo Aleksandrya
Przedbórz
Lublin
Kovel
Chelm
Breslau
Kielce
Oppeln
Czestochowa
Sandomierz
Rovno
Nisko
Nida
San
Vistula
Warta
Vistula
Krakow
Rżuchów
Tarnow
Rzeszów
Jaroslaw
Teschen
Neu Sandez
Przemyśl
Lemberg
Dunajec
Mikołajów
Chyrów
Stryj
Dnester
Bartfeld
Turka
Czernowitz

and fighting elsewhere in France dragged on for several months. This remarkably swift victory was achieved despite the French being supported by a larger population, which should have allowed her to field the larger army, many of whom would also have been veterans of the Wars of Independence in Italy and the intervention in Mexico in 1862–67. Military theorists of all nations – including the victorious Germans – swiftly began to analyse the factors that contributed to this surprising outcome.

One of the stark differences between the combatants was the issue of conscription. France had a large standing army, and could therefore field a substantial force at short notice. However, like all European armies, it also relied extensively on reservists to bring the army up to full strength. Prussia embarked on a modernisation of its army in the middle of the 19th century, and in 1859 Albrecht von Roon was appointed Minister for War. After three years of political wrangling he was able to persuade the Prussian parliament to approve a programme of conscription, with three years' service followed by several years as a reservist.[1] The result was that Prussia was able to mobilise a substantial force of trained soldiers in times of war, though at the outset of hostilities with France, the larger French standing army placed Prussia at a disadvantage. Nevertheless, despite its smaller population, Prussia and the North German Confederation – which rapidly adopted Roon's policy of conscription and reserve service – could ultimately muster a larger force.

Regardless of the size of the reserves available, the efficiency of mobilisation proved to be a crucial factor. Both nations had good railway systems, but although the German network was denser, the key to German success was the efficient mobilisation plan. As a result, German reserves were delivered to the frontier on schedule, while the French system rapidly degenerated into chaos, with over 100,000 troops being left in the wrong locations.[2] Any initial numerical advantage that France might have held evaporated before it could be exploited.

Once the fighting began the conduct of the war raised several further issues. Prussia was unique in the structure of its general staff, itself an innovation in response to a previous war. After the heavy defeat at Napoléon's hands in 1806 the Prussian king Friedrich Wilhelm III established a Military Reorganisation Commission to analyse all aspects of their defeat, and to make recommendations for changes. Prussia had already instigated the assignment of military experts to assist generals – professional soldiers who were there to offset the inexperience of the aristocratic commanders – but the manner in which many senior commanders ignored the advice of their experts played a large role in the Prussian defeat at the hands of Napoleonic France. The Reorganisation Commission evolved into the general staff, a body of officers of the highest intelligence who were responsible for organisation and implementation of military plans, as well as the ongoing analysis of military developments. At every higher level of command, unit commanders – who continued to be selected in the traditional manner, on the basis of a mixture of seniority and patronage – were assisted by a highly trained chief of staff. The latter had the right to dispute any decisions made by the commander, and could appeal to the next higher level of command in the event of such a disagreement. In practice most commanders enjoyed a close and harmonious relationship with their chief of staff, allowing them to delegate much of the routine management of their unit to the staff officer, while the commander concentrated on more pressing matters. During the fighting of 1870–71 the Prussians proved to be far more capable than the French at adapting to changing circumstances, not least because of the smooth functioning of the general staff.

At the front line, differences between the two armies highlighted the importance of up-to-date weaponry. The French rifle was far superior to the German model, and allowed French infantry to sustain higher rates of fire over longer ranges, with considerably greater accuracy. However, the widespread use of muzzle-loading cannon by the French placed them at a disadvantage when compared with the quick-firing breech-loaders used by the German forces.

All of these factors were analysed by each of the European powers, and, to some extent at least, lessons were learned and applied. Analysis of the latter reveals a great deal about the preconceived prejudices and competing interests in the organisations that studied the Franco-Prussian War. The first lesson was the importance of a suitable pool of trained reserves, and the years that followed the war saw a series of changes in most European nations, as all sides attempted to build larger armies. To a certain extent, the growing populations of all states during this period naturally resulted in a larger pool of manpower, but there proved to be unexpected barriers to major changes. The end of the Franco-Prussian War was followed by the brief insurrection of the Paris Commune in March–May 1871, which was bloodily suppressed by the French Army. A bitter mistrust resulted between socialists in French politics and the army, which they perceived – justifiably – as being a bastion of reactionary thought. Many socialist politicians attempted to use the question of conscription to impose a radical change upon the army; it was proposed that conscripts would only spend a year in the army, but would then have a longer reservist commitment. Consequently, the size (and therefore prestige) of the standing army would be diminished, but France would have a larger body of reserves in time of war –to some extent, this would be a return to the concept of the 'citizen army' of the French Revolution. The army establishment fought a long battle against such proposals, resorting to arguments that varied from practical and logical to completely implausible. Reservists, it was maintained, were inferior soldiers to regulars, and an army based primarily on reservists would only be able to fight a defensive war, lacking the unit cohesion and higher level of training required for offensive operations. The army therefore promoted the importance of such offensive operations as a means of opposing greater dependency on reservists. Other nations studied French developments and were influenced in their turn by them, even though the debate in France was distorted by the internal political questions around conscription.

Another consequence of the analysis of the Franco-Prussian War was the creation of detailed timetables for mobilisation, designed to ensure that armies could be deployed in their preferred locations quickly, and brought up to strength faster than their opponents. The speed of mobilisation would potentially give a nation a decisive advantage in the early stages of a war, and large sums were spent on improving railways in key locations. The railway plans for mobilisation became so complex that they imposed a new constraint upon European powers: the arrangements took several weeks to draft, and could not be altered at short notice. Although by 1914 the Germans had embarked upon changes that would have made such plans more flexible, the changes were still in their early stages. Other countries had not even addressed the issues, with disastrous consequences for Germany's main ally, the Austro-Hungarian Empire.

Most nations adopted a system comparable to the Prussian general staff, though few allowed the staff as much independence. But even in these cases, there was often incomplete understanding of the issues involved. The Prussian general staff, which then became the German general staff, was more than a body of highly trained, intelligent officers. Ultimately it developed into part of a revolutionary system of command, though, as will be seen, this development was tortuous, and faced many obstacles from more traditionally minded military thinkers. Helmuth von Moltke (the Elder), Chief of the Prussian General Staff during the Franco-Prussian War, was a major figure in developing the training and ethos of the general staff. He was a leading proponent of the concept that traditional top-down systems of command were too inflexible to cope with the rapidly changing environment of a modern battlefield, which was likely to be far larger than ever before. Consequently, Moltke believed, it was important for subordinate commanders to understand the intentions of higher commands, and the role that their own unit was to play in these intentions. This would afford the subordinate commander the opportunity to improvise and stray outside the original scope of his orders, if by doing so he could still help his higher command achieve its objectives. 'Strategy is a system of ad-hoc expedients,' he insisted, and all levels should be able and willing to adapt to whatever was required by the prevailing circumstances.[3] Even within Prussia, this flexibility was resisted by many – perhaps most – senior figures in the army, who believed that such an approach would lead to chaos. But, unpredictable events were certain to happen, insisted Moltke, and it was impossible to cater for them with rigid hierarchical command structures:

> No plan of operations extends with certainty beyond the first encounter with the enemy's main strength… The situations under which an officer has to act on the basis of his own view of the situation are diverse. It would be wrong if he had to wait for orders at times when no orders can be given. But his actions are most productive when he acts within the framework of his senior commander's intent.[4]

In order to make such a system workable, commanders at lower levels needed the training both to understand the intentions of higher levels, and to be able to show initiative in a reliable manner. The training of all officers, Moltke and his supporters believed, should reflect this. As such concepts spread through the Prussian and later the German military, the training of leaders at all levels incorporated this thinking, and was extended still further to allow for junior commanders to step into the roles filled by their seniors if necessary. As a result, German formations proved to be far more resilient in the face of casualties amongst their commanders than many of those that they fought.

The French had used a form of general staff since the Napoleonic Wars, but its structure and function was radically different from that of Prussia and Germany. French staff officers were little more than the servants of their commanders, responsible for promulgating their orders and instructions. One of the commanders of the armies of Napoléon III, General Patrice de Mac-Mahon, was not unusual amongst senior officers of his era when he declared:

> I shall remove from the promotion list any officer whose name I read on the cover of a book.[5]

Now, in the wake of the Franco-Prussian War, a staff college was created in France, in emulation of the Prussian system, leading first to *l'état-major de l'armée* (the staff of the French Army), and ultimately to *le Grand Quartier général* (the general headquarters). At first, these steps led to a radical change in attitude throughout the French Army, with detailed study of past conflicts as well as analysis of new weapons and tactics, but as time passed, the mood shifted. The momentary enthusiasm for change did not last long, as was the case after other conflicts. The British observer in Manchuria during the Russo-Japanese War of 1904–05 recorded:

> On the actual day of battle naked truths may be picked up for the asking; by the following morning, they have already begun to get into their uniforms.[6]

France was clearly not alone in this trend. Similar processes occurred in both Austria and Russia, where attempts to introduce modern 'scientific' thinking into military education were gradually diluted and eclipsed by a reversion to traditional thinking. In the case of Russia, the growing alliance between her and France ensured that many of the mistakes being made in France were emulated in Russia. Even in Germany, the cradle of a more scientific approach to warfare, the accession of Kaiser Wilhelm II in 1888 brought a radical change to the independence and innovative approach of the general staff, diluting many of the gains of an earlier generation. In addition, as will be described, some of those who followed Moltke the Elder lacked his intellectual capabilities and flexibility.

The failure to grasp the detailed significance of the impact of the Prussian general staff was not the only lesson that was partially heeded. The war saw a series of manoeuvres that left large French armies isolated and surrounded, and it was natural that this was seen as a desirable model for future conflicts. The reality was that much of the German success resulted from catastrophic mistakes by the French, and the evidence that German commanders were able to impose their plans for such encirclements upon a strongly resisting enemy was weak. The issue was further complicated by consideration of the effect of modern firearms on the fighting. The first major clash of the war, at Wissembourg on 4 August, saw an outnumbered French force resist repeated German attacks, mainly as a result of accurate rifle fire from protected positions. Although the Germans won the battle, their losses of over 3,500 were greater than those of the French, which came to no more than 2,100, 900 of which were prisoners. Two days later, German troops again suffered substantial losses from French rifle fire, this time at Spicheren. Later in the month, at Gravelotte, the German assaults against French troops defending favourable terrain resulted in terrible casualties; General Charles Frossard's II Corps lost 621 men defending the Pointe du Jour, but inflicted 4,300 casualties on the attackers, commanded by General Karl Friedrich von Steinmetz. Other German formations, particularly the Prussian Guards Corps, suffered even heavier losses. It was a reflection of the relative advantages enjoyed by the two armies in terms of equipment that most of the German losses were from rifle fire, whereas most of the French losses were inflicted by German artillery.

When he reviewed the conduct of the war, Moltke the Elder remarked specifically on the difficulties of attacking prepared positions:

> My conviction has been won over to the tactical defensive by the improvements in firepower. In the campaign of 1870 we continually took the offensive and took the enemy's strongest positions, but with what sacrifices! It seems to me to be more favourable to go over to the offensive after first parrying the enemy's attacks.[7]

It is interesting to note that immediately after the Franco-Prussian War, most major powers developed plans that were inherently defensive, but with the passage of time other influences crept in – the naked truths began to put on their uniforms. In order to justify the existence of a large standing army, French theorists argued that the defeat of Napoléon III was largely due to an overly passive attitude, and highlighted the successes achieved by the more aggressive policy of the German forces. The failure of the Prussians to break through at Spicheren and Gravelotte was blamed on a reluctance to press home the attack. With the passage of time, further conflicts – the Anglo-Boer War and the Russo-Japanese War – demonstrated once again the superiority of entrenched infantry, these examples were also dismissed on similar grounds.

There were other reasons for the military leaders of all the European powers to favour offensive warfare in preference to defensive fighting. It was more likely that an offensive war would achieve quick results, and thus shorten the length of the war. It also increased the likelihood of being able to impose a solution upon the other side, compared to what could be expected from adopting a defensive posture. The geographical consequences of European treaties also played a part. With potentially hostile neighbours to the east and west, Germany naturally desired to inflict a decisive defeat on one or other opponent, rather than face a protracted two-front war; similarly, France and Russia were aware that their plans for mutual assistance required them to ensure that Germany was not given a free hand to concentrate first on one enemy, then the other – and the only way of achieving this was to plan for offensive operations. Therefore, despite the wealth of evidence that suggested that attackers would be at a severe disadvantage, the strong desire to be able to wage offensive war prevailed in almost every nation.

Many throughout Europe remained convinced that any future war would be short. This directly influenced the size of ammunition stockpiles – there was little point in having large stocks in the event of a short war, nor was there any pressing need to have a munitions and armaments industry capable of major levels of production in a short time. There were some, the great Moltke, for one, who warned the German parliament in 1890 that a future war might last as long as the Seven Years War, or even the Thirty Years War.[8] His nephew, who would oversee the beginning of the First World War, feared that a future war would be prolonged and bloody, but the political unacceptability of such conclusions led everyone to hope – and plan for – a short war. Anything else was simply unacceptable.[9]

Throughout the 19th century, there was a developing debate about the future role of cavalry, and in this respect, the Franco-Prussian War failed to provide any significant lesson. French cavalry inflicted heavy casualties on the Prussians at Mars-La-Tour on 16 August, but failed to achieve any decisive success during the Battle of Sedan a fortnight later. Both sides relied on horsemen to act as the eyes and ears of their armies, but although the Germans appeared to make good use of intelligence gained by cavalry scouts, the French missed several opportunities. Irregular Boer cavalry proved to be superior to British cavalry in South Africa, as a result of which British cavalry training was altered. Horsemen were used more as mounted infantry, the historical function of dragoons, rather than planning to go into combat on horseback, but radical changes in the recruitment and use of cavalry did not occur. This was at least partly due to the presence in all European armies of the sons of aristocratic families in cavalry regiments; the traditionalists in military thinking continued to regard cavalry as the *arme blanche*, inherently superior to infantry, and resisted any attempts to reduce the size of the cavalry arm, or worse still turning it into little more than a mobile version of the infantry.

Consequently, 1914 found all of the future combatants prepared to fight a war that they expected would resemble the Franco-Prussian War: a short conflict, in which speed of mobilisation, offensive operations, and cavalry formations would all play important roles. These expectations were wrong in every respect, and doomed a generation to unimaginable slaughter, ultimately bringing the empires that had dominated Europe for centuries to an abrupt end.

CHAPTER 1

THE GERMAN WAR MACHINE

The years prior to the 1871 unification of Germany brought three short wars in which the Prussian Army – with contingents from other German states – fought brief and successful offensive campaigns against Denmark, Austria, and France. In 1864, the forces of the German Confederation defeated the Danes, reversing the results of an earlier conflict in 1848–51; Denmark was forced to relinquish the provinces of Schleswig, Holstein, and Lauenburg. The Austrians had fought alongside the Prussians against the Danes, but in 1866, disputes between the two powers over the administration of the newly acquired provinces were used by Chancellor Otto von Bismarck to precipitate a new war. The resultant Prussian victory at Königgrätz ended Austrian influence in what would become Germany, and precipitated a crisis in Austria, leading to the creation of the Austro-Hungarian Empire and the Dual Monarchy. In turn the war of 1870–71 with France led directly to the creation of Germany, and firmly established the new nation's place as a Great Power.

The legacy of these successes was that the reputation and standing of the army in the new German nation was extraordinarily high. The quality of the German general staff was widely admired, both within and outside Germany, as was the discipline and fighting power of the army itself. Small wonder that Berlin was frequently regarded as a 'Mecca of militarism', and not always in a critical sense. But, as is often the case, the fear and admiration with which the German Army was regarded by people both outside and inside Germany was not necessarily reflected by the true nature of the army itself.

Despite the three victorious wars, Helmuth von Moltke (the Elder), chief of staff at the time of German unification, was deeply doubtful that future wars could be fought in the same manner, with an emphasis on offensive action.

Nevertheless, he remained convinced that wars per se were inevitable, even desirable:

> Man's life, indeed the whole of nature, is no more than a struggle of the new against the old, and the life of national entities is no different ... it is only the sword that keeps the sword in its sheath.[1]

In an era of social Darwinism, when many European powers believed in the inherent superiority of the white man, this was a widespread opinion. In Germany, it extended to a belief that German triumphs, particularly over France, were both deserved and inevitable:

> There never was a struggle fought for a greater ideal than this; never perhaps did Nemesis strike down the guilty so violently; never perhaps did any army have such warmth, such inspiration, and such a deep poetic sense of the fact that the dreadful work of the battlefields served a higher ethical purpose; never perhaps did the workings of divine providence in the apportionment of rewards and punishment seem in human terms to be so just and logical as on this occasion. Hundreds of thousands perceived this as the poetry of the historical process.[2]

Preventive wars were, in the view of Moltke and most senior German officers, the best way of ensuring Germany's continuing prosperity and success, although the increasing difficulties of mounting swift and successful offensive operations would have to be overcome. Within Germany, many believed that the young nation was surrounded by potential foes, and faced the danger of having to fight on more than one front at the same time. Given the combined strength of these enemies, many felt, Germany's only hope of success in the face of hostile combinations of neighbouring countries was to defeat at least one of her foes in a swift assault before turning on the others; in other words, the way to avoid a war on two or more fronts was to fight a series of short single-front wars. In order to ensure that the German Army was able to switch from one successful campaign to the next in a timely manner, it would be necessary to fight each war as an offensive operation.

In this context, the rapid normalisation of relations between Prussia and the Austro-Hungarian Empire after the war of 1866 was of great significance. Although many in Vienna wished for revenge against Bismarck, there was insufficient unity within the Austro-Hungarian Empire to make further hostilities possible, and the Prussian Chancellor had prudently persuaded his king to bring the war against Austria to an early end; Prussia gained no territory from Austria, and Vienna was unwilling to intervene against Prussia in 1870 unless Bavaria, too, sided with the French. After the defeat of France and the creation of Germany, there was no longer any purpose in attempting to reverse the results of the 1866 war, as there was no prospect of restoring Austrian influence in the affairs of German states. Furthermore, the growing threat to the Dual Monarchy from Italy and in the Balkans forced Vienna to seek a reliable and friendly relationship with its powerful northern neighbour.

Prior to his resignation in 1890, the careful and clever diplomacy of Chancellor Otto von Bismarck ensured that Germany maintained a delicate balancing act with her neighbours, avoiding the need for war. The French were regarded as almost irreconcilably hostile to Germany, not least because of the reparations imposed upon France after the Franco-Prussian War and the loss of her former provinces Alsace and Lorraine to Germany. However, provided that Britain, Russia, and Italy could be discouraged from any formal alliance with France, the implacable hostility of the French towards Germany could be contained, and would not constitute a significant threat. But after Bismarck's departure, the policies pursued by Kaiser Wilhelm II, which were more assertive and in many respects more provocative than any during the Bismarck era, virtually ensured that, sooner or later, Germany would once more have to go to war.

There remained, however, the difficult problem of how to wage a successful offensive war when military developments, in terms of firepower and the mobility provided by railways, favoured the defender so greatly. Infantry firepower combined with even rudimentary fortifications seemed able to bring almost any attack to a bloody standstill, while railways – particularly if configured to allow rapid lateral movement – would allow a defender to move forces to a threatened sector faster than an attacker could march there on foot. It was also to be expected that a retreating opponent would leave the railways in too poor a state for an advancing army to put them to good use. Given the nature of European politics, potential enemies were well known, allowing for the construction of fortifications that were almost impervious to the artillery of any attacking army.

At a tactical level, the firepower advantages of defenders seemed insuperable, and unlike their French and Russian opponents, German officers placed less faith in the ability of their troops to prevail in costly frontal attacks. Instead, Moltke and others suggested, attempts should always be made to outflank the defenders, and to roll up or encircle a strong defensive position. In December 1899, after a series of failed assaults upon the Boer defences at Colenso during the Anglo-Boer War, the British had finally broken through using precisely such

29

a policy. Similarly, at a higher level, there was little prospect of victory in a future war from a frontal clash against an enemy army, particularly if that army was in prepared defensive positions. Instead, attempts should always be made to outflank such defences through movement at corps and army level.

The most dangerous possible combination of enemies that Germany faced was a Franco-Russian alliance. After the Franco-Prussian War, Moltke the Elder planned for such an eventuality by proposing a swift crushing campaign against the French, on the grounds that achieving a rapid success against Russia was difficult; there was every likelihood that the Russian armies would retreat into the vastness of the east, where there were few important military or political objectives within easy striking range for Germany to try to reach. From 1879 Moltke's thinking changed. French fortifications along the shared frontier made the chances of a quick victory against France much slimmer. Also, Russian forces in Poland had been strengthened substantially, allowing for the possibility of a major Russian attack against Germany if the German Army was committed to an attack against France. At the same time, Russian concentrations in Poland now formed an increasingly tempting target for a German attack. Consequently, Moltke now favoured a defensive action in the west, while German troops struck swiftly to encircle and destroy Russian forces in the Warsaw area.

But as Russian military developments around Warsaw continued through the following years, a rapid victory against Russia also began to look less achievable. Moltke continued to favour an attack on Russia, while limited German forces held back the French, but accepted that a deeper advance into Russia would be needed to achieve a decisive encirclement of Russian forces to the east of Warsaw. This would, inevitably, take far longer, raising the spectre of a French victory in the west while German forces were still trying to achieve a resolution with Russia.

Moltke the Elder retired in 1888, his reputation as a quiet, thoughtful man intact; known as a talented linguist, he was once described as being taciturn in seven languages.[3] He was replaced by his deputy, Alfred von Waldersee, a determined supporter of the concept of pre-emptive wars. Waldersee was deeply unpopular with many in Berlin, where even by the standards of the day he was regarded as bigoted and anti-Semitic, and his tendency to develop military attachés at Germany's embassies into almost a separate department of foreign policy earned him a sharp rebuke from Chancellor Bismarck. Nevertheless, his enthusiasm for an early war, particularly against Russia, drew him close to the young Kaiser Wilhelm II. After another depressing meeting at which the kaiser spoke enthusiastically about such a war, Bismarck wrote to Friedrich von Holstein, head of the political department of Germany's Foreign Office:

The young man wants a war with Russia and would like to draw his sword right away. Woe to my grandchildren.[4]

The relationship between the kaiser and Waldersee rapidly ran into more troubled waters when the kaiser used his position to dismiss corps and division commanders, replacing them with his own favourites. Wilhelm II's continued intervention in military matters, a field in which he had no experience or expertise, constantly exasperated the Chief of the General Staff, and, in 1891, Waldersee made the grave political mistake of inflicting a heavy defeat upon the forces commanded by the kaiser in a field exercise. He promptly paid the price. He was swiftly demoted; his replacement was Generalleutnant Alfred von Schlieffen.

In his early years, Schlieffen showed no particular interest in military matters. His first experience of the army came when he served his compulsory military service while studying law; at the end of the year, he became an officer cadet, leading to over 50 years of military service. Schlieffen, like so many of his contemporaries, was convinced that Germany was surrounded by hostile nations, which merely awaited an opportunity to destroy his nation:

> An endeavour is afoot to bring [Britain, France, Italy, and Russia] together for a concentrated attack on the Central Powers. At the given moment, the drawbridges are to be let down, the doors are to be opened, and the million-strong armies let loose, ravaging and destroying, across the Vosges, the Meuse, the Niemen, the Bug and even the Isonzo and the Tyrolean Alps. The danger seems gigantic.[5]

Although he was the leading military thinker of the highly trained German General Staff, Schlieffen was in many respects a lesser figure than Moltke the Elder. He lacked his illustrious predecessor's pragmatic approach to problems; Schlieffen would never have felt comfortable with the suggestion that strategy was merely a system of expedients. During his tenure, the doctrine developed by Moltke to avoid futile frontal assaults by extension of the front line, resulting in envelopment or encirclement, became almost dogmatic, and was taught as the offensive option for almost every setting. Indeed, Schlieffen's book on the subject – based upon Hannibal's famous victory at Cannae – was widely studied in nations across Europe and America. His narrowness of vision was known to his contemporaries. When travelling through East Prussia, his adjutant commented on the beautiful Pregel valley, and after a brief study of the landscape, Schlieffen replied that the river was merely an insignificant military obstacle.[6] It was therefore entirely consistent with this view of the world that he regarded total victory as the only acceptable outcome of war; limited success was merely likely to lead to future wars. Such a total victory was unachievable by defensive warfare, and the German Army should therefore plan to carry out major offensive operations to force a swift, decisive result. He was also unwilling to regard diplomacy as a means of resolving potential conflicts, and based his plans upon the worst possible outcomes, assuming for example that British forces would almost inevitably be committed against Germany in a future war with France.

The differences between Moltke and Schlieffen are striking. Both believed that commanders at lower levels might have to act independently of their superiors, but approached the problem in starkly different ways. Moltke concluded that it was impossible to predict the detailed course of events, and instead suggested that junior commanders, aware of the intentions and objectives of their superiors, should be trained to improvise as required. Schlieffen, too, accepted the inevitability of unpredictable events, but attempted to deal with them by imposing standardised solutions to all such problems, so that superior officers could always predict how their juniors would approach any given problem. In order to ensure this predictability, he was far more inclined to develop meticulous and detailed orders, mapping out the anticipated course of a campaign far more thoroughly than Moltke.

Given these personal views – a desire to wage decisive, offensive wars; a belief that only by outflanking and encircling defensive lines could such wars be won; and the opinion that diplomats would be unable to reduce the scale of the threat to Germany – Schlieffen's solutions to the military problems faced by Germany were predictable. The French defences facing German forces in Alsace and Lorraine were effectively impregnable, and would need to be outflanked. The only way that this could be achieved was via Belgian and possibly Dutch territory. Although this would almost certainly bring Britain into conflict with Germany, such British involvement was probably inevitable anyway, so trying to avoid it by respecting Belgian neutrality was of little value.

The details of the Schlieffen Plan for an offensive against France are not the subject of this book, except in the manner in which the plan influenced German options in the conflict against Russia. At first, Schlieffen concluded that the strength of the French defences would require the Germans to allow France to attack, in the hope that the French Army would be lured out of its fortifications, while the German Army sought the swift victory against Russia that Moltke had envisaged in the Warsaw area. As Russian fortifications around Warsaw grew stronger, Schlieffen abandoned this plan. Believing that the French would have to adopt the same outflanking approach that he favoured, he concluded that a future war would see French troops making use of Belgian territory in an attempt to outflank German defences. In combination with his own strong desire to fight an offensive war featuring outflanking and encircling movements, Schlieffen went on to develop his plan for a sweeping advance through Belgium. In the east, limited German forces would defend against any Russian attack until more forces became available from the west, fresh from their victory over the French. In other words, priority moved from Russia back to France.

It has been argued that the Schlieffen Plan was not a detailed strategy for the defeat of France, but was rather an exercise in strategic thinking.[7] Schlieffen himself accepted that the existing army was not large enough to achieve the plan, and that the roads of Belgium would be inadequate for sufficient troops to march at speed in the great sweeping movement that the plan envisaged. Nevertheless, given the almost certain link between Russia and France in any future war, Schlieffen had to consider how best his forces might force a rapid conclusion on one front, and this was indeed the strategy that was adopted.

Alfred von Schlieffen retired in 1906, and his replacement was Helmuth von Moltke (the Younger), the nephew of the visionary founder of the Imperial German General Staff. Like his namesake, he too believed in the inevitability of wars, and saw them as a means of allowing Germany to achieve its destiny. The German fear of encirclement by hostile enemies had continued to grow throughout the Schlieffen era, and in the early 20th century developed almost into paranoia, comparable in some respects to the attitude on either side of the Iron Curtain during the worst years of the Cold War. By the second decade of the century, a series of steps taken by Russia and France to improve their long-term preparedness gave a further impetus to German paranoia. Moltke repeatedly pressed for a war to relieve the growing tension, on the grounds that the later the war occurred, the less favourable the balance would be between Germany and her enemies. Russia's moves to improve the strength and fighting power of her army led to increasing fears in German military circles that a time would soon come when victory against Russia was almost impossible. Like Schlieffen, Moltke the Younger concluded that a rapid victory against Russia would be unattainable, and that the main effort should be to secure swift victory over France:

> Our foremost intention must be to achieve a speedy decision. This will hardly be possible against Russia. [If this were attempted, the] defence against France would absorb such strength that the remaining troops for an offensive against Russia would not suffice to force a decision upon it.[8]

Nevertheless, Germany continued to maintain a planning option for a strong deployment against Russia until April 1913. After this date, German mobilisation plans were all based upon the bulk of German forces being deployed against France.[9] Only the German Eighth Army with nine divisions – later increased to thirteen infantry divisions and a single cavalry division – would be deployed in East Prussia, to defend against any possible Russian attack. The only variation upon this was that in the event of Russian neutrality, Eighth Army might be available to help in the effort against France, and contingency plans were made for such an eventuality. Significantly, there was no plan for a war against Russia without deployment in the west against France. Moltke the Younger and most of his German contemporaries took it for granted that the vengeful French would take any opportunity to strike at Germany, in the event of a German-Russian war.

To an extent, the German bias towards massive mobilisation against France first enforced a structure on German railways, and was then dictated by the layout of those railways. The far higher density of lines in the west ensured rapid mobilisation against France, but only four double-tracked railway lines ran to the Vistula, and only two of these continued eastwards. Although more eastern routes were planned, these were not available in 1914.[10] There was also a marked disparity in the number of railway platforms available for soldiers to disembark. French intelligence estimates suggested that Germany had 170 suitable platforms along its western frontier, compared with only 125 on the far longer eastern frontier.[11]

The development of the German Army in the years that followed the Franco-Prussian War was marked by many of the same tensions that were seen in the armies of Germany's European rivals. The three arms – infantry, cavalry and artillery – drew selectively upon the events of the war to justify their pre-existing opinions, which reflected prejudices that had their roots in society as well as history. Given the similarity of the debates in Germany and other European powers, it is worth looking in detail at developments in Germany, which mirrored those throughout the continent.

For the infantry, the moment from the Franco-Prussian War that came to symbolise the preferred way of war was the assault by the Prussian Guards at St Privat on 18 August 1870. The French position occupied high ground, with a series of terraces, each extensively fortified with trenches, and dominated by the village of St Privat itself at the top of the slope. Refusing to wait for artillery support, the divisions of the Prussian Guards formed up and set off up the slope, a thin skirmish line leading the way. Behind this was the first wave of troops, formed up in companies, followed by a second wave consisting of battalions in close order.

Within a few minutes, French defensive fire, from a mixture of artillery, rifles, and *mitrailleuse* machine guns, inflicted terrible casualties. With extraordinary resilience, the surviving Prussian officers and NCOs improvised, spreading their men into an ever-wider skirmish line. Supported by the remaining battalion columns, this line ground its way up the slope to St Privat, and at dusk, after three hours of heavy infantry combat, the Prussian Guards' artillery finally made a major contribution to the battle when it reduced the fortified houses of the village to rubble. French losses included over 2,000 prisoners; the Prussians had lost over 8,000 men, most of these in the first half-hour of the attack.[12]

A few days later, the Prussian king issued a special order of the day, praising the courage of his Guards, though he also added:

> I expect from the intelligence of the officers that in future they will succeed in achieving the same results with less sacrifice by means of a smarter use of the terrain, a more thorough preparation of the attack, and by using more appropriate formations.[13]

Although there were experiments with more troops deployed in skirmish lines immediately after the war, conservative elements in the infantry resisted. Such formations, they insisted, would result in senior commanders losing control of their units, as junior commanders improvised in the face of enemy defences. Although this was in keeping with Moltke the Elder's original vision of decision-making delegated to lower levels, the strength of opposition shows how revolutionary this vision was, even in Germany. Sigismund von Schlichting, a regimental commander in Berlin who rose to become the chief of staff of the Prussian Guards, was an enthusiast for devolved command, though he added caveats regarding just how much freedom should be passed to lower commanders. He wrote several articles for army publications extolling his views, drawing additional evidence from the ability of poorly trained Turkish troops to inflict major losses on Russian attacking infantry at the Battle of Plevna in 1877:

> Even in the untrained hands of Turks, so much lead flies that the attacker is devastated – in the face of this firepower, his titanic courage simply sinks into the dust.[14]

A response from the more conservative point of view soon came. Bernhard von Kessel, who had served as an officer in the Prussian Guards at St Privat, stressed the value of close formations in preserving morale and unit cohesion:

Good discipline holds more troops at the ready to be commanded in battle than any formation designed for protection – so look for formations that promote discipline.[15]

Shortly after, the army decided that the debate was over, and ruled in favour of the traditionalists. Despite having experienced the slaughter at St Privat, the majority of senior officers chose to remember that the Guards had successfully advanced in close formation, rather than correctly remembering that it was improvisation in the face of heavy losses, together with belated artillery support, that had saved the day.

Schlichting's campaigns to reform infantry tactics continued as he moved from one command to another, depending on how out of favour he was at the time. He used the independence granted to corps commanders to experiment with men under his own command but traditionalist corps commanders used this same independence to forbid their men from firing as they advanced, on the grounds that this would slow the advance. Eventually, Schlichting's opponents conspired to have him forcibly retired in 1896; however, from the safety of retirement, Schlichting continued to preach reform, writing repeatedly about the superiority of firepower over close-ranked tactics. Offensive operations were still possible, he suggested, but would require the attackers to switch from mass-formation assaults to a more gradual approach, using terrain and field positions to move closer to the defenders and suppress them with superior firepower before attempting to storm their lines.

After the Boer War, there appeared to be a move towards adopting some of Schlichting's ideas, but old habits died hard, and in army exercises in May 1902, Major Hans Krug von Nidda, the Saxon military plenipotentiary, watched in amazement as the Prussian Guards pressed home the final attack in their traditional massed ranks:

The Prussian Guards will probably still make such casualty-generating charges here twenty years from now, no matter how much is written and spoken in the meantime about the modern art of war.[16]

The annual military exercises, in which two or three army corps were selected and allowed to demonstrate their own personal interpretations of current regulations, failed to resolve issues, not least because Kaiser Wilhelm II insisted on taking part, and the umpires were reluctant to rule against him. In 1904, the impetuous kaiser led the concentrated ranks of the Prussian Guards in an assault on IX

Corps, and was allowed to achieve a victory even though he did not wait for artillery support, or even allow his men to open fire. As the kaiser's chamberlain later recalled, an officer on the losing side commented:

Why do you Guardists bother to carry weapons if you don't even need them?[17]

The performance of Japanese troops in the fighting around Port Arthur during the Russo-Japanese War gave contradictory messages. On the one hand, the ultimate triumph of the Japanese seemed to support the prevailing belief in the supremacy of offensive operations; on the other hand, the heavy casualties inflicted by defensive fire suggested that Schlichting's views were worthy of closer examination. Slowly, opinion began to move away from massed formations. But, the independent nature of each German corps ensured that a general move away from massed ranks rushing forward with little preparation took many years to become universal. Even as late as 1907, some corps commanders were still using the old tactics when they took part in the annual exercises.

Of the three sections of the army, the cavalry felt the most threatened by technological developments. The performance of the cavalry during the Franco-Prussian War was limited to – admittedly, effective – scouting, and a single major battlefield intervention. At Mars-la-Tour in August 1870, the German Second Army came under heavy attack from the larger French Army of the Rhine, and was saved from defeat when General Friedrich von Bredow, counterattacked with a cavalry brigade consisting of just two regiments – no more than 800 men. Nearly half were killed in the assault, but the line was stabilised. Further cavalry actions followed, culminating in a major fight between several thousand horsemen from either side at the end of the day. The outcome of the battle was a bloody stalemate, but the memory of Bredow's attack lingered. How much more effective would it have been, argued cavalry enthusiasts, if it had been carried out by an entire division, charging in a 'traditional' formation of three waves, with an initial heavy regiment leading the way, supported by a second wave that would protect its flanks, and a third wave ready to deliver the *coup de grâce* or exploit a breakthrough.[18]

The cavalry of all European armies had always been the home of large numbers of aristocratic officers, and the German Army was no different. In the years that followed the Franco-Prussian War, many of the men who had been middle-ranking officers during the war rose to high command; a decade after the war, two-thirds of German corps commanders were former cavalrymen. Consequently, despite the doubts of many at high level, including Waldersee, about the survivability of dense cavalry formations, the popularity and influence of the cavalry continued to grow. With their selective memory of Mars-la-Tour reinforced by peacetime exercises – in which cavalry divisions manoeuvred and charged on open ground with no inconvenient slopes, rivers, or sunken roads, advancing easily with no regard for the disruption that would be caused in real war by horses and men cut down by defensive fire – the cavalry resolutely turned its face against innovation. One enthusiast, a cavalry veteran of the Franco-Prussian War, wrote:

> The irresistible storming of horses packed in tight formations at full gallop is the main and fundamental strength of the cavalry.[19]

Even during the Napoleonic Wars, relatively primitive firepower had shown the fallacy of such a point of view; only a selective use of evidence made it possible to articulate such a statement in the last quarter of the 19th century. Even more remarkable was this comment by Prince Friedrich Karl of Prussia, regarding horse artillery:

> It is not to be seen as a strengthening of the offensive element.[20]

Nevertheless, some younger cavalry officers were unhappy with this tendency to turn the clock back by more than a century. Friedrich von Bernhardi, a Prussian squadron commander at the time, later pithily pointed out glaring weaknesses in cavalry regulations:

> They contradicted all modern views, assuming that cavalry had to fight on horseback, and mostly against other mounted men, completely ignoring the fact that in the meantime weapons had developed extraordinary capabilities, and that the enemy was free to use them.[21]

Although traditionalists like Prince Friedrich Karl constantly defied instructions from above – the General Staff, at least, could see that modern firepower would reduce any attempt to deploy cavalry en masse to a bloodbath – the tide was turning in favour of innovators. Georg Friedrich von Kleist was another young officer who turned against massed charges, writing that cavalry was far more effective in a scouting and patrolling role.[22] Following the effective use of cavalry as deep raiders by the Russians against Turkey at Plevna in 1877, German cavalry were finally equipped 11 years later with demolition equipment.

After the turn of the century, reformers like Bernhardi – now the chief of staff of XVI Corps – called for cavalry to function as heavily armed 'mounted infantry', capable of fighting equally on foot or on horseback. Their contribution to victory would come before – by scouting and raiding – or after – by pursuit – of the main battle, rather than in the thick of the fighting. After he became Chief of the General Staff, Moltke the Younger decreed that the traditional end to every autumn exercise – a mass cavalry charge – was to be discontinued. Despite this, there was still an old-fashioned three-wave assault in 1906, and diehard cavalrymen dismissed the criticism of foreign observers on the grounds that these comments merely showed how afraid the foreigners were of German lancers. But the star of young reformers like Kleist and Bernhardi was rising, and by 1909 official regulations consigned the three-wave massed charge to the history books. German cavalry might occasionally be involved in mounted action against enemy horsemen, but this would be in the context of scouting and reconnaissance units clashing with their opposite numbers.

The men of the artillery, too, had their moment of glory in the Franco-Prussian War. The massed guns of the army smashed the French forces trapped at Sedan, with the commander of the artillery of the Prussian Guards even warning a senior infantry officer that he would fire on his men if they advanced before the artillery preparation was complete, as the infantry had done at St Privat.[23] Every attempt by the French to fight their way to freedom from the encirclement was broken up by concentrated artillery fire, and the final Prusso-German victory owed much to the dominance of their gunners.

The memory of the massed batteries on high ground overlooking the Meuse valley lingered for years. Although improvements in artillery design allowed for engagement at ever-greater ranges, there was significant emphasis on closing to within about 3,000 ft of the enemy. Mobility was regarded as more valuable than accurate long-range fire. Towards the end of his tenure of office, Moltke the Elder suggested that a small number of batteries might well accompany the infantry forward into close combat, but the bulk should be held further back. Despite this, most field exercises were marked by gunners rushing forward as fast as they could. Whilst such tactics might have prevailed at Sedan, improvements in the range and accuracy of infantry weapons made the rapid advance to close range a decidedly risky proposal.

The problems faced by artillery were compounded by improvements in military fortifications. The Russian artillery at Plevna in 1877 failed to make a significant impact upon the Turkish defences, and the Germans eyed the positions constructed by the French in eastern France, and by the Russians around Warsaw and along the Vistula, with increasing concern. It was easy enough to dismiss the Russian failure at Plevna as being due to alleged timidity on the part of Russian infantry, but the inability of artillery to smash field positions was unarguable.

Towards the end of the 19th century an attempt was made to address this weakness, and experimentation began with howitzers. Traditional artillerists were hostile to these weapons, and the first field trial was rigged to ensure that the new weapons performed badly.[24] Although a second trial had a more positive outcome, a third experiment in late 1888 seemed to confirm that field fortifications were impervious to howitzer fire. Regardless of these disputes, it was increasingly clear that the German Army desperately needed to replace much of its artillery, which was now showing signs of age. One report suggested that nearly half of all German gun batteries were unable to field enough serviceable guns, and perhaps as few as 20 per cent had weapons in good enough condition to sustain fire with high explosive shells for long periods.[25] Experiments with an innovative design of gun were rejected by traditionalists, only for the French to adopt the design and evolve it into their highly successful 75mm quick-firing gun, which provided the backbone of the French Army's artillery during the coming war. In 1900 howitzers finally began to appear in the ranks of the German artillery, not least due to the growing impatience of Schlieffen with the traditionalists, who continued to grumble that the mere presence of a weapon designed to deal with entrenched infantry somehow gave credibility to defensive tactics, and was thus contrary to the spirit of offensive action at all costs.

In the early years of the new century, howitzers began to appear in growing numbers. When the French produced guns with shields to protect gunners from shrapnel and bullets, the Germans were slow to respond. Although many could see the benefits of such protection, the attack-minded traditionalists in the army railed against something that would increase the weight of guns, and thus make them less mobile. A similar argument was used to hold back the development of heavy artillery, designed specifically to breach powerful fortifications, but the increased military budgets that followed the Russo-Japanese War resulted in both gun shields and heavy artillery battalions putting in an appearance.

Arguments about how best to use artillery continued. Slowly and reluctantly, emphasis moved from direct fire to firing from defilade positions. The old mission of the artillery – to suppress enemy artillery first, and then to support the infantry – had to be modified, as enemy gunners were also likely to be firing from defilade (and therefore hidden) positions. But although the increasing presence of howitzers gave the Germans a powerful edge, particularly over the French, the reliance on large numbers of reservist officers – who had little experience of, or interest in, firing from defilade positions – meant that many of the reforms would have limited impacts.

The total strength of the fully mobilised German Army in 1914 amounted to 1,191 battalions, the great majority of which would of course be deployed against France. The Eighth Army in East Prussia would go to war with barely 10 per cent of this total. Compared to the Russian Army, the German divisions were better equipped, particularly with artillery, having eighteen field mortars or howitzers and fifty-four field guns per division. To an extent, it can be argued that this advantage in equipment levels was more an accidental by-product of other decisions than an active choice.[26] A mixture of resistance from the Reichstag on financial grounds, and from the Prussian-dominated officer class of the German Army on social and class grounds, resulted in a limit on the numbers of men being called up for conscription – barely 50 per cent of eligible men were actually conscripted, compared with 85 per cent in France. Firstly, the cost of extending conscription, at a time when Germany was spending so much money on developing a High Seas Fleet capable of challenging the Royal Navy, was regarded as prohibitive by German politicians. Secondly, the officer class felt that any such expansion of the army – and therefore the officer corps – was something that would not be welcome. Prussia had been dominated by the Junkers, landed nobility who continued to control most of German agricultural land east of the Elbe after reunification. Their estates were traditionally passed on to the eldest son in the family, with the result that other sons sought work elsewhere, predominantly in the civil service and army. If large numbers of urban middle-class officers were created to support expansion of the army, the dominance of these traditionally-minded men would be threatened.

Given that a major element of the military budget paid for food and accommodation, such a restriction on conscription meant that money could be spent elsewhere, for example, on more and better artillery. However, there is little to suggest that there was ever any consideration of reducing the level of expenditure per battalion in order to allow the conscription of larger numbers of solders; the German government did not favour quantity over quality when it came to the army and navy. Rather than restricting army numbers to improve levels of equipment, it is likely that the Reichstag was aware that any increase in conscription leading to the creation of new divisions equipped at the same standard as existing units would be prohibitively expensive. An additional factor was that funding for the German Army was agreed on a five-year basis, at least partly to avoid annual wrangling. Once a funding plan was in place, it would take exceptional circumstances to make changes before the next review was due.

The German Eighth Army had six first-line infantry divisions, and four second-line divisions. In addition, it had three divisions composed of troops from the *Landwehr*, comprising reservists aged at least 30, with two brigades of garrison troops, some of whom had received only minimal training. The standard German infantry division consisted of two infantry brigades, each of which had two infantry regiments. Each regiment had two or three infantry battalions. In addition, divisions had an artillery brigade, with two artillery regiments. During peacetime, there was also a cavalry brigade of two regiments, each with two or three cavalry squadrons, but after mobilisation these brigades were removed to form cavalry divisions.

In addition to the regular forces, the second-line reserve divisions, and the *Landwehr*, Germany had a final line of defence. In dire emergencies, all men capable of bearing arms could be mobilised within the ranks of the *Landsturm*. These men may have had no military training, or might have been two or more decades older than when they served in the ranks, but if their homes were threatened by invasion, it was reasoned, they might be able to defend positions, allowing other forces to be deployed elsewhere.

The thirteen infantry divisions and the cavalry division in East Prussia had 774 artillery pieces at their disposal. In all, the troops formed 158 infantry battalions and 78 cavalry squadrons. The commander of the Eighth Army was Generaloberst Maximilian von Prittwitz, the son of a Prussian general, who was 65 years old at the start of the war. Prittwitz's army was formed into three corps, with one stationed in the East Prussian capital Königsberg and the others in Allenstein and Danzig; an additional two corps were to be formed on completion of mobilisation. The commanders of his three initial corps were a typical cross-section of German officers of the time. General der Infanterie Hermann von François, the descendant of French Huguenot refugees, commanded I Corps in Königsberg. His father had served in the Prussian Army as a general, and was killed in action in 1870 in France. His brother served in the German Colonial Army, and was involved in the German wars against the Herero and Namaqua in German South-West Africa (known today as Namibia). Although he was born in Luxembourg, François and his family lived in East Prussia, and his fierce pride for his homeland would play a part in the coming conflict. General August von Mackensen, commander of XVII Corps in Danzig, was the son of a Saxon agricultural administrator, and after service in the Franco-Prussian War commanded several cavalry units. He was widely regarded as an excellent officer; at one stage many thought that he might replace Schlieffen as Chief of the General Staff. General Friedrich von Scholtz, commander of XX Corps in

Allenstein, was also from Saxony, and had extensive experience and training as an artillery officer, having served as a young man in the Franco-Prussian War.

The area Prittwitz's Eighth Army had to defend gave his forces a decided advantage. Roughly in the middle of the frontier area facing Russia were the Masurian Lakes, and a few judiciously positioned fortifications had converted them into a formidable barrier. The Germans correctly anticipated that Russian forces would invade East Prussia directly from the east, attempting to advance along the Pregel valley towards Königsberg, and from Russian-occupied Poland to the south; the latter force would either thrust north towards the East Prussian capital or west towards the lower Vistula. In either case, the presence of the Masurian Lakes between the two Russian axes of advance would make close cooperation between two invasion forces almost impossible. By contrast, the Germans had an enormous advantage in the alignment of their extensive railway network. This effectively functioned as a force multiplier, and would allow German forces to switch easily from one side of the lakes to the other. Such a lateral movement to defeat any Russian invasion in detail was the subject of several pre-war war games, and was a familiar concept to all the German officers in the theatre.

In addition to the fortifications amongst the Masurian Lakes, the Germans had built a series of major forts around Königsberg in the 19th century and had then modernised them over the years. They would ensure that the city could not be taken easily. If a Russian advance along the Pregel attempted to push on towards the Vistula, bypassing the city to the south, large Russian forces would have to be deployed facing Königsberg to prevent the garrison from attacking into the flank of the Russian advance. Similarly, major fortresses had been established along the Vistula, particularly at Thorn (now Toruń). For an army invading East Prussia from Poland to the south, these fortresses again provided the Germans with a secure base from which to launch a flank attack. Combined with the flexibility provided by the German railways, allowing Prittwitz to concentrate against the inner flanks of either Russian invasion force, the Germans could realistically view the coming war with a degree of confidence. Provided that the Russians did not concentrate all their forces against East Prussia – and therefore sent substantial numbers of troops against the Austro-Hungarian Empire – Eighth Army should be able to hold out without conceding too much ground until victory over France was assured. All that was required was for Prittwitz to avoid defeat, and to hold his nerve.

CHAPTER 2

THE RUSSIAN STEAMROLLER

In the decade prior to the First World War, Russian military thinking was dominated by several themes. Some of these were mutually supportive, while others were almost irreconcilable, and the failure to choose clearly between them resulted in the Russian Empire entering the war at a severe disadvantage. In addition, the political infighting within the Russian Army was widely regarded by many senior officers as the most important conflict of all, and the pursuit of this internal struggle fatally weakened the functioning of the tsar's war machine.

One of the conflicting themes facing the Russians was a feeling of encirclement. Somewhat like Germany, Russia perceived itself as surrounded by hostile powers. To the southwest of Russia lay the Ottoman Empire. Ruled by Sultan Abdülhamid II until he was deposed in 1909, this great mass of varying regions had been in decline for a century, steadily losing territory to the Russians in the Caucasus, and in 1878, most of the Balkan region broke away from Ottoman rule. This region constantly drew the attention of expansionists in Russia, who saw it as a natural direction for future conquests; naturally, the Ottoman Empire was therefore regarded as a hostile state, which might attempt to recover some of its lost territories from Russia, if the opportunity arose. There was also a longstanding desire to seize control of the gates of the Black Sea, and the development of the Pan-Slavism movement in the 19th century encouraged Russians to believe that they might be welcomed into the Balkan peninsula by its large Slavic populations. The presence of a well-established Orthodox Christian Church also appeared to suggest that the people of the Balkans would welcome Russian hegemony.

Ambitions in this region, however, threatened to bring Russia into conflict with other European powers. The British and French in particular were strongly opposed to Russia gaining control of the Bosporus and Dardanelles, and the Austro-Hungarian Empire regarded any Russian expansion into the Balkan region as being directly contrary to its own interests and intentions. The Russo-Turkish War of 1877–78 saw Romania, Serbia, and Montenegro achieve international recognition of their statehood, and Bulgaria too established de facto independence. But even as Russian troops marched towards Constantinople, British naval forces deployed to the area to put pressure on Russia to accept a ceasefire.

To the anger and disappointment of the Russians, the Congress of Berlin that followed the end of the war resulted in Bosnia-Herzegovina being occupied by the Austro-Hungarian Empire. Although Russia gained territory, it was thwarted from rewriting the map of the Balkans as it might have wished. Any Russian thoughts of contesting Austrian dominance of the region were effectively blocked a year later by the announcement of the Dual Alliance between Germany and the Austro-Hungarian Empire in 1879. Under the terms of this surprise pact the two nations pledged to go to war against Russia if either came under attack from the armies of Tsar Alexander II.

The Russians were bitterly disappointed by Chancellor Bismarck, who oversaw the 1878 Congress of Berlin – most of the meetings were held in his official residence, the former Radziwill Palace, and proclaiming that he sought no gains for Germany, Bismarck kept tight control over proceedings. The announcement of the Dual Alliance the following year confirmed the Russian view that Germany should be regarded as a potentially hostile power, likely to act against Russia in concert with the Austrians. Nevertheless, Bismarck was able to secure a secret Reinsurance Treaty with Russia in 1887, which stipulated that the two nations would remain neutral in any war involving the other, unless Germany attacked France, or Russia attacked the Austro-Hungarian Empire. As an additional inducement to get the Russians to agree to the treaty, Bismarck included a clause specifying that Germany would remain neutral in the event of a Russian intervention to secure the Bosporus and the Dardanelles. The three-year treaty extended beyond the end of Bismarck's tenure of office, and although the Russians sought to have it renewed, Kaiser Wilhelm II allowed it to lapse. Unable to guarantee peace with Germany via a direct treaty, Russia turned to France, and the two powers drafted the Franco-Russian Alliance, which was finally formalised in 1894. In the event of Germany attacking either power, the other would immediately declare war on Germany. The Dual Alliance and the Franco-Russian Treaty, and the obligations contained within them, would prove to be major mechanisms in the outbreak of war in 1914.

In the last years of the 19th century, the expansion of Russia to the east resulted in a growing demand for a Pacific port that would be usable throughout the year, as Vladivostok, at the end of the Trans-Siberian Railway, was icebound through much of the winter. After China was forced to lease Port Arthur (now known as Lüshun Port), Russian influence began to extend into the Korean peninsula, an area regarded by Japan as vital to its national interests. In the wake of the international intervention to suppress the Boxer Rebellion in 1900, Russian troops occupied Manchuria in strength.

In 1903 the Japanese attempted to negotiate a treaty, whereby they would respect Russian dominance over Manchuria provided Russia accepted Japanese dominance over Korea. Although a degree of agreement was achieved, obstacles remained. For example, whilst Russia insisted that Japanese troops would only be sent to Korea – in the event of an anti-Japanese insurrection – after prior notice to Russia, would be proportionate in numbers to the task at hand, and would thereafter be withdrawn rapidly, there was no reciprocal arrangement regarding Russian troops in Manchuria. Although the Japanese appeared to negotiate in earnest, the Russians repeatedly delayed, and the frustrated Japanese government broke off diplomatic relations in February 1904, followed two days later by a declaration of war. The Russians had negotiated from a position of perceived superiority over their smaller eastern neighbour. Like most European powers, the Russians believed in the inherent superiority of 'the white man' over Asians, and Admiral Yevgeni Alexeyev, the Russian commander in Manchuria before hostilities broke out, treated the Japanese with open contempt with Russian officials even referring to their enemy as 'infantile monkeys'.[1]

In the early hours of 9 February Japanese warships struck at the Russian Pacific Fleet in Port Arthur, torpedoing several ships before the actual declaration of war. Japanese troops slowly closed in on the Russian base, suffering severe casualties as they pushed forward through heavily entrenched Russian positions. The Russian Pacific Fleet attempted to challenge the Japanese Navy for control of the open sea in August 1904, but was defeated at the Battle of the Yellow Sea, during which its commander, Wilhelm Carlovich Vitgeft, who had only taken up his post after the death of his predecessor, Admiral Stepan Makarov, was killed. The siege of Port Arthur proved a difficult and costly endeavour, but after Japanese artillery had destroyed the Russian warships blockaded in the port, the Russian commander, Major-General Anatoly Mikhaylovich Stessel, surprised both his superiors and the besieging Japanese by surrendering in early 1905.

The months that followed saw heavy fighting to the north of Port Arthur. First, General Gripenberg's Second Army attempted to drive back the Japanese in late

January. Then, in late February, the Japanese launched an attack of their own, intended to defeat the Russians before further reinforcements could arrive via the Trans-Siberian Railway. This latter battle, at Mukden, gave a glimpse of the shape of warfare to come. After heavy fighting, the Japanese succeeded in driving in the flanks of the Russian position, but rather than allow themselves to be enveloped, the Russians withdrew. When the Japanese attacked again, with the same outflanking manoeuvre, Gripenberg continued to fall back, but the combination of losses and forced retreats gradually led to the disintegration of his command. Only the heavy casualties suffered by the Japanese – during three weeks of fighting, the opposing armies, numbering 270,000 Japanese and 330,000 Russians, lost 76,000 and 89,000 men respectively – prevented them from turning an important victory into a decisive one.[2] The conclusion of the war came when the Russian Baltic Fleet, which had sailed 18,000 miles to the Pacific, was intercepted and almost completely destroyed by the Japanese in the Tsushima Narrows.

The humiliation of Russia's defeat by an Asian power caused shock throughout the world. Unrest within Russia had already led to the strikes and conflicts known as the 1905 Revolution, and the unpopularity of a bloody and costly war in an obscure corner of the world fuelled anti-government sentiment. This created another concern that dominated the thinking of Russian military planners: the need to ensure that unrest within the Russian Empire was kept under control. Major trouble flared in the western parts of the tsar's empire, with anti-Russian uprisings in Estonia, Latvia, and Lithuania as well as Poland, where Russia was forced to deploy over 250,000 troops to suppress the turmoil.[3]

The Russo-Japanese War and the 1905 Revolution left Russia in a perilous state. The nation's finances were in complete disarray, most of the Russian Navy had been destroyed, and morale in the army had disintegrated. As had been the case in France after the defeat by Prussia, the Russian authorities attempted to learn lessons from their setbacks. Some chose to interpret events in a way that was consistent with their existing beliefs, with absurd results. Many senior figures within the Russian military establishment remained convinced by the inherent superiority of the sword and bayonet over the rifle. General Alexander Suvorov, who died in 1800, had declared in his military manual:

The bullet is a mad thing, only the bayonet knows what it is about.[4]

Even a century after his death, many of Suvorov's beliefs remained firmly entrenched in Russian thinking. Alexei Nikolayevich Kuropatkin, the Russian Minister of War before and during the conflict with Japan, reacted to the finding that Cossack cavalry had been unable to press home their charges against Japanese infantry by concluding that the Cossacks had shown too little courage, rather than had been fought off by superior firepower. In order to ensure that the Cossacks showed the requisite resolution in future, he ordered their carbines to be withdrawn, so that they would have to get close enough to the enemy to use their sabres.[5]

Resistance to creating a Russian equivalent of the Imperial German General Staff had prevented the *Glavny Shtab* ('main staff') from developing into anything more than an administrative component of the Ministry of War. The drive for change, and the resistance to this, came from somewhat unexpected quarters. A large proportion of senior officers in the army were from groups that were not ethnically Russian. The Baltic Germans, for example, had a long tradition of providing the tsar with senior commanders; many had a stronger loyalty towards the tsar himself than to Russia. In troubled times, the tsar turned repeatedly to these conservatively minded men, despite their increasing age and their association with failed policies. By contrast, the Russian Corps of Guards and the cavalry there were large numbers of sons of Russian aristocratic families. Much of the pressure for reforming the existing chain of command came from these men, who might have been expected to represent the forces of reaction and resistance. Instead, it was the 'old guard' of senior ranking officers who saw the development of a strong general staff as a threat to their own dominance, and who resisted at every opportunity.

After the 1905 Revolution, which created the Russian Duma (or parliament), the minister of war became answerable to the Duma rather than directly to the tsar. In order to retain direct control, the tsar agreed to the creation of the *Glavnoe Upravlenie Generalnovo Shtaba,* (abbreviated to *GUGSh*) – the Main Directorate of the General Staff. This body would be headed by a chief of the general staff, answerable to the tsar personally via the new Council of State Defence, rather than to the minister of war. As a result, the old *Glavny Shtab* within the Ministry of War was left purely to deal with minor administrative matters, with its only significant role being to arrange the promotion of officers. This cumbersome and complex arrangement suited the various apparatchiks within the Russian administration, but in no way improved the military functioning of the army.

The first chief of the general staff was Fedor Fedorovich Palitsyn, the son of an aristocratic family who had served in the Russo-Turkish War of 1877–78. He attempted to bring in the sorts of innovations that had changed the armies of Germany and France, and repeatedly highlighted that Russia should pay attention not only to the potential threat from the west, but also from the southeast, where there were 'young, warlike, energetic powers, thirsting for action and conquests'.[6] This was in direct opposition to the Foreign Ministry, which regarded any further adventures in the east as a dangerous distraction. The aristocratic and bourgeois officers who rose to high office in the new general staff under Palitsyn – only graduates of the General Staff Academy were eligible, and few poorer families could afford to put their sons through this – found themselves clashing constantly with senior officers from the old system, with their strong personal bonds to the tsar. As a consequence, the impact of the general staff was far less marked than in France or Britain, and did not even begin to compare with the wide-reaching influence of the Imperial German General Staff.

Nevertheless, the new breed of staff officers laboured to come to terms with the lessons of the defeat in Manchuria. The cavalry, which had functioned particularly badly, struggled to define its role in future wars, and adopted an obstinate resistance to reform. Infantry officers complained that Russian artillery had failed to support them properly, while gunners criticised the infantry for failing to understand modern artillery. The guns of the Russian Army were organised in batteries of eight weapons, and it became clear that as 'fire missions' were assigned to batteries rather than individual guns, the number of batteries available directly influenced the flexibility of the artillery. Modern quick-firing guns in batteries of six could fire as many shells as an eight-gun battery in only a slightly longer time, and it would therefore be prudent to reorganise Russian artillery into six-gun formations, thus increasing the number of batteries and therefore fire missions that could be assigned, but senior artillery officers resisted this. The main reason cited was a lack of funding to expand the number of officers required for such an increase in the number of gun batteries, though it is likely that within the artillery establishment, the desire to maintain eight-gun batteries was strongly influenced by the fact that these were traditionally commanded by officers more senior than those who would command six-gun batteries. A wholesale change to six-gun batteries would thus reduce the number of senior officer posts within the artillery. Other attempts to modernise the Russian artillery were also resisted. Widespread adoption of high-trajectory howitzers was opposed for the same extraordinary reason that surfaced in Germany – that such guns were somehow 'cowardly'. In any event, argued the gunners, storming fortifications was the job of the infantry. Attempts to improve and clarify arrangements between artillery and infantry became bogged down in highly technical meetings, with little clarity emerging. Finally, in 1908, a wrangle between the navy and the army over funding, and between different army departments on how any money diverted from the navy might be spent, created a new crisis, and in its aftermath, Fedor Palitsyn was dismissed.

His replacement as Chief of the Russian General Staff was Vladimir Alexandrovich Sukhomlinov, a cavalry officer who came from the same background as the traditional senior officers of the Russian Army. Of all the figures in the Russian military establishment in the years preceding the First World War, he is perhaps one of the most controversial. He made a great many enemies, and to some extent was demonised after the war by them. Even a century after his tenure of office, it is still difficult to unravel whether he reformed Russia's armies sufficiently to prevent total disaster in 1914, or whether he contributed to their early setbacks. Given the complex relationships that existed within the Russian military establishment, it is likely that only a complex character could have attempted to grapple with reform, and inevitably, such a person would find himself at cross purposes with powerful figures. At an early stage, Sukhomlinov realised that his intention to promote his followers to powerful positions was effectively blocked by the fact that the old *Glavny Shtab*, under the Minister of War, Aleksandr Rödiger, controlled promotions. Consequently, one of his earliest intrigues was to encourage Alexei Polivanov, Rödiger's deputy, to conspire against his master. Evidence was presented to the Duma of Rödiger's incompetence in 1909, and he was dismissed. Aware that Polivanov had strong links with the reformist opposition, Tsar Nicholas II appointed Sukhomlinov as the new minister of war. One of his first acts was to subordinate the General Staff to the Ministry of War, reversing the reforms of just a few years before.

Controlling both the General Staff and the *Glavny Shtab*, Sukhomlinov could now appoint his preferred candidates to important positions within the army. Senior officers with experience of the recent fighting in Manchuria were conspicuous by their absence. In order to prevent a future chief of the general staff from becoming a rival, he was careful to appoint a series of men of limited talents to his former role. In the five years that followed, four men (Myshlayevski, Gerngross, Zhilinski, and Yanushkevich) held the post. This compares with four men (the two Moltkes, Waldersee, and Schlieffen) who held the equivalent post in the German General Staff, and its predecessor in Prussia, from 1857 to the beginning of the war in 1914 – a total of 57 years. Many regarded this transience as one of the key obstacles to reform of the Russian Army:

> Any real possibility of coordinating the numerous and diverse methods of training the armed forces of the country was out of the question. The way one question or

another was dealt with depended upon the competence, proficiency, or even tastes of this person or that; the question would be settled somehow or other, but there was no synthesis upon a scientific basis, as was the case in France and Germany.[7]

Sukhomlinov was also careful to keep a watch on his enemies. Many senior officers actively gathered intelligence on his behalf. One such informant was Colonel Sergei Myasoyedov, an intelligence officer who was also spying for the Germans, and who was protected by Sukhomlinov even when his treasonable activities were detected.[8] Others, such as Prince Mikhail Andronikov, benefited financially from Sukhomlinov's patronage. Sukhomlinov would inform the prince of land that the army was planning to buy, allowing Andronikov to purchase it cheaply, and then sell it to the army at inflated prices.[9]

Like so many of his contemporaries, Sukhomlinov was a firm disciple of the importance of offensive operations. One of his admirers quoted him as saying:

> You should know that the commander who only defends himself loses the battle, whilst he who attacks is victorious, because he is the master of his intentions, carries out his own idea, and is not compelled to deal with the idea of another.[10]

He was also an adherent of the Suvorov school of infantry warfare:

> The authors who have pointed out the nullity and the unimportance of the bayonet in our time, are, without noticing it, making an almost elementary mistake in logic: they only seem to have in view one side of the position, i.e. the firing of the enemy, forgetting that on our side, too, an exactly similar firing exists… The rarity of attacks with the bayonet proves not the nullity of the bayonet, as some are inclined to imagine, but the rarity of an enemy inclined and equally capable for an attack with the bayonet.
>
> Let us imagine an army which relied for its success on the battlefield simply upon firing, and felt pretty safe that it would not allow the enemy to approach up to the distance when the bayonet can be made use of; then imagine that such an army meets an enemy who, although not disdaining to fire, also remembers the bayonet – the first army would be absolutely stunned by an unexpected terrible onslaught, when it really came to a hand-to-hand fight with the enemy.
>
> It cannot be denied that in the present state of armaments the bullet can, at a short distance, be as effective as the bayonet, but this is only possible for a fearless army, i.e. an army capable of making use of the bayonet when, after the firing, it comes to a hand-to-hand tussle with the enemy.[11]

What seems particularly remarkable is that this quotation was recorded in approving terms in 1915. The inability of troops to press home a bayonet charge in the face of rifle and machine-gun fire had been clearly demonstrated in Manchuria, and continued belief in such a doctrine should have been beyond question after the slaughter of 1914.

Other contemporaries were far less flattering. One later wrote:

> At a meeting of the professors of our Staff College, [I] heard War Minister Sukhomlinov blame them for a tendency towards 'innovations' saying that he could not even hear the words 'modern war' without a feeling of annoyance. 'As war is, so it has remained,' he added: 'all these things are vicious innovations; look at me, for instance; for the last 25 years I have not read a single military manual.'... Sukhomlinov inflicted incalculable harm upon the Russian Army. Wherever his influence reached it withered those abundant, but still delicate, shoots of military thought which had sprung up after the Japanese war.[12]

Given his power and importance, it was perhaps inevitable that Sukhomlinov created large numbers of enemies. Maurice Paléologue, the last French ambassador to tsarist Russia, left a particularly vivid personal description of the man:

> There is something about General Sukhomlinov that makes one uneasy. Sixty-two years of age, the slave of a rather pretty wife thirty-two years younger than himself, intelligent, clever, and cunning, obsequious towards the tsar and a friend of Rasputin, surrounded by a rabble who serve as intermediaries in his intrigues and duplicities, he is a man who has lost the habit of work and keeps all his strength for conjugal joys. With his sly look, his eyes always gleaming watchfully under the heavy folds of his eyelids, I know few men who inspire more distrust at first sight.[13]

Unlike the German system, detailed planning for future wars was not the direct responsibility of the chief of the general staff; rather, it was devolved to subordinates. This was partly because any war plan was predicated by arrangements for mobilisation, and these arrangements were complex, bureaucratic, and difficult to alter at short notice. A full mobilisation schedule for the huge Russian Army took up to two years to draft, and it therefore became normal practice for the quartermaster-general's department to redraft these plans in line with the five-yearly military budgeting and planning cycles.[14] The schedule used in 1914 was known as Modified Plan 18, and was due for revision that year.

One of the men who had a strong influence on Russian planning in the years before the war was Yuri Nikoforovich Danilov, who was born in the Ukraine in 1866. As a young man he hoped to become a mining engineer, but was persuaded by his father to join the army.[15] He graduated from the General Staff College in 1898, and after serving under the widely revered General Mikhail Ivanovich Dragomirov (another passionate enthusiast for the bayonet charge), he moved to the general staff, where he became quartermaster-general. One of his responsibilities was war planning, and the careful, cautious Danilov's personality clearly played a part in how he approached this task.

For a variety of reasons, the Russians did not share the German view that the French would take any opportunity that arose to attack Germany. Danilov questioned the accepted wisdom that the bulk of Germany's effort in any future war would fall upon France. Like many in Russia in the first decade of the 20th century, he believed that the French had lost much of their appetite for revenge against Germany, and that either the Germans would be able to go to war against Russia without French involvement, or would choose to defend against the French while unleashing their armies against Russia. Even if the French did enter the war, many believed that they would be swiftly defeated, allowing Germany to turn east in strength. In addition, Danilov and others argued that the Russian Army remained weak after the defeat in Manchuria. As late as 1910, officers like General Alexei Alexeevich Brusilov felt that it would be impossible to fight a major war.[16] Another major factor in Danilov's thinking was a tendency to plan for the worse possible case. For example, he discussed the possibility of Russia having to fight Sweden, Romania, Turkey, Japan, and China at the same time as Germany and the Austro-Hungarian Empire – something that was ridiculed by his critics, one commenting, 'He left out only the Martians.'[17]

Another factor that influenced Danilov's thinking was the fear of a sudden German attack. Much as was the case during the Cold War, military thinkers on all sides repeatedly raised the spectre of a surprise pre-emptive attack by one or more of their enemies. In the case of Russia, Danilov feared that such an assault by the Germans, which could be carried out long before Russian forces had mobilised, would destroy forward deployments and force an early conclusion to hostilities. Accordingly, he selected concentration areas for the Russian Army further to the east, out of range of any such surprise attack.

The western border of the Russian Empire included a large west-facing bulge that mostly consisted of Russian-occupied Poland, and Danilov suggested the uncontested abandonment of this region. The chain of major Russian fortresses along the Vistula would be dismantled, and the bulk of the Russian Army –

fifty-three divisions – would be mobilised to face the Germans north of the Pripet Marshes. Only nineteen divisions would face the Austro-Hungarian Empire to the south. This plan was in stark contrast to the proposals of Mikhail Vasileyevich Alexeyev, who had preceded Danilov as quartermaster-general and was now serving as chief of staff in the Kiev military district. Alexeyev dismissed Danilov's 'worst case' thinking, with the possibility of war against a multitude of enemies at the same time, as an impossible task, and moreover an exceedingly unlikely one:

> The wish to secure all of our borders spreads our forces too thinly and, moreover, completely disregards the role of diplomacy.[18]

Acting accordingly, Alexeyev rejected contingencies such as the need to hold back large forces for the possible defence of St Petersburg from a German seaborne assault, or to defend against a possible Romanian invasion. Instead, he proposed using these forces to secure Warsaw and the Vistula fortresses, establishing sufficient strength to resist a surprise German attack. He also rejected Danilov's proposal for concentrating most of the army north of the Pripet Marshes, as any offensive operation after such a deployment could only be into East Prussia, an area that offered the Germans many defensive options. By having a large force in Poland, Alexeyev argued, there was the possibility of attacking in strength into Austrian-held Galicia. Alternatively, Russian forces would have the option of bypassing East Prussia by attacking west from Warsaw and thus threatening an advance into the heartland of Germany, much as the Red Army did in 1945.

These alternative visions of operations – Danilov's defensive plans, and Alexeyev's proposal for stronger deployments in Poland – first surfaced in the closing months of Palitsyn's tenure of office in 1908. Rather than resolve the debate decisively, Palitsyn chose a compromise between the two proposals. He approved, in general, a more easterly area for initial Russian concentration, but also chose to deploy relatively weak forces around Warsaw. This compromise was inevitably – and correctly – criticised as being the worst of both options.

During peacetime, a substantial part of the Russian Army was deployed around Warsaw, for a variety of reasons. Firstly, despite Danilov's pessimism, there was a longstanding interest in maintaining a capability for early offensive operations against either Germany or the Austro-Hungarian Empire. Secondly, fear of anti-Russian unrest by the Poles required the maintenance of a substantial garrison. Thirdly, the Russians were aware that the inadequacy of their railway system would result in far slower mobilisation than in Germany or Austria-Hungary.

To an extent, the inadequate railways were deliberate policy. Few lines were built in the western fringes of the Russian Empire, so that, in the event of a German attack, the German invaders would struggle to bring forward adequate supplies as they advanced into Russia. But equally, the few railway lines meant that it would be difficult for Russia to move troops west quickly, so it was thought best to station much of the peacetime army in the west, needing only a relatively small movement of reservists to bring the formations up to strength.

However, reforms to the Russian Army resulted in a weakening of the Warsaw deployment. Ironically, much of the planning of these reforms was the result of work done by Alexeyev, who then championed a strong military presence in Poland. In 1910, the Russian Army moved to a system where army units were more strongly associated with specific regions of Russia, and were usually stationed in such regions during peacetime. This was a far simpler arrangement than before, and closely reflected how matters were organised in other European powers. It also ensured that more Russian troops were deployed near major population centres within the Russian Empire, where they had been needed during the unrest in 1905. The disadvantage of the new scheme was that it would take far longer for the Russian Army to move westwards after the completion of mobilisation, thus greatly hindering Alexeyev's plans for possible early offensive operations.

There was widespread criticism of Danilov's 1910 plan from a number of parties. One of the most controversial parts of the plan was the abandonment of the seven major fortresses that protected the Polish salient and its rear area. Four of these (at Zegrze, Novogeorgievsk, Warsaw itself, and Ivangorod) had been intended to protect the forward concentration area of the Russian Army, while the other three (at Brest-Litovsk, Grodno and Kovno [Kaunas][19]), shielded lines of communication from the east. Originally built in the 1880s, these fortresses were widely regarded as obsolete, and would require lavish expenditure if they were to be modernised. For Sukhomlinov and Danilov, this merely confirmed their view that the fortresses should be abandoned and destroyed, but the artillery establishment wished to station large numbers of heavy guns in the fortresses, and objected strongly. They found allies in Alexeyev, who saw the abandonment of the fortresses as a fatal blow for his plans for forward concentration, and General Nikolai Klyuev, Chief of Staff of the Warsaw Military District, who did not want to have his region's prized assets eliminated. Despite the daunting cost of modernising the fortresses (estimated in 1908 at a staggering 800 million roubles – roughly double the entire army budget) and the demands of the artillerists to position 5,000 heavy guns in the fortresses (leaving fewer than 500 for the rest of the army), Sukhomlinov was overruled.[20] The fortresses would stay in existence, even though General Georgi Skalon, Klyuev's commanding officer in Warsaw, simultaneously admitted that while the defence of Poland was almost impossible the abandonment of the salient was also, to him, politically unthinkable.[21] Nevertheless, limited funds prevented a wholesale modernisation of the fortresses, and Sukhomlinov was able to insist that refurbishment of only the rearmost fortresses was carried out.[22]

Sukhomlinov could doubtless console himself that things might have been worse, if the dreams of other fortress enthusiasts had been given free rein:

> On this subject, I recall an absurd project, elaborated ... in 1909 within the walls of the Engineers' Castle [the Mikhailovsky Castle in St Petersburg] under the aegis of a reputable military engineer, an extremely gifted man; amongst other things, he proposed to cover Russian territory with an interlocking network of fortresses. The maintenance of such a labyrinth of fortresses to a roughly modern standard would absorb the entire budget of the Empire, and all the Russian Army would be insufficient to garrison them. But that mattered little to him.[23]

The modernisation programme for the fortresses did not proceed in any systematic manner, and Danilov felt that the end product of this major area of expenditure was no significant improvement in the usefulness of the fortifications. He concluded:

> Seen from a technical point of view, our fortresses thus had no strength and consequently could only be a negative asset. They required strong garrisons, all the stronger due to the technical deficiencies [of the fortresses themselves]; they therefore substantially reduced the efficacy of the field army.[24]

In February 1912, Danilov and Sukhomlinov, accompanied by General Yakov Zhilinski, the current chief of the general staff, met the military district chiefs of staff in Moscow to consider an alternative to Danilov's 1910 plan. Two issues dominated the discussions. Firstly, the Russian Army was widely regarded as having improved its state of readiness for war. Ammunition stocks were at last beginning to improve, and there was a growing feeling that the years of vulnerability after the Russo-Japanese War were coming to an end. Secondly, there was a general view that the strategic situation had changed: the likelihood of Russia having to face the entire weight of the German Army was now regarded as far more remote. It was increasingly clear that the bulk of Germany's forces would be sent west against France. Even if a quick victory over the French were achieved, German losses would be sufficient to weaken them critically:

> Victorious or defeated, [France] will have inflicted such losses on the German Army that it will no longer be capable of a second major effort on a distant front. Thus the mass of Russian armies will find the path open before it. Even in defeat, the French Army will have delivered Europe from German hegemony.[25]

With only a small German force facing them, the Russians did not need to fear a German assault on their concentration areas, and could therefore afford to deploy further forward. Furthermore, it was important that Russia planned for an early offensive operation, for two reasons: the relatively weak German forces gave the Russians an opportunity for an early success, and a Russian attack would force the Germans to divert troops from the west, thus relieving the pressure on France.

However, there remained problems with a possible attack against Germany. The most easterly part of Germany, East Prussia, was rightly regarded as an area that would be easy for the Germans to defend – the presence of the Masurian Lakes would divide any potential Russian attack in two, allowing the defenders to concentrate against each half in turn. Even if East Prussia were captured, the Germans would have the option of withdrawing to their fortified positions along the lower Vistula. A drive towards the west from Poland, ultimately aimed at Berlin, would be vulnerable to attacks on its flanks, unless these were secured by advances both into East Prussia and Galicia. In view of these difficulties, Alexeyev argued, priority should be given to an attack against the Austro-Hungarian Empire. The relatively open terrain of Galicia offered better prospects for a Russian offensive than East Prussia. Furthermore, given the polyglot nature of Austria-Hungary with its deep-rooted ethnic tensions, there was a possibility of pro-Russian uprisings, especially amongst the Slav populations. Russian resentment and dislike of Austria-Hungary had steadily grown after the frustration of Russian ambitions in the Balkan region, and any Russian gains at the expense of Austria-Hungary might resurrect Russia's long-term ambitions relating to Constantinople and the gates of the Black Sea.[26] And, as will be seen, the Russians were in possession of the entire mobilisation plans of the Austro-Hungarian Empire.

There was perhaps a degree of self-interest in Alexeyev's arguments, as any offensive into Galicia would be from his military district. Nevertheless, the discussions in Moscow led to a new war plan, which contained two variations.

Plan A approximated to Alexeyev's preferred option, involving a major effort against Austria-Hungary. In the event of a threat from German troop deployments against Russia, with the bulk of the kaiser's forces attacking eastwards rather than into France, Plan G – a variant of Danilov's original defensive plan of 1910 – would instead be activated.

Plan A stipulated that twenty-nine Russian divisions would be deployed against East Prussia, rather than only twelve, as Alexeyev had wanted. This was partly at the insistence of Klyuev, the Warsaw District Chief of Staff, who was worried that without such a strong defensive force the Russians would be unable to withstand a German attack against Poland. This diversion of forces to face the German Army reduced the offensive power targeted against Galicia, where Alexeyev had intended to execute a grand encirclement of Austro-Hungarian forces by enveloping both flanks. An attempt to sweep past the northwest flank in particular invited the possibility of a German counterattack, and was felt to be too risky. Finally, the requirements of Russia's alliance commitments to France required an early Russian attack on Germany, in order to force German redeployment away from the west. Danilov was cautious about such demands from France, particularly if they required a Russian attack into East Prussia; he had received copies of the reports of a German war game that simulated such an attack, and in which the German defenders successfully used the Masurian Lakes barrier to defeat the Russian invasion in detail. Unfortunately for him, he was not involved in the regular meetings with French staff officers – this role was filled by Yakhov Zhilinski, who was not directly involved in the war planning process. The Russian Chief of Staff repeatedly told his French colleagues that Russia stood by its obligations, and would try to attack Germany no later than the 15th day after mobilisation (M+15). His apparent indifference to whether Russian planners heeded this, might reflect how sincerely he made the commitment to the French. But Zhilinski's assurances to the French were not entirely unreasonable. The forces to be deployed against East Prussia represented the part of the Russian Army that could be expected to be ready for operations at an early stage, and if the bulk of German forces were facing France, there were grounds for optimism about a swift advance across East Prussia to the lower Vistula. Once this was achieved, there would no longer be any German threat to the Russian forces attempting to drive into Galicia.

The consequence of these developments was a further conflict between competing themes: an attack against Austria-Hungary, and an attack against Germany. The former made good strategic sense, while the latter was an obligation of the alliance with France. A failure to assign priority to either resulted in neither being guaranteed sufficient forces to ensure success. In April 1914 Russian staff officers gathered in Kiev to conduct a strategic war game based upon Plan A. The game dictated that German forces in East Prussia attempted a spoiling attack on M+9, and that Russian forces launched a counterattack three days later; the significance of this was that the Russian counterattack was launched before the completion of mobilisation. The attack on East Prussia then developed with an advance either side of the Masurian Lakes. With British forces deploying against Germany in the west, German troops were diverted away from East Prussia, leading to Southwest Front moving forward its timetable for an attack against Galicia, again before mobilisation was complete.[27]

The war game had a decisive weakness, in that logistic arrangements were simply ignored. Officially, this was in order to simplify the conduct of the game, but in reality it was at least partly to spare the blushes of senior commanders, whose poor grasp of such matters was well known. As a result, the limitations of the Russian railway network did not feature as a restricting factor in operations. Also, the Russian mobilisation schedule gave priority to combat soldiers, and personnel intended for logistic units were far down the schedule. This delay in their mobilisation, again dictated by the limitations of the railways, would ensure that any logistical problems that arose at an early stage would be compounded by a shortage of suitable personnel to resolve them.

The insufficiency of the Russian railway system was a recurring theme in the decade before the onset of war. Whilst the total mileage of Russia's railways was impressive, it did not compare well with the density of systems elsewhere, particularly those of Russia's potential enemies in the west. Even without making allowances for the vastness of Russia, the railway was decidedly inferior. There were about 250 miles (402km) of railway per million population in Russia, compared with 600 miles (965km) per million in Germany, and 555 miles (893km) per million in the Austro-Hungarian Empire.[28] The amount of rolling stock was also far lower, the Germans planned to have 250,000 railway wagons available for mobilisation, while Russia, despite having to cope with a far larger area and greater distances, could only muster 214,000.[29] The essential infrastructure of the railways was weak. Signal boxes were further apart, and stations tended to be smaller. The Germans spent large amounts of money ensuring that the stations intended as disembarkation points for mobilisation possessed sufficient platforms for the long troop trains – even if the construction of these platforms provided the French with a clear idea of where Germany intended its concentration points to be. By contrast, some stations earmarked as disembarkation points for the Russian Army were expected to receive twenty trains a day, but their platforms could cope with no more than ten. Watering stations were further apart, and the rail beds themselves were relatively poorly constructed, as were many of the bridges over which the trains ran. Consequently, heavy traffic was certain to result in rapid deterioration of the railways, and the relatively small numbers of skilled railway personnel would be unable to cope with keeping the railways serviceable.[30]

An additional problem was the alignment of the Russian railways. The German and Austro-Hungarian lines were constructed with an eye to mobilisation against Russia (and in Germany's case against France). By contrast, the Russians deliberately chose to limit railway construction in the western parts of the empire, in order to hinder the rate at which a German invasion might progress. By 1914 there were only six double-track railway lines and two single-track lines running into the western frontier area, capable at most of handling 200 trains per day. The German and Austro-Hungarian networks, on the other hand, could deal with double this throughput.[31] Part of the problem, as Danilov wrote after the war, was the difference between peacetime and wartime requirements:

> Apart from the enormous distances, there was another huge difficulty to be surmounted: the important directions from a strategic point of view did not coincide with those required by the economic life of the country. One could almost say that Russia had need of two rail networks: one for times of peace and the material development of the country, and a second for use in a war.[32]

This statement is not entirely accurate, and given the time when it was written, it can be interpreted as an attempt to excuse the failures that occurred in 1914. Anxious to ensure a rapid Russian mobilisation, the French had watched with concern as Russia neglected her railways during the economically and politically troubled first decade of the century. In 1901 France financed a new line running from a point midway between St Petersburg and Moscow to the area to the east of Warsaw but, Russian officials only began to show interest in improving rail infrastructure at the beginning of the second decade. In 1912 the tsar signed an agreement with the French to increase rail lines approaching the western border by a total of nearly 550 miles, but did little to improve lines further to the east. A further agreement was signed with France for the financing of new lines in the Russian interior, but these would take many years to build. Contrary to Danilov's post-war comments, Vladimir Kokovtsov, the Russian prime minister in 1913, ensured that construction of these interior lines tended to proceed fastest where they satisfied peacetime economic requirements, rather than the requirements of mobilisation.[33]

The scale of Russian mobilisation was immense. It would see the peacetime army grow from 1.3 million men to 4.7 million, and over a million horses would be drafted. Over 4,000 troop trains would be needed, and consequently the mobilisation process would take far longer than in Germany or Austria-Hungary. Once the improvements in Russian railways – both towards the frontier and further inside Russia – were complete, Russian mobilisation would only take two or three days longer than German mobilisation. Aware of these plans, the Germans regarded them as a further indication that if war were inevitable, it would be better to fight sooner rather than later.

Despite the controversy that surrounds Sukhomlinov and whether he was an instigator or blocker of reforms, there was certainly considerable activity in the years leading up to the war. In order to increase the number of divisions available to the army, there were proposals to move from the existing structure of each division having four regiments each with four battalions, to a structure of three battalions per regiment. Sukhomlinov also oversaw the creation of a cadre within each division that could be used to help create the nucleus of reserve formations; thus the seventy first-line divisions would furnish personnel to lead thirty-five second-line divisions. This reform, though in keeping with practice in Germany and France, was widely opposed by Sukhomlinov's enemies, who undermined it in numerous ways, ensuring that the reserve divisions received poor-quality cadres and inadequate artillery. Nevertheless, a 'Great Programme' of reforms had commenced by 1913, which would ultimately have converted the army's eight-gun batteries into six-gun units and double the howitzer strength of each division from six to twelve (still short of the German eighteen). The shortage of artillery ammunition that had existed since 1906 began to be addressed, though there were fatal compromises. At a time when the French stockpiled 2,000 rounds per artillery piece, and German experts believed that their army's stocks of 3,000 rounds per gun might be inadequate, the Russians laboured to achieve a figure approaching 1,000 rounds. Much of this ammunition was held in a limited number of artillery parks, and with the relatively poor state of Russia's logistic services, even getting this relatively small amount of ammunition to the guns would pose considerable problems, should the Russian armies move far from their depots. Individual Russian armies were desperately short of ammunition. First Army, deployed to face East Prussia, had only 420 rounds per gun at the outset of the war, with the rest held some distance to the rear.[34]

The comparative lack of development of Russia held back the progress of reform. Iron production in all of Russia in 1910 came to a little over 3 million tons, compared to over 13 million tons in Germany. The lack of development was clearly noted:

> Despite the progress made by our industry, the development of some principle branches remained inadequate. Thus, for example, the output of our metallurgical plants, which even in times of peace, did not remotely correspond to the ordinary needs of the country ... thus the same growing need in the country for all types of machines and tools, resulting in major imports... Furthermore, despite our great wealth in minerals of all kinds, the production of lead, tin, aluminium, zinc and a few other metals necessary for war materiel was almost nil.[35]

The same applied to the chemical industry, on which munitions production critically depended. Furthermore, despite its vast size and long borders, Russia was in a disadvantageous position when it came to contact with the outside world. Many of its borders – most markedly in the north, and in the mountainous parts of Asia – did not allow for easy passage of commerce, with most trade being dependent either on the Black and Baltic Seas or the borders with Germany and the Austro-Hungarian Empire. Railway lines linking the northern ports of Archangelsk and Murmansk with the rest of European Russia were of very limited capacity, whilst that of the Trans-Siberian Railway was far too slow to allow for Russia's future allies to be able to sustain the Russian war effort via Vladivostok.

Other hindrances to the reform programme centred on the inefficiencies of the entire Russian system. Sukhomlinov was rightly criticised for not spending all of his budget in the years before the war. Even where money was spent, the Russian Army appeared to pay more than other nations for basic supplies. Sacks cost twice as much as in Britain, and boots were also more expensive, a problem worsened by a habit amongst soldiers of selling their boots to civilians and then drawing additional pairs from the supply depots.[36] The inability of Russian industry to fulfil contracts also contributed to a constant failure to spend the budget.

As was the case in Germany, Russia's conscription policy could have yielded more troops if it had been used more efficiently. Although conscription was intended to be universal, there were dozens of exemptions. Almost the entire Muslim population of Russia was allowed to pay a tax instead of service with the army, and the non-Slav populations of the far north, Finland, many of those living in Siberia and the Caucasus, recent immigrants, and the clergy were all exempt. About half of those remaining were excused service on the grounds that they were indispensable to their families, a reflection on the largely rural population of Russia. Many of those who might have become officers in the army were given reduced periods of service, for example, if they were studying medicine. There was widespread use – and almost certainly abuse – of further conditional or discretionary exemptions, with the result that the army was far smaller than it might have been:

> In 1914 Russia was only in a position to put into the field *one infantry division per 1,500,000 of her population*, while Germany and France put into the field *one infantry division per 500,000 of population*.
>
> Thus, despite her 170,000,000 population, in terms of her military strength Russia was only equal to 60,000,000 of her allies or foes.[37]

Given the financial pressures on the army budget, especially with nearly half of all expenditure being spent on the controversial fortress programme, it is unlikely that reforms in conscription to the same level as Germany and France would have been affordable. Nevertheless, changes were made, with the annual intake rising to 585,000 in 1914. Unlike recruits in earlier years, these men would remain in the army for three years, and would have a first-line reserve commitment of seven years, followed by a second-line commitment of an additional eight years.

The Guards regiments and the cavalry attracted many of the best officer recruits in the army. However, beyond these units the officers of the tsar's armies compared poorly with those of potential foes. Their pay was inferior, and during the closing years of the 19th century perhaps as many as one-third had not even completed the equivalent of primary school education.[38] Unlike in the armies of Britain, Germany and the Austro-Hungarian Empire, a large percentage of Russian officers up to the rank of colonel were from peasant or commoner backgrounds. The lower levels of literacy in Russia also resulted in non-commissioned officers (NCOs) who were far inferior to those in other countries. In Germany, the policy started by Moltke the Elder of encouraging leaders at every level to be trained to take over from their commanders in the event of casualties resulted in NCOs who were capable of taking command of battalions if required. This was something that the Russians could only marvel at.

Most of the divisions of the Russian Army in 1914 still consisted of four regiments, each with four battalions. In addition, each division had an artillery brigade of six batteries, most of which still had eight guns each. The division had two cavalry brigades, each consisting of two regiments (which in turn had two or three squadrons of men); once war started, these cavalry regiments would be detached and used to form new cavalry-only units, with their own artillery batteries. The equipment of these divisions had slowly improved, but ammunition stocks remained limited by the standards of Russia's potential enemies. But any future war would be short, everyone agreed, and there was therefore little need either to purchase substantial stockpiles or to build up sufficient industrial and chemical capacity for a long conflict.

The forces that faced Germany and Austria-Hungary were organised into several armies, which were in turn deployed as two groups, one in the north facing East Prussia and a second facing Galicia. The original draft of Mobilisation Order 18 effectively defined the troops that would compose these armies. The most northerly was First Army, commanded by General Pavel Karlovich Rennenkampf. He had commanded division and corps-sized units during the Russo-Japanese War, and had played an important part in preventing the collapse of the Russian left flank at Mukden. During this battle, he was accused by General Alexander Vassilievich Samsonov, commander of the neighbouring unit, of failing to support him, leading to a longstanding rift between the two men. Despite his personal successes in the war, Rennenkampf fell from favour as a consequence of the Russian defeat, though his energetic role in suppressing unrest after the 1905 Revolution resurrected his career. His army, which was formed by the mobilisation of the Vilno (Vilnius) Military District, had four infantry corps, with eight first-line divisions. In addition, the army was allocated seven second-line divisions, five cavalry divisions, and an independent cavalry brigade.

Immediately to the south of Rennenkampf was Second Army, commanded by none other than Alexander Samsonov, with whom Rennenkampf had argued in Manchuria. Whilst the stories of the two men coming to blows over the matter are almost certainly exaggerated, relations between them remained poor even in 1914. Their past quarrels undoubtedly played a part, but there were other reasons. Samsonov was a supporter of Sukhomlinov, while Rennenkampf – his Germanic name showing his heritage – was from the traditional group of families that had always supplied the armies of Russia with its senior officers, and was thus from the faction that opposed Minister of War Sukhomlinov. To complicate matters further, Rennenkampf's chief of staff was a member of the Sukhomlinov circle, while Samsonov's chief of staff was a traditionalist and opponent of Sukhomlinov. Formed from the Warsaw Military District, Samsonov's Second Army consisted of five infantry corps with ten first-line divisions, four second-line infantry divisions, and four cavalry divisions. The mission assigned to both Samsonov and Rennenkampf was to attack into East Prussia in order to destroy the limited forces that the Germans were expected to have left to defend the province. Given the expected difficulties with terrain and a railway network explicitly designed to help the German defenders, close cooperation between the two armies would be essential.

To the south of these Northwest Front armies were those of the Southwest Front. Fourth Army possessed eight first-line infantry divisions in four corps, with three second-line divisions and four cavalry divisions. The army commander was another Baltic German, General Anton von Saltza. To his southeast was yet another general from a German family, Pavel von Plehve, commanding Fifth Army. He had eight first-line divisions in four corps, with five second-line divisions and five cavalry divisions. Next in line was Third Army. Its commander was General Nikolai Vladimirovich Ruzsky, who had seen active service against Turkey in 1878 and against the Japanese in 1905. He was an ardent follower of Mikhail Dragomirov, and therefore was strongly filled with the importance of offensive operations, despite which he had a reputation for caution bordering on indecision. His army consisted of sixteen first-line divisions in eight corps, supported by five second-line infantry divisions, and nine cavalry divisions.

By 1913, these original mobilisation orders had been modified. The substantial forces of Third Army were divided into two roughly equal commands: the original Third Army under Ruzsky, and a new Eighth Army led by Alexei Alexeevich Brusilov, the 61-year-old Georgian whose grandfather had fought against Napoléon in 1812. He served with distinction in the war against Turkey, and managed to combine a career as a cavalry officer with initiating substantial improvements in training programmes.

Although considerable forces remained deployed for a strike into Galicia, there were structural weaknesses in these divisions. Most of the troops already positioned in Russian-occupied Poland were allocated to First and Second Armies, and; the armies of the Southwest Front, particularly the two most northerly armies, would only come up to strength when they received their mobilised reinforcements from distant parts of Russia, raised mainly in the Moscow and Kazan Military Districts. Any attempt at early offensive operations against the Austro-Hungarian forces in Galicia was therefore likely to be a perilous business.

The road that Russia followed to prepare and deploy its armies was thus strongly influenced by a multitude of often frequently conflicting factors. Fear of encirclement by potentially hostile powers contrasted with a desire for expansion, and the lure of Pan-Slavism both resulted in and was opposed by increasing tension with the Austro-Hungarian Empire. A healthy respect for the German

Army, bordering on unlimited awe, raised the danger of rapid German mobilisation and an early German assault before the Russian armies could be ready, but early Russian offensive operations against Germany were needed within the terms of the Franco-Russian Alliance. Given the slowness of Russian mobilisation, an early attack on either Austria-Hungary or Germany carried risks – yet the tsar's armies found themselves deploying to attack both at the same time. As will be seen, other tensions – rivalry within the Russian command system, and the general expectation that any war would be short and decisive – would conspire to ensure that any small chance of an early Russian victory disappeared.

CHAPTER 3

AUSTRIA-HUNGARY

The Other Sick man of Europe

In January 1853, prior to the Crimean War, Sir George Hamilton Seymour, the British ambassador in St Petersburg, had one of many meetings with Tsar Nicholas I. In a private conversation that followed, he asked the tsar for greater clarity about Russia's attitude towards Turkey. Speaking in French, the tsar replied:

> We have a sick man on our hands, a man gravely ill, it will be a great misfortune if one of these days he slips through our hands, especially before the necessary arrangements are made.[1]

This is often regarded as the origin of the description of the declining Ottoman Empire as 'the sick man of Europe', but the expression could have been applied with equal accuracy to another empire. Just seven years later, an article in the *New York Times* stated:

> The condition of Austria at the present moment is not less threatening in itself, though less alarming for the peace of the world, than was the condition of Turkey when the Tsar Nicholas invited England to draw up with him the last will and testament of the 'sick man of Europe.' It is, indeed, hardly within the range of probability that another twelvemonth should pass over the House of Habsburg without bringing upon the Austrian Empire a catastrophe unmatched in modern history since the downfall of Poland.[2]

Austria had been under the rule of a single family since the victory of Rudolf of Habsburg over King Ottokar II of Bohemia in 1278. Formally declared the Austrian Empire in 1804, the nation played a leading part in the defeat of Napoléon Bonaparte, and became increasingly involved in the German nationalist movement. In addition to the pressures of German nationalism, the Austrian Empire had struggled to cope with similar nationalist sentiments in many of its non-German provinces. The Hungarians rose up in rebellion as part of the wave of unrest that shook much of Europe in 1848. At first, Vienna was forced to concede several major reforms, not least because the Habsburgs were struggling to retain control of their own capital. However, once they had suppressed unrest in Vienna, the Austrians attempted to restore control over Hungary. Fighting raged into 1849, and it was only with the aid of Russia that the Austrians were able to prevail.

Ultimately, tensions between Austria and Prussia over leadership of the German nationalism movement led to the Austro-Prussian War of 1866. Defeat at the Battle of Königgrätz appeared to trigger the catastrophe anticipated by the *New York Times* six years earlier. In the wake of the disastrous war, there were repeated calls for Hungary to break away from the empire. With his armies weakened by their defeat, the Habsburg Emperor Franz Joseph I decided against risking another major war, and chose to negotiate. The resultant agreement established separate parliaments in Vienna and Budapest, responsible for their own internal affairs and with their own prime ministers. The Habsburg emperor – now with the title Emperor of Austria and King of Hungary – remained responsible for foreign affairs, military matters, and major financial issues. The terms of the agreement were to be renegotiated every ten years. The form of the army was debated at length. In an attempt to appease the wishes of Hungarians for their own army, it was agreed that the field army – now known as the *kaiserliche und königliche Armee* ('Imperial and Royal Army', often abbreviated to *k.u.k.*), rather than the Austro-Hungarian Army – would remain under the direct control of the emperor, but Austria and Hungary would have their own reserve forces, known as the *Landwehr* and *Honvéd* respectively. These would be allowed to wear uniforms and insignia that identified their direct nationalities. In contrast, units in the *k.u.k.* Army – regardless of their Austrian, Hungarian, or other ethnicity – would have no such identifying features.

In this manner, the Austrian Empire narrowly avoided the sort of catastrophe predicted in 1860, though major problems remained. The new Austro-Hungarian Empire, or Dual Monarchy, was home not only to Austrians and Hungarians, but also encompassed populations whose rights were – at least in theory –

protected by the new constitution. The empire comprised many different ethnic populations, including Germans, Hungarians, Czechs, Slovakians, Poles, Ukrainians, Serbs, Romanians, Croatians, Slovenes, and Italians. There were constant wrangles over which of them was to be given the status of having its language recognised as an official language of the empire. But these ethnic tensions, and the fear of further uprisings, often acted as a brake in some areas. Partly to prevent igniting new flames, the Austrian part of the empire tended to have a more accepting attitude to Jews than its neighbours. Although the Jewish population made up only 5 per cent of the total population of the empire, about 18 per cent of officers in the Austro-Hungarian Army reserves were Jewish, with many in senior positions.[3]

As industrialisation and economic growth increased the wealth of Europe, most major powers increased their military spending at least in line with their growing budgets. The Dual Monarchy was an exception. Between 1871 and 1914 Russian military expenditure tripled, while that of Austria-Hungary did not even double.[4] One consequence of this was that, at the beginning of this period, the Austro-Hungarian Empire could field thirty-two infantry divisions to face a likely twenty-nine Russian divisions, but by the eve of the First World War, whilst the *k.u.k.* Army had grown to forty divisions, the Russians were expected to deploy at least fifty.[5] At the heart of the empire's difficulties were the arrangements between the two parliaments. Expenditure on the army had to be approved by both, and whilst the Vienna parliament reluctantly agreed to increases in military spending, this was usually blocked in Budapest. The hostility to the army on the part of the Hungarian politicians, who were elected by a limited franchise in elections that were of dubious honesty, came from several sources. The domination of the army by German-speaking officers was a source of resentment, and there were constant calls for Hungarian to become an official language within the army alongside German. Compromises were arranged by which the language of command remained German, covering about eighty words and phrases essential for manoeuvre and fire control, but adoption of regimental languages, in keeping with the majority ethnicity within each regiment, was allowed for other purposes. Such compromises merely fed the demand for more change. There was also a desire for Hungarian units in the army to be allowed to display Hungarian uniforms and flags, despite the compromise previously worked out over the *Landwehr* and *Honvéd*. It is also striking that the Hungarians, who had resented their 'subjugation' by the Austrians, were far less accommodating of minorities than the Vienna parliament. Despite this unwillingness to fund the army of the empire, the Budapest parliament approved increased spending on *Honvéd* units.

In 1903, an attempt was made to pass a new law that would expand army recruitment and funding, the first such change since 1889. Trying to appease the Budapest parliament, Emperor Franz Joseph I agreed to some reforms, but this encouraged the Hungarians to hold out for greater concessions. After a further two years of wrangling, the emperor lost patience and appointed a minority government led by General Géza Fejérváry. Acting on Franz Joseph's instructions, Fejérváry threatened to introduce universal suffrage, which would have destroyed the monopoly of power held by the Hungarian gentry and their small core of supporters. Although the Budapest parliament agreed to increases in military spending, the bill was still held up repeatedly, and was not finally passed until 1912.

Even this late passage of the bill was only a result of increased tensions in the Balkan region. The opposition parties in the Budapest parliament, stridently nationalistic in tone, saw the threat to the Austro-Hungarian Empire as an opportunity to press for changes to the state that would lead to something resembling Switzerland or the USA. But the governing party decided that the threat to the integrity of the empire was too great, and allowed the bill to pass. The two years that followed were too short a time for the modest changes in the bill to have a significant effect.

As a result of these delays, the army entered the war in 1914 largely under the terms of the previous Common Defence Law of 1889. The restrictions placed upon military spending in this law meant that the army intake per year was limited to a little over 103,000 men, with another 31,000 serving in either the Austrian or Hungarian reserves. Nominally, service was for three years in the army and two in the militia, but financial constraints meant that most conscripts were sent on long-term leave after only two years' full-time service. As the population grew, it became common practice to find reasons to exempt individuals from their obligations; consequently, at a time when the French subjected 0.75 per cent of their population to military training every year, Germany 0.47 per cent, and even Russia 0.35 per cent, the figure for the Austro-Hungarian Empire was a mere 0.29 per cent. The only area where there were encouraging signs was the continued development of the Hungarian *Honvéd*. The Ludovica Military Academy was established in 1872 (though it had existed in a lesser form before that date), and officer cadets of the *Honvéd* received extensive training there in Hungarian. Although artillery units did not exist within the reserves, batteries of primitive Gatling-like machine guns were established in the 1870s, and steadily expanded.[6]

Of all the combatants in the coming war, the Austro-Hungarian Empire was unique in that its population was not inspired by any sense of national cohesion.

Whilst the Russian and Turkish Empires were also homes to many ethnic groups, they at least had the advantage of a single dominant people. The *k.u.k.* Army nominally owed its allegiance more to the emperor than to the state. Demoralised by its defeats in Italy and against Prussia, starved of funds and recruits, both Emperor Franz Joseph and his senior officers held onto the memory of 1848–49, when only the army had saved Habsburg rule during the unrest that swept much of Europe. It was inevitable that its leaders longed for a solution to the army's problems that might also address the declining authority of the empire itself.

The creator of the independent Austrian general staff was Friedrich von Beck-Rzikowsky, who was born in Freiburg in the Duchy of Baden in 1830. He was a division commander at the time of the Second Italian War of Independence, and subsequently spent a considerable amount of time in Prussia. It was there that he became a firm friend and disciple of Moltke the Elder, a friendship that continued even during the Austro-Prussian War. He had a long period of conflict with several ministers of war as he sought to establish an independent general staff, and when he took up the position of Chief of the General Staff in 1881, he was generally regarded as the only man capable of restoring the army to an adequate standard. In addition to reforming the general staff along German lines – to the point where he was accused by some of being a spy and agent of Germany – he instigated major changes to the way in which training and manoeuvres were carried out. He also worked closely with his German counterpart to draw up plans for an offensive war against Russia; while German forces advanced southeast from East Prussia, Austro-Hungarian units would drive northeast from Galicia, with the intention of encircling Russian troops in and around Warsaw. But in his later years in office it became clear that Beck-Rzikowsky was struggling to keep up with advances in technology. Although he remained a firm favourite of the emperor, he retired from service in 1906.

His successor, Franz Xaver Josef Conrad von Hötzendorf (usually known as Conrad), was the son of a retired cavalry officer. Given the dominant role that he played in shaping Austro-Hungarian plans and policy, a review of his career is worthwhile in that it illustrates the factors that helped shape his opinions. His father's own experiences played a major part in shaping Conrad's world view. Conrad senior had served as a cavalryman during the Napoleonic Wars, and was badly injured in a heavy fall while leading his regiment against civilians during the 1848 rising in Vienna. Shortly after, the regiment, which was largely recruited from Hungarians, sided with the Budapest rebels and fought against the Habsburgs. Whilst it was always likely that the child of an elderly cavalry officer – who was 59 when his son was born – would join the army, his mother insisted that he did not join the cavalry, and was always greatly anxious when she knew he was out riding. The rebellion of his father's regiment left Conrad with a firm belief that the army had to be held together, and throughout his life he resisted the demands of Hungarian politicians for greater control of their component of the *k.u.k.* Army.

Conrad attended the newly established War School from 1852, one of only fifty accepted each year from over 1,000 applicants. Here he was strongly influenced by Karl von Gold, a strong advocate of offensive operations.[7] He also had great regard for another instructor, Colonel Johann Waldstätten, who combined an imaginative understanding of the use of terrain with a fervent belief in the importance of the bayonet over accurate rifle fire.[8] Already an accomplished linguist, Conrad added Russian to his repertoire during his time at the War School, and established an early reputation for friendship and popularity with his fellow officers. Few were surprised when he graduated in 1876 at the top of his class, and joined the General Staff Corps.

Conrad was a keen naturalist as a child, and like many of his contemporaries he attempted to apply Darwinist theories to society at large, though he moderated social Darwinist views with those of philosophers like Arthur Schopenhauer. He served as a junior staff officer during the Austro-Hungarian occupation of Bosnia, where he learned yet another new language. By the time of his death he spoke not only German, Hungarian, and Russian, but also French, Italian, Serbo-Croat, Czech, English, and Polish. He was an accomplished sketch artist, and during an attachment to the Mapping Bureau in Vienna he was sent on a covert mission into Russian-occupied Poland, visiting many of the areas where armies would clash in the coming war.

Conrad repeatedly made a mark as an innovator. For example, as a junior officer he wrote an influential paper that advocated the adoption of a British-style officers' mess, with the dual purpose of reducing the costs of board and lodging for junior officers and improving unit cohesion and morale.[9] While serving as a staff officer in Lemberg (modern-day L'viv in the Ukraine), he persuaded his superiors to lease a tract of rough ground that could be converted into a permanent area for training exercises. Throughout this time he remained popular and respected, both with his peers and his superiors. Reflecting his interest in establishing unit-based messes for officers, he remained convinced of the importance of morale, and of the value of understanding individual soldiers and their motivation. An officer who was taught by Conrad in the War School, where he served as an instructor on tactics, recalled him opening the course with the words:

War is conducted by people. Whoever wants to understand war must therefore above all get to know the individual in his reaction to physical and mental influences.[10]

He was completely different from many of his contemporary instructors, engaging his students in novel and interactive discussions, with the result that many remained his friends and acolytes throughout their careers. This was particularly important in the context of the First World War, as many of those he taught in Vienna from 1888 to 1892 had risen to high rank by the time that hostilities broke out in 1914. Of the 100 officers he taught, fifty-one rose to the rank of at least major-general before the end of the First World War, and nine more to the rank of colonel. Five of his former students were appointed as corps commanders, thirty as division commanders, and fourteen as brigade commanders.[11]

Like almost all of his generation, Conrad was a firm adherent of offensive operations. He combined this with his social Darwinist views, defining the aim of warfare as the moral destruction of the enemy.[12] Although he stressed the importance of accurate rifle fire as a means of overcoming defences, he frequently quoted Suvorov's axiom of the superiority of the bayonet over the bullet. He accepted that far more casualties arose from rifle fire than bayonets, but maintained that training with the bayonet ensured that infantrymen were constantly aware of the importance of attacking and closing with the enemy. Similarly, though he acknowledged the value of digging in for defence, he deplored the instinct of many soldiers to dig in whenever possible, as this reduced the desire for further attacks. Like his contemporary the Prussian general Albrecht von Boguslawski, a leading military theorist, he taught that the effort of getting men out of entrenched positions in order to mount an attack was greater than the effort required to get attacking soldiers to press home their assault.

Conrad was aware that his approach to war would result in casualties, and he made no pretence of this. He refused to answer questions about what percentage of losses would make an attack fruitless, preferring to concentrate on the effect of casualties on the morale of the attackers. If a unit had high morale, it could sustain greater losses than a unit with low morale; the 'moral capability' of the troops should be regarded as the resource that was being spent, rather than their numbers. This allowed him to return to a favourite theme: the importance of raising morale amongst the troops, and continuing to mount offensive operations as long as morale remained high enough to do so.

As a result of his prodigious written output and the success of the courses he ran in the War School, Conrad became widely admired as a military writer and tactician, all the more remarkable in that he had never commanded significant bodies of troops in the field. In an attempt to remedy this he requested transfer to a combat formation, and took command of an infantry battalion in 1892. This post gave him full opportunity to put into practice all of his beliefs, a policy he followed as he rose to command a regiment in 1895. He remained convinced of the importance of morale, and his attempts in this direction, including the first provision of a daily hot meal for all soldiers, did much to bind his men to him. He rewrote many of his earlier works on tactics, but did little to change their essential substance. Offensive operations were the only way to win a war, and whilst future wars would result in extremely heavy casualties, these were inevitable and preferable to staying on the defensive.

When he was appointed to command a brigade in Trieste in 1899, Conrad was able to repeat his earlier plan, obtaining land to create a dedicated training area where he put his men through all manner of field manoeuvres. During this period, he took his thinking about offensive operations even further than before, encouraging his officers not to use terrain for concealment and protection, teaching that the primary purpose of allowing troops to lie down was to allow them to use their rifles more accurately rather than to take cover.[13] His only concession to the growing power of defensive firepower was to advise that attacks against machine guns should be undertaken by thinly dispersed, irregular groups of soldiers. During his tenure of office in Trieste he had his first experience of commanding troops in hostile conditions, when he had to order his men to suppress rioting in early 1902. This episode left him with a permanent distrust of Italy. A large proportion of the local population was Italian, and though Slovenes and Croatians as well as Italians were involved in the rioting, Conrad and other Austro-Hungarian officers chose to blame it mainly on the desire of the Italian population to break away from the empire.

During this period the infantry regulations of the army were rewritten, and it was inevitable that Conrad would play a part in this. The commission entrusted with the task was headed by Archduke Franz Ferdinand, the nephew of emperor. Franz Ferdinand carried out a two-step programme, in which a draft manual was circulated for comment before being finalised. Despite his previous views, Conrad contributed to a document that practically ignored the bayonet, and encouraged a degree of flexibility and initiative that was remarkably ahead of its time.

At about the same time Conrad looked at what lessons could be drawn from the British experience in the Anglo-Boer War. He concluded that British casualties and setbacks had been worsened by an adherence to rigid parade-ground discipline at the expense of realistic training in infantry warfare, but pointed out that the Boers, who fought an essentially defensive war, ultimately lost: it was only by mounting offensive operations that victory could be achieved. Whilst acknowledging the losses inflicted by Boer rifle fire, which many cited as a reason why offensive operations should be reconsidered, he argued that, offensive operations being essential, it would be necessary to accept such losses. Moreover, larger forces and greater use of artillery might help reduce casualties. However, another aspect of Conrad's personality was his apparent ability to hold contradictory views at the same time. Although he accepted the need for more powerful artillery components in army formations to suppress enemy defences, he simultaneously opposed the expansion of the artillery arm, preferring to spend the admittedly limited resources devoted to military expenditure on the infantry and cavalry.

After Trieste Conrad commanded an infantry division in Innsbruck. In the wake of a tour of the southern Tyrol his suspicions regarding Italian irredentists seemed to be confirmed, though he made a distinction between pro-Italian intelligentsia and the peasantry and soldiers, whom he regarded as completely loyal to the empire. Shortly after, his wife was diagnosed with and died from stomach cancer. This seems to have had a marked effect on him, leaving him with a more pessimistic outlook on life in general. His brilliant reputation within the army, too, was dimmed a little. The main Austro-Hungarian observer in the Russo-Japanese War, Lieutenant-Colonel Maximilian Czicserics von Bacsány, took the view that the lessons of this recent conflict were far more pertinent to future wars than those of the Franco-Prussian War, which had been the prime influence on Conrad's works on tactics.[14] It was entirely characteristic of Conrad's approach that he raised no objections to Czicserics' theories being tried out by his subordinates, though he personally regarded them as generally confirming his own views. In a future war the extension of the battlefront along the entire front line would make outflanking manoeuvres almost impossible, so attacks would be costly, frontal affairs. The ever-increasing effectiveness of defensive firepower merely accentuated the importance of morale and numbers. The Russians lost the war, Conrad and Czicserics agreed, because they adopted a passive, defensive attitude. This had to be avoided at all costs.

By late 1906 Emperor Franz Joseph had handed over increasing authority to his nephew and heir Franz Ferdinand. The archduke had admired Conrad for many years, and he now summoned him to offer him the post of Chief of the General Staff. In this post Conrad's wider worldview began to have an influence. He regarded the army as an expression of the nation's inner strength, and thus concluded that its success in offensive operations would increase the nation's strength – just as a tactically defensive policy was inferior to an offensive policy, so a passive foreign policy was inferior to an aggressive and assertive one. He therefore repeatedly urged the foreign minister, Alois Lexa von Ährenthal, to plan offensive wars that could be won by the army. Recognition of threats, and a readiness to oppose them, were the only means for a nation's survival:

> The recognition of the struggle for existence as the basic principle of all events on this earth is the only real and rational basis for policy making… Whoever remains blind to the mounting danger, or whoever recognises it but remains too indolent to arm himself, and is too undecided to deliver the blow at the proper moment, deserves his fate.[15]

There was another more personal motive for Conrad to encourage wars of aggression. After meeting Gina von Reininghaus, the wife of an industrialist, Conrad started a long-term affair. With several children, his mistress was unwilling to leave her husband, and in any event the moral standards of the day would have made it very hard for Conrad to marry her without risking public disgrace. In an extraordinary collection of love-letters, most of which he never sent to her, he repeatedly expressed the hope that a victorious war would raise his personal prestige to a level where he could overcome such social approbium.

To date, Conrad's career had brought him into contact mainly with military men, and he found his new role much more difficult. An early opponent was Franz von Schönaich, the War Minister. Fundamentally, the two agreed on the need for greater military funding, but Conrad's lack of political experience and understanding led him to blame Schönaich for the failure of the Vienna and Budapest parliaments to agree increased spending on the army. Nevertheless, he proved to be skilled at establishing new working arrangements, ensuring that he had direct contact not only with the ministers in charge of the *Landwehr* and *Honvéd* but also with military attachés around the world. But in his desire to fight offensive wars, he clashed directly with Franz Ferdinand, who had been instrumental in his appointment. The archduke believed that the army's primary role was to help bolster the state internally, and he therefore was against foreign adventures. Consequently, he did not support Conrad's suggestion in 1907 that Austria-Hungary should take advantage of Russia's weakness in the wake of the Russo-Japanese War and launch an attack on Italy, to settle the lingering issues between the two states – the threat of Russian intervention had always been a brake on any such proposals in the past. The two also disagreed on the development of the Austro-Hungarian Navy. Conrad resented the amount of money spent on a relatively small number of warships, while Franz Ferdinand regarded the development of a modern battle-fleet as a matter of national prestige.

As Chief of the General Staff, Conrad had opportunities to put into effect many of the reforms he had proposed in his numerous publications. Field exercises had long been a target of his zeal, as he regarded them as completely unrealistic. Like other armies, the *k.u.k.* Army had adopted a policy of 'staff rides', in which officers spent long hours in the saddle, riding across the landscape as if accompanied by their various units, with umpires deciding the outcome. The exercises were normally run over three days to a pre-written script; the start line for each army at the beginning of each day was decided in advance, without any regard to the events of the previous day. Conrad replaced this with a continuous exercise that took account of the victories and setbacks of the previous day, but a failure to umpire the exercises properly reduced their value. Casualties were generally underestimated out of a conscious awareness that heavy losses would make offensive operations difficult to sustain. In order to impress Conrad and other senior officers, unit commanders often subjected their men to forced marches that might be sustainable for the duration of a field exercise of a few days but were utterly unrealistic in a prolonged campaign. This led to false expectations of how quickly armies might be able to move.

One of the most important tasks entrusted to Conrad was planning for future mobilisation and war. This was the responsibility of the *Operationsbüro* of the General Staff, and was controlled by Joseph Metzger, a protégé and ardent supporter of Conrad. The empire faced three possible threats: a war in the Balkans, a war against Russia, and a war against Italy. Three plans, prefixed with the letters B, R, and I respectively, had existed for many years to cover these eventualities; Conrad now devised a complex mobilisation system around these. The army would consist of three mobilisation groups, which could be activated in a variety of combinations. The first group, or *A-Staffel*, consisted of nine army corps, with twenty-eight infantry and ten cavalry divisions; the second group, or *B-Staffel*, had another four corps with twelve infantry and one cavalry divisions; and the third group, *Minimalgruppe Balkan*, had three corps with eight infantry divisions. The third group was assigned a defensive role to prevent Serbia and Montenegro from taking advantage of a wider conflict to attack Austria-Hungary, while the *A-Staffel* was envisaged as the main strike force for an offensive war against either Russia or Italy. The *B-Staffel* would be available to reinforce either group. In a rare concession to the value of diplomacy, Conrad acknowledged that a simultaneous war against Russia, Italy, and Serbia was an impossible proposition, and that it was the role of the empire's diplomats to prevent such a catastrophe.

Mobilisation plans involved the call-up of soldiers of any or all of the three groups. The limitations of the Austro-Hungarian rail network resulted in the *A-Staffel* being given priority, as the largest force. This would inevitably result in delays before the *B-Staffel* was available for deployment. Furthermore, in an attempt to simplify their planning task, the officers responsible for organising rail transport decided that all trains would run at the same slow speed. This added new delays to mobilisation, and the complexity of drawing up plans that reflected the flexibility required – with possible options to deploy against Serbia, Russia, or Italy – was such that the task was simply abandoned. Once mobilisation began any redeployment of troops from one front to another would be a difficult and time-consuming exercise.

In the event of a war with Russia the intention was to mass troops in Galicia, around Lemberg (L'viv). From here they could be directed either to attack between the Rivers Vistula and Bug, in order to threaten a southern envelopment of Russian positions in and around Warsaw, or to move northeast towards Dubno, separating Russian forces along the Ukrainian frontier from those in the centre. The predicted deployment of Russian forces, however, would leave the flank of either of these thrusts vulnerable. If an attack was mounted to the north, there was a threat to the eastern flank, while any attack to the northeast faced a threat to its western flank. The only way that either operation could be executed was for both operations to be mounted at the same time. This was clearly beyond the capabilities of the *k.u.k.* Army, and Conrad opted for the attack towards Warsaw. The protection of its eastern flank would have to rely on tardy Russian mobilisation. A further problem was that neither thrust on its own promised to deliver a decisive victory. An advance to isolate Warsaw only made sense if the Germans mounted a similar operation from the north, while an attempt to isolate Russian troops in the Ukraine merely left the advancing *k.u.k.* Army in an increasingly vulnerable salient. The lack of any clear, achievable objective might have led to a rethinking of the entire strategy of mounting an attack in the first place, but for Conrad mounting an offensive operation was such an important objective in itself that any thought of abandoning such a plan was anathema.

Italy was nominally an ally of the Austro-Hungarian Empire, but there were few illusions about the reliability of this alliance in either Vienna or Rome. Conrad and most other senior Austro-Hungarian figures rightly calculated that the only country on which they could rely completely was Germany, and Conrad and the younger Moltke met frequently. Although the Germans promised to support an Austro-Hungarian attack on Russia with an attack of their own out of East Prussia, there was no unified war plan. The commitment of the Germans to an eastern offensive was regarded as far less certain an event in Berlin than in Vienna. Just as there was no comprehensive sharing of information between the Germans and the Austro-Hungarians, there were communications issues within Austria-Hungary itself. In 1911 Italy attacked Turkish possessions in the Mediterranean, seizing control of Libya. Conrad felt that Italian commitment to this adventure was as an ideal opportunity to put into effect his plans for an offensive war against Italy, only to meet resistance at every turn. Unknown to him, Vienna had already conceded Libya to Italy in secret talks in 1902, something that was kept from him by Foreign Minister Ährenthal. In the aftermath of the rows that erupted in Vienna when he became aware of this, Conrad was dismissed as Chief of the General Staff on 2 December 1911. His replacement was General Blasius Schemua.

Schemua's tenure of office proved to be short-lived. In the aftermath of Turkey's defeat by Italy, Serbia, Montenegro, Bulgaria, and Greece formed the Balkan League, and the First Balkan War, between the four nations of the League and Turkey, broke out in the autumn of 1912. At the height of the crisis, Conrad was recalled as the threat of general war grew greater. As before, he advocated aggressive, preventive wars, and was deeply disappointed when the First Balkan War (1912–13) came to an end without Austro-Hungarian involvement. An opportunity had been lost, he felt, for the army to win prestige, which would have helped the entire empire to overcome its internal divisions by taking collective pride in asserting itself on its neighbours. However, a far greater setback to Conrad came with the discovery of a high-placed spy within the military hierarchy.

Colonel Alfred Redl came from a relatively poor background and was twelve years younger than Conrad; he passed through the War School a year after Conrad ceased to be an instructor. Redl developed a reputation as being an expert in Russian matters, and in 1900 he was assigned to the Russian Group of the General Staff's Intelligence Bureau. As an intelligence officer he introduced many innovations, such as covert cameras, recording and keeping fingerprint records of persons who might prove to be useful, and even using wax cylinders to record conversations.

In about 1901 Colonel Nikolai Batyushin, the head of Russian intelligence in Warsaw, learned that Redl, who was in the city at the time, was homosexual. Batyushin blackmailed him into providing information. Whilst blackmail may have been the main initial motive for Redl's treason, lavish payments followed, allowing the colonel to live a lifestyle far beyond the reach of his pay. In 1902 Redl gave the Russians full details of Austro-Hungarian plans for a war against Russia. When the Austro-Hungarian Intelligence Bureau discovered that the Russians had received copies of the plans, the head of the bureau, General von Gieslingen, appointed Redl to investigate the source of the leak. Terrified that his own treason might be uncovered, Redl discussed the matter with his Russian controllers, who gave him the names of several minor Russian agents in Austria. The capture of these agents allowed Redl to remain undetected as a spy, and even enhanced his reputation and access.

By 1907 Redl had risen to be the head of the counter-intelligence arm of the Intelligence Bureau. In addition to war plans, he handed over details of Austro-Hungarian mobilisation schedules and fortifications to the Russians. He betrayed many agents within Russia, who were arrested and executed. By 1912 he owned several apartments in Vienna, an estate outside the city, and a large house in Prague, as well as several of the most expensive automobiles in the world.

Payments were sent to Redl by post, with letters first being sent to Eydtkuhnen, a German town near the Russian border, from there they were posted to the central post office in Vienna, to be collected by a person calling himself Nikon Nizetas – one of Redl's aliases. In 1913, after Redl had been replaced as chief of counter-intelligence by Major Maximilian Ronge, one such letter was opened after Redl failed to collect it. The letter, containing a large amount of money, was passed to Ronge, who initiated an investigation. The letter was returned to the post office and an electric button was installed, to be pressed when such a letter was collected.

In May 1913 a second letter arrived in the Vienna post office. When the alarm button was pressed, counter-intelligence officers attempted to pursue the individual who collected the letter, only to lose him when he boarded a taxi. Just when they were about to give up and return to their office, the police officers were hugely relieved when the same taxi return. The driver informed them that he had taken the man to the nearby Hotel Klomser. Inside the taxi they found a penknife sheath, and showed this to the hotel manager, asking him to inquire of the guests as to whether any of them had lost it. They were stunned when their former boss, Alfred Redl, appeared.

The startled counter-intelligence officers hurried back to their headquarters, where they informed Ronge of their shocking discovery. Ronge briefly spoke to his superiors, and then returned to the Hotel Klomser with his men. Redl had realised that he had been discovered, and greeted Ronge cordially. He was writing some farewell letters, he explained, and asked for a moment to complete them. When Ronge attempted to question him about the extent of his treason, he told Ronge to go to his house in Prague, where he would find the answers to all his questions. He then asked Ronge for the use of a revolver and a single bullet, and shot himself.

Redl's death was unwelcome for various reasons. Franz Joseph, a devout Catholic, deeply regretted his death in a state of mortal sin, while many military figures were frustrated that they had not had the opportunity to question the traitor. Inevitably, the authorities tried to cover up the affair, and equally inevitably, they failed. One of the hotel staff told the press what he had seen, but a far greater leak occurred in Prague. Here, the counter-intelligence officers found a locked safe, and summoned a welder to help them force it. The welder happened to be a footballer in a major Prague club, who missed a match while helping break open the safe. Later, the man was interviewed by a sports reporter about his absence, and he told the journalist what he had been doing at the time. The journalist managed to make the connection with the brief news items about Redl's suicide in Vienna. In the house Ronge's personnel found thousands of secret documents that they had to assume had been shown to the Russians. They also found expensive perfumes, women's clothing, and photographs of Redl and other Austro-Hungarian officers in compromising positions, many of them dressed in women's underwear.

Remarkably, few had ever questioned how Redl came to be so wealthy, apparently accepting his own explanation that he had been left a substantial amount of money by a relative. Considering that he was the son of a lowly railway official, this explanation might have been questioned more closely. It is estimated that the Russians alone paid Redl the equivalent of £2.4 million ($3.8 million) in today's currencies, with additional funds from the French and Italians. Redl had a prolonged affair with an army lieutenant, whom he claimed was his nephew; once again, nobody appeared to question whether this was true. The only person to be punished was the lieutenant, who was sentenced to three months' hard labour and reduced to the ranks.[16]

Conrad was informed that Redl was a spy even as the arrest was being made. He was instrumental in trying to keep the matter quiet. When Franz Ferdinand demanded that senior officers should be sacked, Conrad flatly refused, even threatening to resign himself. He may have had personal reasons for preventing a detailed investigation. One of Redl's emissaries for passing documents to the Russians was Čedomil Jandrić, a friend of Conrad's son Kurt, and it has been suggested that Conrad may have wished to keep the scandal firmly away from his own family.[17] Emperor Franz Joseph himself was profoundly shocked and depressed by the entire affair. He had forbidden his own secret service from using sexual blackmail, and to find that one of his own officers had been recruited by such measures was a further sign that the world was changing in unwelcome ways.

The consequences of Redl's treason have been the subject of debate ever since. He passed full details of Austria-Hungary's mobilisation plans, and wartime deployments, to the Russians, who in turn passed on relevant parts to Serbia. But many of these details could have been anticipated, and the more extreme suggestions – that Redl was responsible for the slaughter of Austro-Hungarian troops in the opening battles of the war – require a link to be made between knowing the plans and taking specific measures to counter them. Whilst the intelligence he passed may have allowed the Serbians to determine the strength of the attack they faced, this can hardly have come as a surprise to them; it is likely that their defensive plans were largely unaltered by this intelligence windfall. Perhaps the biggest military impact was that Conrad ordered a change in the mobilisation plans for the *A-Staffel*, so that if it were deployed against Russia, most of its troops would disembark in western rather than eastern Galicia. The trains carrying the troops into Galicia generally ran from west to east, so this was a relatively simple measure to implement, merely requiring the men to disembark at earlier stations. It proved to have serious consequences in August 1914.

As the First World War approached, Conrad's relationship with Franz Ferdinand deteriorated greatly. The archduke, who became Inspector General of the armed forces in 1913 and would become the commander-in-chief if war broke out, was a traditionalist, insisting on ending the annual field exercises with a grand cavalry charge, which Conrad regarded as 'a spectacle for laymen and children'.[18] Franz Ferdinand also demanded the presence of all senior officers at mass on Sundays, even if this disrupted the field exercise; Conrad refused to attend. By the end of 1913 friends of the two men had to intervene to try to prevent Conrad from submitting his resignation. In spite of this, the chief of staff wrote to Franz Ferdinand in September stating that he felt unable to continue in his role. Franz Ferdinand wrote back immediately, begging him to reconsider. He cited the close relationship that Conrad had developed with the Germans, particularly with Kaiser Wilhelm II, but it took the intervention of Emperor Franz Joseph to persuade Conrad – reluctantly – to withdraw his resignation. Just a month later, when Franz Ferdinand and Conrad joined Kaiser Wilhelm and the younger Moltke in Leipzig to commemorate the famous victory over Napoléon in 1813, the archduke grew resentful of the open friendship between

Conrad and Wilhelm, and publicly criticised his chief of staff, to the consternation and embarrassment of their German hosts.

By the end of the year Conrad was increasingly pessimistic about both his personal prospects and those of the empire. Romania was distancing herself from Austria-Hungary, and it became clear that even neutrality on the part of Romania in any future war between Russia and Austria-Hungary could not be guaranteed. Despite his repeated attempts, he had not succeeded in engineering any of the preventive wars that he regarded as essential to solve the internal divisions within the empire, or to advance his own chance of a happy outcome with his mistress Gina, and he doubted the ability of the empire to survive:

> I believe more and more that our purpose ultimately will only be to go under honourably ... like a sinking ship.[19]

There was a general feeling of pessimism towards the future throughout higher circles in Vienna, and there were even suggestions that Franz Joseph had been cursed. During the strife that preceded the creation of the Dual Monarchy, he had ordered the execution of the son of the Countess Karolyi, who then indeed cursed the emperor in a dramatic manner:

> May Heaven and Hell blast your happiness; may you be smitten in the persons of those you love best; may your children be brought to ruin and your life wrecked, and yet may you live on in lonely, unbroken, horrible grief, to tremble when you recall the name of Karolyi![20]

The emperor's wife, Elizabeth, was assassinated by an Italian anarchist in 1898, a tragedy preceded by other deaths in the imperial family. The oldest child of Elizabeth and Franz Joseph, Sophie, died aged two in 1857, and their only male child, Rudolf, committed suicide with his mistress in 1889. Other members of the Habsburg family also met untimely ends. Maximilian, the brother of Franz Joseph, was executed in Mexico in 1867, and a favourite niece died when her dressing gown caught fire in the palace of Schönbrunn. Combined with the ongoing political tensions within the empire, many believed that the emperor would be the last man to rule, and that he was one of the few forces holding the realm together. This undoubtedly contributed to Conrad's desire to reunite the empire by means of a successful foreign adventure.

Despite this mood of pessimism, there was also a curious feeling almost of complacency throughout the empire. The Czech regions were amongst the most strident to press for additional rights, many of which were conceded by Vienna, but although there were periodic protests, there was little violence, and certainly none on a scale that might have threatened the unity of Franz Joseph's realm. In 1891, Prince Karl Schwartzenberg, a senior Austrian diplomat, discussed the future of the empire's Czech people with the prominent nationalist Edward Grégr, and the latter could not disagree with Schwartzenberg's conclusions:

> What will you do with your country, which is too small to stand alone? Will you give it to Germany, or to Russia, for you have no other choice if you abandon the Austrian union.[21]

This analysis highlighted the fundamental truth of the Austro-Hungarian Empire: for all its problems, it was a well-managed realm, with good infrastructure, a growing economy, and relative freedom of expression and association. Even within the troubled province of Bosnia-Herzegovina, the record of the imperial administration was good, with large sums spent on infrastructure and industrialisation. Nevertheless, the pessimism of individuals like Conrad about the future persisted.

Further discouragement for Conrad followed in May 1914 when he met Moltke the Younger. The German Chief of the General Staff advised Conrad that Germany remained confident that the first part of its war plan, requiring a major attack against France, would be finalised in six weeks, allowing the bulk of German forces to be switched to the east before Russian mobilisation was complete. Conrad had hoped for additional German troops in the east from the outset, as he calculated that the changed political situation in Romania would mean that the Russians would not have to commit so many troops to protect Moldova. The following month he gloomily wrote: 'We are nothing more than a satellite of Germany.'[22] Despite this, he remained committed to an offensive doctrine in the army. Unable to engineer the sort of minor war that he had hoped would strengthen the empire, he now faced the prospect of a major war against Russia – the largest of the potential enemies that Austria-Hungary faced – with limited early support from Germany.

Conrad therefore played a greater part in his nation's preparations for war than any other figure in any country. His influence ranged from training and doctrine, through troop welfare, to planning for mobilisation and deployment for war, and influencing many of the politicians who would make the decisions that would lead to war. It is a testament to his personal charisma and popularity that many ordinary Austrians did not hold him responsible for the disasters that followed, though some politicians had opposing views. Otto Bauer, leader of the post-war Social Democrats, said in 1925:

> If we are listing the five or six men in all of Europe who bear the primary guilt for the outbreak of the war, one of these five or six men would be Field Marshal Conrad.[23]

There can be no question that he repeatedly sought winnable external wars as a solution to Austria-Hungary's internal divisions, and the failure of Austro-Hungarian politicians to deliver such wars contributed greatly to his sense of pessimism for the future of the empire. Nevertheless, his encouragement of an aggressive foreign policy contributed to the increasing tension in the Balkans, and thus to the steps that ultimately led to European-wide war. Immediately after the war, there was a sense that some of Conrad's pre-war predictions had bordered on prophetic. More recently this view has been strongly challenged, and it has been argued that his own actions made the events that he warned of more likely.[24] Whilst his assumptions about the possible hostility of countries such as Romania and Italy may have been correct, there was no inevitability that this hostility would result in war.

Despite Conrad's attempts at modernisation, the *k.u.k.* Army remained in poor shape to fight a major war. Its divisions generally consisted of two brigades, each with two regiments of four battalions. The artillery complement of the division was about forty-two guns of varying calibres, and the total strength of the division came to about 15,000 men. Cavalry was organised into divisions of about 7,000, with twenty-four light field guns and a small number of machine guns. The only area in which the Austro-Hungarian forces might have been regarded as having an advantage was in mountain artillery, where they had pioneered the use of small, mobile guns that could easily be taken apart and reassembled. However, there were no significant mountainous areas where these might give Conrad's men an edge in a war against Russia.

Like many of the German chiefs of staff, Conrad had little time for the massed cavalry formations so beloved by traditionalists. Another area that drew him into conflict with traditional thinking was his early recognition of the potential of aerial reconnaissance, though his efforts in this field resulted in only modest numbers of flying machines being purchased. But despite compiling a detailed analysis of the Franco-Prussian War, he was not a strong advocate of artillery, resulting in this arm – which would be so crucial in the coming war – being comparatively neglected. The artillery, he maintained, made little contribution to the Prussian victory. He noted, for example, that the Prussian Guards prevailed at St Privat without use of artillery support in their attack. His analysis conveniently ignored the intervention – somewhat belated – of the Prussian artillery in the battle. The success of the Prussian Guards, he felt, highlighted the value of the offensive spirit. Such an analysis took no account of the terrible casualties suffered by the attacking infantry, and made little attempt to consider how these losses might have been reduced with proper artillery support.

It is a measure of Conrad's limitations at the highest strategic level that he failed to grasp the impossibility of rapid mobilisation given the state of the Dual Monarchy's railway system. Although the network across Austria, and much of western Hungary, was of a high standard, it deteriorated significantly at greater distances from the centre. Good lines had been created running through the Carpathian Mountains to Galicia, and stations enlarged to allow for longer trains, in the first years of the 20th century. But thereafter growing concerns about a possible war with Italy resulted in most railway expenditure being diverted to the Alpine railways. The expansion of the Russian railway system meant that by the outbreak of war Russia would be able to run over 250 trains a day to the common frontier, whereas Austria-Hungary could only manage 153.[25] For a war with Serbia, the situation was even worse. Only a single railway line ran across Bosnia-Herzegovina, and although two more were approved in principle, wrangles about funding meant that work had not even commenced by the outbreak of war. Despite this, Conrad continued to plan for a strike against Serbia that could deliver a killing blow before Russian mobilisation was complete.

The units of the *k.u.k.* Army would be organised into six armies and the separate *Armeegruppe* Kummer. Many of the formations were commanded by close friends and associates of Conrad. This inner circle, deeply steeped in Conrad's offensive doctrine, formed the men who would have to fight a swift war before Russian mobilisation was complete. Victory depended upon speed of mobilisation and rapid success on the battlefield. The limitations of the railways, and miscalculation at the highest level, hindered the first; the second proved to be as elusive as it was elsewhere during the coming war.

CHAPTER 4

OVER THE BRINK

The events that brought Europe into the First World War have been studied at huge length. The rising tension between Serbia and the Austro-Hungarian Empire ensured that the latter would feel obliged to act after the assassination of Archduke Franz Ferdinand on Sunday, 28 June 1914. Even the Serbs were aware of possible repercussions. It appears that the Serbian government knew of the plans to take the archduke's life, as Ljuba Jovanović, a government minister at the time, later recalled:

> One day, [the Prime Minister of Serbia, Nikola] Pašić said to us ... that there were people who were preparing to go to Sarajevo to kill Franz Ferdinand.[1]

Whilst there were many, particularly amongst the Serbian military, who actively supported the insurgents in Bosnia-Herzegovina, Nikola Pašić was not amongst them. Indeed, it seems that he made attempts to send a warning to the archduke. Jovan Jovanović, the Serbian ambassador in Vienna, was instructed to persuade Franz Ferdinand not to visit Sarajevo, and a week before the assassination, he met Leon Biliński, the Austro-Hungarian Finance Minister. Jovanović advised against the imminent visit, on the grounds that it was too close to the anniversary of the battle of Kosovo, an event of great importance to Serbs, and might be inflammatory. The message was far too ambiguous; there was no clear articulation of any threat, and to cancel the visit on the basis of this warning might even have been seen as a sign of weakness. As a result, Biliński did not pass the message on.

The impact of such a high-level assassination has been compared with the sense of shock in the USA after the attacks of 11 September 2001. Franz Ferdinand had been a very reserved person, without much popular support, but his death was regarded as a blow directed at the heart of the Empire. There was universal agreement within Austria that a response was needed, and in the second decade of the 20th century it was inevitable that this would involve military action. If such action came, Conrad would effectively be the commander of Austro-Hungarian forces. Franz Ferdinand, the commander designate, was dead, and any successor appointed by the emperor would inevitably defer to the prestigious Chief of the General Staff. Conrad pressed for immediate mobilisation, but was widely opposed by civilian figures, not least because they felt that public opinion needed to be prepared for war first. Nevertheless, Heinrich von Tschirschky, the German ambassador in Vienna, sent a telegram to Bethmann-Hollweg:

> Here, I hear even from serious-minded persons that matters must be settled once and for all with Serbia. One needs to give the Serbs a list of demands, and if these are not accepted, proceed energetically. I use every opportunity to urge quietly but forcefully against taking hasty measures.[2]

The kaiser added some comments in the margin of the telegram: 'Now or never' and 'The Serbian issues must be tidied up, and soon.' Next to Tschirschky's comments about urging caution, he wrote 'Who authorised him to say this? This is stupid!' It seemed that it was purely a matter of timing.

Reaction elsewhere in Europe was different. The Serbs distanced themselves from events; for years, the Prime Minister, Nikola Pašić, had tried to disassociate himself from the activities of more radical Serbian groups, mainly within the army, who actively fomented trouble across the border. There was widespread jubilation in Belgrade and other towns, which predictably caused great anger in Vienna. The Russians dismissed all suggestions that there was any Serbian involvement, and the ambassador in Belgrade even wrote to St Petersburg reporting that the local population were behaving with great sympathy for the victims of the assassination. In France, the assassinations were initially overshadowed by local news. The country was dealing with the trial and acquittal of the wife of the former Prime Minister Joseph Caillaux, who had shot and killed a newspaper editor who published love-letters from her to Caillaux when he was still married to another woman. What comment there was, suggested that the Austro-Hungarian Empire had brought its troubles upon itself by its treatment of Serbs. The London press tended to take a different view, agreeing that Vienna had a right to demand a thorough enquiry and more stringent control of militant groups by Serbia.[3]

The attitude of Russia and France in particular as the crisis developed was shaped considerably by their initial responses. Both countries accepted without question the denials of involvement from Belgrade, and also seemed to regard Franz Ferdinand as a leading light in the pro-war movement within the Austro-Hungarian Empire. The reality was that the archduke had been a strong voice calling for restraint in recent crises, and was also increasingly hostile to Conrad – had he not been assassinated, it is highly likely that he would have dismissed the Chief of the General Staff and appointed someone less bellicose to the post. He also made no secret of his intention on becoming Emperor of moving to a more federal model of government, with minorities such as the Romanians, Ukrainians, Czechs, and most importantly the Serbs and Croats, having their own regional assemblies. Had this happened, it would have weakened Serbia's claim to be the only voice of the Serbs in particular and the South Slavs – as the Slavic people of the Balkans were frequently called – in general. One diplomat remarked on the irony of the situation:

> Through his death he has helped *us* find the energy [for war] that he would never have found as long as he lived![4]

The importance of these nuances was that by accepting Serbian innocence and regarding Franz Ferdinand as an aggressor, it was natural for France and Russia to regard the entire crisis as an excuse by Austria-Hungary to pick a fight with Serbia. And given that both France and Russia regarded Vienna as little more than Berlin's puppet, it was equally natural to suspect that Germany lay behind the entire scheme.

The key to the issue was inevitably the attitude of Germany, and an early indication came on 1 July 1914. Victor Naumann, a German journalist and close friend of Gottlieb von Jagow, the German foreign minister, met Alexander von Hoyos, a senior figure in Leopold von Berchtold's Austro-Hungarian foreign ministry in Vienna. He told Hoyos that, in Germany's opinion, it was time to settle scores with Serbia, and that the Austro-Hungarian Empire could rely on German support. This was welcome news for Hoyos, who was a member of a grouping within the Foreign Ministry that believed strongly that an aggressive foreign policy, backed if necessary by military force, was the only way of preventing the demise of the Austro-Hungarian Empire. Tschirschky, the German ambassador in Vienna confirmed this in a conversation with Emperor Franz Joseph and Berchtold the following day.[5] Aware of the magnitude of the decisions that lay ahead, the emperor decided that he needed confirmation and dispatched Hoyos to Berlin. There, Hoyos passed the letters to the Austro-Hungarian ambassador, Count László Szőgyény-Marich de Magyar-Szőgyén et Szolgaegyháza, who took them with him to Potsdam, where he met Kaiser Wilhelm on 5 July.

The documents that Szőgyény presented to Wilhelm addressed issues that stretched further than the assassination. A letter from Franz Joseph to the kaiser – written before the assassination – expressed the fear that unless Austria-Hungary dealt with Serbia, the Dual Monarchy was unlikely to survive because of constant Serbian interference in Bosnia-Herzegovina. A setback here, the Austrians felt, would encourage other nationalities within the Dual Monarchy to demand freedom, bringing the entire empire to an end. The kaiser gave his personal support for action against Serbia, with the caveat that he should consult Chancellor Friedrich Bethmann-Hollweg. Later that day, he met both the Chancellor and Minister for War Falkenhayn, and they agreed that Vienna was clearly preparing to settle matters with Serbia. They also concluded that if this were done quickly, the likelihood of Russian involvement was minimal.

Hoyos had a discussion with Arthur Zimmermann, under-secretary in the Foreign Office in Berlin; after reading copies of the letters from Franz Joseph, Zimmermann apparently told Hoyos that Germany's support was certain, but contrary to the opinion of Wilhelm, Bethmann-Hollweg, and Falkenhayn, Zimmermann felt that there was a high probability – Hoyos quoted him as saying 90 per cent – of a European war.[6]

The following day there was a further meeting, involving Wilhelm, Hoyos, Bethmann-Hollweg, and Szőgyény. The Germans confirmed their support for Austria-Hungary, effectively giving their allies a 'blank cheque' for action against Serbia, and whatever may ensue.[7]

It seems that most senior figures in the German military, including Moltke the Younger, were on leave at the time. Kaiser Wilhelm summoned Generalleutnant Hermann von Bertrab, who was the quartermaster-general of the *Reichsamt für Landesaufname* (roughly the German equivalent of the British Ordnance Survey), to inform him that, in the kaiser's opinion, any conflict would be limited to Serbia and the Austro-Hungarian Empire, but the kaiser had given an assurance that Germany would support its ally and stand by its alliance obligations. This government department was only peripherally involved in military matters, and it seems that there was little discussion with other senior members of the general staff. Indeed, Moltke was advised that there was no need for him to return from leave, and his deputy, Generalmajor Georg Graf von Waldersee, was told that he, too, was free to depart for a few days in the country.

Back in Vienna, Conrad met Franz Joseph on 5 July, the day that Szőgyény first met Wilhelm. Although the decision-making process within Austria-Hungary was in the hands of civilian politicians and the emperor, Conrad's pre-war efforts to persuade his peers that war was both desirable and inevitable ensured that many of those involved in discussions were keen to promote his ideas. The Council of Joint Ministers, involving officials from both Austria and Hungary, met in full session on 7 July. Only István Tisza, Prime Minister of the Hungarian government, was against war, maintaining that Russia would attempt to intervene and that this in turn would rapidly lead to a general war throughout Europe.[8] Conrad was invited to outline his war plans, and made clear that he fully expected Russian intervention. This did little to calm the general belligerent mood, though Tisza persuaded the Council that rather than an immediate declaration of war, Serbia should be sent a series of demands. A declaration of war after failure to satisfy these demands, he argued, would be easier to justify on the diplomatic scene than a more precipitate commencement of hostilities. With the exception of Tisza, everyone agreed that the demands would have to be so severe that Serbia was unable to agree to them – a purely diplomatic victory was not sufficient.

Although the kaiser had told the general staff in Berlin that there was little prospect of a war involving Germany, a few precautionary steps were taken. Intelligence on the capabilities and intentions of the probable enemies of the German and Austro-Hungarian empires was gathered through a variety of agencies. Like all European powers, Germany relied on her diplomats, military attachés, and individuals such as journalists to gather information. In addition, a branch of the general staff – Section IIIb – had been created to gather data via espionage. Specially appointed *Nachrichtenoffiziere* were assigned to army corps on Germany's frontiers, with responsibility for managing agents across the border. On 16 July Section IIIb was advised to increase its information-gathering activities in the east. However, there was no sense of urgency; the signal that was sent from Section IIIb to the *Nachrichtenoffiziere* in the east informed them that, in view of increasing tension between Russia and Austria-Hungary, surveillance should be at a somewhat higher level than was normal in peacetime, but there was no need at present for 'special measures of any kind'.[9] A week later, as tensions heightened, the Austro-Hungarian government made a request to Berlin for any intelligence information that might be available, and Waldersee, who had just returned to the capital, ordered a further escalation in surveillance.[10]

The kaiser gave his approval for action against Serbia on 5 July, but a delay of over two weeks followed before an ultimatum was sent to Belgrade. Whilst it is possible that this was due to the time it took to persuade Tisza and the Hungarian government of the need to go to war, a more persuasive explanation relates to the Austro-Hungarian policy of granting summer leave to soldiers, so that they could help gather the harvest. Seven of Conrad's sixteen army corps had granted such leave and any attempt to go to war immediately would either have an impact upon harvest yields, or would necessitate commencing hostilities while large numbers of men were still away from their units.[11] Another reason for the delay was the presence of the French president and prime minister in St Petersburg. The ultimatum would be delivered after they had left. It was a sign of the continuing tensions inside Russia that on the same day that military bands were playing the Marseillaise to celebrate the presence of the French head of state, Cossacks were suppressing striking workers singing the same tune in the suburbs of St Petersburg.[12]

At the beginning of the crisis, there had been a degree of consensus in Vienna and Berlin that if military action was to be taken, then it would be best if it was done as soon as possible. Now, due to Tisza's insistence on the ultimatum, due to the delays around the French presence in St Petersburg, and due to the issue of harvest leave, there was no possibility of rapid action. Whilst the first two factors were avoidable, it seems strange that troops were allowed to go on harvest leave after the assassination occurred. Conrad must have known about the benefits of an early military move, and it would have been straightforward for him, as Chief of the General Staff, to issue a precautionary order telling his corps commanders not to allow troops to go on harvest leave, but no such measure was taken. As a result, any lingering possibility of acting quickly, before Russia and France could intervene, disappeared completely.

Whilst it seems that the Austro-Hungarian leadership was convinced of the necessity for war, it was important to prevent other European powers from becoming aware of this. Foreign Minister Leopold von Berchtold suggested that both Conrad and General Alexander von Krobatin, the Minister of War, went on summer leave, as if there were no immediate plans for hostilities.[13] During the period of delay, the ultimatum to Serbia was modified, deliberately ensuring that it would be almost impossible for Serbia to comply. The officials of Austria-Hungary went to great lengths to tone down newspaper coverage of the crisis, but despite their best efforts, news leaked out. Within days, the Russians – and therefore the French – became aware of the plans to issue an unacceptable ultimatum to Serbia. Whilst some of these leaks originated in Vienna, perhaps the most damaging one came via Berlin. The German Foreign Ministry sent a telegram to its ambassador in Rome to advise him of the plan, and he passed the information to the Italians, who were nominally members of the Central Alliance.

The Italians promptly sent coded telegrams to their delegations in Russia, Romania, and Austria, unaware that Austro-Hungarian intelligence officers had cracked their codes. It was a source of great irritation to the Austro-Hungarian officials that not only had their closest ally Germany behaved in such a casual manner, but the Italians had demonstrated once more that they were members of the Central Alliance in little more than name. But the real consequence was that the entire world, including Serbia, knew about the unacceptable nature of the ultimatum even before it saw the light of day.

The days that followed are perhaps one of the most intensely studied short periods of history. Numerous theories have been suggested to explain the growing avalanche that propelled Europe and the world into war, ranging from a Russian desire to force a conflict to the mechanistic effect of mobilisation schedules which, once initiated, were hard to alter.[14] Others suggest that the eagerness of military figures to press forward with the war option resulted in civilian authorities effectively being sidelined.[15] It seems likely that there were many factors at work, and that individuals in each European capital failed to understand the impact their actions would have upon their neighbours.[16]

In order to understand some of the events that followed, it is worth considering the manner in which all European powers prepared for war. Although the expression 'mobilisation' is used to describe the entire process, it occurred in three distinct phases. The first was a state of increased vigilance, in which frontier units were brought up to strength, officers were brought back from leave, and guards placed at key installations such as railway bridges and ports. The second was mobilisation itself, which saw reservists called into the army. Finally, the mobilised armies were concentrated at the borders, preparatory for the commencement of hostilities. If any of these phases were put into effect by a European nation, its potential enemies would have to consider whether they could afford to be left behind in terms of the overall timetable for preparation for war.

The ten-point ultimatum to Serbia was finalised in a meeting in Vienna on 19 July, in Berchtold's residence. Mobilisation plans were considered in detail, and Conrad outlined Plan B (a war against Serbia). Plan R (mobilisation against Russia) was for the moment regarded as no more than a contingency. At first glance this seems remarkable, given that Conrad had told his colleagues that he fully expected Russia to try to intervene, but it is likely that Conrad was gambling on a quick, decisive campaign against Serbia before Russian mobilisation was complete. There was also a widespread belief that the reputation of German military power, coupled with Germany's 'blank cheque' to Austria-Hungary, might be sufficient to deter the Russians from risking a conflict. Berchtold was increasingly anxious about the reliability of the Italians, particularly after the incident involving the intercepted coded telegrams, and Conrad made it clear to everyone that if Italian military intervention was a serious threat, then war was impossible – he would be hard-pressed enough to fight against Serbia and Russia, without the demands of diverting troops to the Alps. The men present at the meeting must have been aware that Italy was almost certain to renege on its alliance obligations. General Alberto Pollio, Chief of the Italian General Staff and one of the few figures in the Italian establishment regarded as pro-Austrian, had died of a heart attack just three days after the Sarajevo assassination. The best that the Austro-Hungarian high command could hope for was that Italy would remain neutral.

But if there were last-minute doubts in Vienna, there seemed to be none in Berlin. Strategic concerns that Russia's military expansion programme, coupled with the construction of new French-financed railroads in Poland, led many to believe that the passage of time would only worsen the balance of power against Germany. If an Austro-Hungarian attack on Serbia resulted in war with Russia, then better it should come now than in a few years' time. If Russia failed to come to Serbia's aid, the Entente against Germany would become strained, and might even collapse.[17]

In St Petersburg, the discussions between the French and Russians were dominated by the importance of maintaining the alliance between the two nations. Prime Minister Viviani became increasingly agitated and upset by the bellicose talk around him, but most of the others involved in the discussions had no such doubts. At a reception, President Poincaré met the Austro-Hungarian ambassador, Fritz Szapáry, and treated him with a degree of brusqueness that surprised many of those present. Inevitably, the conversation turned to the recent assassinations, and Szapáry replied that an enquiry was under way. Poincaré responded by reminding everyone present about two infamous incidents in recent years when Vienna had been shown to be using bogus material against Serbia. The implication was clear: regardless of the outcome of the Austro-Hungarian enquiry, the French intended to dismiss any suggestions of Serbian involvement.[18]

The Austro-Hungarian ultimatum was presented on 23 July, just hours after the French president and prime minister had left St Petersburg by ship. The Serbs were given only forty-eight hours to consider the document. Despite several government officials stating that they felt that Serbia would have to fight, the general mood was one of despondency. In October 1913, Russia had urged Serbia to accept Austro-Hungarian demands for a withdrawal of Serbian troops from

Albanian territory, and there was therefore little confidence that the Russians would back the Serbs in this current crisis. A telegram was sent to Miroslav Spalajković, the Serbian ambassador in St Petersburg, asking him to determine Russia's position. As the deadline ticked away, a series of telegrams arrived in Belgrade from Spalajković, successively strengthening the resolve of the Belgrade government with assurances of Russian support. After a hectic discussion on the wording of the response to the Austro-Hungarian ultimatum, a formal reply was agreed just before the deadline passed, and presented to the Austro-Hungarian ambassador. With a mixture of qualifications and evasions, Serbia accepted all but one demand from Vienna: the requirement for the involvement of Austro-Hungarian police officials in enquiries within Serbia into the assassination plot and other anti-Austro-Hungarian schemes was unacceptable within the terms of the Serbian constitution.

In the words of Alexander Musulin, an Austro-Hungarian diplomat who had been involved in the drafting of the Vienna ultimatum, the Serbian response was 'the most brilliant example of diplomatic skill' that he had ever come across.[19] Even with the points on which the Serbs agreed to help Vienna, the onus would be upon the Austro-Hungarian authorities to produce sufficient preliminary evidence, and in all likelihood the production of any such evidence would only lead to further unproductive negotiations. But on the face of it, Serbia was able to demonstrate to the diplomatic community – particularly to Russia, France, and Britain – that it was trying its best to accommodate Austria-Hungary's harsh demands.

Concluding that war was inevitable, Serbia initiated mobilisation on 24 July, and in the days that followed, further enthusiastic telegrams from Spalajković promised a huge Russian assault against Austria-Hungary. It seemed to many in Belgrade that events were moving in their favour, and that the coming war would result in the dissolution of the Dual Monarchy and the realisation of the dream of a Greater Serbia, incorporating all the South Slav people. The Austro-Hungarian emperor authorised implementation of Conrad's Plan B on the evening of the Serbian response to the ultimatum. In order to allow for all harvest leave to run its course, the first day of mobilisation was set for 28 July.

Aware that he needed to deliver a killing blow to the Serbs before the Russians could intervene, Conrad moved to strengthen the forces committed against Serbia. Plan B called for the *B-Staffel* and *Minimalgruppe Balkan* to deploy seven corps, but Conrad now added III Corps from *A-Staffel*. In an attempt to avoid giving the Russians any excuse to declare war prematurely, he expressly ordered that no preparations were to be made for war in Galicia.

On the same day that Serbia responded to the Austro-Hungarian ultimatum, Section IIIb of the German General Staff sent further instructions to its intelligence officers. Agents known as *Spannungsreisende* ('travellers during tension') were to be dispatched across the border. A mixture of army reservists, commercial travellers, and others, they would make journeys through Russia and France, and attempt to observe whether any preparations for war were taking place. Almost immediately the intelligence officer in Königsberg advised his superiors that his men had detected an unusually long exchange of coded signals between the Russian station in Bobruisk and – probably – the Eiffel Tower in Paris. This was followed by a report from the German military attaché in St Petersburg, who informed Moscow that officer cadets had been collectively commissioned, and troops at a nearby training area had suddenly been ordered back to barracks.[20]

Clearly, the Russians were making their own preparations. The first phase – the declaration of the increased vigilance in 'the period preparatory to war' – had been ordered into action on 25 July, even as Section IIIb ordered the dispatch of *Spannungsreisende*. Orders to this effect were sent out the following day, and it appears that in some areas local officers took action above and beyond the originally intended scope of these preparations. The Serbian chargé d'affaires in Berlin, passing through Russian-occupied Poland on 28 July, noted that there were widespread signs of troop movements and preparations, including the declaration of a state of siege in Brest-Litovsk.[21] But although Tsar Nicholas ordered over a million reservists to join their units before the Belgrade government had even rejected the ultimatum, this should not be regarded as an intention to go to war.[22] On 25 July, at a meeting in St Petersburg, Chief of the Imperial Russian General Staff Vladimir Sukhomlinov told the tsar that although Russia was not ready for war, preparations for war might act as a deterrent to Austro-Hungarian action against Serbia.[23] It seems that from the start the Russians used preparations for mobilisation, and mobilisation itself, as a means of exerting pressure on Vienna.

This was not a view shared by others. George Buchanan was the British ambassador in St Petersburg in 1914, and he had previously struggled to make sense of Foreign Minister Sazonov's statements during the First Balkan War. Sazonov's predecessor, Alexander Izvolsky, had agreed to support the Austro-Hungarian annexation of Bosnia-Herzegovina in 1910, already occupied by the troops of the Dual Monarchy for over thirty years, in return for Austro-Hungarian diplomatic support for Russian naval access to the Bosporus and Dardanelles, with the support of the tsar but without the assent or knowledge of the Russian government. The outcome was a disaster for the Russians, with Vienna successfully annexing Bosnia-Herzegovina and Izvolsky left denying that he had been involved in secret talks. As a result, Izvolsky was sacked, and Prime Minister Stolypin appointed Sazonov in his place. This seems to have been inspired more by Stolypin's desire to ensure personal control of the Russian government – Sazonov was his brother-in-law – than due to any particular talents on the part of Sazonov, who was widely regarded in the Russian establishment as a mediocrity. When Stolypin was assassinated in 1911, Sazonov was left without a strong mentor to guide him, and soon found himself in difficulties. He encouraged the Serbs and Bulgarians to take up arms against Turkey in the First Balkan War, but he then baffled and irritated the governments of both Balkan nations by advising them that they should not count on Russian backing if they ran into difficulties.[24] He oscillated on almost a daily basis between supporting Serbian dreams of securing a port on the Adriatic coast and discouraging the Serbs from such a path, which was certain to antagonise Vienna and might result in Austro-Hungarian intervention in the war. Despite regarding Sazonov as a personal friend, Buchanan sent an exasperated report to London late in 1912:

> Sazonov is so continually changing his ground that it is difficult to follow the successive phases of pessimism and optimism through which he passes.[25]

Now, on 25 July, with tensions rising, Buchanan met Sazonov for the second time in as many days due to the crisis.

> I could but repeat what I had said to the Emperor [Tsar Nicholas] ... that we could play the role of mediator to better purpose as a friend who, if her counsels of moderation were disregarded, might be converted into an ally, than if we were at once to declare our complete solidarity with Russia. I, at the same time, expressed the earnest hope that Russia would give His Majesty's Government time to use their influence as peacemaker and that she would not precipitate matters by mobilising. Were she to do so Germany would, I warned him, not be content with a counter-mobilisation, but would at once declare war on her. Russia, Sazonov replied, could not allow Austria to crush Serbia, but I might rest assured that she would take no military action unless absolutely forced to do so.[26]

Sazonov added that Russia was ready to face the risk of war, confident of French support.[27] The following day, acting on the instructions of Chancellor Bethmann-Hollweg, the German ambassador in St Petersburg, Friedrich von Pourtalès, dispelled any doubts that Sazonov might have had regarding the likely German reaction to signs of Russian mobilisation:

Preparatory military measures on the part of Russia aimed in any way at us would compel us to take measures for our own protection, which would have to take the form of mobilisation of the army. Mobilisation, however, would mean war.[28]

Sazonov appears to have sought confirmation, asking whether the Germans really regarded mobilisation as automatically resulting in war. Pourtalès replied that there might be a theoretical difference, but once the 'machinery of mobilisation' was put into effect, it could not be stopped.[29] It is difficult to know whether Sazonov really believed that there was no clear link between mobilisation and war. There had been a partial mobilisation of Russian and Austro-Hungarian troops during the Balkan crises without a war ensuing, but the terms of the Russo-French alliance had changed since then, giving Russia a stronger guarantee of French support regardless of the reason for the outbreak of war. It is also probably relevant that, insofar as such a thing existed, Russian doctrine for the period prior to war was to try to achieve as much mobilisation as possible without triggering a reaction by the other side, particularly given the slower timetable of Russian mobilisation. It was therefore in Russia's interests to persuade Germany in particular that the Russians did not automatically regard mobilisation as leading to war.

But the German ambassador had left the Russians in no doubt: if they mobilised, the Germans would not allow them to gain a time advantage, and would mobilise in turn. In response to this warning, Sazonov sent a telegram to the Russian Embassy in Paris, alerting them to the German warning, and making it clear that war was now inevitable.

The Germans could see Russian preparations were proceeding, and Sukhomlinov tried to calm them, telling Major Bernhardt von Eggeling, the German military attaché in St Petersburg, on 26 July that no steps had yet been taken for mobilisation, and that the troop movements that were clearly visible had more to do with unrest within Russia itself, as witnessed by the recent strikes in St Petersburg. Eggeling reported to Berlin:

I consider the wish for peace genuine, military statements in so far correct, that complete mobilisation has probably not been ordered, but preparatory measures are very far-reaching. They are evidently striving to gain time for new negotiations and for continuing their armaments. Also the internal situation is unmistakably causing serious anxiety.[30]

The precise details of mobilisation of the Russian Army now became the subject of considerable argument. Foreign Minister Sazonov and the tsar met several senior figures, including the Russian chief of staff General Nikolai Yanushkevich and Minister for War Sukhomlinov, on the day the Austro-Hungarian ultimatum was sent to Serbia. At this meeting the notion of a partial mobilisation – with troops destined for the Austro-Hungarian front only – was first raised, probably at the suggestion of Sukhomlinov and Sazonov. Yanushkevich had discussed such a possibility with General Sergei Dobrorolsky, the head of the General Staff's mobilisation section, a few days before. At this meeting Dobrorolsky objected strongly to the entire concept; on the grounds that plans for hostilities required the mobilisation of sixteen army corps, whereas the proposed partial mobilisation would only create thirteen corps. In particular, although the Warsaw Military District would not take part in a partial mobilisation, it was essential to protect the northern flank of any operation against the Austro-Hungarian Empire.[31] Sukhomlinov must have known that without the Warsaw troops being mobilised, any military operation against Galicia would be fraught with difficulties. This gave further weight to the view that he and others regarded the process of mobilisation as a means of exerting diplomatic pressure, rather than an inevitable prelude to war.

The degree to which the Austro-Hungarians were strongly influenced by Germany is controversial. It was a widespread opinion in France, Russia, and even Britain that the Germans were controlling events in Vienna, and that the Germans were therefore responsible for the entire crisis, but there is little firm proof of this. What is clear is that Russia was strongly influenced by its ally France. Although the French President Raymond Poincaré and Prime Minister René Viviani were out of contact for several key days aboard the warship *France* on their way home from St Petersburg – an isolation that was made worse by the Germans repeatedly jamming radio transmissions – they managed to send telegrams both to Paris and St Petersburg, particularly when they went ashore in Sweden on their way home. On 27 July Viviani urged the French ambassador in Russia, Maurice Paléologue, to ask the Russians to take every opportunity to seek a peaceful solution. Paléologue, who had repeatedly encouraged quite the opposite, is reported in some accounts to have spoken to Sazonov on the following day, assuring him of France's complete readiness to fulfil her alliance obligations.[32] In his own memoirs, he painted a somewhat different picture of what he told the Russian foreign minister:

> However great the danger may be and however remote the chance of salvation, you and I ought to leave nothing undone to save the cause of peace. I do want you to realize that I am in a position which is unprecedented for an ambassador. The

head of the State and the head of the Government are at sea. I can only communicate with them at intervals and through very uncertain channels; as their knowledge of the situation is incomplete, they cannot send me any instructions. The ministry in Paris is without its chief, and its means of communication with the President of the Republic and the President of the Council are as irregular and defective as mine. My responsibility is thus enormous and that's why I ask you to pledge yourself henceforth to accept all the proposals France and England may make to you to save peace.[33]

Paléologue also wrote that Sazonov appeared to be wavering, and that strong reassurances of French support were required to stiffen his resolve, but other accounts suggest that Sazonov needed little encouragement. Louis de Robien, a French diplomat, witnessed a heated lunch in which Paléologue, Sazonov, and Buchanan, the British ambassador, all took a hard line against Austria-Hungary and Germany, egging each other on in a manner that shocked the 26-year-old Robien.[34] Meetings between Russian government officials followed, and there was general agreement on the need to remain firm. In any event, many argued, war was inevitable, and there was little to be gained by delay.

The Austro-Hungarian Empire finally declared war on Serbia on 28 July. Throughout the crisis, the inability of Vienna to move faster had been a repeated cause of irritation in Berlin, where officials, both military and civilian, believed that the best chance of preventing a general war and keeping the crisis localised was to proceed quickly. Conrad had advised against an early declaration of war, after telling his colleagues that he would not be ready to start hostilities until the second week of August, but he was overruled by Berchtold, who wanted to pre-empt any last-minute diplomatic moves.

St Petersburg felt obliged to make a response, partly to show solidarity with the Serbs, and partly to exert some pressure, even at this late stage, on Vienna. It can be argued, and indeed Conrad expected, that it would have served the Russians better to wait until the *k.u.k.* Army was fully embroiled in a war with Serbia before mobilising.[35] As a result of Redl's betrayal of Austro-Hungarian mobilisation plans, the Russians were aware of the alternative mobilisation scenarios, and as a result, it would have been in Russia's interests for Conrad's armies to be completely committed on the Serbian front before Russian forces moved against Austro-Hungarian troops in Galicia. The Russians were fully aware from the exchanges between Pourtalès and Sazonov that general mobilisation would result in war, and were anxious to avoid being blamed for such a war. Several senior Russian figures met to discuss what to do. Grand Duke

Nikolai, the uncle of the tsar, was in favour of general mobilisation, while others wished to mobilise only against the Austro-Hungarian Empire. They concluded that they would draw up two orders, one for partial mobilisation and one for general mobilisation, and present them to the tsar for a final decision. Sazonov sent a telegram to Berlin, warning that Russia would declare partial mobilisation on 29 July. In an attempt to head off a German response, Tsar Nicholas sent a telegram to the kaiser:

> The military measures which have now come into force were decided five days ago for reasons of defence on account of Austria's preparations. I hope from all my heart that these measures won't interfere with your part as mediator which I greatly value.[36]

However, regardless of the tsar's views, Yanushkevich sent a further message to the commanders of Russia's military districts, advising them that general mobilisation would be ordered on 30 July, and that they should prepare accordingly.

On 29 July the tsar was given the two mobilisation orders, and signed them both. Immediately, the military authorities set to work, drafting the detailed telegrams required to initiate mobilisation. Again, Pourtalès went out of his way to ensure that the Russians were fully aware of the German point of view, in a further exchange with Sazonov on 29 July:

> The danger of all military measures lies in the countermeasures of the other side. It is to be expected that the General Staffs of eventual enemies of Russia would not want to sacrifice the trump card of their great lead over Russia in mobilisation and would press for countermeasures.[37]

In Serbia, hostilities commenced. Although the Austro-Hungarian Army was far from ready to invade Serbia, artillery batteries on the Austro-Hungarian bank of the River Danube opened fire on the Serbian capital Belgrade, supported by Austro-Hungarian monitors on the river itself. News of the bombardment spread rapidly, increasing further the growing tension. At this last moment, Bethmann-Hollweg seems to have had doubts about the wisdom of allowing a conflict between Serbia and Austria-Hungary to drag the rest of Europe into a war. He sent a telegram to Vienna, trying to seek a way out from the slide to hostilities, and urging the Austro-Hungarian government to enter into serious dialogue with Russia:

The refusal of all exchange of views with St Petersburg would be a grave error, since it would provoke armed intervention by Russia which it is, more than anything, to Austria-Hungary's interest to avoid. We are, of course, prepared to fulfil our duty as allies, but must decline to let ourselves be dragged by Vienna, wantonly and without regard to our advice, into a world conflagration.[38]

Numerous factors have been suggested as causing this change of heart. The kaiser seemed to be having doubts about war, believing that the Serbian acceptance of almost all of Vienna's ultimatum could be negotiated into a major position of advantage – Wilhelm had a long history of making bellicose statements, only to shrink back from them when the possibility of conflict actually increased. The British foreign secretary, Lord Grey, had informed the German ambassador in London late on 29 July that Britain would not stay neutral in any war between France and Germany. In Berlin, Erich von Falkenhayn, the minister of war, favoured pre-mobilisation measures in response to the Russian move; only Moltke the Younger showed any enthusiasm for reacting by ordering general mobilisation. He even went so far as to send telegrams to Conrad in Vienna, urging the Austro-Hungarian Empire to move to general mobilisation, in direct contradiction of the messages being sent by Bethmann-Hollweg. Unless the Austro-Hungarians mobilised fully and thus tied up significant Russian forces, his own plans for a major offensive against France would be almost impossible to enact. Anxious to avoid being labelled as the aggressors, the German government wished to delay its own mobilisation until Russia had already done so. After all, the faster pace of German mobilisation would eliminate the slight advantage that the Russians could gain by initiating events.

Late on 29 July there was a further discussion in St Petersburg, involving Chief of the General Staff Yanushkevich, Foreign Minister Sazonov, and Minister of War Sukhomlinov:

After examining the situation from all points, both the Ministers decided that in view of the small probability of avoiding a war with Germany it was indispensable to prepare for it in every way and in good time, and that therefore the risk could not be accepted of delaying a general mobilisation later by effecting a partial mobilisation now. The conclusion reached at this conference was at once reported by telephone to the tsar, who authorised the taking of steps accordingly. This information was received with enthusiasm by the small circle of those acquainted with what was in progress.[39]

The tsar gave approval for general mobilisation, but was himself involved in an exchange of telegrams with the kaiser, in which both men continued to profess a desire for peace. Whilst the telegrams have often been regarded as last-minute interventions by two sovereigns, the reality is that the telegrams were drafted by officials, still seeking to portray their own nations as acting in the interests of peace. Acting on one such telegram from Wilhelm, Tsar Nicholas cancelled the authorisation for general mobilisation, insisting on partial mobilisation only. By this stage it seems that the meeting with Yanushkevich and Sukhomlinov had dispelled any lingering doubts in Sazonov's mind, and he was now firmly in the camp of those who favoured general mobilisation, not least because Dobrorolsky and others involved in mobilisation planning insisted that partial mobilisation at this stage would disrupt and delay full mobilisation at a later stage. Furthermore, the military men pointed out, if partial mobilisation was intended as a prelude to war with Austria-Hungary, it made no sense without mobilisation in Warsaw, which would be interpreted by the Germans as mobilisation against them.

Herein lay part of the reason for the confused signals of the preceding days. For some, particularly the tsar, mobilisation – or the threat of it – was a means of exerting diplomatic pressure, and not necessarily an automatic step towards war. The professional soldiers (and the increasingly hard-line civilian politicians) saw things very differently, and were frustrated at the idea of mobilising only partially, only to have to order general mobilisation at a later date, with its timetable badly disrupted by the earlier partial mobilisation. True to his dual role as both a military man and a politician, Sukhomlinov gave ambiguous signals, supporting both points of view at different times. This difference of opinion was not confined to Russia, but appears to have been strongest in St Petersburg. In Berlin, there was little doubt that mobilisation in Germany was a clear step towards war, and consequently all key figures interpreted mobilisation in Russia in the same manner.

Another difficulty faced by the Russians was the comparatively poor quality of their leadership at this stage. Sukhomlinov was disliked by a large part of the officer corps, and included the future commander-in-chief Grand Duke Nikolai Nikolaevich, uncle of the tsar, amongst his enemies. Yanushkevich, the chief of the general staff, was more of a courtier than a military figure. He had not commanded any unit larger than an infantry company, and repeatedly showed his poor understanding of even straightforward military matters, owing his current post to a mixture of patronage by the tsar and the desire of Sukhomlinov to ensure that anyone in the post of chief of the general staff was too weak to threaten his own position, though he was one of the few senior Russian figures to understand the importance of logistics.[40] After agreeing with Sazonov about partial mobilisation earlier in the crisis, Yanushkevich ignored the protests of Dobrorolsky that such a step was almost impossible to implement in a militarily effective manner.[41] The problems that might have resulted from a partial mobilisation, in terms of disrupting a future general mobilisation, are difficult to assess. After the war Sukhomlinov stated that such a transition would have been difficult, but not impossible, but the concept had never been tested, not even as a staff exercise. One might question why Sukhomlinov had not actually conducted such an exercise; it was an eventuality that might easily have been anticipated. The difficulties of waging war against the Austro-Hungarian Empire without the involvement of the Warsaw Military District are far easier to assess, but even this difficulty only mattered if mobilisation was an automatic step towards war. If it was intended merely as a means of increasing pressure on Vienna, such difficulties remained only theoretical.

By 30 July, though, Yanushkevich had become convinced of the need for full mobilisation. He met Sazonov and Sukhomlinov again, and they attempted in vain to persuade the tsar by telephone to restore the order for full mobilisation. During the afternoon Sazonov had an audience with the tsar. After a lengthy discussion he finally persuaded him that war was imminent and unavoidable, and that the personal telegrams from the kaiser were at odds with what was actually happening. With great reluctance Nicholas agreed to full mobilisation. Sazonov telephoned the news to Yanushkevich immediately.

Bethmann-Hollweg had been urging Vienna to launch only limited operations against Serbia, stopping after the capture of Belgrade, but when news of Russian general mobilisation reached Berlin on 31 July, the mood changed once more. The kaiser gave approval for general mobilisation, to the relief of Moltke and Falkenhayn. The following day, there appeared to be a further shift: even as German troops began to move towards Belgium and Luxembourg, the kaiser received a telegram from Britain, which he interpreted as offering a guarantee of French neutrality. Wilhelm immediately demanded that German troops should be mobilised purely for a war against Russia, only to be told by Moltke that this was simply impossible. Wilhelm accepted this, but ordered that whilst mobilisation could proceed as planned, troops would not be allowed to move west; on completion of mobilisation, they would instead be transferred east. An immediate message was sent to prevent German troops entering Luxembourg. Moltke pleaded that the railways of Luxembourg had to be secured to make possible a deployment against France, even if such a deployment was not followed through. Kaiser Wilhelm, but brusquely dismissed his arguments.[42]

Further telegrams from the German ambassador in London followed. After initially suggesting that Britain would remain neutral Foreign Secretary Edward Grey seemed to be backing away from this position, and it became clear that he had made his previous statements without consulting the French. Nor, it seemed, had he consulted others in London. Wilhelm sent a telegram to King George V, accepting the guarantee of French neutrality, and this resulted in Grey being summoned to Buckingham Palace. By the end of the day, the British proposal – or more accurately, Grey's unilateral proposal – had disappeared. Moltke had been reduced to tears of frustration by the last-minute complications, but was now given permission by Wilhelm to proceed without restraint.

When the French refused a German demand that they renounce their treaty obligations with Russia, and instead mobilised their own armies, the last diminishing possibility of avoiding a general war disappeared. German troops crossed into Luxembourg during the evening, and Germany declared war on Russia. It is perhaps characteristic of the unpredictable sequence of events that Austria-Hungary and Russia, whose relationships were at the heart of the escalating crisis, only found themselves at war on 6 August, when Vienna issued a declaration of war. This was two days after Britain and France had entered the conflict, and nearly a week after Germany had declared war on Russia.

The obligations of interlocking treaties now imposed themselves upon the plans and intentions of the military commanders. Russia had mobilised with a view to attacking Austria-Hungary in support of Serbia, but as German mobilisation would result in a major German attack on France, the Russians had to devote the main strength of their regular army to launching an early attack on East Prussia in an attempt to draw off German troops from the Western Front. In the same way, the *k.u.k.* Army had been preparing for a major attack on Serbia, but Moltke demanded an early Austro-Hungarian attack on the Russians in order to prevent Russia from concentrating overwhelming force against East Prussia. While Russian general mobilisation plans had always assumed a major effort against Germany, Conrad had deliberately put into action his plan for a Balkan war. Indeed, by diverting additional troops to the Balkan theatre, he had weakened what forces might be available for the defence of Galicia. On 31 July Emperor Franz Joseph ordered a general mobilisation, bringing the remaining units of *A-Staffel* up to full strength.

Conrad now struggled to catch up with events. With troops already moving towards the Serbian frontier, he had to switch from concentrating the bulk of his strength against Serbia to deploying most of his men against Russia. He decided to leave *Minimalgruppe Balkan* with three corps to attack Serbia, while the rest of the army would deploy according to the original Plan R, which called for a major offensive against Russia. In order to do this he needed to re-route the four corps of *B-Staffel*, and the extra corps from *A-Staffel* that he had already committed to the Serbian front, and send them all to Galicia. Late on 31 July he met Colonel Johann Straub, head of the Austro-Hungarian general staff's Railway Bureau. Straub advised him that it was impossible to re-route these units without the entire railway system degenerating into complete chaos. If an attempt were made, said Straub, the troops involved would end up stranded in the railway network, unable to intervene on either the Serbian or the Galician front. The only units that could be diverted without too much difficulty were III Corps – originally part of *A-Staffel* before Conrad assigned it to the Serbian front – and two Hungarian reserve cavalry divisions.[43]

Nevertheless, there was a pressing need to divert forces to Galicia. Those that could be redirected were ordered to do so. On the advice of Major Emil Ratzenhofer, head of the Russian Group within Straub's Railway Bureau, Conrad ordered that the other four corps that made up *B-Staffel* should be allowed to complete their concentration as planned. They would then be re-embarked and sent by train to Galicia. Ratzenhofer assured Conrad that they would reach Galicia on 23 August, broadly the same date that they would have reached the area if they had been originally mobilised for deployment there. Even at first glance, this seems a remarkably optimistic suggestion, and it is astonishing that Conrad accepted it without further questioning. Unfortunately, he failed to inform General Oskar Potiorek, who had overall command of the forces deployed against Serbia. Potiorek was determined to deliver a lethal blow against Serbia at the earliest opportunity, and as will be seen, he proved reluctant to release the forces he had expected to be at his disposal.

The news of mobilisation, and the coming of war, was greeted with mixed reactions by the people of the three empires. In the Dual Monarchy the nationalist tensions that had threatened to tear Franz Joseph's realm apart seemed to ease, with men of all ethnicities responding to their mobilisation orders. The writer Stefan Zweig, who was 33 at the time, later remarked that with the coming of war, the people of the empire felt that they belonged together – something that they should have felt during peacetime.[44] In Russia, too, there seemed an outpouring of patriotic sentiment, though it often took an unpleasant turn, and there were worrying undercurrents:

> On 2 August, there was a meeting in the Winter Palace, where the government, the Senate, the Duma, the military, and the civil servants assembled to hear the

declaration of war. The great square in front of the palace was not sufficient to hold the crowd that assembled to give free voice to its sentiments... However, alongside this brave outlook, there were, alarmingly, muffled notes of censure. During the formal session of the Duma, a deputy from the left had to be silenced by the President, because his words were defeatist...

At the start of mobilisation, there was disorder amongst the reservists at several locations; as at Barnaul [the administrative centre of Altai Krai, in southern Siberia], they sometimes were of a serious character; one had to resort to serious measures, including the use of arms, to suppress them. They were blamed on drunkenness, but this explanation was not sufficient. An imperial order forbade all sales of alcohol during mobilisation ... the masses were already deeply restless. Amongst the crowds of reservists, there was an ill will that incited them to pillage and disorder.

Even in St Petersburg, the enthusiasm that filled the populace ended in a monstrous form. On the evening of 4 August, the German ambassador took his leave. I personally witnessed this disgusting tableau of the unfettered brutal, dangerous instincts of the mob. Fires were lit inside the embassy; the great Germanic figures that the German architects had used to embellish the façade were dragged down by the mob, who hurled them into the facing canal. The police did not intervene, probably for fear of being accused of lacking patriotism. There was talk of the murder of an ordinary elderly German, who the mob had accused of espionage.

Bit by bit, other signs of the disquiet and anxious state of the masses appeared. The patriotic manifestations and declarations of enthusiasm seemed little more than a poor façade, behind which hid a less attractive reality... The Russian people were not psychologically ready for war. The great mass of peasantry could not give a clear account of why they had been called to war, nor why the war was taking place. The peasant came to the colours because he was generally used to doing everything that the authorities told him to do.[45]

General Danilov, quartermaster-general at the time, wrote these observations after the war, perhaps with the benefit of hindsight, went on:

The popular state of mind of our nation, politically naïve and inadequately educated, could not hold. It was susceptible to the same sudden changes as that of a young child that laughs frequently before bursting into tears. The concept of imperial unity was more or less foreign to the masses; given the diversity of races, and the enormous distances, the dispersed population, and the difficulties with communications, it was very difficult to get them to understand. The Russian-speaking population had no clear sense of national unity. 'We are from Viatka, or Tula, or Perm – the Germans will never come as far as us' – this was often the reasoning of our peasants with regard to the danger that threatened the state.

The sense of duty was no healthier amongst the intelligentsia; one saw the proof of this in the number of 'draft-dodgers'. The mobilisation bureau was inundated with demands for exemptions or reprieve. Even worse, this state of affairs led neither to repression on the part of the authorities, nor disapproval on the part of society; in this sphere, there was an almost criminal sense of indulgence. The draft-dodgers were often protégés; one watched them strengthen their illegal position even further.[46]

Danilov went on to comment that there had been no attempt to prepare the Russian people for the rigours of a prolonged war, and no such attempt was made when it became clear that the initial optimism about a quick war was completely misplaced. Much the same could be said about the army in 1914:

[The army] received the declaration of war with calm and assurance. The officer cadre was universally filled with great enthusiasm, but nobody, even in the highest posts, was able to give a precise account of the difficulties that had to be overcome. One viewed the future with a rosy glow, one left one's home, one's family, with the expectation of returning at Christmas, victorious of course. Nobody predicted the four years of arduous life, full of privations and mortal danger, or the long months of living like a troglodyte in trenches; still less did anyone anticipate the terrible experiences of the revolutionary era and the terrible humiliation of the Fatherland.[47]

Such a view was common in any army in Europe in the summer of 1914.

Others recalled a less ambiguous enthusiasm after the initiation of mobilisation:

Those who had witnessed the mobilisation for the Russo-Japanese War could not help being amazed at the immeasurable difference in feeling in all classes of the Russian nation. Many of the reservists in obscure provinces appeared before the Recruiting Commissions and asked not to have to undergo medical examination, declaring that they were perfectly fit, desiring thereby to facilitate the work of the Commissions and to help in speeding up mobilisation.[48]

Like much of Europe, Germany had enjoyed a memorable summer, as many later recalled:

> The summer was more beautiful than any other and promised to become even more so; we looked at the world without a care. I remember how right at the end I went through the vineyards in Baden with a friend and an elderly farmer said to us: 'So, we haven't had a summer like this for a long time. If it goes on, we're going to make an exceptional wine. People will always remember this summer!'[49]

Soldiers assembled according to the great mobilisation plans, and marched off with confidence and optimism. Elfriede Kuhr, who was twelve years old, witnessed the departure of 149th Infantry Regiment from her hometown of Schneidemühl on 4 August. Although the town was closer to the Russian frontier than the border with France, the requirements of the Schlieffen Plan resulted in the regiment being destined for the west. She wrote in her diary:

> There came the 149th, shoulder-to-shoulder, and poured onto the railway platform like a grey wave. All the soldiers had long chains of summer flowers around their necks and chests. There were even bunches of asters, wallflowers and roses in the rifle barrels, as if they wanted to shoot the enemy with flowers. The expressions of the soldiers were stern. I had expected that they would be laughing and jubilant… The hurrahs rose to a crescendo, the faces of the soldiers appeared at the open doors, flowers were thrown into the air, and all of a sudden, many people in the square began to cry.
> 'Auf Wiedersehen! Auf Wiedersehen in the homeland!'
> 'Don't worry! We'll soon be back home!'
> 'We'll celebrate Christmas with Mother!'[50]

With a mixture of misgivings, but also a sense of inevitability and even optimism, the entire continent went to war.

CHAPTER 5

THE FIRST BATTLES

STALLUPÖNEN AND GUMBINNEN

The conflict that erupted on Russia's western borders broke into two distinct theatres: the northern theatre, where Russian forces attempted to fulfil their treaty obligations with France by putting pressure on the Germans, and the southern theatre, where the forces of the Austro-Hungarian Empire attempted to put pressure on the Russians, in a similar attempt to relieve pressure on their German allies. The first month of the war was in many respects atypical of the conflict that followed. To an extent, it followed the pattern that most military theorists had predicted, and featured major offensive operations by all sides. Again, as Conrad and others had anticipated, these offensive operations resulted in heavy losses for the attacking forces. But, contrary to their expectations, commanders of all the armies that mobilised in 1914 found that their offensives failed to achieve the stunning successes required to bring the war to a swift and successful conclusion.

For the Russians, the first matter that required urgent resolution was the appointment of a commander-in-chief. Traditionally, this was a role that belonged to the tsar. Although there appears to have been some speculation about whether he might choose to take up the post, the reality was that he had very little military experience.[1] But if the tsar was not to lead the armies of Russia, who was the right man? Danilov later wrote:

Public opinion recognised only one candidate: Grand Duke Nikolai Nikolaevich. A man of action, straightforward, decisive, with an imposing demeanour, the Grand Duke had passed all the courses in the School of War, fought in the war against Turkey, and his military career, which commenced as a subaltern, had led him to command the troops of the Guards and the military district of St Petersburg. Those who knew him best, particularly amongst the officers, had concerns about his temper and sometimes brusque manners, but these traits had become less pronounced with age, while the sincerity and noble gentlemanliness of his deeds increased his popularity.[2]

The grand duke was 57 years old at the outbreak of war, and made no secret of his dislike of Germany. He was a strong adherent of the alliance with France, regarding an early attack on Germany by Russia as essential for two main reasons. Firstly, it would reduce pressure upon Russia's ally. Secondly, with the bulk of German troops committed to the Schlieffen Plan, there would be a window of opportunity for the Russian Army to achieve a potentially decisive victory. Despite Danilov's glowing description, Grand Duke Nikolai's suitability for the post of supreme commander was limited. He had never commanded armies in the field, and much of his reputation was centred on being a sound administrator and reformer, particularly of training, rather than as a decisive leader. Furthermore, he had played no part in devising the Russian mobilisation or war plans, and would now have to implement them despite lacking clear knowledge of their details. Finally, he would have to act through intermediaries that he had not selected.

But there was no other candidate who was likely to do better. Some suggested that the role should be assigned to Minister of War Sukhomlinov, but Danilov's opinion of his suitability was shared by many:

He was certainly a capable man, but somewhat thoughtless, I would say too insubstantial for this post. Very competent in his time, the general had slowly lost interest in military affairs; he was now no longer up to date in the profession and did not see any value in new concepts... Allowing his juniors great freedom in their work, which, poorly directed, frequently suffered from a lack of coherence, General Sukhomlinov jealously and stubbornly defended certain principles ... of organisation and training which, for one reason or other, seemed to him unassailable. It was only with the greatest difficulty that one was able to get him to change his mind, which sometimes made the position of his assistants completely untenable. Strongly egotistical, he was never able, or indeed wished, to rise above personal grudges.[3]

It has been argued that Sukhomlinov deliberately declined to put himself forward on the grounds that the war was anticipated to be a short one; the post would be one with little power associated with it, and, moreover, it would carry considerable risks in the event of setbacks.[4] All rumours and speculation ceased on 2 August, when the tsar announced the nomination of the grand duke as supreme commander. Yanushkevich was the Chief of the General Staff, but true to form, Sukhomlinov had ensured in his selection that the post was filled, as before, by someone who could not threaten his own position. The real centre of authority in the Russian high command (or *Stavka*) was the quartermaster-general, Yuri Danilov. When *Stavka* moved to the town of Baranovichi, selected for its good railway connections in all directions, Danilov and his staff occupied the only suitable building, leaving Yanushkevich and others to live in their – admittedly opulent – railway carriages.[5]

In the opening days of the war – as there had been during the preceding years – concerns were raised in Russia that the Germans might use their vast naval superiority to land troops anywhere along the Baltic coast, and even threaten St Petersburg. Consequently, substantial forces that might have been deployed on the front line in East Prussia, Poland, and Galicia were held back to counter any such danger. News that Britain had declared war on Germany was therefore greeted with relief, as the threat of the Royal Navy would, it was hoped, keep the German fleet busy defending the North Sea approaches to Germany. But whatever the requirements of coping with the British fleet, the kaiser's navy was able to assign several warships to the Baltic theatre, under the command of Vizeadmiral Robert Mischke, and a mixed force of warships bombarded the port of Libau, on the Latvian coast (now known as Liepāja). The light cruiser *Augsburg* also laid a minefield outside the port, but it was poorly marked on German charts, and caused more problems for the German warships in the coming months than to any Russian seaborne traffic. From Libau, the German ships – two light cruisers, three destroyers and a minelayer – proceeded along the Baltic coast, striking at several targets, including the historic Kõpu lighthouse on the Estonian island of Hiiumaa. A few days later Mischke's force encountered two Russian armoured cruisers, *Admiral Makarov* and *Gromoboi*. Both sides believed that the other was more powerful – the Russians mistakenly believed that the German vessels included two armoured cruisers in their ranks – and withdrew.

Konteradmiral Ehler Behring replaced Mischke as commander of the German flotilla; he continued the aggressive patrolling policy of his predecessor, though with worse fortune. On 26 August the light cruiser *Magdeburg* ran aground near Odensholm (now the Estonian island of Osmussaar, off the northwest coast of Estonia). Attempts to tow her back into deeper water were unsuccessful, and came to an end when the Russian cruisers *Bogatyr* and *Pallada* intervened. They subjected the stranded *Magdeburg* to a short bombardment before boarding her.

The loss of the *Magdeburg* – she was partly scrapped by the Russians – was bad enough, but far more importantly her crew was unable to destroy her codebooks before the Russians took control. Three of these, as well as the current cipher key, were captured. The Russians passed one codebook to the British, who successfully used it to good effect through much of the war in operations in the North Sea, including the battles of Dogger Bank and Jutland.[6]

The land forces on Russia's western frontiers fell into two groups: Yakov Zhilinski's Northwest Front, facing the Germans, and General Nikolai Ivanov's Southwest Front, deployed against the Austro-Hungarian Army in Galicia. On 5 August the French ambassador Maurice Paléologue had an audience with the tsar, in which he pressed for urgent action:

I summoned up all the vigour at my command to represent the terrible danger France would have to face in the first phase of the war:

'The French army will have to face the formidable onset of twenty-five German corps. I therefore beg Your Majesty to order your troops to take the offensive immediately. If they do not do so there is a risk that the French army will be crushed. Then the whole German mass will turn *en bloc* against Russia.'

He replied, emphasizing each word:

'The moment mobilisation is complete I shall order an advance. My troops are most enthusiastic. The attack will be pressed with the greatest vigour. No doubt you know that the Grand Duke [Nikolai] is extraordinarily forceful.'[7]

Russian mobilisation appears to have proceeded without any major problems. Despite Danilov's observations about draft-dodgers amongst the ranks of the intelligentsia, the Russian general and military historian Nikolai Golovine recorded that 96 per cent of those liable for service reported to their mobilisation centres.[8] The armies of Zhilinski's Northwest Front, facing East Prussia, started the process of mobilisation already at two-thirds strength, and began probing operations almost immediately. On 3 August, Second Army's 4th Cavalry Division crossed the frontier to the east of Lyck, and penetrated a short distance inland. The Russian horsemen reported that the Germans had evacuated the frontier area, and had set fire to a number of villages before they left.[9] A Russian cavalry officer observed several such fires:

At daybreak, to our great astonishment, we saw a large number of fires ahead, the heavy smoke from which, in the calm morning air, rose in thick black columns. By the positions of the smoke columns I could tell that they agreed with the movements of the three cavalry columns I had sent out. Naturally, the first thought was that my cavalry units were burning the farms in their locality, destroying the forage and unthrashed grain. As this did not fall in with my plans, I immediately sent them orders to stop this incendiarism. But before I received the reply from the commanders of these columns I was able to satisfy myself that it was not any of their work. What the actual cause of these fires was we never found out, but as we advanced further into East Prussia we nearly always saw the same picture. In conjunction with the approach of any considerable body of Russian troops, thick columns of smoke started from some store filled with forage or straw, usually from the farms nearest to the head of the column. In this the very line of direction and speed of our columns was seen from a great distance off. Naturally the only thing to do was to adopt some kind of repressive measures, although this caused us a great deal of trouble. With the slightest sign of an advance by us, the local population fled towards the west, carting away their most valued possessions. This appearance was so general that it could only have been due to arrangement by the German authorities. The only human beings we at any time saw in these deserted villages were very old women and men who could barely drag one foot after the other. Very often we met, but oftener observed disappearing in the distance, cyclists who were without exception boys from 12 to 14 years of age.[10]

In an area in which peacetime crime had been at above-average levels, largely due to the proximity of the border and cross-border smuggling activity, it is possible that some of the fires were started by looters, or by the Russians themselves.

The Germans meanwhile mounted a raid into Poland further west, towards the tip of the great salient of Russian Poland, but after a few skirmishes they too fell back. Neither side was prepared to commit large-scale cavalry forces at this stage, though, as will be seen later, the Austro-Hungarians thought otherwise. A young officer of the Uhlans, Manfred von Richthofen, who would later achieve fame as 'the Red Baron' in a completely different arm, led a cavalry raid into Poland, and captured the village of Kieltze.[11]

On 7 August Yanushkevich told the two front commanders that he intended to create two new Ninth and Tenth Armies to the west of Warsaw, with a view to mounting an offensive directly towards Berlin. There was a considerable amount of logic in this plan, as this new group would start its offensive from the most western point of the Russian Empire. However, the fact that this point was at the tip of a large salient meant that the flanks of this new group would be vulnerable, until Zhilinski's and Ivanov's fronts had eliminated the forces facing them. Pavel Rennenkampf's First Army would lose the Guards Corps and I Corps, but would receive XX Corps from Fourth Army as a replacement but as the latter corps had a larger proportion of reservists than the two corps being transferred to the new armies, the readiness of First Army for immediate operations would be compromised. Further south, the loss of XX Corps left Fourth Army, facing the Austro-Hungarians, short of troops.

Nevertheless, on 10 August *Stavka* was able to declare that First Army would have a little over five divisions of cavalry and ninety-six battalions of infantry at full strength by the end of the following day. The situation for Second Army, *Stavka* reported, was even more optimistic. With the transfer of one of its corps to the new forces gathering west of Warsaw, it would no longer have to await the arrival of all its reservists, and would therefore have 112 infantry battalions and four cavalry divisions available. The total strength of the two armies – 208 infantry battalions, and over nine cavalry divisions with 192 squadrons – would face an estimated German strength of 100 first-line battalions, together with reserve and *Landwehr* formations. The *Stavka* statement summarised the political and strategic requirement for an attack against East Prussia at the earliest opportunity, and therefore ordered First Army to attack north of the Masurian Lakes, aiming to tie down the bulk of the German forces. Meanwhile, Second Army would advance to strike the German forces from the south. The intention was to force a decisive action between the lower Vistula and the Masurian Lakes:

> Close touch must be established between the First and Second Armies by advancing a sufficiently strong covering force opposite the Masurian Lakes front.
>
> The general idea of the operations would thus consist of the envelopment of the enemy from both flanks... In the opinion of the Supreme Commander-in-Chief the offensive of the armies of the Northwest Front should commence from the 14th day of mobilisation.[12]

The estimate of relative troop strengths was reasonable, but several factors resulted in the disparity between the two sides being far less. For many years the Russian Army had treated its reserve formations as inferior units, building their peacetime regular cadres from personnel who for one reason or another were regarded as unsuitable for first-line service. Poorly equipped compared to the first-line divisions, and with poor quality officers, the reserve divisions fulfilled all the suspicions of the senior command whenever they were called up in peacetime, thus perpetuating the problem. As a result, Rennenkampf eventually advanced into East Prussia with only slightly more than six infantry divisions, leaving six second-line divisions languishing inside Russian territory. The Russian Army was also accustomed to ensuring that its fortresses were fully garrisoned, reducing still further the number of troops available for an offensive. By contrast, the German Army treated its reservists in almost the same manner as regular units, not least because of the high quality of their peacetime cadres. Additional German units were created by stripping fortresses of their garrisons and artillery.

The timetable dictated by *Stavka* was ambitious, but almost immediately was made even more so by moving the proposed date of the offensive forward one day. Whilst this resulted in several units being under strength, the biggest problem lay with logistics units. The Russian mobilisation timetable had assigned these units a low priority, meaning that even if mobilisation had been completed prior to an advance, the units required to resupply the advancing armies would barely have arrived before they had to commence work. Now the attacking armies would have almost no logistic support.

As if these problems were not sufficient, both First and Second Armies faced serious problems related to their senior personnel. Rennenkampf was a man from the old inner circle of generals descended from Baltic German families, and deeply hostile to Sukhomlinov. Zhilinski, commander of the Northwest Front, was from the opposite camp. Rennenkampf's own chief of staff, General Georgi Mileant, was also a Sukhomlinovite. Relations between the two men were so bad that they communicated with each other exclusively by writing; Rennenkampf refused to acknowledge information that was received first by his chief of staff, and treated Zhilinski with contempt, sending him almost no information about his intentions and activity. Matters were no better in Second Army, where Samsonov – a Sukhomlinovite – had General Pyotr Ivanovich Postovsky, from the opposing camp, as his chief of staff.

Rennenkampf's army crossed the border in strength on 15 August, intending to advance along the railway line that led through Stallupönen and Gumbinnen. In theory this would allow supplies to be brought forward, but the Russian railways operated a different gauge, meaning that it would take considerable time to adapt captured railway lines to allow for Russian rolling stock to be used. The alternative would require the capture of German locomotives and wagons, and the laborious transfer of men and materiel from Russian trains to German trains at the border. Concerned about his right flank, Rennenkampf ordered his cavalry commander, General Huseyn Khan Nahitchevanski, to screen to the north with four divisions of cavalry, and to outflank any opposing German forces, aiming to seize the town of Insterburg. Nahitchevanski was a 51-year-old veteran of the Russo-Japanese War, in which he had served with some distinction, but the intervening years had not been kind to him. He suffered badly from piles, restricting his ability to spend time in the saddle, and he spent much of the coming campaign completely out of touch with both his units and higher command.

On the German side of the frontier was the Rominte Heath, an area of tangled undergrowth and small copses. The Germans knew that it was most likely that the Russians would advance either north or south of the heath, rather than on both sides, and were anxious to determine the location of the leading Russian elements. Given that an advance south of the heath would lead to the difficult terrain around the Masurian Lakes, it was anticipated that the main Russian attack would come to the north, aiming to reach the Pregel valley, which then led west to Königsberg. The nearest German units belonged to I Corps, commanded by Hermann von François. Before the war, he had written about the possibility of a forward defence of East Prussia, close to the border. He argued that an aggressive posture could derail Russian plans for an early advance, thus buying precious time for the workings of the Schlieffen Plan, which required several weeks for the bulk of the German Army to defeat France before turning east.[13] Maximilian von Prittwitz, the commander of the German Eighth Army, was nervous about any such proposal, and instead ordered François to concentrate along the line of the River Angerapp, some distance to the west of the frontier. To a large extent, this was driven by an awareness of the danger to the German positions posed by Samsonov's Second Army in the south. If large parts of Eighth Army were drawn into heavy and prolonged fighting near the eastern frontier, then regardless of the success of such a battle, there was a strong likelihood of Samsonov simply marching into the rear of Prittwitz's forces. A position on the Angerapp would be able to deal equally with a Russian advance either to the south of Rominte Heath, or to the north.

For François, defending the line of the Angerapp – thus giving up all of East Prussia to the east of the valley – was unacceptable, especially given his personal view that an aggressive forward defence was not only possible, but desirable. He was also an ardent enthusiast for the beliefs of the elder Moltke when it came to developed decision-making, and was therefore perfectly happy to take matters into his own hands. François began to edge forward from his positions on the Angerapp, advancing his units in increments – first a battalion, then another, with some guns in support. By 13 August, most of his corps was deployed roughly in a line from Goldap in the south to Stallupönen in the north, about 20 miles (32km) east of the Angerapp valley. The following day, concluding from his reconnaissance reports that the Russians intended to advance exclusively north of the Rominte Heath, Prittwitz ordered the rest of his army to move to the line of the Angerapp.[14] Meanwhile, François ordered his cavalry to probe along the frontier, in an attempt to determine the exact location of Russian forces.

Eighth Army Headquarters was operating with only partial information. Prittwitz had at his disposal a resource unknown to any general in earlier wars: the aircraft of *Flieger Abteilung 16*, which flew reconnaissance missions to the south. The pilots informed him that Samsonov's Second Army was still concentrating, but appeared to be doing so at a faster rate than expected. However, information was fragmentary, partly due to the primitive nature of aerial reconnaissance, and partly due to deteriorating weather conditions.[15] Information from François' I Corps was also incomplete. Aware that his chief of staff, Oberst Walter Schmidt von Schmidtseck, disapproved of his rather cavalier attitude to Prittwitz's orders, François left his corps headquarters, together with his chief of staff, in Insterburg, at the northern end of the Angerapp position, and effectively forbade Schmidtseck from giving a clear report of I Corps' positions to Prittwitz.

Late on 15 August François' men were involved in a sharp exchange with Russian forces to the northeast of the town of Stallupönen (renamed Ebenrode in 1938, now Nesterov). François was with his leading units, perhaps at least partly to avoid having to explain to Prittwitz why he had advanced beyond the Angerapp, and witnessed the attempts of his men to fire on a water tower, which was being used by the Russians as an observation point for their artillery:

> From a haystack to the northeast [of Stallupönen] in Szuggern, I saw the artillery duel and our infantry advancing in stages. The Russians were again busy with their torches, and the sky north of Eydtkuhnen [a village right on the frontier] was painted red by the flames of burning villages. As the heavy howitzer battery ... trotted forward, I accompanied it into its firing position, and forward of that found a good observation point. The battery commander promised to fulfil his mission quickly. The shells landed right next to the tower. As the hundredth shot was fired, I ordered them to stop. The last shot didn't hit the tower either, but landed on the neighbouring gasworks, hurling its roof into the air in a huge explosion. Eydtkuhnen was taken at 1 a.m. The enemy pulled back to the frontier in order to offer strong resistance from deeply dug positions. Their strength was estimated at one division.[16]

This estimate is very likely an exaggeration; the Russian forces were little more than First Army's reconnaissance elements.

The following day saw little action. Suddenly aware of just how far east I Corps had deployed, Prittwitz ordered François to pull back to Gumbinnen, leaving only small reconnaissance units further forward. This would still place François some distance to the east of the rest of Eight Army on the Angerapp, but the aircrews of *Flieger Abteilung 16* had informed Prittwitz that large numbers of Russian troops appeared to be advancing west directly towards the Angerapp valley. Consequently, Prittwitz reasoned, it might be prudent to leave I Corps in the Gumbinnen area, from where it might be able to strike into the flank and rear of any Russian thrust against the Angerapp. But far from concentrating around Gumbinnen, François decided to keep his men further east. The 1st Infantry Division remained in Stallupönen, with 2nd Infantry Division divided between Goldap and Tollmingkehmen, covering the northern side of the Rominte Heath. Anxious to cover as broad an area as possible, François was left with only a battery of howitzers as reserve, based in Gumbinnen.

On 17 August Rennenkampf pushed forward again, once more towards Stallupönen. François was visiting one of his front-line battalions to give his congratulations to Major Schmidt, an infantry officer who had fought with particular distinction on 15 August, when the assault intensified:

Smoke and fire on the horizon, more than before, were today's signs. I was still talking to Major Schmidt when heavy gunfire broke out in front of the position. A cyclist brought a message that the Russians were advancing and had already pushed into Mecken, south of Bilderweitschen. I went to the same haystack near Szuggern, which had given me a good overview of the fighting two days before. Without binoculars, we could see an extended skirmish line moving towards Szuggern, but we too were spotted and had to leave the area. In Stallupönen, I encountered General [Richard] von Conta [commander of 1st Infantry Division] who had already received reports that several enemy columns were marching against Stallupönen, and that his troops were engaged in combat.[17]

The nearest reinforcements were elements of General Adalbert von Falk's 2nd Infantry Division in Tollmingkehmen, about 11 miles (18km) away. François summoned them by telephone, as well as ordering his only reserves, the howitzers in Gumbinnen, to move forward to Stallupönen. By late morning, four battalions of 2nd Infantry Division, together with supporting artillery, had reached Göritten. Meanwhile, François had taken up a post in the church tower in Stallupönen, from where he could see that the battle was now raging on a front of over 9 miles (14km). To his irritation, a local civilian official decided that the church bell should be rung to warn locals to flee, resulting in an unwelcome deafening addition to the increasing sounds of battle.

The Russian advance consisted of all three of Rennenkampf's infantry corps. His XX Corps, with 28th and 29th Infantry Divisions, was north of the road from the frontier, with III Corps (25th and 27th Infantry Divisions) on the road itself and to the south. Further south was IV Corps, with 40th and 30th Infantry Divisions, advancing towards the Rominte Heath. An independent rifle brigade deployed on the extreme southern flank, supported by a single cavalry division, while the bulk of Rennenkampf's cavalry remained to the north.[18] This advance in strength should have brushed aside François' thinly spread troops, but there was little coordination between the three corps. III Corps crossed the frontier early in the morning, with the flanking corps only entering German territory nearer midday. This was partly due to the Russian policy of deploying into line at the first threat of enemy contact, which resulted in a slower advance, but it has also been suggested that coordination within the Russian Army was further hampered by the simple fact that many officers, and most NCOs, were strangers to the concept of mechanically measured time, with few of them having much familiarity with watches and clocks. Consequently, there was a poor understanding of the requirement to advance at a given time.[19] Nevertheless, the German 1st Infantry Division soon found itself in an increasingly tough battle for Stallupönen, though the arrival of I Corps' howitzers at midday provided a welcome boost. François was still in the church tower, watching the battle:

> At this moment – about 1pm – an envoy from General Prittwitz arrived by car, and told me, in a loud voice in view of the large number of officers present: 'The commanding officer orders the immediate breaking off of the engagement and a retreat to Gumbinnen!' I replied to him: 'Tell General von Prittwitz that General von François will break off the engagement when the Russians are defeated.'[20]

It was a rather vainglorious moment, though entirely in keeping with François' character. It seems that Prittwitz had contacted I Corps Headquarters in Insterburg during the morning, and had finally learned from Schmidtseck that François' troops were deployed far further east than Prittwitz had imagined, at least 24 miles (38km) in advance of any other elements of Eighth Army – hence the urgent order for an immediate retreat to Gumbinnen. It seems that the wording of the reply was toned down before it reached Prittwitz, who was told that François said that he was not able at the moment to break off combat. In

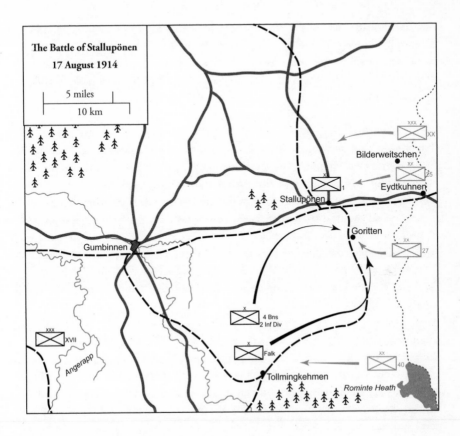

The Battle of Stallupönen
17 August 1914

5 miles

10 km

any event, disengagement in the midst of a fight against superior enemy forces would have been a hazardous business, especially given the fact that both flanks of the position at Stallupönen were being enveloped.

François was aware that the four battalions of Falk's 2nd Infantry Division in Göritten seemed to be under increasing pressure, and he decided to investigate, leaving the defence of Stallupönen in the hands of General von Conta. He discovered that 2nd Infantry Division had its hands full dealing with Russian forces advancing on a front from the Rominte Heath in the south to the Stallupönen area in the north. But the advance was disjointed, and a gap of several miles had opened up between the Russian 27th Infantry Division and 40th Infantry Division to its south. Coordination between the two divisions, from different infantry corps, was almost non-existent, offering ample opportunities for German counterattacks. Immediately north of the Rominte

Heath, Falk had gathered together a force a little larger than a regiment. Much as generals had done for centuries, Falk had followed the sounds of heavy fighting, in this case towards the north. As a result, when François arrived, he was leading an attack towards Göritten into the exposed flank of the advancing Russian 27th Infantry Division;

> The attack led directly into the rear of the Russians across open land, crossed by the main road and railway line, which the Russians had crossed in the same direction when attacking towards Göritten ... dead and wounded Russians littered the field. A badly wounded Russian colonel – the commander of 105th Infantry Regiment – sat on the edge of the ditch by the side of the road; Russian medics had already dressed the gaping wound in his chest. I will never forget his expression, full of pain and grief.
>
> As soon as the Russians became aware of the attack in their rear, they surrendered by the company. About 3,000 men were captured in this position alone. We could see the Russians fleeing east at Göritten, and their artillery fell silent along the entire front. The battle was won.[21]

Colonel Komarov, the wounded man that François saw sitting by the side of the road, did not survive.[22]

It had been a battle out of the 19th century, with the opposing forces clashing on a relatively small battlefield, broken into a series of smaller engagements by a series of low hills. Through a mixture of poor coordination by the Russians, good judgement, and good initiative shown by his subordinates, particularly Falk, François had won a remarkable victory. This brought Rennenkampf's advance to a halt within a few miles of the frontier. The battle was not without setbacks; to the north of Stallupönen, the Russian 29th and 25th Infantry Divisions combined their forces to drive back elements of Conta's 1st Infantry Division at Bilderweitschen, capturing several prisoners and eight guns. Nevertheless, François had good reason to be pleased with the outcome, and the performance of his men. His losses amounted to about 1,300 casualties; Russian dead and wounded numbered about 5,000, in addition to the haul of prisoners from the counterattack at Göritten.

Conta and François briefly discussed pursuing the Russians right to the frontier, but decided against such an action. Instead, orders were given to withdraw on Gumbinnen. Returning to his corps headquarters, François found a further message waiting for him, tersely demanding why he had deployed his corps in battle contrary to his orders:

I reported my reasons to General von Prittwitz by telephone. In response to the reproaches that he heaped upon me, I replied that he would think differently about the battle at Stallupönen in the morning. I was then able to advise him that the Russians, their strength estimated at two corps, had been pushed back across the frontier. The haul of prisoners exceeded 3,000.[23]

While the unrepentant François reported to his superiors, the Russian high command waited in frustration for news of developments:

General Headquarters [*Stavka*] at first only received very brief and incomplete reports of this engagement, which occurred near Stallupönen. They were limited to saying that ultimately, the Germans were forced to withdraw after losing several guns, while some of our units had suffered heavy losses under heavy artillery fire… In reality, as one learned later, there had been serious errors in the leadership of our troops and in reconnaissance in this first engagement, errors that resulted in a heavy tactical setback and the almost complete annihilation of one of our most valorous regiments which the Germans had opportunistically attacked in the flank and rear. Thus we saw on the first day of fighting, the reopening of the old wound that had long poisoned the wellbeing of our army, a tendency to dissimulate facts. During the course of the war, this malady, never eliminated, repeatedly prevented us from seeing the situation clearly and correcting such errors in a timely manner, as they were detected.[24]

These criticisms seem to be entirely justified. Coordination between units in Rennenkampf's First Army was poor. The fact that 29th Infantry Division's commander, General Anatoly Nikolaevich Rozenschield-Paulin, took it upon himself to turn his units to support the neighbouring 25th Infantry Division in a flank attack was regarded as noteworthy and remarkable, rather than what one would expect of any infantry commander in his position. With most of his cavalry covering his northern flank, Rennenkampf had little or no reconnaissance information about German dispositions, and thus missed an opportunity to concentrate his forces and overwhelm François' dispersed formations.

François chose this moment to settle scores with his own chief of staff, Schmidtseck. Learning that the latter had ignored orders not to communicate I Corps' deployments to Eighth Army Headquarters, François wrote to the kaiser, requesting that he be assigned a new chief of staff, as he no longer trusted Schmidtseck. The hapless chief of staff had done nothing wrong – he had a right under German army protocols to share concerns with higher authorities – but this was to no avail in the face of a complaint from a successful superior. A replacement was assigned shortly after.

The orders to I Corps to withdraw towards Gumbinnen were carried out in good order after the day of hard fighting, and without interference by the Russians. Unfortunately, the withdrawal order did not reach two companies of German soldiers from 1st Infantry Division, who had held out all day near Bilderweitschen. In the pre-dawn darkness of 18 August, the Russian III Corps probed forward, encountered the Germans, and began to encircle them. The senior German officer present refused to retreat, insisting that he had received no orders, and rejected a call from the Russians to surrender. As ammunition began to run out, the Germans finally decided that they had to withdraw, and managed to use the remaining time before dawn to break contact and retreat in good order, taking with them a small group of Russian prisoners they had captured the previous day.[25]

The success of Falk's flanking attack, marching north from the direction of the Rominte Heath, persuaded Rennenkampf to extend his own line to the north as he resumed his cautious advance. His orders were to turn the northern flank of the German Eighth Army, preventing it from falling back on Königsberg, and he ordered General Huseyn Nahitchevanski to advance with his cavalry around the north of the battlefield of Stallupönen and on to Insterburg. There were a few skirmishes between Russian and German horsemen on 18 August, but the following day scouts advised Nahitchevanski that German troops had arrived by train and were heading for Kraupischken. This was a vital crossing point over the River Inster, which flowed southwest towards Insterburg. Nahitchevanski acted with unaccustomed energy, advancing on Kraupischken and storming the hastily prepared German defences. The Germans withdrew across the river to the northwest bank, from where they could dominate the lower southeast bank. After this limited success, Nahitchevanski reverted to his previous caution, and made little attempt to use the mobility of his forces to find a way past, either during the battle or after.

Rennenkampf, who had made his reputation as a dashing cavalry commander on the Chinese frontier at the turn of the century, had already been critical of the handling of his cavalry, which had failed to intervene during the fighting at Stallupönen. He sent an exasperated message to his cavalry commander, ordering him to reconnoitre immediately towards Insterburg and Gumbinnen, and to exert better control over his subordinates:

As before, I remain convinced that these operations were quite unsuccessful. The central column (1st Guards Cavalry Division), having encountered the enemy

124

frontally, quite correctly deployed. The flank divisions of Belgard [3rd Cavalry Division] and Raukh [2nd Guards Cavalry Division] should then have been dispatched in full force to take the enemy in flank. From General Raukh's statement, I know that he dispatched part of his division with the artillery; but General Belgard literally astonishes me. Is it possible that a general who has risen to be appointed commander of a division can be ignorant of the fact that in outflanking operations he must take his three batteries with him? The enemy, taken by artillery enfilade fire from both flanks, would have been annihilated. The whole of his 12 guns would have fallen into your hands with ease, but as it was you only took two, at the cost of heavy casualties. The heavy responsibility for all these losses lies upon your division commanders... If those in command are not worthy of their appointments, you must in duty bound have no pity, otherwise all responsibility would devolve entirely upon you. I have given ... many criticisms with regard to your absolutely unsatisfactory reports. I know nothing, or at any rate too little, about your operations, and about your losses almost nothing.[26]

Given Rennenkampf's own reluctance to keep *Stavka* informed of his own setbacks and losses, the last point seems unintentionally ironic. Nahitchevanski, a descendant of Tatar horsemen, was struggling to cope with a war that seemed to offer him no opportunities for the glorious application of horsepower and steel that his ancestors had enjoyed. On the one occasion that he actually managed to get his men into a charge, leading to the capture of a couple of German guns at Kraupischken, his commanding officer lambasted him, rather than congratulating him for his exploits. Increasingly bewildered, he ordered his men to retreat, claiming that artillery ammunition had not been sent forward to replenish his troops. Pre-war exercises might have highlighted that many senior officers regarded the task of ensuring their own supplies was a matter beneath them, but in such exercises logistic arrangements were ignored in order to spare their blushes. Trying to find out what First Army's cavalry was doing, Rennenkampf's aides finally found Nahitchevanski sitting in tears in his tent, unable even to mount his horse due to the pain from his piles.[27]

As François had predicted, Prittwitz took a slightly different view of events once he received the details of the Stallupönen engagement. His strategic problem was that he knew only too well that he was facing two Russian armies, and his only hope of success was to defeat them in detail. In view of the success of I Corps, he now decided to venture out of his positions along the Angerapp. I Corps was ordered to stay around Gumbinnen, but in order to guard against the northern flank being turned, François was ordered to withdraw his

2nd Infantry Division into reserve. To replace Falk's men in their positions south of Gumbinnen, François was assigned approximately a division of reservists from the Königsberg garrison.

There was now a pressing need for Prittwitz to force a decision with Rennenkampf's army. The intrepid pilots of *Flieger Abteilung 16* were still monitoring Russian movements, and reported that there remained a large gap between the southern flank of Rennenkampf's First Army and the Russian Second Army, which had finally begun to move forward from Poland. Originally, Prittwitz had intended to hold the line of the Angerapp and allow Rennenkampf to suffer heavy casualties while trying to force the position. But he now received additional intelligence, in the form of a radio intercept, that Rennenkampf had ordered his men to halt their advance on 20 August for a day's rest. The onus for driving matters to a conclusion now lay with the Germans.

The intercepted Russian radio message had been transmitted without any coding; the Germans were aware that their opponents had concerns about the ability of their officers to cope with codes, and it is well known that Russian communications were often compromised as a result. Whilst this has frequently been stated as a major advantage for the Germans, it should be pointed out that the Germans, too, had problems with codes. As has already been described, the Russians acquired a complete set of German naval codebooks in the first month of the war, and many army signals were sent without any coding. The pressure of time often meant that risks were taken and signals were simply transmitted *en clair* by both sides.

While Prittwitz and his chief of staff, Georg von Waldersee – son of Alfred, the former Chief of the General Staff – debated the relative merits of whether and how to attack the Russians, a message arrived from François during the afternoon of 19 August. Russian forces were moving closer to Gumbinnen, he reported, and he expected to come under attack the following day. However, scouts reported that the northern flank of the Russian advance was exposed, and François suggested that he move 2nd Infantry Division to his own northern wing, to take the Russians in their flank. To support this, he requested that Prittwitz bring XVII Corps and I Reserve Corps forward in support.

The flank of the Russian First Army was exposed as a consequence of the failure of Nahitchevanski to follow orders. After further reconnaissance reports had confirmed that Samsonov's Second Army was slowly advancing on Ortelsburg, Prittwitz decided, albeit reluctantly, that François' assessment and intention was correct. He visited Mackensen in Darkehmen, where he irritably informed the commander of XVII Corps that 'I Corps had made a soup for us, and we will now have to eat it up'.[28] XVII Corps was to move up in support of I Corps, while I Reserve Corps covered the army's southern flank. If the Russians turned to face François, XVII Corps would take them in the flank. The weakness of the plan, however, was that the three German corps would arrive on the battlefield in echelon, with I Corps entering combat first, followed by XVII Corps, and I Reserve Corps not even expected to take part in the main battle. Prittwitz was in danger of mounting as disjointed an advance as Rennenkampf had on 17 August.

Falk's 2nd Division was ordered to make a night move into positions to the north of Gumbinnen, so that he could advance at 4 a.m. on 20 August. His troops set off at 9 p.m. the previous evening, but almost immediately a messenger arrived and reported that Russian forces had broken through the northern flank of 1st Infantry Division. Falk immediately deployed his troops for a counterattack. By the time he learned that the message was a false alarm, valuable time had been lost. It was not the only false alarm. Earlier in the evening, German soldiers had opened fire on an unexpected aircraft, before realising it was one of their own; the noise of the gunfire panicked some supply troops, who rode off to the rear in disorder. Now, another such scare cost Falk two hours. He telephoned François and told his corps commander that he doubted that he would be in position in time for an attack at 4 a.m. François replied that he had to be ready at all costs.

The soldiers of 2nd Infantry Division marched through the Zülkinner Forest in the darkness, with visibility worsened by fog, to their starting positions. 1st Infantry Division's artillery opened fire at 3.30 a.m., and as the Russian gunners slowly began to respond, Falk's men launched their attack. Opposing them was the Russian XX Corps, aligned to face south as part of Rennenkampf's plan to bypass and turn the northern flank of the German position. Now the Russians found that they had been outflanked. The Russian 28th Infantry Division had made little provision for a German advance against its flank, believing that it was protected by the mass of Nahitchevanski's cavalry, which had been tasked with at least determining if German troops were in the Zülkinner Forest, even if seizure of the forest was not possible. But Nahitchevanski had already withdrawn, leaving behind only a weak brigade; it was easily driven off by the German 1st Cavalry Division.

The initial German surge captured the village of Mallwischken, and a Russian counterattack was repulsed. Much of the Russian 28th Infantry Division was scattered or destroyed, losing perhaps 60 per cent of its combat strength.[29] One unit, carrying the standard of the division's 111th Regiment, retreated all the way to Kovno, deep inside the territory of the Russian Empire. But as the German infantry moved beyond the support of their artillery, and as Russian resistance stiffened, the advance slowed. A Russian artilleryman described the fighting:

> Our infantry held out long and stubbornly. No individual firing could be heard; it was as though a gigantic kettle was boiling. Ever nearer and nearer... And then machine-gun bullets began to whistle into the battery. Under a terrible fire, its ranks thinned by half and with nearly all its officers casualties, 28th Infantry Division slowly retreated behind the line of the artillery... The main road ran less than a verst [about 0.6 miles, or 1km] in front of the batteries, and in a minute's time, as far as the eye could reach, a grey wave of dense German columns poured across the road. The batteries opened fire, and the white stretch of the road became grey with the numbers of the dead. Then a second wave of men in spiked helmets; again rapid fire, and again all lay on the road. Then a German battery audaciously galloped out and took up a position in the open, and at the same time an aeroplane with black crosses flew over our batteries. The German infantry pushed on against the batteries and outflanked the 4th [at the northern end of the artillery position], which poured shrapnel into them at point-blank range, but a German machine-gun opened fire against its rear, and it was wiped out. The German infantry got up to 500–600 paces in front of the batteries and lay down, firing. The batteries could only maintain a desultory fire against the enemy, as there was hardly any ammunition left.[30]

Rennenkampf's First Army had started the war with roughly 420 rounds of artillery ammunition per gun, rising to 737 as mobilisation progressed. Although this was to prove hopelessly inadequate, such realisations lay in the future; during a whole year of fighting in the Russo-Japanese War, Russian artillery had averaged less than 1,000 rounds per gun. For the anticipated short war, 737 rounds per gun were thought to be adequate. The reality was that the guns rapidly ran short of ammunition, especially as even the limited supply available was only brought forward slowly.

1st Infantry Division joined the attack, and although heartened by a steady stream of prisoners from the fall of Mallwischken, the Germans were dismayed by the accuracy and weight of Russian artillery fire. Casualties were modest by comparison to the slaughter on the Western Front, or indeed in the east in later battles, but for men in their first month of war, they were serious enough to reduce the German advance to a crawl. To his alarm, François learned that the improvised division from Königsberg, commanded by Generalleutnant Georg

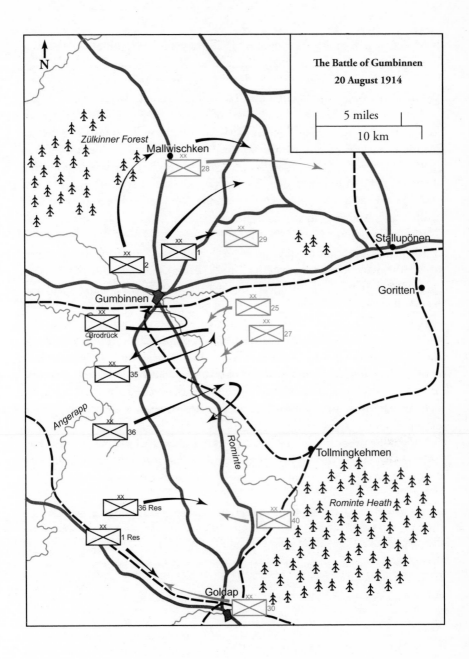

N

The Battle of Gumbinnen
20 August 1914

5 miles

10 km

Zülkinner Forest

Mallwischken

28

29

Stallupönen

2

1

Gumbinnen

Goritten

Brodrück

25

27

35

Angerapp

36

Rominte

Tollmingkehmen

36 Res

Rominte Heath

1 Res

40

Goldap

30

Brodrück, which should have been in defensive positions south of Gumbinnen, had also attacked. Unsurprisingly, the mixture of reservists and garrison troops made little headway, and merely suffered heavy losses as they ran into Russian positions alerted by the fighting further north. Although disadvantaged by the collapse of 28th Infantry Division, the other unit of the Russian XX Corps, Rozenschield-Paulin's 29th Infantry Division, fought well, repulsing all attacks against its lines. Matters were made worse for the Germans by confusion between their infantry and artillery. Many of the losses of Brodrück's division were from shrapnel fired by the guns of other German units.[31] 1st and 2nd Infantry Divisions also suffered casualties from the indiscriminate firing of 2nd Infantry Division's artillery, even resulting in a temporary retreat.

Further south, the German XVII Corps, commanded by General August von Mackensen, was meant to move up in support of François during the preceding night. The march of approximately 15 miles (24km) to the starting positions for the planned attack on 20 August should have been straightforward, but was repeatedly held up by German refugees trying to escape towards the west. In light rain, the soldiers – damp, tired, and dispirited – struggled into their forming-up areas. At the outset, Mackensen was worried about a lack of information about the Russian forces that he might face. At 8 p.m. on the evening of the approach march, he received an optimistic report from François, advising him that only weak Russian units would oppose him. As the evening progressed, further updates arrived, gradually increasing the reported strength of the Russians south of Gumbinnen.[32]

While his subordinates struggled to round up stragglers and sort out their units, Mackensen tried in vain to determine what was going on. From high ground near the River Rominte, he peered through the morning mist:

> At dawn ... as the Rominte valley and the neighbouring land gradually appeared before my eyes, I could see that the enemy had left the vital crossing unopposed for my corps. As far as Grünweitschen, only patrols or pickets were visible in the foreground. From the north, apparently in front of I Corps, sounds of battle could be heard at first light, and then rapidly intensifying artillery fire.[33]

The sounds of fighting to the north in I Corps' sector were a clear sign that the battle had started, but Mackensen still had no clear idea of what Russian forces faced his own corps. There were no orders from Prittwitz, and – remarkably for a man who was a former hussar – Mackensen made no attempt to send his small force of cavalry forward to reconnoitre.[34] As it began to grow light, he decided that he was most likely confronted by only the flank guard of the Russian First Army, which appeared to be heavily engaged around Gumbinnen. Believing that I Reserve Corps was protecting his right flank, he ordered his two divisions, 35th Infantry Division in the north and 36th Infantry Division in the south, to advance northeast.

The troops of XVII Corps were in confident mood, despite their hard approach march. They had been told that they were striking against the enemy's flank and rear, and were keen to get into action:

> The attack order was received with jubilation that was hard to suppress, and the ammunition wagons almost stormed with shouts of 'hurrah!' Finally, finally it was beginning! Night march, fatigue – now, just onwards![35]

Mackensen's advance began at 4.30 a.m. and made good progress, crossing the Rominte and reaching the road running south from Gumbinnen by mid-morning. The southern division of the corps encountered increasingly strong Russian resistance, and launched an attack without waiting for its artillery to deploy and prepare the way. In difficult terrain the attack disintegrated, with disproportionately high casualties amongst the officers, who were trying to lead from the front in the best traditions of peacetime training. The Russians, from III Corps' 25th and 27th Infantry Divisions, had been moving forward themselves. They reacted to the encounter battle better than their German opponents, rapidly improvising a strong defensive line. A German platoon commander later described the fighting:

> It was like hell opening out before us. Fire from the village of Warschlegen, from the right flank by the windmill, from the village of Sodehnen, and a no less heavy fire from the left ... no enemy was to be seen; nothing but the fire of thousands of rifles, of machine-guns and of artillery... Units quickly thinned out. Whole ranks already lay dead. Groans and cries resounded over the whole field. Our artillery was late in opening fire... Some batteries came into action in the open upon the heights, but almost immediately we saw shells bursting between the guns, the ammunition wagons disappearing in all directions, and loose horses galloping riderless over the battlefield. Ammunition-wagons in the batteries were blown into the air. The infantry were pinned down by Russian fire; the men lay with their faces to the ground, no one daring so much as to raise his head, let alone firing a shot himself. It was the same picture in the 128th Regiment. The

village of Ribinnen was taken by them, but then a storm of fire broke over them, and very soon the regiment reported that its strength was spent.[36]

35th Infantry Division to the north made good headway at first. As resistance began to strengthen, a messenger arrived from I Corps, urging XVII Corps to turn north: the Russians were tied down by I Corps, and this would take them in the flank and rear. Without waiting for approval from Mackensen, Generalmajor Johannes von Hahn, commander of 87th Infantry Brigade, the most northern part of the corps, decided to change the direction of his advance, veering to the north. If the message from I Corps had been correct, it would have been an excellent move. But instead, the attack ran into the point where the Russian 25th and 27th Infantry Divisions joined. Both Russian divisions withdrew a short distance, resulting in Hahn's brigade advancing into a salient, where it came under heavy artillery fire from three sides.

After two further attempts to rally and push forward, the Germans began to retreat during the afternoon. An officer on Mackensen's staff saw the first signs of the growing setback:

> In the early afternoon, the first signs of retreat from Grünweitschen began to be seen. At first, we saw individuals, then small and large bodies of troops crumbling, some of them passing the location of the corps commander. Officers of the staff halted them and organised them into a firing line, facing the enemy again, even if they weren't sent back to the battle-line. The commander himself also went amongst the men, encouraging them with quiet, earnest words about their duty. It was particularly striking when an artilleryman appeared on a horse and reported that he was the survivor of a battery that had been destroyed. Following the arrival of reports from all parts of the front, but particularly the northern flank of 35th Infantry Division about the unhealthy battle situation and of retreating elements, the mood in headquarters grew grimmer. Naturally, it didn't help when an enemy battery began to fire on the location of headquarters... There was unrest amongst the staff and a distinct movement towards the rear. But it was rapidly stopped by the outstanding personal conduct of the corps commander. General von Mackensen had his white horse brought forward onto the high ground, mounted up, and road with his chief of staff to an isolated farmhouse, where he took up position and the staff also followed.[37]

The Russians attempted to pursue the retreating Germans, trying to turn their flanks, only to have their own attack brought to a halt by artillery fire. But

XVII Corps' infantry was now in full retreat, the artillery swept along by the disintegrated remnants of infantry battalions and companies. It was impossible to maintain order, and the survivors streamed back in chaos to the line of the River Rominte. Some continued as far as the Angerapp. Of his 30,000 men Mackensen had lost over a quarter. The Russian 27th Infantry Division alone claimed to have captured twelve artillery pieces, twenty-five ammunition wagons, and about 1,000 prisoners.[38]

The most southerly part of Prittwitz' army, General Otto von Below's I Reserve Corps, was ordered to advance towards Goldap, and to cover the southern flank of XVII Corps. When his cavalry reported that there appeared to be no Russians to his front, Below decided to turn his corps north, in an attempt to help Mackensen by launching a flank attack on the Russians who were putting up such strong resistance. Unfortunately for Below the reconnaissance carried out by his cavalry was inadequate, and General Korotkevich's 30th Infantry Division, the most southern formation in Rennenkampf's main battle line, advanced from Goldap into the flank of the German 1st Reserve Division. Both sides suffered heavy losses from artillery fire, and bitter fighting raged through much of the day. Weaker in artillery than a regular division, the German unit rapidly lost many of its guns to efficient and accurate Russian counter-battery fire. Driven partly by self preservation – the closer they were to the Russians, the less likely they were to come under Russian artillery fire – the German infantry continued to press forward. During the afternoon, the German 36th Reserve Division was able to push in the centre of the Russian line. For a moment it seemed possible that the Germans would be able to drive Korotkevich from the field, and then turn north to support Mackensen, but by throwing his last reserves into action, the Russian commander was able to stabilise his position.

A short distance to the south of I Reserve Corps was the German 3rd Reserve Division, commanded by Curt von Morgen. It had enjoyed a relatively quiet start to the war, covering the line of the Masurian Lakes. At about 4.30 p.m. its commander received a telephone call from Prittwitz, ordering him to strike against the flank of the German forces facing I Reserve Corps. As dusk fell Morgen's leading elements reached high ground south of the battlefield, from where they could see the smoke of exploding shells. It was too late to intervene, but Morgen was confident that his approach had not been detected, and he looked forward to striking a blow against the Russians the following day.[39]

It had been a day of mixed fortunes. Despite suffering losses, François' two divisions had been largely successful. Mackensen's corps, by contrast, had been effectively knocked out of action; its troops streamed back in disarray, with

Mackensen and his staff swept along in the flood. I Reserve Corps to the south had acquitted itself well, but had ended just short of a decisive success. On the Russian side, their northern flank had taken a beating, but was still intact. In their centre, 27th Infantry Division had demonstrated a high level of coordination between its infantry and artillery, as well as with its neighbouring divisions, resulting in the defeat of the German XVII Corps. And if the Russian IV Corps had failed to turn the southern flank of the German position, nor had it been defeated. The German hopes of a swift victory, allowing them to turn triumphantly against Samsonov's Second Army in the south, looked increasingly forlorn. As darkness fell, the normally cautious Prittwitz pondered whether he had been wise to listen to the urgings of François, and a crisis of confidence developed that threatened to have wide-ranging consequences.

CHAPTER 6

CRISIS OF COMMAND

Maximilian von Prittwitz had originally intended to defend the line of the Angerapp valley. He had been drawn into attacking Rennenkampf's First Army partly because he felt that he had to strike a blow before the Russian Second Army moved against his rear, and partly because of the success of his subordinate, Hermann von François, at Stallupönen. At first on 20 August the mood in Eighth Army's headquarters was optimistic, but as the day progressed, the stream of reports about the collapse of Mackensen's XVII Corps, and the apparent inability of either flank corps to advance, seemed to bring about a major change. Prittwitz's earlier message to *Oberste Heeresleitung* (*OHL* – the Supreme Army Command), that the battle was proceeding well and looked likely to bring about a major success, began to look increasingly premature.

The news from the south was also alarming. In order to concentrate as much of his army as possible against Rennenkampf, Prittwitz had left only Friedrich von Scholtz's reinforced XX Corps to cover the border between East Prussia and Russian-occupied Poland. In the early afternoon the German radio station in Posen (now Poznań) intercepted a signal from Samsonov's Second Army, giving its strength as five corps and a cavalry division – a far larger force than the German corps facing it. When this intelligence was passed to Eighth Army, Prittwitz telephoned Emil Hell, Scholtz's chief of staff. Hell seemed to be very confident. He told Prittwitz that XX Corps' own aerial reconnaissance confirmed that at least six Russian divisions were about to cross the border, but he and Scholtz believed that they would be able to hold their positions while Prittwitz completed his victory at Gumbinnen.[1]

By late afternoon Prittwitz had become more concerned about his prospects of victory. When he telephoned François at 5 p.m., the ebullient corps commander told his superior that he had enjoyed a successful day, taking over 6,000 prisoners and eight Russian guns. Prittwitz's response filled him with dismay: XVII Corps was unable to advance (in fact, it was barely functioning as an organised body by this time). Given the threat to XX Corps from the south, Prittwitz added that he might need to withdraw behind the Vistula.

François was aghast, and asked for more time. On 21 August he maintained, his corps would be able to continue to turn the flank of the Russian position, thus clearing the Russian forces in front of XVII Corps. Prittwitz was unconvinced, but promised to phone back later. François began to plan for a resumption of the battle in the morning, but back at Eighth Army Headquarters, Prittwitz received more alarming news. Aerial reconnaissance from Graudenz (now Grudziadz) reported that a large body of Russian infantry was marching towards Mlawa, and there were signs that an even more substantial force was following it. The significance of this report – confirmed by a later flight by aircraft from XX Corps – was that Mlawa lay far to the west of the small covering force assigned to cover the western flank of XX Corps. If the Russians had a large body of troops this far west, they would be able to turn north and cut off all of Eighth Army from the Vistula.

Prittwitz now telephoned Moltke in Koblenz, who had his hands full with the campaign in the west. He told Moltke that the attack at Gumbinnen had failed, that XVII Corps had effectively been knocked out, and that he intended to break contact with Rennenkampf's army and retreat to the Vistula. Moltke was, predictably, furious. The entire strategy of defending against a Russian attack on East Prussia had been based upon the principle that a smaller German force would be able to use internal lines of communication and movement to defeat each of its opposing armies, by concentrating first against one, then the other. If Eighth Army retreated to the line of the Vistula, the two Russian armies would be able to combine their strength, and such a strategy would unravel completely. Moltke told Prittwitz that the proposed retreat was out of the question. With equal anger, Prittwitz responded that he would need reinforcements; at this time of year the water level of the Vistula was low, and his forces were too few to defend such a long front. The mood and confidence of the commander of Eighth Army were not improved by Moltke's reply. He would just have to manage, replied the chief of the general staff, whose own campaign against France was not proceeding as well as he had planned and hoped. Testily, he told Prittwitz that the commander of Eighth Army could not expect Moltke to plan his campaign for him from Koblenz.[2]

Max Hoffmann, who was deputy chief of staff in Eighth Army Headquarters, later recalled the evening of 20 August. When news arrived of the Russian forces approaching Mlawa, Hoffmann suggested, not entirely seriously, that perhaps the staff should keep the message from Prittwitz, in an attempt to persuade him to renew the fighting at Gumbinnen:

> At that moment, the Commander-in-Chief [Prittwitz] and the Chief of Staff [Alfred von Waldersee] came out of their quarters next to the office, and I saw from their faces that they had already received the message. General von Prittwitz asked us to come into the office with them. 'Gentlemen,' he said, 'I see you have also received the message, and you know that the Russian Army from Warsaw will advance on our rear if we continue the battle, and cut us off from the Vistula. The army shall therefore break off the fight and retire behind the Vistula.' General [Paul] Grünert [Quartermaster-General of Eighth Army] tried to explain his and my different standpoint: that the battle near Gumbinnen was in a favourable position; that in two or three days we would be able to make an end of the Russian Army from Vilna [Rennenkampf's First Army]; and that there would then be sufficient time to turn on the enemy from Warsaw. Until then General von Scholtz and his [XX] corps would have to manage for themselves. General von Prittwitz cut short General Grünert's discourse abruptly, and said that he had decided to retire beyond the Vistula, and only he, and the Chief of Staff, were responsible for tactical decisions, and not the first officer of the General Staff [i.e. Hoffmann], nor the Quartermaster-General. This was followed by orders given to me by Count Waldersee to make the necessary dispositions for the retreat of the army beyond the Vistula. I explained that I considered it would be impossible for the army to retire beyond the Vistula and I therefore requested to be instructed how the Commander-in-Chief wished the retreat to be effected. Then the question of how the retreat was to be carried out was discussed. General Grünert and I showed ... that a simple retreat beyond the Vistula would be impossible, as in order to retire in that way we would have to fight the left wing of the Russian Warsaw Army, which was nearer to the Vistula than we were. Therefore, it would be necessary to stop the advance of the Warsaw Army, and the easiest way would be by an offensive thrust at the left wing of that army. General von Prittwitz, who as well as General Waldersee had for a moment lost command over his nerves, saw the necessity of the measures we proposed. However, he stuck to his opinion that it was necessary to break off the battle against Rennenkampf, but he gave up the intention of retiring beyond the Vistula, and agreed with our opinion, that it was necessary to take up the offensive against the left wing of the Warsaw Army.[3]

There are differing accounts of the events of that evening. Waldersee and Grünert are sometimes given credit for persuading Prittwitz not to retreat to the Vistula, with Hoffmann reduced to raging with impotence at what he believed to be his commander's errors.[4] Nor is it completely clear whether the discussion in Eighth Army's headquarters took place before or after Prittwitz's telephone call to Koblenz. The outcome, though, was largely as Hoffmann described. Prittwitz was persuaded not to abandon East Prussia, and to concentrate instead against Samsonov's Second Army.

Prittwitz's apparent loss of nerve had fatal consequences for his career and reputation, as will be described later. At the time, given what he knew, should he have acted differently? Whilst François and Hoffmann were keen to resume the battle at Gumbinnen the following day, such a policy was by no means certain to achieve success. François' I Corps had sustained substantial losses, and despite its commander's confidence, was not guaranteed to roll up the Russian position from the north. Below's I Reserve Corps in the south had fought well, but its divisions were badly positioned to cooperate. In the centre, although Mackensen's officers were pulling the battered XVII Corps back into shape, there was little prospect of the corps resuming offensive operations. At 9 p.m., presumably before the exchange between Prittwitz, Hoffmann, Waldersee, and Grünert, the commander of Eighth Army spoke by telephone to Mackensen. He was told that 35th Infantry Division was in no state to remain east of the Rominte, but 36th Infantry Division was still in good shape. However, the losses suffered during the day, particularly amongst officers, meant that XVII Corps would not be able to renew its attack. According to Mackensen, Prittwitz replied:

The situation has changed completely. [There are] new troops in the north. I know absolutely nothing about the location of the [1st] Cavalry Division. Likewise, [there are] fresh [enemy] forces from the reserve formations – about a corps – at Lyck. The Narew [Second] Army is advancing with powerful forces on Ortelsburg and Soldau. Therefore, I will pull back behind the Vistula.[5]

But Rennenkampf's troops were also in poor shape. Artillery ammunition was running low, and the medical services of First Army were hopelessly inadequate to cope with the casualties that had been suffered during the day's fighting. Nevertheless, whilst a German victory was possible, it seems likely that the Germans would have paid a substantial price for it, and might then have lacked the strength to deal with Samsonov's army.

Although it seems reasonable to conclude that Prittwitz was right to break off the battle at Gumbinnen, the abandonment of East Prussia – the homeland of such a large proportion of Germany's senior officers – would have been a major blow to German morale, and as was proved in the days that followed, Prittwitz's plan was an overreaction to events. It has been argued that the 65-year-old Prittwitz was merely a tired, elderly commander at the end of a difficult day, who temporarily allowed events to get out of proportion.[6] Unfortunately for him, the actions of those both below and above him in the chain of command did not help his cause. On 21 August, even as Eighth Army began to issue orders for redeployment to the southwest so that it could concentrate against the western flank of Samsonov's army, Moltke telephoned Prittwitz. Their conversation was as tetchy as that of the previous evening, and Moltke appeared to be just as displeased by the new plans of Eighth Army as he had been by the proposal to withdraw to the Vistula. He certainly made his anger clear to those around him in *OHL*. Generalmajor Karl von Wenninger, the Bavarian military plenipotentiary in Koblenz, sent a message back to Munich:

> I may add, extremely confidentially, to the official reports: the unhappy combination (Prittwitz–Waldersee) is causing great concern here.[7]

Others at *OHL* also commented on Moltke's clear dissatisfaction with events in the east. As the day progressed numerous telephone calls were made to the lower formations of Eighth Army, enquiring about their opinions on the situation. The replies from the commanders of Prittwitz's four corps were broadly the same: none of them felt that Eighth Army had been defeated.[8]

François was singularly unhappy with the refusal of his army commander to allow him to continue the battle:

> [Early on 21 August] the field table on which I had given the orders for attack was still in the schoolmaster's garden. There, I was overcome with pain, and I shed tears of bitter disappointment and rage, tears for poor East Prussia, whose population I had grown to love and was proud to defend. The brave Major von Massow (first general staff officer [i.e. deputy chief of staff in I Corps]), who was an outstanding pillar of strength to me during these days and the days of Tannenberg, tried to console me. But the best consolation was in work. We weren't yet behind the Vistula, nor had we yet broken contact with the Russians.[9]

François did more than immerse himself in the work of issuing orders to his corps. In his memoirs he states that he received a signal from *OHL* during the early evening of 22 August, asking his opinion about the situation, but it is clear from other sources that he had already given his views the previous day.[10]

Meanwhile, the quartermaster-general of the German Army, Hermann von Stein, made enquiries of his own. He spoke to Waldersee, and objected to the proposal to move Eighth Army to the west of Samsonov's Second Army before attacking the Russian left flank. Instead, he suggested, Eighth Army should concentrate immediately west of the Masurian Lakes, and should attack the Russian right flank. Waldersee tried to make the case for his army commander's plan, but Stein was unconvinced.[11] The two men were not on good terms. At the beginning of the war Waldersee had been disappointed to be assigned to what he regarded as a secondary theatre, and Stein had made little secret of his disdain for Waldersee's role. The Chief of Staff of Eighth Army knew that Stein was an influential figure who was trusted by Moltke, and he could probably guess that the quartermaster-general's misgivings would be passed along the chain of command without delay.[12]

François was not the only commander who felt frustrated by the turn of events. Morgen had deployed his 3rd Reserve Division during the night for an assault against the southern flank of Rennenkampf's army, and was issuing final orders at a final meeting with his subordinates:

> When I was giving attack orders at 3 a.m. on 21 August, Eighth Army's devastating order to retreat arrived. As I told my Chief of Staff that I wanted to ignore the order in light of the unusually good situation [his division remained undetected by the Russians] and therefore wished to link up with General von Below, commander of I Reserve Corps, a report arrived from the latter that he had already pulled out in accordance with Eighth Army's orders. I had to grit my teeth and bow to the inevitable. I felt ashamed in front of my men, who were burning with passion to get into action, and the fleeing civilian population wailed at us.[13]

Later in the day, when he became aware of the general situation, Morgen remained convinced that the decision to retreat was unsound:

> These reasons [the retreat of XVII Corps and the threat of Samsonov's Second Army] were in my opinion not so cogent as to obviate the use of an attack in Eighth Army's good position. On the north flank, I Corps had fought successfully, XVII Corps was able to hold in the centre, even if it had been necessary to pull back behind the Angerapp. But on the southern flank of the battlefield, there was an encouraging prospect of enveloping the left flank of the Russian Niemen [First] Army. The Narew [Second] Army was still some distance away and could be held off by XX Corps for however long it took to achieve a decision against

the Niemen Army. After this, the entire Eighth Army could turn against the Narew Army.[14]

Meanwhile, the staff of Eighth Army began to put the new plans into action. XX Corps, already on the southern border, was ordered to concentrate around Hohenstein, while François' I Corps would be dispatched by train to an area immediately to the west of XX Corps. The 3rd Reserve Division, which was pulling back to Angerburg, would join XX Corps. Brodrück's division, built around the garrison of Königsberg, would cover the withdrawal of I Corps, falling back to the line of the River Deime. I Reserve Corps and XVII Corps – rapidly recovering from its mauling on 20 August – were to withdraw westwards. The intention of Eighth Army was to use I Corps to attack the left flank of the Russian advance. If I Reserve Corps and XVII Corps were able to disengage from Rennenkampf's army without being pursued, they too would be available for action against Samsonov. When he passed these orders on, Waldersee was explicit in his instructions to Scholtz: XX Corps was to remain on the defensive until François was ready on his western flank. A costly frontal attack on the Russians was to be avoided.[15]

The change of emphasis of Eighth Army – from facing east against Rennenkampf to facing south against Samsonov – was something that had been rehearsed by the Germans many times in war games. Its success would depend upon whether the two Russian armies could cooperate, and just as the Germans were experiencing a crisis in their higher levels of leadership, so the Russians had problems with their own command. Ever since he had crossed the border, Rennenkampf had been urging Zhilinski to ensure that Samsonov attacked from the south; this would create precisely the sort of pressure that caused so much concern to Prittwitz. Samsonov, though, had his own troubles. The Russians had deliberately not constructed railways and good roads to the southern border of East Prussia from Warsaw, in order to hinder any German offensive. They now found that the lack of good lines of communication meant that their own advance was slow. In addition, Samsonov was hamstrung by the tardiness of Russian mobilisation. The longer he delayed his own advance, the greater would be his strength.

There were also problems with the inner flanks of the two Russian armies. The distance between the two starting positions of the Russian armies, and the fact that their lines of advance would leave the Masurian Lakes between them, ensured further difficulties in coordination. Matters were made worse by Samsonov extending his own axis of advance further west. On the one hand it created a serious crisis in Prittwitz's headquarters; on the other hand, the two Russian armies were left even further apart, with both of Samsonov's flanks exposed to German counterattacks.

With the Germans now reversing their strategy, leaving a minimal force to screen Rennenkampf while they concentrated against Samsonov, the priorities for the Russians were reversed. It was now necessary for First Army to keep pressing forward, in order to tie down German forces. But Rennenkampf made little attempt to pursue as the Germans withdrew. Losses in First Army had been substantial, food and ammunition were running short, and the German withdrawal was greeted with relief. As his corps began to withdraw the day after it was driven back in disorder, Mackensen surveyed the battlefield where he had lost so many men:

> From first light, I watched the withdrawal of the individual columns from Plicken Hill, and with my staff I was probably the last to leave the high ground west of the Rominte. There were no Russians visible, as far as the eye or field glass could see. Even their positions of yesterday, behind the Schwentisch Stream, seemed empty. Reports from the right flank of Russian movements towards the rear confirmed this. Only a badly hit opponent would behave like this. I had the strong impression that my corps had not been outfought, nor had it suffered such heavy losses. In complete calm and good order and without any interference by the enemy, it made its withdrawal.[16]

Regardless of the strategic necessity to keep up pressure on the Germans, Rennenkampf felt that his divisions were in too disorganised a state to conduct a hot pursuit, it was always possible that the German retreat was a feint, and any hasty Russian advance would be punished severely. One of his divisions had been knocked out for the time being by François, and others had suffered serious casualties. And there was still the issue of the Russian cavalry. Despite Rennenkampf's irritated messages, Nahitchevanski still showed little inclination to support the Russian advance in an adequately assertive manner.

There was also the question of the character of the Russian Army. Its commanders were aware that their strongest characteristic was an ability to endure, and to defend tenaciously; ambitious and rapid advances were things for which it was not renowned. It would be better, Rennenkampf concluded, to allow his formation to gather their strength before they tried to push forward again. Zhilinski, who had done little to hurry forward Samsonov's Second Army, now did little to put pressure on Rennenkampf. Although he was nominally in command of both armies, his ability to exercise this authority was limited, both in terms of his own personality and the command arrangements in the Russian Army.

Much has been made of the enmity between Rennenkampf and Samsonov as a possible reason for their failure to cooperate better. It is certainly true that there was bad blood between the two men, dating back to the failure of Samsonov to support Rennenkampf during the Battle of Mukden in the Russo-Japanese War, but accounts of a physical fight between them on a railway platform are almost certainly not true. They were representatives of the two factions within the Russian Army that were most opposed to each other, but it seems unlikely that either man would endanger the entire campaign to settle a personal score, or to denigrate an opposing faction in the army.[17]

Moltke made another telephone call to Eighth Army's headquarters on the evening of 21 August, his third conversation with Prittwitz in twenty-four hours. In his own account Moltke appears to have conflated this call with the conversation the two men had had the previous evening, but while tempers were controlled far better, Prittwitz seems to have done little to restore his superior's faith in his abilities.[18] He first told Moltke that the German 1st Cavalry Division, operating on the northern flank of his army, was missing presumed destroyed, only to contradict himself moments later. The division was in fact alive and well; after admittedly being out of contact for a day, it had sent an officer to I Corps early on 21 August to report that it had successfully driven back the Russian cavalry, and had captured several hundred prisoners.[19]

It is not clear exactly when Moltke decided to change the command of Eighth Army. Prittwitz had not been his own choice for command in East Prussia, and at some stage on 21 August his confidence in the elderly general was irreparably damaged. Waldersee, too, would have to go; a good chief of staff should have prevented the panic that seemed to have gripped Eighth Army Headquarters late on 20 August. It is also possible that Stein's views about Waldersee influenced Moltke's judgement. The question that remained to be settled was about their replacements.

Fortunately for the German high command, the solution – at least with regard to the post of chief of staff – was at hand. Erich Ludendorff was born near Posen in 1865, and at an early stage showed a flair for mathematics, combined with a formidable work ethic that would stay with him throughout his life. He entered the General Staff aged 29, and served as a senior officer in the Mobilisation Section from 1904 to 1913. He had risen to the rank of Generalmajor by the outbreak of the war, and was assigned to the post of Deputy Chief of Staff with Second Army.

Prior to the war he had spent considerable time studying the layout of Belgian fortifications around Liège, and when the commander of the German 14th Brigade was killed in a futile assault on the fortress on 5 August, Ludendorff took command. The eleven days that followed made his reputation. He showed a mixture of direct aggression and attention to detail as he surrounded the fortress, reducing its protective forts one by one, and finally took the citadel on 16 August.

On 22 August, while he was conducting another siege, this time at Namur, Ludendorff received an important message from Moltke:

> You are assigned a new and difficult task, perhaps even harder than the assault on Liège… I know no other man in whom I have such limitless faith as I have in you. Perhaps you will still be able to save the day in the east. Don't be angry with me for recalling you from a post in which you are perhaps close to a decisive moment that God willing will be crucial. This, too, you must sacrifice for the Fatherland. The Kaiser, too, has faith in you. Naturally, you cannot be held responsible for what has already happened, but with your energies you can still avoid the worst. Therefore, take up your new post, which is the greatest that can be granted to a soldier. You will not betray the trust placed in you.[20]

Another letter, from General Hermann von Stein, expressed the same sentiment: the task was a hard one, but Ludendorff was the man for the job. As he prepared to leave for Koblenz, the messenger who had brought him the letters informed him that the new commander of Eighth Army would be Paul von Hindenburg, though nobody seemed to know where he might be. Hindenburg – whose full name was Paul Ludwig Hans Anton von Beneckendorff und von Hindenburg – had briefly been considered as a possible candidate for the roles of Chief of the General Staff and Prussian War Minister, but declined both, saying that he would not make a good courtier. He retired in 1911, but German planners kept his name as a suitable army commander in the event of war. Listening to the news as a civilian, he later wrote, the war seemed to be going well, with news of the fall of Liège and victories on the East Prussian frontier, though the old soldier – with an illustrious war record of his own, including serving as a young officer in the Prussian Guards on the bloody slopes of St Privat – was keen to take any opportunity to serve his nation:

> At 3 o'clock in the afternoon of August 22 I received an enquiry from the Headquarters of His Majesty the Emperor as to whether I was prepared for immediate employment.

My answer ran: 'I am ready.'

Even before this telegram could have reached Main Headquarters I received another. It was to the effect that my willingness to accept a post in the field was assumed as a matter of course, and that General Ludendorff was to be assigned to me. Further telegrams from Main Headquarters explained that I was to leave for the east immediately to take command of an army.

At 3 o'clock in the morning I went to the station, imperfectly equipped, as time had been short, and waited expectantly in the well-lit hall. It was only when the short special train steamed in that I wrenched my thoughts away from the hearth and home which I had to leave so suddenly. General Ludendorff stepped briskly from the train and reported as my chief of staff of Eighth Army.[21]

Ludendorff had come via Koblenz, where he had met Moltke. The Chief of the General Staff, Ludendorff recorded, looked tired as he described the situation in the east. The kaiser, who was also at *OHL*, took the opportunity to speak personally to Eighth Army's new chief of staff, and to present him with the *Pour le Mérite* in recognition of his key role in the capture of Liège. Ludendorff took the opportunity of being in *OHL* to issue his first instructions to his new army: I Corps, XVII Corps, and Brodrück's division were to treat 23 August as a day of rest, so that they could recover their strength. The remaining garrisons along the Vistula were ordered to concentrate their troops in the southwest corner of East Prussia. Although they were mainly reservists and *Landsturm*, they still created a substantial body of men when massed together – a force that might be able to make a decisive influence in the coming battle. In addition, I Corps would detrain somewhat further east than originally ordered. This would place it far closer to the expected area of battle, and it would thus be available sooner. The change also made any thoughts of withdrawing beyond the Vistula less likely to be carried out.[22]

From Koblenz Ludendorff travelled east, collecting his new army commander in Hannover. Their encounter on the railway platform was the first time that the two men had met. As they trundled through the night, Ludendorff briefed Hindenburg on the situation, and the orders he had already dispatched. After discussing matters for less than an hour, the 66-year-old Hindenburg went to bed.[23] It was the start of a long relationship between the two men, one that would dominate German policy for much of the war.

This was the first occasion that any army commander was dismissed during the First World War, and matters were not handled remotely tactfully, at several levels. The kaiser grumbled that, despite being officially the commander-in-chief, he had merely been required to rubber-stamp decisions about the new appointments, rather than being consulted about them. But as Hoffmann later wrote, Prittwitz and Waldersee were also treated poorly:

> The form of their recall was uncommonly rough. The subordinate generals in command heard of it sooner than the Commander-in-Chief. Orders were sent by the General Headquarters [i.e. by Ludendorff from his brief time in *OHL*] to the generals in command without the Commander-in-Chief being informed. For example, I Reserve Corps and XVII Corps were ordered to take a day's rest; the necessity of this order may easily be doubted. The Headquarters [of Eighth Army] had moved on the morning of 21 August to Bartenstein and on 22 August to Mühlhausen, in East Prussia. The reports that came in announced that the retirement of the troops before the Vilna Army [Rennenkampf's First Army] had been effected surprisingly well. Colonel Hell, the Chief of Staff of XX Corps, reported that the corps had been successfully concentrated in the neighbourhood of Hohenstein, and he received the order to draw up the corps on the line Gilgenburg–Lahne. He expressed his doubts about the left flank of the corps as it would take days to transport by rail the troops that were still on frontier duty, and therefore requested that the 3rd Reserve Division should not be sent to the right wing of XX Corps, as the headquarters [of Eighth Army] had ordered, but to have it sent to the left wing in the neighbourhood of Hohenstein. This the headquarters approved of. It was only in the afternoon of 22 August that the headquarters heard of the change in the higher command when a telegram sent to the Chief of the Field Railway announced the arrival of an extra train with the new Commander-in-Chief and the Chief of Staff. It was only a few hours later that His Majesty's order arrived, which placed General von Prittwitz and General Waldersee on the unattached list. General von Prittwitz bore this stroke of fate in an extraordinarily noble manner, and he took leave of us without a single word of complaint on his hard destiny. On the evening of 22 August, a telegram from Ludendorff announced his arrival in Marienburg on the following day with the new Commander-in-Chief who expected to find the chief commanders there.[24]

For Prittwitz it was the end of a military career that had started with service as a junior officer in the 3rd Guards Grenadier Regiment, and had included action in the Austro-Prussian and Franco-Prussian wars. He retired to Berlin, where he struggled to persuade anyone who would listen that he had never intended to retreat beyond the Vistula, merely that he wished to fall back towards the river, and raised the question of how it could be defended. He died of a heart attack in

March 1917. There was little time for the men he left in his wake to reflect upon his departure. They had their hands full with the redeployment of troops to face the threat from Samsonov's Second Army. However many times they might have rehearsed such an operation, the reality was now upon them, with the clear danger that if they failed, there would be little prospect of preventing a Russian conquest of East Prussia, and even a thrust towards Berlin.

CHAPTER 7

TANNENBERG

Writing after the war, Hindenburg summarised the task that faced the new command of Eighth Army in the days after the retreat from Gumbinnen in vivid terms:

> We had not merely to win a victory over Samsonov. We had to annihilate him. Only thus could we get a free hand to deal with the second enemy, Rennenkampf, who was even then plundering and burning East Prussia. Only thus could we really and completely free our old Prussian land and be in a position to do something else which was expected of us – intervene in the mighty battle for a decision that was raging between Russia and our Austro-Hungarian ally in Galicia and Poland. If this first blow was not final the danger for our homeland would become like a lingering disease, the burnings and murders in East Prussia would remain unavenged, and our Allies in the south would wait for us in vain.

It was thus a case for complete measures. Everything must be thrown in which could prove of the slightest use in manoeuvre warfare and could at all be spared. The fortresses of Graudenz [Grudziądz] and Thorn [Toruń] disgorged yet more *Landwehr* fit for the field. Moreover, our *Landwehr* came from the trenches between the Masurian Lakes, which were covering our new operations in the east, and handed over the defence there to a smaller and diminishing number of *Landsturm*. Once we had won the battle in the field we should no longer need the fortresses of Thorn and Graudenz, and should be freed from anxieties as regards the defiles between the lakes.[1]

A decisive knockout blow against the Russian Second Army was certainly a desirable objective, but contrary to Hindenburg's statement it was probably not

148

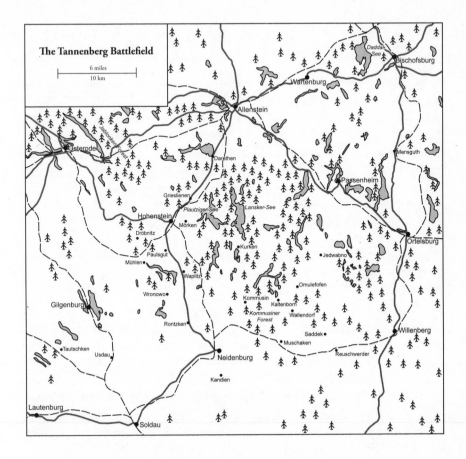

a necessity, provided events went as expected in the west. The Schlieffen Plan had expected territory to be conceded in the face of superior forces while the war against France was fought to a successful conclusion. Then the victorious armies of Germany would turn east, and deal with the Russian threat, if necessary retaking territory that had been lost. When Hindenburg took command, the great plan to knock France out of the war within six weeks seemed to be progressing well. In this context, the purpose of Eighth Army was to delay the advance of the Russians as much as possible, and ideally to use the barrier of the Masurian Lakes to prevent the two Russian armies from coordinating their forces. A series of battles not dissimilar to the actions at Stallupönen and Gumbinnen would have sufficed to buy sufficient time for reinforcements to arrive from the west. But in the event of the Schlieffen Plan failing to deliver a rapid victory over France, the Germans had no secondary strategy. Everything was staked upon the success of the enveloping movement through Belgium and northern France.

Similarly, there was no need for Samsonov to try to win a decisive victory on his own. It would have sufficed for either of the two Russian armies to engage and tie down the German forces in East Prussia; the other Russian Army would then have been free to operate against the rear of the German positions. It is arguable that the Russians lacked the skill, or perhaps even the will, to carry out such a coordinated operation. However, it could simply have been achieved almost by default, provided that First and Second Armies attempted to advance in directions that generally converged.

This proviso was missing in August 1914. The original Russian plan had been for Second Army to move into East Prussia in two groups. II and VI Corps were to advance on Lyck and Johannisburg, while XIII and XV Corps marched on Ortelsburg and Rudczanny, and from there towards Rastenburg. This ensured that there was close contact with First Army to the north, but only the two corps marching through Ortelsburg and Rudczanny would turn the flank of the Masurian Lakes position. On 10 August *Stavka* suggested that Second Army might choose to advance northwest rather than north, taking its centre of gravity away from the line of the lakes altogether. Zhilinski adopted this new plan, instructing Samsonov of the change three days later. As a result, Second Army's II Corps would advance directly towards the lakes and try to keep contact with First Army. VI and XV Corps, reinforced by a division of XXIII Corps, were ordered to advance northwest towards Rudczanny and Passenheim, where they would change their line of march to a northerly one, aiming for Seeburg and Rastenburg. I Corps, on the left (western) flank of Second Army, received the other half of XXIII Corps as reinforcements, and would protect the open western flank.

Only three days after this change of plan, Samsonov announced a further adjustment. The starting point of the advance of the main group of three corps was moved further west, so that the Russians would then march due north towards Rudczanny and Passenheim after they had crossed the border. The left flank of the main group, XV Corps, would now be much closer to I Corps to the west. The advantage of this new shift of the centre of gravity was that it increased the chances of the Russian forces being able to slip past the western flank of any German units deployed against them; the disadvantages were that an additional two days of marching would be required before the border was crossed, and far from moving on a convergent axis with First Army, Samsonov was actually moving further away. None of this would have mattered too much if Rennenkampf succeeded in holding a large portion of the German forces in the east. Samsonov would have easily outnumbered any defenders he faced, and could have enveloped them with ease, concentrating his forces only if he felt the need. But with the failure of Rennenkampf to advance and thus hold back at least one or two corps of Eighth Army, Samsonov's plans represented a dangerous dispersal of his troops over a broad front.

Zhilinski expressed his doubts about Samsonov's proposal:

> You have extended your left flank … and consequently the front of the three corps of Second Army during the march to the frontier will cover 60 versts [38 miles, or 61km], which I consider excessive.[2]

The new starting points for Second Army's advance into East Prussia were some distance from the concentration centres where reservists joined their units. The urgency of intervening in order to force Germany to reduce the pressure on France meant that many divisions had not yet received their full complement of troops. One estimate suggests that VI Corps was seven battalions below strength, XV Corps was four battalions short, and XIII Corps one battalion short.[3] It would take up to five days of hard marching before the troops even crossed the border – at a time when the French were clamouring for early pressure on Germany, in the hope that Moltke would be forced to divert troops to the east. Such an approach march would have been hard enough for regular troops, but some of Samsonov's formations, such as Klyuev's XIII Corps, contained a majority of reservists, and logistic arrangements were hopelessly inadequate. Stragglers fell out of line at every opportunity, in search of food or water, or to nurse aching feet. When the infantry reached their starting positions, they found that they had to wait until sufficient numbers of these stragglers could catch up before any invasion could be attempted.

Zhilinski pressed Samsonov to hurry up on 19 August, telling the commander of Second Army that his delays were causing problems for Rennenkampf. Samsonov's reply was terse:

> The army has been advancing without a pause since the receipt of your orders, traversing daily more than 20 versts [nearly 13 miles, or 21km] of sand, and consequently further acceleration is impossible.[4]

The frustration of both men – Zhilinski and Samsonov – was genuine, but there was a distinct lack of any acceptance of responsibility. Zhilinski should have been aware of the slow rate of Russian mobilisation, particularly of logistics units without which a sustained campaign would be impossible. Samsonov had deliberately increased the length of his approach march, even though he had been thoroughly briefed on the transport difficulties he faced, and the poor roads that he would have to use.

The breadth of the starting line also created communication problems. Although the Russian Army possessed formations responsible for setting up wire communications, they were often ill-trained, and their supplies were inadequate for the task. As a result, the Russians had to resort to wireless communication. This created a new dilemma. There had been insufficient attention to radio procedures in exercises before the war, and both encoding and decoding signals proved difficult, sometimes impossible. As the troops gathered along the East Prussian frontier, staff officers were alarmed to discover that the different corps had been assigned different coding ciphers, making coded communication between them almost impossible.[5] Consequently, Samsonov concluded that he would have to take the risk of using uncoded radio messages. Whilst there was a possibility that the Germans might intercept them, all other options seemed completely impractical.

Major-General Alfred Knox was a British liaison officer in St Petersburg at the start of the war, and travelled south with Grand Duke Nikolai to join the newly created *Stavka*. From there he took every opportunity to visit units close to the border. On 20 August, while returning to his quarters, Knox encountered a Russian troop column marching towards the front. His description encapsulates the lack of any sense of urgency in many such columns:

> On our way back we ran into the corps transport, which had been overtaken by ambulance transport and which was marching on a double front, blocking the *chaussée*. However, everyone remains good-humoured and quiet throughout. There is an extraordinary calmness and absence of shouting, and also of the abuse which we sometimes see in the management of our transport. The Russian has no very high ideal of efficiency to strive after, so he is content with a little, and takes it for granted that everyone is doing his best, as indeed he probably is.[6]

The staff of Second Army came from the Warsaw Military District. On mobilisation, Zhilinski commandeered the best officers in the district's staff for his Northwest Front, leaving Samsonov with a decidedly mixed bag. To make matters worse, Russian officers were generally not aware of their wartime staff appointments until the war began, and therefore had not had the opportunity to acquaint themselves with their roles, or with their future colleagues. Given all its handicaps, it was small wonder that, in the words of one of the participants, Second Army's move towards the frontier often bore more resemblance to a chaotic pilgrimage than an organised military advance.

Even as the invasion began, Samsonov received unwelcome news. He had assumed that I Corps, reinforced by 3rd Guards Infantry Division, would be under his command and would protect his flank to the left. He now learned that these formations would not be directly subordinated to him, but would be commanded directly by Northwest Front. He would have no ability to issue orders to them, and would instead have to pass requests to Zhilinski's headquarters.

The Russian Second Army finally crossed the border in strength on 21 August. VI Corps was ordered to take Ortelsburg, while I and XV Corps moved up to a line from Neidenburg to Soldau. XIII Corps was initially held back between the two, with the intention of supporting either if German resistance proved strong. One of the first East Prussian towns to fall to Samsonov's forces was Neidenburg, which was occupied by XV Corps on 22 August. General Nikolai Nikolayevich Martos, the corps commander, ordered his artillery to bombard the town after elements of the Orenburg Cossack Regiment reported that they had come under fire from civilians; perhaps a third of the town centre was reduced to ruins. The truth behind the incident that triggered the bombardment was slightly different. The Cossacks attached to Russian infantry divisions were usually reservists with relatively poor levels of training. A group of them encountered about thirty German infantrymen just outside the town. The Germans, mounted on bicycles and led by Leutnant Burscher von Saher, rapidly dismounted and took cover, and when the Cossacks attempted to charge them, they opened fire and killed several riders. The rest withdrew in haste, and Saher led his men into Neidenburg. Near the railway station they came across a full squadron of Cossacks, who were preparing their midday meal. After another brief burst of fire, the Germans found themselves – briefly – masters of the town. Before withdrawing, they gathered together some loot from the railway station square, including the meal that the Cossacks had been preparing, but much more significantly a map that showed the main Russian troop positions. The map was swiftly passed on to Eighth Army Headquarters. Meanwhile the Cossacks rode back to join their comrades in XV Corps. Given the suddenness of the German attack, it is perhaps understandable that many simply did not see who had fired on them, and assumed that the marksmen were civilians.[7]

Martos reached Neidenburg on the heels of his troops:

Accompanied by my staff I entered the town with the leading units; the houses on the outskirts of the town were burning, and I took up my quarters in the house of the local justice.

A town commandant was appointed by me and measures were taken to establish order. The Germans, especially the inhabitants of the neighbouring villages, had commenced looting. Our wounded were taken into the finely appointed town hospital, already occupied by some wounded German soldiers; the doctors and the administration were placed under our control…

During the further advance to Hohenstein we saw rich manorial estates which had been looted by the peasants, and valuable, but heavy, appointments (such as mirrors, sideboards, wall tablets in marble inscribed with genealogies etc.) had been smashed or spoiled. I am setting down these facts, as at that time the German press attributed all this to the Russian soldiers. I can give absolute assurance that the troops of XV Corps took no part in any looting. Thanks to the activity of the military police, order was quickly established in the town and was maintained the whole time until the departure of our troops.[8]

There can be no doubt that some Germans in this border region took advantage of the situation to indulge in some looting; equally, it is highly unlikely that no members of the Russian Army were involved in such activities. Martos had a reputation as a disciplinarian, and during the brief time that XV Corps was in the area his military police conducted public floggings of soldiers caught looting, and a few men were actually executed for more serious crimes.[9]

Ludendorff and Hindenburg reached Marienburg, where Eighth Army's headquarters was now based, early in the afternoon of 23 August:

We had a cool reception in Marienburg. For me, it was like another world, to come into this depressed environment from Liège and the rapid advance in the west. Everything changed quickly. Morale climbed.[10]

To a large extent, it seems that the panic of the previous days had already passed, and matters were in hand to redeploy Eighth Army to face south. After a slow start, I Corps had entrained, and made excellent use of the railway line running southwest to start concentrating near Deutsch Eylau, in support of XX Corps. The annotated map recovered by Saher in Neidenburg helped the new command of Eighth Army a great deal. Whilst the document could have been an attempt at deliberate misinformation, it was broadly in line with what the Germans had expected, and it seemed reasonable to regard it as accurate. The main concern was not with Samsonov's forces but with Rennenkampf's First Army. If it pressed forward rapidly, XVII Corps and I Reserve Corps might have to be committed to prevent it from pressing into the rear of the German forces deploying against Samsonov. But with every passing hour, it became clear that Rennenkampf was moving slowly, if at all. The failure of Rennenkampf to act with more alacrity raised concerns and criticism in the Russian chain of command. Some of his officers rallied to his support:

> As having taken part in this operation, I can testify to the fact that both the First Army commander and the corps commanders … got out of the infantry units every last effort that they could possibly have made under the conditions ruling First Army's advance. Further, as regards speed, it was impossible to do more without reaching the point where an army begins to break up to a serious degree through losses in stragglers. The orders issued by the army commander and the corps commander during those memorable days – 'The more sweat, the less blood' and 'Victory for the Army depends on your legs' – speak for themselves.[11]

More than one officer gave testimony similar to this, but none of it was backed up by what actually happened: the formations of First Army moved slowly and cautiously. Regardless of whether the Russian First Army could have pressed forward more energetically, given its supply problems, the facts on the ground were that the retreating Germans came under no significant pressure. Ludendorff and Hindenburg decided to screen Rennenkampf with only 1st Cavalry Division, Brodrück's division created around the Königsberg garrison, and two Landwehr brigades. XVII Corps and I Reserve Corps, which had been allowed to rest for the day, were ordered to press on. Their objective was set as Bischofsburg. The result would be that two German corps – François' I Corps and Scholtz's XX Corps – would be on the western flank of the Russian Army, while the other two corps – Mackensen's XVII Corps and Below's I Reserve Corps – would be facing the eastern flank. The possibility of breaking both wings of Samsonov's force, and potentially encircling it, now presented itself.

During the evening of 22 August, Samsonov issued instructions for the following day. The ease with which his troops had taken Neidenburg and the other border towns surprised him. Cossack patrols had implied that there was a more substantial German presence in the area. He ordered VI Corps to remain near Ortelsburg, on the right flank of his army. XIII Corps was to move northwest, to a point midway between Ortelsburg and Neidenburg, and XV Corps was to push north towards Hohenstein. Meanwhile, I Corps – no longer under

Samsonov's direct command – was to stay in Soldau, on the deep left flank of Second Army. When he received a copy of the orders, Zhilinski was unhappy. He had expected a faster advance, and wanted Samsonov to try to pursue a converging line of march with respect to Rennenkampf. Instead, Second Army's formations closest to First Army would mark time at Ortelsburg, while the centre – XIII and XV Corps – moved northwest and north respectively.

In the path of XV Corps were the troops of Scholtz's XX Corps. Since its inception two years before, the corps had always been intended to defend this part of Germany; Scholtz and his officers had trained hard in the area. As the Russian 8th Infantry Division advanced in four brigade columns, it ran into prepared defences occupied by a regiment from 70th *Landwehr* Brigade and 37th Infantry Division, straddling the main road to Hohenstein. Martos was close behind his leading units:

> I heard artillery fire, and at first supposed that small German rearguards were delaying our advance. However, the cannonade quickly increased, and it then became apparent from reports arriving from units and from staff officers sent out by me, that the Germans were occupying in considerable force a position, previously fortified in peacetime, on the line of the villages Orlau–Frankenau, and that the Chernigov Infantry Regiment [part of 8th Infantry Division], which had been marching at the head of the right-hand column, after occupying a village … without serious opposition had got into a very difficult position: the village lay low and was swept by frontal and flanking fire. It was stated in the report that Colonel Alexeyev, the regimental commander, had been killed. At the same time it became apparent that the left-hand column of the corps (Colonel Novitsky's 1st Brigade of the 6th Infantry Division) was opposed by insignificant enemy units. The Orenburg Cossack Regiment, which had been moving in advance of the corps, having stumbled upon the position, had withdrawn behind the infantry and the whole unit was in reserve.[12]

Martos ordered Novitsky to hold firm on the left, while he moved the Cossacks forward to support the 30th Poltava Infantry Regiment, the other half of 8th Infantry Division. He noted, quite accurately, that the Cossacks were unlikely to take any aggressive steps, but he hoped that their appearance would at least give the Germans pause for thought. Bitter fighting raged all along the line, with scenes from a previous century. At one stage German infantry attacked with the regimental band playing; officers fought each other with swords, even as bullets cut them down; soldiers fought furiously for possession of the regimental colours

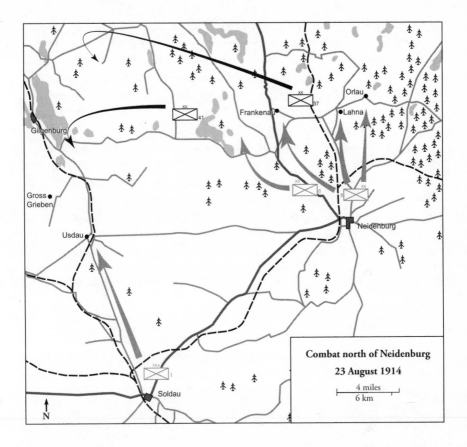

Combat north of Neidenburg
23 August 1914

4 miles
6 km

of the Russian 29th Infantry Regiment – although the Germans managed to capture and hold the staff, the flag itself disappeared, and was later found wrapped around the corpse of a Russian officer from the regiment.

The Russian attempts to take Orlau pushed the German defenders to the limit, but were ultimately beaten off. The village of Lahna was held by troops from the 1st East Prussian *Jäger* Battalion (Yorck von Wartenburg). Renowned marksmen, they inflicted terrible losses on the attacking Russians. About 500 Germans were deployed in Lahna at the beginning of the day; fewer than 50 were left to withdraw from the blazing village by dusk.[13]

As the bloodied soldiers of both sides attempted to reorganise after dusk, the commanders took stock. At first Scholtz planned a counterattack to retake Lahna, but as reports came into his corps headquarters, it became clear that his units were in no state to mount such an attack. In any case, Hindenburg and Ludendorff intended to use XX Corps, together with I Corps, to launch a major attack against the western flank of Samsonov's army, and there was no prospect of François' divisions being ready before 26 August. Scholtz was therefore ordered to conserve his strength, and to pull back his left flank. As Hindenburg later wrote, this move drew Samsonov's men even further west, exposing their right flank to the massing forces of XVII Corps and I Reserve Corps.

Late on 23 August, Martos was confident that he was about to win a major victory. He ordered his men to infiltrate forwards so that they would be able to launch an attack at first light. As dawn spread across the landscape, battle was resumed, with orders from Scholtz to his units to withdraw to the northwest arriving too late to be put into effect. The chief of staff of the German XX Corps, Emil Hell, had doubted that 37th Infantry Division would be able to disengage from the battle without being overrun, but a combination of exhaustion, casualties – particularly amongst the officers – and the supply problems that crippled both Rennenkampf's and Samsonov's armies prevented the Russians from pursuing their foes, as Martos described:

> The Germans apparently were not expecting an attack, and after stubborn resistance at strong points, began to retreat from them in disorder, abandoning their wounded. The whole of the battlefield was covered with corpses and dead horses, articles of equipment, rifles and abandoned vehicles, amongst which were several damaged motors. Two guns and several machine guns were captured by the 2nd Brigade of 6th Infantry Division. In addition, several officers and about a hundred men were captured. The German officers, in accordance with warnings received from above, expected to be shot immediately, and were overjoyed to learn that their lives were not in danger... The retirement of the Germans was so rapid that the troops of the corps, being at the point of exhaustion, could not pursue them far.
>
> Unfortunately the infantry regiments of the corps had suffered heavy losses; three regimental commanders had been killed, the best battalion commanders had become casualties, killed or wounded.[14]

Knox visited the scene of the battle the following day:

> The Russians used the spade freely in the attack. I saw rifle trenches scooped out within 130 yards of the defenders' trenches. The German machine-guns were deadly, mowing down rows of Russians immediately they raised themselves in the potato-fields to fire or to advance. The Russian artillery quickly silenced the German guns... The Russians estimate their loss in this action of 23–24 August

at 4,000 men and that of the Germans – but this is mere guesswork – at 6,000. One Russian regiment had nine company commanders killed out of 16, and one company which went into action 190 strong lost all its officers and 120 men killed.

The sight of the corpses was awful. We saw German and Russian wounded being carried from a field on which they must have lain for at least 36 hours.[15]

At first Scholtz feared that his losses were greater than the Russian estimate of 6,000, but as the day progressed, stragglers continued to arrive, and 37th Infantry Division began to regain its strength and confidence. Fearing an imminent attack along his front, Scholtz requested permission to pull back further. Aware that François' I Corps would not be able to take up positions on Scholtz's right for another two days, Ludendorff urged the commander of XX Corps to hold on if at all possible.

Aided by intercepted Russian radio signals, Ludendorff and Hindenburg continued to draw up plans for their counterstroke. Initially, Ludendorff contemplated an attack that would strike the most western part of Samsonov's army – I Corps, at Soldau and Usdau – from the west, but concluded that he lacked the numbers to carry out such an operation. Instead he suggested that these Russian forces should be masked, and the main effort, by François and Scholtz, should be from Gilgenburg towards Neidenburg. In his memoirs he talked of a vision of a huge encirclement of the Russian Second Army, with XVII Corps and I Reserve Corps driving in the Russian right flank. But it is not clear if this was the intention from the outset, or whether Ludendorff and Hindenburg merely planned powerful flanking attacks, which in themselves would inflict major losses on the Russians. On 24 August, the two generals visited Scholtz. Hindenburg found the confidence of the officers at XX Corps Headquarters refreshing, after a journey in which he had been forced to pick his way past columns of civilians fleeing the Russians.[16]

François personally drove west by road from Insterburg, travelling via Königsberg. He took the opportunity to visit the battlefield of Gross-Jägersdorf, where in 1757, Hans von Lehwaldt and 28,000 Prussians had attacked a Russian Army perhaps twice as large commanded by Stepan Apraksin, though in his memoirs François exaggerated the odds, suggesting that the Russian Army exceeded 100,000 men. Although the Prussians were defeated, they inflicted heavier losses on the Russians than they suffered themselves, and withdrew from the battlefield in perfect order. The comparison with the performance of his own corps at Stallupönen and Gumbinnen was not lost on François. He drove on to

Marienburg, where he met Hindenburg. He had served as the latter's chief of staff in IV Corps in 1903, and consequently the men knew each other well. Ludendorff, too, was no stranger to François. The two men had shared accommodation many years before as junior staff officers. Eighth Army's chief of staff quickly outlined his plans to François, which met with the latter's approval.[17]

Throughout this period, Ludendorff and Hindenburg had to be aware of the threat posed by Rennenkampf to the east; the Russian First Army was, according to Ludendorff, an ever-present storm cloud on the eastern horizon. Although German civilians reported that Russian troops were moving forward, they still appeared to be doing so slowly. There was certainly no pressure on the paper-thin line of troops that Eighth Army had left facing east. For the moment, at least, XVII Corps and I Reserve Corps remained available for operations in the south, even though their march away from Gumbinnen was relatively slow – railway capacity was being used to move I Corps, and the two corps travelled southwest along dusty roads under hot summer skies. The allocation to Eighth Army of the *Landwehr* Division von der Goltz, which had been on coastal defence duties in Schleswig-Holstein, came as welcome news to Ludendorff. Although the men of the *Landwehr* were not in the same class as regular army soldiers, they at least provided a reserve that could be used in an emergency to hold up Rennenkampf. Ludendorff ordered the division to detrain around Osterode, from where it could be deployed either south to support operations against Samsonov, or east to delay Rennenkampf.[18]

The first troop trains – only eight, to the disappointment of François – arrived in Deutsch Eylau during the afternoon of 24 August. Immediately, the first infantry regiment to arrive was assigned to support XX Corps. The following day, I Corps established its headquarters in Montowo, where Hindenburg and Ludendorff visited François. They informed him that he was to attack towards Usdau on 26 August:

> I suggested that, as a result of the detraining points being some distance to the rear and the delays in transport, the corps was widely dispersed and had not yet completed detraining. As a result of the assignation of 1st Grenadier Regiment to XX Corps, I was short of infantry, and I had only six batteries of field artillery. The heavy artillery, all light munitions columns, the artillery commanders, and all of my cavalry were still travelling by rail. Ludendorff replied that as further trains were expected to arrive before the attack, the attack itself had to go ahead.
>
> 'If it is so ordered,' I replied, 'of course an attack will be made, and the troops will obviously have to fight with bayonets.' Hindenburg remained silent.[19]

Conrad von Hötzendorf, Chief of the Austro-Hungarian General Staff and architect of the armies with which the Dual Monarchy went to war.

Oskar Potiorek was military governor in Bosnia-Herzegovina in 1914, and commanded Austro-Hungarian forces during the disastrous invasion of Serbia.

Dankl was one of the very few senior Austro-Hungarian commanders to come out of the opening months of the war with his reputation enhanced.

Rising from a humble background, Böhm-Ermolli was an unusual senior officer in an era where aristocracy and gentry still dominated the higher echelons of Europe's armies.

During the opening campaigns, Boroević established a reputation for strong-mindedness and determination, earning him rapid promotion.

Hindenburg (left), Kaiser Wilhelm (centre), and Ludendorff (right). Paired together by chance in 1914, Hindenburg and Ludendorff came to dominate the German conduct of the entire war.

Serving as Minister for War at the beginning of the conflict, Falkenhayn became Chief of the German General Staff after the Battle of the Marne, and had to deal with the consequences of a prolonged two-front war.

Commander of Eighth Army at the beginning of the war, Prittwitz was the first army commander on either side to lose his post.

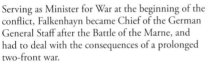

Popular with his men, Mackensen – photographed here in 1915 – was one of the most capable commanders in any army during the entire war.

Gallwitz was another effective German commander on the Eastern Front, with a reputation for determination and stubbornness.

Moltke was Chief of the General Staff at the outbreak of the war, and a proponent of fighting a war before Russia's rearmament programme was complete. The defeat at the Battle of the Marne cost him his health and his post.

Photographed here in 1917, Brusilov was one of the most successful Russian commanders of the war. Despite his innovative approach, his battles also proved to be amongst the bloodiest and most costly for the Russian Army.

A controversial figure, Sukhomlinov was responsible for many of the best – and worst – aspects of the Russian Army at the outset of the war.

The two masterminds of German policy in the east, Ludendorff and Hindenburg, photographed here with the staff of Eighth Army.

Grand Duke Nikolai (right) with Tsar Nicholas (left). Appointed as commander-in-chief at the beginning of the war, Nikolai struggled to assert his authority over his front commanders.

Rennenkampf led the Russian First Army into East Prussia at the beginning of the war, but his failure to cooperate with Samsonov contributed greatly to the defeat at Tannenberg.

It is almost certain that the staff of Eighth Army had already briefed Hindenburg and Ludendorff about François' cavalier attitude during the days of Prittwitz's command. They took this opportunity to make clear to the commander of I Corps that they expected their orders to be carried out. After being assured that everything would be done to expedite the arrival of the rest of his corps, François conceded. He would attack towards Usdau on 26 August from the northwest, while XX Corps supported him by attacking south.

There was considerable confusion in the Russian camp. Samsonov was of course aware of the strength of resistance that XV Corps had faced when Martos forced the Orlau–Lahna line. The Germans had withdrawn to the northwest, but aerial reconnaissance by planes from the Russian I Corps had spotted the arrival of the first elements of the German I Corps. Nevertheless, Zhilinski at Northwest Front Headquarters continued to insist that the Germans were retreating from their positions facing Rennenkampf towards Königsberg. By now, he had also been informed that some German troops had withdrawn to the southwest, and were concentrating around Rastenburg. Accordingly, he ordered Samsonov to attack northwest to secure the line from Allenstein to Osterode. I Corps would be sufficient to provide protection for the left flank; in order to cover against any German attack from Rastenburg, VI Corps should take up positions around Bischofsburg.

The result of this was that Samsonov was left to advance with only Martos' XV Corps on the left and Klyuev's XIII Corps on the right. Expecting orders to march north, Klyuev had already ordered one of his divisions to march to Omulefofen, but the tired men now had to retrace their steps and prepare for a thrust towards Wartenburg.[20] Klyuev sent a messenger to Samsonov, reminding his superior of how German war games before the conflict had envisaged a powerful thrust from the west; in order to counter this, he argued, both XV Corps and XIII Corps should strike west, rather than northwest. Already labouring under a mass of criticism from Zhilinski for his slow progress, Samsonov was advised by his staff that any attempt to wheel the entire army to the west would result in further delays. His chief of staff, Postovsky, sent a telegram to Northwest Front Headquarters, pleading for a day's halt – the supply lines were inadequate for the army, and time was needed to bring forward food and ammunition. The reply was not encouraging:

> With regard to a halt, the Front Commander states that the Second Army offensive has progressed considerably more slowly than he expected. The enemy had already left Insterburg on 23 August, and is therefore at least two marches

away from that town. In view of this, the Front Commander finds it impossible to sanction a halt until the line Allenstein–Osterode has been reached, as only then will it become possible to threaten the enemy's line of retreat to the lower Vistula.[21]

A request to turn the axis of advance west, to face the attack that Samsonov increasingly expected, was submitted in person by Samsonov's quartermaster-general, Filimonov. Zhilinski dismissed him with a demand that the advance into the heart of East Prussia had to continue. He added disdainfully that it was cowardice to imagine enemies where there weren't any.[22] It is curious that, at the same time that he was hounding Samsonov to show more energy, Zhilinski appears to have done little to enliven Rennenkampf; since the fighting at Gumbinnen, his forces had advanced less than 30 miles (50km) in five days, in the face of no opposition. Zhilinski was, like Samsonov, a member of the pro-Sukhomlinov circle, but on this occasion there was no sign of any preferential treatment of a fellow member of the same faction. Believing that two German corps – XVII Corps and I Reserve Corps – were falling back towards Königsberg, Rennenkampf continued to edge west towards the East Prussian capital, rather than southwest towards the area where Second Army was attempting to advance.

In his memoirs, François wrote that he discussed the planned attack against Usdau with his division commanders during the afternoon of 25 August. If he did so, it must have been in the most general of terms. Formal orders for the attack arrived from Eighth Army Headquarters shortly before midnight, requiring the attack to commence at 4 a.m. the following morning, with the intention of taking Usdau by midday. François continued to doubt that this was possible:

> I could understand the desire for a rapid advance. But an attack with inadequate resources raised very serious concerns. At that moment, I Corps' fighting strength was still missing 16 field artillery batteries, seven light artillery munitions columns, four heavy field howitzer batteries, all our cavalry, and all the infantry ammunition columns.
>
> Up to 21 August, the battle losses of the corps in terms of dead and wounded were about 1,400 men, or about 3.5 per cent of the wartime strength of the corps of 40,000 ¼ My repeated request by telephone [for a delay] was in vain.[23]

François issued orders to his corps shortly after midnight, less than four hours before Ludendorff's start time for the attack. 1st Infantry Division was to

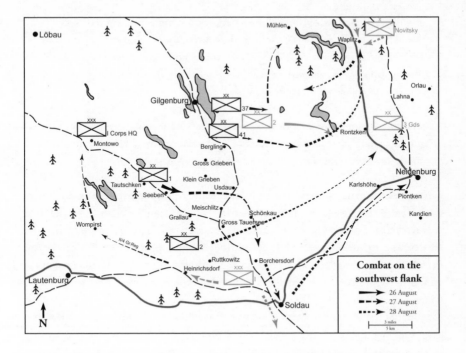

Combat on the southwest flank

→ 26 August
⇢ 27 August
⇢ 28 August

3 miles
5 km

N

commence the advance, with 2nd Infantry Division setting off three hours later in support on its southern flank. Whatever briefing he may have received during the afternoon had clearly not alerted the commander of 1st Infantry Division, General Conta, to the likelihood of such an early start, and his men were bedded down for the night. Now, in darkness, they assembled and started to move forward across broken, unfamiliar ground towards their forming-up areas for the attack.[24]

As the sky began to lighten on 26 August, François became aware of the sounds of fighting from the direction of 1st Infantry Division. Accompanied by his son, a young lieutenant, he made his way to Conta's headquarters:

> I found him in a small copse east of Tautschken, that the enemy was spraying with shrapnel. One officer of the division staff was wounded. The division had crossed the Welle [a small river immediately west of Tautschken] and begun the battle. General Conta had only eight battalions and four field batteries at his disposal. The artillery munitions columns were totally absent. The Russian artillery was significantly superior, and the Russian infantry had dug in on high

ground at Seeben. Continuing the attack without effective artillery support
would be tactically reckless. I refrained from giving the order to attack, informed
2nd Infantry Division accordingly, and once more sent a request to Army
Headquarters to be allowed to set the time for the attack myself. In reply, I
received the following transmission:

'The Army Commander cannot leave the decision about the start time of the
attack to the commander of I Corps, because the decision on this matter rests on
considerations other than just those of I Corps. For the time being, the time of
attack [on Usdau] remains midday.'[25]

Written confirmation arrived shortly afterwards; Ludendorff and Hindenburg
were determined to keep a tighter control over François than Prittwitz had
achieved. But François was correct in his assessment. He had learned from the
battles against Rennenkampf that without adequate artillery, any attack on
prepared positions was doomed to failure. Hoping that more of his artillery –
and, just as importantly, his artillery munitions columns – would arrive, François
issued orders for an attack towards Usdau, but gave a start time of 1 p.m. to allow
for the infantry to be fed. Even as he was setting out from Löbau for Gilgenburg
at first light, Ludendorff had received an erroneous report that Usdau had already
fallen, only to be disappointed when he learned of the slow progress of I Corps.
As François continued to delay, he raged in frustration – but there was nothing
he could do. Dismissal of François was pointless, as there was nobody at hand
who could take his place and be expected to be more reliable.

The staff of Eighth Army had promised François that they would expedite the
arrival of the missing elements of his corps, and the German railway system did
its best to oblige, as Walther von Stephani, the staff officer responsible for rail
movements in the area, later recorded:

When the main body of the 1st Division was already in action, the 1st Battalion
of the 3rd Grenadier Regiment arrived in Montowo. After the hasty off-loading
of the transport and horses at this station, the train with officers and other ranks
was sent on in the direction of Tautschken. Owing to this measure the appearance
of the battalion on the battlefield was hastened by half an hour. What a different
picture, compared to the previous day, presented itself to one's gaze. Peace and
quiet had then reigned over Tautschken. Now the guns were thundering. Rubble
thrown up by the Russian shells was rattling right and left of the train. The driver
calmly ran the engine, paying no attention to any of this, as though he had spent
his whole life in the midst of whistling bullets and bursting shells. I ordered him

to stop before reaching the bridge. The battalion detrained and immediately went into action.[26]

Abandoning the usual rules about spacing between trains and maximum speeds, the trains rushed men towards the battlefield as fast as they could. Seeben finally fell to 1st Infantry Division in mid-afternoon. Usdau remained in Russian hands, but François concluded that his men had done as much as could be asked of them. They had secured a start line from where a full attack against the main Russian position could be launched the following day.

Leonid Artamonov, the commander of the Russian I Corps that fought against François, had made little use of reconnaissance immediately before the battle began. Nevertheless, he accurately predicted that his positions would come under attack, and had advised Samsonov accordingly the previous day. Artamonov had a high reputation before the war as a leading military thinker, but his performance during this campaign was lacklustre. As the day drew to a close, he cautiously concluded that he had weathered the German attack. The main threat, he decided, lay at the southern end of his line, and he planned for a counterattack on 27 August to drive back the Germans.

Immediately to the north of François' troops were the divisions of Scholtz's XX Corps. They had largely recovered from the fighting north of Neidenburg, and now faced the Russian 2nd Infantry Division, from XXIII Corps, and all of XV Corps. The chief of staff, Emil Hell, showed admirable sangfroid by ordering the corps artillery to fire on his own house in Gross Grieben after the Russians occupied it, but the main German line came under little pressure in front of Gilgenburg. As the day progressed, it seemed to the Germans that the Russian 2nd Infantry Division, linking the left flank of XV Corps with the right flank of I Corps, was struggling to keep in contact with either of its neighbours, and Ludendorff ordered Scholtz to attack. In mid-afternoon, the German 41st Infantry Division and half of 37th Infantry Division moved forward across broken ground.

The northern half of the attack, carried out by 37th Infantry Division, rapidly found a gap between the two brigades of the Russian division, and exploited the exposed flanks. 41st Infantry Division encountered tougher resistance when it ran into the Russian 6th Infantry Division, and German losses were made worse by part of 59th Infantry Regiment getting caught in artillery fire from the division's own guns. Unable to send a message back to tell the artillerymen to cease fire, the German soldiers pressed on, suffering still more casualties from the defensive fire of the Russian infantry. The Russian trenches were eventually cleared in the early evening; the German regiment had lost 550 men.[27] Elsewhere, the German gunners worked more closely with their infantry, emulating their fathers who had fought against France in 1870–71. The ground was too broken for effective long-range fire, and the batteries deployed right in the front line, with the leading infantrymen, blasting Russian positions at short range. The machine gunners, too, accompanied the attacking troops, and reduced the few attempts by the Russians to launch counterattacks to a bloody shambles.[28]

One of the regiments of the Russian 2nd Infantry Division, the 7th Reval Infantry Regiment, started the day advancing confidently. Coming under increasingly heavy German fire, it managed to reach the first line of German trenches, only to be attacked in its flank by the German 37th Infantry Division. In bitter fighting the regiment lost nearly 3,000 men – 75 per cent of its strength – and was effectively wiped out as a combat formation. Split in two, 2nd Infantry Division fell back in disarray.[29]

The German 3rd Reserve Division was on the left flank of XX Corps, and had been ordered to advance to retake Hohenstein. Like other division commanders, Generalmajor Curt von Morgen had received details of the radio intercepts that described planned Russian movements, and knew that the Russian XV and XIII Corps were operating to his front. Reasoning that his division might find its own left flank threatened by XIII Corps, he decided to hold back. From the vantage of high ground, he could see the fighting between the Russian XV Corps and the German XX Corps developing, and concluded that it would be better to wait until the Russians were completely committed. He would then advance and try to turn the northern flank of XV Corps.

Opposing Morgen's division was Klyuev's XIII Corps. Klyuev had originally been ordered to march on Allenstein, but given the general shift of the axis of advance to the west, he waited on 26 August for new orders. When the original orders were confirmed in the middle of the day, he set off for Allenstein, advancing across a narrow neck of land between two lakes, the Plautziger-See and the Lansker-See. One consequence of this was that, as fighting erupted in front of XV Corps, there was little that Klyuev could do to move to support Martos, as the Plautziger-See lay between the two corps. The line of march ran through woodland, and there was only a single good road, adding to the delays. By the end of the day Klyuev was still short of Allenstein, though he had cleared the lakes. He now signalled Second Army Headquarters that he intended to march to support XV Corps on 27 August, but shortly after lost contact with Neidenburg.[30]

On the other side of the battlefield, to the east, Lieutenant-General Alexander Blagoveschensky's Russian VI Corps, supported by 4th Cavalry Division, was meant to be protecting the right flank of Samsonov's army, and had reached Ortelsburg. Communications between the elements of Second Army were generally problematic, and VI Corps was no exception. Orders had been sent to the corps by radio ordering an immediate advance to Bischofsburg. When this message was intercepted, Ludendorff immediately took steps to hurry his own forces to reach the town as soon as possible. As Samsonov's army changed its axis of advance from north to northwest, revised orders were issued – this time by telegraph – ordering VI Corps to leave only a screening force in Bischofsburg, while the rest of the corps moved to Allenstein. Shortly after, communications broke down completely. Unable to contact Samsonov, Blagoveschensky sent a liaison officer to report personally to his army commander on 25 August. The officer told Samsonov that the corps was approaching Bischofsburg, but could provide no more details, as his journey to Second Army Headquarters had been very time-consuming. Samsonov's staff tried to contact Blagoveschensky by radio during the following night, and finally managed to make contact shortly before dawn on 26 August. In response to a request for an update, Blagoveschensky's staff sent an encoded signal – which Second Army Headquarters was unable to decipher.[31]

During 25 August, one of Blagoveschensky's formations, 16th Infantry Division, occupied Bischofsburg, while 4th Infantry Division took up positions a little further north at Rothfliess, and 4th Cavalry Division was centred on Sensburg. All three units were significantly below strength, being at least a regiment short. In keeping with his new orders, Blagoveschensky ordered 16th Infantry Division to move to Allenstein, but neglected to inform 4th Infantry Division of the change of deployment.[32] Meanwhile, the German XVII Corps and I Reserve Corps were approaching, and were preparing to make their presence felt. It had been a long march, under blazing skies, as Mackensen later recalled, only made possible by the efforts of an unlikely team of heroes:

> For me, the march of the corps' infantry was unforgettable, conducted in a timely manner during the hot August days of 1914, from the Rominte through Friedland to Bischofsburg to take part in the decision at Tannenberg... Without field kitchens, this achievement of long marches through the day and into the night would not have been possible. This impression, and similar experiences in other theatres of the war, changed the controversial view about the proliferation of rear area units to an awareness of their indispensable contribution to war. Both during

these days and later, I personally ate my fill on many occasions of their satisfying, tasty meals.[33]

By the afternoon of 25 August, despite losing large numbers of exhausted, footsore men, the two corps were approaching Bischofsburg. Acting on the intercepted orders instructing VI Corps to take Bischofsburg – the change to march on Allenstein was sent by telegraph, and therefore escaped German interception – Ludendorff telephoned instructions for an attack on the town. Mackensen, the senior corps commander in the German force, issued orders late that night. XVII Corps was to press forward quickly down the main road to Bishofsburg, and given the urgency that Ludendorff had imparted in his telephone call, the XVII Corps commander stressed the importance of rapid, early progress. He was alarmed to discover, too late to intervene, that Below had ordered his I Reserve Corps to attack on the right of XVII Corps, but planned to start his advance in mid-morning, to allow his tired men a better chance to rest and recuperate. There was now a danger that the German attack would be delivered piecemeal, with the possibility that the Russians could defeat each corps in turn.

A further dilution of the attack force would have occurred if Mackensen had acted on a further order from Ludendorff, which arrived after the demand for an early advance on Bischofsburg. Eighth Army Headquarters continued to keep a wary eye on Rennenkampf's First Army, and ordered Mackensen to detach a division to cover his rear area. Aware that his divisions, depleted by their long march, would need all their strength for the coming battle, Mackensen decided to ignore the instruction.[34] In any event, it was the Russians, and not the Germans, who dispersed their troops. Blagoveschensky's cavalry remained massed around Sensburg, removed from his command and under direct command of Second Army, instead of providing the Russian corps commander with some much-needed reconnaissance. In the absence of such information, Blagoveschensky unaware of the imminent arrival of large numbers of German troops from the northeast, accepted the information from higher commands that the defeated German formations retreating from Gumbinnen would be marching directly to the west, across his front. Accordingly, he left a single brigade of infantry from 4th Infantry Division deployed around Lautern, a little to the north of Bischofsburg, with the second brigade in Gross-Bössau, midway between Lautern and Bischofsburg. 16th Infantry Division was ordered to march towards Allenstein. With the rest of Samsonov's army moving away towards the northwest, VI Corps had to try to keep in contact, if it was to protect the right flank of the Russian advance.

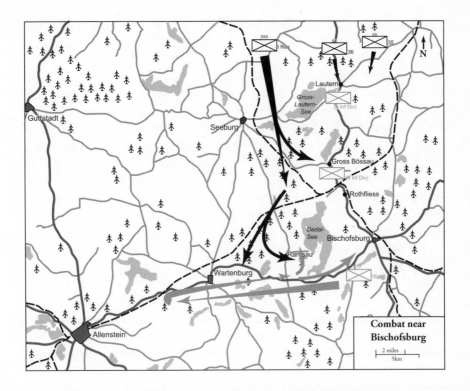

Combat near
Bischofsburg

2 miles
5km

Mackensen chose to bring both divisions of his corps into line for the attack towards Bischofsburg, with 36th Infantry Division on the right and 35th Infantry Division on the left. It was less than a week since the entire corps had been driven back in near-rout at Gumbinnen, and the commander of 36th Infantry Division, Konstanz von Heineccius, was in no mood for another such experience. Cautiously, his men probed forward through the morning mist, and when they encountered the Russian defences around Lautern, they decided that prudence was the order of the day, and dug in. Meanwhile, exhausted after its long march, 35th Infantry Division was in no state to launch itself into an immediate attack, and stopped a little to the north to rest and reorganise before moving forward. Russian troops probing forward from Lautern soon discovered that the area to the east of 36th Infantry Division was as yet unoccupied by German troops, and began to outflank Heineccius' men, only to be driven to ground by accurate artillery fire.[35]

XVII Corps might be stuck, through a combination of stout Russian defences, reluctance to repeat the rash attacks of Gumbinnen, and the exhaustion of 35th

Infantry Division, Below's I Reserve Corps was still moving forward, to the west of Mackensen's corps. Making excellent use of his cavalry to monitor Russian troop movements, Below advanced south, to the west of the large lakes near Lautern – the Gross-Lautern-See and Dadai-See – and cut the road from Bischofsburg to Wartenburg. Below sent a brigade of *Landwehr*, reinforced by 69th Reserve Brigade (part of 36th Reserve Division) to mask the Russian brigade at Gross-Bössau, to the east of the lakes. The Russians were moving forward to support the position at Lautern, and fighting suddenly erupted as the two forces collided. At first, the skill with which the Russians immediately went to ground brought the Germans to a halt. It was only when the supporting German artillery moved into the German front line and drove the Russians out of their positions that the attack finally moved forward. Late in the day, a final German charge secured Gross-Bössau.

Further north, running low on ammunition, the other brigade of the Russian 4th Infantry Division came under renewed attack, preceded by a powerful artillery bombardment. Although the infantry of 35th Infantry Division continued to lag, its artillery was now able to join the battle in earnest. The advancing Germans swiftly overran the exhausted defenders. The survivors of the Russian brigade reeled back, sweeping up both the other brigade and the rear area formations in a rout that continued until they reached Ortelsburg. By the end of the day, 4th Infantry Division, which had until then experienced almost no significant fighting, had lost seventy-three officers, 5,283 other ranks, and two of its artillery batteries – over half its infantry strength.[36] XVII Corps' losses, all from 36th Infantry Division, amounted to fewer than 200 men, reflecting the caution with which the Germans had advanced. I Reserve Corps had a harder time, losing nearly 1,600 men.

When he became aware of the heavy fighting to the north of Bischofsburg, Blagoveschensky attempted to send reinforcements. 16th Infantry Division, marching towards Allenstein, was ordered to turn around and retrace its footsteps. Laboriously, the weary Russian troops rearranged themselves and set off. As they approached the southern end of the Dadai-See, further orders arrived, dividing the division in two. Half was to proceed to Bischofsburg, while the other half turned north towards Ramsau. In the early evening, as 4th Infantry Division's battle reached a climax, this second column was spotted moving south by Below's I Reserve Corps. In an encounter battle the speed of reaction was critical, and Below's cavalry reconnaissance gave him a decisive edge. His troops deployed rapidly, taking the Russian force in its flank and rear and driving it back in disarray.

As the day drew to a close, Hindenburg and Ludendorff waited for hard news. The slowness of François' attack had left Eighth Army's chief of staff raging impotently, but it seemed that I Corps was at last in position to deliver a decisive attack on 27 August. Much more alarming was the news from beyond the battlefield. Aerial reconnaissance had spotted more Russian troops detraining at Mlawa, and Ludendorff feared that by effectively delaying the flank attack on Samsonov's army for a day, François might have exposed the German army to a Russian flank attack.

As the officers in Eighth Army Headquarters sat down to eat their dinner, news of the outcome of the fighting in Bischofsburg had still not arrived, but there were worrying reports that Russian troops, thought to be the left flank of Rennenkampf's army, had reached Gerdauen, in the rear of XVII Corps and I Reserve Corps. Ludendorff and Hindenburg left the room to discuss matters in private. The details of their conversation remain unknown, but Hindenburg's memoirs contain an oblique reference:

> It was now apparent that danger was threatening from the side of Rennenkampf. It was reported that one of his corps was on the march through Angerburg. Would it not find its way to the rear of our left enveloping force [XVII Corps and I Reserve Corps]? Moreover, disquieting news came to us from the flank and rear of our western wing [I Corps]. Strong forces of Russian cavalry were in movement away there in the south. We could not find out whether they were being followed up by infantry. The crisis of the battle now approached. One question forced itself upon us. How would the situation develop if these mighty movements and the enemy's superiority in numbers delayed the decision for days? Is it surprising that misgivings filled many a heart, that firm resolution began to yield to vacillation, and that doubts crept in where a clear vision had hitherto prevailed? Would it not be wiser to strengthen our line facing Rennenkampf again and be content with half-measures against Samsonov? Was it not better to abandon the idea of destroying the Narew [Second] Army in order to ensure ourselves against destruction?[37]

Given that none of the others present at dinner that evening – including Hoffmann, who wrote extensively about the battle – later mentioned anyone having such misgivings, it is reasonable to assume that this passage relates to Hindenburg's private conversation with Ludendorff. The author of a book published in 1928 about the battle described Ludendorff as being almost overcome with nerves and indecision that night, apparently basing this claim on a private conversation he had with Hindenburg shortly before the latter's death.[38]

Ludendorff always denied this, accusing the author of defamation. Hindenburg's account continued:

> We overcame the inward crisis, adhered to our original intention, and turned in
> full strength to effect its realisation by attack. So the order was issued for our right
> wing to advance straight on Neidenburg, and the left enveloping wing 'to take up
> its position at 4 a.m. and intervene with the greatest energy.'[39]

News from Mackensen and Below arrived shortly after, improving the mood at Eighth Army Headquarters. The commander of XVII Corps, though, was nervous about the possibility of substantial elements of Rennenkampf's army moving into his rear. When orders arrived from Eighth Army in mid-evening, requiring a resumption of the advance the following day, Mackensen considered his options. It was possible that two Russian corps – II Corps, which had been detached from Second Army in a futile attempt to form a link between the two Russian armies, and IV Corps, the most southerly of Rennenkampf's formations – were perhaps a day's march from his rear. The options for Mackensen were limited, and he decided to do all he could to finish off the Russians to his front. The *Landwehr* brigade that had fought at Gross-Bössau was in poor shape, and was ordered out of the front line. On 27 August, Below would march towards Allenstein with his I Reserve Corps, while Mackensen's XVII Corps pursued the retreating elements of Blagoveschensky's VI Corps south.

On the other side of the front line, in his headquarters in Neidenburg, Samsonov was also desperate for hard information. He dined that evening with his staff and Knox, the British military attaché, in the house of the town's German governor:

> The Chief of Staff [Postovsky] said that the whole of Second Army was making a
> wheel to the left pivoted on XV Corps. He spoke of general complaints of the
> enemy's use of hand-grenades. It is curious that we heard nothing of them in
> Frankenau yesterday.
>
> Samsonov was worried because he had not yet received a letter from his wife.
>
> There was a dramatic incident in the middle of the meal. An officer brought
> in a telegram for the Chief of Staff and said that the GOC [General Officer
> Commanding] I Corps wished to speak on the telephone with the Army
> Commander or the Chief of Staff. He said he was hotly engaged. General
> Postovsky put on his pince-nez, read the telegram, and he and General Samsonov
> buckled on their swords, said goodbye to the Commandant, and left at once...

Anders [a staff officer assigned to look after Knox] came back from the Army Staff at 9 p.m. and told us something of the situation:

General Artamonov with the HQ of I Corps at Usdau is in occupation of a line westnorthwest of that village. He telephoned to Samsonov that he expected to be attacked by two or three divisions advancing from the northwest, and aerial reconnaissance had revealed another division advancing against him from Lautenburg. He asked for the 2nd Infantry Division. Samsonov told him that the brigade of the 3rd Guards Infantry Division at Soldau would be under his orders, and sent an officer in an automobile to turn back the 2nd Infantry Division from Martos' left to cover Artamonov's right flank. He told Artamonov to hold on to the last man.

Martos reports that his Cossacks entered Hohenstein but were driven out, and he is preparing to attack it with infantry. Klyuev with XIII Corps, has passed the defile of Lansk (southeast of Hohenstein) which was only slightly defended…

Postovsky is nervous; he is generally nervous, and goes by the name of 'the mad Mullah.' Samsonov is content and satisfied.[40]

It is clear from this account that Second Army Headquarters was not yet aware of the losses sustained by 2nd Infantry Division; nor was there yet any news of the disaster that had befallen VI Corps. Artamonov's corps had come under attack, but seemed to have held off the German forces facing it. Samsonov's orders for the following day therefore assumed that Second Army would proceed with its attack as planned:

VI Corps, leaving a screening force at Bischofsburg, is to march on Allenstein, to cooperate with XIII and XV Corps in striking a blow against the left flank of the enemy; XIII and XV Corps are to continue their offensive, aiming at the occupation of the line Allenstein–Osterode; I Corps is to continue in the execution of its present task of safeguarding the left flank of the army.[41]

The following morning – 27 August – finally saw François fully prepared for battle:

The fighting for the positions on high ground at Usdau, which would have a decisive influence on the outcome of the Battle of Tannenberg, began at 4 a.m.

The detraining of the troops was over. During the night, the divisions had been able to unite their troop formations. The artillery commanders and artillery, with their munitions columns, were present, supplies secured. Now I Corps had its full fighting strength and could go into action with a strong will for victory and cheerful confidence.

The road to Battle Headquarters ran over the Seeben Heights. [We saw] deeply dug rifle trenches, with chairs and benches, items of equipment and entrenching tools. A few dead Russians. Under all these things there was also a small, woollen, well-made lion – a child's toy – presumably stolen in Soldau. This was something for my drivers, Koglin and Dannenberg; two outstanding men, who gave me the most loyal service throughout the entire war. They put the little lion on the radiator of the staff car as a talisman, and thus it accompanied us over the battlefields of Russia, France, Galicia and then back to France, greeted everywhere by the troops and local populace with friendly laughter. With every victory, the drivers gave it a higher rank insignia, and thus it rose rapidly from rifleman to officer. Every man in the unit knew the 'Lion of Seeben' and in Austria it became a war anecdote in the newspapers.

Reports of the commencement of the attack began to arrive at Battle Headquarters from 5 a.m. 2nd Infantry Division was to advance on the right through Gross Tauersee. Detachment Schmettau (six battalions, a cavalry squadron, three batteries) that had been subordinated to me from XX Corps, reported that it expected to be able to set off for Usdau from Bergling no sooner than 5.45 a.m, as its troops had not yet assembled. The Army Commander wished for a strong screen against Soldau, where according to radio intercepts elements of the Warsaw Guards [3rd Guards Infantry Division had been held in reserve in Warsaw] were to have arrived. Likewise, the 2nd Infantry Division of the Russian XXIII Corps was to be deployed for an attack from Meischlitz–Grallau railway station towards Grieben. The last report contradicted this, as Grallau railway station and the road halfway to Meischlitz was held by our 2nd Infantry Division.[42]

The Russian 2nd Infantry Division was in no state to take part in any fighting, still less mount an attack. François continued to monitor his corps:

All troop movements were under way, there was silence from Army Headquarters and I could make my customary tour of the troops; General Staff officers von Massow and Schubert as well as Rittmeister von Brandenstein and Leutnant von François accompanied me. I encountered General von Falk at Treppau railway station. Despite heavy Russian artillery fire, the right flank of his [2nd Infantry] division was progressing well with its attack on Gross Tauersee; but beyond, east of Heinrichsdorf, one could see troops marching back. We thought they were a troop redeployment behind the front and were not concerned. At 8 a.m.,

1st Infantry Division reported that Usdau had been taken. I climbed into the car to travel there; the escort car followed. A little past Meischlitz, we came under rifle and machine-gun fire, and shortly after also rifle fire from Usdau. The report of the capture of Usdau was therefore wrong. We had to bale out of the cars, and I sent them back to Grallau railway station. The officers stayed with me. The entire railway embankment was occupied by the Russians, one could see their heads bobbing up and down, and behind them on Hill 203 was Russian artillery, which found our cars a welcome target. But nothing came of it, we just had to return to the railway station on foot, often taking cover in the roadside ditch. I now drove to General von Conta on the high ground southwest of Usdau. Someone had mistaken an isolated farm to the west of Usdau for the beginning of the village, and hastily given an erroneous report of its capture. But now, at 11 a.m., one actually saw our 2nd Infantry Brigade taking the village of Usdau by storm from the direction of Klein Grieben. The Russians fled to the east and towards Borchersdorf. I followed the troops through Usdau, which had been reduced to burning ruins, and early in the afternoon we stood on the high ground north of Borchersdorf. The Russians were everywhere hurrying towards Soldau in retreat.[43]

The Russian forces facing the German 1st Infantry Division were from 24th Infantry Division. The collapse of the 2nd Infantry Division to the north the previous day left the Russian I Corps' position exposed, and Conta's 1st Infantry Division rapidly extended its line to outflank the Russians. Artamonov deployed his only reserves comprising a single brigade from 22nd Infantry Division, but the gap in the Russian line was too wide – Generalleutnant Max von Schmettau's forces, assigned to François overnight, simply extended the line of the attack further north. Unlike their German opponents, the Russians had received no supplies during the night. Hungry and almost out of ammunition, they had no choice but to fall back towards the south, widening the gap in Samsonov's front that had been created the previous day by the collapse of 2nd Infantry Division.

The southern flank of I Corps' advance was exposed, and in an attempt to protect it, François had ordered 2nd Infantry Division's 3rd Brigade, together with a *Landwehr* brigade, to guard against a Russian attack. Artamonov had already decided that the best way of holding his positions was to try to outflank the Germans, and dispatched the other half of 22nd Infantry Division, reinforced by the newly arrived 1st Rifle Brigade, to attack towards Heinrichsdorf. Originally, the former formation had been intended to reinforce the northern flank of

Artamonov's position; its absence ensured the success of the German outflanking attack. The German *Landwehr* brigade held up the first Russian drive towards Heinrichsdorf, but the southern flank of Falk's 2nd Infantry Division found itself under heavy attack. With its own supporting artillery outgunned by the Russian artillery, and unable to bring forward ammunition, the German 44th Infantry Regiment and 4th Grenadier Regiment fell back in haste. It was this withdrawal that François had seen east of Heinrichsdorf.

Most of the retreating German troops rapidly rallied, and stopped the Russian attack in its tracks. On his own initiative, Conta had already begun to turn elements of 1st Infantry Division to face the south, and a new battle line quickly formed, facing southeast.

But not all of the retreating troops from 2nd Infantry Division had been halted to form the new battle line. A battalion of 4th Grenadier Regiment was on the extreme flank of the German position:

> The commander was of a sensitive and nervous disposition that had already caused concerns in peacetime. Now, he stood alone with his battalion under heavy artillery fire, with his machine guns destroyed by direct hits. He could see nothing of his division through the intervening trees. He believed that they were retreating, and the reports that he received from the Mülmann detachment [the *Landwehr* brigade] were unfavourable. As strong Russian forces could now be seen moving near Ruttkowitz, the major's nerves failed. He imagined that his battalion had been abandoned in grave danger and marched through Wompirst to Montowo.[44]

As the battalion fell back, it streamed through rear area units, sweeping them up in the process. Rumours spread about the scale of the German retreat, amplified at every turn. In the afternoon Ludendorff and Hindenburg returned to Löbau to some unwelcome news:

> On our return, news arrived that I Corps had been defeated. The remnants had fallen back to Montowo. The report was hard to believe. But a telegraph report from the railway commandant confirmed that troops from I Corps were gathering there. Later it became clear that there was only one battalion, which had found itself in a difficult position and had given way.[45]

Other staff officers found themselves caught up in the middle of the confusion, and did what they could to restore order:

In Löbau we came upon columns and transport trains of I Corps, which, to our surprise, were going the other way and had turned their horses' heads northwards. When in my astonishment I questioned the leader, Cavalry Captain von Schneider, that officer explained that an order had come to make everything ready for a retreat to the north. When I got to my office, I was called to the telephone: the commander of the ammunition column and transport trains of I Corps reported from the station [at] Montowo and gave me the following information: '2nd Battalion of the Grenadier Regiment has just reached Montowo, quite disorganised. The commander of the battalion reports that I Corps has been completely defeated and it, as well as XX Corps, is retiring. He has only been able to save himself and his battalion from the general disaster by making a rapid retreat. For all eventualities, he has given orders to the column to turn around with the horses' heads to the north.' I did not doubt that this must be one of the numerous panics that so often occur – but possibly after we had left the field of battle I Corps had had to sustain a counterattack. I next ordered the commander of the battalion to come to the telephone, and I was very peremptory. I ordered him to turn his battalion around and to continue to march until he came upon the enemy. Then the Second Aide-de-Camp of the Army Command, Captain Caemmerer, who afterwards became so well known as the personal aide-de-camp of Field Marshal Hindenburg, was sent in a car with the order to drive on until he came upon either German or Russian forces. Nevertheless, the next hour, while awaiting Caemmerer's return with his report, was a very trying one.[46]

The unfortunate major did what he could to make amends, ensuring that he and his men were in the forefront of I Corps' operations the following day. For what remained of 27 August, fighting died down in the sector held by the respective I Corps of both armies. Artamonov's counterattack had petered out, and François was content to prepare for an advance on Neidenburg after a night's rest.

The confusion and alarm caused by Artamonov's limited attack, and the success of François' operation, demonstrate the vulnerability of both armies to such moves against the exposed flanks of positions. Even at this stage of the overall battle, Artamonov might have turned the tide of battle in Samsonov's favour, but his forces were hamstrung by their parlous supply problems. In any event, the Russian I Corps simply lacked the strength both to defend against the German 1st Infantry Division – especially given the hole in the Russian front to the north – and at the same time to gather sufficient strength for its own attack. Artamonov was personally criticised for his failure to manage his corps better. He was accused of spending too much time in the front line, interfering with lower level commanders, instead of coordinating events from above. But whatever the truth of this accusation, he was acting on incomplete and inaccurate information, having been told by Second Army Headquarters that 2nd Infantry Division was protecting his northern flank. By the end of the day his men were falling back through Soldau, a withdrawal that became increasingly chaotic as François' artillery spotted the movement and subjected it to a heavy bombardment.

Immediately to the north, Scholtz's XX Corps had been ordered by Eighth Army to attack once more. 3rd Reserve Division, which had spent the whole of 26 August waiting in vain for an opportunity to attack the northern flank of the forces facing Scholtz, was to move forward first, in an attempt to draw Russian reserves into action. The two divisions of Scholtz's corps would then attack in the south. The gap that yawned ever wider between the Russian XV Corps facing Scholtz and I Corps, being driven south by François, actually had an unsettling effect on the Germans. 41st Infantry Division advanced cautiously into almost open ground, while 37th Infantry Division, weakened by the detachment of Schmettau's battalions that had been sent to I Corps, came up against the remnants of the Russian 2nd Infantry Division. Fighting in wooded terrain, the Germans failed to detect the weakness of the Russian line; although 2nd Infantry Division collapsed and fell back to Neidenburg, Scholtz did not pursue. Instead, he turned his attention to Mühlen, from where came reports of an energetic Russian attack against General Unger's *Landwehr* units, mainly made up of the garrison of Graudenz.

At first, in discussion with Hindenburg and Ludendorff, Scholtz contemplated attacking into the southern flank of the Russian forces pressing towards Mühlen. News then arrived that the Russians had broken through the German lines and had taken the village. Immediately, Scholtz ordered 37th Infantry Division to move to support the *Landwehr* units. This left only Generalmajor Sontag's 41st Infantry Division available to threaten the southern flank of the Russian attack. Sontag had spent most of the day worrying about the lack of contact with I Corps to his south, and was not reassured by reports of François' successes. Now, he was ordered to move forward, possibly exposing his left flank to the Russians who were pressing so hard at Mühlen. Instead of driving forward energetically, he edged forward, constantly worried about reports of Russian cavalry in the scattered woods to his front. By dusk Sontag had covered only 2 or 3 miles (3 to 5km), perhaps half the distance he had been ordered to advance.

The news of a Russian breakthrough at Mühlen almost coincided with the alarms from the southern flank of I Corps, and proved to be just as illusory. One *Landwehr* unit had retreated in some disorder under heavy fire from Russian artillery, but soon rallied. General Unger, the commander of the *Landwehr* forces, remained confident that his men could hold their positions. The Russian artillery fire slowly slackened, through a combination of ammunition shortages and prudent use by Unger of his own guns. When the Russian 6th Infantry Division launched a major attack in mid-afternoon, it was halted with ease, and about 1,000 prisoners taken.[47]

The situation for the Russian Second Army was thus steadily worsening. Its left flank had been driven away to the south, and in the centre Martos' XV Corps had been partially defeated, and had made no progress in its own attacks towards Gilgenburg. Even if these attacks had succeeded, they would merely have moved the Russian forces into a more exposed position. The other corps deployed in the Russian centre, Klyuev's XIII Corps, had spent 26 August without engaging the Germans. Communications problems left Klyuev with little knowledge about what was happening. He had been ordered to take Allenstein to his north, but could hear sounds of heavy fighting from Martos' front to the southwest. Attempts to communicate by radio with Blagoveschensky's VI Corps on his right failed. As Samsonov's headquarters had discovered, VI Corps was using a different codebook from the one used by the rest of Second Army.

The men of XIII Corps had marched almost continuously since mobilisation, and their rations were exhausted. Whatever the requirements of higher commands, Klyuev was aware that his men would not be able to function as an effective fighting force unless they received food; and he was anxious to seize a major town, so that he could requisition rations. Reconnaissance reported that there were no German forces in Allenstein, which XIII Corps had been ordered to capture. The general orders for Second Army also stated that VI Corps was meant to be heading for Allenstein; Klyuev was therefore anxious that his troops might become entangled with Blagoveschensky's columns. He urgently sought clarification from Second Army Headquarters during the night of 26/27 August. When he received no reply, he sent a message to Martos asking whether XV Corps required assistance. By dawn on 27 August, no reply had been received, and Klyuev ordered an advance to Allenstein. Within minutes of the troops setting off, a telegram arrived from Martos, requesting support. Klyuev ordered his left hand formation, 1st Infantry Division, to divert to Hohenstein, while 36th Infantry Division concentrated in Stabigotten, midway between Hohenstein and Allenstein. These orders had barely been issued when another message arrived from XV Corps. This stated that Second Army had ordered XIII Corps to assign a brigade to XV Corps, while the rest of XIII Corps was to march to Allenstein.[48]

Klyuev dispatched 1st Infantry Division's 2nd Brigade to the southwest. The tired, hungry infantrymen marched through the day, and formed the most northern part of Martos' doomed attack at Mühlen towards the end of the 27th. Their contribution to the battle was negligible, and they fell back to the east in confusion. Meanwhile, the rest of XIII Corps occupied Allenstein without a struggle. Shortly after the Russians seized the town, a Russian aircraft landed, bringing news that a large force of infantry was marching down the road from Wartenburg towards Allenstein. Klyuev and his staff were aware that Blagoveschensky was meant to be approaching Allenstein from this direction, and assumed the troops that had been spotted were part of VI Corps. The pilot was given dispatches for Blagoveschensky, and ordered to land and make contact with the column of troops. At the same time a mounted patrol was sent to make contact with the column too. The aircraft disappeared into the summer sky, and no more was heard from it. The cavalry patrol approached the marching column and came under small arms fire. It promptly turned around and galloped back to Allenstein, but the commander of the Russian 36th Infantry Division, which had sent out the cavalry patrol, refused to be alarmed. There had been so many examples of nervous soldiers firing on their own sides that he simply assumed that this was another such case.[49] In fact, the troops were the leading elements of Below's I Reserve Corps.

Despite marching hard for ten days, XIII Corps had made almost no contribution to the battle. Martos had sent a messenger back to Second Army Headquarters early on 27 August demanding that Klyuev's corps support his northern flank. As a result, the solitary brigade from XIII Corps joined his attacks without achieving anything. Towards the end of the day, Martos received further orders from Second Army:

General Postovsky [Chief of Staff of Second Army] transmitted to me the following orders from the Army Commander: on the morning of 28 August, XV Corps was to march on Allenstein to cooperate with XIII and VI Corps. He added that a strong concentration would thus be formed for a blow against the Germans. I replied that it was impossible to carry out these instructions, as all the units of the corps were engaged in fierce fighting, and the enemy was receiving continual reinforcements, and that an aviator who had returned a short time previously reported a continuous movement of German troops towards the east. When Postovsky nevertheless began to insist on the execution of these orders, I declared to him finally that the Army Commander could appoint a general to take over the corps, and relieve me of my command. 'I will report our

conversation to the Army Commander,' replied Postovsky, 'and in an hour's time
I will call you up on the telephone.' However, he did not.[50]

At the eastern edge of the battlefield, Mackensen and Below had been ordered
to pursue the defeated VI Corps south on 27 August. At first their advance to
Bischofsburg was as cautious as XVII Corps' attack the previous day – or 'feeble'
in the words of a Russian staff officer who, with elements of the Russian 16th
Infantry Division, was part of the rearguard of VI Corps. But they soon
discovered that Blagoveschensky did not intend to hold Bischofsburg, and had
fallen back further south.[51] From the German perspective, the nature of their
victory the previous evening was still not clear, and Mackensen fully expected to
meet further tough resistance. Instead his men found Bischofsburg free of
organised Russian units, though there were many stragglers in the town. By the
time they had been rounded up, the total haul of prisoners exceeded 3,000, in
addition to over forty guns captured.[52]

Shortly after midday, fresh orders arrived for the two German corps, which
had been dispatched at 7.30 a.m. XVII Corps was to continue to advance south,
to Mensguth and Passenheim, with I Reserve Corps advancing southeast, into
the area between Allenstein and Passenheim. From here it would be available for
deployment either against Allenstein or towards the south. Mackensen's divisions
improvised a flying column under the command of Oberstleutnant von Löen,
led by XVII Corps' two cavalry regiments and supported by infantry using
whatever means of transport they could commandeer; 50 of the infantrymen
were mounted on bicycles.[53] Mackensen, who had spent the previous night in
full uniform, half-expecting hostilities to resume at any moment, accompanied
36th Infantry Division. An officer on his staff remarked on the commander's
effect on his men:

> Everywhere, where he appeared, his inspiring words, his energetic manner, and
> his constant care inspired and invigorated, so that everyone gave of his best.[54]

The leading elements reached Passenheim in the middle of the following night.
The Russians had continued to retreat in haste. An ammunition column, and
the pay-chest of VI Corps – a total of 200,000 roubles – were amongst the
booty.[55]

As another day of hard fighting drew to a close, the respective headquarters
attempted to determine what had happened, and what to do next. Samsonov
issued further orders to his scattered formations:

I Corps must at all costs maintain its position in front of Soldau, in order to safeguard the left flank of the army. XXIII Corps (2nd Infantry Division and those units of 3rd Guards Infantry Division which have come up) must at all costs maintain their position on the front westward of Frankenau...

XIII and XV Corps, under the general command of General Martos, at dawn are to assume an energetic offensive in the general direction Gilgenburg–Lautenburg, with the object of attacking in flank and rear the enemy forces opposite XXIII and I Corps.

VI Corps is being transferred to the Passenheim area.[56]

News of the disaster at Bischofsburg reached Samsonov only a full day after events, and even then it was not clear to Samsonov whether the setback was large or small. XXIII Corps had been divided into its constituent divisions at the outset of the campaign, and an attempt to reform it now was pure wishful thinking; 2nd Infantry Division remained in no shape to resume combat, and elements of 3rd Guards Infantry Division were spread over a large area. The fulfilment of Samsonov's orders – XIII and XV Corps advancing sufficiently far to outflank and defeat the German forces facing I Corps – would require an advance several times greater than any that had been achieved to date. But Samsonov continued to operate in an intelligence vacuum. There was almost no information from higher commands about the situation facing Rennenkampf, and Samsonov had to assume that at least part of the German forces in East Prussia were being tied down by the Russian First Army, or at least herded back towards Königsberg. Most of the heavy fighting that his men had undertaken was in the west, and it seemed logical to assume that the main strength of the German forces lay there. Consequently, concentrating against them was not an unreasonable assumption. It was only in combination with the disastrous situation on both flanks that Second Army's orders assumed the nature of a suicide note.

After writing these orders, Samsonov sent a telegram report to Zhilinski at 11.30 p.m. in which he declared that he wished to dismiss Artamonov for retreating 'without sufficient reason'.[57] His replacement was General Dushkevich, formerly the commander of 2nd Infantry Division. The following morning, Samsonov sent a further signal to Northwest Front Headquarters, stating that he intended to join the staff of XV Corps to take personal command of the battle. Such a trip to a front-line unit was, in the case of the German Army, an everyday event, and the headquarters staff were expected and required to ensure that all functions continued smoothly in the absence of the commander. The quality of staff officers in the Russian Army, though, was not as high.

The mood in Eighth Army Headquarters was not as jubilant as might be expected. Reports suggested that Rennenkampf's units had reached Rastenburg, and were therefore edging ever closer. Anxious to avoid the two eastern corps being caught between the two Russian armies, Ludendorff ordered that their combined forces attack Allenstein the following day, in order to accelerate the collapse of Samsonov's army. Below was to lead off the attack by midday at the latest, while Mackensen was to send part of his corps in support; XIII Corps was not to wait until XVII Corps' units were in position. The rest of XVII Corps would continue to press south. Unfortunately, Ludendorff only had direct contact with Below, and assumed that the latter would pass the orders on to Mackensen. But the only message passed to XVII Corps, by Below's chief of staff, stated that the entire XVII Corps was to aid I Reserve Corps in the assault on Allenstein.

Many reasons have been suggested for this change of emphasis, from simple error to a deliberate attempt by Below to ensure that his I Reserve Corps would be fully supported by Mackensen's corps. It may be relevant that Below tasked Posadowsky, his chief of staff with passing the message to Mackensen, rather than entrusting it to a lower-ranked officer. Mackensen was deeply unhappy about the order:

> Since the evening of 25 August, Passenheim and Jedwabno seemed to me the appropriate operational objectives, given the general situation. These considerations had driven me on, led me through the fighting at Lautern on 26 August, and on 27 August with my leading elements even further to Raschung. My intention was to reach Jedwabno with the corps on 28 August, and to send a detachment to reach Ortelsburg. The appropriate orders had been issued. Then Oberst Graf Posadowsky, send from I Reserve Corps, dealt 'a lethal blow,' and called on XVII Corps to march through Wartenburg on Allenstein! This line of march was so contrary to my understanding of the situation and the orders I had received to date from Army Headquarters that I was reluctant to comply. But I had no opportunity to clarify matters with Army Headquarters, as I was no longer in direct contact. Posadowsky's explanation that his request originated in an order from Army Headquarters, which he was passing on, finally left me with no choice to agree to march the corps towards Allenstein and leave only reconnaissance and screening elements in the direction of Jedwabno–Ortelsburg. My aversion to marching on Allenstein and a distinct mistrust in the order brought by Posadowsky affected me so strongly that I would have acted contrary to it and stuck to the planned march on Jedwabno, had it not been the trusted person of Posadowsky, with whom I had worked before, standing before me.[58]

Mackensen was not the only man in XVII Corps Headquarters to have misgivings about these new orders. Karl von Dunker, who was Mackensen's chief of staff, later wrote:

> I had never seen General von Mackensen in such a rage. He and his staff had the feeling that the order from Army Headquarters, as issued, could not be followed. The younger general staff officers were particularly opposed. But Graf Schwerin [a major on Mackensen's staff] and I could do nothing, when the commander told us with a heavy heart to comply with the orders.[59]

On the other side of the battlefield, François prepared for a resumption of operations. As it grew light, the soldiers of I Corps moved through the morning mist to their starting positions. François' orders issued during the evening of 27 August called for a resumption of the assault on the Russian I Corps:

> As soon as daylight permits, the Russian batteries spotted in front of Soldau are to be suppressed ... the infantry of the divisions and both Mülmann and Schmettau Detachments are to occupy jumping off lines for an attack on Soldau. I will order the timing and details of the attack at 6 a.m. from Hill 202 west of the main road at Usdau.[60]

As it grew light, François became aware that the Russian positions around Soldau were far less substantial than he had expected. His own reconnaissance found few defenders, and aerial reconnaissance reported large numbers of Russians retreating to the south. Immediately, François altered his plans. Oberstleutnant Freiherr von Schäffer was to take the combined cavalry of 1st Infantry Division and the Schmettau detachment – the forces immediately available next to François' battle headquarters – down the Neidenburg road in order to cut the lines of retreat of the Russian troops facing XX Corps to the north. A battery of artillery, together with the bicycle battalion of 43rd Infantry Regiment, was ordered to follow.

The Russian rearguard in front of Soldau consisted of troops from five infantry regiments, with some six batteries of artillery in support.[61] The men were from different formations – three regiments from the independent 1st Rifle Brigade, one regiment from 3rd Guards Infantry Division, and one from 22nd Infantry Division – and were short of ammunition. Nevertheless, ably led by General Otto Sirelius, the Russians put up determined resistance, and it took until late morning for 1st Infantry Division and the Mülmann detachment to secure

Soldau. Confident that the Russian I Corps had been effectively driven out of the battle, François issued further orders. Schmettau's detachment and 2nd Infantry Division were to march on Neidenburg, securing the road from Neidenburg to Willenberg. After Soldau was secure, 1st Infantry Division would move to Neidenburg and form the main corps reserve. Mülmann would hold the line of the River Neide at Soldau.[62]

Immediately to the north, the battle in the centre also resumed. Scholtz had concluded that the Russian forces facing him were approaching the end of their strength, and ordered Sontag's 41st Infantry Division to infiltrate forward through what remained of the Russian positions. When it reached the main Neidenburg-Hohenstein road, it was to turn north and march through Waplitz to Paulsgut, placing it in the rear of the Russian troops that had tried to storm Mühlen the previous evening. Once the Russian flank and rear had thus been turned, the *Landwehr* forces around Mühlen, supported by XX Corps' 37th Infantry Division, would advance, driving the Russians onto the guns of 41st Infantry Division.

The task of infiltrating through the Russian lines and seizing Paulsgut would have been a challenge for fresh troops, but 41st Infantry Division was tired after several days of fighting. Moreover, three of its twelve battalions were elsewhere; two were with Schmettau in the south, and one was collecting wounded and equipment from the battlefields of the last two days. Orders arrived late, and in the darkness the men proceeded in fits and starts. At about 2 a.m., Martos later wrote, his officers became aware of the German movement, though he described this as being due to sporadic shots being fired. German accounts, in contrast, describe how the advancing soldiers were ordered to unload their weapons, precisely to avoid giving away their locations. In any event, at first light the leading elements were approaching Waplitz from the south when they came under increasing Russian fire. One of Sontag's three regiments managed to penetrate into Waplitz, but as the morning mist cleared, increasing Russian artillery fire drove most of the division to cover. A river ran through Waplitz, and the leading German troops now found themselves on the north side of the main bridge, unable to withdraw due to heavy fire on the bridge itself. This also prevented reinforcements from reaching them; one attempt by a company of pioneers was rapidly reduced to a bloody shambles, with no men getting more than halfway across the bridge.

Martos had transferred the only reserves available to XV Corps, a brigade led by Colonel Novitsky, to the area, and together with what remained of 2nd Infantry Division, this force now applied increasing pressure to the Germans.

The spearhead that had penetrated into Waplitz was forced to surrender, having exhausted its ammunition. The remaining two regiments began to fall back, with the waters of the Mühlen-See to the west and Russian troops to the north and east. It was only when 41st Infantry Division's artillery deployed in the open and fired on the Russian lines – and drew fire upon itself to spare the retreating infantry – that Sontag was able to salvage his regiments. Casualties were heavy, with nearly 2,500 men missing. German accounts reported that about 300 men surrendered to the Russians in Waplitz; Russian accounts put the number nearer 1,000.[63]

The German plan of operations had called for the main battle line of XX Corps to attack once 41st Infantry Division was established in the rear and flank of the Russian defences. As the morning mist dispersed, and with it any chance of creeping forward under cover, Morgen ordered a brigade of his 3rd Reserve Division to seek out the northern flank of the Russian position, and his main line pressed forward shortly after. It was a battle in which traditional Russian strengths in stubborn resistance were decisively effective. The main advance ground to a halt with heavy casualties, and the brigade sent through the Jablonken Forest to seek the Russian northern flank ran straight into troops from the Narvsy and Koporsky Regiments of XIII Corps. Although these regiments had spent the entire campaign on exhausting marches, they had seen little action, and now threw themselves into close-quarter fighting in the forest. Despite being surprised by the presence of the Germans, they put up tough resistance. Slowly, they were driven back, eventually into Hohenstein, but a breakthrough eluded the Germans. Immediately to the south, Morgen's other brigade pushed through Dröbnitz, with the division staff hard on the heels of the infantry. Morgen's mood was one that would have resonated with many of his fellow commanders:

> These were still good times for senior officers. Without being tied to the telephone, one stood on the 'commander's hill', overlooking most of the battlefield, sending orders via mounted staff officers and receiving reports from messengers and liaison officers.[64]

The Goltz *Landwehr* Division, attacking Hohenstein from the north, was also held up with heavy losses.

News began to arrive at Eighth Army Headquarters of the defeat of 41st Infantry Division as the morning progressed. Shortly after 9 a.m., Ludendorff sent out fresh orders to François:

41st Infantry Division has been driven back by the enemy to Wronowo. I Corps is to send the division assembled at Schönkau immediately to Rontzken to prevent a breakthrough by the enemy, and to launch an attack.

The troops of the Schmettau Detachment are likewise to move in the same direction. The Army Commander desires that the ordered movements are started immediately, all haste is required. Report when the division is on the march.[65]

Further orders followed at midday, requiring all of I Corps to support 41st Infantry Division; perhaps in recognition of François' previous disregard of instructions, the orders concluded with the sentence: 'I Corps can do to the Army the greatest service by following these orders precisely.'[66] The exhortation was wasted. Even if 41st Infantry Division had been driven back, François reasoned, the capture of Neidenburg would make any tactical victory by the Russians almost irrelevant. Falk's 2nd Infantry Division was already engaging elements of the Russian 3rd Guards Infantry Division around Kontzen, and appeared to be advancing well. 1st Infantry Division was ordered to rest and replenish, prior to further fighting. But other than this, François made little attempt to comply with Ludendorff's wishes.

In any event, the crisis rapidly resolved. Although Sontag sent an alarming message to XX Corps Headquarters confirming the mauling his division had received, adding that he thought his division would struggle to hold its ground, no Russian attack developed. The units deployed against him, particularly those from 2nd Infantry Division, were too weak as a result of their losses on previous days. Despite stubborn resistance, the German 3rd Reserve Division slowly moved forward as XV Corps was ground down. Martos' troops had been in almost continuous combat, bearing the brunt of the fighting on the Russian side; ammunition, food and reserves were all at an end. Large numbers of prisoners were taken, and by nightfall the leading elements of the German division had reached the area where 41st Infantry Division had been driven back in the morning. They even managed to liberate about 200 of the prisoners that the Russians had taken in their early success. A brigade of the Russian 1st Infantry Division, from XIII Corps, which had been ordered forward the previous day to try to seek out the northern flank of the German position, found itself caught between the *Landwehr* advancing from the northwest and the 3rd Reserve Division advancing from the southwest. The Russians resisted as long as they could, but with both their flanks bypassed, they were forced to fall back at dusk – especially as the German 37th Infantry Division hurried forward during the afternoon after a slow start, reaching Hohenstein after a draining march along dusty roads in the burning heat. Goltz's *Landwehr* division, though, had a harder time, coming up against fresher troops from XIII Corps, and was forced to give up its early gains.

Samsonov had joined Martos in the centre, and personally congratulated the commander of XV Corps on the defeat of the German 41st Infantry Division. It was only now that Martos learned fully about the defeat of the Russian I Corps, and the resulting exposure of Second Army's left flank. He advocated an immediate retreat by both his corps and XIII Corps, but Samsonov's chief of staff, Postovsky, pressed for a delay until all the troops of XIII Corps had arrived, still hoping for a victory. By mid-afternoon the leading elements of Klyuev's corps arrived and were suddenly subjected to German artillery fire. The infantry broke and ran, though some were gathered together by Samsonov's staff officers and organised into a reserve behind XV Corps. Orders were sent to Klyuev urging him to hurry forward with the rest of his troops, but as dusk fell Postovsky abandoned his resistance to a retreat. Orders were issued for the Russian centre to prepare to pull back to Neidenburg.

François had decisively turned the left flank of Samsonov's army, and pressed forward towards Neidenburg during the afternoon of 28 August. The well-rested 1st Infantry Division and the Schmettau detachment led the way, and the two cavalry regiments of I Corps reached the outskirts in the face of only minimal resistance. The Russian defence of the town was in the hands of 6th Cavalry Division and the Keksgolmski Regiment of 3rd Guards Infantry Division, commanded by General Stempel, but although these units fought well against Falk's 2nd Infantry Division, preventing it from reaching Grünfliess, they could do little to prevent the advance on Neidenburg. Acting on a report from an aviator that the Russians had withdrawn from the town, François decided to investigate personally, driving with his staff to Karlshöhe, immediately west of the town:

> Neidenburg wasn't visible from there, so with a few officers of the staff I climbed up Signal-hill 215. I looked around with my field glasses, and was just drawing the attention of my companions to some earth-brown lumps in a potato field, when bullets whizzed past our ears and we had to take cover. The fire grew steadily stronger, and the striking rounds scattered sand in our faces. Then the vanguard squadron of the 10th Mounted Jäger Regiment, which had been dispatched to Neidenburg, appeared, drew up and attacked the Russians through our position; [we saw] fleeing infantry, trying to get to Neidenburg, which was still in Russian hands. I ordered the commander of the Mounted Jägers, Oberstleutnant Berring,

who reported to me immediately after the attack, to move south of Neidenburg through Piontken with his regiment and then on to Willenberg.[67]

François waited until troops from the Schmettau detachment arrived, and then entered Neidenburg, thus severing the lines of communication of the remaining elements of Samsonov's army. During the evening Schmettau pushed on to Muschaken, and 1st Infantry Division took up positions in Neidenburg itself, even as Samsonov was ordering a general retreat to the town.

In Allenstein, Klyuev was not aware of the defeat of Blagoveschensky's VI Corps, and that any troops approaching him from the east were likely to be German, not Russian. Indeed, the orders he had received included information that VI Corps was to proceed to Passenheim. At first light on 28 August, XIII Corps set off westwards from Allenstein, leaving a single battalion in the town to wait until all corps transport had left; after this it too was to head west towards Hohenstein, even if VI Corps units had not arrived to relieve it. Just as the battalion was preparing to leave, the German 36th Reserve Division arrived – the vanguard of Below's I Reserve Corps. In a swift action, the Russians were overwhelmed. Crucially, they were unable to alert the rest of XIII Corps.[68]

The rest of XIII Corps ran into German troops at Grieslienen, and an untidy battle commenced as Klyuev's men deployed off the line of march. As the fighting grew heavier, the last formation in the Russian column, 143rd Dorogobujsky Regiment from 36th Infantry Division, suddenly came under attack from Below's vanguard. The Russians succeeded in holding off the Germans, but the corps transport column, sent to the south of Allenstein, was overrun and captured. Both actions – in a battle in which similarly named units fought each other, the German 36th Reserve Division fought the Russian 36th Infantry Division, while the 1st Reserve Division captured XIII Corps' transport column – the Russians resisted fiercely. Driven from the transport column, the troops assigned as escorts retreated to the village of Darethen, where they resisted long into the night.

By the end of the day, Klyuev was still relatively isolated. His leading elements had been in action around Hohenstein, and his rearguard had successfully fended off Below's corps. German cavalry patrols were operating between his positions and XV Corps, somewhere to the south. After a discussion with his staff, Klyuev decided that his men should rest for the night, and at first light on 29 August, they would attempt to launch an attack to link up with XV Corps. At midnight orders finally arrived from Samsonov, telling Klyuev to retreat to Kurken. Klyuev wanted to withdraw to the east of the Plautziger-See, where although the roads were smaller, there was less danger of the Germans interfering. However, concluding that Second Army Headquarters must have a clearer picture of the overall situation than he did, he decided to follow orders, which would require him to attempt to march south to the west of the Plautziger-See, with the German forces in and around Hohenstein on his western flank.

One half of the encirclement of Samsonov's Second Army was effectively complete. The other half would depend on Mackensen, who had been so reluctant to turn his corps towards Allenstein. During the morning of 28 August he received a further message from I Reserve Corps to the effect that the Russians were marching from Allenstein to Hohenstein. I Reserve Corps had been ordered to pursue them, and in the absence of orders to the contrary, Below suggested that XVII Corps do the same. Having received no direct orders for more than a day, Mackensen told Hauptmann Bartenwerfer, one of his junior staff officers, to fly to Army Headquarters to get definitive instructions. Before Bartenwerfer could complete the journey, though, telephone contact was re-established. As soon as he became aware of the change in emphasis in the orders that had been passed to XVII Corps, Ludendorff issued clarifying orders. XVII Corps was to resume its drive to Ortelsburg:

> As strong forces as possible are to be dispatched to Jedwabno, to intercept all Russian units that emerge from the Allenstein–Hohenstein woodland … pursue to the last gasp. A great success [can be achieved] if pursued energetically. Onwards![69]

Under the relentless sun, soldiers and horses dropped out of the marching columns of XVII Corps with increasing frequency, but the pursuit continued unabated. Dunker, the junior staff officer in Mackensen's headquarters, later recalled the march:

> I saw the staff halt on a woodland road to allow an infantry regiment of 35th Infantry Division to march past. Shrouded in thick clouds of dust, the troops passed singing, their demeanour showing no sign of fatigue from their tremendous marches. Such was the impact of the words 'victory and pursuit.'[70]

The lead elements reached Ortelsburg at 3 a.m. the following night, on the heels of the retreating Russians. They had outstripped their supply columns, and officers did what they could to feed their men. Leutnant von Althoff, serving with 35th Infantry Division's 176th Infantry Regiment, purchased all the bread he could find in Rummy with his own funds, loaded it onto a captured Cossack horse, and hurried it to the troops of the vanguard.[71]

Ludendorff ended the day in confident mood:

> West of Hohenstein, 3rd Reserve Division had gained ground, just as 37th
> Infantry Division did later, and von der Goltz's *Landwehr* Division had penetrated
> into Hohenstein. The enemy front seemed to be breaking up… We did not have
> a clear picture of the situation with individual units. But there was no doubt that
> the battle was won.[72]

Earlier in the day, Eighth Army's chief of staff had appeared less certain. During
the morning a message arrived that Rennenkampf's army was finally approaching
from the east. Ludendorff apparently declared that the fight with Second Army
would have to be abandoned, but Hindenburg took him aside for a private
conversation. When the two men rejoined the rest of the army staff, Hindenburg
announced that nothing had changed; the attacks against Samsonov were to
continue.[73] It was only when further radio intercepts confirmed that
Rennenkampf's First Army was still advancing slowly towards Königsberg, and
was at least 40 miles (64km) away, that anxieties were completely allayed.

The Russian front was far from broken, though gaps were beginning to
appear. Several days of intense battle had left Martos' XV Corps almost completely
exhausted. After trying in vain to reach Neidenburg, Samsonov and his staff
spent the night in Orlau, where the advancing XV Corps had driven off the
German XX Corps only a week before. Unable to contact Martos, Samsonov sent
orders for a general withdrawal to Klyuev, adding that, for the moment, the
commander of XIII Corps was responsible both for his corps and XV Corps, as
well as the fragments of XXIII Corps. XV Corps' 6th and 8th Infantry Divisions
had already started an orderly withdrawal before the end of 28 August, and did
so without close pursuit by the Germans. XXIII Corps was in control of the units
facing south, from the area where the German 41st Infantry Division had been
defeated the previous morning to the western approaches of Neidenburg. As they
arrived, the leading elements of XV Corps extended this line to the east. News
now arrived that Martos had been killed, and General Fittinhof, the commander
of 8th Infantry Division, took over command of XV Corps.

Martos was still alive and in good health, though not in good spirits or
circumstances. The previous night he too had tried to reach Neidenburg, as
ordered, to take command of the defence of the town, not knowing that it was
already in German hands. He and his staff took shelter in the Kommusiner Forest,
to the northeast of Neidenburg, where patrols informed them that the Germans
were already in the town. After ordering units to set up a defensive line facing

south as they arrived, Martos decided to visit the front line, unaware that the soldiers had failed to follow their orders. As soon as they left the woods, the Russian party came under German artillery fire. Some men were killed, the others scattered, and Martos and a small group managed to escape back into the forest. Here, during 29 August they eventually ran almost straight into a German machine gun. The burst of gunfire scattered them and killed Major-General Machugovsky, Chief of Staff of XV Corps. Accompanied by a single captain and two Cossacks, Martos continued to try to find a way to safety. Late on 29 August he led his group south, navigating by starlight, until they encountered another German patrol near Muschaken, where they were taken prisoner.[74]

François' troops were slow to get into action on 29 August. Falk's 2nd Infantry Division advanced cautiously northwards, with troop commanders unwilling to take risks. By the end of the day the German infantry had moved only 3 miles (5km). 1st Infantry Division was delayed by alarming reports of strong Russian columns approaching Neidenburg from the north. François watched as the Russians – mainly rear area units trying to reach safety, accompanied by several batteries of artillery – were brought under fire and scattered.[75] Aware that he had to be watchful both to north and south, François was nevertheless determined to push on eastwards to complete the encirclement of Samsonov's army. He ordered one of his cavalry regiments to patrol south towards the Russian frontier, while the other set off along the road to Willenberg. Accompanied by Schmettau's detachment, the horsemen of the 10th Jäger Regiment reached Willenberg in the early evening. Schmettau's infantry had covered a remarkable 39 miles (63km) in two days, often fighting their way past Russian units. Around Willenberg they found many Russians only too keen to surrender, and the haul of prisoners increased by the hour.[76] By the end of the day, elements of 1st Infantry Division were deployed along the road between Neidenburg and Willenberg, where they too added to the number of captured Russians.

On the Russian side, Klyuev ordered his men to break contact with the Germans around Hohenstein during the night of 28/29 August. Moving under orders of strict silence, they assembled for a night march through Mörken. Almost inevitably, they started off down the wrong road, and valuable time was lost while the correct route was identified. The leading elements passed through Mörken during the night, but at first light a German machine gun position in the village – the gunners had either not noticed the retreating Russians earlier, or had fallen asleep, or perhaps decided not to risk engaging an unknown number of Russians in the dark – opened fire. This inevitably drew the attention of other German units, and a fierce battle rapidly developed as the Russians attempted to march east. Surrounded on three sides, Klyuev's rearguard – the Kashirsky Regiment, commanded by Colonel Kakhovsky – was almost completely destroyed, but the rest of the column managed to slip away.[77] The road that they were following had several potential choke points, where vital bridges had to be crossed. At Schwedrich, Klyuev's men had another hard fight, as German forces pressed in from the west. The last elements of XIII Corps crossed the bridge even as it burned down around them, and followed their comrades to Kurken. The pursuing men, from Morgen's 3rd Reserve Division, overran XV Corps' baggage column, much to the delight of the men, who regarded their loot as a just reward for several days of hard fighting.[78]

In Kurken further orders awaited Klyuev. He was to proceed to Khorjele via Willenberg, as Neidenburg was now in German hands. The problem XIII Corps now faced was that there were no good roads that led to Willenberg, and progress along the narrow woodland tracks southeast of Kurken would be slow and difficult. But even as Klyuev prepared to set out, he received orders to take up positions facing Neidenburg. Aware that such a deployment, which would involve potentially crossing the rear area of XV Corps, would be extremely difficult for his exhausted men, Klyuev obeyed reluctantly.

Once more the soldiers of XIII Corps set out on a difficult night march late on 29 August. Most had not eaten for two days, and they had spent almost the entire campaign on tiring marches. Klyuev's corps had been reduced to only four regiments, two from 1st Infantry Division, and two from 36th Infantry Division. When they ran into the rear area units of XV Corps at Kommusin, the traffic jam that Klyuev had feared became a reality. Staff officers struggled to sort out the men of the two formations, and directed XIII Corps east along the woodland road to Kaltenborn. They found the village was in German hands, but the garrison proved to be no more than a small force of hussars, numbering fewer than 100. Short of ammunition, the Germans fought until first light, and then withdrew.[79]

As it grew light on 30 August, the Russian forces were grouped into three columns. The western column was marching towards Muschaken, the central one (led by Klyuev) headed towards Saddek, and the eastern one tried to reach Wallendorf. Klyuev's column rapidly broke up, and surrendered piecemeal during the day. The eastern column also disintegrated, but substantial elements managed to infiltrate past the outposts of the German 1st Infantry Division along the Neidenburg–Willenberg road. Combined with elements of XV and XXIII Corps, perhaps a total of 14,000 Russian soldiers managed to reach safety. The western Russian column ran into German troops in prepared positions during the afternoon. In a last desperate charge the Russians managed to drive off the Germans, even capturing some guns, but as officers struggled, with limited success, to reorganise the column and to press on, repeated German assaults continued to spread chaos, and the last remnants were rounded up by German cavalry the following morning.[80]

While François was closing off the Russian lines of retreat from the west, Mackensen was still pressing forward from the northeast. As tired as the Russians they were pursuing, the men of XVII Corps pressed on, reaching Jedwabno during the afternoon and liberating several hundred German soldiers from XX Corps who had surrendered to the Russians in previous fighting. There was almost no significant Russian resistance, and it was pure fatigue that brought the Germans to a halt, just north of the Neidenburg–Willenberg road. Here they linked up with patrols from François' I Corps. The encirclement was complete.

After his meeting with Martos, Samsonov and his immediate entourage continued their journey, as his chief of staff later recorded:

At about noon on 29 August General Samsonov left 2nd Division and rode towards Willenberg, where he expected to find VI Corps. At all the crossings over the swampy streams along the road German units with machine guns were encountered. The Army Commander ordered his Cossack convoy to charge the machine guns at one of these swampy defiles. The gallant Colonel Vyalov of the General Staff led the Cossacks to the attack, but unfortunately the attack failed. General Samsonov reached Willenberg, but found the town occupied by the Germans. Only a few of the Cossack convoy remained with the Army Commander, who stayed till evening in a wood near Willenberg with seven officers of the General Staff and one NCO. It was essential to get out of the area of the German positions by night. This was impossible on horseback. When complete darkness arrived the group of officers and the Army Commander travelled on foot through swamps and forests, often encountering German patrols and being fired on by them.

Before we reached Willenberg, General Samsonov had requested me not to seek to prevent him from putting an end to himself, and had only changed his mind after warm protests on the part of the officers accompanying him. About 1 a.m. the group, after a short rest in a wood, moved on to continue their journey but General Samsonov had hidden himself from his companions. Shortly afterwards a shot was discharged in the woods and all realised that with this shot had ended the life of the noble Army Commander, who did not wish to survive the disaster which had overtaken his army. The whole group of officers decided to remain where they were until morning in order to find the body of their commander as soon as it was light, and to carry it away from the enemy lines. Unfortunately they failed in this. With the first beam of the rising sun German riflemen approached and opened fire on the officers. The searchers had to abandon General Samsonov's body.[81]

Samsonov was buried near Willenberg. His widow later obtained permission from the Russian and German governments to visit the area, and had his body repatriated to be interred in the family vault in the village of Akimov in the Ukraine.

Russian forces outside the encirclement made two attempts to reach their comrades. On 29 August the Russian 4th Cavalry Division, which together with Blagoveschensky's VI Corps had been tasked with protecting the eastern flank of Second Army, probed into Ortelsburg, held at that time by only a small force of German cavalry. Generalmajor Hennig, commander of 35th Infantry Division, personally drove in search of reinforcements, coming under fire from Russian troops to the north of the town. By the time he encountered half a dozen companies of 176th Infantry Regiment hurrying down the road from the north, news of the fighting in Ortelsburg had already reached the marching column. A spearhead had already been dispatched, passing Hennig on a parallel road north of Ortelsburg. The expression 'marching' is used here in its loosest sense; the footsore soldiers walked along in groups rather than ranks, and had abandoned many of their packs and other items during their long journey, but they still had their rifles. Hennig hurried back to Ortelsburg at the head of the column. Ahead of him the spearhead from 176th Infantry Regiment, mounted on a mixture of horse-drawn wagons and bicycles, rushed a small Russian defensive position north of Ortelsburg and entered the town at 7 p.m. The remaining Russian cavalry put up no significant resistance and withdrew to the southeast. Hennig and the rest of the troops from 176th Infantry Regiment appeared two hours later.[82]

During the evening Blagoveschensky gathered together something approaching a division of infantry and attempted to recapture Ortelsburg. Early the following morning two squadrons of the 10th Jäger cavalry regiment, sent north by Schmettau, arrived as welcome reinforcements for the Germans in the town. The first probing attacks began shortly after dawn, and rapidly developed into heavy fighting. Despite having no artillery or machine guns, the troops of 176th Infantry Regiment, who had enjoyed only a single day of rest in the previous eleven and had been marching almost continuously the rest of the time, held on grimly. Pressure was particularly strong from the northeast, eventually driving the defenders from a seminary on the edge of the town. As the Russians attempted to penetrate further, infantrymen occupying the church tower near the market square stopped them, until artillery made the position untenable.

As soon as he became aware of the crisis, Mackensen sent what help he could, even creating an improvised battalion using the German soldiers from XX Corps that his men had liberated the previous day, hastily arming them with captured Russian rifles. Within Ortelsburg the German defenders had deployed their last modest reserves by midday, and were carefully counting their dwindling stocks of ammunition, when artillery fire at the southern edge of the town heralded the arrival of the first German forces hurrying to the battle.

Elements of 176th Infantry Division that had passed through Ortelsburg the previous day and were part-way down the road to Willenberg, were making use of abandoned Russian equipment for their own use, and were able to rush back as reinforcements:

> When this order reached us, we were having a brief rest on the main road between Willenberg and Ortelsburg on high ground near Kutzburg, from where we could see immeasurable loot that had fallen into the hands of I Corps. During the entire war, we never saw again such a collection of vehicles, guns, horses and other war materiel, both functional and destroyed. It practically invited exploration. My men waited for the merest hint that they could take possession of it. In no time, I had myself a ready made mounted company, looking anything but Prussian. The tall men of 1 Company made an entertaining picture on small Cossack ponies, their legs reaching to the ground in many cases. But I allowed these magnificent riflemen a little rest for their aching knees for once, and in any case, in this manner we reached our new objective significantly more quickly.[83]

The reinforcements that arrived in early afternoon at the southern end of Ortelsburg rapidly moved through the eastern parts of the town and launched a surprise attack on the Russians, who soon disengaged and fell back to the northeast. Further reinforcements continued to arrive, until all of 176th Infantry Regiment was present. Fighting continued until dark, particularly to the north, but the crisis was over. The Russian troops continued to fade away to the northeast, and then to the east.[84]

Blagoveschensky's withdrawal owed as much to orders from above as it did to German pressure. He had been told to gather his corps at Willenberg, and broke off the attack to conserve what little fighting power remained in his corps. As his men moved south towards Willenberg, any further attack was cancelled: they were to continue south until they crossed the frontier into Russian Poland.

On 30 August it was the turn of the Russian I Corps. After François drove them back from Soldau, some of its units rallied and approached Neidenburg. Otto Sirelius, the Finnish officer who had ably led the Russian rearguard at Soldau, advanced towards the town with two regiments of 3rd Guards Infantry Division, seven battalions of 1st Rifle Brigade, and an artillery brigade. The rest of I Corps was to follow, but made little attempt to do so.

Sirelius reached Kandien, south of Neidenburg, early on 30 August. A little further north, in Neidenburg, François and his staff had spent an interesting breakfast poring over captured Russian documents. As he crossed the market square to examine some of the guns that had been captured, François saw a German aircraft overhead. The plane flew lower, and then a message was dropped:

Aircraft A29, Leutnant Hesse. Course: Eylau – Soldau – Mlawa – Neidenburg. [Message] dispatched Neidenburg, 30 August, 9.15 a.m.

To: Commanding General I Corps.
    Columns of all weapons [marching] from Mlawa to Neidenburg, spearhead 9.10 a.m in Kandien, tail elements 1km [0.6 miles] north of Mlawa.
    Second column [marching] from Slupsk to Mlawa, spearhead 8.45 a.m. at edge of Mlawa, tail elements in Wola.

[Signed] Körner, Observer.[85]

François wasted no time, alerting Major Schlimm, the commander of the detachment on the southern side of Neidenburg, and also sending a message to 2nd Infantry Division and the Mülmann detachment, asking for all available forces to be hurried to the new battle. For the moment he left 1st Infantry Division to hold the cordon between Neidenburg and Willenberg, judging that this was more than enough to keep the division occupied. The messenger sent to Schlimm returned with the news that the defence of the southern approaches of Neidenburg was limited to a single battalion of 41st Infantry Regiment; a second infantry division was dispersed on different duties in the town, such as guarding prisoners, while the artillery that should have been with Schlimm had been ordered to move to a different location, apparently by error.

François managed to locate an additional battalion of infantry and an artillery battery to the east of Neidenburg, and sent them to reinforce Schlimm. In the early afternoon he received reports of the capture of General Martos, and sent a car to collect him. After a brief conversation François sent Martos on to Eighth Army Headquarters. Ludendorff treated the captured officer disdainfully, but Hindenburg greeted him courteously, and congratulated him on the tough battle that his men had fought. In a letter to his wife Hindenburg commented that Martos wept when he shook his hand.[86]

The aviator's report about the advance of the Russians also reached Eighth Army command, and Ludendorff immediately dispatched whatever forces were to hand. Still keeping a nervous eye to the northeast, he had begun to pull units out of the battle in case Rennenkampf should put in an appearance. Now he ordered the Goltz *Landwehr* Division, 3rd Reserve Division, Unger's fortress troops, and elements of both XVII and XX Corps to head for Neidenburg. Fighting intensified throughout the day, as German formations arrived and attempted to intervene. Schlimm's detachment held on until dusk, when it was forced back, and during the evening, the Russians reoccupied Neidenburg.

Throughout the night reinforcements continued to arrive for François. By contrast, the second column of troops from the Russian I Corps made very little progress towards Neidenburg; the few troops that did approach came under heavy artillery fire from German guns to the southwest of the town, and suffered substantial losses. At first light on 31 August the German 41st Infantry Division, now attached to François' I Corps, entered Neidenburg almost unopposed. With 2nd Infantry Division threatening Neidenburg from the east, and the Mülmann detachment approaching from the west, Sirelius decided that the risk of being surrounded was too great, and slipped away in the darkness. Later Sirelius would be criticised for failing to make more of his initial success, but orders had already arrived from Zhilinski's Northwest Front, pulling I Corps back to the south.

Could more have been done to save the encircled troops? An earlier advance by I Corps on Neidenburg, even if only by one day, might have made a difference, as the trapped Russian units had not yet lost all cohesion. Writing after the war, Golovine criticised Klyuev in particular for surrendering when he commanded more firepower than the Germans had deployed in his path. But such criticism ignores the fact that the exhausted troops of XIII Corps had been marching for over a week, had not been fed for two days, and were utterly demoralised. In addition, Klyuev had spent most of the battle receiving frequently contradictory orders, and almost constantly lacked a clear idea of the overall situation. It is hard to conceive of how his men could have been organised and motivated to fight a decisive battle against the German 1st Infantry Division, strung out in their path.

Many of the trapped Russian units fought to the bitter end. After the fighting in Neidenburg was over, François visited the battlefield where 1st Infantry Division had blocked Russian attempts to escape across the Neidenburg–Willenberg road:

> There seemed to be no end to the long columns of prisoners coming back. At Muschaken-Buchallowen and Reuschwerder [there were] large prison camps, and parks for artillery and vehicles. I greeted nine Russian generals who were passing in a wagon, and sent them to Neidenburg in my escort car. Across the battlefield [were] dead Russians and Germans in large numbers, and wounded awaiting aid, dead horses, and often entire horse teams still harnessed, tangled together. The battlefield at Muschaken was particularly striking. There was a heavy Russian battery in a copse with its train shot away. The field in front of it was covered in [corpses wearing] field grey, killed trying to storm the battery, still holding their rifles with fixed bayonets. In front of them all was the brave leader, Hauptmann Schoen, well known to me. Amongst the guns were dead Russians, artillerymen and infantry, including the gigantic figure of the commander of the Russian 24th Infantry Regiment. Even in death, one could see dramatically the course of the German assault on the battery.[87]

Ludendorff spent the last two days of the battle oscillating in mood. He signalled *OHL* that a great victory had been achieved, but then advised Moltke that the haul of prisoners might be rather less than expected, given the failings of his corps commanders. At first, German signals referred to the Battle of Allenstein, or Gilgenburg–Ortelsburg, but at Hoffmann's suggestion the name Tannenberg was adopted. Although the village lay just outside the battleground, its name was famous to all Germans as the scene of the defeat of the Teutonic Knights in 1410. It was fitting to name this new victory after a place where Germanic military power had been humbled so many centuries before.

Tannenberg ranks as perhaps the only clear-cut military victory of the German Army in the entire war. Estimates of Russian losses and prisoners vary, but the German figure of 92,000 prisoners and 300 guns seems reasonable. In addition, the Russians lost perhaps 70,000 killed or wounded, compared to total German losses of fewer than 15,000.[88] The figures are not seriously disputed by Russian sources, though there may have been large numbers – perhaps tens of thousands – who were counted amongst both the wounded and prisoners. Even before the war was over the legend of the battle was growing, fed by several factors. The main German protagonists – Hindenburg and Ludendorff in particular, but also François, Hoffmann, and Mackensen – ensured that their personal roles in the battle received prominent attention, and Ludendorff in particular fostered the view that he had masterminded a modern Cannae. On the Russian side there were attempts to allocate blame for the defeat. Samsonov, by shooting himself, provided a convenient scapegoat, as he was unable to defend himself, but other factors were also cited: the pressure from France for an early Russian intervention, resulting in both First and Second Armies attacking before they had completed mobilisation; poor supply arrangements; the failure of Zhilinski's Northwest Front to coordinate matters better; Rennenkampf's failure to advance swiftly in support of Samsonov; and the failures of individuals within Second Army, particularly the commanders of the two corps on the flanks, Artamonov and Blagoveschensky.

Max Hoffmann attempted to claim, with at least a degree of truth, that he had helped write the orders that placed François' I Corps on Samsonov's western flank, and thus created the conditions essential for the German triumph, prior to the arrival of Hindenburg and Ludendorff. But this was only in the context of an orthodox attempt to put pressure on an exposed part of the line, and, in itself, would have had little major consequence. Artamonov's corps should have withdrawn east, not south; if it had done so, François would have been unable to exploit the hole in the Russian lines that appeared as a result of the collapse of the Russian 2nd Infantry Division. Similarly, Mackensen's pursuit of the defeated Blagoveschensky ensured that Samsonov's army was encircled and not merely driven back; this advance, though, owed as much to Blagoveschensky's failures as it did to German successes. The chaotic nature of communications played a large part, with the Russian VI Corps frequently operating on out-of-date orders, and with Samsonov unaware of what was happening on his eastern flank until it was too late, but it should also be pointed out that German communications problems caused difficulties for Mackensen.

Samsonov attempted to bring his forces to bear against what he perceived as the main German force, in the centre. He could not ignore this group, but nor was there any need for him to attack so repeatedly. Had he adopted a defensive posture facing west with Martos' XV Corps, he could have pushed north with XIII and VI Corps, ensuring a link up with Rennenkampf. However, this is to be wise after the event, and in any case, the almost universal belief in the necessity for offensive operations ensured that such a policy was almost unthinkable. By constantly shifting the axis of his advance to the west, he inadvertently aided the German attempts to surround his army.

Whilst Artamonov and Blagoveschensky failed in several respects – particularly when the commander of VI Corps failed to inform Samsonov in a timely manner that he had been driven back from Bischofsburg, and that the rear area was therefore badly exposed – communication problems bedevilled matters for the Russian commanders. Without good communication links with the various corps under his command, Samsonov had to rely on the men on the spot making good decisions, and both Artamonov and Blagoveschensky fell short in this respect. By contrast, François and Mackensen showed great energy and good judgement in leading their men. But the biggest failing in command on the Russian side must rest with Zhilinski at Northwest Front Headquarters. He made little attempt to hurry Rennenkampf forward, and appears to have indulged in a degree of mutual deception: Rennenkampf suggested that at least two German corps were retreating towards Königsberg, and Zhilinski colluded in this belief, without making any attempt to acquire hard evidence. It was not until 27 August that Zhilinski urged Rennenkampf to move southwest in order to support Samsonov, by which time even if Rennenkampf's southern wing had moved forward in forced marches, it would have arrived too late.

Writing after the war, Alfred Knox summed up his own views, based upon both his observations and those of senior officers he later met:

> Rennenkampf and Samsonov had made their reputation as commanders of cavalry divisions in the war against Japan. Their experience, however, as cavalry leaders in the Far East was of no value as a preparation for the control of large armies in an essentially different theatre under totally dissimilar conditions. They had to contend with men who had made a lifelong study of war in this theatre and under the existing conditions.
>
> Samsonov's all-prevailing idea was to try to see the battle with his own eyes. He was probably worried, too, by instructions from Bialystok [i.e. from Zhilinski at Northwest Front Headquarters]. Hence the mad decision, taken in the early hours of the 28th, to cut himself off, not only from his base, but also from half his command, to send all such paraphernalia as wireless apparatus back to Russia, and to get on a Cossack saddle and ride forward to take his fortune in his hand under conditions resembling those to which he had been accustomed in Manchuria.[89]

Knox added that many Russian officers later admitted that the Russian Army of 1914 did not know how to wage modern war; in that respect, they were surely no better or worse than any other army in Europe at that time. If the German officers had used the preceding years to consider how they would fight a war against Russia in the terrain of East Prussia, then the same opportunity existed for the Russians. Compared to the Germans, they had at least been involved in a major war far more recently.

The contrast in the account of the battle in the memoirs of Ludendorff and François is striking. The former pays little attention to the occasions when the commander of I Corps refused to follow orders, while François predictably describes each occasion with relish, not least because on almost every occasion François' judgement was correct. If any individual can be credited with the victory, it should probably be the independent-minded East Prussian François. But it was Ludendorff who, in combination with Hindenburg, received widespread acclamation for masterminding the great triumph. A close reading of the accounts of the battle, though, reveals both sides of Ludendorff's character. His huge capacity for work was undoubted, and he ensured that Eighth Army Headquarters had a far better grasp of the overall situation than Samsonov's Headquarters. He was also fortunate in that the German system of command and training ensured that the subordinate formations understood their tasks, and – particularly in the case of François – were able to put matters right when Ludendorff's orders were wide of the mark. There were several moments – particularly when the battle against Martos' XV Corps tilted first one way then the other, and whenever there were rumours of the approach of Rennenkampf's army – when Ludendorff showed a far more nervous side to his character. Perhaps the greatest advantage the Germans had in their command arrangements was that Hindenburg was able to provide the gravity and steadfastness that Ludendorff sometimes lacked.

Ultimately, Tannenberg was a flawed victory. Samsonov's army was almost destroyed, but there was little opportunity to exploit this. Rennenkampf's forces remained at large, and had occupied perhaps half of East Prussia. In any event, the scale of Russian mobilisation ensured that Second Army could be rebuilt rapidly. A few months later, Curt von Morgen recalled the words of a Russian medical officer captured at Tannenberg, who spoke to the commander of 3rd Reserve Division:

> You have won a great victory, which would force a small nation to end the war. But Russia has 170 million inhabitants and can put 17 million soldiers in the field.[90]

If a quick victory over Russia was to be achieved, the Russian First Army would also have to be crushed just as decisively. Ludendorff and Hindenburg now set about trying to achieve this.

CHAPTER 8

THE ILLUSION OF VICTORY

GALICIA, AUGUST 1914

The Austro-Hungarian Empire, whose conflict with Serbia lay at the heart of the tensions that plunged the continent into war, initially intended to strike a swift blow against Serbia before the Russians could complete mobilisation, but to the frustration of many, particularly in Berlin, numerous factors interfered. When hostilities did begin, Conrad and his colleagues found themselves coerced by Germany to alter their plans and attack Russia. This was in order to reduce pressure on Germany, thus allowing her to complete a planned victory over France. Indeed, even in the absence of alliance obligations, the improved speed of Russian mobilisation meant that it would be simply foolhardy to neglect the Russian front. Any delay in overcoming Serbia might give the Russians time to seize considerable amounts of territory, and perhaps even threaten the Carpathian passes, which would give them access to Hungary. This change of emphasis put the Austro-Hungarians in a difficult position.

Conrad's plans for war against Russia required all thirteen corps of *A-Staffel* and *B-Staffel*, in order to mount an attack out of Galicia. The mobilisation against Serbia had diverted five of these corps to the south, and although one – III Corps – could be redirected fairly easily, Conrad allowed himself to be persuaded to allow the other four to proceed to their Plan B mobilisation points before they were put on trains heading back to Galicia. The details of Austro-Hungarian mobilisation provide an excellent example of the ability of Conrad and his associates to distance themselves from reality.

From the moment of the archduke's assassination in Sarajevo – indeed, even in the years preceding the First World War – Conrad and many other Austro-Hungarian figures had been keen to strike a blow against Serbia, which was perceived as the source of unwelcome agitation in the Balkans. Conrad made no secret of his belief that Russia would almost certainly intervene in the event of a war between Vienna and Belgrade, yet he chose to plan for a decisive strike in the Balkans, believing – with no real foundation – that such a campaign could be completed before Russian mobilisation was completed. At the same time, Conrad was aware that Germany would deploy most of its strength in the west against France, and therefore wished for an early Austro-Hungarian offensive against Russia, in order to relieve pressure on the German defences in East Prussia. For an ardent disciple of the offensive spirit like Conrad, this was not an unwelcome proposition, but it created two problems. Firstly, it was simply not possible to mount an offensive against Serbia at the same time as launching an early attack on Russia. Secondly, an attack on Russia made little strategic sense in the absence of a German offensive from the north. Unless the intention of an attack on Russia was to draw the tsar's inadequately mobilised armies into a hopeless defence of the Polish salient, by launching a great pincer movement, the Russians would be able to do what they had always done in the event of war: trade space for time, allowing their greater numbers to gather in the interior of Russia. Whilst Moltke told Conrad what the latter wanted to hear about the possibility of a German attack against Russia, any competent strategist should have been able to deduce that Germany would not have the resources for such an operation until the end of the campaign against France. The tragedy for the Austro-Hungarian Empire was that, despite his renown as a prolific writer on tactical and operational doctrine, Conrad was not a strategist.

Implementation of mobilisation against Russia while sending sufficient troops south to crush Serbia was a great enough challenge for the planners of the Austro-Hungarian general staff's Railway Bureau, but Conrad's decision to redirect troops back to the Galician front from the Serbian front made matters far worse. The head of the bureau, Colonel Johann Straub, declared that such a change was impossible, and would result in thousands of troops being stranded in the rail network, unavailable for deployment on either front. As an alternative, as has already been described, Major Emil Ratzenhofer, head of the Russian Group of the general staff's Railway Bureau, assured Conrad that the new plans could still be implemented, provided that the relevant formations were allowed to proceed to the Serbian front first, where they would be placed on trains and sent back to Galicia. He declared that this could be accomplished by 23 August, but the basis of these assurances seems to have been little more than wishful thinking. By that date none of the four corps had arrived in Galicia. Two corps arrived in piecemeal fashion in the first week of September, while Oskar Potiorek, commanding the forces facing Serbia, contrived to ensure that at least one corps remained with him permanently, and another was greatly delayed in its redeployment.[1] Any hope of achieving this radical redeployment was further hindered, probably fatally, by the inflexibility of the Railway Bureau. During the years of peace there had been little meaningful liaison between the officers of the bureau and the civilians who ran the railways. Indeed, the military planners treated the civilian railwaymen with barely disguised contempt. Consequently, once mobilisation began, they made little use of the expertise and experience of the civilian railway officials. In an attempt to simplify planning, the Railway Bureau ordered all mobilisation trains to travel at the maximum speed that the least powerful trains could manage, on the worst railroads. As a result, the improved double-track lines running to the front line were seriously under-utilised. At a time when the civilian railway officials had regularly run trains of 100 axles, the military planners refused to allow trains with more than fifty axles. There were prolonged stops, often for inexplicable reasons. The headquarters of Third Army left Bratislava at 6 a.m. on 5 August, and reached its destination in Sambor exactly five days later. On this journey of about 390 miles (630km) they averaged only 78 miles (125km) a day, or less than 7 miles (11km) per hour. The journey of Fourth Army Headquarters from Vienna to the River San took four times as long as the same journey made during peacetime.[2]

The plans for a war against Serbia called for three armies to be deployed in the south. Sixth Army, with XV and XVI Corps, would concentrate around Sarajevo and Mostar; Fifth Army, with VIII and XIII Corps, would concentrate along the line of the River Drina, north of Zvornik; and Second Army, with IV and IX Corps, would be further north, facing Serbia along the line of the River Sava. The independent VII Corps would be closest to Belgrade.[3] VIII Corps was one of the formations that had been earmarked for deployment in Galicia, but Conrad agreed to allow it to remain in the south, partly because it contained large numbers of Czech soldiers, and it was felt in Vienna that they would be more likely to fight well against Serbia than against Russia. The two corps of Second Army and the independent VII Corps were the other formations that should have been sent north to Galicia, but to do so immediately would have left a large portion of the front line facing Serbia unprotected.

The declaration of war and full mobilisation resulted in the activation of the *Armee-Oberkommando* (*AOK*, or Army High Command). It had always been intended that the commander of this body, and therefore the overall commander of Austro-Hungarian forces, would be Archduke Franz Ferdinand; the cousin of the emperor, Archduke Frederick, was appointed in his place. Conrad was his chief of staff, and rapidly became the de facto commander of the army. Partly in expectation of a short war, the Austrian government effectively subordinated itself to *AOK*, though in Budapest Prime Minister Tisza worked hard to preserve as much autonomy as he could.

Moltke repeatedly encouraged Conrad to attack Russia as early as possible. On 2 August he wrote to his Austrian counterpart:

> The Commander-in-Chief [the kaiser] has ordered that the strongest possible forces should tie down the northern and western Russian armies, thus drawing them away from the Austrian Army and facilitating its early battles.
>
> Should the Russians launch an early attack against East Prussia with forces substantially stronger than the German *Ostheer* [Army of the East], then the victory of the Austro-Hungarian Army will be facilitated, all the more if the Austro-Hungarian Army advances sooner against Russia.
>
> If such an early and powerful Russian attack against Germany north of the Vistula is not successful, then the German Commander-in-Chief will advance against Russia with the German *Ostheer*, in whatever direction brings the greatest benefit to the Austrian Army...
>
> The German army corps marching on Kalisz–Czenstochau will in any case begin an advance on Radom–Nowo-Alexandriya via Kalisz–Czenstochau on the 12th day of mobilisation. The commander of this army corps is ordered to advance relentlessly into Russia and to join up with the left flank of the leftmost Austrian army. When approaching strong Russian forces, the commander will be careful to ensure tactical cooperation with the leftmost Austrian army.
>
> The Austrian army can therefore count with certainty on strong support for its campaign against Russia from all of Germany's forces deploying in the east. The overall success will be so much the greater, the earlier and more relentless the advance against Russia is.[4]

The logic of the eventual victory being all the greater if the Austro-Hungarian advance began earlier only applies in the greater scale of events – such an early offensive would allow Germany time to defeat France before turning east. But in any event, Conrad was keen to take the offensive and needed little urging. He had repeatedly shared with his German counterpart the concept of a huge pincer operation to isolate the Russian salient west of Warsaw. Consequently, he chose to

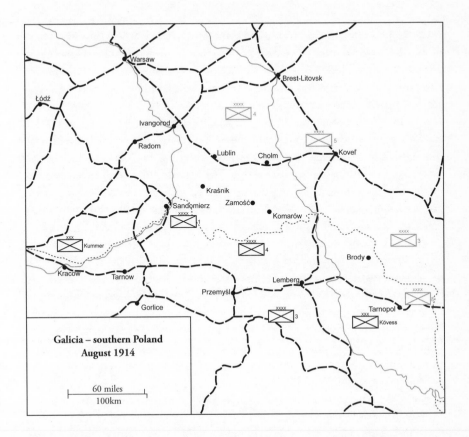

Galicia – southern Poland
August 1914

60 miles
100km

interpret this letter as an indication that Germany would assist him in such an operation, even though a casual glance at the strength of German forces in East Prussia would have revealed that such an operation was not remotely possible. Over the next two weeks, however, as Rennenkampf's army penetrated into East Prussia and the threat from Samsonov developed, Conrad tried repeatedly and in vain to persuade the Germans to mount what he regarded as their promised supporting attack. Even when it became clear that Germany lacked both the intention and manpower for delivering a northern component to such an operation, Conrad chose to press ahead, even though the value of a thrust from the south – without a complimentary thrust from the north to complete the encirclement – was limited. At best, it might inflict substantial losses on the partially mobilised Russian forces; at worst, it was an advance of no strategic importance that would expose the *k.u.k.* Army to a crushing Russian counterattack.

In Galicia the Austro-Hungarian planners expected major Russian cavalry raids, which would attempt to disrupt the concentration of the newly mobilised armies. In anticipation of this, XI Corps, mobilising around Czernowitz, Brzeżany and Lemberg, was ordered to withdraw if faced with powerful Russian attacks. But the massed cavalry raids failed to appear, and on 8 August General von Kolossváry, commander of XI Corps, concluded that he would be able to hold his positions until the arrival of the bulk of Conrad's armies. The following day Russian forces crossed the frontier east of Lemberg, but were rapidly engaged by the Austro-Hungarian frontier forces. The Russian 9th Cavalry Division was involved in a running two-day fight near Tarnopol, and the reinforced Austro-Hungarian 4th Cavalry Division, commanded by Generalmajor Edmund Ritter von Zaremba, defeated a similar penetration near Brody.[5]

It was now the turn of the Austro-Hungarian Army to test its cavalry on enemy territory. Given his pre-war contempt for massed cavalry manoeuvres, it is perhaps a little surprising that on 11 August Conrad ordered ten cavalry divisions to cross to the eastern bank of the Vistula and carry out a reconnaissance in force, prior to the main Austro-Hungarian advance. To an extent this was forced upon him, given that despite his pre-war recommendations the Austro-Hungarian Army had not invested heavily in aircraft. Although there were forty-two aeroplanes allocated to the Galician front, fewer than half were fit for service. For the men of the cavalry this was an opportunity to demonstrate that their way of war still had relevance, and they crossed the border with enthusiasm on 15 August. Their orders were to penetrate as far as Lublin and Koveľ. But within two days, it became clear that this was likely to be beyond them. The Austro-Hungarian cavalry divisions had limited firepower; regardless of their mobility, even modest forces were able to fight them off without difficulty, much as the Austro-Hungarian border units had fought off the Russian raids.

The only notable moment of the entire operation occurred at the village of Jaroslawice, to the east of Lemberg. On 19 August Zaremba and his 4th Cavalry Division were in Brody, where they received a report that a powerful Russian force had advanced to Salozce, about 15 miles (24km) to the south. Zaremba immediately dispatched a squadron of the 1st Lancer Regiment as a vanguard, and cautiously followed with the rest of his division, reinforced by two *Landwehr* battalions. Shortly before midnight he received orders to engage the Russian force, now reported as having reached Zborow.

The Russian force had been tentatively identified as consisting of 9th Cavalry Division, which was commanded by Lieutenant-General Prince Begeldeyev. Expecting support from the nearby 8th Cavalry Division and 11th Infantry

Division, Zaremba gave his men a brief rest when they reached a plateau midway between Salozce and Zborow. His *Landwehr* battalions, tired after a 20-mile (32km) forced march under the hot sun the previous day, were left struggling to catch up.

The Russian force, actually Lieutenant-General Keller's 10th Cavalry Division, had eighteen squadrons, each of about 150 men, with eighteen field guns and twelve machine guns. The Austrians facing them had twenty squadrons, each perhaps a little larger than their Russian equivalents, with eight field guns and eight machine guns. Both sides were expecting reinforcements. The Russian 9th Cavalry Division was nearby, and Begeldeyev (who in addition to commanding his division was also the commander of the cavalry corps to which both divisions belonged) was hurrying forward with his men, together with a small force of infantry. Zaremba and his chief of staff, Oberstleutnant Maxon de Rovid, had been assured that 8th Cavalry Division and 11th Infantry Division were approaching to encircle the Russians. At first Zaremba paused on the edge of the open plateau, hoping that the two *Landwehr* battalions would arrive, but then there was a sudden loud explosion from the direction of Zborow – the sound of Russian cavalry destroying the railway line in the village. The Austro-Hungarian officers, however, concluded that it was the sound of artillery fire, and that 11th Infantry Division was already engaged in combat. Immediately, Zaremba ordered his 15th Dragoon Regiment – in which Conrad's son Herbert was an officer – to move forward, followed by the rest of the division fifteen minutes later.

East of Jaroslawice, Zaremba drew his men into a battle line, even though there were no Russian forces in sight. The exhausted *Landwehr* soldiers, when they finally arrived, blundered into a Russian force and were put to flight. While Zaremba waited in vain for a suitable target for a traditional massed cavalry charge, he suddenly came under artillery fire as the Russians followed up the flight of the *Landwehr*. Ignominiously, Zaremba's horsemen withdrew through Jaroslawice, where the retreat descended into chaos as they encountered a modest stream. The wooden bridges over the stream soon collapsed, forcing the horsemen to ford the stream or to try to jump from one bank to the other. After struggling through Jaroslawice, 4th Cavalry Division turned once more to face the Russians. A confused battle commenced, with units from both sides charging their opponents in a series of wild attacks, sabres and lances featuring prominently. Eventually, after the fighting had swung back and forth, the Russians prevailed, through a mixture of luck and good judgement culminating in the arrival of reinforcements. The engagement cost the Austro-Hungarians nearly 1,000 men; Russian losses were fewer than 200. It would rank as the largest cavalry-versus-cavalry battle of the entire war. It is perhaps fitting that it was inconclusive, and had no real impact on the rest of the campaign.[6]

The Austro-Hungarian cavalry reconnaissance in force achieved very little. Almost no worthwhile information was gathered, and little was accomplished by way of raiding operations. The biggest outcome was the loss of large numbers of horses, leaving many regiments almost unable to function for the rest of the year. The only consolation was that Russian cavalry deployed in a similar manner had suffered just as badly. However, most of the Russian cavalry had been held back, and would therefore be in better shape for the coming conflict.

Conrad and the rest of *AOK* moved to the huge fortress of Przemyśl on 17 August. Some 30 miles (50km) west of Lemberg on the banks of the River San, the town had been heavily fortified by the Austro-Hungarian Empire in order to protect the approaches to the Carpathian passes. It was also substantially provisioned, so that a garrison could survive a prolonged siege if necessary. In addition to the central fortress, twenty-five smaller forts and twelve major artillery emplacements surrounded Przemyśl. Provided that it was garrisoned adequately, the Austro-Hungarians believed, it would constitute a formidable obstacle to any Russian advance. The quarters occupied by *AOK* were, by the opulent standards of Grand Duke Nikolai's train in Russia – and the future accommodation of *AOK* itself – very Spartan. The thick-walled rooms were lit by petroleum lamps, and all ranks, from private soldiers to generals, slept on straw mattresses.[7] But expecting a short war, the staff officers made the best of things as they went to work.

For operations against the Russians Conrad had several armies at his disposal. The most western, deployed immediately east of Sandomierz, was Viktor Dankl's First Army, with I, V and X Corps; these consisted of a total of ten infantry divisions, two cavalry divisions, and an independent infantry brigade. A little further east, along the frontier north of Przemyśl, was Fourth Army, under the command of Moritz von Auffenberg, composed of II, VI, IX and XVII Corps, with nine infantry divisions and two cavalry divisions. To the east of Przemyśl was Third Army, commanded by Rudolf Ritter von Brudermann; he had III, XI and XIV Corps, with eighteeen infantry divisions and four cavalry divisions.

On the extreme western flank of the Austro-Hungarian forces was an independent *Armeegruppe* (army group) commanded by Heinrich Rittmeister Kummer von Falkenfeld (shortened to Kummer), with two infantry divisions and a cavalry division. The eastern flank should have consisted of Second Army, but it was still en route from the Serbian front; in its place, near Tarnopol, there was another *Armeegruppe*, consisting primarily of XII Corps under Hermann von Kövesz. The troops of Second Army would arrive over the coming weeks.

Before he left Vienna for the front, Auffenberg, together with other senior officers, met Archduke Frederick. The nominal supreme commander did not make a good impression on the Fourth Army general:

> On 31 July I was ordered to attend an audience with Archduke Frederick, now appointed Army Supreme Commander. He made a short speech, lacking content, and on this occasion, as always, the illustrious gentleman gave the impression of an ordinary talent. It did not create any extraordinary feeling of confidence to know that he was in command of two million people, even though it was known that the Archduke was only acting in a representative role. The merit-worthy role was assigned to his senior staff, above all the Chief of the General Staff, Conrad von Hötzendorf. But from the outset, there was a series of minor and more major events that gave one a sense of insecurity.[8]

The archduke and Auffenberg met again briefly on 8 August, as the latter left for Galicia. Few words were exchanged, but as will be seen later, whatever passed between the two men was not entirely without consequence.

As his army prepared to advance, Auffenberg visited many of the units that would be serving under his command. His comments about some of his cavalry speak volumes about the reluctance of some sections of the army to change old habits:

> On 24 August, I went to Plazow-Narol. Along the way, I visited the newly arrived troops of 10th Cavalry Division. Splendid hussar regiments. Officers and men in perfect condition, everything spotless, braids and cords as shiny as on parade. I advised them to make themselves less conspicuous. At first, they were reluctant. Then they did it anyway. There was much to unlearn in this war! I hoped for a great deal from this division, and it was attacked and dispersed a few days later in its encampment. The fortunes and misfortunes of war![9]

In an attempt to nullify the fact that the spy Alfred Redl had betrayed Austro-Hungarian mobilisation plans to the Russians, Conrad ordered the debarkation points for the Galician armies to be shifted further west than originally intended. Given that the railway line bringing the troops to the front ran from west to east, this was easily accomplished; the troops merely detrained at earlier stages. This certainly took the Russians by surprise, as they expected the main Austro-Hungarian concentration to be east of Przemyśl. Almost at the last moment Conrad changed his mind, and ordered the Galician armies to concentrate at locations some distance to the east of their detraining zones. It was now impossible to alter train timetables, and the troops of the Austro-Hungarian Army dutifully trudged through the Galician countryside, often marching alongside the railway lines that should have carried them in the first place. It is estimated that the average distance between detraining and concentration was as much as 100 miles (161km).[10] Conrad's armies would thus start the campaign at a considerable disadvantage. Their cavalry was already exhausted by its ineffectual reconnaissance in force, and the infantry, too, was drained by a long march under the summer sun.

The Russian forces deployed against Austria-Hungary were the armies of General Nikolai Ivanov's Southwest Front. As with all command arrangements in the tsar's armies, those on the Southwest Front were certain to make matters far more complex than they needed to be. Ivanov, the front commander, owed his post to the patronage of Sukhomlinov, and had little aptitude for high command. Mikhail Alexeyev, his chief of staff, was from the opposite camp, and the two men were barely on speaking terms, often issuing completely contradictory sets of orders and instructions. Their undisguised criticism of each other might, in any other army, have resulted in embarrassment and discomfort in the headquarters, but such matters were so commonplace in the Russian Army that the rest of the staff seems to have been unaffected.

The most westerly of Southwest Front's forces was Fourth Army, commanded by Anton Jegorowich von Saltza. It comprised the Grenadier Corps, XIV and XVI Corps, for a total of six infantry divisions and three cavalry divisions, as well as independent infantry and cavalry brigades. Immediately to its east was Pavel von Plehve with Fifth Army, made up of V, XVII, XIX and XXV Corps, with ten infantry divisions and five cavalry divisions.

There was a gap of 45 miles (72km) between Plehve's eastern flank and the next Russian Army. Nikolai Vladimirovich Ruzsky's Third Army was some distance further east, with IX, X, XI and XXI Corps, for a total of twelve infantry divisions and four cavalry divisions. On Ruzsky's eastern flank stood the Russian Eighth Army, commanded by Alexei Alexeevich Brusilov, consisting of VII, VIII, XII, and XXIV Corps, for a total of ten infantry and five cavalry divisions. Based upon the mobilisation plans and other documents provided by Redl, the Russian plan for war assumed that the main Austro-Hungarian concentration would occur east of the River San. Consequently, the plan of campaign for 1914 would be an attempt to surround and destroy this concentration. As the two Russian armies would be operating in pairs, the gap between the pairs was regarded as acceptable; it would allow a broader overall frontage, so that the attacking armies could work their way around the outer flanks of the Austro-Hungarian armies that faced them. As the Russian forces advanced on converging paths, this gap would diminish and ultimately disappear.[11]

Conrad's initial decision to detrain the mobilised armies further west upset the Russian plan substantially. Even his change of mind, requiring the troops to march dozens of miles east, did not result in the concentration far to the east of the San that the Russians had expected. The result was that Conrad would attack northwards somewhat further west than the intelligence gained by the Russians had suggested. Consequently, Saltza's Fourth Army, on the western end of the Russian line, would face a substantial Austro-Hungarian force, while the two eastern armies of Southwest Front would start the campaign some distance from the main battle area. There was therefore an opportunity, albeit a limited one, for Conrad to strike a powerful blow against the Russian Fourth and Fifth Armies, before Third and Eighth Armies could march to their aid. In addition, the western flank of Saltza's Fourth Army, and therefore of the entire Southwest Front, was dangerously exposed, as the Austro-Hungarians were concentrating further west than anticipated. Partly to offset this, *Stavka* proposed sending the newly forming Ninth Army in the Warsaw area into line on the western flank of Saltza's army, but the forces massing around Warsaw were also earmarked for a major offensive against Germany. When Ivanov became aware of Conrad's deployment further west than anticipated, he altered his plans slightly. On 23 August his chief of staff Alexeyev issued orders to the western pair of armies, altering their proposed axis of attack slightly to the west. It was a modest change, and did little to improve either the protection of Saltza's western flank, or to address the fact that the bulk of the Austro-Hungarian forces were not where they were supposed to be.

During the afternoon of 21 August a messenger arrived in Przemyśl. He informed Conrad that the German forces in East Prussia had been defeated at Gumbinnen, and intended to withdraw behind the Vistula. Even though this news made a German offensive against Russia even less likely, Conrad was spurred to launch an attack of his own, in order to draw Russian strength away from his ally. When further reports clarified that the German Eighth Army was concentrating against Samsonov, Conrad seems to have hoped that, having disposed of the Russian Second Army, the Germans would continue to drive south, thus resurrecting his vision of a joint pincer against the Polish salient. At first the Austro-Hungarian *AOK* was reassured by aerial reconnaissance that there appeared to be no Russian troops approaching the eastern flank of their line. In reality, the eastern pair of Southwest Front's armies were moving mainly at night and resting during the day; the Austro-Hungarian aircraft had simply failed to spot them.[12] However, there were reasons for optimism. Even if a major Russian force should appear in eastern Galicia, elements of Eduard von Böhm-Ermolli's Second Army were beginning to arrive from the Serbian front. They would, Conrad hoped, be able to hold off the Russians long enough for his more western forces to win a decisive victory.

On 22 August Saltza's Fourth Army cautiously moved into Galicia, taking up a line facing south about 20 miles (32km) southeast of Lublin. To their south the Austro-Hungarian armies also began to move, clearing the River Tanew in the early hours of the following morning. The first serious fighting took place near the town of Kraśnik. At about 9 a.m. on 23 August the leading elements of Dankl's First Army, General Karl Freiherr von Kirchbach's I Corps, ran into the Russian 18th Infantry Division, part of XIV Corps, near the village of Zaklików. The Russians were outflanked and outnumbered, and although fighting lasted all day, they were driven back. A little to the west the Russian 13th Cavalry Division encountered the Austro-Hungarian 3rd Cavalry Division, and at first had the better of the engagement, but the arrival of Austro-Hungarian infantry swung the battle against the Russians. By the evening the western flank of Fourth Army, and therefore the entire Southwest Front, was falling back in some disarray.

The centre of Dankl's First Army consisted of V Corps. At midday, elements of its 14th Infantry Division clashed with the Russian 45th Infantry Division, the other half of Fourth Army's XIV Corps. Although the Russians had a temporary numerical advantage, the Austro-Hungarian troops were positioned on high ground at the edge of dense woodland, and held off the Russian attacks with ease. As the attacks slackened, the Austro-Hungarian officers – true to the doctrine bred into them by Conrad – ordered their men to advance. By the end of the day they had reached and secured the village of Polichna, though the official Austro-Hungarian history of the war conceded that they paid a heavy price for their success.[13] The rest of V Corps joined the attack, rapidly gaining ground, and on the Austro-Hungarian right, X Corps was able to cross the Tanew without hindrance.

By the end of the day Dankl's army was ready for a further advance. Aware that he had effectively outflanked the Russian Fourth Army, he sought to exploit this, ordering I Corps and the western half of V Corps to press forward. Following the military maxim of reinforcing success, Conrad ordered Kummer's independent army group, operating west of the Vistula, to secure crossings over the river near Sandomierz, and then to reinforce Dankl's left flank. Meanwhile, the advancing columns of the rest of Saltza's army, XVI and Grenadier Corps,

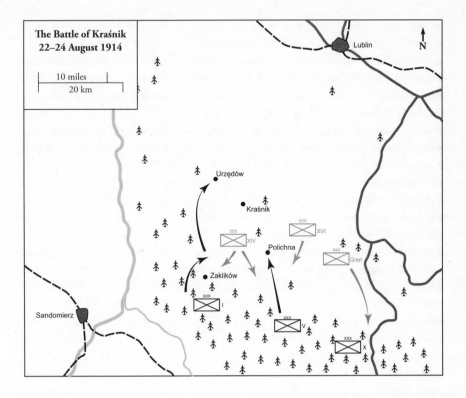

The Battle of Kraśnik
22–24 August 1914

10 miles
20 km

N

Lublin

Urzędów

Kraśnik

XIV

XVI

Polichna

Gren

Zaklików

I

Sandomierz

V

X

had been spotted moving towards the eastern part of Dankl's line. The nearest units of Dankl's eastern neighbour, Auffenberg's Fourth Army, were ordered to cooperate to bring these columns to battle.

The defeat of the Russian XIV Corps confirmed Saltza's fears about his western flank. In order to move units to reinforce the threatened area, he would need to shift forces from his centre and the eastern flank of Fourth Army. He therefore requested support from his eastern neighbour, Fifth Army. Accordingly, Plehve ordered his western unit, Lieutenant-General Dmitri Petrovich Zhuyev's XXV Corps, to cooperate with Saltza's units. At Southwest Front Headquarters, Ivanov assumed that the rapid advance of the Austro-Hungarian western flank might mean that the eastern flank of the attacking Austro-Hungarian forces was exposed. He therefore ordered the other two corps of Plehve's army to advance and try to turn the eastern flank of Dankl's army. As this western movement of Fifth Army threatened to widen the gap between the two halves of Southwest Front, the two eastern armies were ordered to move west. At the same time two formations that were yet to arrive in the area – XVIII and III Caucasian Corps – were assigned to reinforce the western flank.[14]

Ivanov's plan called for Fourth Army to hold its current positions, while Fifth Army – eventually supported by Third and Eighth Armies – turned the eastern flank of the Austro-Hungarian line. Unfortunately for the Russians, the undefeated elements of Fourth Army, the Grenadier Corps and XVI Corps, were not told of the change of plan. Other than sending a brigade to support the battered XIV Corps, the two formations assumed that their previous orders – to continue to advance south – still applied. On 24 August the two Russian corps encountered the Austro-Hungarian V and X Corps, and heavy fighting continued all day. During the afternoon it seemed as if the Russians might break through between the two divisions of X Corps, but an intervention by 9th Cavalry Division, fighting dismounted, brought the Russian attack to a halt. It was now the turn of the Austro-Hungarians to advance. The exposed eastern flank of the Grenadier Corps came under attack, and the Russians streamed back in retreat, leaving dozens of prisoners and nineteen guns in the hands of the Austro-Hungarians. Further west, the left flank of the Austro-Hungarian V Corps exploited a gap between the Russian XVI Corps and XIV Corps, sending the former streaming back to Kraśnik. On the western flank, I Corps continued to drive back the defeated XIV Corps, reaching Urzędów during the evening.[15]

Dankl was very satisfied with the performance of his army, and called for more of the same for the following day. While his centre and right stood firm, I Corps was to continue to roll up the Russian western flank, moving around the north of Kraśnik. However, the long march from detrainment to concentration area, followed by hard fighting, had taken its toll, and the planned dawn attack had to be put off. When the battle-weary men of I Corps finally moved forward at 10 a.m., they met no resistance. Similarly, patrols sent out by V and X Corps found abandoned and broken equipment, but no Russians. Saltza had taken advantage of the lack of Austro-Hungarian activity at dawn, and had withdrawn during the night to Lublin.

It was a very auspicious start to the war for Conrad's armies. Austro-Hungarian casualties amounted to about 15,000, whereas the Russians lost over 25,000, including 6,000 prisoners. Dankl was regarded as a hero, though he had to wait until 1917 for formal recognition, when he was awarded the Commander's Cross of the Military Order of Maria Theresa, and raised to the status of Graf von Kraśnik. However, even in the days immediately after the victory, there were many who criticised Dankl for not pressing the retreating Russians harder. His methodical, careful approach was felt to be too cautious. Without such an approach, though, it seems unlikely that his army would have been able to get the better of the Russians.

On the Russian side, internal politics played an inevitable part. Saltza was a member of the anti-Sukhomlinov group, and supported by Geysmans, commander of XVI Corps, he complained that Voyshin, commander of XIV Corps, had failed to fulfil his orders. Southwest Front's chief of staff Alexeyev, acting in conjunction with Yanushkevich in *Stavka*, had Voyshin dismissed. Unhappy with this act, front commander Ivanov – who was of course a Sukhomlinovite – responded by sacking Geysmans, and assigning Voyshin to command of XVI Corps in his place.

Saltza had rightly warned his superiors of the threat from the west, but in the tsar's armies in 1914, being right was not always a good thing. Angered by Saltza's criticism of Voyshin, Ivanov made no attempt to defend Saltza, and the hapless commander of Fourth Army was dismissed. To an extent, this was a move instigated by Grand Duke Nikolai in *Stavka*, seeking to put men that he knew and trusted into important positions. The new commander was Alexei Evert, an experienced artilleryman, and a close ally of the grand duke and his anti-Sukhomlinov faction. His first act was to divert as much of his army's strength as possible to the western flank, in an attempt to prevent Dankl from outflanking him again. Prince Georgi Evseevich Tumanov, commander of Fourth Army's cavalry, skilfully kept the Austro-Hungarian cavalry at bay until the arriving elements of XVIII Corps could establish a firmer line extending to the Vistula late on 27 August.

In his memoirs Auffenberg wrote that he only learned the details of Conrad's plans – for his army to advance alongside Dankl's troops – early on 25 August, or after the main battle was already over.[16] It seems remarkable that these details were kept from such a senior commander until such a late stage. But to a large extent, Conrad was himself operating in something of a vacuum. The orders sent to Auffenberg included an assessment of Russian strength, suggesting that there would be between eight and ten front-line corps deployed between the Bug and the Vistula, but they were not expected to be ready for combat before the beginning of September. The reality was very different. By the time this message reached Auffenberg, his troops had already taken prisoners from a Russian reservist formation, not expected at the front for at least another two weeks. Auffenberg had already made his own plans for operations, and now rushed to rewrite them in light of Conrad's instructions.

Plehve's Fifth Army advanced in an attempt to find and turn the eastern flank of the Austro-Hungarian forces that had defeated Saltza. Trying to retain contact with Saltza's Fourth Army, Plehve deployed XXV Corps to the west of the rest of his forces, with XIX, V and XVII Corps advancing down the valley of the River

Bug, between Hrubieszów and Vladimir-Volynsk. The frontage assigned to XXV Corps was considerable – over 10 miles (16km) – and steadily grew as the Russian Fourth Army began to retreat further northwest towards Lublin. Late on 25 August Austro-Hungarian reconnaissance patrols correctly identified the advancing Russian units, and reported that there were large gaps emerging in the Russian front as XXV Corps struggled to retain contact on both its flanks with friendly forces. The following morning, the Russians continued to advance down the main road towards the south, but their exposed western flank came under repeated attack by the extreme eastern wing of X Corps and part of Blasius Schemua's II Corps from Auffenberg's Fourth Army. The leading Russian units managed to reach Zamość, but as Fourth Army continued to retreat towards Lublin, pressure on the western flank steadily worsened. During the afternoon, with fighting now raging on a broad front, the Russians withdrew towards Krasnostaw before the road could be cut. Dust clouds covered the battlefield, and troops on both sides began to fall out of line suffering from the effects of heat and dehydration, adding to the heavy losses from combat.

The other three corps of Plehve's army advanced in echelon, with XVII Corps in the east following the Bug to Sokal. Zhuyev, commander of XXV Corps, wrote a note to the nearest friendly unit calling for help, concluding that if Vladimir Gorbatovsky's XIX Corps arrived in good time, victory over the enemy was assured. However, the letter was captured by Austro-Hungarian patrols, and did not reach its destination.[17] But although Gorbatovsky had already decided to try to link up with Zhuyev, he was unable to extend his line towards the west until he had dealt with the forces facing him. At midday XX Corps ran into the left flank of the Austro-Hungarian VI Corps at Tarnawatka. The troops facing the Russians were from a Hungarian *Honvéd* division, and were soon put to flight, with many being taken prisoner. A little to the east V Corps ran into Austro-Hungarian defences during the afternoon. As darkness fell, Plehve took advantage of the lull in fighting to take stock. The pressure on XXV Corps was consistent with the Austro-Hungarian advance towards Lublin, and Plehve continued to believe that he could turn the eastern flank of his opponent. Despite its losses, XXV Corps was ordered to attack again the following day, while XIX and V Corps thrust southwest against what he believed was the eastern flank of the Austro-Hungarian forces facing him. XVII Corps was to move away from the Bug and close up with the two central corps, with the intent of being available to turn the flank of the Austro-Hungarian position if XIX and VI Corps did not succeed in doing so alone. This does not appear to have been based upon any firm reconnaissance information; it seems that Plehve merely assumed that the flank of Auffenberg's Fourth Army was in that area.

27 August began well for the Russians, when a Cossack detachment, armed with machine guns, surprised and routed an Austro-Hungarian Hussar regiment from 10th Cavalry Division on the eastern end of the battlefield. Moreover, news arrived of the approach of columns of the Russian Third Army, hurrying west to link up with Plehve's Fifth Army. It seemed that the eastern flank of Auffenberg's army might indeed be turned, just as the Russians had planned. Throughout the day, Auffenberg paced the gardens of the stately home where he had established his headquarters, waiting impatiently for hard news, while just a few miles away his men fought and died in their thousands. Fortunately for the Austro-Hungarian forces, an army detachment of troops built around Archduke Joseph Ferdinand's XIV Corps, consisting of four infantry divisions, was available as reinforcements. Together with additional independent formations, this detachment moved into position for an attack the following day. In the centre, VI Corps engaged the Russian XVII and V Corps, effectively tying them down; unable to break through, their eastern flank was now overlapped by the archduke's divisions. As darkness fell, the commanders of the infantry fighting in the central area counted the heavy cost of the day's actions, which had seen no significant movement in the front line.

On the western flank, the Russian XXV Corps once more attempted to reach Zamość. However, as had been the case the previous day, its own western flank remained badly exposed, and the Austro-Hungarian II Corps swiftly scattered the Russian infantry probing towards the town. Two days' fighting had resulted in little substantial movement on the battlefield, but the strength of XXV Corps was now greatly reduced. On the other hand, the other three corps of Plehve's army were close enough to each other to be able to coordinate an attack the following day, and the Russian general remained confident that the tide would now turn in his favour. His orders for 28 August for XIX, V and XVII Corps remained the same, with one small variation: XVII Corps was to release a brigade, which would cross behind the front line to provide reinforcements for XXV Corps in the west.

During the night, V Corps attempted to move forward in order to surprise the Austro-Hungarians, and stumbled into 15th Infantry Division, part of VI Corps. A brutal fight broke out in the darkness, with much of the Austro-Hungarian division destroyed or put to flight; some of its artillery, attempting to flee through a swamp, had to be abandoned. The Russians took 4,000 prisoners and captured twenty guns, but were unable to achieve a decisive success when the attack ran into the rest of the Austro-Hungarian VI Corps. Alerted by the earlier fighting, these units put up a far tougher fight, and brought the attack to a halt. The following day, reports reached Auffenberg and Conrad that Brudermann's Third Army to the east was retreating in the face of superior enemy forces. Conrad suggested transferring Archduke Joseph Ferdinand's group to help support Third Army. The group had already spent at least a day being dispatched first towards Third Army, then back towards Auffenberg's Fourth Army, and was now once more ordered to turn southeast. Auffenberg objected, on the grounds that the removal of the four divisions would eliminate any chance he might have of victory; in any case, it would not arrive in time to offer significant support to Third Army. Furthermore, the archduke reported that his leading elements were already encountering Russian troops, and it would therefore be difficult for them to turn away in the face of the enemy. Conrad eventually agreed, and dispatched whatever cavalry he could find, together with his last reserves, to try to prevent any further retreat by Brudermann's units.

Bloody fighting continued in the central area through much of 28 August, with little ground changing hands as first one side, then the other, attempted to advance across the open, flat fields of grain. Swept by artillery and machine-gun fire, the lines of infantry melted away, adding to the mounds of corpses. Late in the afternoon the archduke's divisions and the Austro-Hungarian XVII Corps – confusingly deployed opposite the Russian corps bearing the same number – began to make their presence felt on Plehve's exposed eastern flank. Hearing the roar of cannon where VI Corps was struggling to hold back the Russian attack, Feldmarschalleutnant Lukas, commander of XVII Corps' 19th Infantry Division, took it upon himself to march to the battlefield, and thrust into the eastern flank of the Russian V Corps. This disrupted the Russian attack, which had begun to make headway against the Austro-Hungarian 15th and 27th Infantry Divisions, both from VI Corps. Shortly after, the archduke's four divisions, which had moved forward in the early morning and then paused to rest, burst upon the flank and rear of the Russian XVII Corps. Joseph Ferdinand's troops happened to be advancing in the one part of the battlefield where there was sufficient cover to mask an attacker's movements, and as his men pressed forward in broken country, dotted with numerous copses, they took the Russians completely by surprise. As had been the case in the early battles in East Prussia, some units attacked impetuously, often without waiting for their artillery to take up positions, and others ran into better-prepared Russian defences. Nevertheless, as darkness fell, the Russian XVII Corps was in full flight. As reports of the

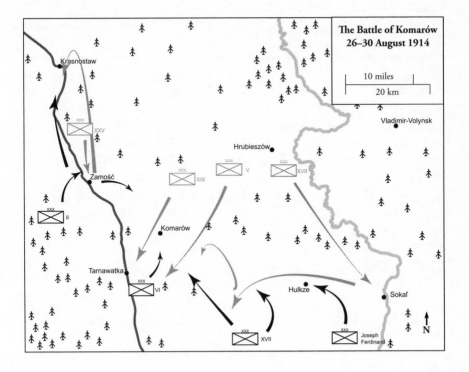

archduke's success reached him, Auffenberg began to consider whether there was the possibility of encircling the forces opposed to him, given that he had broken both their flanks.

If such an encirclement was to be achieved, the task facing Auffenberg's units was harder than the task that faced the Germans who encircled Samsonov's army. When François and Mackensen broke the flanks of the Russian Second Army, the defeated Russian formations were some distance from the central bulk of the army, and compounded matters by retreating away from the centre, thus facilitating the German encirclement. Nor did they show any enthusiasm for immediate counterattacks. In Galicia, by contrast, Schemua's II Corps had lost contact with the retreating Russian XXV Corps on the western flank during the night, and at first had little idea of where the Russians had taken up new positions. On 29 August, hoping that the right flank of the neighbouring First Army was close enough to offer support, Schemua left a reinforced infantry division facing north, towards Krasnostaw, and turned the rest of his force to face east. Compared to the previous days, progress was slow. Feldmarschalleutnant von Stöger-Steiner's

4th Infantry Division, guarding to the north, advanced cautiously, encountering little resistance but also making little headway.

On the other flank, Archduke Joseph Ferdinand resumed his attack, swiftly seizing the village of Hulkze, where his men captured twenty-four guns. But unlike the German flank attacks in East Prussia, the force he defeated withdrew towards the Russian central formations, and remained intact. In the centre, some elements of VI Corps made steady progress in the face of determined Russian resistance, but others ran into prepared positions occupied by the Russian XIX Corps, and although the attack gained ground initially, it was driven back to its start line.

Auffenberg had moved his headquarters further forward, and took the opportunity to visit some of the nearby units. He then saw first-hand the price that his men were paying for their successes:

> On the way back, I encountered a column of wounded. A *Honvéd* infantryman from 16th Regiment had been shot straight across the face. Both eyes had been lost. I took the poor, helpless man by the hand, and tried to find words of comfort. He replied briefly and from the heart: '*Hazá ért!* (For the Fatherland!)' I was deeply moved.[18]

Whilst the day had not produced a decisive victory, Auffenberg still had reasons to be satisfied that he was making progress. The following day 4th Infantry Division came under heavy attack as the remnants of the Russian XXV Corps made a determined effort to drive the Austro-Hungarian force back. Fortunately for Stöger-Steiner, his left flank regiment overlapped the Russian attack, and was able to take it in its flank. Again, there was a substantial difference between here and East Prussia, where, once defeated, the Russian flank corps remained inactive for several days. More importantly for Auffenberg, 4th Infantry Division was unable to march east, as it had been ordered to do, to help complete the encirclement of the Russian forces. While bitter fighting continued in the centre, Archduke Joseph Ferdinand made a further effort to turn the eastern flank. After their losses of the previous days, his men made limited progress in the face of determined resistance by the formations of the Russian XVII Corps. The Russians might have suffered serious losses, but their officers had worked industriously through the night to reorganise their men and to take up defensive positions. Meanwhile, as the archduke turned his forces northwest, aerial reconnaissance reported a Russian column approaching from the east – a report that later proved to be false. Although Auffenberg had deployed a reinforced cavalry screen to protect his eastern flank, Joseph Ferdinand decided that he had to take further measures, and reluctantly ordered his last reserves to face east. Auffenberg had nothing to offer the archduke; his own reserves were completely committed. If he was to win a victory, his depleted formations would have to do so without reinforcements.

In any event, Plehve's men had had enough. On 30 August the Austro-Hungarian 24th Infantry Division, part of First Army's X Corps, entered Krasnostaw from the west. With their western flank now completely exposed, the battered Russian forces around Komarów found themselves in serious danger of complete annihilation. After dusk a Russian counterattack drove back some parts of Archduke Joseph Ferdinand's force. Heavy fighting raged immediately to the south of Komarów, where the Russian V Corps held off the Austro-Hungarian forces as long as it could. To the west of the town, elements of the Austro-Hungarian II Corps under the command of Archduke Peter also came under pressure, preventing it from completing an encircling movement, but as soon as their lines of retreat were secure, the Russians withdrew. Plehve ordered XXV Corps to retake Krasnostaw at all costs, but the reality was that the Russian formation was completely exhausted, as was most of Fifth Army.[19]

The failure of Archduke Peter to complete the encirclement of the Russian forces was a source of particular disappointment for Auffenberg. The archduke, commanding the 25th Infantry Division, had at his disposal some twenty-four battalions with 100 guns, opposed by perhaps twenty Russian battalions, supported by three artillery batteries, each of eight guns. The archduke's own account of the fighting stressed the Russian superiority in artillery as the main reason why he was driven back. Numbers can be misleading, and it is highly unlikely that at this stage of the battle, either side was able to field full-strength units, with adequate supplies of ammunition for sustained combat. The men on both sides were exhausted from several days of combat under a hot summer sun, with few supplies of food or water reaching the front lines. The simple facts of the matter were that the Austro-Hungarian forces failed to make any headway in their own attack, and were then driven back by the Russians towards the area held by 4th Infantry Division. At the very least, it seems that the archduke's contingent lacked adequate command and control to make the most of its forces, though the modest advantage implied by a count of battalions and guns should be set against the growing evidence, even at this early stage, of the superiority of defensive firepower. Nor did the *k.u.k.* Army have any doctrine of infiltrating past established defences; Conrad's rules of warfare centred only on the physical destruction of any foe that was encountered.

Between the armies of the Dual Monarchy and the Germans in the north was the open space of Poland, covered by minimal forces. At the beginning of the war, the Silesian *Landwehr* had been mobilised as a corps, and General Remus von Woyrsch was brought out of retirement to take command. He had served at Königgrätz, where he was taken prisoner by the Austrians, and was adjutant of an officer cadet school at the outbreak of the Franco-Prussian War. By making energetic requests, he managed to ensure that he was recalled to serve with the Prussian Guards during the war, and was wounded in the bitter fighting at St Privat. In 1911 he retired from the army at the age of 64, but volunteered for service in August. His new command consisted of 3rd and 4th *Landwehr* Divisions, and he led them forward to Petrikau (now Piotrków Trybunalski) and Radom by the end of the month against minimal resistance. Woyrsch wrote in his own account that the only forces he encountered came from the Russian 14th Cavalry Division.[20] This march, by men past normal military service, was a substantial achievement under hot skies and across the poor roads of Poland. On 31 August Woyrsch intended to rest his men. However, the reconnaissance aircraft attached to his corps alerted him to the presence of strong Russian columns approaching Radom. Although these columns failed to materialise, Woyrsch was aware that the Russians facing him from the far bank of the Vistula were slowly increasing in strength. His corps was subordinated to Dankl's First Army, and received a request to cross the river in support of the operation against Lublin. Woyrsch was reluctant to do so, as he still regarded the primary function of his divisions to be the defence of Silesia. Eventually, on 1 September, he prepared to move to the right bank of the river.

Although Auffenberg wanted to pursue the defeated Russians aggressively, he knew that his men were badly in need of rest and reinforcements. Supplies of all sorts were almost exhausted, and prolonged fighting would be difficult to accomplish. In any case, events elsewhere intervened, as will be described next. The victory at Komarów was incomplete, inasmuch as Plehve escaped being encircled and thus saved much of his army, but his losses were considerable. The Austro-Hungarians took over 20,000 prisoners, and captured 150 guns. But the battlefield losses of both sides were heavy. True to Conrad's doctrine, the Austro-Hungarian infantry threw itself into attacks that resulted in terrible casualties.

The fact that victories at Kraśnik and Komarów were perhaps the high point of the entire war for the *k.u.k.* Army speaks volumes for the magnitude and frequency of the setbacks that followed. It is worth considering whether Conrad could have achieved more in these battles, or whether he might have exploited their successes more effectively. In order for either battle to have resulted in a greater victory, the Austro-Hungarian armies involved would have required substantially greater assets, but the decision to send so many troops to the Balkans ensured that the forces facing Russia would be weaker than Conrad had originally intended. This decision was compounded by the change in concentration areas, first requiring troops to detrain further west than planned, and then requiring them to march on foot most of the way to their original concentration areas. This ensured that the troops started the campaign already tired and degraded.

Once the fighting began, Conrad's armies began to discover the same truths that were being learned throughout the continent. Defensive firepower was exceedingly hard to overcome, unless an open flank could be found, or artillery could be used effectively to suppress defensive fire. Moreover, the pre-war doctrine of offensive operations frequently resulted in casualties so great that the formations involved were unable to exploit whatever successes they achieved. In the 19th century, the previous practice of holding substantial units in reserve during battle had gradually been replaced by a tendency to deploy every available rifle in order to maximise striking power, but this ensured that if the troops in the front line were able to achieve a success, and were too weakened themselves to exploit it, there were insufficient reserves available to launch follow-up attacks. In any event, even if such reserves were available, the speed of movement after troops had detrained remained walking pace, giving plenty of time for defenders to reorganise and restore their lines.

Consequently, it is difficult to see, given the experience and knowledge that existed at the time, how the Austro-Hungarian armies might have done better in these battles, once the initial decisions about mobilisation and concentration had been made. At an operational level, could the victories have been exploited differently? Here, it is possible to consider real alternatives, but again, only with the benefit of hindsight. Conrad believed that he could deliver a deadly blow against the Russians, and that his alliance obligations required him to make every effort to do so. However, it has been suggested that he had doubts about the chances of success; he later stated that he ordered the advance with a heavy heart.[21] But if the armies in Galicia had concentrated on defending their territory, much as Eighth Army did in East Prussia, they might have achieved more in the long term. Had Conrad followed the victories of his western armies with a concerted effort to halt the Russian armies in eastern Galicia, he might then have been in better shape to cooperate with Hindenburg for a decisive autumn offensive. Instead, he chose to press forward in the hope of achieving an immediate strategic triumph, and ultimately met with disaster.

Many critics of Conrad suggested that resolute defence, without any offensive operations at all, would have served the long-term interests of the Dual Monarchy better than a rash offensive.[22] However, as has already been described, huge importance was placed at the time on the value of offensive operations as a means of securing control of events. It must be noted that few, if any, of the later critics of Conrad and other offensive-minded generals made any such criticisms before the First World War.

Perhaps the best that can be said from the Austro-Hungarian point of view for the opening rounds in Galicia is that the Russians were forced to divert reinforcements to the area, preventing them from assembling a powerful attack group around Warsaw that might have threatened an advance on Germany. To a large extent, Hindenburg's victory at Tannenberg had already made any such advance effectively impossible, but at the outset of the war, Conrad had no way of knowing that Samsonov's army would be almost annihilated. Under considerable pressure from Moltke to launch an early attack in order to reduce pressure on Germany's *Ostheer*, Conrad followed his instincts and delivered the best that he could.

CHAPTER 9

THE BATTLE FOR THE MASURIAN LAKES

In East Prussia the victory of Eighth Army over the Russian Second Army might have eliminated the possibility of a German retreat to the Vistula, but there remained the substantial forces of Rennenkampf's First Army in the eastern half of the province. With their southern flank secure, Hindenburg and Ludendorff now turned their attention back to the east.

On 31 August, even as mopping-up operations were proceeding against the remnants of Samsonov's forces, a signal arrived in Hindenburg's headquarters from *OHL*:

> XI Corps, Guards Reserve Corps, and 8th Cavalry Division are placed at your disposal. Their transport has begun. The first task of Eighth Army is to clear East Prussia of Rennenkampf's army.
>
> It is desired that with such troops as you can spare you should follow up the enemy you have just beaten in the direction of Warsaw, bearing in mind the Russian movements from Warsaw on Silesia.
>
> When the situation in East Prussia has been restored you are to contemplate employing Eighth Army in the direction of Warsaw.[1]

The three formations assigned to Hindenburg were in the process of being redeployed from the Western Front. This move has frequently been quoted as justification for the Russian advance against Germany prior to the end of Russian mobilisation: by doing so, and thus ultimately sacrificing Samsonov's Second Army, Russia forced Germany to weaken its forces in the west, and consequently failed to win the decisive victory that it sought against France. In other words, the precipitate Russian attack, at the urging of the French, achieved precisely the purpose that had been intended. Guards Reserve Corps was part of the German Second Army, on the right wing of the great drive through Belgium, and XI Corps was with the neighbouring Third Army; both units fought in Belgium before being sent east. Whilst their presence would have been very welcome in France during the Battle of the Marne, it is by no means clear whether they would have given the Germans a sufficient advantage to alter the outcome. Nevertheless, the reinforcements gave a powerful boost to the Eighth Army in East Prussia, and taking into account the destruction of the Russian Second Army, the Germans were now for the first time in a numerically advantageous position across the entire theatre.

Hindenburg and Ludendorff could not fail to be aware of the repeated requests by Conrad for a German offensive towards the south or southeast, to complement the push by Dankl and Auffenberg from the south. In his memoirs, Ludendorff described what he clearly saw as the inescapable logic of the German position, which prevented such a move:

The difficult situation of the Austro-Hungarian Army at the end of August in the face of great Russian superiority of numbers could not be mistaken. The Chief of the General Staff, General Conrad, suggested – with justice, from his point of view – that we advance over the Narew. Given the continuing weakness of Eighth Army compared with Rennenkampf's forces, this was not achievable. An advance towards Mlawa–Pultusk would be brought to a halt by a simultaneous advance by Rennenkampf towards a line from Allenstein to Elbing. There was therefore no choice but to deal first with the Russian Army of the Niemen [Rennenkampf's First Army].[2]

It could be argued that the Germans had left Rennenkampf facing only a paper-thin screen while they dealt with Samsonov, and might do so again, but a repeat of this would have been foolhardy. A drive to link up with Conrad's forces would have lengthened the front line far beyond the ability of the Eighth Army to cover, and would have invited disaster. However much Conrad might have wished otherwise, a German drive into Poland was simply impossible with their current resources.

As the magnitude of the disaster that had befallen Samsonov's army became clear, Rennenkampf ordered his men to pull back from their most advanced positions. First Army took up a line running from the Deime valley in the north, through Wehlau and Nordenberg, to the northern shore of the Mauer-See, immediately to the west of Angerburg. A German garrison still held the town of Lötzen, at the end of the narrow land bridge that separated the Mauer-See and the Löwentin-See. II Corps, which had tried in vain to act as a link between the Russian First and Second Armies during August, had now moved northwest, and faced the German garrison.

This left a substantial gap between II Corps and the remnants of Second Army, now commanded by Sergei Scheidemann, the former commander of II Corps. In order to fill this gap, *Stavka* ordered the creation of a new Tenth Army, which would be built around four formations en route to the front – XXII Corps from Finland, III Siberian Corps, I Turkestan Corps, and II Caucasian Corps. The first to arrive was the Finnish corps, which deployed in and to the west of Lyck. General Vasili Pflug, the commander of the new army, found himself in a position that was even worse than that of Scheidemann when he had attempted to cover the gap with a single corps; in August, II Corps had at least been flanked by powerful Russian armies ready to advance. Now, First Army had been ordered to dig in, and Second Army barely existed as a fighting force.

Other Russian forces had also arrived at the front. Rennenkampf's reserve divisions, left behind during August as they were deemed to be inferior to regular formations, were now used to create a new XXVI Corps on the northern flank, while two others were kept in reserve, giving Rennenkampf a total strength of fourteen infantry divisions.[3]

Ludendorff now reversed his previous policy of leaving only weak forces facing east while Eighth Army concentrated in the south. Instead, limited forces commanded by General Hans von der Goltz were left around Soldau, with orders to advance on Mlawa, while the rest of the army turned on Rennenkampf. The bulk of Rennenkampf's army remained north of the Masurian Lakes, in keeping with his belief that the Germans had been withdrawing towards Königsberg. Hindenburg and Ludendorff decided to divide their forces into three. One element – with Guards Reserve Corps, I Reserve Corps, XI Corps, and XX Corps – would face the strong northern flank of the Russian First Army. A second group – Mackensen's XVII Corps – would use the position at Lötzen. A third force – François' I Corps reinforced by 3rd Reserve Infantry Division – would deploy against the weak southeast wing of the Russian forces around Lyck. If the southern flank could be turned, the entire Russian line might be rolled up from the south, possibly with an outcome similar to the August battles against Samsonov. Given the widespread disdain shown by the Germans for Samsonov's use of uncoded radio messages, it is worth noting that the Russians became aware of the imminent arrival of Guards Reserve Corps when they intercepted an uncoded German radio message sent from Königsberg.

Goltz reported the first success of the new campaign on 4 September. Rejoicing under the title of *Führer der ostpreussischen Südarmee* ('Commander of the East Prussian Army of the South'), he attacked towards Mlawa on 3 September with his forces – mainly with 1st *Landwehr* Division and 35th Reserve Infantry Division, which comprised his original command – and took the town the following day. Positioned on the railway line from Warsaw, Mlawa was a natural starting point for any Russian advance against the southern frontier of East Prussia, and its capture therefore did much to safeguard the southern flank of the German Eighth Army. The following day François issued new orders to his corps, starting with a proclamation that was entirely in keeping with his character:

> Soldiers of I Corps!
>
> We have liberated the southern part of East Prussia from the enemy. Now we approach our corps' home area, and the Russian hordes that have driven our families from our homeland and have burned down our homes. Now comes the reckoning. Remain true to our resolve: 'Invincibly forwards for our Kaiser, our Fatherland, and our Homeland!'
>
> God is with us.[4]

I Corps was to advance either side of the Spirding-See, with Falk's 2nd Infantry Division marching through Nikolaiken while 1st Infantry Division skirted the southern shore of the lake. The 3rd Reserve Infantry Division would operate on the extreme south, covering the frontier with Poland. The approach to the lake was through difficult terrain, dotted with small lakes and patches of dense woodland. To the relief of the advancing Germans they encountered no resistance. Most of their movement difficulties were caused by bridges destroyed by the German *Landsturm* in an attempt to prevent a Russian advance, and the dense woodland hid them from Russian patrols. Fortunately for 2nd Infantry Division, an energetic bridging column conducted a forced march along the woodland roads to reach the vital town of Nikolaiken on 6 September, and then spent the night labouring to repair the bridges in the town. The following day Falk's men marched across without hindrance. Meanwhile, the leading elements of 1st Infantry Division reached Johannisburg, where they encountered the first Russian resistance.[5]

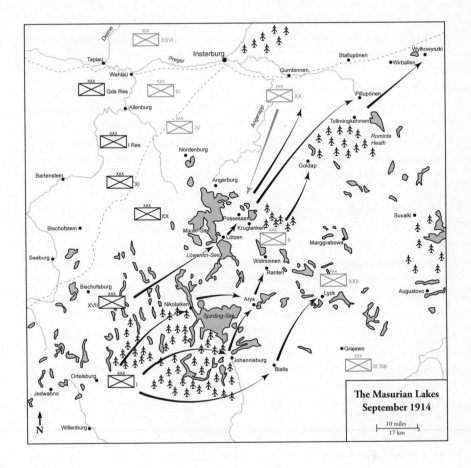

The Masurian Lakes
September 1914

10 miles
17 km

From the Pregel valley to the Mauer-See, the German forces – from north to south, Guards Reserve Corps, I Reserve Corps, XI Corps, and XX Corps – moved forward to engage Rennenkampf's men. The intention of the Germans was to put strong pressure on the Russians, partly to tie them down, but also to exploit any weaknesses. Although they had shown little appetite for a rapid advance, the Russians proved – as usual – to be tough opponents when fighting a defensive action. As both German and Austro-Hungarian soldiers had already discovered, their ability to dig in at short notice gave them a decided advantage. III and IV Corps successfully fended off the German attacks, even mounting counterattacks of their own. The contrast between the two armies was striking, and as was frequently the case, the observations of a Russian officer on the strengths and

231

weaknesses of the Germans say a great deal about the corresponding qualities of Russian troops:

> [The Germans] showed a certain impetuosity, and one could notice the personal initiative, not only of the smaller units, but even of small bodies of infantry, even when they were without officers. On the other hand, in defensive open fighting they did not distinguish themselves by any extraordinary tenacity of purpose, and when they began to retire after a battle their power of resistance dwindled to vanishing point.[6]

Although Ludendorff expressed disappointment at the lack of progress in the north, the reality was that the German battle plan depended for success on events in the south. Here, François travelled to Johannisburg to see first-hand how things were progressing on 7 September. Prisoner interrogations confirmed that most of the Russian defenders had been Finnish, newly arrived in the theatre. Reconnaissance suggested that these men were merely outliers of a stronger concentration further east, around Bialla, and 3rd Reserve Infantry Division was ordered to press forward to engage these units, supported by a brigade from 1st Infantry Division. To François' satisfaction, Bialla was reached just before midday, and secured before dusk after a brisk attack. Morgen reported only light casualties, but had taken several hundred prisoners and captured eight Russian guns.[7] The rest of I Corps marched towards Arys, where further Russian resistance was encountered. With daylight running out, François ordered a pause, while the detached brigade from 1st Infantry Division rejoined Conta's men in preparation for a formal attack on 8 September.[8]

The following day dawned clear and warm. Fortunately for the men of 1st Infantry Division, their approach to Arys lay across an area frequently used by the division in peacetime for training. Almost every tree and bush was familiar to the troops; in mid-July they had conducted an attack across the exact terrain, and they now made swift progress, their familiarity with the terrain being put to good use as they used the cover provided by the gentle hills and small woodlands to good effect. With strong support from 2nd Infantry Division, advancing from the west, the Germans made short work of the Russian defenders. German losses were modest. The Russians left several hundred dead and wounded on the field, and perhaps a thousand prisoners.

Most of the troops that François' corps had encountered were from the Finnish XXII Corps, deployed in late August from Grodno. Documents captured during the fighting against Samsonov's army had given details of the forces gathering in Grodno, including III Siberian Corps, and the Germans therefore had good intelligence on what further reinforcements might be available to the Russians. Depending on where it deployed, III Siberian Corps might interfere considerably with the German battle plan. As a result the loss of contact between I Corps Headquarters and 3rd Reserve Infantry Division on 9 September caused momentary concern. For the moment, though, the ebullient François remained confident that his corps would achieve its objectives. After the victory in Arys 1st Infantry Division had marched northeast to reach Ranten, about 6 miles (10km) away, and on 9 September continued its advance. In its path was Vasilli Gurko's 1st Cavalry Division. His original mission had been to protect the southern flank of Rennenkampf's army, but he had now been ordered to Grajewo, as part of the new Russian Tenth Army. Whilst his men were en route, his scouts informed him of the German advance. He was expecting infantry reinforcements, but for the moment, was on his own:

> Considerable German forces had occupied the small German town of Widminnen to the east of Lötzen … apparently with the intention of turning Rennenkampf's left flank. I was thus between two fires; I had either to follow exactly the orders I had been given by the commanders of both armies, or, on my own initiative, and despite orders, to move forward on the flank of II Corps and sustain the first blow of the German column until the promised assistance arrived. When this infantry did arrive I should have at once retired, for in fighting strength my cavalry could not compare with an infantry division.
>
> I did not hesitate as to the course I should take. Strong bodies of cavalry were sent to capture the necks between the lakes to the east of Widminnen, so far occupied only by weak cavalry patrols. Simultaneously I rode off to choose a position, close to the isthmuses, near the Kruglanken-See, which was comparatively easy to defend with small bodies of troops. My division at this time consisted of four regiments, the Moscow Lancers having returned to me from IV Corps.[9]

Gurko was correct in his assessment that the Germans were attempting to turn Rennenkampf's left flank. However, he did not realise that the flank had effectively been turned already, and there was no need for the German column – from 1st Infantry Division – to press further east. Consequently, although he was gratified at preventing German cavalry from infiltrating between the lakes, and commented that the Germans made only modest attempts to force their way through his men, his intervention did little to prevent François from continuing his advance towards the north and northeast.

The German cavalry operating in the area were 1st and 8th Cavalry Divisions, the latter newly arrived from the west. They had been subordinated to François' corps, and he ordered them to advance into the rear area of Rennenkampf's army. To the north of I Corps was Mackensen's XVII Corps, which moved forward through the fortress of Lötzen to add pressure to Rennenkampf's southern flank. The garrison of Lötzen was under the command of Oberst Busse, who had rejected Russian calls for his surrender in late August, and had then fought off a Russian attempt to take the fortifications. Built in the mid-19th century, the Boyen Fortress remained a formidable obstacle, and without heavy siege guns the Russians could do little about the German troops. As Mackensen's divisions moved east, they ran into strong resistance from II Corps. The hilly landscape and numerous lakes made it difficult for XVII Corps to manoeuvre, and progress was slow. The day before, XVII Corps' divisions had received a welcome boost:

> My troops have just had their first replacements sent to them and are once more at full fighting strength. But there are many wartime volunteers amongst them, with barely five weeks' training behind them. I would have wished for these young people to undergo longer training. Courage and enthusiasm alone are not sufficient. Tight discipline, fitness and marksmanship can't be learned quickly, and they form the basis for the wartime skills of the infantry.[10]

During the morning of 9 September Mackensen reported that his men had reached Kruglanken, but this proved to be an error. It took most of the day for XVII Corps to reach and capture the town, as the Russians were forced to give way in the face of I Corps' advance from the south. Much of the fighting centred on the village of Possessern, to the northwest of Kruglanken. By the end of the day Mackensen was confident that he had achieved a decisive breakthrough.

Rennenkampf's left flank was clearly in trouble, but the rest of his line was holding back the German forces. He ordered XX Corps and 54th and 72nd Infantry Divisions, all held in reserve, to move up in support, but there was no prospect of them reaching the threatened flank until 11 September. His entire position would be transformed if the new Tenth Army could attack from the south, but Zhilinski advised Rennenkampf that far from advancing from Lyck to Widminnen and thus into the rear of François' I Corps, the only element of Tenth Army that had reached the front line – XXII Corps – was in no state for such an attack. Concluding that the reinforcements being dispatched to his southern flank would arrive too late, Rennenkampf ordered his entire army to withdraw to the east.

On 10 September François was relieved to hear from 3rd Reserve Infantry Division, which had been heavily engaged by elements of the Russian XXII Corps near Lyck. The left flank of Morgen's division found itself in danger of being outflanked, and the Germans soon realised that the Russians outnumbered them. Towards evening the Russian artillery intensified its fire, but to Morgen's relief the anticipated Russian assault failed to develop. Overnight he prepared his men to renew their attacks, but the Russians had had enough, and began to withdraw. To Morgen's satisfaction, his men captured a message written by General von Brincken, commander of XXII Corps:

> I cannot carry out my orders to march against the flank of the Hindenburg Army, as I was attacked at Lyck and beaten.[11]

Confident that he had already smashed one of XXII Corps' Finnish divisions in earlier fighting, François ordered 3rd Reserve Infantry Division to drive back the Russians, to proceed through Marggrabowa, and then, in cooperation with the two cavalry divisions, to march north in order to cut across Rennenkampf's lines of communication. It was a risk to use the division intended to protect the southern flank of the German advance in this manner, but as had been the case in earlier fighting, François was prepared to take risks. His main force, consisting of 1st and 2nd Infantry Divisions, encountered diminishing resistance, and continued to take prisoners all day. Content at the progress his corps was making, François drove to view the areas where both his and Mackensen's divisions had fought over the previous two days:

> There could be no doubt that the Russians had suffered a heavy defeat and were hurrying away in headless flight. At Gross-Babkensee there was an entire tent camp laid out with all its baggage and plenty of rations. Everywhere across the landscape were abandoned weapons and stranded munitions and baggage wagons. Near Siewen, a farmer told me that Russian artillery had deployed on his land south of Siewen. There, I found a fully camouflaged Russian battery – eight guns and eight ammunition wagons – in earthworks with shelters and shields, technically complete. In the battery commander's dugout was a table, still laid out with breakfast cocoa, eggs and ham. The battery commander was lying by his guns with two lieutenants, apparently shot by their own men, who had then made off with the horses. The battery was so inconspicuous in the terrain that our men had not noticed it.[12]

Aerial reconnaissance reports reached Ludendorff and Hindenburg early on 10 September, suggesting that the Russians had begun to withdraw during the night, and that many of the front-line positions were now weakly, if at all, held. Immediately, Ludendorff issued orders for an energetic pursuit. The entire line was to press the retreating Russians, while Mackensen and François drove north, either side of the Rominte Heath, in an attempt to cut off Rennenkampf's units before they could reach the frontier. The tangle of trees, scrub, and the low hills of the heath, a popular area for hunting, was to be avoided if possible – speed was of the essence, and even token Russian resistance in such terrain would be difficult to overcome. Even as orders were issued, news came of a surprise Russian attack: General Aliev's IV Corps had launched a powerful assault on the German centre. There was consternation in Eighth Army Headquarters when the news arrived. After their hard marching and fighting in the south against Samsonov's Second Army, the German divisions had rushed north with little time for rest or reorganisation. Their ability to sustain high-tempo operations was probably approaching its limit, particularly in those units that had not been given a boost in morale by recent successes. I Corps in particular could be relied on to continue advancing and fighting until the men dropped through exhaustion, but in the centre XI Corps had endured tough resistance from the Russian forces opposing them. In an attempt to bolster the weakening centre, Ludendorff issued revised instructions to the two corps on the southern flank. They were to march more directly north, so that they could thrust into the flank of the Russian IV Corps as it tried to advance.[13]

The change of plan reached François shortly after midday on 11 September, as he and his lead elements cleared Russian forces from the town of Goldap. Slightly uncharacteristically, François obeyed the instructions, turning his divisions away from their drive towards the frontier. As the day progressed, Ludendorff received further reports, suggesting that the threat to his centre was not as great as he had feared. It now appeared that the Russians had broken off their attack, and were hurrying east. As the day grew to a close, Ludendorff sent a stream of messages to François, urging him to revert to his previous orders and to cut off the Russian retreat.

It was too late. A precious half-day had been lost, and Rennenkampf's men wasted no time in making their escape. On 12 September the two divisions of the German I Corps found themselves advancing almost amongst the retreating Russians. Conta's 1st Infantry Division fought a tough battle to beat off Russian units trying to escape towards the east. François' corps then deployed in a line facing north, immediately north of the Rominte Heath, and towards the evening managed to press forward to Pillupönen. Meanwhile Cossacks attempting to escape across the Rominte Heath attacked the rear area units of François' corps, killing several officers.[14]

Mackensen's XVII Corps had exploited its earlier successes in a more northerly direction than I Corps, cutting the road from Angerburg to Goldap late on 11 September. The volunteer drafts that had restored the ranks to full strength featured conspicuously in encounters with Russian forces along the road, making up with enthusiasm and energy what they lacked in skill. The following day 35th Infantry Division reached Tollmingkehmen, to the northeast of Goldap, while 36th Infantry approached the area where the division had lost so many men on 20 August. This time the experience was completely different:

> The number of prisoners climbed once more into the thousands, and many guns were captured. The roads of march were increasingly littered with the retreating enemy's military equipment, discarded items of uniform, weapons, ammunition and abandoned vehicles. As the former dry weather turned to rain, the heavy, wet East Prussian soil hindered the advance along the country roads and required considerable exertions by the men and horses.[15]

Meanwhile, there had been further developments on the Russian side. On 11 September Grand Duke Nikolai visited Zhilinski's headquarters in Bialystok, to enquire why Tenth Army had not intervened from the south to outflank the German forces:

> A discussion with General Zhilinski convinced the Grand Duke that the armies of Northwest Front had not been led well. The circumstances for an energetic thrust by Tenth Army against the rear of the Germans who were turning First Army's left flank existed; instead of organising this attack at all costs, the Front commander had accepted as final a report from the commander of XXII Corps that his unit was temporarily incapacitated… However, aside from this corps, General Zhilinski still had the 8th Light Infantry Division (from III Siberian Corps) which was just arriving at the front and was closely followed by 7th Infantry Division from the same corps. After deciding against ordering an attack by Tenth Army, General Zhilinski had dispatched XXII Corps to Augustovo and the units of III Siberian Corps to Grajewo, the motivation behind these orders being the necessity to give the corps of the new army time to organise themselves properly.[16]

To an extent Zhilinski was condemned regardless of what he did. He had ordered Samsonov to press forward even though his units were still completing their concentration, and the result was complete disaster. Now, when he tried to give newly arrived formations time to regroup, he was criticised for showing too little urgency. He was the victim of the ongoing struggle between the Sukhomlinovite camp and its opponents. The Sukhomlinovites had tried to use the growing debacle in East Prussia as an excuse to get Rennenkampf dismissed, but his sympathisers in high places succeeded in protecting him; in revenge, they ensured Zhilinski shouldered the blame. Regardless of the details of the case, Grand Duke Nikolai decided that he was responsible for the failure of Northwest Front to perform adequately, and dismissed him. His replacement was a curious choice: Nikolai Ruzsky, who had commanded Third Army in Galicia.

Three days after his meeting with Zhilinski, Grand Duke Nikolai ordered a conference with both his front commanders. Ruzsky told him what he had already realised: the armies of Northwest Front were in no shape for further offensive operations. Ivanov, by contrast, was bullish about the prospects of further success, and requested reinforcements. The grand duke was not enthusiastic. Instead, he ordered Fifth Army to be moved from its current position in Galicia to an area north of Warsaw, where it could protect the southern flank of Northwest Front. From north to south the Russian front line now consisted of First, Tenth, Fifth, Ninth, Fourth, Third and Eighth Armies, with Second Army still reforming. Two other armies – Sixth Army in the north, and Seventh Army in the south – were tasked with protecting Russia's coastlines.

On the battlefield François' men continued to fire on retreating Russian columns, taking prisoners in large numbers. On 14 September the Germans pursued the last elements of Rennenkampf's army over the frontier, with Conta's 1st Infantry Division reaching Wyłkowyszki, about 10 miles (16km) inside Russian territory.

According to the local population, the great retreat began during the night of 9–10 September. In Stallupönen, the Russian columns were at first in good order, but after the rush of men from the south, chaos broke out. The main road was no longer sufficient for the masses. Everyone pressed on, footsoldiers, riders, and columns of wagons rolling along and beside the road to Wyłkowyszki in disordered crowds. The local clergy in Wyłkowyszki explained that crowds had moved through the town for three days and nights, hungry and exhausted, without discipline. The road was a picture of the wildest flight. Where small streams crossed the field next to the road, there were hundreds of stranded vehicles, some plundered, others still loaded. Food, munitions, aircraft, medical supplies, weapons, and baggage of all kinds in huge quantities littered the fields.[17]

I Corps had taken 13,000 prisoners in eight days of fighting, and had captured 90 guns. Although the Russian XXVI and III Corps, and parts of IV Corps, managed to retreat fairly intact, the rest of Rennenkampf's army disintegrated. Russian losses exceeded 125,000 dead or wounded, with at least 30,000 men taken prisoner. German losses, mainly in the units that had launched frontal attacks against Rennenkampf's centre, amounted to about 40,000 dead or wounded.

It seemed to be another decisive German victory. Russian forces had been driven from German soil, and had suffered heavy casualties. But for the lost half-day, I Corps might have been able to achieve an even greater success. Yet despite its losses, the Russian First Army was still intact. Besides, pressure was developing elsewhere, particularly in view of setbacks in Galicia, where the intial promise of a major Austro-Hungarian victory had rapidly evaporated. As early as 10 September Hindenburg sent a telegram to *OHL*:

> It seems to me questionable whether Rennenkampf can be decisively beaten as the Russians have begun to retreat early this morning. As regards plans for the future there is a question of concentrating an army in Silesia. Can we rely on further reinforcement from the west? We can dispense with two corps from this front.[18]

The Germans were now in a position to strike south across the Narew into Poland, but such a thrust would be about as pointless as the Austro-Hungarian advance of earlier weeks had been – it only made sense as part of a pincer operation from both north and south. By this date Conrad's battered armies were forced not only to abandon their drive north, but also to withdraw from most of Galicia. As a result there was a threat to German territory in the southeast, where, if the Russians advanced to Krakow, they could potentially push on into the resource-rich territory of Upper Silesia. On 15 September a new German Ninth Army was created, with its headquarters based in Silesia, to counter any such threat. Ludendorff was designated its chief of staff, and left for his new command. The new army would be built around several of the units that had fought in the First Battle of the Masurian Lakes – XI, XVII, XX, and Guards Reserve Corps. Three days later, Hindenburg was assigned to command Ninth Army, with General Richard von Schubert taking command of what remained of Eighth Army. Schubert had previously commanded XIV Reserve Corps in the west, and was a newcomer to the Eastern Front. He inherited an army primarily consisting of François' I Corps, with additional firepower provided by von der Goltz's *Landwehr* Division and 3rd Reserve Infantry Division.

For the moment, the pursuit of the defeated Russians continued, with the intention of doing as much damage to Rennenkampf's First Army as possible. General von Morgen's 3rd Reserve Infantry Division continued to advance on the southern flank of Eighth Army, seizing Augustovo and Suvalki, and capturing welcome supplies in the Russian barracks in the latter town on 13 September, while I Corps drove on to the east. The Germans now faced the same problem that had confronted every invader of Russia: the terrain was so vast, the Russians could simply continue to retreat until the invaders had outstripped their lines of supply. Given that the intention of the advance was to ravage the retreating Russians, Schubert felt that it was important to define a distinct endpoint of the advance, in order to prevent his army being drawn further east than was necessary. Accordingly, the goal set for Eighth Army was the valley of the River Niemen, perhaps 50 miles (80km) inside Russian territory. Such an advance would potentially expose the southern flank of Eighth Army to an attack as the Russian Tenth Army built up its strength; in order to prevent this, a force was organised to attack the Russian fortress at Osowiec, between Grajewo and Bialystok. Construction of the fortress started in 1882, and continued until the outbreak of the war; it covered nearly 2 miles (3.2km) along its long axis, and was as formidable as any defensive position of its era. German infantry reached the area on 21 September, swiftly driving the garrison into the fortress. The artillery train, including several powerful 8-inch siege guns, laboured forward along poor roads in heavy rain, and started to fire on the defences on 26 September. After two days the German infantry made an assault, but were beaten back with substantial losses. To make matters worse for the Germans, the Russian counterattack brought Russian artillery in range of the German gun lines, forcing the German gunners to withdraw. It was effectively the end of the German attempt to take Osowiec, and the German infantry settled down to mask the garrison. Whilst this prevented any threat to the German advance on the Niemen, the failure to take the fortress was nevertheless a disappointment. It was effectively the first setback endured by Eighth Army since the fighting at Gumbinnen. At different times during the following weeks, both the kaiser and the tsar visited the battlefield at Osowiec.[19]

The line of the Niemen was protected by two further Russian fortresses: Kovno in the north, and Grodno in the south. The German forces that laboured across the increasingly muddy autumnal landscape were hindered more by poor roads than by Russian resistance, and additional problems were created by the difference in railway gauge – Russian railways were of a wider gauge, and the rails had to be re-pinned before German trains could run on them. When his men reached the Niemen, Schubert decided to make an attempt to force the line of the river by establishing a bridgehead at Olita (Alytus). The rationale behind this is not obvious. It would have been sufficient to occupy the line of the river, and await reinforcements; even if Eighth Army were able to force a crossing, it probably lacked the strength to deal with either of the Russian fortresses. The attempt to cross the river was fraught with difficulties. The eastern bank was higher than the western bank, giving the Russian defenders a marked advantage, and the length of the German supply lines was now taking its toll. Two pontoon bridges were established across the Niemen on 25 September, but Russian artillery destroyed them as soon as German troops attempted to cross. Two days later the Germans tried again, with the same outcome.

Casualties on both sides, while not heavy, were still substantial. One of the most noteworthy was Prince Oleg Konstantinovich, a great-grandson of Tsar Nicholas I. The 22-year-old was an officer in the Life Guards Hussars Regiment; although he had been offered a post as an orderly officer in higher headquarters, he requested permission to stay with his regiment. Here, he was tasked with maintaining the regimental diary, and spent his days dreaming of glory and longing for a post in the front line. Reluctantly, his commander allowed him to return to his platoon, where on 27 September he was involved in an action against the Germans in Pilviškiai, a village some 24 miles (39km) southwest of Kovno. He was badly wounded and was taken to Vilnius, where he underwent surgery the following day. He died a day later, the only member of the Romanov family to be killed during the war as a result of wounds received in combat. His family came together to mourn their loss, an experience that they shared with hundreds of thousands of other families across the continent.[20]

As September drew to a close, the Russian Tenth Army began to exert itself. Pflug had been replaced as commander by Thaddeus von Sievers, who had earned praise for commanding X Corps as part of Ruszky's Third Army in Galicia. The names of both Pflug and Sievers, as well as other generals like Plehve and Rennenkampf, show the degree to which families of Baltic German descent dominated the Russian military hierarchy. The Russian forces, primarily III Siberian Corps, marched first to Osowiec, where they drove off the German forces, mainly comprising Goltz's division, and then pressed on towards Augustovo and Suvalki. Confused fighting raged for several days in the woodland between the two towns.

Morgen was now in command of an improvised corps (I Reserve Corps), consisting of his former 3rd Reserve Infantry Division and 36th Reserve Infantry Division. He ordered the latter formation under General Kruge to hold Augustovo, while 3rd Reserve Infantry Division attacked the Russians in their flank. Kruge was forced out of the town, and the flank attack failed. Nevertheless, reinforced by a *Landwehr* brigade, Morgen was confident that he would be able to hold onto Suvalki, until he received a message from the neighbouring 2nd Infantry Division that it was withdrawing towards the west. It was now pointless to hold the town, and Suvalki was abandoned on 3 October.[21]

Increasingly concerned that his Eighth Army was threatened from the south, Schubert gave orders for a withdrawal towards the frontier. Unfortunately for him, I Corps was enjoying some local successes, and – in much the same way that he had dealt with disagreeable orders in the past – François was unwilling to accept such an order. Instead he sent a telegram to *OHL*, advising the higher command that Schubert was badly advised. By this time François' reputation was riding high, particularly with the kaiser. Wilhelm ordered Schubert's dismissal, and replacement by François himself.

The change of command could do little to alter the reality on the ground. The Russians were aware that several German formations had left Eighth Army, and attempted to take advantage of this by exerting as much pressure as they could. François had no alternative but to order a withdrawal in the face of growing Russian pressure. Throughout the second half of September Schubert had urged François to prepare defensive positions east of the East Prussian frontier. François had refused, repeatedly replying that he had successfully defended East Prussia by local offensives against advancing Russian forces, and that he therefore saw no need for defensive lines. Now, when such a line might have been of use, he had to accept a war of movement, and by the second week of October Russian forces had once more occupied Lyck and the southeast corner of East Prussia. The Russian advance was finally brought to a halt along entrenched lines that ran from northwest of Lyck to Wirballen. The Russians shelled Wirballen heavily, and then made several attempt to storm it, as witnessed by an American correspondent who was in the German lines. His graphic account of the fighting captures the full horror and futility of assaults on prepared positions. Even here, on the Eastern Front, the combination of trenches, artillery and machine guns imposed their implacable, cold logic upon any lingering hopes that offensive spirit could win the day.

The German artillery today beat back, in a bloody, ghastly smear of men, the Russian advance.

Yesterday I saw an infantry engagement. Today it was mostly an artillery encounter. The infantry attack is the more ghastly, but the artillery the more awe-inspiring. This was the fifth day of constant fighting and still the German trenches hold.

Today's battle opened at dawn… [W]hen dawn once again revealed the two long lines of the Russian and German positions, the Russian guns began to hurl their loads of shrapnel at the German trenches…

We went to one of the German batteries on the left centre. They were already in action, though it was only 6 o'clock. The men got the range from observers a little in advance, cunningly masked, and slowly, methodically and enthusiastically fed the guns with their loads of death.

The Russians didn't have our range. All of their shells flew screaming 1,000 yards to our left. Through my glasses I watched them strike…

While we watched the Russians seemed to tire of shooting holes in an inoffensive hill. They began to try chance shots to the right and to the left … I saw one [shell] strike a windmill, shattering the long arms and crumpling it over in a slow burning heap. Then we beat a retreat, further toward the centre…

Back behind us, on the extreme left, I was told the Russians were attacking the German trenches by an infantry charge, the German field telephone service having apprised the commanders along the front. With glasses we could see a faint line of what must have been the Russian infantry rushing across the open fields…

[A]s we arrived at the right wing we witnessed the last of a Russian infantry advance at that end. The wave of Russians had swept nearly to the German lines, situated between two sections of field artillery, and there had been repulsed. Russians were smeared across in front of these pits, dead, dying or wounded – cut down by the terrible spray of German machine-guns.

I got up to the trenches as the German fire slackened because of the lack of targets. The Russians had gone back. Strewn in the trenches were countless empty shells, the bullets of which had, as it looked to inexpert eyes, slain thousands. As a matter of fact, there were hundreds of dead in the field ahead.

German infantrymen spat on their rapid firers as we reached the trench and delightedly called our attention to the sizzle that told how hot the barrels were from firing.

The men stretched their cramped limbs, helping a few wounded to the rear, and waited for breakfast… Meanwhile men with the white brassard and red Geneva Cross were busy out in the open, lending succour to the Russian wounded. The battle seemed to have come to a sudden halt.

But even as I was getting soup, the artillery fusillade broke forth again. From 9 o'clock to noon the Russians hurled their heavy shells at the German trenches and the German guns. The German batteries replied slowly.

There was mighty little fuss and feathers about this business of dealing death from guns. The crew of each piece laughed among themselves, but there were none of the picturesque shouts of command, the indiscriminate blowing of bugles, and the flashy waving of battle flags that the word battle usually conjures up. It was merely a deadly business of killing.

Over to the right, a scant 300 yards away, the Russians had apparently succeeded in getting the range. As I watched through the glasses I saw shrapnel burst over the battery there and watched a non-commissioned soldier fall with three of his comrades. I was told that one had been killed and three wounded. The Red Cross crew came up and bore away the four – the dead and the live – and before they were gone the gun was speaking away with four fresh men working it…

Yesterday, my first day at Wirballen, I saw the third attempt of the Russians to carry the German centre by storm. Twice on Wednesday their infantry had advanced under cover of their artillery, only to be repulsed. Their third effort proved no more successful…

At a number of points along their line, observable by us, but screened from the observation of the German trenches in the centre, the Russian infantry came tumbling out, and, rushing forward, took up advanced positions, awaiting the formation of the new and irregular battle line. Dozens of light rapid-firers were dragged along by hand. Other troops – the reserves – took up semi-advanced positions. All the while the Russian shrapnel was raining over the German trenches.

Finally came the Russian order to advance. At the word, hundreds of yards of the Russian fighting line leaped forward, deployed in open order and came on. One, two, three, and in some places four and five successive skirmish lines, separated by intervals of from 20 to 50 yards, swept forward. Some of them came into range of the German trench fire almost at once. These lines began to wilt and thin out. Others were able to make a considerable advance under cover. The smoke of the burning village gave a grateful protection to several regiments…

On came the Slav swarm – into the range of the German trenches, with wild yells and never a waver. Russian battle flags – the first I had ever seen – appeared in the front of the charging ranks. The advance line thinned and the second line moved up. Nearer and nearer they swept toward the German positions.

And then came a new sight. A few seconds later came a new sound. First I saw a sudden, almost grotesque, melting of the advancing lines. It was different from anything that had taken place before. The men literally went down like dominoes in a row. Those who kept their feet were hurled back as though by a terrible gust of wind. Almost in the second that I pondered, puzzled, the staccato rattle of machine-guns reached us. My ear answered the query of my eye.

The crucial period for the section of the charge on which I had riveted my attention probably lasted less than a minute. To my throbbing brain it seemed like an hour.

Then, with the withering fire raking them, even as they faltered, the lines broke. Panic ensued. It was every man for himself. The entire Russian charge turned and went tearing back to cover and the shelter of the Russian trenches…

After the assault had failed and the battle had resumed its normal trend, I swept the field with my glasses. The dead were everywhere. They were not piled up, but were strewn over acres.

More horrible than the sight of the dead, though, were the other pictures brought up by the glasses. Squirming, tossing, writhing figures everywhere! The wounded!

All who could stumble or crawl were working their way back toward their own lines or back to the friendly cover of hills or wooded spots.

But there appeared to be hundreds to whom was denied even this hope, hundreds doomed to lie there in the open, with wounds unwashed and undressed, suffering from thirst and hunger until the merciful shadows of darkness made possible their rescue by the Good Samaritans of the hospital corps, who are tonight gleaning that field of death for the third time since Sunday.[22]

After weeks of fighting, and hundreds of thousands of dead and wounded, the two sides faced each other across a front line that was little different from that occupied on the eve of the Battle of Gumbinnen in the first days of the war. Any decision in the war in the east, it seemed, would have to be forced elsewhere.

CHAPTER 10

THE REALITY OF DEFEAT

GALICIA, SEPTEMBER 1914

The opening rounds of the fighting in Galicia had clearly gone in favour of Conrad and his armies, but in a contest against a heavyweight like the tsar's army, there was still a long way to go. Two Russian armies had been defeated and driven back, but two others remained active. Moreover, neither of the defeated armies had been destroyed. Given the sheer scale of Russian mobilisation, they had suffered a setback, no more.

Stereotypes often exist for good reasons. The frequent description of the Russian Army as a steamroller was, in this case, entirely appropriate. Subtlety and daring might be beyond its expertise and skill, but given time, it could recover from tactical or even operational setbacks. Its sheer scale meant that, unless it was forced to deal with such setbacks across its entire front, it was able to mount attacks elsewhere that allowed its defeated elements time to regroup. And, as it now demonstrated, it was also perfectly capable of moving quickly, though this appears to have been very much dependent on local commanders.

In Galicia the weakness of the Austro-Hungarian position lay in the east. An entire army – Böhm-Ermolli's Second Army – was still missing, either still deployed in the Balkans or languishing on painfully slow troop trains. The change in concentration areas to a more westward position was only partly reversed late in the day, and the remaining troops were still somewhat further west than originally planned. By contrast, the Russians had two powerful armies deployed for an early advance into eastern Galicia.

In the north, Nikolai Ruzsky's Third Army concentrated around Rovno and Dubno, from where it was only a short march from Brody, with IX, X, XI, and XXI Corps, a total of twelve infantry divisions and four cavalry divisions. Like most of his generation, Ruzsky had served in both the Russo-Turkish War of 1877–78 and the Russo-Japanese War of 1904–05. In the latter conflict he had been the chief of staff of Second Manchurian Army. He had a reputation for caution, sometimes bordering on indecisiveness, but he was also a firm member of the pro-Sukhomlinov circle in the Russian Army, and owed his current post at least partly to Sukhomlinov. His caution would not have been a significant problem if his superior had been a suitably aggressive character, but Nikolai Ivanov, the commander of Southwest Front, also had 'a certain penchant for hesitation'.[1] Aware of this, Grand Duke Nikolai resolved to keep a close eye on matters, visiting Ivanov in Rovno on 18 August to ensure that the Southwest Front would conduct itself with appropriate vigour.

A little further south of Ruzsky, concentrating around Proskurov, was the Russian Eighth Army, commanded by Alexei Brusilov, with VII, VIII, XII, and XXIV Corps, for a total of ten infantry divisions and five cavalry divisions. In some respects Brusilov was a typical product of the Russian Empire, having been born to a Russian father and a Polish mother in Georgia. He would be the fourth generation of his family to rise to high rank in the tsar's armies; his grandfather saw action against Napoléon during the campaign of 1812. A tutor described the young Brusilov as clever and gifted, but prone to laziness; perhaps this lack of application lay behind his failure to secure a place in the top class of the Imperial Corps of Pages – an academy for the sons of the nobility and senior officers in St Petersburg – in 1872. Instead, Brusilov joined a regiment of dragoons, where his aptitude soon earned him promotion. He saw action against Ottoman Turkey in the 1877–78 war, earning several medals, and then spent many years in the Cavalry Officer School in St Petersburg, overseeing the modernisation of the cavalry arm. His insistence on training officers to operate in all weather was innovative at the time, and attracted the disapproval of aristocratic families, who made representations to the tsar about the risks being taken with the lives of their sons. When the tsar spoke to Brusilov about the matter, he replied that he would be happy to discontinue such training provided that the tsar would guarantee that the enemies of Russia would only ever attack when the sun shone.[2] The July Crisis broke when he was on holiday in Germany. He managed to return to Vinnitsa before the declaration of war, when he was appointed to command Eighth Army.

Facing the two Russian armies was the Austro-Hungarian Third Army under Rudolf Ritter von Brudermann. Like Brusilov he was a cavalryman, and in 1906 became Inspector General of the Cavalry. Unfortunately, he was an ardent enthusiast for old-fashioned cavalry tactics, and placed little or no value on new weapons like machine guns, preferring that the cavalry should, as had always been the case in the past, intervene in battle on horseback by the application of sabre and lance. Conrad seems to have been aware of his limitations, not least of which was that he had never commanded troops in battle. Although he was unable to prevent him from being given high command when war broke out, the chief of the general staff assigned him to an army that would take a defensive posture. Third Army consisted of III, XI, and XIV Corps, with eighteen infantry divisions and four cavalry divisions. In addition, it was supported by the *Armeegruppe* (army group) of Hermann von Kövess, which consisted primarily of XII Corps.

The Russians had always expected eastern Galicia to be the centre of concentration for all the Austro-Hungarian armies, which would then attack to the east and northeast. Consequently, Third and Eighth Armies were originally ordered to adopt a defensive posture in order to bring this attack to a halt, while Fourth and Fifth Armies launched a counterattack from the north. The more westerly deployment of Conrad's armies, together with their unexpected drive towards the north, resulted in Ivanov making radical changes to his plans. The two eastern armies were now ordered to move west as fast as possible, in order to take advantage of the Austro-Hungarian weakness in eastern Galicia, and also to reduce the pressure on Fourth and Fifth Armies.[3]

At first the Austro-Hungarian forces failed to spot the imminent advance of Ivanov's eastern armies. Although Kövess had detected the approach of the leading elements of Brusilov's Eighth Army, he reported on 19 August that he did not regard them as posing any threat. Inexplicably, this report took two days to reach Conrad. On the same day a reconnaissance pilot flew over Russian territory to the east, also failing to spot significant Russian forces. Reassured by these reports, *AOK* confirmed to Kövess during the afternoon of 21 August that there were no significant Russian forces between the Dniester, Tarnopol, and Proskurov.[4]

As his western armies moved north, Conrad had to protect their eastern flank, and therefore ordered Brudermann's Third Army to perform this task by moving north. As Third Army thus edged closer to Auffenberg's Fourth Army, its southeast flank would in turn be exposed; in order to cover this, Kövess was ordered to advance to the east of Lemberg towards Przemyślany. The headquarters of Böhm-Ermolli's Second Army was expected to arrive at any moment, followed by the first of the troops rerouted from the Serbian front. In principle, it should have been perfectly possible for Kövess to protect the eastern flank of the *k.u.k.* Army. The terrain around Lemberg was ideally suited for defensive operations, especially against an enemy advancing from the east; three rivers ran from north to south through small, deep valleys, and amongst low hills studded with copses. But a deliberate defence was anathema to the doctrine that Conrad had instilled into his officers, and no attempt was made to take advantage of the landscape.

The first inkling of the threat from the east came late on 21 August, even as confident orders for a general advance to the north were being issued: substantial Russian infantry and cavalry forces were reported to have crossed the frontier between Brody and Tarnopol. For the moment, though, Conrad remained certain that these were not powerful formations, and continued to plan for a general advance to the north, with only XII Corps –11th Infantry Division and three cavalry divisions, all depleted by their abortive raids over the frontier – facing east. These units were about to receive the full weight of two Russian armies.

By 24 August *AOK* estimated the Russian forces advancing from the east as numbering ten divisions of infantry and cavalry. Although Kövess had now been reinforced by 43rd Rifle Division – a unit made up of Austrian *Landwehr* – the continuing delays in the arrival of Second Army were now becoming serious. In an attempt to shore up the forces facing east, Conrad ordered Brudermann to take XII Corps under his command, and to deploy two of his own Third Army corps alongside it. This, he hoped, would take care of the Russian forces advancing from Brody. Meanwhile, there were disturbing reports of further Russian columns advancing south of Tarnopol. Conrad ordered Böhm-Ermolli to defeat these with his Second Army as it arrived. News had reached *AOK* in Przemyśl that Hindenburg and Ludendorff were turning south against Samsonov, resurrecting Conrad's hopes of a joint pincer movement against Russian Poland. This was not the time, he felt, to divert significant forces to the east to cover what might prove to be an imaginary threat.[5]

Meanwhile, the forces screening the Russian advance from the east were getting their first taste of battle. Pál Kelemen, a Hungarian hussar from Budapest, had not been part of the first wave of mobilisation, and had thus missed out on the abortive cavalry missions. Near the town of Stanislau (now Ivano-Frankivsk), his first encounter with the reality of war was the same as that of so many soldiers – confusion and disorder:

> We slept in tents. At 11.30 p.m.: alarm! The Russians were approaching the town.
> I thought that everyone showed little anxiety. I threw on my clothes and ran out
> to join my troop. Infantrymen had been deployed on the road. [There was] the

thunder of cannon. About 500m further forward was the chatter of rifles. Automobiles roared past. The lights of their carbide lamps disappeared in a long line down the road from Stanislau to Halitsch [now Halych].

I passed the pickets, climbed over a hedge-covered fence, past the ditches by the roadway. My troop was waiting for me, mounted up, and we were ready for further orders.

As morning dawned, the population streamed out of the town in long columns. On carts, on foot, and on horseback. Everyone did what they could to save themselves. Everyone had taken what they could carry with them. All their faces were marked with fatigue, soot, sweat and panic, terribly downcast, [with] pain and suffering. Their eyes were full of fear, their movements hesitant; a dreadful terror gripped them all. It seemed as if the cloud of dust they stirred up clung to them, and they couldn't shake it off.

I stayed next to the road, sleepless, and watched this infernal kaleidoscope. There were even military vehicles, and in the fields soldiers could be seen retreating, infantry fleeing in panic, unsaddled horsemen. Nobody seemed to have their full kit. The crowd of exhausted people streamed through the valley.[6]

At first there seemed the real prospect of further Austro-Hungarian victories to the north. After its success around Kraśnik, Dankl's First Army began to feel its way forwards towards Lublin. But a steady stream of reinforcements had restored much of the fighting strength of the Russian Fourth Army; when Dankl renewed his attack on 27 August, his units ran into Russian lines invigorated by fresh formations. Nevertheless, the losses of the previous days were not without consequence, and during the afternoon the Russian XXV Corps was driven back, leading to a general withdrawal. The 28th of August found Dankl's troops less than 10 miles (16km) from the centre of Lublin, but their own losses were steadily mounting, and as was the case with every army of the era, the task of keeping them supplied adequately to allow an advance to continue proved to be an impossible one. Reluctantly, Dankl had to grant his units a brief rest.[7]

As Stavka became increasingly aware of the weakness of the Austro-Hungarian forces in eastern Galicia, and in light of the constant pressure from the French for an early drive on Berlin – and therefore a swift end to the fighting against the Dual Monarchy – Grand Duke Nikolai urged the Southwest Front to advance 'at a higher tempo'.[8] Ruzsky was forced to give his men a day of rest on 25 August, if only to allow supplies to catch up, but this gave Brusilov, who had started further east, an opportunity to draw up his army level with its neighbour. Confident that sufficient ammunition had been brought forward, Ruzsky now ordered his units to prepare to advance into the area immediately north of Lemberg, while Brusilov advanced to the south of the city.

Meanwhile, Brudermann was issuing his own orders. Still confident that only weak Russian forces were advancing from the east, he concluded that III and XII Corps were sufficient to hold them at bay. Consequently, he ordered XI Corps to move north, on the eastern flank of the neighbouring Fourth Army. Kövess' units had been marching west through the heat and dust of late August from the frontier in the face of the Russian advance for three days, averaging perhaps 18 miles (30km) a day; their commander felt that they, like so many other formations, were in urgent need of a rest. The Austro-Hungarian cavalry, too, was feeling the strain, both from its failed raid into Russian territory and the constant skirmishing with Russian cavalry. There was a sharp engagement near Czernowitz, where the advancing Russian forces ran into a brigade of *Landsturm*. While they exchanged fire, part of the Austrian 43rd Rifle Brigade arrived and took the Russians in their flank, forcing them to retreat. The engagement, and the ease with which Austro-Hungarian reservists fought off their opponents, only served to bolster the belief in *AOK* in Przemyśl that the Russian advance was not a major threat. Although Brudermann had been informed of strong Russian forces assembling northeast of Lemberg, he merely ordered the reinforced XII Corps to strike at them should they advance. The main axis of operations remained to the north, to protect the eastern flank of Auffenberg's army.[9]

Brudermann had no clear idea of the strength of the Russian forces now in eastern Galicia, but he was anxious to strike a blow at those nearest to him before they could be reinforced. To this end, his chief of staff, Generalmajor Pfeffer, telephoned Conrad on 25 August to suggest an attack against what were assumed to be two or three isolated Russian divisions that had advanced into the area near Złoczów. Conrad assented, though with hesitation. He was still determined to push on towards the north, and did not welcome anything, however temporary, that diverted troops in any other direction.

An important factor that should be considered here is whether Conrad should have been more aware of the true strength of the forces facing Brudermann. Whilst aerial and other reconnaissance gave only a partial picture of Russian forces, intelligence had come from other sources. As early as 14 August the Austro-Hungarian consul in the Romanian city of Jassy had sent a telegram to Conrad with an accurate report of the strength of the two eastern armies of the Southwest Front.[10] Before the war several analyses had been made of the defensive potential of the terrain to the east of Lemberg, but it seems that Conrad's obsessive belief in the superiority of offensive operations to solve all military problems prevailed. Rather than allowing the Russian armies to bloody themselves against prepared positions, he preferred to seek a decisive blow against them by way of an attack that turned their northern flank.

Brudermann planned to attack eastwards with much of his strength. XII Corps would advance south of Złoczów towards Remizowce, while III Corps attacked towards Złoczów itself. A little further north, XI Corps would protect the northern flank of the assault. Given the estimate of only two or three Russian infantry divisions, this amounted to sufficient strength to achieve a quick, crushing success. This would free Brudermann to turn his attention to the north, even though the formations deployed to the attack were weary from long marches. On the same day as these plans were drawn up, Böhm-Ermolli arrived in Stanislau with his staff to form the headquarters of Second Army, which for the moment existed more on paper than in reality. During the day elements of Kövess' former army group – effectively the only combat elements of Second Army – clashed with Russian troops from XXIV Corps, part of Brusilov's Eighth Army, to the southeast of Lemberg. The results were mixed: a division of Hungarian reservist cavalry retreated in disorder, while the reliable 43rd Rifle Brigade withdrew to Czernowitz, confident that it had done its duty.

Early on 26 August, as the sun rose into a cloudless summer sky, Brudermann's Third Army attack began. General Emil von Colerus ordered the lead formations of his III Corps, 6th and 28th Infantry Divisions, to move forward at 7.30 a.m., an hour earlier than planned. Almost immediately, they encountered the leading elements of the Russian XI Corps. The attack was broadly along the main road running east from Lemberg, and although 28th Infantry Division made good headway north of the road, 6th Infantry Division encountered tough defences to the south, and was soon brought to a halt. In several of the battles in Galicia, the Austro-Hungarian commanders had been dismayed by the relatively poor performance of their artillery, and this was no exception. Indeed, the men of 6th Infantry Division complained that their artillery barely featured during their battle.

III Corps had a third unit, the reservist 22nd Rifle Division, which was meant to be protecting the southern flank of 6th Infantry Division. The attack of the main divisions, launched an hour earlier than intended, took the reservists by surprise, and as its columns hurried east, they found the roads blocked by rear area elements of 6th Infantry Division. Consequently, as the Russians responded to the Austro-Hungarian advance, they exploited the open southern flank of 6th Infantry Division; during the afternoon the Austrian troops were forced to withdraw to their starting position in Gologóry. South of the village was the

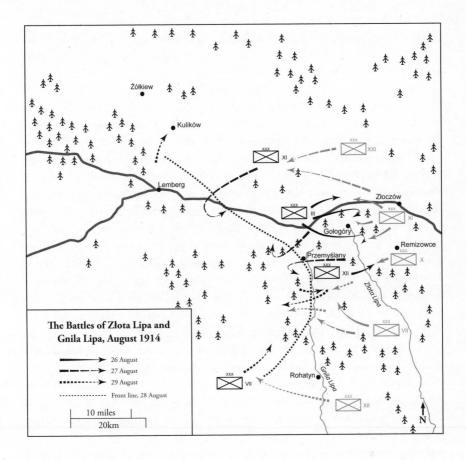

The Battles of Złota Lipa and
Gnila Lipa, August 1914

➤ 26 August
➤ 27 August
➤ 29 August
Front line, 28 August

10 miles
20km

Złota Lipa, a small river; as 22nd Rifle Division struggled forward, it found that
it had to cross this stream to attack the Russians. The men pushed forward,
leaving most of their inadequate artillery behind, and were soon under intense
pressure. As darkness fell, the decision was made to withdraw them behind the
Złota Lipa, but executing the order in darkness proved to be an almost impossible
task for the exhausted reservists. Only a small proportion of the division managed
to reach their designated positions; the rest were scattered over a large area, with
many taken prisoner.

A little further south, Kövess' XII Corps also moved forward. Confident that
the Russian forces facing him were both weak and disorganised, Kövess ordered
only 16th Infantry Division to advance on Remizowce, keeping the rest of his
units – some of which had suffered losses in the last few days – in reserve. At first

the division encountered limited resistance, but shortly after it had crossed the Złota Lipa it became clear that it was badly outnumbered. In reality, the 'weak and disorganised' forces facing it were the three infantry divisions of the Russian X Corps. Worried about his southern flank, Kövess could spare little by way of reinforcements for his hard-pressed division. The northern flank of Brudermann's attack, where XI Corps advanced as cover against any Russian intervention from the north, also encountered substantial Russian forces. Reports from all areas of the front began to arrive in *AOK* during the afternoon. Although Conrad considered diverting the forces under Archduke Joseph Ferdinand to the east, he remained determined – as did Brudermann – that Third Army could and would achieve a decisive success on 27 August. To this end, new orders were issued for a resumption of the attack the following morning. However, during the night details emerged of the losses suffered by the attacking units, particularly those of III Corps – one regiment had completely disintegrated and fled back to Lemberg before it could be rallied – and there was a change of heart. It was now eminently clear that the Russian forces opposing Brudermann were more than a few isolated divisions, and Conrad ordered a withdrawal to a line roughly level with Lemberg. However, as 27 August dawned and the Russians failed to press their advantage in the east, Conrad and Brudermann once more changed their minds. They would try again to mount an attack towards the east.

The Austro-Hungarian attacks of 26 August might not have achieved their objectives, but they had an effect on Ruzsky, who ordered his men to proceed cautiously – hence the apparent pause in the fighting in front of Brudermann's army. Further south, Brusilov felt few such restraints. On his northern wing VII Corps was advancing and meeting almost no resistance, and Brusilov ordered it to turn north, so that it could attack the southern flank of the troops facing Ruzsky. At the same time Ruzsky ordered his own northern flank to strike with five infantry divisions from XI and XXI Corps. The Austro-Hungarian XI Corps came under heavy attack, and several reservist formations broke and fled. General Kolossváry, the corps commander, managed to establish a front facing north and east, but was greatly relieved when the Russians failed to press their advantage against his weakened corps.

Despite their successes, all was not well in the Russian camp. Ivanov, the commander of Southwest Front, remained anxious about the gap between his eastern and western armies, particularly as the latter two formations had been forced to retreat to the north. On 26 August he had repeated his orders to Ruzsky that he should attempt to move his troops to the northwest, in order to establish contact with Plehve's retreating Fifth Army formations. Whilst Ruzsky could claim on 26 August that he was dealing with the Austro-Hungarian attack, thereafter he had plenty of opportunity to follow orders; instead, he continued to concentrate on advancing on the Galician capital Lemberg. Throughout 27 August his troops moved forward, at first cautiously and then with growing confidence, directly towards the city. On the southern end of the battlefield, too, Brusilov's VII Corps, temporarily transferred to Ruzsky's army, worked forward, and by the end of the day, despite his intentions to press forward with an attack, Brudermann ordered his army to fall back to a salient stretching from just outside Lemberg to the stream of the Gnila Lipa, near Przemyślany. To his relief, they were able to do so during the following night and the morning of 28 August with little intervention by the Russians. Colerus was concerned that his weakened III Corps might not be able to withdraw in good order if the Russians pursued too closely; in order to buy a little space and time for the withdrawal, he ordered a limited attack on the Russians early on 28 August. German liaison officers who were present recorded that the Austrian troops involved carried out the attack with skill and determination; the rest of the corps was then able to fall back in good order.[11] A little further south, though, Russian cavalry slipped past the withdrawing infantry and penetrated into a rear area, causing panic amongst the supply elements of XII Corps before being driven off.

Even at this stage *AOK* struggled to obtain good intelligence about the strength of the forces threatening Lemberg. Although it was clear that the Russian units now crossing the Złota Lipa were substantially stronger than originally thought, the magnitude of the Russian strength remained apparently unknown, despite the excellent intelligence received before the fighting began. The reality was that whilst the Austro-Hungarian units in the area amounted to about thirteen infantry divisions, the Russians had twenty-two.[12] More details did not appear until the afternoon of 28 August, when a reconnaissance flight reported that, in addition to the units that had driven back Brudermann's army, more columns were approaching from the southeast. These were the leading divisions of the Russian VIII and XII Corps, further elements of Brusilov's army. The only units available to block them were the few formations of Böhm-Ermolli's Second Army. Hastily, a group of units, mainly reservists, amounting to perhaps three infantry divisions was scraped together under the command of General Otto Meixner von Zweienstamm and dispatched to the area west of Rohatyn. A second group was also assembled on the Dniester near Halitsch. The consequences of the confusion about Austro-Hungarian mobilisation, resulting in Böhm-Ermolli's men being sent south to face Serbia, were now being felt in full measure.

Conrad remained determined to carry out his offensive towards the north. In a forlorn attempt to obtain German cooperation, he wrote to Moltke on 28 August stating, 'Our most urgent requirement is that German forces reach the area of Siedlce as early as possible.' The town, which lay some 50 miles (80km) east of Warsaw, could only be reached by the Germans if they mounted their own offensive from the north. This meant resurrecting Conrad's hopes of a huge pincer operation to isolate the Warsaw salient. It is striking that even at this stage, when it must have been clear to Conrad that the Germans were showing no inclination to mount such an attack, he still clung to this plan. Indeed, on subsequent days he sent further telegrams to his German counterpart, congratulating him on the successes of German forces in Belgium and France and suggesting that the time had come for a German assault on Russia. This was despite the fact that Fleischmann, the Austro-Hungarian liaison officer with Hindenburg's Eighth Army, had already informed Conrad that Hindenburg intended to follow up his success against Samsonov's Second Army by turning east against Rennenkampf, rather than pressing on south to link up with the Austro-Hungarians.[13]

In the other camp, there were continuing tensions about the extended front. To the west, Evert, Fourth Army's commander, continued to express concerns for his western flank, and as previously noted, he ordered XVIII Corps, sent to him as reinforcements, to concentrate close to the Vistula. Despite this, he advised Ivanov that he might have to retreat further. Ivanov urged him to hold his positions, and after discussions with Grand Duke Nikolai, all plans for the new Ninth Army to advance west towards Germany were abandoned. Instead, the remaining two corps would be sent south to reinforce the western flank of Southwest Front. The news from the neighbouring Fifth Army was, at first, rather better, with Plehve confident that he was making headway. However, following the intervention of Archduke Joseph Ferdinand's troops and the turning of Plehve's eastern flank, Plehve had to advise Ivanov that there was no longer any prospect of him attacking and turning the eastern flank of the Austro-Hungarian troops facing Evert's Fourth Army. Nevertheless, Plehve reassured his commander, he would at least be able to hold his front.

Regardless of his concerns for the western flank, Ivanov's main preoccupation was with Ruzsky's Third Army, on two accounts. Firstly, Ruzsky had fulfilled his reputation for extreme caution, and had advanced far too slowly even for the liking of his front commander. As early as 23 August, Chief of the General Staff Yanushkevich had been advising Ivanov that the Austro-Hungarian forces were concentrating further west than expected. Ivanov in turn passed this on to Ruzsky and Brusilov but Ruzsky continued to behave as if he was faced by the massed strength of Conrad's forces.[14] On 28 August Ivanov repeated his orders for Third Army to move further northwest, but Ruzsky simply ignored him and continued to concentrate on Lemberg. Indeed, he ordered a pause for two days while the Austro-Hungarian fortifications around Lemberg were reconnoitred. In exasperation, Alexeyev sent Ruzsky a telegram:

> At the present moment the outcome of the first period of the campaign does not depend on your operations against Lvov [Lemberg] and the Dniester, but on the issue of the battle on the front Lublin–Kholm–Hrubieszów. Even the taking of Lvov would not compensate us for the loss of the battle in the north.[15]

Ivanov, too, was growing increasingly impatient, to the point where he abandoned some of his own cautious tendency. Ordering Ruzsky to cancel his two-day pause, he told his subordinate that it was the duty of the front commander to assign tasks to each army, and the duty of each army commander then to pursue the appointed task. Despite this, Ruzsky continued to insist on a pause in operations, forcing Ivanov to accept what seemed to be inevitable. From his distant headquarters, Grand Duke Nikolai also intervened:

> General Ruzsky's delay, whatever its causes, is recognised as entirely inadmissible, as it gives the enemy a breathing space, and will allow him to transfer forces from Lvov to the north. General Ruzsky must hold the enemy before him by the throat, pressing him incessantly, and developing turning movements with his right wing to the north of Lvov.[16]

On 30 August Nikolai issued further orders, which arrived in Ivanov's headquarters the following day:

> In view of a great check in the Second Army [in East Prussia], and of the necessity of finishing with the Austrians before the arrival from the west of German reinforcements, the Commander-in-Chief has ordered the Armies of the Southwest Front to pass to the most decisive action against the Austrians on the whole of your front, expressing his firm will that the forces of General Evert and Lechitsky [commander of Ninth Army] should advance wherever possible in the most determined way, so as to crush the enemy. In those sectors where the situation renders an offensive impossible, the troops must hold their positions to the last man. Tomorrow morning the Commander-in-Chief intends to be in Rovno to explain the present order.[17]

Meanwhile, events were progressing in eastern Galicia. Aware that Brudermann's northern flank was threatened, Conrad responded in characteristic manner by ordering an attack on the Russians to drive them back all along the front. To this end, two cavalry divisions, reinforced by four battalions of reservist infantry, were ordered to advance to Żółkiew to try to turn the Russian northern flank. They managed to reach Kulików on 29 August, but could go no further. Reinforcements had arrived for Brudermann's forces in the shape of the Kaiser Rifle Brigade, and Colerus distributed its personnel to the battered divisions of III Corps. However, these reinforcements were of little value when the Russians to the east of Lemberg mounted a crushing artillery bombardment. Once again the Austro-Hungarian gunners were outclassed, matters worsened by poor supply arrangements. The seam between III and XII Corps came under heavy pressure, and only by rapid deployment of newly arrived reserve battalions was Brudermann able to hold the front. By contrast, the southern flank of XII Corps made some headway at first, but by the end of 29 August, the intervention of the Russian VII Corps from the south drove the Austro-Hungarian forces back over the Gnila Lipa. Believing that all was lost, many units simply melted away, their survivors fleeing far to the rear. An attempt by those elements of the Austro-Hungarian Second Army's VII Corps, newly arrived from the Serbian front, to mount a counterattack from the south achieved little of significance. In any event, the arrival of the Russian XII Corps, another of Brusilov's formations, in its rear brought any prospect of success to an end.

Communications in the Austro-Hungarian Second Army were not good, partly due to its piecemeal arrival from the Serbian front. Böhm-Ermolli received little information about the progress – or otherwise – of VII Corps, and at the end of the day assumed that all was going well. He merely reiterated his orders for a further attack to drive back the Russian forces threatening the southern flank of Brudermann's army. Meixner, the commander of VII Corps, was similarly uncertain about the whereabouts of his formations, and attempted to advance both north and east. Neither attack made much headway; the latter ran into far stronger Russian forces advancing westwards, and was put to flight.

Fighting extended right along the front line on 30 August. Everywhere, the Russians pressed forward against their opponents. In some areas the Austro-Hungarians were able to mount effective counterattacks, but these were too few, and too isolated, to be exploited into full-scale successes. The decisive moment of the day came when Kövess' XII Corps was overwhelmed by a major attack and driven back in disorder. At first Brudermann tried to limit the damage to his position by issuing orders to pull back the southern flank of his army, but as the northern flank also began to come under pressure, he had to consider a more substantial withdrawal. Back in Przemyśl, Conrad had been inspired by the success of Hindenburg in East Prussia, and now planned to attempt something similar to restore his own position. As soon as it had successfully defeated the Russian forces around Komarów, Auffenberg's Fourth Army was to turn southeast, in order to attack the exposed northern flank of the Russian forces around Lemberg. It would take another day or two for Auffenberg to complete his operations in the north, and Brudermann was therefore given permission to shorten his front and to withdraw to a line extending due south from Lemberg. Orders were issued to this effect late on 30 August.

The two-day battle along the Gnila Lipa had cost Conrad's armies another 20,000 casualties, and the loss of 70 guns. While the slow process of Russian mobilisation continued to run its course, bringing new formations to the front line to replace those that had been mauled by the early Austro-Hungarian successes, the armies of the Dual Monarchy received only a few battalions of reservists. All of this could have been anticipated; the decision to allow so much of Second Army to spend the precious weeks of early mobilisation travelling first to Serbia, and then – slowly – back to the north, did much to eliminate any advantage that faster mobilisation might have given to the Austro-Hungarians.

But if the Austro-Hungarians squandered their early advantage, the Russians did their best to repay the compliment. Ruzsky continued to prevaricate, advancing with astonishing caution, and Brudermann was able to pull his army back to its new positions almost unmolested. Conrad's spirits lifted when news arrived from Auffenberg's headquarters that the Russian forces involved in the fighting around Komarów had been destroyed, and that it would therefore be possible for the victorious Fourth Army to attack towards Lemberg as planned. Consequently, Conrad concluded that Brudermann could abandon Lemberg for the moment, if required. The aged fortifications were of limited military value, and any political damage resulting from the loss of the city would be short-term, rapidly offset by a dazzling victory as Auffenberg crushed the Russian troops advancing from the east.

The last day of August passed with comparatively little fighting. In the southeast Brusilov's army continued to move forward through the province of Bukovina, and the weak screen of Austro-Hungarian units facing him fell back. The Austro-Hungarian governor of Bukovina left on 31 August, by which time rumours were circulating widely about the mistreatment of civilians – especially Jews – at the hands of the Russians. Given the events of the coming decades, it is remarkable to note that the Austrians had a better record of tolerance towards communities like the Jews than some of the 'subordinate' nationalities of the Dual Monarchy, perhaps because those nationalities at least partly defined themselves in terms of excluding those they regarded as outsiders. Regardless of such nuances within the Austro-Hungarian Empire, the pogroms against Jews in the tsar's empire were well known, and the most lurid stories were therefore granted a degree of credibility. Affluent Jews began to leave Czernowitz, the largest town in Bukovina, even before the governor had done so. However, there was widespread consternation at the end of August when news arrived that the railway line running west from the town had been cut by Cossack patrols. Further transport problems were caused by the destruction of bridges over the River Pruth by the rearguard of 35th *Landsturm* Infantry Brigade. Stripped of even its police force, Czernowitz was declared an open city, and several thousand Jewish families fled along the roads running south as the Russians arrived in early September.

Dr Salo Weisselberger, the Jewish town mayor, remained behind with most of the population. The first Russian troops to arrive were Cossacks from the Ural Mountains, commanded by General Aryutinov. To the dismay of Weisselberger and others, Aryutinov demanded the payment of a large sum in gold to the Russian authorities; he took twenty-three citizens hostage, both to ensure good order and to force the payment of the demanded gold. It seems that in this part of Europe discipline amongst the occupying forces was not as good as elsewhere. Compared to the punishments meted out by Samsonov for infringements in East Prussia, there was little attempt to restrain Aryutinov's Cossacks from taking whatever they wished. Moreover, it seems that some local elements took advantage of the situation to turn on the Jews. Many of the Jews who had fled took up arms against the Russians in the southern edge of Bukovina, which remained unoccupied. Weisselberger himself was arrested, and deported to Siberia. While some locals joined the Cossacks in their attacks on the Jews, others stood by their neighbours. Vladimir von Repta, the Greek Orthodox Archbishop of Bukovina, intervened to prevent the burning of the synagogue. He had the Torah scrolls transferred to his own residence, kept them safe until the end of the war, and then returned them to the Chief Rabbi.[18]

Meanwhile, Conrad issued further orders to prepare for what he hoped would be a decisive blow by Auffenberg's Fourth Army. A further advance towards the north was of little value, given that the Germans showed no sign of mounting a matching attack from the north. Leaving only four infantry divisions and two cavalry divisions facing north, under the collective command of Archduke Joseph Ferdinand, Auffenberg was to turn and march southeast. His orders were to be ready for battle in the Uhnów–Bełżec area, about 25 miles (40km) north of Lemberg, by 3 September. But even before Auffenberg's men could reach this start line, events around the Galician capital moved forward. Late on 1 September panic swept through some Hungarian reservist units north of the city, and they abandoned the front line, fleeing back to Lemberg. The cause of this was the advance of a Russian column through the woodland northwest of the city. Already faced with a large hole in his line to the south, where XII Corps had been withdrawn – the gap was intended to be filled by further units of Second Army as they arrived – Brudermann concluded that there was no prospect of his army holding its positions. At 2 a.m. on 2 September he signalled *AOK* that he intended to withdraw behind the Wereszyca, where he felt he stood a better chance of being able to hold his front line. Whatever Conrad's views about such a retreat, he had no choice but to agree; it was clear that Brudermann could only hold his current line with substantial reinforcements, which simply were not available. When Brudermann added that even this retreat might not be enough if his army came under prolonged pressure, Conrad again had to concede that his subordinate was probably right.

The last Austro-Hungarian troops abandoned Lemberg on 2 September. The ever-cautious Ruzsky had reached the outskirts of the Galician capital the previous day, and spent the first two days of September sending out small reconnaissance units to check whether the extensive – though elderly – fortifications around Lemberg held any surprises. Finally, a day after the last defenders had left, he entered the town. It was hardly in keeping with Grand Duke Nikolai's instructions to keep at the throat of his enemy. Like many cities across the eastern parts of the Austro-Hungarian Empire and the western parts of the Russian Empire, Lemberg had a very mixed population. The 1910 census recorded that 51 per cent of the population were Catholics, 28 per cent Jews, and 19 per cent were members of the Ukrainian Orthodox Church. As a consequence, a sizable part of the population welcomed the Russian troops as they arrived, though as was the case in Bukovina, others – particularly the Jews – chose to leave.

It was the end of Brudermann's command of Third Army. He had risen to high rank through a mixture of good fortune and patronage, and prior to 1914 had never commanded troops in battle. As Inspector General of the Cavalry, he had resisted instructions to give cavalrymen uniforms that paid more attention to the needs of camouflage than display, and like many officers of the era he had remained wedded to a desire to see cavalry operating in dense formations, delivering an attack that owed more to weight of bone, muscle, and steel than to firepower. It was inevitable that he would struggle to adapt to the realities of war, and almost all of his decisions during the fighting east of Lemberg ended disastrously. Nevertheless, he made those decisions with the full knowledge of Conrad, who failed to pass on intelligence to Brudermann about the true strength of the Russian forces in eastern Galicia. It seems that, to some extent, Conrad used Brudermann as a convenient scapegoat for failings that were as much due to him as they were to the commander of Third Army. He was dismissed from his post on 3 September. After a short period without a post, Brudermann requested permission to retire from military service, and this was granted in late November. His replacement as commander of the battered formations of Third Army was Svetozar Boroević, a Croatian who had seen action in Bosnia and had commanded VI Corps during August. He had a very different personality compared to Brudermann, and had impressed Auffenberg, his former army commander:

> He was as gifted as he was determined – a steely sort of leader. Ambitious in the
> extreme, he subordinated all to his aims and intentions. Completely unhindered
> by any emotional baggage, he pursued his path through thick and thin, which he
> did not doubt would lead him to his objective.[19]

Conrad's armies now prepared for his counterattack, designed to restore the advantage to the forces of the Dual Monarchy. But the move of Auffenberg's army towards the southeast rested upon the assumption that the Russian Fifth Army had been decisively defeated. The reality was that although Auffenberg had mauled many of its formations, the Fifth Army remained a powerful force. In addition, Auffenberg's men were weary from their exertions against Plehve's Fifth Army, and as with all armies of the era, the Austro-Hungarian logistic services failed to deliver sufficient ammunition and supplies to restore their fighting power. The slower pace of Russian mobilisation now became something of an advantage. Forced to retreat along their axis of supply, the units of Fifth Army received a steady stream of reinforcements, and were rapidly reinvigorated. In addition to Auffenberg's attack, Second Army, which now had a few more divisions in its strength – even though large elements were still detained on the Serbian front – was ordered to attack from the south, in the hope of achieving an encirclement to match the German success at Tannenberg. Meanwhile, Ivanov finally prevailed upon Ruzsky to turn northwest, so that he could march to the aid of Plehve's army. Unwittingly, the Russians and Austro-Hungarians thus created the circumstances that would lead to a head-on collision between Auffenberg's Fourth Army and Ruzsky's Third Army.

In northwest Galicia the Austro-Hungarian advance towards Lublin had reached its high-water mark on 1 September. The following day, even as the exhausted troops of Dankl's divisions gathered their strength for a further effort, troops from the Russian III Caucasian Corps, together with 2nd Grenadier Division and 1st Guards Infantry Division, massed for a major counterattack. Originally, these forces were to deploy to the west of Lublin, but as the greatest threat to the city appeared to be from the southeast, where the inner flanks of Dankl's and Auffenberg's armies had cooperated most effectively, they detrained to the east of Lublin and attacked from there. The blow fell on 24th Infantry Division and 2nd Infantry Division. Promised reinforcements had not arrived, and the Austro-Hungarians were desperately short of ammunition, having been in near-continuous combat for eleven days. Reluctantly, they fell back, hoping that they might be able to restore their forward momentum the following day. 24th Infantry Division came under heavy attack again on 3 September, and at first managed to fend off the Russians. After another day of bloody fighting, both sides found themselves roughly where they had started. On 4 September further Russian attacks towards the southeast from Lublin increased the pressure on Dankl's First Army. A gap had opened between V and X Corps, and the weakened 3rd Cavalry Division was ordered to plug this at all costs until reinforcements arrived. On the extreme western flank Kummer's group bloodily repulsed a Russian outflanking attack, but such local successes could not disguise the fact that the initiative lay firmly with the Russians, who now significantly outnumbered their opponents, and were able to exploit to the full the open terrain, which gave the Austro-Hungarian defenders few natural features that could hold up their opponents. By 4 September Dankl had thirteen infantry divisions, two cavalry divisions, and five brigades of *Landsturm* reservists with which to confront twenty-two infantry divisions and two cavalry divisions. In addition, many of the Russian units had only just arrived at the front, whereas almost all the Austro-Hungarian divisions were badly worn down by heavy fighting. With Auffenberg's army turning away to the southeast, Dankl had to pull back X Corps on his right flank, something that did not escape the notice of Plehve's most westerly units. Some elements of X Corps had not pulled back in time, and were overwhelmed by Russian formations from XXV Corps. Under heavy artillery fire X Corps began to give way, and Dankl had no choice but to order a further withdrawal of his eastern flank.

5 September saw X Corps retreating steadily, but the heavy fighting had taken its toll on the Russian XXV Corps, and as the day progressed the pace of the Russian pursuit eased somewhat. For X Corps, whose divisions were generally reduced to only one-third of their establishment strength, this came as a welcome

relief. On Dankl's other flank, too, the Russians did not press as hard as they had done on preceding days. More seriously, the gap between Dankl's eastern flank and Auffenberg's army yawned ever wider, and the Russian XIX Corps advanced almost unopposed to capture Zamość; Joseph Ferdinand's divisions, which had been ordered to fill the gap, were still some distance to the east. Despite having made this advance, the Russians failed to exploit their advantage. Dankl's battered, exhausted formations plodded back to the south, and the momentary opportunity for the Russians to trap and destroy them vanished as quickly as it had appeared. Further east the Russian Fifth Army moved into a position where it could threaten the rear of Auffenberg's forces, which had so nearly destroyed the Russians just a few days earlier.

As Ruzsky turned to the northwest, he found new reasons for delay, informing Ivanov that he was increasingly concerned about the seam between his southern or left flank and the nearest troops of Brusilov's Eighth Army. There was little to fear, given the losses suffered by Brudermann's Third Army, but it took further strong words from Southwest Front Headquarters to persuade Ruzsky to follow instructions. Facing him were Auffenberg's IX, VI, and XVII Corps, deployed from west to east from Niemirów to Rawa Ruska. Conrad was deeply worried that the Russians would drive into the gap between Auffenberg's southwest flank and Third Army's northern flank, and ordered Auffenberg to keep this flank of his army strong. The consequence was that the eastern flank of Fourth Army, which was completely exposed, was far weaker than Auffenberg might have wished.[20]

On 6 September Feldzugmeister von Friedei ordered his IX Corps forward into the woodland south of Niemirów on the western flank. VI Corps, under Feldmarschalleutnant von Arz, was in the centre, and XVII Corps, commanded by Feldmarschalleutnant Křitek, was on the eastern flank to the southeast of Rawa Ruska. Even as the three corps moved off, Auffenberg became aware of the sounds of artillery fire to the north, where the supposedly defeated remnants of Plehve's army had retreated. Unable to find out more about what was happening, he had to hope for the best and concentrate on his attack. XVII Corps reported the presence of a Russian division to its east, but the other two corps initially encountered little resistance.

The troops opposing Křitek's XVII Corps were from the Russian IX Corps. At first the Austro-Hungarian units made good progress, but the threat to the flank remained. VI Corps encountered the Russian X Corps during the fternoon, and intensifying Russian artillery fire brought Arz's men to a halt. Although IX Corps on the western flank continued to report little resistance, the sandy roads took their toll on Friedei's tired men, and their advance, too, slowed.

Auffenberg was frustrated by lack of information. The hills and woods on his eastern flank made it difficult to assess the threat from the Russian division that had been reported there, and intelligence from all three corps of the forces they faced was patchy at best. There remained the worrying sounds of fighting to the north, and Auffenberg's anxieties were deepened by the receipt of an indecipherable coded telegram from Archduke Joseph Ferdinand. In fact, the distant sound of artillery from the north marked the beginning of the southward advance of Plehve's Fifth Army. Nevertheless, both Auffenberg and Boroević issued orders to their armies. As Fourth Army's western flank approached from the north, Third Army's northern flank would establish contact; then the entire Third Army would commence its own advance. The immediate objective for Fourth Army was to secure the town of Magierów and the high ground immediately to the north, while the eastern flank was to advance to the southeast, in order to cut off the expected line of retreat of the Russian forces facing Fourth Army. Unable to obtain any clear idea of what was happening to the north, Auffenberg could only hope that the forces covering his rear – predominantly the troops under Archduke Joseph Ferdinand – would be sufficient to deal with any advance by the supposedly defeated Russian Fifth Army.

The Russian high command was equally unsure about the overall situation. Ivanov had finally prevailed upon the reluctant Ruzsky to turn towards the northwest, but he had expected Auffenberg's army still to be facing north. Consequently, Third Army was expected to encounter few Austro-Hungarian troops until it reached the rear area of the Austro-Hungarian Fourth Army. However, fortune was on the side of the Russians. As Auffenberg and Ruzsky collided, the right flank of the Russian Third Army, formed by XXI Corps, extended beyond the left flank of the Austro-Hungarian Fourth Army, and in a battle of roughly equal forces, this small advantage would prove critical. During the night of 6/7 September, two battalions of Austro-Hungarian troops moved out towards the west to protect Auffenberg's open flank. In confused woodland fighting they initially made headway, but were then enveloped and overwhelmed. Their commander Oberst Brosch, a personal friend of Auffenberg, was amongst the dead. The complete destruction of Brosch's battalions prevented any news of the setback – and therefore the magnitude of the threat to Auffenberg's eastern flank – from becoming known to the Austro-Hungarian high command until the following afternoon.

A little further north the advance of the Russian XXI Corps from the east was spotted by elements of Archduke Joseph Ferdinand's forces. The archduke, who was close at hand, immediately marched to intercept the Russians at Waręż on 6 September, but soon discovered that the Russians were present in greater strength than expected. Aware that this Russian force posed a serious threat to Auffenberg's rear, the archduke summoned more troops from his command. At the same time, though, his men had to cope with the southward advance of Plehve's revitalised Fifth Army. It was impossible for the battle-weary and badly depleted Austro-Hungarian divisions to perform both tasks. To make matters worse, Conrad now ordered Joseph Ferdinand to march to the aid of Dankl's hard-pressed First Army. Far from being able to perform this multitude of tasks, the archduke became acutely aware of his own precarious position, with the Russian XXI Corps to his east, the advancing forces of Plehve's Fifth Army to the north, and a threat from the west as Dankl retreated towards the south.

Auffenberg was reduced to little more than a spectator as Conrad issued orders to the units that were supposed to be protecting Fourth Army's rear, as he recorded in his diary:

> Our left is weak, and will be hard put to hold off a major assault. But First Army command and *AOK* repeatedly call for help from Joseph Ferdinand's group. *AOK* in particular waxes eloquent on this. Yet this was a force above all intended to protect my rear, without which I would never have marched south. Do they not understand that?[21]

Instead of being protected by the considerable forces of the archduke, Auffenberg was to be left with only a single weak cavalry division covering his rear area. But even these orders from Conrad were rapidly countermanded. Instead, Joseph Ferdinand was instructed to send two divisions to protect Auffenberg's left rear, while three divisions were to be sent to support Dankl. Aware that the Russian advances from the north were increasingly rendering Conrad's orders both out of date and irrelevant, Joseph Ferdinand did what he could to protect Fourth Army, trying to concentrate his troops directly to the north of Rawa Ruska.

On 7 September Auffenberg learned that he had been awarded the Military Order of Maria Theresa, regarded as the highest honour that could be awarded to an Austro-Hungarian commander, and the Grand Cross of the Order of Leopold, for his victory at Komarów. The battle that was rapidly developing left him no time to celebrate. The significance of the loss of the two battalions that had been overrun during the night on the eastern flank became increasingly clear as the morning progressed, and Křitek's XVII Corps found itself under mounting pressure as increasing numbers of Russian troops from XXI Corps emerged from the woods and hills that had masked their approach. At first Křitek tried to advance, as he had been ordered, but Feltmarschalleutnant Wittmann, commanding the units on the eastern flank, reported Russian units moving further and further north. By the end of the day Křitek had been forced to adopt an almost semicircular line, facing south, east, and even north. One of the few crumbs of comfort for Auffenberg was the success enjoyed by the cavalry on the eastern flank. To his satisfaction they had dismounted and taken up defensive positions in trenches, from where they beat off repeated Russian attacks. Prior to the war he had tried in vain to persuade the cavalry to modernise both its tactics and equipment to make such battles part of the cavalry's standard repertoire. Elsewhere, Russian resistance slowed Auffenberg's advance to a crawl. There could no longer be any doubt; far from advancing into the exposed flank of the Russian Army that had taken Lemberg, the Austro-Hungarian Fourth Army faced a head-to-head frontal battle. Still seeking an attacking solution to his problems, Conrad ordered Auffenberg's army to tie down the Russian forces facing it, while Second Army, at the southeast end of his line, now took the offensive against Brusilov's Eighth Army.

Whilst this change of emphasis took account of the diminishing chances of Auffenberg mounting a successful counteroffensive from the north, it also required Second Army – still not at full strength – to attack across difficult terrain. The insistence on offensive operations ignored the reality that the land to the south of Lemberg was perfectly suited for defensive action. The three rivers running from north to south in their deep ravines, the small areas of woodland, and the hilly terrain created conditions in which relatively small forces could at the very least inflict time-consuming delays on an attack. During the fighting in late August Conrad's repeated attacks on the advancing Russians prevented his troops from using the ground to their advantage, and the new operational plan repeated this. The relative ease with which the Russians advanced over the same terrain was largely due to their opponents' own failed attacks leaving them in no state to mount an organised defence. Writing after the war, Auffenberg summed up his feelings at the time:

> One can twist and turn, as one will, but this originally unplanned attack with a strong, decisive southern flank had no tactical or strategic benefits, and was only chosen because there simply wasn't any alternative. With no success on the left, one tried on the right, once the seed had been sown of risking a battle. One wanted to parade the recapture of Lemberg before the public.[22]

The Russians, too, were modifying their plans. Brusilov was ordered to attack south of Lemberg between Janow and Gródek, with a view to breaking the

Austro-Hungarian line and driving the southern part away to the south. This was at least partially to alleviate Ruzsky's fears for his left flank. As it happened, Böhm-Ermolli managed to get his attack underway first, though a mixture of factors – delays in the arrival of troops from the Serbian front, and casualties amongst those who had already been facing the Russian Eighth Army in battles for the past two weeks – resulted in only modest gains on 8 September. Other, deep-seated problems also played a major part:

> Unfortunately, the Austro-Hungarian infantry had still not abandoned their peacetime doctrine of attacking. They stormed forward impatiently, without waiting for their artillery to make an impact, and making negligible efforts to coordinate with flanking units, and not infrequently ran into an enemy who proved to be tough, resilient and battle-hardened. This is what happened here. After initially making considerable gains, first the *Honvéd*, then 34th Infantry Division, and finally all of VII Corps were forced to retreat in the afternoon.[23]

The retreat of VII Corps threatened to become a rout, and General Karl Tersztyánszky, who had been promoted on the battlefield to command of IV Corps, was ordered to take command of the sector. Most of his troops were south of the Dniester, and he immediately issued orders for the bulk of IV Corps to cross the river. However, just as the terrain had favoured the Russian defenders, so it now came to the aid of VII Corps and the first battalions of IV Corps to reach it. The Russian counterattack rapidly broke down. Similar events took place further north, with the fragile morale of the attacking Austro-Hungarian troops rapidly evaporating when they ran into determined Russian troops. Even if the overall advance was minimal, Brusilov's own offensive plans had to be abandoned. For the moment, all his energies turned to containing the attacks by the Austro-Hungarian Second and Third Armies.

From the perspective of the Russians, Brusilov's Eighth Army had to do no more than hold his ground. Ruzsky's Third Army continued to face Auffenberg in an increasingly bloody stalemate, but all the time, Plehve's Fifth Army closed in on the rear of Auffenberg's Fourth Army. Ultimately, time was on the side of the Russians. Unless Conrad and his army commanders could achieve a striking success, Fourth Army would eventually find itself almost surrounded.

As was the case almost everywhere in 1914, a striking success proved beyond the reach of the *k.u.k.* Army. Fighting continued to rage along Auffenberg's entire front on 8 September, and the dismounted cavalry divisions trying to protect his eastern flank struggled to hold back the Russians. Amongst their losses on

8 September was the young Herbert Conrad, son of the chief of the general staff, near Rawa Ruska. He was buried on the battlefield, and the following day, when his unit was forced to concede ground, his unmarked grave passed into Russian hands. His father was deeply affected by the death of his son, even if the developing crisis left him little time for personal grief. A year later, he wrote to his mistress Gina von Reininghaus, that 'this shadow will always hang over my life'.[24]

Auffenberg had passed the stage where he felt that he could achieve victory. Aerial reconnaissance reported that the roads running north from Lemberg were packed with Russian troops hastening to assemble against his exposed flank. Even without the intervention of Plehve's Fifth Army, the Austro-Hungarian Fourth Army was outnumbered nearly 2:1 in infantry, and 3:2 in artillery. Glumly, he recorded in his diary that he had been ordered to renew his attacks, even though he rated the chances of success as minimal.[25] Reports from everywhere brought bad news; the rear areas were choked with wounded, and one infantry division sent a messenger to tell Auffenberg that it had almost no officers left. Ammunition was also running short, but for the moment, his men continued to hold the line. Casualties mounted on both sides, in numbers that dwarfed even the most pessimistic pre-war estimates. But the battle was being decided elsewhere; to the north, Plehve's V and XVII Corps now reached Komarów. Archduke Joseph Ferdinand could send only a single division to block their further advance.

For Conrad all depended on whether Second and Third Armies could achieve a decisive victory in the south. Although they gained considerable ground on 9 September, and Brusilov was forced to pull back XXIV Corps, there was still no sign of a decisive outcome. During the evening Ivanov's chief of staff spoke to Brusilov by telephone, urging him to hold on. By contrast, Conrad was beginning to accept the inevitability of defeat. While First Army was ordered to fall back to the line of the River San, Conrad personally travelled to the Wereszyca Front in an almost desperate attempt to urge Second and Third Armies to save the day. Despite their best efforts, the task was beyond them. Many units reported that they were down to less than 25 per cent establishment strength, and even these were desperately short of supplies. Nevertheless, the slow Austro-Hungarian advance – and the failure of Ruzsky's troops to advance towards Rawa Ruska – continued to create anxieties in the Russian ranks. Ivanov urged Plehve to accelerate his advance. Böhm-Ermolli continued to believe that he was within reach of the outskirts of Lemberg, and that if he could maintain his advance for another day, it would be possible for Third Army to his north to begin to advance, thus relieving the frontal pressure on Auffenberg's Fourth Army. But such a task was beyond the strength of his depleted battalions. On 10 September *AOK* received the text of a radio intercept, ordering Plehve's V and XVII Corps to advance and cut the roads running west from Rawa Ruska, thus putting them directly on Auffenberg's line of retreat. Still hoping that Second Army would achieve a miracle in the south, Conrad ordered Auffenberg and Joseph Ferdinand to counterattack with all available forces. But the divisions of the archduke's group had been in almost continuous action for eighteen days, and they barely had the strength to hold their positions, still less to mount a counterattack. Finally, during the afternoon of 11 September the exhausted men of Second Army, after three days of hard fighting, reached the objectives that had been assigned for them for the first day of their attack. When they reported that they could go no further, Conrad reluctantly gave the order for a general withdrawal of all his armies.

On his own initiative Auffenberg had already ordered many of his rear area units to start moving westwards on 9 September. Nevertheless, the order to retreat came as a bitter blow to a man whose army had spilt so much of its blood in the fighting around Rawa Ruska. He ordered his cavalry, which had fought so hard to hold his eastern flank, to proceed immediately to the west, in an attempt to ensure that the roads that would be vital for a retreat were kept open. In an increasingly chaotic stream, under skies that suddenly turned to rain, the Austro-Hungarian troops wearily marched west towards the River San. Although the Russians had created a winning position, they now failed to exploit it:

> Our armies' heavy losses and fatigue unfortunately prevented us from pursuing the enemy closely. The commander of Southwest Front deemed it indispensible to give the troops a period of rest, to replenish them and reorganise rear areas. The supply services remained far behind the troops, who were short of bread and particularly of salt.[26]

In truth, Ivanov's armies were now as exhausted as their Austro-Hungarian counterparts. Nevertheless, Ivanov made little effort to urge them onwards, at a time when one more effort might have dealt an irreparable blow to Conrad's forces. A more forceful commander might have ignored these problems in an attempt to secure a decisive victory, in the manner of Mackensen's determined drive to complete the encirclement of Samsonov's Second Army. Instead, troops were allowed to rest, reserves and supplies were brought forward, and in the case of Ruzsky's army considerable efforts were spent – or wasted – on rebuilding and strengthening the fortifications around Lemberg. Nevertheless, there could be little doubt about who had triumphed. A Russian officer described the moment when his men, part of Third Army, finally took possession of a fiercely contested valley:

> When we attacked at 3 o'clock in the morning, the gorge contained 15,000 Austrians, a large proportion of whom were mowed down by the artillery fire which ploughed through the valley in the darkness. The Austrians surrendered and we entered the gorge to receive their arms, while their general stood quietly on a hill watching the scene. Eight of his standards being turned over to the Russians was more than he could bear, for he drew a pistol and shot himself.[27]

The official communiqué issued by Conrad's *AOK* tried to put the best possible light on matters:

> In the fighting around Lemberg, our troops on and south of the Grodek road succeeded in driving back the enemy in a tough five-day battle, taking 10,000 prisoners and capturing numerous guns. But this success could not be fully exploited, as our northern flank at Rawa Ruska was threatened by greatly superior forces and new Russian forces advanced both against Dankl's army and into the area between this army and the Lemberg battlefield. In view of the enemy's great numerical superiority, it was necessary to assemble our armies, which had been locked in heroic combat continuously for three weeks, in a suitable area and prepare them for further operations.[28]

The most important question was where this suitable area lay, and whether the shattered armies could reach it. The line of the San proved to be indefensible, not least because the Germans recommended a line further west, where they would be able to offer more immediate support. A retreat further west, though, would force Conrad to abandon the huge fortress of Przemyśl. After discussions with Ludendorff, Conrad left a garrison of six divisions in the fortress and allowed it to be encircled. His armies continued their retreat.

There were major changes in command in the aftermath of the fighting. Zhilinski, commander of Northwest Front, was removed from his post following the failure of the Russian First and Second Armies in East Prussia. His replacement, slightly surprisingly, was Ruzsky, whose conduct of operations with Third Army had been so dilatory that even the cautious Ivanov had grown impatient. It seems that Sukhomlinov's powers of patronage remained strong enough to protect those he regarded as his supporters. The new commander of Third Army was the colourful Radko Dimitriev, who had commanded VIII Corps in Brusilov's

Eighth Army. Born in modern-day Bulgaria, he took part in a popular rising against Turkish rule in 1876, aged only 16. Following the suppression of the rising he left his homeland for Russia, where he served with the Russian Army before returning to Bulgaria. In 1886 he was involved in a plot with fellow pro-Russian officers to force the abdication of Prince Alexander of Battenberg. He was exiled again, spending ten years in Russian military service, from where he continued to be involved in attempts to topple the Bulgarian government. In 1898 he returned once more to Bulgaria, rising rapidly to become Chief of the General Staff in 1904. He was in Russia at the outbreak of the First World War, acting as Bulgarian military plenipotentiary, and immediately rejoined the Russian Army. After enjoying some success with VIII Corps, he was now given his most important command yet.

There were mixed opinions in Russian circles about how best to deal with the fortress of Przemyśl. *Stavka* was concerned about the army's shortage of heavy artillery, and doubted that it would be possible to reduce the fortress rapidly. Perhaps emboldened by the successes of his armies, Ivanov contrastingly reported that the garrison was weak, and that Przemyśl could be captured with relative ease. Brusilov, whose army bypassed the town, was of a similar opinion:

> The investment of Przemyśl was entrusted to the new commander of Third Army, Radko Dimitriev, who when he was in command of VIII Corps of my army, and earlier, in the Turco-Bulgarian War, had struck me as a strong-minded, quick-witted and capable officer. I did not doubt for a moment that at this juncture he would display these same military qualities and would attempt to take Przemyśl without more ado, which would have freed our hands, established us firmly in eastern Galicia, and given us an opportunity of pushing onward without meeting any resistance and without leaving behind us an enemy fortress and a besieged city. Indeed, after such a succession of defeats and heavy losses, the Austrian Army was so demoralised and Przemyśl so little prepared to stand a siege (for its garrison, composed of beaten troops, was far from steady), that I was absolutely convinced that by the middle of October the place could have been taken by assault without any serious artillery preparation. But the days passed and no effort was made to take Przemyśl.[29]

The reality was a little different from Brusilov's optimistic view. The Austro-Hungarian troops had strengthened the considerable fortifications around the town with an additional 30 miles (50km) of trenches and hundreds of miles of barbed wire, to create a total of seven defensive rings around

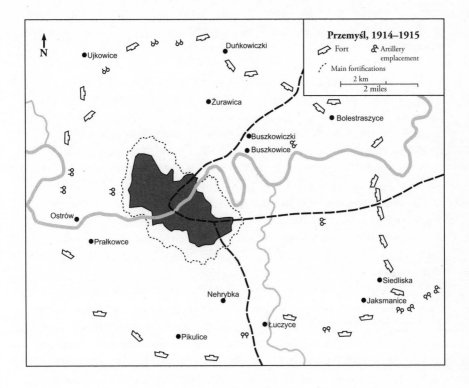

Przemyśl. When Dimitriev reached the area on 24 September, he surrounded the town with six divisions, and after a brief – and ineffectual – bombardment by his artillery, he ordered his men to storm the defences, much as Brusilov had expected. Contrary to the expectations of both Brusilov and his former corps commander, the garrison, commanded by Feldmarschalleutnant von Kusmanek, put up a tough fight. After three days, and 40,000 casualties, Dimitriev had to abandon the assault. His divisions, already weakened by the fighting east of Lemberg, sat back to nurse their wounds. Inside the fortifications the garrison – for whom no fewer than fifteen languages were required to ensure all personnel understood their orders – glowered back defiantly.

Life within Przemyśl rapidly settled into a routine. Despite being provisioned for a long siege, there were problems with supplies for ordinary soldiers, who appeared to have plenty of money, but little on which to spend it. One of the 18,000 civilians who were trapped in the fortress along with over 120,000 soldiers was Helena Jabłońska, a middle-aged widow, who kept a diary throughout the siege. During October she commented on the apparent shortages of food for the garrison, and the increasing effect of disease, both features that would have been familiar to veterans of sieges throughout history:

> Soldiers are out on the streets begging. A few of them were trying to thrust ten, fifteen crowns at me to buy some bread, a few rolls, some chocolate. One offered me five crowns to bring him a glass of tea, saying I had to bring it and that he would wait. He was Romanian. I went back home and fetched the food I had made for Pegan, potato broth and some rice, and gave it to him. He was so happy he shouted for joy and tried to thrust two five-crown notes into my pockets. I did not accept them, of course. He must have thought this was still too little, for he pulled out a silver watch and wanted me to take it. Other soldiers crowded around me, taking out their money and waving it at me. I hurried home again and fetched a hunk of bread, a few apples, a few boiled potatoes and half a kilo of sugar, which were all I had left. They gobbled it all up and wanted to pay. You can make a fortune, but seeing it all is enough to break your heart.
>
> The municipal authorities try to regulate prices but then all the goods vanish. All shops are closed, so you have to go round the back. The Jewish women in basements rip you off the worst. People say they purposely rent basements with windows onto the street, so that they can pass goods out through a crack, never showing more than a few items at a time, a few bread rolls or eggs. You see whole groups of soldiers huddled around these little windows...
>
> Vast numbers of wounded are being brought in. Many of them die from severe blood loss, but the death toll would not be half as great were it not for cholera. It is spreading so fast that the cases outnumber those wounded and killed in battle. Everything has been infected: carts, stretchers, rooms, wardens, streets, manure, mud, everything. Soldiers fall in battle, and it is impossible to remove the bodies and disinfect them. They don't even bother.[30]

The siege saw a remarkable innovation: the world's first airmail service, carried out by a mixture of fixed-wing and balloon vehicles, as well as pigeons. One flight crashed in Russian-held territory; the letters were sent to Russia for censorship, and were then passed on to their addressees.[31]

Meanwhile the San line was abandoned even before all the Austro-Hungarian armies had reached it. The retreat continued to the valleys of the Dunajec and Biała Rivers, where, in mid-September, the two sides finally halted. The Russian armies that had first been driven back in western Galicia, and had then mounted an assault across the entire front, were as battered and weakened as the Austro-Hungarian armies that they had pursued. In the words of a Russian commentator:

The success was dearly bought ... the victor was indistinguishable from the defeated; he lacked the strength to exploit the advantages of victory through a vigorous pursuit.[32]

On the Austro-Hungarian side, the disappointment that accompanied the defeat in Galicia, made all the worse by the initial successes at Kraśnik and Komarów, rapidly turned into a search for a scapegoat. On 29 September Auffenberg was stunned to receive a letter from Archduke Frederick, the nominal supreme commander of the *k.u.k.* Army:

> Personal contact with Fourth Army has made me realise that quite extraordinary demands will be made of the army leadership in the near future.
>
> The condition of the army makes it imperative that in the forthcoming days of decision, there stands at the summit a commander who not only has the full confidence of the army but who also can lead the army in combat in the most complete physical and mental freshness, with a strong will and belief in victory.
>
> Since, to my bitterest regret, I have gained the impression that your Excellency's capabilities and resilience have suffered as a consequence of the fate that has befallen Fourth Army in these difficult days of trial, I call upon you to give to your Fatherland the greatest sacrifice that a soldier can be asked to make, that is, to report sick and to resign the command of Fourth Army.
>
> In the fullest appreciation of your long, honourable service in the armed forces, your quite extraordinary recognition and – equally outstanding – magnificent performance against the enemy, I hope that you will recover your full health as quickly as possible.[33]

It was a hard pill for Auffenberg to swallow. He had commanded Fourth Army to what he personally regarded – with some justification – as the greatest victory ever won by Austria against Russia at Komarów, and had then overseen an almost 180 degree reorientation of his units. At Rawa Ruska he and his men, although outnumbered, had done all that could be expected of them. Finally, he had conducted a fighting retreat to the line of the San, constantly in danger of being completely cut off and surrounded. His entry in his diary is full of the bitterness of a man who feels deeply wronged:

> Who can have arranged this shocking act of arbitrariness and injustice? Elements of the high command are probably involved. In whose way was I standing, that the whole pack is now snapping at my heels? Being separated from my army is hard for me. It was so resolute in all the changing situations in which it found

itself, and will soon be a suitable instrument again despite all the setbacks that it has suffered. I wish it success with all my heart.[34]

Conrad sent a senior officer to visit Auffenberg that night, to explain that the chief of the general staff had not personally been involved in the decision. Auffenberg was left to speculate on why he had been treated in this manner. Brudermann, too, had been sacked, but the only criticism that could possibly be laid at the door of Auffenberg and his Fourth Army was that they had not prevailed at Rawa Ruska; given the weakened and tired state of his men, this could hardly be seen as a surprise. Indeed, even if they had been entirely fresh, a head-on clash with Ruzsky's army – which outnumbered them and was able to outflank them to the east – would surely have had exactly the same outcome. A clue lies in the letter that Archduke Frederick sent to the Austrian emperor on 30 September. In this, the archduke described how he had felt concerns about Auffenberg's lack of confidence in the war from the outset, and that Auffenberg had failed to complete his victory at Komarów, and had perhaps even overstated the magnitude of the triumph. Even after it had become clear that Plehve's army was far from annihilated, Frederick continued, Auffenberg had done nothing to remedy matters. Therefore, he concluded, he and Conrad had agreed that, given the loss of confidence in Auffenberg amongst the senior officers of Fourth Army, it was best for him to be removed from his post. He would be replaced by Archduke Joseph Ferdinand, 'who had led his corps and army group in an outstanding manner'.[35] The fact that Joseph Ferdinand's forces had lost 80 per cent of their strength was not mentioned.

Such a judgement of Auffenberg seems flawed. He had done little to exaggerate his victory at Komarów, and the decision to turn Fourth Army to the south was Conrad's, not his. The reference to Auffenberg's apparent mood prior to departing Vienna is intriguing. Did he say or do anything that caused offence to Archduke Frederick?

Another interesting facet is Conrad's part in the affair. It seems odd that he was not party to the decision to remove Auffenberg from command; after all, the dismissal of Brudermann was largely at his instigation. He and Auffenberg had known each other since their time as classmates in 1871. If he did know what was about to happen, he did little to protect his friend. There may have been an element of self-protection involved. In Germany the disastrous setback at the First Battle of the Marne plunged Moltke into a nervous breakdown, and led to his dismissal. Conrad may have feared that his own position was under threat. On 7 October, Conrad wrote to the emperor's Chief of Military Council, General Bolfras and gave a description of events:

> When we reached the area where the troops could be given rest and we could make preparations for a renewed offensive, I asked his Imperial Highness to visit the troops … apart from the journey to the departing German *Landwehr* corps, which I had to do for the sake of appearances, I did not accompany his Imperial Highness on any of these trips, primarily as I did not have the time, secondly because I wished that his Imperial Highness would be able to act as the army's Commander-in-Chief, and thirdly I am opposed to personal intervention. His Imperial Highness visited the troops alone, accompanied only by his Imperial Highness Carl Franz Joseph and his staff. When his Imperial Highness returned from visiting Fourth Army, he told me, to my great astonishment, that it was necessary to dismiss Auffenberg. This did not seem practical to me, especially in view of the consequences and in consideration of Auffenberg's achievements. When I found an opportunity to speak to his Imperial Highness about it and asked what grounds he had, his Imperial Highness replied that, based upon numerous reports and even from senior, earnest, clear-thinking generals, as well as other sources of information, and also on the impression that Auffenberg had made upon him, that he was very sceptical and pessimistic about matters. His Imperial Highness also sent to me Oberst Baron Mor, to give me details in this regard.
>
> I then replied to his Imperial Highness that this was a most important matter, but that his Imperial Highness clearly had no confidence in Auffenberg with regard to the planned new offensive. His Imperial Highness replied to me that he could not in good conscience, as the Commander-in-Chief of the Army, agree to Auffenberg continuing in command of Fourth Army.
>
> In this situation, I had no choice but to accept his Imperial Highness' words, the more so because following the experiences of Lemberg, it seemed that the situation after the battle of Komarów, which was actually a victory, reports had been too optimistic.[36]

It is hard to see where this idea – that Auffenberg had somehow overstated his success at Komarów, and had thus misled Conrad into directing Fourth Army towards Rawa Ruska – originated. Auffenberg himself appeared to be in no doubt that Plehve's army might have suffered heavy losses in the battle, but had escaped a far greater defeat due to the failure of Archduke Peter to prevent their withdrawal. The complete about-face imposed upon Fourth Army was necessitated by the growing pressure on the Lemberg front, and originated with Conrad, not Auffenberg. It is interesting, in light of Archduke Frederick's comments that he had had misgivings about Auffenberg from the outset, to speculate what words passed between Auffenberg and Archduke Frederick in Vienna before the departure of the general for the front. It was on this occasion that Auffenberg commented on the very ordinary impression made by the archduke. The fact that Auffenberg was so critical of Archduke Peter's performance may have helped precipitate, or may have been the consequence of, Archduke Frederick's move to dismiss him. The precise motives of all those involved will probably remain a subject of speculation. The power and influence of members of the aristocracy in the Austro-Hungarian Empire is beyond doubt.

Auffenberg, who was aged 62 when he was dismissed, played no further part in the war. In April 1915 he was awarded the honorific 'von Komarów' in recognition of the victory that he had won the previous year. But in the same month he was arrested on charges of showing classified documents to a friend when he had been Minister of War in 1912. The allegation was that his friend, an impoverished colonel, had intended to use the information for personal financial gain. For Auffenberg this was an even greater humiliation than his dismissal from command. His house was searched and his personal documents examined in detail, but eventually the charges were dismissed in court. In his memoirs Auffenberg claimed that Archduke Frederick was behind these charges, further adding to the question of the personal enmity between the two men.[37] For the rest of his life Auffenberg continued to argue that he had been badly treated in 1914 and 1915, and that there were no grounds for the accusations that he had somehow exaggerated his successes against Plehve's army. The failure to complete the victory at Komarów, he insisted, was down to Archduke Peter, who should have prevented Plehve's retreat.

Conrad had his own problems. In addition to seeing his hopes and dreams of a decisive victory over Russia disappear, he was also mourning the death of his son, which may have contributed to his acquiescence in the dismissal of his old friend. Conrad was not the only person who was mourning the loss of a loved one. Casualties in the first six weeks of the war had been terrible – it is difficult to find an adjective that does justice to the losses. Conrad's armies had lost 324,000 men, of whom 130,000 had been taken prisoner, out of an initial strength of 950,000.[38] The Russians had committed about 1.2 million men to the campaign, and lost 225,000, including 40,000 prisoners. With nearly 400,000 dead or wounded in just four weeks – the serious fighting did not begin until at least mid-August – this amounts to nearly 20,000 per day, as high a casualty rate as any theatre in an exceptionally bloody war. Loss of equipment was also serious. Although the Austro-Hungarian armies captured over 100 Russian guns, they lost more than 300 of their own. Some of the fears about the reliability of the Dual Monarchy's polyglot army were realised during the retreat from Galicia, when entire units of Slav soldiers surrendered en masse, making little attempt to fight. Although both sides were able to make good their losses in the weeks that followed, many of the dead comprised experienced and irreplaceable officers and NCOs. Neither army would ever again field forces with such a strong core of well-trained personnel. Given the great numerical superiority enjoyed by the Russians, the losses of the *k.u.k.* Army were not only numerically greater, but proportionally far more serious.

Throughout Europe, and indeed the wider world, September seemed to mark a distinct turning point. The apparently implacable advance of German armies across Belgium and northern France had been brought to an abrupt halt, and although Hindenburg and Ludendorff were triumphant in East Prussia, the battles in Galicia more than offset the German successes at Tannenberg and the Masurian Lakes. Newspapers throughout the world reported the Austro-Hungarian setbacks, and it is striking that although the deadly effect of machine guns is often mentioned, there is a particular emphasis on battles being won by the use of the bayonet. At least in the minds of newspaper editors, the power of cold steel remained strong in the imagination of the public.[39]

Whilst Auffenberg shouldered the blame for the loss of Galicia, there can be little doubt that the main burden of responsibility lay with Conrad. The army had operated according to his doctrines, which deliberately ignored the value of firepower and in particular artillery, and completely rejected notions of success through defensive action. To make matters worse, Conrad interfered with the mobilisation process, resulting in Second Army spending much of the campaign travelling between theatres, and the Galician armies first detraining at locations further west than expected, then being required to march east towards their originally intended detraining points. Furthermore, his insistence on attacks on the Lemberg front, across terrain that was so manifestly in favour of the defender, was wildly optimistic at best. Indeed, his theories of offensive action had failed completely, but he remained resolutely determined not to alter his policies. Both he and his subordinates – and, for that matter, senior officers on all sides – continued to believe that offensive operations would bring success. To an extent, this was inevitable, given the prevalent cult of the offensive that had prospered so strongly, and had defied all logic, for the previous forty years. Part of the reason behind its persistence in the face of persuasive evidence to the contrary, particularly in Germany and Austria-Hungary, may lie in the influence of Romanticism in central Europe during the 19th century. With its deliberate rejection of scientific rationale, it encouraged a mindset in which notions about the value of intangibles such as morale, national and racial superiority, and aggressive spirit came to be regarded as being at least as important as cold calculations about rates of fire and the calibre of artillery. Having grown up steeped in such imagery, it is not surprising that Conrad's generation clung to their views, even as contrasting evidence – in the form of appallingly heavy casualties – mounted up all around them. Hundreds of thousands of men would continue to die in the battles that followed, as the theories about the importance of offensive operations were repeatedly put to the test.

CHAPTER 11

A BLOODY SIDESHOW

THE SERBIAN FRONT

The world had been plunged into war because of the assassination of Archduke Franz Ferdinand, which led to the declaration of war on Serbia by the Austro-Hungarian Empire. Yet although this conflict, long in gestation, lay at the heart of the greater struggle that engulfed Europe, it rapidly assumed a secondary role in the war.

Oskar Potiorek, who took command of Austro-Hungarian forces on the Balkan front, was a contemporary of Conrad, and in many respects his rival. He had been a candidate for the post of chief of staff in 1906, as he was already deputy chief of staff and would have been preferred by the emperor. However, Conrad was the nominee of Archduke Franz Ferdinand, whose will prevailed on this occasion. Potiorek was appointed as the military governor of Bosnia and Herzegovina in 1911, where he soon acquired a reputation for being tough on Serbs who objected to Austro-Hungarian rule. In 1913 he invited Archduke Franz Ferdinand to visit Bosnia, in order to watch the annual military manoeuvres; the date of the visit was set as June 1914.

During the fateful visit, Franz Ferdinand, accompanied by his wife Sophie, drove through the streets of Sarajevo. As he was doing so, Nedeljko Čabrinović, a would-be assassin, threw a bomb at the convoy. The driver of the car carrying the royal couple and Potiorek spotted the bomb and accelerated; the device bounced off the folded canvas roof and rolled under the following car, where it exploded, injuring several occupants. The 19-year-old Čabrinović took a cyanide pill and leaped into the nearby River Miljacka. Unfortunately for him the cyanide was insufficient to kill him and only made him violently sick. Furthermore, as a result of the dry weather the river was just a few inches deep. He was promptly arrested.

Another member of the same terrorist cell, Gavrilo Princip, heard the explosion and hurried to the scene, expecting to see the wreckage of Franz Ferdinand's car. Instead, he witnessed the arrest of his accomplice, by which time Franz Ferdinand was too far away for him to open fire with his revolver. Deciding that it was likely the royal entourage would return by a similar route, he sought a position where he could sit and wait to see if he would get a second chance.

At the official reception for the royal couple Franz Ferdinand asked if he could visit those wounded in the grenade attack. Andreas von Morsey, a member of the archduke's staff, expressed his doubts about the safety of such a visit, as did Baron Rumerskirch, the archduke's chamberlain. Potiorek, who was present, later testified that he advised the archduke that another attempt was unlikely, but could not be ruled out entirely.[1] According to other accounts, he dismissed such concerns. He rejected calls for troops to be deployed as a cordon along the roads, stating that there was insufficient time to get them all into the correct uniforms. In any event, he continued, it was inconceivable that there would be a second assassination attempt on the same day. 'Do you think that Sarajevo is full of assassins?' he asked. The only concession that Potiorek was prepared to make was to alter the route, avoiding the centre of Sarajevo. Unfortunately – and inexplicably – he failed to inform the drivers of the cars of the change.[2]

Whilst the archduke was determined to visit the wounded, he was also concerned for the wellbeing of his wife and sent Morsey to tell her that she would not be going to the hospital. Although she was shaken by the morning's attack – she had been cut slightly on one cheek by a splinter – Sophie calmly rejected the suggestion, telling Morsey that she would accompany her husband wherever he appeared in public.[3] In any event, it was the couple's wedding anniversary, and she was determined that they were going to spend it together.

The archduke's car was second in the convoy, and when the leading car failed to take the revised route, it simply followed, driving straight past Princip, who had given up all hope of getting into a position where he could make an assassination attempt. Potiorek, who was sitting with the archduke, berated the driver, telling him to stop and change course. The car had no reverse gear, and was slowly pushed backwards, and Princip stepped forward and fired the fatal rounds that would lead to a world war. Like his fellow conspirator Čabrinović, Princip took cyanide that failed to kill him. Given that it was the testimony of the assassins that implicated Serbia and thus led to the Austro-Hungarian ultimatum, it is fascinating to speculate what might have happened had their cyanide actually worked.

Potiorek was not hit by any of the bullets fired by the young Serb, though Princip later claimed that the round that struck Sophie had been intended for the governor of Bosnia and Herzegovina. Although physically unharmed, Potiorek was affected in several other ways by the assassination. From the moment he was appointed governor in Bosnia and Herzegovina he undermined the civilian authority, headed by Leon Biliński; for example, police matters should have been under the control of Biliński's administration, but Potiorek interfered repeatedly, usually to the detriment of the Serbian population. He had ignored repeated warnings about security in Sarajevo, apparently fearing loss of personal prestige if the archduke's visit was cancelled, and his role in the events of 28 June was critical in allowing Princip an opportunity to fire the fatal shots. According to some, he scoffed at suggestions about further assassination attempts, refused to deploy troops along the roads that were to be used during the visit, and completely bungled the change of route. He was heavily criticised by many at the time, as was Edmund Gerde, the police commissioner in Sarajevo. However, Emperor Franz Joseph did not utter a word against Potiorek; there appears to have been a close friendship between the two men. Despite rumours that circulated at the time, Potiorek was neither asked for his resignation, nor did he volunteer it.[4] When war came, he was nominated as commander of the forces facing Serbia. Like his great rival Conrad, he was strongly in favour of war with Serbia, perhaps with the added edge of feeling that such a war might give him a chance to redeem himself for the deaths in Sarajevo. This desire for personal revenge was probably a significant factor in some of the decisions that Potiorek made in the campaign that followed.

As war loomed Potiorek was appointed commander of Sixth Army, but with overall control of the Serbian front. His own army, positioned along the upper River Drina, consisted of XV and XVI Corps, but was weakened by Potiorek's insistence on deploying troops in the interior of Bosnia in case of a pro-Serbian insurrection. There is little evidence that any such insurrection was ever planned, and the absence of these divisions from the front line would leave the *k.u.k.* Army fighting with a self-imposed handicap. His chief of staff was Eduard von Böltz. Erik von Merizzi, who had originally been earmarked as Sixth Army's chief of staff, was one of those wounded in Čabrinović's grenade attack on Archduke Franz Ferdinand in Sarajevo, and was still recovering in hospital.

Alongside Potiorek's army was Liborius Ritter von Frank's Fifth Army, with VIII and XIII Corps, deployed further along the Drina valley to the River Sava at Zvornik. The rest of the front was assigned to Böhm-Ermolli's Second Army, mainly concentrated northwest of Belgrade, with the independent VII Corps on the eastern flank, facing Serbia from Pancsova (now Pančevo).

Opposing these forces was the Serbian Army. The Belgrade government ordered the nation to mobilise for war on 25 July, and the process was complete by the end of the month, with about 450,000 men reporting for duty. A little over half of these formed the operational elements of the army, with the rest being deployed on rear area duties. The combat elements were organised as First Army, commanded by Petar Bojović; Second Army, under Stepa Stepanović; Third Army, under Pavle Jurišić Šturm; and the independent Army Group Užice, commanded by Miloš Božanović. Although many of the men who swelled the ranks had personal experience of fighting from Serbia's involvement in the First and Second Balkan Wars of 1912–13, the army itself was still feeling the effects of these conflicts. The relative poverty of Serbia meant that it had not been possible for the state to finance the army adequately to make good its material losses in the wars. Only 180,000 rifles were available at mobilisation, and although more were ordered from Russia, they did not arrive until the second half of August. There were insufficient uniforms for all men, and very few were issued with boots. Artillery ammunition stocks per gun were barely 10 per cent of those of other armies at the beginning of the war. Moreover, with only a single shell factory, producing perhaps 100 shells per day, the army would rapidly run out of ammunition once fighting began. A single gun was capable of firing more rounds than this every day.

The leading figure in the Serbian Army was Radomir Putnik, who had been chief of the general staff since 1903. At the beginning of the war he was in Budapest, and was detained by the Austro-Hungarian authorities. In a characteristic gesture more in keeping with a previous era, Emperor Franz Joseph ordered his release.[5] On his return to Belgrade, Putnik – who was 67 years old – offered his resignation on grounds of age and ill health. He was persuaded to stay, if only to oversee matters at a strategic level.

It had always been Conrad's intention to increase the odds in favour of his forces by exploiting diplomatic tensions in the Balkan region, but Bulgaria and Romania showed little inclination to join a war against Serbia. In late July the Greek government announced that any Bulgarian attack on Serbia would trigger an alliance between Serbia and Greece. Indeed, there were fears in Vienna that Romania might ally herself with Russia and Serbia. Franz Joseph spoke to Ottokar Graf Czernin, his ambassador to Bucharest, when the latter was passing through Vienna in late July, urging him to ensure that Romania would at least stay neutral. An agreement existed between Vienna and Bucharest for mutual aid in the event of a war with Serbia, but Czernin found that other factors were at work in the Romanian capital. The Italians, who were growing increasingly lukewarm towards Austria-Hungary and Germany, argued successfully that Vienna's ultimatum to Belgrade had been delivered without any consultation of nations such as Italy and Romania, and therefore those nations should not feel bound to Vienna. For Romania, the death of Archduke Franz Ferdinand had been a major blow. The archduke had been friendly towards her, and many in Bucharest had held out a hope that when Franz Ferdinand succeeded as emperor, he might look kindly on their ambitions to incorporate Transylvania into Romania; at the moment, this territory lay within the Hungarian part of the Austro-Hungarian Empire. These ambitions had resulted in hostile feelings between Hungary and Romania. After Vienna's ultimatum to Serbia, the Romanians began to wonder whether they might achieve their territorial ambitions more easily by joining those opposed to Austria-Hungary than by staying on good terms. Czernin attempted to influence King Carol of Romania directly, placing the elderly monarch under great personal pressure:

> The last weeks of his life were a torture to him; each message that I had to deliver he felt as the lash of a whip. I was enjoined to do all I could to secure Romania's prompt cooperation [in the war with Serbia], according to the terms of the alliance, and I was even obliged to go so far as to remind him that 'a promise given allows of no prevarication: that a treaty is a treaty, and his honour obliged him to unsheathe his sword.' I recollect one particularly painful scene, where the King, weeping bitterly, flung himself across the writing-table and with trembling hands tried to wrench from his neck his order *Pour le Mérite*. I can affirm without any exaggeration that I could see him wasting away under the ceaseless moral blows dealt to him, and that the mental torment he went through undoubtedly shortened his life.[6]

For the moment though, Czernin informed Vienna, Romania would stay neutral, and it was also likely that Greece could be kept out of any war, provided that Bulgaria and Turkey also stayed neutral. It seemed to Vienna that the only prospect of Romania – and particularly Bulgaria – becoming involved in a war with Serbia was if the *k.u.k.* Army achieved an early success, but this was the reverse of what had been hoped for. The intention had been that the involvement of Serbia's neighbours in the war would divert Serbian troops away from the forces facing the *k.u.k.* Army, making its early success easier. If the other Balkan nations were going to await such an early success, the task for Potiorek would be far harder to accomplish.

The terrain facing the three Austro-Hungarian armies should have imposed its own logic on the battlefield. The most straightforward route for an invasion was from north of Belgrade, with relatively open ground on either bank of the Danube. Furthermore, the presence of the Austro-Hungarian Danube Flotilla effectively ensured control of the river, facilitating any crossing. In particular, the Morava valley, running south from the Danube to the east of Belgrade, was an ideal invasion route, and had always been Conrad's preferred option in the event of a war with Serbia. Further west, the valley of the Drina was deep, with mountainous and densely forested terrain on either side, particularly to the east. Any attempt to cross the river would be difficult, and any attempt to exploit such a crossing even harder. The Austro-Hungarian high command can have had no illusions about the difficulties that lay ahead if they chose to invade across the Drina. The terrain was well known to them, as the official Austrian history of the war later recorded:

> The Serbian military leadership was able to look forward to the future with confidence, all the more so given that the character of the land was suited to their apparent plans for a defensive posture. The threatened borders were protected by watercourses, behind which the troops of the third mobilisation wave [roughly the equivalent of Austrian *Landwehr*] took up positions almost as they were mobilised. A series of great mountain ranges runs across the interior from southeast to northwest with parallel ridges ... each lower than the preceding one, with spurs running out towards the Sava and Danube. Nearly two-thirds of the operational area is covered by woodland with dense undergrowth. The courses of the Sava and Danube are flanked by flood plains. If one takes account of the numerous fruit plantations, one could say that the entire land is more or less covered with trees...
>
> The land is sparsely settled. Accordingly, the transport network of unimproved roads is extremely poor. Only the main roads through the valleys and a few important mountain passes are worthy of the name; but even these become bottomless after prolonged rain. In the area in which combat activities would take place, railways were almost completely absent.
>
> Taking into account that especially in summer there are water shortages on the often-parched mountains, one must conclude that Serbia is an extraordinarily difficult war zone, requiring particular organisational and technical preparations by an attacker. To this end, only troops trained in and equipped for mountain

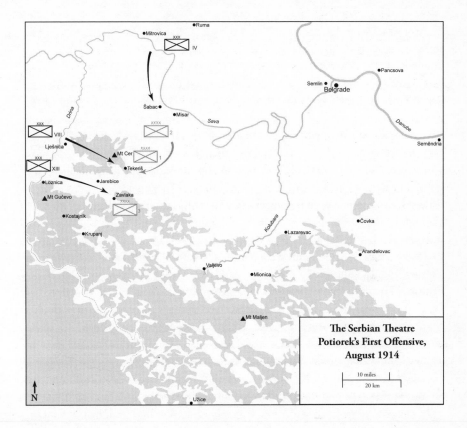

The Serbian Theatre
Potiorek's First Offensive,
August 1914

10 miles
20 km

N

warfare could be considered. Troops accustomed to the central European areas of military manoeuvres faced almost insurmountable difficulties for their mobile artillery and heavy equipment trains. Significant advantages accrued for the country's defenders, familiar with the peculiarities of the landscape.[7]

Potiorek had to wait until early on 6 August to receive official confirmation that he was the overall commander of the Serbian front. Before the war he had taken part in a war game in which the Austro-Hungarian Army, massed east of Sarajevo near the lower Drina, inflicted a major blow on Serbian forces attempting to advance from the Belgrade area in a northerly direction. He remained wedded to this idea of a flank attack, and planned to advance across the Drina using eleven brigades of experienced mountain infantry from XV and XVI Corps, intending to capture Užice some 15 miles (24km) east of the border. Elements of

Second Army would mount what was little more than a demonstration along the River Sava, in the hope that Serbian forces would be drawn north. Fifth Army would then attack across the lower Drina to take the Serbs in their western flank, driving on towards Valjevo. He submitted these plans to Vienna on 4 August. The intention to switch Second Army to Galicia as soon as possible might have rendered these plans obsolete, but the attraction of striking a telling blow against Serbia remained a strong one, particularly for a man driven by a strong desire for personal revenge at the earliest opportunity. Unfortunately, the war game on which these plans were based had treated the mountainous terrain east of the lower Drina as an area through which advancing troops had to proceed only a little slower than usual, thus completely underestimating the difficulties faced.[8]

Fighting broke out along the border with both Serbia and Montenegro over the next few days. The Kingdom of Montenegro, a close ally of Serbia, had an army that could only really be regarded as a militia; locally organised Austro-Hungarian frontier guards, supported by units of gendarmes, were sufficient to protect the frontier, though a sizable force of Montenegrin and Serbian troops penetrated as far as Višegrad. Meanwhile, messages arrived from Vienna, expressing doubts about Potiorek's plans, not least because Conrad and *AOK* simply could not make sense of them. Potiorek was basing his strategy on a counterthrust into the flank of an attacking Serbian force, even though there was little sign of the Serbs mounting any such attack. Locally, Potiorek's fellow army commanders also had concerns about the plans. In particular, Böhm-Ermolli, whose Second Army was intended to be transferred to Galicia as soon as possible, repeatedly asked for clarification about how far he should go in supporting Fifth Army's crossing of the Danube. The more he committed to supporting the crossing, the harder it would be for him to extract his troops and send them north. In any event, *AOK* instructed him with unambiguous clarity:

> In no circumstances should Second Army be drawn into events south of the Sava–Danube [line].[9]

Potiorek's instructions to Fifth Army were remarkably optimistic. Frank's troops were to begin their attack on 12 August across the lower Drina, and – in the expectation of weak resistance – were to advance in five days to the area around Valjevo – a distance of 60 miles (100km) across difficult terrain. Sixth Army would cross the middle Drina and secure bridgeheads by 17 August. Unfortunately for Frank, his army's concentration was hampered by railway difficulties, and he requested a delay of two days for the start date. Potiorek refused to change his plans, reassuring Frank that Serbian resistance would not be serious. In any event, he concluded, the greater the body of troops committed by the Serbs against Frank's Fifth Army, the greater the chances of success for his own Sixth Army, attacking from the southwest. The basis for these assessments of Serbian strength is not clear. The Austro-Hungarian forces had little firm information about Serbian deployments, with the few aerial reconnaissance flights over the area proving unable to spot concentrations of troops in the hilly and wooded landscape. The first hard information came on the eve of Fifth Army's attack, when reports arrived that the main strength of the Serbian Army was concentrating on the lower Drina. These reports were incorrect, but they gave Potiorek a further reason to hold onto the units of Second Army.

Both Potiorek and Conrad were anxious to engage the Serbs as soon as possible, in order to win a decisive early victory. On 9 August Potiorek sent a message to Frank, making his intentions clear:

> Our objective at present is not a lasting gain of territory. Rather, we need an early, comprehensive, decisive victory over the Serbs.[10]

A letter from Conrad to Potiorek, written on the same day, reinforced this point of view:

> We have now reached the situation where we can in no circumstances endure a setback in the Balkans and where a victory is now of the greatest value, as it would be expected to bring the still hesitating states of Bulgaria and Romania into our camp, an objective which I am striving to achieve with all means available, so that – the sooner the better – the Bulgarians will conduct a powerful assault...[11]

Plans on the other side of the border were rather more realistic. Whilst a Serbian–Montenegrin advance on Sarajevo was considered, the reality was that the Serbian Army would try to tie down as much of the *k.u.k.* Army as it could, keeping it as far away as possible from the critical front facing Russia. Serbia's ultimate salvation would depend upon a Russian victory, not a triumph by her own troops. The attack towards Višegrad was not a serious invasion, merely an exercise in disruption.

Handicapped by a shortage of bridging equipment – one of the reasons that he had asked in vain for a delay in the start date of operations – Frank began to cross the Drina on 12 August. His XIII Corps succeeded in securing a bridgehead, but the dense woodland rendered its artillery of limited value. VIII Corps had occupied a small island in the river as a preliminary step, and now struggled to secure a crossing in the face of tough Serbian resistance. The haste with which Frank's subordinates attempted to make up for the delays in mobilisation and concentration merely served to spread confusion in the rear area, with supply columns becoming hopelessly entangled with each other in the approaches to the crossings. Almost no supplies reached the front line during the next two days. To the northeast, Second Army managed to secure crossings over the Sava with relative ease at Mitrovica, aided considerably by the guns of the Danube Flotilla. The following day VIII Corps finally had a bridge across the Drina, but progress on the Serbian bank was painfully slow. The men struggled forward under a blazing sun through thick undergrowth, taking almost all day to reach the high ground around the town of Lješnica, barely 2 miles (3km) east of the river. Before them lay the mass of Mount Cer, which would prove to be the decisive battlefield of the campaign. XIII Corps, which had crossed further south – confusingly, at the town of Loznica – also struggled to make headway, finally reaching Jarebice. However, IV Corps from Böhm-Ermolli's Second Army fared better, managing to take Šabac.

Putnik had expected a major Austro-Hungarian attack from the north, and at first dismissed reports of crossings over the Drina as a diversion. By the third day of the campaign there could be no further doubts that these crossings constituted the main Austro-Hungarian advance, and he began to move more forces forward. Šturm's Third Army faced Potiorek's Sixth Army and VIII Corps from Frank's Fifth Army, while the other two Serbian armies moved against XIII Corps and the crossings secured by Second Army. An attempt to recapture Šabac failed when Austro-Hungarian troops, supported by the heavy guns of the Danube Flotilla, counterattacked into the open western flank of the Serbian troops, who withdrew into fortified positions about 5 miles (8km) to the south. Although the Serbian attack failed, it was not without consequences. Fearing a further attack, Böhm-Ermolli reluctantly sent reinforcements into the bridgehead, thus committing more of Second Army's troops to the Serbian campaign, almost at the very moment when they were meant to be heading to Galicia.

Whilst Serbia was looking to Russia for salvation, the Russians – and also the French – were anxious for the Serbs to play their part in the defeat of the Central Powers. Messages reached Belgrade from Grand Duke Nikolai urging the Serbian high command to mount attacks on Austro-Hungarian territory. Not only would this divert Austro-Hungarian troops from other theatres, it might also trigger a general uprising in the Balkans. Moreover, given the fragile nature of, and ethnic tensions within, the Austro-Hungarian Empire, there was hope that this might precipitate a wider series of revolts. Some of this belief was derived from the widespread conviction in Russia that fellow Slavs would rise up to overthrow their rulers in support of Russia, and it is not clear how much this was actually supported by hard intelligence. The Serbian response was that their attack on Šabac was the prelude to just such an operation, and that the Russians would greatly help matters if they delivered the 120,000 rifles that had been ordered for the Serbian Army.[12] However, the growing fighting along the Drina persuaded Putnik that the Austro-Hungarian seizure of Šabac was merely a diversion. Regardless of the wishes of the Russians, an offensive into enemy territory would have to wait until the threat on the Drina had been neutralised. A single division was left to mask Šabac, while the rest of the Serbian Second Army force-marched to the southern flank of Potiorek's Drina bridgeheads.[13]

There were high hopes that Frank's divisions would be able to penetrate deeper into Serbia on 15 August, and objectives about 10 miles (16km) distant were set for the various formations. Reality – in the shape of almost impossible terrain, tough resistance, and shortages of ammunition, food, and water – soon asserted itself, and it took until after midday on 15 August for XIII Corps' troops to receive sufficient supplies for them to advance. Thunderstorms hindered both the movement of troops and the transmission of orders, and very little progress was made. It was only in the south that XV Corps, part of Potiorek's Sixth Army, made any significant gains. Nevertheless, by the end of the day Frank was cautiously optimistic. He had made sufficient headway on both his flanks to feel sure that the Serbian troops facing him – now firmly identified as coming from Šturm's Third Army – would have to fall back. Nevertheless, Frank remained concerned about his own northern flank. This could only be secured, he told both Potiorek and *AOK*, by a further advance by Second Army, particularly as the diversionary attack at Šabac had tied down only minimal Serbian forces.

This requirement for further involvement by Second Army raised many concerns in Vienna. On the one hand, it remained imperative that a victory was secured over Serbia; on the other hand, delays in dispatching Second Army to Galicia would increase the possibility of setbacks on the more important Russian front. Unhappily, Conrad had to agree a compromise, allowing IV Corps and 29th Infantry Division to remain in the Balkan theatre. By the time this decision reached Böhm-Ermolli, he had already concentrated IV Corps in Ruma, some 15 miles (24km) north of Šabac, in preparation for entrainment for Galicia. More time was lost as the troops were ordered to head back to the front line.

Meanwhile, off the coast of Montenegro, the Austro-Hungarian Navy attempted to blockade the coast. Two ships – the protected cruiser *Zenta* and the destroyer *Ulan* – were bombarding the small port of Antivari (now known as Bar) when a large Anglo-French force, including two Dreadnought battleships and no fewer than ten pre-Dreadnoughts, surprised them. It was clear to Paul Pachner, the captain of the *Zenta*, that his two ships were hopelessly outgunned, but he chose to engage the battleships with his own vessel in order to buy time for the escape of the *Ulan*. Half the crew of the *Zenta* perished with their ship in the unequal struggle that followed. Pachner and the surviving members of his crew swam ashore, where they were interned until 1916.

After a long and difficult march, the Serbian Combined Division, part of Stepanović's Second Army, reached the town of Tekeriš late on 15 August. Urged on by the army commander, the Serbian division launched an immediate attack on the leading elements of the Austro-Hungarian forces advancing in the other direction: the two divisions of VIII Corps, 21st Rifle Division in the north and 9th Infantry Division in the south. Fighting continued until dawn on 16 August, when the arrival of additional Serbian forces, including artillery, swung the balance in Stepanović's favour. But just as it seemed that a Serbian victory was imminent, the main body of 21st Rifle Division arrived. Supported by the artillery and an infantry regiment of 9th Infantry Division, a counterattack was launched, driving the exhausted Serbs from the battlefield. The satisfaction at this success, though, was tempered by events immediately to the north; a flanking column of 21st Rifle Division was attacked by Serbian cavalry, which overran an infantry battalion and captured two batteries of artillery. Nor were the Austro-Hungarian forces able to exploit the withdrawal of the Serbian Combined Division. Bloody fighting between 9th Infantry Division and Colonel Ilija Gojković's 1st Morava Division continued all day, with neither side able to make any headway. It was only further south that XIII Corps was able to make limited progress around Zavlaka.

The heavy losses suffered by VIII Corps on the slopes of Mount Cer had a major impact. Supplies were still not reaching the front line in adequate quantities, and Feldmarschalleutnant Przyborski, commander of 21st Rifle Division, sent a message to VIII Corps Headquarters that the position on Mount Cer was untenable, and that his division was withdrawing. This order was not passed to all parts of the division, and by sunset 41st Rifle Brigade, commanded by Generalmajor Panesch, was still holding the vital high ground. As soon as he became aware of this, General Artur Giesl Freiherr von Gieslingen, the commander of VIII Corps (and brother of Wladimir von Gieslingen, head of the Austro-Hungarian Intelligence Bureau), ordered 9th Infantry Division to provide both supplies and reinforcements for Panesch's men. By doing so, he hoped it would be possible to prevent the abandonment of the positions on Mount Cer. But it was already too late, and by the time this message reached the front line, Panesch had finally received Przyborski's orders to pull back, and had withdrawn under cover of darkness.

The troops of Second Army made a determined attempt to enlarge their bridgehead around Šabac on 16 August, partly to tie down Serbian forces, and partly to advance and link up with Frank's Fifth Army; the three Austro-Hungarian armies were still not in physical contact with each other, and were effectively fighting different battles. The Serbian defences had already been pulled back, and at first the Austro-Hungarian 7th Infantry Division made good progress, taking the high ground at Misar, to the southeast of Šabac without a fight. The neighbouring 29th Infantry Division, attempting to thrust along the road towards the southwest, was surprised by a powerful flank attack in heavily wooded terrain. Confused fighting raged all day, with both sides repeatedly firing on their own men. As casualties accumulated, the commander of 29th Infantry Division, Feldmarschalleutnant Graf Zedtwitz, concluded that his men were facing a powerful Serbian force. Zedtwitz decided that he had accomplished his mission of tying down the Serbs, even if he had been unable to link up with Fifth Army, and withdrew to Šabac. On 17 August the Serbian Šumadija Division attacked the Šabac perimeter, reaching and destroying the pontoon bridge across the Sava. The advance of the Serbs created panic amongst the rear area units crowded into Šabac, and Böhm-Ermolli ordered General Karl Tersztyánszky, commander of IV Corps, to launch an immediate counterattack with those elements of his corps that were available. By the end of the day both sides were back in their starting positions. The numbers of dead and wounded had grown further, and there seemed even less prospect of Second Army being able to disengage and head for Galicia.

Despite the withdrawal of 21st Rifle Division from Mount Cer, Frank remained hopeful that he would be able to turn the southern flank of the Serbian position. The Serbs, too, were aware of their weakness in this area, and had already ordered reinforcements to this location. These included a regiment of cadets, force-marched to the region but not expected to arrive for three days. The threat to the Serbian Third Army was more pressing, and rather than risk his flank being turned, Šturm ordered a withdrawal from Jarebice of about 3 miles (5km) to high ground around Zavlaka. The key to the entire position, though, was the mountain itself, and in particular the high ground overlooking the flank of the Austro-Hungarian 9th Infantry Division. Here, and along the entire front of Fifth Army, bitter fighting raged all day. Despite heavy losses, neither side could secure a lasting advantage.

As he left for the north, Böhm-Ermolli signalled Frank that he had left behind IV Corps, with which Tersztyánszky would plan to attack towards Fifth Army on 18 August. Frank replied that he would be unable to contribute anything by way of an attack from the southwest with VIII Corps; 21st Rifle Division was still too disorganised after its withdrawal from Mount Cer, and 9th Infantry Division was threatened on three sides. Nevertheless, Frank continued, XIII Corps would do its best to attack. He was either unaware that one of XIII Corps' division commanders had advised the corps commander that his unit was in desperate need of rest and resupply, or he chose to ignore the warning.

The fighting on 18 August centred on three locations. At the southern end of the battlefield elements of the Austro-Hungarian XIII Corps attempted in vain to locate and turn the flank of the Serbian 2nd Morava Division near Zavlaka. Although 36th Infantry Division succeeded in gaining ground north of the town, its own left flank – and therefore the left flank of the entire corps – was now exposed, as a gap of 6 miles (10km) lay between XIII Corps and VIII Corps. Reluctantly, XIII Corps pulled back to its start line. In the centre of the battlefield 9th Infantry Division continued to contest the slopes of Mount Cer with the Serbian Combined Division. The deadlock was broken when the Serbian 1st Morava Division moved forward to join the attack. Both flanks of 9th Infantry Division were forced back, and during the night the centre too was ordered to withdraw. In the north IV Corps' attack from Šabac was delayed, as a result of the damage done by the last Serbian attack to the pontoon bridge across the river, which hindered the build-up of Tersztyánszky's forces. Finally, 31st Infantry Division attacked in mid-morning with powerful artillery support, and drove back the Serbian 1st Šumadija Division; confident that he had defeated the Serbs, Tersztyánszky advised Frank that he would be able to advance further on 19 August, and that Fifth Army should make every effort to reach out to link up with him.

From his headquarters in Przemyśl, Conrad followed developments with impatience. The increasingly bloody fighting in northwest Serbia seemed to be going nowhere, while Potiorek's own command – Sixth Army – was achieving equally little, mopping up a few Montenegrin and Serb penetrations into Austro-Hungarian territory. Potiorek assured *AOK* that Sixth Army would imminently cross the border and advance on Užice. Once the Second and Fifth Armies had united their forces in the north, the three armies would combine in a killing thrust into the heartland of Serbia. After all, he maintained, given the decisive success achieved by IV Corps outside Šabac, it was clear that the Serbs were approaching the end of their strength.

The reality was somewhat different. Although their resources were stretched, the Serbs still had reserves available, and remained focussed on the centre of the long battlefield. Early on 19 August the Combined Division once more attacked the Austro-Hungarian 9th Infantry Division, finally driving it from its trenches. Desperately, the troops of VIII Corps tried to hold their positions in the hope of linking up with IV Corps, which was to strike towards them from Šabac. But by the end of the day, the entire corps was forced to retreat. This in turn left XIII Corps' northern flank exposed, and as dusk fell all of Frank's army withdrew towards the west.

In the north Tersztyánszky found that the Serbs were far from beaten, and his assault on the 1st Šumadija Division failed to make a decisive breakthrough. The fighting was as confused as on earlier days, with the Austro-Hungarian divisions reeling under the shock of ever-greater casualties in difficult terrain. Progress was far slower than the Austro-Hungarians had expected, and towards the end of the day, IV Corps called a halt to give its battered units a chance to regroup. It was time for the entire Austro-Hungarian high command to consider its options. Frank felt that he had no choice but to pull back across the Drina. Without his army advancing east, there seemed little point in Tersztyánszky's IV Corps continuing its efforts at Šabac. Despite the political consequences, Conrad had to accept that the offensive would have to be abandoned in its entirety. Sixth Army was ordered to place strict limits on any counterattacks it might make.

The effective cancellation of the invasion of Serbia, by Conrad in *AOK*, hit Potiorek hard. He had still hoped to renew the attacks in the next day, with the added benefit of troops that he was transferring from his own Sixth Army to Fifth Army. At the very least, he insisted, IV Corps should remain in Šabac, holding a bridgehead that could be used for future offensives. A dispute now developed over the control of IV Corps. *AOK* had assigned Tersztyánszky's troops to Frank's Fifth Army, at the same time as ordering IV Corps back to the northern bank of the Sava. Perhaps in reaction to what he regarded as interference in his overall command of the Serbian front, Potiorek sent instructions to Frank forbidding his headquarters from communicating directly with *AOK*. In future, all such communications would have to be passed through Potiorek's headquarters.

The outcome of this dispute was that Tersztyánszky found himself with contradictory orders. Late on 19 August he had begun preparations to evacuate Šabac, in accordance with instructions from *AOK* and Fifth Army, but a message then arrived from Potiorek telling him to prepare to resume his attacks. This message was in turn countermanded almost as the troops were preparing to launch a dawn attack, and succeeded by instructions from Frank for a retreat north of the Sava. By the end of 21 August the last elements of Frank's battered divisions had crossed back over the Drina. The Serbian troops facing them were too weakened to put up more than a token pursuit. In Šabac, Tersztyánszky had finally received consistent instructions, telling him to maintain a foothold on the southern shore of the river, but to pull back the bulk of IV Corps to the northern shore. On 21 August the Serbian First Army attacked the perimeter. Although they were driven off to the south by a counterattack, the attack from the west made better progress. Once more, contradictory orders abounded; unaware of the success of the counterattack against the Serbian forces attacking from the south, Tersztyánszky ordered an evacuation of the bridgehead, only to countermand the order a few hours later. To make matters worse, instructions now arrived from Potiorek authorising a withdrawal only if IV Corps were faced with clearly superior forces. Tersztyánszky knew that the Serbian forces pressing his perimeter were not 'clearly superior' to his corps, but much of his corps was now on the north bank, and therefore unable to take part in the fighting. Given that Fifth Army's retreat across the Drina effectively left him fighting a lone battle within Serbia, he decided that there was no point in holding on to Šabac. Nevertheless, bitter fighting continued through 22 and 23 August. The following day, when Serbian scouts cautiously moved forward, they found that IV Corps had withdrawn.

Potiorek had always had a close relationship with Emperor Franz Joseph, and put it to good use. He advised Vienna that the morale of his troops remained 'outstanding', despite their heavy losses and their clear defeat.[14] He made representations that his offensive had been greatly hindered by confusions over command, at a time when the emperor had already become aware that news about the Balkan front travelled first to Przemyśl and thereafter to Vienna, taking up to four days to reach the capital:

> I need a guarantee of complete authority over [Tersztyánszky's corps], so that *AOK* gives me a free hand in future for the task that it has assigned to me, namely to prevent the advance of the Serbian Army into the Empire, does not influence individual actions, and discontinues direct communication with commands subordinated to me.[15]

Consequently, Conrad received an order from the emperor on 21 August:

> As I regard it as necessary for combat units fighting in the Balkans to be under a single command, I delegate that Feldzugmeister Potiorek is given independent

high command over all army corps fighting against Serbia and Montenegro, and that I do not regard any diminution of [the troops deployed in the Balkans] as of any value.[16]

In other words, command of the Balkan front was no longer subordinated to *AOK*. Any sense of personal triumph that Potiorek felt had to be tempered by the reality on the ground. Contrary to all expectations, his forces had been soundly beaten by the poorly equipped and numerically weaker Serbian forces. Casualties on both sides during the nine days of fighting were substantial. The *k.u.k.* Army lost 8,000 dead and 30,000 wounded, with another 4,500 taken prisoner, amounting to about 21 per cent of the troops deployed. Serbian casualties were about 3,000 dead and 15,000 wounded. But the political damage suffered by the Austro-Hungarian Empire was far greater than its material losses. Any hope of an immediate involvement of other Balkan states diminished hugely.

One of those who saw the terrible price paid by both armies was Henry Barby, a French journalist accompanying the Serbian troops:

> The region where the tough battle of Cer and the Jadar gorge was fought was filled with graves and the stench of the dead… It was impossible to approach the crest of the Cer via the terrible slope. There, the number of dead was so great that Second Army was forced by lack of resources and time to abandon burying them all.
>
> The killing had been equally terrible before Third Army, where, in a single field, at Bela-Zerkva, there were 694 Austrian corpses.[17]

Several factors contributed to the failure of the *k.u.k.* Army. In his haste to exact revenge for Sarajevo, Potiorek attacked sooner than was absolutely necessary, and showed shockingly bad judgement in the location of his attacks. To make matters worse, the three attacking armies were too far apart to cooperate effectively, allowing the Serbs to concentrate their forces at key locations. This lack of coordination was worsened by several factors. Firstly, Second Army was only in the area temporarily, despite Potiorek's attempts to detain it as long as possible. Secondly, Sixth Army did not complete its concentration until after the initial offensive of Frank's Fifth Army had already begun. Thirdly, several formations were not even deployed in the front line, but were held back for fear of pro-Serbian revolts across the region.

Potiorek's plan of campaign was clearly deeply flawed, but it should be remembered that he made *AOK* aware of his intentions before the assault began.

Conrad did not countermand his orders, as he was entitled to do, though he did question them. At least a degree of blame, therefore, must rest with Conrad. Barby offered a pithy summary of events:

> The history of Austria-Hungary provides a remarkable collection of defeats, and the reign of Franz Joseph was particularly rich in military disasters. But until today, the old monarch could always claim that he had only been defeated by the Great Powers, by France in 1850, by Prussia in 1866. Today, it is Serbia, one tenth of the size and population, that inflicted the first resounding defeat of this war.[18]

The fighting around Mount Cer saw a notable first. Miodrag Tomić was a young infantryman of 23 when he was sent to France in 1912 to become one of Serbia's first military pilots. He flew in the 1913 Second Balkan War against Turkey, dropping a number of small bombs and conducting reconnaissance flights, and piloted one of only three aircraft owned by Serbia in 1914. Whilst conducting a reconnaissance flight over the Drina, he encountered an Austro-Hungarian plane, and was startled when the Austro-Hungarian pilot opened fire on him with a pistol. It was – probably – the first exchange of fire between aircraft in history.[19]

As the Serbs retook territory from their enemies, they reported coming across examples of atrocities against civilians. Barby, the French journalist, was outside Šabac on 18 August when he encountered three civilians, fleeing towards the south. They told them what had happened in their village, at the bottom of the hill:

> 'The Chvabas [Serbian slang for Austro-Hungarian troops, akin to the use of the word 'Boche' on the Western Front] massacred the women! They set fire to the houses! They forced themselves upon young women!'
>
> At first, we were incredulous. However, Gentchich [a Russian journalist] decided that we had to go and see. I was tempted to point out that we could wait until the enemy had pulled back a distance, but he was already heading towards the village with the three peasants. I followed…
>
> On the lower side of the road, a peasant of about 50 years was lying on his stomach, his arms stretched out. His fingers still twitched, moved by reflexes. He had been knocked down by blows from a rifle butt!
>
> The village appeared to be deserted and uninhabited. White cloths fluttered at the doors of almost all the buildings and in many houses that had open windows, I saw furniture that had been turned over and broken. A little further,

we were drawn to a house by a sad, rattling groan … we entered. What horror! Lying on the ground, a woman, dying in a pool of blood. Her torn chest was no more than a bloody wound!

Later, in another house, a second woman lying amid the debris of furniture. She had been bayoneted. The poor woman who had died held a dead child in her arms, stabbed right through with the same weapon.

I felt as if life had suddenly become a dreadful nightmare … my entire being was revolted and suffered before such crimes.

But that was not all. The columns of smoke that we had seen from the top of the hill came from several houses that had been set ablaze and had burned out.

During this time, one by one, some of the inhabitants appeared. Cautiously at first, then with greater confidence, they approached and surrounded us. Almost all of these unfortunates were crying. Last night, it seemed that the hatred of the Austro-Hungarians was suddenly unleashed.[20]

There were other accounts of similar deeds, as indeed there were from other fronts at the time. The German invasion of Belgium was rapidly given the title 'the rape of Belgium', and stories soon circulated that gave this title a literal meaning. Whilst there is no doubt that many atrocities occurred – hundreds of civilians were shot in places like Leuven and Dinant – there is equally no doubt that some of the more lurid stories that were printed in newspapers were complete fabrications.[21] It served the purposes of all sides to claim that their enemies behaved with complete brutality. German accounts of the behaviour of Russian troops in East Prussia, particularly Cossacks, have always been vehemently denied by Russian sources. Many Austro-Hungarian troops may have been driven to commit crimes in their desire for revenge on the nation they blamed for the assassination of Franz Ferdinand, and others simply behaved as soldiers have done in similar circumstances throughout history, venting their rage and terror on those around them.

Nevertheless, it seems that Potiorek's forces behaved with particular brutality. Barby, who recorded that he saw many of the atrocities committed by the Austro-Hungarian Army, came to a clear conclusion:

The Austrian Army seems to have regarded devastation as a particular objective, and began its work of devastation as soon as it entered Serbia.

What cruelties, what infernal orgies, did the soldiers and officers not carry out? How many times did I stand frozen in horror before the results of the criminal intoxication, incendiarism or sadism of these soldiers of a country so proud of its civilisation!

It was what Austria wanted, a great and mighty nation surging over a small country, the ruin of Serbia, which it pursued systematically by steel and fire, by pillage and incendiarism in the towns and villages, and also by extermination, by the massacre of the Serbian people.

Austria did not hesitate because she believed she would succeed in her criminal work before Serbia could defend herself and could reveal the horror of the crimes to the world.[22]

In support of his assertions, Barby published the text of a document issued by the headquarters of the Austro-Hungarian IX Corps, one of Second Army's formations that was in the area briefly before being sent to Galicia. The document was entitled 'Instructions regarding the conduct to be followed with regard to the Serbian population':

The war brings us to an enemy country inhabited by those with a lively, fanatical hatred of us, a country where murder, as was demonstrated by the catastrophe in Sarajevo, is considered permissible, even in the upper classes, who glorify it as a heroic deed.

One can show no humanity or kindness to such a population. Such feelings would be harmful, because the way in which they may possibly arise in time of war could, here, put our troops in grave danger.

Accordingly, for the duration of hostilities, I order the greatest severity and firmness, and wariness, with regard to the inhabitants.

Above all, I will not allow us to take prisoner any locals who are encountered armed, singly or in groups, who are not wearing uniforms. They must be executed on the field of battle.

Anyone showing clemency will be punished with the greatest severity.[23]

It was common practice in many European armies to regard combatants who were not in uniform as irregulars, not protected by the usual rules of war. In the case of the Serbs, a large proportion of their mobilised forces received very little by way of uniforms, due to shortages in the Serbian Army. The Serbs can hardly be blamed for deploying these ill-equipped men in defence of their nation in the face of such a mortal threat. However, the Serbian government would have been aware of the likely manner in which these men would be treated by the Austro-Hungarians. Indeed, when Russian troops in East Prussia encountered armed German civilians, they often executed them without compunction, but criticism of this was limited to the German press. Barby quoted further details of the order issued to the troops of IX Corps, stipulating that hostages were to be taken in every village, and executed in the event of troops coming under fire from civilians. Again, this practice was almost identical to that of the Russians in parts of East Prussia.[24]

None of this can detract from the fact that Austro-Hungarian forces undoubtedly executed and mistreated civilians. Given the manner in which European troops behaved around the world when dealing with populations that they regarded as their cultural and racial inferiors, it can be argued that the Austro-Hungarian troops treated the Serbs – who they saw as a lesser people, further tainted by their assumed collective responsibility for the events in Sarajevo – badly out of a sense of superiority. Nor is it surprising that the enemies of the Central Powers did all they could to amplify the atrocities to the maximum extent possible. However, this seems at odds with the way that minorities were treated within the Austro-Hungarian Empire generally, or at least the Austrian portion – even the Magyar nationalists in Hungary may have tried to marginalise minorities in a political sense, but there was very little persecution or ill-treatment. The behaviour of the *k.u.k.* Army in Serbia seems to have been very different from what had gone before.

The Serbs themselves did not have a good record in terms of atrocities. As a result of the First Balkan War, in which Bulgaria, Serbia, Greece, and Romania gained territory from Turkey, and the second Balkan War, in which Bulgaria lost some of its new acquisitions to its former allies, Serbia took control of considerable areas with Muslim populations, including Kosovo, the scene of recent tensions. British observers in Macedonia reported that the Serbs treated the inhabitants of the area badly, with widespread reports of killings, rapes, the destruction of entire villages, arbitrary detention, and beatings for little or no reason. The vice-consul in Monastir added to his report:

> It is already abundantly evident that the Moslems under Servian rule have nothing whatsoever to expect but periodical massacre, certain exploitation and final ruin.[25]

Vienna, too, received reports of death and destruction in the territories seized by Serbia from the Ottoman Empire. In 1913, the consul-general in Skopje wrote describing how ten villages had been destroyed, with the men lined up and shot, the villages set ablaze, and women and children who attempted to flee being bayoneted by the waiting Serbian soldiers, though the reports are unclear whether these were regular troops or militia. In Albania, following a local revolt against Serbian rule, 300 civilians were beaten and stabbed to death at night. The consul-general concluded that the manner in which the killings were organised suggested that they were not spontaneous local acts, but had been ordered from higher authorities. This is something that is impossible to confirm or deny, and assuming that the killings were in response to orders, it is difficult to know where these orders originated. To a large extent, the Belgrade government struggled to control Serbian combatants, particularly as a large proportion of those involved in the two Balkan Wars were irregular groups of partisans. But the objective of unifying all Slavs in the region under Serbian rule was something that lay at the heart of the Serbian nation, and there was no acceptance of any minorities. Bosnians, Croats, and others, regardless of religious or other affiliations, would simply be forced to become Serbs. Any who opposed or resisted would be crushed without mercy.

After the evacuation of Šabac there was a brief lull in the fighting. The Serbs were pressured by Grand Duke Nikolai to mount an offensive of their own, in an attempt to prevent further Austro-Hungarian forces from being transferred to Galicia. The Serbian high command responded that, despite the numerical superiority of the Austro-Hungarian forces, the Serbian Army would be prepared to mount an offensive – provided that it had sufficient bridging equipment to build crossings over the Sava and Danube, and provided that it received enough weapons to allow it to arm all the men who had been mobilised in July.[26]

Bojović's First Army regrouped and assembled along the Sava. It had been ordered to cross the river during the night of 5/6 September, and once it had established a bridgehead, it was to push north through Mitrovica in order to sever communications between the Austro-Hungarian forces that had fought at Šabac and those along the Drina. The orders went on to suggest that First Army would attempt to overrun all of Syrmia – the relatively flat, fertile area between the Sava and Danube Rivers – but given that Bojović's army amounted to only three divisions, this was an unlikely objective. The other two Serbian armies were ordered to hold the line of the Drina, and to prevent any interference by the bulk of Austro-Hungarian forces. At the same time, the Serbian forces around Užice, in conjunction with Montenegrin forces, would invade southern Bosnia.

Before dawn on 6 September the Serbian First Army, with substantial artillery support, secured a bridgehead across the Sava. Resistance from a Hungarian reservist formation was minimal, and a pontoon bridge was established during the morning. A little further west, the 1st Timok Division, part of Second Army, also secured a bridgehead; however, a shortage of bridging equipment meant that it was not possible to deploy a bridge until the following day. Given their modest resources, the local Austro-Hungarian forces had never intended to mount a determined defence of the river, and instead relied on the presence a substantial force under Feldmarschalleutnant Alfred Krauss, primarily 7th and 29th Infantry Divisions, to provide sufficient weight for a counterattack against any bridgehead. While Krauss organised his forces, one of his units – 74th Infantry Regiment – took it upon itself to launch an immediate counterattack. Slowly, other units joined in, and 1st Timok Division sustained heavy losses, leading it to abandon its bridgehead. Over 4,600 men were left behind, doomed to become prisoners, when the Austro-Hungarians reached and destroyed the pontoon bridge.[27]

Further east, the Serbian 1st Dunav Division from First Army was having a better time, and succeeded in enlarging its bridgehead. But early on 8 September the main bulk of the Austro-Hungarian forces intervened. To some extent at least, Potiorek had anticipated a Serbian attack into Syrmia; he had planned to counter it by repeating his earlier attack across the Drina, with the intention of taking the attacking Serbian forces in their western flank. Whilst this plan was not without merit, it ignored the fact that the terrain on the eastern side of the Drina was ideal for defensive fighting, and that even if substantial Serbian forces were committed to a northern drive over the Sava, the rest of the Serbian Army would still be sufficient to defend the hilly and heavily wooded terrain. A day later than originally planned – due to delays in getting adequate artillery into position – 42nd Infantry Division, part of XIII Corps, secured a crossing over the Drina. However, 36th Infantry Division's attempt to cross the river failed with heavy casualties. VIII Corps, a little further north, did rather better at first, where the Serbian defences were substantially weaker. Nevertheless, in the difficult terrain it proved almost impossible to push the Serbs back, and the crossings remained within artillery range. Pressure on VIII Corps' bridgehead steadily increased, as more Serbian troops joined the battle. By the end of the day, the crossings had been abandoned. Each side lost perhaps 4,000 men.

At the southern end of the battlefield Sixth Army enjoyed a far more successful day. The Serbian Third Army put up tough resistance, but the Austro-Hungarian attack, led by well-trained mountain troops, gradually worked its way up the steep hillsides and drove off the defenders. On 9 September, while Frank's Fifth Army licked its wounds from the previous day's abortive attempt to secure crossings, Potiorek's own army, with XV and XVI Corps, battered its way forward, slowly gaining ground in a tough battle of attrition.

With the southern flank of his position under pressure, Putnik rushed whatever reinforcements he could scrape together to the area. One early consequence was that the planned Serbian penetration into southern Bosnia, in conjunction with the Montenegrin Army, was reduced substantially in strength.

Partly due to the arrival of the Serbian reinforcements, and partly as a consequence of the terrain, Potiorek's army's progress was both costly and slow. Nevertheless, XVI Corps began to envelop the southern flank of the Serbian position, forcing Putnik to draw troops away from the bridgehead in Syrmia with the intention of using them to launch his own flanking attack from the southeast. Fighting north of the Sava continued for several days, with both sides enjoying moments of success, before the Serbs finally pulled back before dawn on 14 September. Two days later elements of Krauss' corps began to cross to the southern bank. Potiorek now began to hope for successes on both flanks of the battlefield, with XVI Corps driving forward in the south at the same time that Krauss advanced from the north.

In the mountains to the east of the Drina the weather was now deteriorating, with heavy, cold rain that turned to snow over higher ground. On 14 September Frank made another attempt to secure crossings over the lower Drina. For several days his troops took heavy losses – 21st Rifle Division reported over 2,000 casualties in just two days – in the face of well-prepared defences. 42nd Infantry Division, made up largely of Croatians, was almost routed by the Serbian 2nd Drina Division. XVI Corps, at the southern end of the battlefield, tried in vain to secure the high ground at Kostajnik. The Serbs now launched their own counterattack in the south with the regrouped First Army. Potiorek urged Krauss to advance as rapidly as possible from the Sava crossings, in an attempt to draw off Serbian forces, or even to break through into the rear of the Drina defences. Before Krauss' forces could launch their assault, they came under heavy attack themselves in heavily wooded terrain. For a moment, it seemed as if the Austro-Hungarian troops would be forced back to the river, but the last reserves saved the day, and the Serbs pulled back and dug in. They might not have crushed Krauss' bridgehead, but they had effectively stopped its enlargement.

Serbian pressure on Potiorek's southern flank grew steadily, and on 17 September Sixth Army had to begin a withdrawal. Unlike the previous occasion when Austro-Hungarian troops were forced back to the Drina, they did not pull back across the river; instead, they withdrew to positions where they could conduct a defence, and dug in. On 18 September, the Serbs attacked again, convinced that they would be dealing with little more than an Austro-Hungarian rearguard. After bloody fighting all day, their attacks were fought off. Further attacks followed in the next few days, with heavy casualties on both sides, for almost no gain. Sixth Army's losses since it had crossed the Drina in early September exceeded 20,000 men, but elements of XVI Corps clung to the vital high ground of Mount Gučevo that dominated the southern end of the battlefield;

Samsonov's Second Army was effectively destroyed at Tannenberg, and he shot himself in the last days of the battle.

With a reputation for caution, Ruzsky rose to command Northwest Front, as much due to his political connections as to any military skill.

Commander of Northwest Front at the beginning of the War, Zhilinski was unable to coordinate his two subordinate armies in their invasion of East Prussia.

Putnik was reluctant to take command of the Serbian Army at the beginning of the war, but went on to coordinate a remarkable victory over the Austro-Hungarian forces in late 1914.

Gavrilo Princip (left), the man who fired the fatal shots that started the slide towards war, photographed here with two fellow Serbian activists.

Serbian gunners struggling with exhausted horses in winter conditions.

Encouraged by Tsar Nicholas to fight like lions, Serbia's army was forced to recruit both the very old and the very young into its ranks.

This photograph in 1914 shows the complete absence of helmets at this early stage of the war.

When the Germans retreated back to the line of the Masurian Lakes in autumn 1914, they rapidly constructed a line of defences to rival the trenches seen throughout the Western Front.

German soldiers shelter inside a farmhouse during the Battle of Tannenberg.

Russian soldiers in a hastily scraped trench in Galicia.

Russian dead at Tannenberg.

Austro-Hungarian soldiers wounded during the fighting in Galicia. Medical support was swamped by the huge numbers of casualties, and wounded men were frequently abandoned when either side retreated.

German troops advancing during the Tannenberg campaign.

Mobile communications were unreliable and difficult to maintain at this early stage of the war. Telephone sets like this one required the extensive laying of cables, which were frequently cut by artillery fire or enemy patrols.

German soldiers with machine guns are pictured here in their lines at Johannisburg in the winter of 1914.

successive attacks and counterattacks merely added to the piles of corpses, without any significant gains for either side. On 24 September fighting finally died down as exhaustion and supply shortages took their toll. Barby described the battlefields when he visited them at the end of the month:

> No description – because there are no suitable words – can give an idea of the fields of carnage that lie along the Drina, the battlefields of Gučevo, along the Boragna and the Jarogda, where blood continues to gush…
>
> This chaos of mountains, constantly shaken by a hurricane of infernal bullets, has become a realm of death. Everywhere, the carcasses of horses and cattle, also everywhere the cadavers of soldiers, which one often does not find until long after they have fallen, and at times, in pursuit of one's pious duty, one has to dispute possession with the voracious, hungry boar that roam everywhere.
>
> In the forests that cover the region, there are daily reports of groups of wounded, Serbs or Austrians – sometimes both Serbs and Austrians – who are lost, and die of starvation or lack of medical help.[28]

Fighting now erupted around Belgrade, where Serbian forces briefly established a bridgehead across the Sava and threatened to capture Semlin (now Zemun). A dramatic intervention by three monitors of the Austro-Hungarian Danube Flotilla, commanded by Linienschiffsleutnant Richard Wulff, resulted in the Serbian pontoon bridges being destroyed.

Both sides were in desperate need of a pause. Although fighting continued in southern Bosnia, where Serbian and Montenegrin troops clashed repeatedly with their Austro-Hungarian opponents, the shortage of artillery ammunition for both armies, together with the first heavy snow of the winter, forced a lull in the battles east of the Drina. Swollen by rainwater and melting snow, the river rose, destroying several of the makeshift bridges that carried supplies to the Austro-Hungarian Fifth and Sixth Armies. Although supplies began to run short for these troops, the situation was even worse on the Serbian side of the front line. Soldiers faced each other in trenches that were half-full of water, husbanding their limited supplies of ammunition. From time to time one side or the other launched a local attack, none of which achieved anything other than further casualties. Losses accumulated on both sides for several weeks, while the front line barely moved.

But whilst there were supply shortages on both sides, the resources of the Austro-Hungarian Empire dwarfed those of Serbia, and gradually, the advantage began to tilt in favour of Potiorek's units, particularly in the field of heavy artillery.

The one area of military equipment in which the *k.u.k.* Army enjoyed a distinct advantage over its enemies was in the field of mountain artillery. The Austro-Hungarian lightweight howitzers were far more practical compared to the Serbian antiquated heavy guns, which were difficult to move in the mountainous terrain and of limited efficacy. Between 6 and 9 November XIII Corps, on the right flank of Frank's Fifth Army, began to make significant headway. Although neither flank of the Austro-Hungarian Army was able to achieve the envelopment that Potiorek continued to seek, the Serbs were forced to abandon their fortifications. Heavy rain turned all roads to quagmires, limiting the movements of both sides. By the time they reached their new lines, many of the formations of the battered Serbian Third Army were reported to be entirely unfit for any major fighting.[29] On 9 November elements of the Austro-Hungarian XIII and XV Corps finally reached the Loznica–Krupanj road, which had been their initial objective in the first week of the August invasion. Valjevo, another early objective of the war, fell to Potiorek's forces in mid-November. Through the near-constant rain and snow, the Serbian armies fell back to the line of the River Kolubara. Bojović, the commander of the Serbian First Army, was forced to step aside due to illness, and was replaced by General Živojin Mišić, who had previously served as Putnik's deputy.

Potiorek and his staff were aware that ammunition was running very low for the Serbian forces, and that without adequate artillery support, they would be unable to hold the line of the Kolubara for long. Nevertheless, the pursuing forces needed a pause. When the weather improved markedly on 16 November, Potiorek ordered Fifth and Sixth Armies to secure crossings over the Kolubara. Despite resisting as resolutely as their limited artillery ammunition allowed, the Serbs were forced to pull back towards the line of the River Ljig. On 17 November the good weather came to a sudden end; with heavy rain, the rivers swelled and overran, and the Austro-Hungarian supply lines once more broke down.

Nevertheless, Potiorek had grounds for being optimistic. His troops had finally broken out of the mountainous northwest corner of Serbia, and interrogations of prisoners suggested that morale in the Serbian ranks was beginning to crumble. On 20 November Potiorek advised Vienna:

> [There are] confirmed reports, that the Serbian Army [is] severely degraded, [with] a shortage of food, clothing and artillery ammunition.[30]

The Austro-Hungarian military attaché in Bulgaria also sent encouraging news: Paris had advised the French ambassador in Sofia that the French government regarded Serbia as approaching the end of her strength. In light of this, Potiorek reasoned, his battered, tired troops needed to make just one last effort to knock the hated Serbs out of the war.

Accordingly, Frank's Fifth Army was to prepare for an offensive in the north against Belgrade. At the same time, Sixth Army would advance to Aranđelovac, in order to prevent the Serbs from sending troops north to Belgrade and to cut the line of retreat for any Serbian units committed to battle in the capital. Heavy fighting erupted all along the line as the Austro-Hungarian forces made their assaults. In vain, front-line commanders asked for a pause in operations, at least until supply columns could reach them. Casualties continued to mount as Potiorek's men slowly advanced. On 23 November, convinced that he was facing the main strength of the Serbian Army, Potiorek urged XV and XVI Corps forward; XV Corps would then turn northeast, to meet up with the southern flank of Fifth Army (XIII Corps), which would be advancing towards the southeast. As the weather turned colder and heavy snow fell, Fifth Army's troops finally took control of Mount Maljen, at the southern end of the battlefield, where they had spilt so much blood over the previous two days. A further success was achieved at Čovka the following day, where VIII Corps captured 1,300 prisoners and four guns. The centre of the Serbian line appeared to be giving way. On the Serbian side, General Mišić repeatedly requested a further withdrawal for his First Army at the southern end of the battle line. The front line was simply too long for his depleted formations, he insisted, and an orderly withdrawal would give his men a much-needed breathing space. Putnik refused at first, pointing out that a retreat by First Army would necessitate withdrawals by the other two armies, and would also result in the abandonment of Belgrade. Mišić was adamant. In any event, he told Putnik, he had already given orders for his forces to pull back. Putnik had no choice but to accept the withdrawal.[31]

But if the Serbs were at their last gasp, Potiorek's men were in little better shape. Battalions were reduced to the strength of companies, and supplies of all sorts remained desperately short. Nevertheless, as the Austro-Hungarian troops – clad in threadbare uniforms they had worn since the summer, and in boots often reduced to fragments of leather – laboured forward again, they found that the Serbs had pulled back. On 30 November Sixth Army was ordered to halt. Potiorek now came under pressure from an unexpected source. The Germans were anxious to secure a rail link with Turkey, and this necessitated the capture of Belgrade. The German Minister of War Falkenhayn even offered to send a German division to Serbia, but Conrad refused to allow this; if German troops were to be deployed to help the *k.u.k.* Army, he insisted, it would be in Galicia, not Serbia. Regardless of whether German troops would be available, Potiorek ordered Fifth Army to march on Belgrade. Prisoners told their Austro-Hungarian captors that the city was being abandoned, with Serbian troops pulling back to the southeast. Even as Frank's men hurried through the winter snows to secure the great prize, they found that the small Austro-Hungarian garrison on the far side of the Danube had already sent troops into the city. Belgrade was declared captured on 2 December.

Potiorek immediately issued further orders. Only weak units were to be left in the Serbian capital; the rest of Fifth Army was to march on Semendria (now Smederevo), about 20 miles (32km) further east. By doing so, Frank would drive back the Serbian Second Army, and would then be able to turn south into the rear of the main Serbian forces. Final victory would then be assured.

Unfortunately for Potiorek, the Serbs might have been greatly weakened by the bitter fighting in terrible weather and difficult terrain, but help had arrived just in time. Ammunition supplies from France and Russia had finally been unloaded in Salonika, and transported from there to Serbia. Potiorek had been aware of the arrival of munitions in Salonika, but had relied on reports that the railway bridge over the Vardar gorge had been destroyed, cutting the line. Although these reports were true, the destruction of the bridge occurred after the trains carrying munitions had already passed. In addition, unlike their enemies, the Serbs were retreating into their homeland, and thus did not suffer from lengthening supply lines. They were also aware from interrogation of prisoners that the ordinary Austro-Hungarian troops were exhausted, poorly clothed, and short of all manner of supplies. On 1 December Mišić issued a proclamation to his men:

> The difficult and miserable situation of the enemy must now be exploited. He must be attacked everywhere and in every place, and given no rest or peace until he is destroyed and driven from our homeland. Now we will use all our strength, all our courage and all our self-sacrifice, as the most favourable opportunity has arisen to defeat the enemy troops that have penetrated into our land.[32]

Without waiting for approval, Mišić gave orders for an attack on 2 December. At this stage he would have had limited information about Austro-Hungarian movements, but his attack happened to fall at the very moment when a gap had opened in Potiorek's ranks; Sixth Army was still in its positions to the south, and Fifth Army was concentrating around Belgrade. While one of his divisions tied down the flank of Sixth Army, Mišić burst through a 6-mile (10km) sector of front with his other three divisions on 3 December, inflicting heavy casualties on XVI

Corps. Later the same day, the neighbouring Third Army also attacked. Although it gained only modest ground, it tied down Austro-Hungarian units that might have been rushed to the aid of XVI Corps.

Frank's troops in Belgrade had been granted a rest day, but this was hastily cancelled when news arrived of the general Serbian offensive in the south. Preparations for the planned advance of Fifth Army were accelerated, and the following day both VIII and XIII Corps launched powerful attacks – but the key battlefield remained in the south. Although the 'Užice Army' – the relatively small mixed force that had conducted forays into southern Bosnia, and was now on the extreme southern flank of the Serbian line – was unable to force the fortified lines held by the Austro-Hungarian forces, Mišić's First Army continued to advance. Although his right flank was thrown back by an energetic counterattack, Mišić pushed on, knowing that gains on the rest of his front would make any local Austro-Hungarian success irrelevant. Further north, the Serbian Third Army and the Austro-Hungarian XIII Corps fought a bitter engagement around Žička, with heavy losses on both sides, but little change in territory.

For Potiorek all now depended on whether the hard-pressed XVI Corps could hold out while Frank's Fifth Army launched its decisive attack from the north. His daily telegrams to Vienna give little impression that a crisis was looming; either he remained supremely confident, or he chose not to inform his superiors about the details of the situation.[33] The problem for Frank was that he had intended to use both VIII Corps and Krauss' troops, now known as the Combined Corps, in his attack, but the latter force was still en route for the area. In the meantime the balance of power had shifted firmly in favour of the Serbs. The comparatively ample supply of ammunition to the Serbian forces allowed their artillery to fire without restraint, for the first time in weeks. XVI Corps was driven back in increasing disorder, and XV Corps to its north forced to yield its southern flank to maintain continuity. Potiorek received encouraging reports from elements of XVI Corps during the night of 5/6 December, suggesting that the Serbian advance was being held up. He urged Krauss to rush his Combined Corps into action, adding:

> The main objective for the Combined Corps must be the Topola area. The decision of the current struggle between the two armies depends on the force of this corps.[34]

This might have been true, but the men of the Combined Corps were too tired by their long march in difficult weather to exert much force. In any event, XVI

Corps was unable to resist. Almost out of ammunition, with its units hopelessly entangled with each other as a consequence of their disorderly retreat, there was no prospect of it continuing to hold up the Serbian First Army, regardless of the optimistic message sent late on 5 December. As a result, Potiorek reluctantly ordered its withdrawal behind the Kolubara. The order came too late to prevent further heavy losses, when a regiment of the Serbian 1st Dunav Division, bypassing the retreating Austro-Hungarian troops, took up position overlooking the road to Mionica, and shelled the long columns of rear area units struggling westward. Racing to catch up with events, Feldzugmeister Wurm, commander of XVI Corps, ordered his remaining battle-worthy troops to take up positions either side of Valjevo.

The 7th of December brought a much-needed respite for XVI Corps. Like armies on all fronts in the First World War, the Serbian First Army found that even if a local success was achieved, troops rapidly outstripped their supply lines, and had to pause while food and ammunition were brought forward. With XVI Corps driven back, XV Corps now came under increasing pressure. The crossings over the Kolubara and Ljig became a series of miniature battles, with small Austro-Hungarian units fighting desperately to hold them while stragglers made their way to comparative safety.

It was now the last possible opportunity for Fifth Army to come to the rescue. Frank's exhausted men struggled forward, but a decisive victory was beyond their strength, especially in the face of the rejuvenated Serbian artillery. On 8 December, having been resupplied overnight, Mišić's First Army resumed its attacks at the same time that Second Army launched a powerful attack on VIII Corps north of Lazarevac. Despite heavy fighting, the Serbs were unable to retake Valjevo; however, they did establish a bridgehead over the Kolubara, threatening to outflank the defenders. The struggle for the town was renewed the following morning, and by the afternoon it was clear that Sixth Army would not be able to hold its positions. Potiorek had no choice, and had to allow XVI and XV Corps to retreat towards the west. XIII Corps, which had been part of Sixth Army for much of the campaign, was returned to Fifth Army, and allowed to retreat north to the Belgrade area, where a bridgehead was to be held.

By the end of 9 December, Potiorek's chief of staff Generalmajor Böltz had come to the conclusion that Sixth Army's units required several weeks to recover their fighting strength, and that they should attempt to withdraw completely from Serbia. Potiorek, for perfectly understandable reasons, was reluctant to agree to this, but had to accept reality. He now finally sent a report to Vienna that revealed the true nature of events:

I report that I must withdraw XV and XVI Corps, which have been in almost continuous combat for a month and whose offensive was weakened through a lack of replacement drafts and limited ammunition supplies after they reached the area east of Valjevo, to the Šabac area, as they cannot hold the Kolubara at Valjevo. Recovery will take three weeks.[35]

Following the generally confident reports of previous day, this telegram must have come as a huge shock to Chief of Military Council Bolfras and others in Vienna. Having finally given their pursuers the slip, the shattered remnants of XV and XVI Corps crossed the river into Syrmia on 12 December.

All eyes now turned to Belgrade. Pressure on Fifth Army began to build late on 11 December, when an attack late in the day nearly broke through the Austro-Hungarian lines. Both Second and Third Armies now concentrated on the Austro-Hungarian 'bridgehead', and there were numerous penetrations the following day. Frank's troops pulled back to a new defensive line with difficulty. On 13 December pressure continued, with setbacks all along the front. Alarmed by the sudden string of disastrous reports, AOK sent an urgent telegram to Potiorek, urging him to avoid the defeat of Fifth Army; after the near-complete collapse of Sixth Army, this would leave Syrmia almost defenceless.[36] Potiorek passed on the message to Frank, adding that he would allow Fifth Army to give up Belgrade when it was no longer possible to hold it, and a withdrawal over the Sava could safely be carried out. Although Frank replied to the effect that he would do what he could, the message was delayed in transit. The following day, as fighting flared once more around the perimeter, Potiorek spoke to the commander of Fifth Army by telephone to seek clarification of what was happening. The two men agreed that Belgrade could not be held, and orders were given for a retreat.

Late on 14 December, after exhaustion had brought a pause to the bitter fighting, Frank's Fifth Army withdrew across the river. Under the protective guns of the Danube Flotilla, the rearguard pulled back across the pontoon bridges, which were safely dismantled, and all permanent bridges blown up. The Serbian campaign was over.

Casualties on both sides had been terrible. Perhaps 450,000 Austro-Hungarian troops had been committed to the Serbian front; of these, over 224,000 were dead, wounded or prisoner. Serbian losses numbered 170,000, but as a percentage of their forces were far heavier. Typhus spread through both armies at the end of the campaign, adding to the death toll; General Michael von Appel, commander of XV Corps in Sixth Army, was one of those to die of illness during the winter. In addition, a large part of Serbia had been reduced to ruins. Thousands of civilians perished in the winter that followed, from a combination of illness, hunger, and exposure.

It was inevitable that there would be an inquest into the Austro-Hungarian disaster. Archduke Karl was appointed to oversee the investigation, during which Potiorek refused to assign any blame to his subordinates. The responsibility lay entirely with him, he insisted. Late in December, Potiorek was invited to submit his resignation. Almost suicidal with despair at his failure to avenge Sarajevo, he obliged, and was allowed to retire. He survived until 1931; one of his prized possessions at the time of his death was the couch on which Franz Ferdinand had been placed after he was shot. Frank, the commander of Fifth Army, was also dismissed. Potiorek's Sixth Army was disbanded, and Tersztyánszky, who had commanded IV Corps in August, replaced Frank as Fifth Army's commander. Overall command of the Balkan theatre passed to Archduke Eugen von Habsburg-Lothringen. In peacetime, he had commanded XIV Corps, and had retired from military service in 1911, officially for health reasons, though there had been suggestions of friction between him and Franz Ferdinand. At the beginning of the war, he volunteered for service, but was given an unimportant welfare role. Now, he found himself in command of the shattered *k.u.k.* troops along the Serbian border.

The mistakes made by Potiorek were numerous. He chose to attack before mobilisation was complete, and selected completely unsuitable terrain for his initial invasion. The original invasion resulted in three Austro-Hungarian lines of advance, unable to support each other. Even after he was forced into an ignominious retreat, Potiorek attacked in exactly the same location, condemning his men to several weeks of bloody fighting in the mountains east of the Drina. It was widely accepted that railways were essential for the supplies of armies; the Russians even avoided building railway lines that might be used by the Germans in an invasion of Russia, even though this complicated mobilisation and concentration of the Russian Army. Despite this, Potiorek's line of advance did not follow any railways, ensuring that when his men were finally successful in driving back the Serbs, they inevitably suffered from supply problems. Potiorek attempted to blame Conrad for the failure of the initial invasion, citing the withdrawal of Second Army at a critical moment. Whilst this might have been true at a tactical level, the planned transfer of Second Army to Galicia was something that Potiorek had known would happen, and it was irresponsible in the extreme for him to make plans that stood in the way of this transfer.

On the Serbian side, the cost of their astonishing victory had been severe. Their casualties had left the ranks of Serbia's armies full of replacements, many of them in their teens. Material costs had also been considerable, but Serbia had done what it believed was necessary: it had survived until the end of the year, by which time the Russians had confidently predicted they would have won the war. Indeed, the British, French, Russians, and the Germans had all expected that they would enjoy a victorious homecoming by Christmas. The reality was completely different.

CHAPTER 12

MUD AND BLOOD

AUTUMN IN POLAND

When Ludendorff left East Prussia for his new assignment, he was intended to become the chief of staff of a new Ninth Army, with General Richard von Schubert as commander. However, partly at Ludendorff's suggestion, there was a radical change of plan. Schubert would take over a much-reduced Eighth Army, while Hindenburg, taking with him the bulk of Eighth Army's strength, would join Ludendorff in Silesia to take command of Ninth Army. In addition, Hindenburg would have overall responsibility for Eighth Army. Ludendorff arrived in Breslau (now Wrocław) early on 16 September to the news that the new army would consist of XI, XVII, XX and Guards Reserve Corps, with 35th Reserve Division and Graf von Bredow's *Landwehr* Division as additional forces. Hindenburg arrived the following day, and after further discussions Ludendorff travelled to Neu-Sandez (now Nowy Sącz) to meet Conrad von Hötzendorf and the Austro-Hungarian high command.

There were changes elsewhere in the German command structure. The First Battle of the Marne in the west was, taken on its own, little more than a tactical victory for the French, but its strategic implications were enormous, bringing to an end any hopes of a swift victory for the Germans in France, which would have allowed them to switch their armies to the east. As his plans and hopes turned to ashes, Moltke collapsed under the strain, and was relieved of his post. He was assigned to a staff post in Berlin, but his health continued to decline. He died in June 1916.

Opinions of Moltke have varied greatly. In many respects he was unfortunate, in that his name inevitably invited unfavourable comparisons with his illustrious uncle. He deliberately rejected plans for a war solely with Russia, arguing that it was inconceivable that France would not intervene in the west, and he has thus been blamed for ensuring that Germany became embroiled in a war with both France and Russia at the same time.[1] He has also been criticised for not keeping tight control of the armies that swept through Belgium, and for allowing the gap to develop in the German lines that the French exploited in the First Battle of the Marne. Given the technology of the age, and the scale of the troop movements in the campaign, it is hard to imagine how anyone could have maintained control, and in any case, such tight control was contrary to the German way of war. Writing at the height of the Marne fighting, he stated in a letter to his wife:

> I am often overcome with horror when I think about [the war], and I feel as if I should answer for this appalling situation, yet I could have done no other than I have.[2]

Moltke's replacement as chief of the general staff was Erich von Falkenhayn, who was currently serving as the minister for war. He held both posts until Adolf Wild von Hohenborn took over his ministerial duties in early 1915. Falkenhayn was the man who now had to devise a plan for Germany to continue the war, after the failure of the strategy that had been designed to ensure a swift victory. In particular, he had to deal with the grim certainty of a two-front war, which the Schlieffen Plan had been designed to avoid.

As Ludendorff travelled through the comparatively rich Silesian countryside and on into Galicia, he was struck by the contrast:

> Upper Silesia, with its high culture, had been unknown to me before. In Galicia, I saw the nature of the most neglected land in Europe and I got a taste of the Polish economy. Particularly backward were the Polish Jews ... it is not just the fault of these people, but also of their administrators.[3]

Ludendorff was not alone in regarding the Jews of Eastern Europe as being particularly lowly. In a brief incursion into Poland before his corps was sent to take part in the Battle of Gumbinnen, Mackensen made similar observations. Anti-Semitism was widespread in Europe, particularly in Germany and Russia, even though thousands of Jews served loyally in the armies of the two nations. Whilst this clearly has resonances with German behaviour towards Jews in a later war, it should be remembered that Alfred Knox, the British military attaché who accompanied Samsonov's army into East Prussia, made similar comments. While such comments are judgemental to a modern eye, they would have been unremarkable at the time, and represented attitudes that were widely shared.

In Neu-Sandez Ludendorff met Conrad for the first time. Whilst he clearly warmed to Conrad as an individual, his assessment of the Austro-Hungarian high command was very astute:

> General Conrad had not had a high opinion of our peacetime training. Now he confessed that he was open to our principles. In particular, he said, he could not place too great a value on what built men's morale. The *k.u.k.* General Staff had too many theories and was a stranger to military service. There was too much command from on high, and any enthusiasm for independent action was suppressed.
>
> The staff personnel were well trained, but there was a huge excess of officers.[4]

Conrad had always shown a somewhat contradictory attitude to independent action by subordinates. On the one hand he had acknowledged the benefits of devolved decision-making on the lines proposed by the elder Moltke, but on the other hand his insistence on attack at all costs, even prescribing at a tactical level how this should be carried out, ensured that any subordinates who used their theoretical independence of action would do so in an entirely predictable way. His pre-eminent status in the *k.u.k.* Army before the war ensured that all young officers tried to emulate him, and followed his teachings with painstaking detail, further stifling any genuine innovation. The sometimes chaotic and contradictory attitude of German corps commanders in peacetime exercises at least allowed different theories to be displayed, and subsequently criticised. In the Austro-Hungarian Empire, the almost slavish following of Conrad's doctrine ensured that only one tactical doctrine prevailed.

Another factor that contributed to the gulf between expectations and reality in the *k.u.k.* Army was that plans were based upon peacetime exercises that rarely lasted more than a few days. During those exercises, commanders pushed their troops to the limit, in a manner that would be unsustainable for more than a short period, especially given the supply difficulties of wartime. Nor was there any appreciation of the fact that troops who were already tired from long marches were unlikely to be able to endure the physical and mental strain of intense combat. Rather than accept that these pre-war assessments were inaccurate, Conrad persisted in blaming his subordinates for failing to execute operations according to hopelessly optimistic timetables.

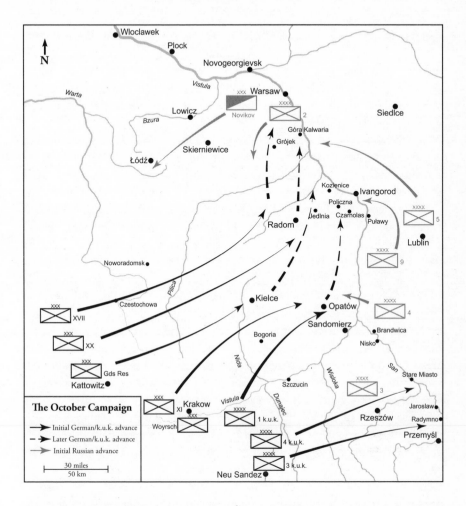

The October Campaign

→ Initial German/k.u.k. advance
--→ Later German/k.u.k. advance
→ Initial Russian advance

30 miles
50 km

Regardless of his criticisms of the Austro-Hungarian general staff, Ludendorff became a close personal friend of Conrad. The two men discussed the current situation, and the likelihood of a further Russian attack towards Krakow, which would in turn raise the possibility of a Russian advance into Silesia. There would also be a possibility of the Russians turning south through the Moravian Gap, a break in the Carpathian Mountains that led directly into Austria itself. Several Siberian divisions were now gathered around Warsaw, and it seemed likely that these would march southwest to support a westerly drive by the forces of Southwest Front. In order to oppose this, Conrad and Ludendorff agreed, the *k.u.k.* Army would extend its northern flank north of the Vistula, and the

German Ninth Army would then take up positions alongside. At the same time, Conrad's armies would attempt to counterattack in Galicia. If the Russians attempted to hold onto all their gains in Galicia, they would run the risk of defeat west of the Vistula and ultimately at Warsaw. If they diverted troops to defend Poland, the Austro-Hungarian armies in the south might reverse their defeats of preceding weeks.

By the end of September Ninth Army was fully assembled and in position; in addition to the forces previously assigned, it had also been allocated 8th Cavalry Division. XI Corps was deployed immediately to the north of Krakow, with the bulk of the army, including Mackensen's XVII Corps, to the northwest of Katowice. The cavalry, supported by Bredow's *Landwehr* Division, was deployed on the extreme left flank. In addition, linking the right flank of Ninth Army with the Austro-Hungarian forces, was the *Landwehr* Corps commanded by General Remus von Woyrsch. The 68-year-old veteran of Bismarck's wars against Austria and France had led his two *Landwehr* divisions across Poland – against almost no resistance – as far as the Vistula to link up with the left flank of Dankl's First Army during the Austro-Hungarian advance in August. He had then played a substantial part in holding off the Russians as they drove Dankl back. During the Austro-Hungarian retreat, Woyrsch and his men lost contact with the German high command; Ludendorff and Hindenburg even received a message saying that the corps had been annihilated, and its commander killed. Now, having received a battalion of elderly howitzers as reinforcements, Woyrsch was once more ready for an advance.

The advance of the German Ninth Army began with the leading elements setting out on 28 September, followed by the bulk of the troops two days later. It encountered minimal opposition. On its right flank, Dankl's weakened First Army crossed the Vistula and kept step. The main obstacle encountered by the Germans came in the form of poor roads, reduced to rivers of mud by the weather. 35th Infantry Division reached Przedbórz late on 30 September the small Polish town did not make a good impression on the German infantry, who described it as giving 'an impression of concentrated filth and stench'.[5] Five days later the division reached Radom, where it expected to encounter the first serious resistance of the campaign. As soon as the German heavy artillery was brought to bear, though, the Russian infantry withdrew from their positions and abandoned the town. The march through the muddy countryside resumed, as Mackensen recorded in his diary:

> The graceless countryside, the grubby villages and people look even less inviting in the hideous rainy weather. Russia is in every respect a backward, ugly country. The

towns, too, have degenerated into filth and disorder. Even the streets of a town as important as Radom paint a picture that would be impossible in Germany, quite apart from the numerous Jews who live in this town. The roads of this country defy all description. One has the impression that the authorities have not been accustomed to do anything at all to help traffic. Even the few so-called hard roads between the larger areas are neglected. In this respect, it is readily apparent that our conduct of the war is seriously affected.[6]

The casual inability to distinguish between Poland and Russia is a recurring theme of German accounts of the era, but it should be remembered that Poland had not existed as a national entity for over a century. Just a few days earlier the Russians had published a proclamation that says much about their attitudes to Poland:

People of Poland! The hour when the dreams of your fathers and grandfathers will be realised is at hand. It has been 150 years since the living body of Poland was cut into pieces, but its soul is not dead. It lives in hope of witnessing the hour of the resurrection of the Polish people, of their fraternal reconciliation with Great Russia … the frontiers will be erased, those frontiers that have cut the people of Poland into pieces… [Poland] will find its unity under the sceptre of the Tsar of Russia. Under this sceptre, Poland will be reborn, free in its religion, language, and its own administration.[7]

The proclamation conveniently glossed over the fact that Russia had been a leading player in the dismemberment of Poland, and even this promise of a new Poland was explicitly couched in terms that ensured that Poland remained subordinated to Russia. Unsurprisingly, the proclamation had little or no effect on inciting Poles in German and Austro-Hungarian territories to rise up in revolt. Attempts by Polish groups in Paris to seek clarification on what was meant by 'own administration' – one translation of the proclamation used the expression 'autonomy' – merely revealed that the Russian administration had contradictory views regarding Poland. Many remained deeply hostile to the concept of any independence at all, not least because it was feared that if Poland were granted a degree of autonomy, there would inevitably be demands from regions such as the Baltic for similar recognition.

As the October rains continued to pour down, the German forces approached the Vistula valley, and Ninth Army Headquarters was established in Kielce. To the disappointment of Hindenburg and Ludendorff, the Russians put up only token resistance before withdrawing over the Vistula. Having advanced with so little fighting, the Germans faced a problem of what to do next. Simply forcing a crossing over the Vistula would merely invite ever-lengthening lines of communication, without necessarily bringing the Russians to battle. In the end it was decided to move most of Ninth Army to secure the Vistula north of Ivangorod, while a crossing over the river would have to wait until the Austro-Hungarian forces succeeded in making headway.

The reason for the lack of Russian resistance was because the Russians did not intend to contest the region with the limited forces they had in the area. There appears to have been no clear idea in the Russian camp of how to exploit the victory in Galicia. The fortress of Przemyśl continued to defy the besiegers, and Ivanov made plans to replace the forces surrounding the city with reserve divisions. This would allow him to send his more experienced armies west towards Krakow. Alternatively, he suggested a major concentration of forces on the Vistula with the intention of penetrating into central Poland, from where the Russians could either threaten to turn south to Krakow – and thence towards Vienna – or northwest towards Berlin. Aware that Ruzsky's Northwest Front was in no position to protect the northern flank of such an advance, *Stavka* was not enthusiastic. But as the situation in the north stabilised, there was further pressure from Russia's ally in the west. The Russian ambassador to Paris cabled Sergei Sazonov, the Russian foreign minister, to report that there was growing public criticism of Russia's efforts, and that it would be prudent to appease these comments by making a greater effort against Germany.[8] As confidence about a thrust into Poland grew, both front commanders were ordered on 28 September to prepare for major offensive operations. Ruzsky's Northwest Front would attack from Warsaw towards Kalisz in central Poland, while Ivanov's Southwest Front would muster at least ten corps along the Vistula as a supporting advance. In the meantime, Ivanov had proposed a major withdrawal by his forces, so that they could concentrate in anticipation of a joint Austro-Hungarian and German offensive in Galicia. Once this offensive had left the woodland around the River San, Southwest Front would then counterattack in force. There was no evidence to support suggestions that the Central Powers were planning any such major attack, and Grand Duke Nikolai brusquely overruled Ivanov, ordering him instead to concentrate his forces on the Vistula as ordered. This was not dissimilar to Ivanov's original proposal, and he now ordered the bulk of the units under his command – Second, Fourth, Ninth, and Fifth Armies – to concentrate along the Vistula. Two armies would be left in Galicia, Dimitriev's Third Army and Brusilov's Eighth Army, with the latter commander in overall charge. Inevitably, if the Austro-Hungarian armies advanced, this force would have to fall back, but this was accepted as a necessary evil. Brusilov would not have enough men to hold all the ground that had been gained, particularly at the end of such long supply lines that ran across most of Galicia, terrain that had been ravaged by the fighting of the previous weeks. The new emphasis on operations across the Vistula, ultimately leading to a major thrust into the heart of Germany, made this a sacrifice worth making. Once the 'Russian steamroller' of at least four armies had assembled, it was argued, it would be unstoppable.[9]

The redeployment of Plehve's Fifth Army from Galicia to the area around Warsaw proved to be a laborious business, effectively removing the entire army from the front line for several weeks. Even if Ivanov had been inclined to attack, the absence of Plehve's troops ensured that the Russian forces left in Galicia were too weak to mount a major thrust. Nevertheless, Brusilov dispatched a cavalry force to probe the Uzsok Pass, one of three major routes through the Carpathian Mountains. Fighting continued in the region during the last week of September before the Russians withdrew.

While Ludendorff and Hindenburg planned and executed their advance across southern Poland, Conrad struggled to find out what the Russians intended to do. For possibly the first time in the war, cavalry units succeeded in achieving one of their expected roles – Russian cavalry managed to screen the Russian armies from Austro-Hungarian reconnaissance. The first hard intelligence came late on 27 September, when a radio intercept suggested that the Russian Ninth Army was withdrawing towards the east. The Austro-Hungarian armies had used their days of rest to good effect, absorbing reinforcements to refill their depleted ranks. In a similar manner, Conrad's own belief in the virtues of offensive operations began to make itself felt again, and he speculated on various possibilities. If the Russians were to push west in Galicia towards Silesia, they would expose both their flanks to counterstrokes – from the south by the Austro-Hungarian forces, and from the north by Hindenburg and Ludendorff. If they attacked the Germans, the Austro-Hungarian armies could engage their flank. If they turned south to try to force the Carpathian passes into Hungary, they would leave their west flank and rear open to counterstrokes.

The arrival of reinforcements might have restored Conrad's battered divisions to something approaching their establishment strength, but nothing could disguise the loss of experienced officers and NCOs, and the terrible conditions during the retreat had also taken a severe toll. Cholera became almost epidemic in some encampments; Second Army's IV Corps had over 2,000 men struck down with the disease in the last two weeks of September, two-thirds of whom did not survive.[10] Nevertheless, on 1 October Dankl's troops advanced across the Vistula, reaching Bogoria without encountering any significant resistance.

South of the Vistula, Conrad's armies found that the Russians had already commenced a withdrawal prior to the Austro-Hungarian advance. Immediately, Conrad's thoughts turned to the possibilities of major offensives, reaching as far as Lublin or even Lemberg. In addition to sending Dankl's First Army to advance either side of the Vistula, the other Austro-Hungarian armies were also to launch attacks. If the Russian forces remaining in Galicia could be pinned down, First Army was to turn the western flank, while Second Army turned the eastern flank. If all went well, and the two Austro-Hungarian armies moved swiftly, there was the possibility of an encirclement to equal Hindenburg's achievement at Tannenberg. The disaster of August would be reversed.

Given how much difficulty the Russians faced in marching through this area, even without any enemy resistance, such dreams were optimistic in the extreme, and both sides rapidly ran into difficulties. Early October saw major troop movements, with the Russians struggling to redeploy their armies in line with the plans of *Stavka*. Throughout the region heavy rain resulted in swollen rivers, particularly the San, which often swept away the temporary bridges erected by the army. Additional problems were created by the reluctance of the two Russian fronts to cooperate effectively. Once Fifth Army began to arrive in its new location, to the southeast of Warsaw, it was reliant upon Northwest Front for its supplies. Ruzsky refused to allocate it any priority, preferring to divert all resources to his own armies, with the result that Plehve's four infantry corps and three cavalry divisions, already seriously degraded by the difficulties of their march from the south, remained unfit for combat. Danilov later summarised the root causes of this lack of cooperation and coordination:

> For a very long time, our plans for campaigns in the event of a war on our western frontier divided our field army into two great fronts, operating in many respects independently – the German front and the Austrian front. This division necessitated a reduction in the authority of the Commander-in-Chief and his influence on the conduct of operations; on the other hand, it gave the Front commanders such great independence that their conduct would eventually be able to compromise not only the unity of action of the groups, but even the outcome of the war. The Front commanders had been granted too much power, even if it was limited by the directives of the Commander-in-Chief. But these directives, given the vast scope of each Front and the numbers of units in the line of battle, clearly could not encompass these vast operations and the problems of coordination. In fact, this division into two Fronts in the west corresponded more with the concept of two distinct wars – one against Germany, the other against

Austria – than with the concept of a single war, conducted against the monolithic block of the Central Powers … every tentative attempt during times of peace to modify this established division of our field army into two was defeated, particularly as the established arrangement was ingrained amongst military leaders. It would be even harder to reform the organisation of higher commands during wartime, as it would require the abolition of important and responsible posts, and the concentration not only of the direction of combat operations, but also of rear area arrangements, in the hands of the Commander-in-Chief.[11]

Whilst Danilov's comments are certainly true, there is little to suggest that the expertise existed within Russian military circles for such a centralised system of command. There was also the problem created by geography – the great Pripet Marshes effectively divided the western frontier of Russia into two zones, leading almost inevitably to two completely separate arrangements for military operations. The same geographical constraints ensured that supply lines lay within two distinct jurisdictions, leading directly to the problems faced by Fifth Army in securing supplies from a different command network.[12]

The most significant fighting west of the Vistula occurred near Opatów. A mixed force of Russian infantry and cavalry found itself facing the junction of the German and Austro-Hungarian forces, and after an initial skirmish, Carl Gustaf Mannerheim, the Finnish commander of the Russian force, ordered his cavalry to withdraw across the Vistula. Unfortunately, he failed to inform General Delsalle, the commander of his infantry that he was withdrawing; in any case, his artillery severely damaged the bridge as it crossed, leaving it almost impossible for the infantry to follow. Perhaps half the Russian infantry managed to escape to alternative crossing points, for example at Sandomierz; the rest, numbering about 7,000, were killed or taken prisoner.

With growing confidence Dankl urged his troops forward. His I Corps and a mixed group under Feldmarschalleutnant Wieber were operating on the left bank of the Vistula, and he ordered them to press on towards Sandomierz. At the same time, his other two corps were to pursue the retreating Russians on the right bank, and would attempt to reach the San crossings as fast as possible, ideally before the Russian units had completed their own retreat across the river. From there V Corps would continue along the Vistula to support the strike against Sandomierz, while X Corps was to be ready to turn southeast. Hindered by a mixture of bad weather and Russian resistance, it took Wieber's cavalry, operating in conjunction with I Corps' infantry, until early on 6 October to secure Sandomierz. By then the Russians had completed an orderly withdrawal across the river. Nor did the Austro-Hungarian V Corps enjoy better success on the other bank, running into the Russian XIV Corps in prepared positions. Although V Corps was able to advance, it could not interfere with the Russian withdrawal from Sandomierz.

Dankl's advance on either bank of the Vistula placed his army about two days' march ahead of its neighbour to the south. Conrad moved what reserves he had to protect the exposed eastern flank, and ordered Dankl to concentrate on clearing the area where the San ran into the Vistula. There were a few sharp actions, but the Russians made little attempt at stopping Dankl. By 8 October his men, tired by their march through difficult terrain along muddy roads already heavily degraded by the constant movements of troops over several weeks, were lined up along the lower San. The retreating Russians had destroyed all the bridges.

Dankl's First Army was not the only Austro-Hungarian force that was moving forward. Under its new commander Archduke Joseph Ferdinand, Fourth Army marched on Rzeszów on 4 October. By the end of the following day the leading elements were within 10 miles (16km) of Rzeszów. There had been little resistance, but the disappearance of the Russian Fifth Army was having an effect on Conrad's plans. *AOK* was unaware that the Russian force was actually struggling along muddy roads towards Warsaw, and constantly fretted about a sudden Russian counterattack, particularly against the exposed southeast flank of Dankl's First Army. Consequently, Archduke Joseph Ferdinand held an entire corps behind his own northern flank, ready to intervene wherever it might be required. Inevitably, this left the rest of the army weakened, reducing its chances of pinning down the retreating Russians.

On the southern flank of Fourth Army, Boroević drove forward with his Third Army directly towards Przemyśl. In anticipation of significant Russian resistance, Boroević kept his army grouped tightly together. This actually delayed the advance. Although the expected resistance failed to materialise, progress remained very slow; the rain, together with the heavy traffic created by so many units struggling forward over only a few routes, reduced the roads to almost impassable mud. On Boroević's right flank the Austro-Hungarian Second Army was also advancing, and beginning to move ahead; in an attempt to catch up, Boroević ordered his units to send 'flying columns' forward. Although there were a few encounters with Russian cavalry, there appeared to be no major attempt by the Russians to prevent the Austro-Hungarian advance.

Rzeszów was recaptured without a fight late on 7 October. Finally concluding that the Russians were not going to stand their ground, Archduke Joseph Ferdinand ordered a rapid march to the San at Radymno. This would effectively isolate Przemyśl from the north. The only significant resistance to Conrad's armies came in the south, where Böhm-Ermolli's Second Army struggled to drive Brusilov's forces from the Uzsok Pass. In the Carpathians the heavy rain that was falling across the entire region turned to snow, adding to the misery of the troops of both armies. Pál Kelemen, the Hungarian cavalryman, wrote in his diary:

There was only a single intact building in the mountain pass, a small tavern … a field telegraph had been set up in the main room; the staff officers of the cavalry corps were quartered in the next room. At 11 p.m., I entered and made my report to headquarters, that at the moment there was no progress. Then I lay down on a mattress on the first floor and slipped under my woollen blanket.

The wind howled through the dilapidated roof and rattled the windows. Outside, it was pitch black. Inside, the only light came from the flickering flame of a solitary candle. The telegraph was in constant use, transmitting orders for the morning's attack. In the hallway and the attic lay rows of men who had not been able to keep up with their units – the weak, the ill, the lightly wounded, who would resume their retreat in the morning.

I was half-awake, exhausted, a few officers were lying around me on straw sacks. The frozen, shivering men near the house had made a fire with the timbers from a neighbouring stable, and the flames, flickering in the night, attracted yet more soldiers.

A sergeant entered and asked permission to bring one of his comrades into the warmth: he was barely conscious and would certainly die in the cold outside. They laid him next to the door on straw, curled up, the whites of his eyes showing from time to time, his head drawn in between his shoulders. His coat had been shot through with bullets at several points, and the hem had been burned in some encampment. His hands were stiff with cold, and a scruffy, unkempt beard covered his haggard, tormented face…

At dawn I was wakened by the sound of men making ready to march onwards, and confused and dazed, I looked around this lowly dormitory. The grey-blue morning light leaked in through the frosted windows and filled every corner of the room. Only the soldier who had been carried in the previous evening was still lying there, his face turned down, towards the wall.

The door of the back room opened, and one of the adjutants, Prince Schönau-Gratzfeld, entered, freshly shaved, in pyjamas, blowing smoke from a long Turkish pipe into the stale, sour air.

He noticed the soldier who lay motionless in his corner, went over to him, but then recoiled in horror. Indignantly, he ordered that the corpse of the man, who apparently had died of cholera, was to be removed immediately. He then withdrew to the back room with an outraged expression. Two men dragged out a portable rubber bathtub, marked with an aristocratic crest and filled with warm water.[13]

The attitude of the aristocratic adjutant to the dead soldier was not unusual in an era of huge social divisions, and he was certainly right to demand the removal of a cholera victim, but the *k.u.k.* Army appears to have had a particular problem in this respect. Despite Conrad's pre-war writing about the importance of officers living together in order to build camaraderie, there was no attempt made to build good relationships between officers and other ranks. An additional problem arose as a result of the heavy losses suffered in the opening battles in Galicia. The core of experienced officers, many of whom were multilingual, was gone, and replacement officers frequently did not speak the same language as their men, and showed little inclination to learn a new language in the midst of war. As the war continued, soldiers repeatedly commented on the gulf between classes within the army, and in particular the almost complete absence of senior officers and staff from front-line positions. Commanders of other armies, too, spent much of their time away from the front line, causing resentment amongst those who struggled to implement their often completely unrealistic plans. With their boots and uniforms wearing out, and supplies rarely keeping up with their movements, the front-line soldiers of the Russian and Austro-Hungarian forces endured the mud and cold while their commanders – above the level of the most junior officers – commandeered comfortable accommodation in rear areas. Most of the troops had never trained in such conditions, and their ordeal was made worse by the loss of so many familiar faces around them. The replacement drafts were in an even worse situation, often rushed through training and then thrust into an utterly alien environment.

Prince Schönau-Gratzfeld might have treated his men with contempt and cared little for their welfare, but other officers were also struggling with the nuances of leadership. One such was General Orlov, who replaced Dimitriev as commander of VIII Corps in Brusilov's Eighth Army:

He was a man of intelligence, with a thorough knowledge of his profession, ingenious, and hard-working; yet his men hated him and did not trust him. From the very beginning of the campaign I had been always hearing complaints that he was an impossible leader and that the troops under him were thoroughly miserable. I attempted to find out for my own purposes what was at the bottom of this, and discovered that his officers disliked him because he was sparing of rewards, very rarely spoke to them, and, in their opinion, looked down on them. The men disliked him because he generally did not give them the usual greeting, never went around the cookhouses, did not sample the food, never thanked them for what they had done, and altogether appeared to ignore their existence. In actual fact he took a great interest in both officers and men, attempted by all the means in his power to achieve results with the least possible bloodshed, and was constantly offering me the most happy suggestions for the improvement of food and kit; but he scorned to let his men know it, or else did not understand how to tell them. I have known other commanders who took no sort of trouble about anything and yet were loved by their men and called 'father.' I warned General Orlov of this weakness, but my words had little effect; he did not know how to win the affection of those under him.[14]

Even here in the Carpathian passes, once they were threatened with a possible encirclement the Russians withdrew. Everywhere, the Austro-Hungarian armies approached the San. On 8 October the incessant rain finally ceased. Joseph Ferdinand's Fourth Army continued to advance either side of Rzeszów, driving before it the rearguard of Third Army. Sensing that his northern flank faced weaker forces, Joseph Ferdinand urged II and XIV Corps, supported by three cavalry divisions, to turn the Russian right flank. At the same time, Boroević was to attack from the south towards Jaroslaw, in the hope of encircling the retreating Russian forces. But Dimitriev had no intention of allowing his army to be trapped in this manner, and withdrew as fast as he could. The leading elements of XIV Corps overtook the Russian 13th Infantry Division, catching it in the process of crossing the San at Stare Miasto and Leżajsk; about 1,300 Russians were captured, but it was the only significant success of the encirclement attempt. Further south XVII Corps reached and captured Jaroslaw on 11 October. Fatigued by the muddy roads and already beginning to suffer from supply shortages, the Austro-Hungarian forces stopped along the river. Since they had begun their advance, Conrad's armies had taken about 5,000 prisoners; but it is notable that they recorded only six guns in their haul of booty. The Russians had carried out a very efficient withdrawal in difficult conditions.[15]

Attention now shifted to Przemyśl. On 5 October General Shcherbakov, commander of the forces encircling Przemyśl, had commenced assaults with what amounted to perhaps a little over seven infantry divisions, in an attempt to seize the fortress before the advancing Austro-Hungarian forces could reach the area. The main attack was on the southeast sector of the defences, around the village of Sedliska, with a major attempt being made to storm the fortifications early on 7 October. This part of the outer defences was in fact the strongest, but Shcherbakov deliberately chose to attack here, reasoning that the capture of the most formidable positions would precipitate a collapse in the garrison's morale. The leading formation in the Russian assault at this key area was 19th Infantry Division, part of XII Corps. Despite heavy casualties, the Russians captured some of the Austro-Hungarian positions, resulting in the garrison moving its limited reserves to the area. Shcherbakov and Brusilov had anticipated this, and had prepared other elements of XII Corps to attack north and south of 19th Infantry Division to take advantage of the weakening of the perimeter elsewhere. With Austro-Hungarian forces approaching the city from the south and west, the two Russian commanders paused to consider whether they could continue. They agreed that it would take another five or six days to reduce the fortress, and there was little prospect of the advancing Austro-Hungarian armies being held off for that long. In any event, the fighting would leave the Russian forces seriously weakened and unable to hold Przemyśl. Reluctantly, the assault was cancelled, and the battered regiments of 19th Infantry Division withdrew to their starting positions.[16]

Boroević originally intended to march his Third Army towards the besieged city on both banks of the San, but the destruction of bridges by the retreating Russians made cooperation between forces either side of the river difficult. In any event, the best road for his army was on the northern bank, and he directed III and IX Corps along this route. The Russians put up limited resistance, and it rapidly became clear to Boroević that the Russians did not intend to contest the lifting of the siege. At midday on 9 October a cavalry patrol from XII Corps reached and entered Przemyśl. The main body of Third Army reached the city three days later. The siege was, for the moment, ended.

Further east, Böhm-Ermolli's Second Army was also continuing its advance out of the Carpathians. The right flank of Second Army, commanded by General Tersztyánszky, marching on Stary Sambor (now Staryi Sambir) encountered a large body of Russian infantry dug in around the town of Turka. On 8 October the Austro-Hungarian soldiers laboured up the slopes held by the Russians through falling snow. Visibility was very limited, greatly reducing the efficacy of the artillery of both sides. Although 38th Infantry Division – the central body of Tersztyánszky's forces – managed to gain control of the high ground immediately south of Turka, the flanking formations, which it had been hoped would encounter little resistance, were unable to make sufficient headway. The isolated soldiers of 38th Infantry Division had to pull back, so that the entire force could regroup and attack again the following day. In the meantime 1st

Cavalry Division was ordered to bypass the western flank of the Russian defences with a view to cutting the only good road leading north from Turka. But as had previously been the case, the Russians – under the command of General Kornilov – did not wait to be encircled, and pulled out during the night.

Further north, the Russians were now in their new positions along the Vistula. Fourth Army held the line of the lower San and the Vistula with XIV, XVII, and Guards Corps. To its north, as far as Ivangorod, was Ninth Army with XVI, Grenadier, and III Caucasian Corps. Fifth Army should have been the next in line, but its exhausted units were still assembling around Lublin. The rejuvenated Second Army, consisting of I, XXVII, and II Siberian Corps, was closest to Warsaw. On 10 October orders were issued for a general attack. Fourth Army was to secure bridgeheads across the Vistula, while II and XXIII Corps, temporarily holding the zone intended for Fifth Army, would perform a similar task further north. Fifth Army would then deploy into this second bridgehead. While Second Army and General Novikov's cavalry divisions screened the northern flank, the mass of Russian forces would then roll west.

The Germans had made a tentative attack on the Russian defences to the west of Ivangorod, but did not make a serious attempt to storm the fortifications, opting instead to bombard them from a distance. Late on 9 October the Russian Grenadier and XVI Corps began to cross to the left bank south of Ivangorod. Both attempts failed in the face of powerful German resistance, with heavy losses. At the crossings at Puławy the German artillery followed the retreating Grenadiers and bombarded both the temporary bridges and the town beyond. The significance of this was that the main railway line to Ivangorod from the south ran through the town. The line was now only usable at night, and even then the sound of rail traffic attracted German bombardment. As a consequence, the redeployment of Fifth Army became even more protracted.[17]

The Russians already had a bridgehead across the river at Ivangorod, and III Caucasian Corps crossed to the left bank on 12 October. Although it received support from elements of XVII Corps, it was unable to push back the Germans at Kozienice, at the northern end of the bridgehead. Further north, although XXIII Corps succeeded in crossing the Vistula, it was unable to link up with the Russian Second Army defending the southern approaches to Warsaw, because the Germans were themselves advancing towards the Polish capital. On the same day, Ivanov met Grand Duke Nikolai in Chełm. Ivanov complained that the failure of Second Army to advance as planned had left both XXIII and XVII Corps in vulnerable positions. Nikolai responded by urging Ivanov to do all he could to bring Fifth Army into line as soon as possible. Once this was achieved,

Second and Fifth Armies would be able to drive forward together, with the intention of turning the northern flank of the German line. There then followed a discussion about command arrangements for the forces on the left bank of the Vistula. Grand Duke Nikolai suggested that Ivanov's chief of staff, Alexeyev, should be given command of Second Army, and even of all forces that were operating across the river. Ivanov replied that he would only accept this if Danilov was assigned as his chief of staff to replace Alexeyev. Unwilling to lose Danilov from his current post as quartermaster-general, Grand Duke Nikolai dropped the matter. It says much of command assignments in the Russian Army that both Alexeyev and Danilov were present at the meeting, but neither was invited to join the discussion.[18]

Grand Duke Nikolai remained preoccupied with the command of the forces that were to steamroller their way across Poland. The alacrity with which Ivanov, the commander of Southwest Front, blamed the command of Second Army (from Northwest Front) for the current problems seems to have made up the commander-in-chief's mind. Operations involving both fronts ran a high risk of being undermined by the constant lack of cooperation between the two commands. On 13 October Grand Duke Nikolai issued an instruction placing both Second and Fifth Armies, which were to provide the main force for the advance into Poland, under the command of Northwest Front. The role of Southwest Front was changed; instead of overseeing the main effort, it was to mount powerful attacks across the Vistula to tie down as many German and Austro-Hungarian formations as possible.

The precise timing of the commencement of the new Russian offensive was subject to interference by the Germans. On 8 October Mackensen had received instructions from Ninth Army Headquarters that he was to turn north and advance directly on Warsaw over the River Pilica. In the expectation that Russian resistance would remain light, XVII Corps – reinforced by XX Corps and *Landwehr* – was to attack the city itself on 11 October. It was hoped that by securing Warsaw Mackensen would gain not only an important political objective, but he would also secure Ninth Army's northern flank. Given that the supply lines for any Russian forces directed against the southern border of East Prussia ran through the Warsaw area, the cutting of these lines would also protect German territory from further invasions. Mackensen was under no doubts about the magnitude of the task he had been handed, as he wrote in his diary on 9 October:

> I have been given a new, difficult task. There is much at stake, and the success of the operation assigned to me will require much good fortune.[19]

The following day Mackensen's forces ran into the first serious resistance. Near Góra Kalwaria, 35th Infantry Division encountered Siberian troops for the first time. The neighbouring 36th Infantry Division fought its way through Grójek, while Bredow's *Landwehr* Division achieved the greatest success on the western end of the line, capturing over 2,000 prisoners and six guns. Everywhere, the Germans were within 15 miles (24km) of Warsaw, and it seemed possible that they would achieve a remarkable victory. However, pressure remained strong on the right flank of the German line, closest to the Vistula. Although 35th Infantry Division had pressed north from Góra Kalwaria, Russian forces were now spotted concentrating in the area. As a result, Mackensen hurried reinforcements from XX Corps to the area.

On 11 October the situation changed completely. A set of orders was found on the corpse of a Russian staff officer on the battlefield, revealing details of the Russian forces that were gathering along the Vistula. For the first time, the Germans became aware that they were facing no fewer than four Russian armies, which intended to roll up the German line from the north. This put the entire campaign in a different light. It was clear that these Russian armies had been sent to the area from Galicia – hence the speed and comparative ease with which Conrad's armies had advanced. It now became the intention of Hindenburg and Ludendorff to try to tie down as much of the Russian strength as possible, thus allowing the *k.u.k.* Army to achieve a victory against weaker forces in the south.

At first Mackensen continued to advance towards Warsaw, though predominantly with units further west. On the eastern flank XX Corps arrived and took up covering positions, and on the evening of 11 October Mackensen wrote to his wife proudly that he and his men were holding the most important sector of the battlefield.[20] His advance towards Warsaw took the Russians by surprise. Endless delays in getting Fifth Army to its designated sector ensured that there was no prospect of the great Russian offensive into Poland starting until 18 October, and the presence of German troops barely 6 miles (10km) from the southern edge of Warsaw caused a degree of panic, with refugees, stragglers, and wounded streaming into the city. The Russian forces facing XX Corps withdrew across the Vistula on 12 October, and although the front line remained relatively quiet, Mackensen could not fail to notice the steady build-up of Russian troops facing him. At first he was reluctant to abandon the ground that had been won in the last few days. Traugott von Sauberzweig, a staff officer currently serving as Ninth Army's quartermaster-general, later recorded:

I personally travelled to the positions of XVII Corps near Warsaw every day and convinced myself that despite all that had been done to strengthen them, they could not be held against a substantially superior enemy. The necessary reserves were lacking. General von Mackensen lamented loudly to me that he would have to give way in the face of the overwhelming Russian superiority. The popular, venerable General contemplated with warm compassion the great efforts that a retreat would require from his brave West Prussians, and the losses that would thus have been in vain.[21]

Mackensen himself later described the situation in slightly different words:

When the Commanding Officer expressly gave me a free hand to stand my ground or to retreat, I saw it as my most important task to act in the best interests of the overall operation. Thus came my answer: I would stand my ground. The more the Russians were concentrated around Warsaw, the greater would be the consequence of this decision. But I cannot deny that in view of the daily increasing Russian superiority, I felt a sense of responsibility, which also placed a growing strain on my nerves.[22]

How much of this is rationalisation after the event, and how much was a genuine calculation at the time, is hard to say. It can be argued that Mackensen did not want to retreat, for the reasons that Sauberzweig described, and later justified his decision on strategic grounds. Similarly, although Ludendorff and Hindenburg later requested that Mackensen hold on as long as possible, the commander of XVII Corps and its attached forces had already made a decision by then to cling to his positions.

Despite their growing strength, the Russians limited themselves to an increasingly heavy bombardment of Mackensen's positions on 14 and 15 October. Attacks began in earnest on 16 October along the entire front. In view of the overall strategic plan – that the Germans would tie down as much Russian strength as possible, while Conrad's armies tried to win a decisive victory in the south – Ludendorff advised Mackensen that an Austro-Hungarian success in Galicia was unlikely to occur quickly. Ludendorff had already suggested to Conrad that the Austro-Hungarian First Army, much of which was already on the left bank of the Vistula, should concentrate in support of Mackensen before Warsaw. Conrad refused, stating that he did not want to see his own front line broken up; his preferred solution was to extend First Army's positions northwards, allowing the Germans in turn to shift their strength to the north. Such a move would take too long, Hindenburg had decided, and had already issued instructions for preparations for a general withdrawal to the southwest. All roads and railway lines were to be destroyed as the Germans withdrew, to limit the ability of the Russians to follow. In order to allow time for preparations to be completed, Mackensen was informed, his forces would have to hold their positions for another two days:

> It was a dramatic scene when the bringer of the Commanding Officer's message asked if General von Mackensen could hold until 18 October, and weighed down with this, the latter answered: 'I will hold until 19 October!'[23]

By the following day pressure on Mackensen's line was growing stronger. Despite his unwillingness to send First Army north, Conrad had allowed his 7th Cavalry Division to be dispatched to Mackensen's aid. The horsemen arrived in time to engage, though not completely halt, large Russian cavalry forces that slipped past Mackensen's western flank. At the same time, the Russian forces across the Vistula on Mackensen's other flank were also increasingly active. At last, XIX Corps, part of the much-delayed Fifth Army, crossed the river and allowed the Russians to extend their bridgehead.

With cavalry operating beyond his lines to the west and a growing pressure from the east, Mackensen faced a serious danger of envelopment. On 18 October a German and Austro-Hungarian cavalry group managed to extend the overall line to the west, but it was clear that substantial Russian forces had already bypassed the German line. Attempts to drive back the Russian XIX Corps made no headway, and soldiers of both sides struggled and died in the mud and rain. Swollen by several weeks of downpour, the waters of the Vistula swept away the single pontoon bridge on which XIX Corps relied for its supplies, which at least prevented the Russians from increasing the strength of their forces facing Mackensen.

Elsewhere along the Vistula, Ivanov tried in vain to get the 'steamroller' across the river. Fourth Army continued to reinforce the bridgehead at Ivangorod, but despite repeated efforts, they could not expand it westward. It was only at Warsaw that the Russians had sizable forces west of the Vistula, but in spite of their steadily growing numerical superiority in this sector, there was still no overwhelming assault. It seems that Sergei Scheidemann, the commander of Second Army, remained concerned that the German forces facing him were preparing to renew their own advance on Warsaw, and held back forces in defensive positions. Throughout 19 October Mackensen's men were able to hold their positions, but by the end of the day, with Russian cavalry that had bypassed the western flank of the position now threatening to move southeast against his lines of communication, Mackensen ordered the instructions he had previously prepared for a withdrawal should be executed. It was not a moment too soon. Grand Duke Nikolai had grown tired of Scheidemann's excuses, and insisted on a general offensive for 20 October.

Far to the south Conrad had hoped for an advance across Galicia towards Lemberg, with a view to reversing all his setbacks of the late summer and early autumn. On 10 October he ordered Third and Fourth Armies to secure crossings over the San. Böhm-Ermolli's Second Army would protect the eastern flank of the general advance. But as was the case in so many parts of the Austro-Hungarian Empire, the gap between ambitions and intentions on the one hand, and reality on the other, was vast. Despite attacking with all the élan and vigour that Conrad could have wished for, his armies had failed to achieve decisive breakthroughs in August. Now, having lost their best officers, and with their ranks filled with replacement drafts, the Austro-Hungarian divisions struggled through the sodden landscape to fulfil their commanders' instructions. Wherever they ran into Russian resistance, the advance rapidly ground to a halt. On either side of Chyrów (now Kyriv), VIII and XII Corps from Second Army battled in vain on 11 and 12 October to make any headway; again and again, Austro-Hungarian officers rallied their men and attempted to close with the enemy in the best tradition of Conrad's teachings, only to be slaughtered by Russian defensive fire. Despite their numbers being depleted by the transfer of troops to the concentration along the Vistula, the Russians opposing Conrad's armies seem to have had little problem holding off the Austro-Hungarians. Such fighting highlighted the traditional strengths of Russian troops – the alacrity with which they dug in, and their ability to endure hardship and to defend positions tenaciously.

All along the San valley Conrad's troops tried in vain to secure meaningful bridgeheads. Even the short advance in pursuit of the retreating Russians had stretched supply lines to breaking point, especially given the heavily damaged state of the roads after so many armies had marched to and fro, and the almost ceaseless rain. Russian artillery covered almost all of the main river crossing points, and in the hope that a brief pause might improve his chances of success, Archduke Joseph Ferdinand postponed by a day the major assault across the San planned for 13 October. Despite this, the outcome was no different. Closer to the Vistula, First Army attempted to force crossings over the lower San. The entire area had been reduced almost to a swamp, and the troops struggled to move bridging equipment forward under fire from long-range Russian guns. Elements of 24th Infantry Division, from X Corps, managed to cross, but had to be withdrawn when it proved impossible to reinforce them. Finally, on 12 October, Conrad ordered First Army to cancel all further attempts to cross the river.

The staff at *AOK* now had detailed information regarding the forces facing them. Although the thirty-six Austro-Hungarian divisions outnumbered the estimated twenty-six Russian divisions in Galicia, the Russians had the advantage of being the defenders. Moreover, the historical weakness of artillery in the *k.u.k.* Army resulted in the Russians actually having a greater number of guns than Conrad's divisions. Unable to force the San River line, Conrad turned to the extreme southeast, and urged Böhm-Ermolli to make another effort to turn the southern flank of the Russian line. The commander of Second Army replied that a further attempt at mounting a major advance 'would result in the complete exhaustion of the striking power of the troops'.[24] But the whole thrust of the campaign was for the Germans to hold as many Russian divisions as possible along the Vistula, while the Austro-Hungarians inflicted a telling defeat on the Russians in the south. This meant that Conrad's armies were obliged to deliver, regardless of what it might cost them. In addition, the Germans were calling for reinforcements to be sent to the left bank of the Vistula. As a result, on 11 October Conrad agreed to dispatch First Army's V Corps to Ożarów. Instead of forcing its way over the San, the rest of Dankl's First Army would wait until Fourth Army had crossed the river.

Brusilov was under pressure from Ivanov to resume offensive operations; such a move, Ivanov argued, would prevent the *k.u.k.* Army from reinforcing the Vistula front. Aware that his men were exhausted by their withdrawal across terrain already devastated by previous troop movements, Brusilov responded that his army was in no state to mount an attack. The railways around Lemberg, damaged during the fighting in August, were still in a chaotic state. Despite repeated requests from Brusilov for the problem to be resolved as a matter of urgency – his entire command depended on this hub for the transit of their supplies – Ivanov's quartermaster-general, who was responsible for rail movements, proved unable or unwilling to help. An exasperated Brusilov assigned Alexander Dobryshin, who was responsible for railway matters within his own army, the task of sorting out the mess. As he later noted, he had no authority over the Lemberg area, but Southwest Front's quartermaster-general was as indifferent to Brusilov's intrusion into the railway problem as he had been to Brusilov's requests for a resolution of the problem.[25]

The second-line Russian troops that had formed the bulk of the besieging forces at Przemyśl were now organised into a new Eleventh Army, commanded by General Andrei Nikolaevich Selivanov. He had served in the war with Japan without particular distinction, but had been an energetic commander during the suppression of unrest after the war. Brusilov's opinion of him was not favourable; he later described him as rigid and inflexible.[26] While he took control of his forces, Brusilov surveyed his command. Dimitriev's Third Army was in position to hold the line of the San, but had required reinforcements in the shape of VII Corps. This left Brusilov's own Eighth Army, covering the ground to the south of Przemyśl, in a weakened state, particularly as this was the area where the Austro-Hungarian forces had the best chance of success, as a further advance would not require a difficult river crossing. An increasingly frustrated Brusilov made repeated requests for reinforcements, fearing that his army would be surrounded and destroyed west of Lemberg. Ivanov's response was to order rear area units to prepare to evacuate the city, but no reinforcements were sent to Eighth Army. Although Brusilov found this inexplicable, there was a degree of logic behind the decision. The decisive battle was about to be fought along the Vistula, and if it was a success, Galicia would be little more than a sideshow. Indeed, an Austro-Hungarian success in this area might draw Conrad's armies further east, leaving them too far away to intervene when the Russian steamroller smashed its way across Poland to the Moravian Gap and beyond. Despite this apparent neglect, it seems that Dobryshin was able to untangle some of the supply problems around Lemberg, and ammunition and reinforcements began to arrive at the front line. Like commanders in most armies at the time, Brusilov expressed dismay at the poor physical quality and training of the replacement drafts.

On 13 October Böhm-Ermolli's troops at the southern end of the long front made an attempt to drive the Russians north. From its positions in the Carpathian foothills, VII Corps moved two divisions forward to try to gain sufficient space to deploy its full strength; the troops were brought to a halt by heavy artillery fire. Elsewhere, too, along a sector of front line perhaps 15 miles (24km) wide, Austro-Hungarian forces attacked, took heavy casualties, and were either driven to take cover, or on the rare occasions they succeeded in penetrating into the Russian positions, were driven off by counterattacks. The following day Böhm-Ermolli visited VII Corps and watched as another attack faltered in the face of the tough Russian defences. Concluding that VII Corps was unlikely to be able to force the issue alone, he ordered a pause while the neighbouring IV Corps attempted to advance. However, IV Corps also failed to make headway. It was only nearer Przemyśl that III Corps penetrated the Russian positions; by good fortune, it attacked one of the weaker second-line divisions of the newly formed Eleventh Army. The Russian infantrymen abandoned their positions and withdrew in disorder, but the Austro-Hungarian forces then moved into dense woodland, where they lost their bearings and were unable to exploit their success. Brusilov rushed his few reserves to the area, and officers from a cavalry division restored order to the routed infantry. A combined counterattack recaptured the original positions; the front line had not moved at all.[27]

At Stryj, the Austro-Hungarian Second Army had one of its few successes, driving back the Russians towards Mikołajów. Brusilov had no reserves left, but ordered 58th Infantry Division to move from Eleventh Army's positions on the San to the threatened area. The regiments of 71st Infantry Division, retreating from Stryj, rallied around the new division as it was rushed to Mikołajów by rail; a swift counterattack not only prevented the fall of Mikołajów, but even retook Stryj. On 14 October Brusilov widened this local counterattack into a general drive towards the south.[28] It is striking to note that whenever Conrad's forces ran into Russian defences, their attacks rapidly ground to a halt. By contrast, when Brusilov ordered his men forward, the Austro-Hungarian defences were rapidly stretched to breaking point. On the first day many of Böhm-Ermolli's divisions were forced to abandon their positions, and on 15 October the positions around Chyrów came under increasing strain. Only by committing their last reserves were Second Army's corps commanders able to halt the Russian attacks. By the end of the day it was increasingly clear that unless Boroević drove southeast with his Third Army, Böhm-Ermolli would be forced to retreat.

VII Corps came under severe pressure on 16 October. A timely counterattack by III Corps, part of Boroević's army, restored the situation for the moment, and in order to improve coordination at the key part of the battlefield, Conrad ordered VII Corps to be transferred to Third Army's command. Both VII and III Corps were ordered to counterattack again on 17 October, but as was almost always the case in 1914, the Austro-Hungarian advance was rapidly driven to ground by Russian artillery and rifle fire. The relative weakness of artillery in the *k.u.k.* Army was worsened by ammunition shortages, and by the end of the day the initiative had passed back to the Russians. On the extreme eastern flank of the battlefield, confused movements in hilly terrain left both sides struggling to determine the exact position of the opposing forces. Taking advantage of a gap that opened in the Austro-Hungarian lines, the Russian 4th Rifle Brigade launched an attack into the flank of one of IV Corps' divisions, forcing the entire corps, under the command of General Karl Tersztyánszky, to abandon its attempts to outflank the Russian positions.[29]

With Second and Third Armies unable to achieve a decisive success, Conrad was left with only Joseph Ferdinand's Fourth Army. From 14 October troops from the Austro-Hungarian XVII, II and XIV Corps all attempted to force crossings over the San. Only the latter corps was able to secure a bridgehead on the first day near Rżuchów, and the assault formations from 8th Infantry Division suffered terrible casualties as their boats came under heavy fire. The bridgehead itself was constantly swept by Russian artillery and machine-gun fire, and every attempt to reinforce the troops clinging to the right bank failed.[30] Desperate to achieve a success, Joseph Ferdinand ordered XVII Corps to make another assault at Jaroslaw, and late on 15 August a bridgehead was secured. Joseph Ferdinand now asked Boroević to attack with his IX Corps, to support XVII Corps from the south. The corps commander suggested that his troops should move north and cross the river via XVII Corps' bridgehead, but Boroević insisted that IX Corps should make its own crossing. This was partially due to the fact that moving IX Corps to Jaroslaw would leave Third Army's lines dangerously overstretched.

Late on 17 October the remnants of 8th Infantry Division's forces on the east bank of the San at Rżuchów were withdrawn. The division had lost over 2,000 men in three days. IX Corps duly made its attempt to cross the San, and again, with limited and inadequate artillery support, the crossing failed with heavy losses. Joseph Ferdinand attempted to reinforce his surviving bridgehead at Jaroslaw, but although his men were able to repulse determined Russian counterattacks, they failed to enlarge their foothold. Before XI Corps could launch its supporting attack, the Russian VIII Corps attacked further south, putting serious pressure on the line held by Boroević's Third Army. XI Corps finally began its own attack on 18 October, and despite heavy losses, achieved little.

Faced with failure along the San and southeast of Przemyśl, Conrad turned his attention elsewhere. He had been unenthusiastic about transferring large bodies of Austro-Hungarian troops to the Warsaw area, fearing that they would thus come under the command of German officers. He remained determined to win a decisive victory on his own terms, and there were probably many reasons for this. There was a strong sense that a subordination of Austro-Hungarian divisions to German command would be a serious blow to the prestige of the Dual Monarchy. As Conrad told Oberstleutnant Kundmann, one of his adjutants, he felt badly let down by the Germans, firstly for their failure to deliver their promised quick victory in France, and secondly by their failure to provide the northern half of a combined operation against the Warsaw salient.[31] He had also always regarded an Austro-Hungarian military success as a vital step in restoring the credibility of the Austro-Hungarian Empire, and of thus overcoming what he saw as its slow decline. Another factor in Conrad's thinking was the failure of the Germans to reduce the Russian foothold on the west bank of the Vistula at Ivangorod. The Germans had not made a determined effort to do so, but their lack of success was highlighted, perhaps exaggerated, by Hauptmann Fleischmann, the Austro-Hungarian liaison officer in the area.[32]

Conrad now proposed to move the bulk of Dankl's First Army across the Vistula, so that it could concentrate against the southern flank of the Russian bridgehead. It was clear that the Russians were intent on crossing the river here, he argued, and Dankl would be able to attack them before they had completed their crossing, taking advantage of the disruption to obliterate the bridgehead and inflict major losses on the Russians. Conrad's new plan explicitly called for the Russians to be allowed to begin to cross the river in strength before the counterattack was launched. Ludendorff was unenthusiastic about the proposal. At best the Central Powers could achieve what amounted to only a tactical victory, and even this would be gained by the risky manoeuvre of allowing the leading Russian elements to cross the river unhindered. He and Hindenburg still preferred to concentrate Austro-Hungarian and German forces for a thrust against Warsaw.[33] A final appeal came from Kaiser Wilhelm to Emperor Franz Joseph, urging the Austro-Hungarians to agree to the German proposal for a concentration against Warsaw. The elderly emperor instructed Frederick to do whatever was possible. Strongly influenced by Conrad, Frederick decided not to agree to the German plan.

Given the lack of success of Austro-Hungarian forces in the past few weeks, Conrad's plan demonstrated a remarkably enduring confidence in the ability of the *k.u.k.* Army to mount attacks. On the other hand, given the heavy losses suffered by his forces when attempting to force the line of the San, Conrad may have considered that the Russians would be equally handicapped. Elsewhere, the tide was turning against Conrad's armies. Having held off the attacks along his front, Brusilov moved onto the offensive. Stryj was retaken by 79th Cavalry Division on 22 October. With some of his forces assigned to Boroević's Third Army, and the rest ground down by casualties and illness and the constant supply shortages, Böhm-Ermolli pleaded in vain for reinforcements. In any case, regardless of the merits of the request, Conrad had no reinforcements to send to him.

It was now the turn of Fourth Army to feel the weight of the Russian forces. After the failure of his bloody attempts to secure crossings over the San, Joseph Ferdinand left XVII Corps to hold its bridgehead at Jaroslaw, with II Corps on the line of the river to the north. Beyond II Corps a mixed force of infantry and cavalry held the river as far as XIV Corps. VI Corps was to form an army reserve behind the front. Opposing Joseph Ferdinand was Dimitriev's Third Army, with XXI, XI, IX and X Corps. He ordered each corps to prepare operational groups that would be used to secure crossings over the San, and the first assaults were made on 17 October, even as Joseph Ferdinand's troops were giving up their own attempts to force a crossing. Further attacks followed over the next few days; attempts by Joseph Ferdinand's forces to destroy the bridgeheads were largely in vain. For *AOK* this was a most unwelcome development, as increased Russian pressure in Galicia would make it impossible to move all of First Army to the west bank of the Vistula. An irritated Conrad sent a signal to Third Army Headquarters:

> The fact that the enemy could cross the San at four locations in the face of the troops of Fourth Army is hardly explicable other than that they were permitted to cross with the intention of then crushing them. It is not sufficient just to push the enemy back to the river, he must be destroyed, which is the next task of Fourth Army, for which it has its own ten divisions available... By the evening of 20 October, there must be no enemy forces on the left bank of the San.[34]

Far from being able to wipe out all the bridgeheads by the end of 20 October, Joseph Ferdinand had to report the appearance of a fifth Russian bridgehead on that day. A further unwelcome development was the surrender of several battalions of 36th Infantry Regiment to the Russians near Radymno; the troops were Czech soldiers, and clearly did not wish to fight for the Austro-Hungarian Empire. There had long been concerns about the loyalty of Slav troops in the *k.u.k.* Army, and this report, following similar though smaller incidents in September, increased fears that the fragile unity of Franz Joseph's empire was coming under increasing strain. Nevertheless, other units that might have been expected to show limited loyalty, such as the Czech and Galician troops fighting in XVII Corps, acquitted themselves in an exemplary manner.

Despite Conrad's orders, the Russian bridgeheads continued to hold out against Austro-Hungarian attacks. The heavy losses suffered by the *k.u.k.* Army, particularly amongst officers, began to play an increasing part in influencing events. Many of the battalions of XVII Corps were now commanded by lieutenants, with companies under the control of half-trained officer cadets. However, the Russians were in barely any better a position. Despite succeeding where the Austro-Hungarian troops had singularly failed, Dimitriev's battered regiments could do little to exploit their success. Nevertheless, their very presence on the west bank of the San hindered Austro-Hungarian attempts to send troops north towards Ivangorod, or southeast to support Böhm-Ermolli.

On the west bank of the Vistula, Conrad's plan for an ambush of the Russian forces attempting to cross at Ivangorod began to unfold. Late on 20 October German and Austro-Hungarian troops abandoned their positions and withdrew to the west, in an attempt to entice the Russians into what they hoped would become a killing ground. Further north, Mackensen had begun to pull back from his positions before Warsaw; Scheidemann's troops followed cautiously. As reconnaissance reports about the withdrawal of the forces of the Central Powers began to arrive at *Stavka*, Grand Duke Nikolai urged both front commanders to take full advantage. He wanted to ensure that his mass offensive struck before the enemy could escape, and also before German reinforcements from the west could arrive. Evert, commander of Fourth Army, required no urging, and was already taking advantage of the Austro-Hungarian and German withdrawal before Kozienice. To his south, Ninth Army began to hurry its troops into the Ivangorod bridgehead, and to make preparations for crossings along the Vistula as far south as Sandomierz.

Dankl planned to strike at the Russians on 22 October. The previous evening, he received reports that only Russian reconnaissance units had ventured forward, making a counterthrust unlikely to have the desired effect. Nevertheless, Feldzugmeister Puhallo struck at the southern flank of the Ivangorod bridgehead as planned with the three infantry divisions of V Corps. At first the advance proceeded well, but in the late morning came news that the Russians had established a bridgehead behind his eastern flank. Hastily, reserves were dispatched to the area, but the bulk of V Corps, with I Corps alongside, continued towards Ivangorod. Shortly after crossing the road running from Radom in the west to Góra Puławska on the Vistula, they ran into Russian columns marching south. A general engagement erupted.

It was an encounter battle, in which speed of response was critical. The Russian Guards Corps had been delayed in its crossing of the Vistula, and there was a wide gap in the Russian line at Czarnolas. Elements of 33rd and 14th Infantry Divisions attempted to exploit this, swiftly driving back the weak Russian positions and thrusting forward to Policzna, where they ran into the first units of the Guards Corps. In the face of strengthening Russian resistance, the advance broke down. Similarly, the march of I Corps to the west also faltered in the face of powerful defensive fire. It was only at Jedlnia, at the western end of the Austro-Hungarian advance, that events proceeded according to plan. A swift attack on the village threw the Russian III Caucasian Corps back into the path of the Russian XVII Corps, hurrying to the front. General Kirchbach, commander of First Army's I Corps, urged the German Guards Reserve Corps to join the attack, so that the Russians could be driven back to the river and destroyed. To his bitter disappointment, the commander of the Guards Reserve Corps, General von Gallwitz replied that the Russian advance from the north had prevented him from gathering his corps for a powerful attack, and an assault with the modest forces available would be pointless. As darkness fell, fighting died down.

For the following day, Dankl remained confident that he would be able to win a major victory. Puhallo drew forces away from his eastern flank in order to reinforce his main drive northwards, with the intention of breaking up the strong Russian line in his path. To the west, it was hoped that the entangled units of III Caucasian and XVII Corps could be destroyed before they could reorganise. The Russians, though, had plans of their own. The Austro-Hungarian attack had come as an unwelcome surprise, but, despite their losses, the two corps at the western end of the line were still in good shape. The rest of the Guards Corps had now arrived, and filled the gap that Puhallo's V Corps had exploited the previous day. Meanwhile all of XXV Corps crossed the Vistula across newly built pontoon bridges at Nowo-Alexandrya (Pulawy), and was thus poised on the eastern flank of Dankl's First Army. The Grenadier Corps and XVI Corps were still crossing the river, but the numerical advantage was now in favour of the Russians, and increasing steadily. Conrad's plan to crush the Russians in the process of crossing the river, always a risky venture, would now face the combined strength of the Russian Fourth and Ninth Armies.

Meanwhile, there was a significant change of personnel on the German side. Karl Litzmann had come out of retirement at the beginning of the war, and was now assigned to take command of 3rd Guards Infantry Division, part of Gallwitz's Guards Reserve Corps; the previous commander had been, Hanz Fritz von Bonin. Although he regarded Gallwitz as an old comrade, Litzmann noticed that his welcome was a little muted – perhaps, he speculated in his memoirs, Gallwitz had hoped for a younger man than the 64-year-old Litzmann.[35] Gallwitz need not have worried; Litzmann would rapidly prove to be one of the best commanders on the Eastern Front. After his slightly chilly reception at corps headquarters on 22 October, Litzmann travelled on to his division on a borrowed horse, as it was impossible to make the 12-mile (20km) journey by any other means, such was the state of the muddy roads. It wasn't an enjoyable journey:

> My nag was dreadfully unpleasant and I had completely stopped riding for years
> ... the continued trotting was a terrible ordeal for me. In addition, the horse
> slipped in the swampy ground and struck me in the mouth with the back of its
> neck, leaving blood streaming down my face. This wasn't a good start.[36]

When he reached his new division, the outgoing commander gave him a welcome present: his three good horses. Litzmann noted that these mounts stayed with him throughout the war, carrying him safely across numerous battlefields without a repeat of the mishap of his journey of 22 October.

There were serious differences of opinion between the Germans and their Austro-Hungarian counterparts both about recent events and how to proceed. The failure of the German Guards Reserve Corps to strike at the Russian troops at the western end of the Ivangorod bridgehead caused considerable resentment, while the Germans learned of the very limited progress of the *k.u.k.* Army with a mixture of resignation and irritation. Hindenburg advised Dankl that it would not be possible for his troops to remain before Warsaw unless Dankl could reinforce them. Dankl replied that this would only be possible after the successful conclusion of the fighting around Ivangorod. The prospects of such a successful conclusion grew worse by the hour. Russian forces had established a new bridgehead over the Vistula at Kazimierz, behind Dankl's eastern flank.

The day after he took command of his division, Litzmann attempted to advance on Kozienice from the west. By the end of the day, 3rd Guards Infantry Division had succeeded in advancing perhaps 6 miles (10km) towards the town, through boggy woodland that constantly hindered movement. The opposing Russian forces contested the ground, but fell back whenever their positions came under serious threat. Casualties were heavy on both sides, with one of Litzmann's battalions reduced to barely two companies. As dusk fell, it became clear to the Germans that there was a dangerous gap in the front line of one of Litzmann's two brigades, and Hauptmann von Schauroth, a young adjutant, was dispatched from the regiment on one side of the gap to locate the regiment on the other side:

Schauroth took Leutnant von Pachelbl from the Guards Fusilier Regiment as an assistant and now tried to locate the Lehr Regiment. He thought he had found it when, on riding into a burning village, he saw light glinting off the bayonets of a column of troops who were marching through. He rode up to these troops and asked loudly for the general, who he thought had to be with the Lehr Regiment. The column stopped at his shout, and in this moment Schauroth realised: Russian hats! A tricky situation: the two officers were alone, between the houses and the fence of enemy bayonets. The only option was reckless audacity. Schauroth drew his sword from its sheath, jumped into the column with Pachelbl and shouted to them in Russian: 'Drop your rifles!' Some of the Russians obeyed, others hesitated. One Russian raised his gun to shoot. But faced by Schauroth's sword and ferocious expression, he too threw down his rifle. It was unbelievable: with Pachelbl leading, Schauroth at the end, a Russian column was led from the open battlefield.[37]

The intrepid German officers captured two Russian officers and 120 other ranks in their escapade, and even made contact with the Lehr Regiment and succeeded in closing the hole in the German lines.

On 24 October Dankl made a determined attempt to clear up the smaller bridgeheads that threatened his flank. The assault on Góra Puławska made good progress at first, but as usual, when the attacking infantry encountered prepared defences, they were halted with heavy losses. As the day progressed more and more Russian forces crossed the river at Góra Puławska, mainly from XIV Corps, and the front line moved away from the river, pushing Dankl's exhausted and depleted troops back to their starting positions.

The Russians finally advanced in strength on 25 October, using the wooded terrain to good effect to prevent the Austro-Hungarian forces from determining their precise positions. For the moment it seemed as if Dankl's line would hold, and with further troops expected – X Corps, part of his army, had finally crossed the Vistula and was making its way north – he continued to believe that a decisive blow could be dealt against the Russians, particularly if the German Guards Reserve Corps was able to join the attack. From the Russian point of view, the day's fighting might not have resulted in a decisive victory, but nor had it been disastrous. Alfred Knox, who had accompanied Samsonov during Second Army's invasion of East Prussia, was now with XIV and XXV Corps. His opinions of the Russians were mixed:

> On the 25th progress was facilitated by the fire of fortress artillery [brought from Ivangorod] and heavy field artillery from the right bank and by the progress of the 1st Division of the Guard on the right of the corps. There were continual hand-to-hand combats, and the Austrians suffered enormously. The two corps have taken 5,000 prisoners in four days. 70th Infantry Division … delivered a spirited attack across the open. This division has lost 2,700 rank and file and 47 officers in the three days' fighting 23rd–25th. Its GOC on the night of the 10th went into the trenches and told the men that the bridge at Nowo-Alexandriya in their rear had been burned! He led them personally, and personal leading is what the reserve divisions require…
>
> The moral of all this is that the Austrians are being pushed back with loss, it is true, but they are escaping us. The letting slip of chances like this makes one despair of a really decisive success.[38]

As had been the case in East Prussia, a speedy advance was simply not the way that the tsar's soldiers waged war. But their traditional strengths of stubborn defence and good fieldcraft contributed greatly to the failure of Dankl's divisions to smash the Ivangorod bridgehead. When they attacked, the Russians found, like all armies in Europe in 1914, that even hastily prepared positions could only be overcome at great cost. When penetrations were achieved, local counterattacks frequently restored the line, as Oberst Feldtkeller, commander of 176th Infantry Regiment, recalled:

> As usual, regimental headquarters was a shabby hovel, this time right behind the front. In desperate need of fresh air, I arose after an unsettled night at first light and went outside. Hauptmann Jahns was with me, and a cold autumn fog enveloped us. Suddenly, infantry shots rang out. Without any doubt, they were coming from a direction that could only mean that the Russians must have broken into the positions of the *Landwehr* division on our left. We had to deal with it quickly. I gathered together all the men of the regimental staff – clerks, orderlies, etc – then, together with the weak reserve platoon that had just arrived, I sent them to the forward line, later sending a further half-platoon. Under the sharp leadership of assistant regimental adjutant, Oberleutnant Röbrich, and the orderly officer, Leutnant Mende, these rapidly gathered troops went forward against the Russians. The mischief was put right by this energetic move.[39]

Despite the bloodshed in the clashes around the Ivangorod perimeter, the outcome of the campaign was being decided elsewhere. Just as frontal assaults were almost always unsuccessful, the efficacy of attacks on exposed flanks remained critical. Hindenburg and Ludendorff had to continue to withdraw Ninth Army to the southwest, for fear of its western flank being turned; this in turn exposed Dankl's western flank, particularly when Gallwitz pulled the Guards Reserve Corps back towards the southwest on 26 October. On the other end of the battlefield west of the Vistula, the Russian forces that had crossed the Vistula at Kazimierz began to put increasing pressure on Dankl's right flank. In these circumstances, a continuation of the attacks on the Ivangorod bridgehead was pointless. Even if Dankl were to succeed, he ran the risk of finding Russian forces behind both flanks. The news that the Russians had established yet another bridgehead over the Vistula eliminated any remaining hope of a successful outcome for the Austro-Hungarian attack. By the end of the day, V Corps had been forced to retreat, and although it had not yet come under heavy pressure, I Corps could not stay in its positions with its flanks exposed. A few days later Dankl wrote to his wife:

It was a great blow to morale. I had to use all logical arguments to persuade myself to retreat. Despite all the pressure of events, I held on for one more day in the hope that the situation would turn, but then there was no point, the Germans had already withdrawn, we had to follow.[40]

Both the German and the Austro-Hungarian commanders attempted to emphasise that they had been forced to retreat because their allies had not delivered what was required. Ludendorff stressed that the Germans had tried to tie down as many Russian forces as possible, in order to give Conrad's armies the best chance of victory, and that once the retreat began, the Guards Reserve Corps, on the eastern end of the German line, suffered repeatedly due to the failure of Dankl's retreating troops to provide any serious resistance.[41] Despite taking an estimated 12,000 Russian prisoners, First Army had lost over 40,000 men, and had failed to eliminate any of the Russian bridgeheads across the Vistula.[42] As they fell back, the Austro-Hungarians abandoned many of their wounded, lacking the time or the means to evacuate them. Knox was with a Russian force that entered Zwoleń:

> The place is infected with typhoid. The church is full of Austrian wounded – nearly all Magyars, who cannot speak German. I found a hospital assistant who looked blank when I tried him in a succession of German, French and Russian, but who spoke English, as he had been in America… These poor people have been without anything to eat for two to three days; the smell in the church is dreadful. The poor fellows were no doubt quite healthy three months ago. Now they have been torn from their homes and dragged to a foreign country, made to stand up before the enemy's bullets, and finally left by their own people, mutilated, to die of starvation. This is war![43]

The German retreat across Poland was accompanied by a ruthless scorched earth policy. Bridges, roads, and railways that had been repaired – in some cases, constructed for the first time – during the German advance just a few weeks before were now destroyed. Ludendorff and Hindenburg had two purposes in ordering such a policy. Firstly, it would greatly hinder the ability of the Russians to pursue them. Secondly, it would eventually bring the Russian advance to a halt:

> Experience had taught us that a modern army can move about 120km from the end of its rail lines. If this was true and we succeeded in destroying the railway lines as I hoped, we could then reckon that the Russian masses would have to halt before reaching our frontiers, even without the use of force.[44]

The result was that, even if the Russians had been so inclined, an energetic pursuit such as that carried out by Mackensen and François after Rennenkampf's army was defeated in East Prussia was simply impossible. The combination of winter weather and poor roads ensured that the Germans were able to withdraw safely and intact. Nevertheless, the Russians reached Łódź on 30 October, though as Ludendorff had predicted, lengthening supply lines took a heavy toll.

The retreat took a toll upon the Germans, too. The muddy roads had been badly damaged by the German advance, and now deteriorated even further, as Litzmann's troops found out to their cost:

> The withdrawal of 3rd Guards Infantry Division was initially along very poor roads and required great exertions by the troops. The vehicles often became stuck in the mud and had to be laboriously set in motion again by the efforts of the men. Hundreds of horses lay dead of exhaustion at the sides of the road. I was amazed by my tirelessly efficient pioneers. A half-company went in advance of the division, to make the roads reasonably usable; the other half followed behind us, in order to destroy all bridges and selected roads. These splendid chaps gave themselves no rest and were always of good cheer.[45]

In Galicia and Poland, the Austro-Hungarian armies proved unable to hold the ground they had gained. The extreme eastern flank of the Austro-Hungarian line was forced back after being outflanked, and though Böhm-Ermolli tried to concentrate sufficient forces for what he hoped would be a stabilising counterattack, his army was in constant danger of being driven back on the Carpathians. On 26 October Boroević made one last attempt to seize the initiative, ordering an attack along the entire front of his Third Army. Artillery ammunition was in short supply, and consequently the preliminary bombardment was modest. The soldiers, many of them suffering from cholera, climbed out of their trenches and hurled themselves at the Russian positions. Thousands died, for no gain. Joseph Ferdinand's Fourth Army also made a concerted attempt to eliminate the Russian bridgeheads across the San. Although limited progress was gained, it was at an unacceptable price. Matters were made worse by a further incident when Czech troops appeared to surrender to the Russians without putting up a fight. By the end of 26 October Křitek's XVII Corps alone reported that it had lost over 10,000 troops since the beginning of the month, through a mixture of enemy action and illness.[46]

Amidst the steady stream of reports of Austro-Hungarian setbacks, the attacks and counterattacks by the troops of Böhm-Ermolli and Brusilov continued unabated. On 31 October, after four days of almost constant fighting, Second

Army managed to drive the Russians back to Terszów in the Carpathian foothills, and for a moment, it seemed as if Böhm-Ermolli had finally turned the Russian flank. As he followed up his apparent success, his troops ran into yet another Russian defensive line late on 1 November; after their setback the previous day, the Russians had simply withdrawn to a new position.

Although Conrad had placed great importance on the battles at the southeast end of the line, events elsewhere were now making them irrelevant. Grand Duke Nikolai's 'steamroller' was now moving at last across Poland, with Second Army in the north, and Fifth, Fourth and Ninth Armies lined up to the south. In order to protect the southern flank of this great force, Ivanov ordered Otto von Krusenstern, a Baltic German officer from an Estonian family, to form a new group of three infantry divisions and a Cossack division. This group was to cross the lower San and turn the flank of the Austro-Hungarian Fourth Army, thus opening the way for Dimitriev's forces to advance. Even as this new group was deploying, Dimitriev ordered XXI Corps on his right to expand its bridgehead at Nisko. Late on 29 October the Russians attacked the Austro-Hungarian XIV Corps and captured Rakławice. Further attacks by the Russian XI and IX Corps developed over the following two days, forcing Joseph Ferdinand to cancel plans to divert troops from his front to the hard-pressed First Army. As Dimitriev's XXI Corps and Krusenstern's group prepared to make a major thrust, the Austro-Hungarians intercepted radio messages that alerted them to the developments. As a result, an additional reservist formation, 39th *Honvéd* Infantry Division, was assigned to XIV Corps. It was immediately deployed in the front line, so that the battered 3rd Infantry Division could be pulled back. The reservists had barely arrived when they were engulfed in a major Russian attack, and the exhausted men of 3rd Infantry Division were thrown into a counterattack, restoring the front. However, when Krusenstern's group attempted to force a crossing over the lower San at Brandwica, it ran into Generalmajor Ludwig Fabini's 8th Infantry Division. Fabini had been made aware of the wireless intercept, and his troops rapidly crushed the attempted crossing.[47]

Conrad had finally accepted that there was no prospect of snatching an unlikely victory from the jaws of defeat at the last moment, and was now concerned with the line to which his armies should retreat. Failure to hold the line of the San would inevitably result in a resumption of the siege of Przemyśl. He was therefore reluctant to allow Dankl's First Army to retreat further south than the mouth of the San, as such a retreat would expose the left flank of Joseph Ferdinand's Fourth Army. However, the line to which Dankl would have to retreat was at least in part dependent on where Hindenburg and Ludendorff planned to withdraw. As early as 28 October the two German commanders had revisited a proposal they had discussed even before the Austro-Hungarian attack on the Ivangorod bridgehead failed, and had decided to use the excellent German railway network to switch at least two corps of Ninth Army to the north. They would concentrate around Thorn (Toruń), and from there would be able to thrust into the northern flank of the Russian advance. To a large extent, Conrad and *AOK* remained unaware of these plans, and urged Hindenburg to halt his retreat sufficiently far north to allow the San line to be held. Having finally arrived in the rear of First Army, X Corps was deployed against the Russian forces threatening to turn Dankl's eastern flank from the numerous Vistula bridgeheads. But Dankl had serious doubts that he would be able to perform the task required of him in either Hindenburg's or Conrad's plans. He advised Conrad on 28 October that his divisions were reduced to between 7,000 and 8,000 men, that ammunition remained in short supply, and that it was questionable, to say the least, whether his troops – amounting to a little over eleven divisions – would be able to hold a front line of up to 54 miles (87km) against strong Russian forces. He advised that such a line would hold for two or three days at most before being shattered. He urged Conrad to allow him to retreat in contact with the Germans, covering the northern approaches of Krakow. Such a retreat, replied Conrad, would force the armies on the right bank of the Vistula to pull back on the Carpathians, something that he wished to avoid. He had resigned himself to the likelihood that Przemyśl would once more be encircled, and had ordered the fortress to be resupplied. He also sent an urgent message to Falkenhayn in the west, requesting a rapid transfer of troops to the Eastern Front.[48]

Falkenhayn was still determined to force a decision in the west, and since 20 October the German Fourth and Sixth Armies had been battering the British, French, and Belgian line at Ypres. Despite suffering heavy casualties, the Germans remained close to achieving a breakthrough that might outflank the entire Anglo-French line. In such circumstances the diversion of substantial forces to Poland was not something that Falkenhayn wished to contemplate. His response to Conrad's telegrams was curt: he was prepared to discuss matters with his Austro-Hungarian counterpart, but he wanted Conrad to travel to Berlin. When it came to reinforcements, he ordered the transfer of three cavalry divisions to Hindenburg's command. In the circumstances, it was impossible for Conrad to travel to Berlin, and finally learning of the plans of Hindenburg and Ludendorff to divert troops to an attack from Thorn, he conceded that he would have to pull his own forces back to the Dunajec–Biała line, from where they had advanced at the beginning of the month. He pressed Hindenburg not to withdraw further forces from the left flank of First Army. Reluctantly, the German commander agreed to allow XX Corps, in addition to the already earmarked Guards Reserve Corps, to hold a line between Kielce and Noworadomsk for the time being.

Another formation that would remain with Conrad's armies was Woyrsch's *Landwehr* Corps. On 2 November, when the corps withdrew to Czestochowa, the elderly corps commander mused on the events of the weeks since he and his men had passed through the town heading west in the early days of the war:

> Thus, I rode grim-faced into Czestochowa, this time from the east, the same town I had cheerfully entered from the west 11 weeks before. 41 moves of location, and about 1,200km [745 miles] of actual marching lay behind the personnel of corps headquarters. Naturally, the troops had done more, but instead of accommodation, they had had to spend the nights under the open sky. What hadn't I experienced in this time! How my *Landwehr* Corps had changed – not in courage and self-belief, there were no troops better than them in that respect in the army – but rather in terms of changes in officers and other personnel. Tarmawka, the fighting on the Vistula, and at Rawa had torn sad holes in the old core cadres.[49]

As the Russian advance approached the River Opatówka, Ludendorff's prediction that it would be brought to a halt by supply problems was borne out. The Germans had comprehensively disabled the railway lines as they retreated, as Knox observed:

> Between Radom and Pinchov the railway has been thoroughly destroyed. All the water-supply arrangements, all the points, besides every bridge and long stretches of embankment, have been destroyed by explosives placed at a few yards' intervals.[50]

Aware that the Germans had retreated faster than his armies could pursue them, and that it was likely that Hindenburg and Ludendorff would repeat their earlier use of railway transport to redeploy their forces, Grand Duke Nikolai ordered Fourth and Ninth Armies to force the line of the Opatówka. Once more the Austro-Hungarians intercepted a radio message that alerted them to this, though on this occasion it was at least encrypted. Dankl warned Conrad that his army was outflanked to the west, and that if his men were unable to hold their positions, they would be forced back on the Vistula at Szczucin, some 30 miles (50km) east of Krakow. Such a development would leave Krakow exposed, and Dankl was ordered to avoid being pinned against the Vistula at all costs. When the main Russian blow fell, however, the greatest impact was against Dankl's right wing, nearest the Vistula, where X Corps was forced back by the Russian Guards Corps. The hasty retreat of X Corps exposed the right flank of V Corps in Dankl's centre, and it now came under heavy attack by the Russian XXV Corps. Although the front line in I Corps' sector on the left remained quiet, the Russians were clearly massing here for an attack, and rather than stand and risk major losses amongst his already badly depleted formations, Dankl ordered a withdrawal to the River Nida.

On the other bank of the Vistula, Conrad's armies had succeeded in holding off the Russians, though at a high cost. Now, with the threat of Russian forces from the left bank crossing into their rear, Conrad had no choice but to order a general retreat. As October drew to a close, it seemed as if the war was turning against the Central Powers. Despite huge bloodshed, the Western Front appeared to be heading towards a complete stalemate, and although the Austro-Hungarian armies remained in the field alongside the German Eighth and Ninth Armies, it seemed only a matter of time before the Russians were able to regroup and resupply. Thereafter, they would be able to press into Hungary across the Carpathians, or by taking Krakow they would threaten both Austria and Silesia. East Prussia would be left isolated.

Like Conrad, Ludendorff was summoned to Berlin. Here, he met Falkenhayn at the end of October:

> In Berlin, I felt as if I had entered another world. The difference between the immense tension that I had endured since the beginning of the war and the crowds in Berlin was huge. There was a general drive to dissipation and indulgence. There was no concern about our difficult military situation. It made an unpleasant impression, and I felt a foreigner. I was relieved when I returned to [Czenstochau] and found myself in the ranks of my comrades again.[51]

Falkenhayn had advised Ludendorff that there was still hope that a decisive victory would result from the fighting at Ypres. On 1 November Berlin announced that Hindenburg had been confirmed as overall commander on the Eastern Front, once more with Ludendorff at his side. In order to allow Hindenburg to concentrate on the entire front, Mackensen was promoted to command Ninth Army. At the same time, Kaiser Wilhelm sent a telegram to Emperor Franz Joseph, requesting that all forces on the left bank of the Vistula – in other words, Hindenburg's forces and Dankl's First Army – should be under a united command. Following Conrad's advice Franz Joseph turned down the request, replying to Berlin that the closest cooperation between Dankl's army and neighbouring German forces was assured, making any change in command arrangements unnecessary. It seems that Conrad was still feeling resentful towards the Germans. He had sacrificed tens of thousands of his men by drawing the main weight of the Russian Army into Galicia, so that the Germans could win a decisive victory in France, only to find that the Germans were unable to deliver their part of the bargain. The recent fighting in Poland had also been a great disappointment, with *AOK* convinced that the failure of Dankl's troops outside Ivangorod had everything to do with the lack of cooperation by the German Guards Reserve Corps and nothing to do with their own failings.

But if the German military leadership was determined to impose a German commander upon the Eastern Front, others in Berlin had a different solution. The official Austrian history of the war describes how Arthur Zimmermann, who was *Unterstaatssekretär* (junior state secretary) in the Foreign Office in Berlin, suggested to Gottfried Hohenlohe, the Austro-Hungarian ambassador, that a diplomatic solution to the issue might be to appoint Archduke Frederick as supreme commander on the Eastern Front, with Ludendorff as his chief of staff. Conrad would then command the Austro-Hungarian forces, while Hindenburg or another German general commanded the German forces. A telegram outlining such an arrangement reached Conrad at his headquarters in Neu-Sandez on 4 November, and his response was cool. Such an arrangement, he maintained, would leave all operational decisions in Ludendorff's control, and that he would see no option but to offer his resignation. After discussions with Archduke Frederick, Franz Joseph sent assurances to Conrad that his confidence in his chief of staff remained undiminished. Zimmermann's suggestion – apparently made without the knowledge of Falkenhayn, Hindenburg, or Ludendorff – was quietly dropped.[52]

It is striking that Conrad only learned of Hindenburg's plan to move troops north on 3 November. Always an enthusiast for offensive action, he immediately proposed launching a matching attack from the south. This was a triumph of optimism over reality, given that all of his armies were depleted in every respect – casualties, ammunition, food, health, and morale. Whilst the Russians pursued the Germans slowly, they succeeded in pressing Dankl's First Army much harder. By 5 November Dankl reported to *AOK* that he expected to come under heavy attack the following day, preventing him from retreating towards the west and keeping in contact with units to his left. At the same time, Conrad's liaison officer with Hindenburg reported that the Guards Reserve Corps, which Conrad had hoped would protect the left flank of First Army, was being ordered to pull back towards the Silesian frontier. In the circumstances, to allow First Army to come under massive attack ran the risk that Dankl would be driven back on the Vistula, leaving the way open for the Russians to march on Krakow. Conrad therefore ordered Dankl to retreat immediately towards the city. This ran the risk of opening a gap between Dankl's army and the Austro-Hungarian forces on the right bank of the Vistula, and they were accordingly ordered to retreat west. Second Army would fall back on the Carpathians, from where four of its divisions, and additional troops from Third Army, would be transported by rail to the west, in order to link up with the Germans, allowing the bulk of Ninth Army to be redeployed around Thorn. The troops left behind to cover the Carpathian passes would fall under Third Army's command. All the gains of the October campaign were to be abandoned, and a new line would be held through the winter, running along the Carpathians and then to Krakow.

In the Carpathian foothills, Böhm-Ermolli's divisions slowly withdrew from the ground they had gained at such cost. Pál Kelemen, the Hungarian cavalryman, was caught up in fighting near Turka on the eastern flank. Before dawn on 4 November, he and his hussars led their horses on foot along a frozen road with the last elements of the retreating army:

A couple of abandoned army wagons stood on the roads, without crew or horses. We had just passed them when I felt a hard blow on my left knee, and at the same time my horse became startled. I thought that I had ridden into something in the darkness. I felt my knee and then instinctively raised my gloved hand to my face. It was warm and moist, and I now felt a sharp, throbbing pain.

Mogor rode next to me and I told him that I thought I had been hit. He rode right out and saw that my horse was wounded too, a small one in the loin. But both horse and rider could continue. In any case, there was nowhere here to lie down. There was no aid station in the area. And to seek out the infantry first aid station in the front line, which was under heavy fire, was much more dangerous than to ride further back…

In the east the sun rose with bright colours. The sky lightened, the snow-covered mountains stood sharp against the dark green pine forests. I had the feeling that my leg was swelling … my face was white, and I held the reins with a stiff hand. My horse, a sensible, intelligent animal, picked its way through the mounds of snow with sure steps.

Finally we reached the southern end of the pass. Here, on the side sheltered from the wind, the road was not so icy, and as the sun lit up the valley before us in all its glory, we saw the first remote houses at the edge of a village.

> In the open marketplace we encountered Vas, who asked us with concern why we were so late… During the night, the village school had been hastily converted into an aid station, and with Vas on one side and Mogor on the other, I road to the door of the schoolhouse.
>
> Now my eyes began to swim. I could no longer climb down from the saddle; my left knee had become stiff. Two medics helped me from the saddle and Mogor led the horse away. Carefully, they helped me down; as my left knee touched the ground, one could hear the blood that had pooled in the saddle gurgling. I couldn't stand. With the casualness of youth, Vas held his pocket mirror before my eyes, and I saw a strange, yellow, aged face.[53]

Third and Fourth Armies also began to withdraw from the San, pursued only slowly by the Russians. Aware that Dimitriev's forces were short of supplies, Křitek decided to make one final attempt at ending the campaign with at least a local success, and gathered together the units of his XVII Corps for a united attack. On 4 November his troops caught the Russians by surprise, and drove them back to the San at many points. Some 2,000 prisoners were taken. In addition, twenty-four Russian guns were overrun, but Křitek's men lacked the means to drag them away and had to content themselves with rendering them unusable. The following day, both XVII and the neighbouring IX Corps were able to withdraw unmolested.[54]

An inevitable consequence of the Austro-Hungarian retreat was that Przemyśl would once more be besieged. On 4 November civilians were ordered to leave, to reduce demands on the limited supplies held in the city. Helena Jabłońska, who had endured the first siege, watched the preparations:

> This morning the gendarmerie and police were sent out, and ordered everyone to pack up immediately, with barely time to throw some clothes into a bundle, take their children by the hand, throw their belongings on their backs and run, shoved along cruelly by rifle butts, no rest allowed. They even dragged the sick out of their beds, including a woman with a five-day-old baby. They hurried along an old crippled man wrapped only in shawls, with no warm clothing, as though he were no better than swine… Children are separated from their families. Everyone has become heartless. A mother with two children boarded the train and her three-year-old child was left behind when it moved off. She wanted to jump off, but it was too late.[55]

With other civilians she left the city and travelled by cart to Olszany, less than 5 miles (8km) from the fortress, to find the town devastated by fighting. With rumours of Cossack patrols everywhere, she turned back to Przemyśl. On 10 November she learned that the city was once more surrounded.

The German and Austro-Hungarian campaigns of October achieved no lasting gains. Casualties were substantial, with the two nations losing nearly 90,000 men; by contrast, Russian losses were about 70,000. Hindenburg and Conrad attacked without any clear objective or purpose, and when the Russians failed to stand and fight west of the Vistula, the campaign increasingly became an attempt to seek some form of decisive success, whether it was by taking Warsaw, crushing the Ivangorod bridgehead, or by turning the eastern flank of Brusilov's army. On their part, the Russians did little better. Their redeployment of forces along the Vistula was a considerable achievement, given the difficult conditions, and the 'Russian steamroller' was finally unleashed, but without any clear direction. Merely getting the steamroller moving was regarded as an end in itself; however, lacking an attainable objective, the massed armies merely ran out of steam on the Polish plain. Although Grand Duke Nikolai urged his front commanders to attack and advance with determination, he found himself struggling with the consequences of diverging axes of advance, and grew increasingly worried about the threat from East and West Prussia. This was not helped by Ruzsky's instinct for caution; he constantly overestimated the danger of a German blow from the northwest at a time when the German forces in that area were minimal. As the grand duke struggled to reconcile the fear of a German counterstrike with his own desire to push on towards German territory, the detailed orders emanating from *Stavka* were often contradictory, urging first a drive across Poland towards Silesia, followed by increasing concern about the flanks. By the end of the first week of November Ivanov recorded:

> Frankly speaking, it is impossible to detect in Stavka's instructions either an exact task or a fixed objective.[56]

This was perhaps more than a little unfair. Ivanov had assured Nikolai that the Austro-Hungarian forces along the San were at their last strength, but had then singularly failed to break through. Now he found himself having to deal with impatient demands from *Stavka* to finish the Galician campaign as quickly as possible. But with both flanks potentially exposed, and at the end of lengthy supply lines, and advancing across devastated terrain, the Russian steamroller ground to a halt in early November. Both sides paused for breath, and planned for one final effort to end the war by Christmas.

CHAPTER 13

ŁÓDŹ

The German forces on the Eastern Front remained weaker than Hindenburg, Ludendorff, or Conrad would have liked, but at last some reinforcements were available. Like other countries, Germany experienced a huge groundswell of popular patriotism after the outbreak of war, and large numbers of men who would not have been called up for military service presented themselves as volunteers. In the autumn of 1914, they were organised into new formations, creating six new reserve corps numbered from XXII to XXVII, each with two or three infantry divisions. They were weaker than a regular army corps, with fewer machine guns, cavalry, and artillery, and they lacked the training and field experience of their regular equivalents. Nevertheless, they represented a useful asset for an army that had prepared for a short war, and now faced the prospect of prolonged hostilities.

XXV Reserve Corps was created as a paper entity at the outbreak of war, but did not receive any troops until the formation of 49th and 50th Reserve Infantry Divisions. Between them they consisted of twenty-six infantry battalions, a total of about 32,000 men; by contrast, Mackensen's XVII Corps numbered about 40,000 at mobilisation. Under the command of Generalleutnant Reinhard Freiherr von Scheffer-Boyadel, the corps was sent to East Prussia as reinforcements for François' Ninth Army. Scheffer had retired from the army in 1913, having previously been chief of staff in the Guards Corps and quartermaster-general in the German general staff. He was widely regarded as a capable, tough officer.[1]

Other troop formations were improvised out of the fortress garrisons along the eastern borders of Germany. Whilst he welcomed these new regiments and divisions, Ludendorff had no illusions about the fighting abilities of these garrison divisions, which drew much of their strength from *Landsturm* formations:

These divisions were later given numbers like the active divisions, but this did not alter their character. Fighting and marching made demands on them that were different for units made up of younger men. Frequently, in the urgency of the moment, these distinctions were not possible. These troops did more than could reasonably be expected of them; they gave their best for the defence of the homeland and thus their homes, women and children.[2]

Two such divisions were created in the area of Soldau, grouped initially as *Korps Zastrow* and later renamed XVII Reserve Corps. The addition of numerous battalions of *Landwehr* to the garrison of Thorn (35th Reserve Division) created *Korps von Dickhuth*. In a similar manner, the Posen garrison had already been deployed in the advance to the Vistula, on the left flank of Hindenburg's army, as part of *Korps Frommel*. The *Landwehr* units in this corps lacked field kitchens, and their officers decided that an early objective was to capture some from the Russians, something they achieved with alacrity. Eventually, an entire *Korps Posen* was created, followed later by *Korps Breslau*.[3]

With these units it was possible to create a line – albeit a thin one – along the eastern borders of Germany. Mackensen's Ninth Army was dispatched by rail from its positions covering Silesia and sent towards Thorn, while Böhm-Ermolli's Second Army began to arrive to replace it. Beyond this line, the Russian armies that had finally rolled across Poland paused for breath. *Stavka* was acutely aware of the need to force a conclusive battle upon the Germans before they withdrew to their frontiers. It would be much harder to achieve a decisive victory once on German soil, at the end of long supply lines running across a devastated Poland. Nevertheless, the speed of the German withdrawal, the inability of the Russians to pursue at a similar pace, and attrition all brought Grand Duke Nikolai's steamroller to a halt. The fighting of the previous months had taken a heavy toll, and many formations had lost up to half their regular cadre. The consumption of ammunition, for small arms but particularly for artillery, had been far higher than pre-war estimates, and was far beyond the ability of Russian industry to replace. Contracts had been placed with foreign firms, but there was little prospect of these being delivered in a timely manner. British and French firms were fully employed supplying their own armies, and both Britain and France had placed substantial orders with American firms before the Russians realised that they had a problem. Even if foreign producers had fulfilled their orders on time, there would still have been huge problems getting the ordered material to Russia. Historically, most of Russia's trade had been via Germany or the Baltic Sea, and both routes were now closed. The railway from Murmansk and

Archangel, so important in a later war, had very limited capacity at this time, as did the great Trans-Siberian Railway. The inability of western firms to deliver, and the grossly inflated prices that they charged, contributed greatly to the growing distrust of the Western Powers in Russia as the war continued.[4] But other factors in the shortages were entirely Russian. For the first few months of the war, senior Russian artillery commanders insisted that sufficient ammunition had been sent to the front, but that it was being wasted, or had been stockpiled by local commanders.[5] Almost from the outset of the war, front-line commanders were painfully aware that ammunition consumption was far greater than had been anticipated. The Russians estimated that they had used an entire year's ammunition production since the war began, and although substantial stocks of ammunition were indeed held in 'artillery parks', usually in the frontier fortresses, many were now either depleted or were being held back by fortress artillerymen who feared that they would not have sufficient stockpiles to be able to hold their fortresses if the need arose. By the second week of November artillery units in the armies earmarked for the drive on Silesia had sufficient ammunition for only four days' fighting.[6]

Another increasingly difficult shortage related to rifles. As the war continued, the scale of Russian mobilisation, and the casualties suffered, was far greater than had ever been expected. Indeed, throughout the war, Russia struggled to manufacture enough rifles to equip all her armies. Eventually, in an attempt to alleviate the shortage, Russian ammunition factories were ordered to produce bullets and cartridges that were compatible with captured Austrian weapons. Polish civilians were offered money for any weapons that they recovered, but it was typical of the inefficiency of the Russian Empire that although a suitable proclamation was issued, funds were not made available to pay for any weapons recovered. As a result, the Poles rapidly lost interest in the scheme.

Meanwhile, the war was spreading. After its defeat in the Balkan Wars of 1912–13, Turkey had formed a close relationship with Germany. A substantial German military mission in Turkey, headed by Otto Liman von Sanders, with Colonel Friedrich Bronsart von Schellendorf as his chief of staff, had helped modernise Turkey's army and war plans. Sanders' role was far in excess of what might be expected of the head of a military mission, notably when he was put in command of the Turkish I Corps in Istanbul. This resulted in diplomatic protests, particularly from the Russians. German diplomats tried to defuse the crisis by asking Sanders to accept command of another unit, but he refused on the grounds that if he was to function as head of the military mission, he had to be in Istanbul, and therefore any troops he commanded had to be in the Turkish capital – which was precisely the basis for Russian objections. The matter was finally settled when the kaiser promoted Sanders to the rank of general. It was normal for German officers in Turkey to function at one rank higher than their German rank, and consequently he was now too senior to command a corps, and became instead Inspector General of the Turkish Army.[7]

Sanders and Schellendorf were often at loggerheads, but worked effectively to modernise the Turkish forces. Schellendorf was later a key figure in the Turkish persecution of Armenian Christians, and his comments on the subject in 1919 carry a chilling shadow of what was to follow in a later war:

> Like the Jew, the Armenian outside his homeland is like a parasite, absorbing the wellbeing of the country in which he is established. This also results in hatred that has been directed against him in a medieval manner as an unwanted people, and has led to his murder.[8]

Sanders and Schellendorf were instrumental in a secret treaty drawn up on 2 August between the two nations, requiring Turkey to declare war on Russia should Germany become involved in such a conflict. The sultan, however, did not sign the treaty, making its legality dubious. In any event, Turkey was not ready for war in August, and the German mission worked to prepare Turkish forces for operations both against Russia – in Anatolia and the Caucasus – and against Britain, in Egypt. Confident that the Central Powers would win a swift victory, the Germans made little attempt to force implementation of the secret treaty. Although the revised war plans were complete by early September, the sultan still tried to maintain a neutral stance, despite the urging of his pro-German generals. Turkish mobilisation began in August, but proceeded in a chaotic manner through the following weeks. Finally, on 29 October, Turkish officers led a force of several warships – including the two former German vessels *Goeben* and *Breslau* – to the Russian Black Sea port of Novorossiysk. A 30-minute bombardment ensued, resulting in widespread destruction. Russia declared war on Turkey on 2 November, followed a few days later by Britain and France.

This had major consequences for the Russians. Whilst Grand Duke Nikolai had reasons to be satisfied with the outcome of the current campaign – the Austro-Hungarian armies had once more been driven back on the Carpathians, Krakow seemed within reach, and major Russian forces were in position close to Germany's borders – he had to make allowances for possible Turkish attacks on Russia. Consequently, he was anxious to achieve as swift a victory as possible. If this could be accomplished, there was the prospect of considerable gains at the expense of Turkey, perhaps even the capture of Istanbul, which was a long-term Russian goal. In the past the British and French had steadfastly opposed any Russian attempt to seize the Bosporus, but if Russia could deliver victory against Germany, there was surely no possibility of the Western Powers thwarting Russian ambitions at the mouth of the Black Sea.

Within the Russian camp, there were different opinions on how to proceed. All agreed that a swift blow was needed, before the Turks could put significant pressure on Russia's southern flank. Inevitably, there was a desire by the front commanders to ensure that they individually had a pre-eminent role in what they hoped would be the decisive campaign of the war. Ruzsky wished to take command of the assault on Silesia and the Warta valley, using Second, Fifth, and Fourth Armies, while Tenth and First Armies subdued East Prussia. Ivanov and Alexeyev, in Southwest Front, wanted to knock the Austro-Hungarian Empire out of the war, and proposed a drive on Krakow with Fifth, Fourth, and Ninth Armies.

On this occasion, Grand Duke Nikolai chose to side with Ruzsky. Fourth Army was to be transferred to Northwest Front, which would conduct the drive southwest into Silesia, and directly west across the Warta. Tenth Army would hold the line facing the Masurian Lakes, while Rennenkampf's First Army deployed on its left flank, threatening the southern approaches of East Prussia. In the south, Eighth Army was to try to force the Carpathian passes, while Eleventh Army besieged Przemyśl, and Third Army advanced towards Krakow. The new drive was to commence on 14 November, by which time it was hoped that Southwest Front would have completed its operations in Galicia. But as had been the case during the fighting on the Vistula, logistic difficulties interfered with this timetable, with Fourth Army reporting that a shortage of food would delay any advance by at least a week. The railways had been badly damaged by the enemy, insisted Evert, and without supplies his men would be unable to push on. Nikolai ordered supplies to be moved forward by motor vehicle. If he was aware of the shortage of such vehicles, and the badly degraded state of the roads, he simply ignored these details.[9]

In any event, the Germans had no intention of waiting for the Russians to make the next move, though their attempts at concentrating sufficient forces had an unexpected effect on the command arrangements on the Eastern Front. The rapid retreat across Poland had done no damage either to Ninth Army's morale or to its commander's reputation, as the Russians discovered from letters captured during their advance.[10] Hindenburg and Ludendorff had decided that the best way of defending Silesia was to strike against the Russian forces from the northwest. To this end, Mackensen's Ninth Army moved XI, XVII, and XX Corps and 3rd Guards Infantry Division to the Thorn area, where they were joined by reinforcements from First Army. One of the formations transferred by François to Mackensen was I Reserve Corps; the other was XXV Reserve Corps. It seems that Ludendorff requested that François should send his old command, I Corps, to Mackensen's army, but the independently minded François decided to keep control of his veterans, sending the new (and relatively poorly equipped) reservists instead. Bearing in mind the series of insubordinate acts by François before and during the Tannenberg campaign, it is unsurprising that this proved to be one insubordination too many. Hindenburg dismissed him from command of Eighth Army; he was replaced by Otto von Below, who had commanded I Reserve Corps at Tannenberg. Curt von Morgen, the commander of 3rd Reserve Infantry Division at Tannenberg, now took command of I Reserve Corps. Additional reinforcements, in the shape of five cavalry divisions, arrived from the Western Front.

It was estimated that some 800 trains would be required to move all of Mackensen's troops into position. As it had on every occasion, the *Reichsbahn* rose to the challenge, running over eighty trains a day. General von Woyrsch was left to command the German forces that linked Mackensen's army to the Austro-Hungarian forces near Krakow. Despite Conrad's enthusiasm for joining in the attack on the Russians, Ludendorff recorded that it was only one day before the planned start of the operation that it became clear that an Austro-Hungarian attack would not take place.[11] Although more troops were expected from the west, Ludendorff and Hindenburg decided they could not wait until they arrived. There was a risk that the Russians would become aware of Mackensen's redeployment, and would move sufficient numbers of troops into the area to make a successful attack impossible, or would commence their drive towards Silesia and across the Warta.

On the Russian side, the main problem was dealing with the consequences of the German scorched earth policy. Quartermaster-General Yuri Danilov took personal control of improving supplies, ensuring that depots were established throughout the area. Acting on reports that bread was often mouldy by the time that it reached the front line, he ordered bakeries to be established at corps level.[12] Ammunition and replacement weaponry remained problematic. Whilst he was aware that this was a very limited supply, Ruzsky – under pressure from the grand duke – was unwilling to delay the start of operations to allow for larger stocks to be brought forward. To add to the frustration of Russian commanders throughout the chain of command, there was little clarity about the coming operation. Neither the start date, nor the precise details of objectives, had been passed down by either Ruzsky or Grand Duke Nikolai, and it was therefore impossible to assess whether the stocks of ammunition and food would be adequate for the coming battles. As a consequence, unsure of where they should concentrate their forces in preparation for an advance, army and corps commanders left most of their troops deployed fairly uniformly along the front. By contrast, Hindenburg and Ludendorff ruthlessly depleted their front in order to concentrate adequate striking power for the drive on Łódź, with a total of fifteen infantry divisions and five cavalry divisions massed under Mackensen's command. Facing them would be about twenty-four Russian infantry divisions and eight cavalry divisions. Belatedly, Grand Duke Nikolai ordered Ruzsky to commence concentration for the advance on Silesia and the Warta, but the cautiously minded commander of Northwest Front made little attempt to implement the order.

On 10 November, while the Russians continued to vacillate about their planned offensive, Mackensen held a final conference with his corps commanders. The German operational plan was a simple thrust from the Thorn area towards the southeast, in order to cut the lines of communication between Łódź and Warsaw. This would isolate the city, and allow for an operation to destroy the troops trapped within it. Scheidemann's Second Army was concentrated around Łódź, and German reconnaissance had correctly identified its most northerly formation as II Corps, near the town of Leczyca, some distance behind and to the northeast of XXIII Corps. Rennenkampf's First Army was deployed to the east of II Corps, along the line of the Vistula as far as Wloclawek. It was handicapped by having units on both shores of the Vistula, with limited crossing points available to transfer them if required. However, many of the elements of V Siberian Corps, which should have held this segment of the front, had not yet deployed, giving the Germans an opportunity to strike while the defences were weak:

> It depends on a swift and energetic offensive, with a determined march to reach its objectives on the first day. Wherever the enemy is encountered, attack without delay, don't break off the final attack at dusk but renew the attack. In the face of entrenchments, deploy troops no stronger than necessary, and envelop them with strong forces.[13]

In the best traditions of the elder Moltke's teachings about devolved command, Hindenburg and Ludendorff had given Mackensen only the broadest of

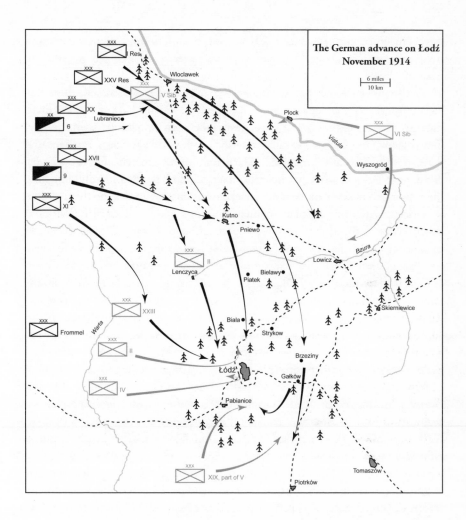

The German advance on Łódź
November 1914

6 miles
10 km

I Res
XXV Res
V Sib
XX
6
Lubraniec
Wloclawek
Plock
VI Sib
Vistula
Wyszogród
XVII
9
XI
Kutno
Pniewo
Bzura
Lowicz
II
Lenczyca
Bielawy
Piatek
Skierniewice
XXIII
Biala
Frommel
Warta
II
Strykow
Brzeziny
Łódź
Gałków
IV
Pabianice
Tomaszów
XIX, part of V
Piotrków

instructions, leaving detailed deployment to him. Two of his cavalry divisions
had already set off towards Kutno, which would put them on the flank of the
Russian II Corps. The following day the rest of Ninth Army set off. Its first
objective was to overwhelm V Siberian Corps before it could deploy along the
Vistula; to this end, I Reserve Corps and XXV Reserve Corps were tasked with
pinning the Russians in their positions, while XX Corps marched on Lubraniec,
from where it would attack into the flank of V Siberian Corps. The other
formations of Mackensen's army, XVII and XI Corps, were to march towards
Konin. In order to strengthen XXV Reserve Corps, Mackensen had assigned

several machine gun teams to its strength from the Thorn garrison, as well as a solid cadre of NCOs and officers who had already experienced war on the Eastern Front.

With Russian forces still deploying westwards from Wloclawek, there was little resistance to the deployment of XVII and XI Corps. However, the leading units of both reserve corps ran into resistance from V Siberian Corps almost immediately. The German cavalry combined well with XX Corps to drive back Russian units around Lubraniec. Mackensen now ordered the two cavalry divisions to advance directly eastwards, to ensure that the Russians did not close the gap between Rennenkampf's First Army and Scheidemann's Second Army.

Belatedly, Rennenkampf's reconnaissance forces had detected the threat to V Siberian Corps, and he requested permission to move VI Siberian Corps to support his left flank. *Stavka* refused, but Rennenkampf took steps to move bridging equipment to the area so that the corps could operate on either bank of the Vistula as required. V Siberian Corps had begun to dig defensive positions on 10 November, but shortages of shovels ensured that only limited progress had been made when the Germans attacked, particularly as Leonid Sidorin, the corps commander, prevaricated about exactly where priority should be given. As a result, none of the positions were remotely ready.[14] Badly outnumbered by the concentrated German forces, V Siberian Corps was forced back.

On 12 November Russian resistance strengthened. Although the two German reserve corps made progress against the main Russian defences, attempts to turn the southern flank of the Wloclawek position were frustrated. As the day continued, weight of numbers – and of German artillery – began to tell, and after suffering heavy losses, including over a thousand prisoners, Sidorin's troops fell back to the southeast. A substantial gap opened between V Siberian Corps and II Corps nearer Łódź, and on 13 November Mackensen's troops advanced into open space. The Russians were still not aware of what was happening, as the Germans discovered from an intercepted wireless transmission. Although they knew that Sidorin had been driven back, General Mikhail Bonch-Bruevich, quartermaster-general in Northwest Front, mistakenly assessed the attacking German forces as perhaps only two divisions, attributing the German success to the fact that V Siberian Corps was made up of second-line (and therefore inferior) divisions.[15] Although II Corps was ordered to move northeast, and VI Siberian Corps was ordered to move up to support V Siberian Corps, the transmission confirmed that the drive on Silesia was nevertheless to continue, commencing on 14 November. The northern flank was to be protected by Rennenkampf's First Army, extending its line along the Vistula. Mackensen didn't hesitate to take advantage, issuing orders for 14 November for his entire army to advance. XI Corps would strike against the northern flank of XXIII Corps, which would now be exposed by the shift of II Corps to try to cover the gap to Rennenkampf's army. XVII and XX Corps would try to envelop and overwhelm II Corps, while I Reserve Corps and the cavalry, now grouped together into a corps commanded by Manfred von Richthofen (whose nephew and namesake had already distinguished himself leading a cavalry raid in the opening days of the war, and would go on to great fame as a pilot), were to waylay and hold up any attempt by VI Siberian Corps to extend its line towards the west.[16]

Any illusions that the Russians had about the strength of the German forces were dispelled on 14 November as heavy fighting erupted. The Russian XXIII Corps was taken completely by surprise by XI Corps and forced to retreat in almost continuous combat throughout the day and evening. II Corps came under heavy attack by the two German corps tasked with driving it back, but managed to hold most of its positions, with help from the remnants of V Siberian Corps. Reports reaching Mackensen suggested considerably greater German success than was actually the case. Nevertheless, the men of his former command enjoyed at least local successes, as one officer later recalled in a description of an attack late on 14 November:

> With the usual flank guards, the battalion set off at 6.30 p.m. on the road to Pniewo. As a result of the ease with which we overcame the Russian outposts, we had become rather careless and weren't thinking about encountering strong resistance. We were soon to have our illusions dispelled. 8 Coy encountered a strongly held Russian trench about 300m ahead, from where it suddenly came under a hail of heavy machine gun and rifle fire. In their agitation, the Russians fired too high, otherwise not a single man from the leasing company would have survived. Luckily, there was a wide ditch next to the road, in which the company took shelter in seconds. I lay pressed into the earth, surrounded by 8 Coy, and it was good to see how despite the constant fire from the Russian trenches, 8 Coy deployed from column into battle order in the ditch. One group after another leaped out in turn, the following companies sequentially deployed on our left, and a few machine guns soon opened fire. Given the disparity in strength between the Russians and us, there was no possibility of a firefight, but the heavy fire from the Russian trenches slackened a little. From 7 p.m. to 10 p.m. the battalion was held in this uneven firefight without artillery support. Finally, the first shells flew over us and struck the Russian trenches. Our artillery with rapid shell- and

shrapnel-fire also hit the Russians' rear positions, which were clearly visible on the flat landscape. The Russians endured this bombardment, which was strongly supported by the infantry, for only a short time, and then began to withdraw, first individually, then in groups, finally en masse. Our machine guns and rifles fired as best they could, shrapnel exploded amongst the Russian masses, and soon the withdrawal turned to wild flight. II Battalion was the first to move forward from its trench, and several hundred prisoners, and machine guns and other military equipment were captured.

The losses of II Battalion and particularly 8 Coy were heavy ... the pursuit continued to Masew, which the battalion reached at 8.30 a.m. [on 15 November]. In addition to fighting, the physical strains of these days were particularly severe. The companies had been two days without sleep or [hot] food.[17]

VI Siberian Corps, trying to move west to cover the gap that had opened up between First Army and Second Army, was on the right bank of the Vistula, and ran into huge problems attempting to cross the river. There was a very limited ferry operating across the river, which rapidly broke down, and although a pontoon bridge was established, this too was damaged when artillery attempted to cross. As the units crossed, they were dispatched west in a trickle; Morgen's I Reserve Corps was kept busy throughout the day, fighting off a series of attacks, but was never seriously threatened.[18]

Danilov was deeply critical of the command arrangements on the Russian side:

Each of our corps was superior to a German corps in terms of battalions, resulting in the two sides having broadly equal numbers. But in a war of movement, the side that has the greater flexibility of organisation always has a huge advantage over its opponent; this was precisely the organisation of the Germans who had concentrated their forces, while ours were dispersed. German artillery was more numerous than ours; the fighting quality of their reserve divisions was far greater than that of ours, of which V and VI Siberian Corps were formed. But the most important factor was that command of the attacking German troops was always in the hands of a single commander, whereas our corps came from two neighbouring armies and had no direct coordination ... it must be said that the tendency to obey the letter of every order, even when contrary to one's instincts, was unfortunately ingrained in our army; consequently, I cannot place too much blame on the commander of Northwest Front; but it is clear that our interests would have been better served if command of the corps involved had been temporarily assigned to General Ruzsky himself or to one of the army commanders, or even to one of the front line corps

366

commanders. This would have ensured the unity of action so indispensable in military matters and prevented the tendency of each corps to withdraw towards its own army, greatly facilitating the enemy's ability to penetrate the seam [between the armies].[19]

The German XVII and XX Corps continued to drive back the Russian forces that were meant to be covering the seam between First and Second Armies on 15 November. General Alexei Churin's II Corps almost disintegrated towards the end of the day, falling back in disarray to and through Kutno, losing thousands of prisoners in the process. Some of Richthofen's cavalry, pursuing hard, seized Kutno at dusk, capturing a further 1,500 Russians, many of them men who had been wounded in the previous days. Amongst those involved in the fighting was a Latvian officer, Jucums Vācietis; he would later be appointed the very first commander-in-chief of the Red Army. The following day the German cavalry patrolled aggressively to the east of Kutno, and rounded up more prisoners. They must have been both surprised and delighted to find that one of them was Baron Korff, the civilian Russian governor of Warsaw.[20]

Despite these setbacks, Ruzsky remained convinced that the German forces driving into the seam between First and Second Armies were limited to a few reservist formations. He remained determined to conduct the offensive operation that he had proposed to, and that had been accepted by, Grand Duke Nikolai. Dismissing the German attackers as 'reservist rabble', he ignored intelligence that had identified elements of all the major German formations in the area, and impatiently ordered V and VI Siberian Corps and II Corps to destroy the Germans without further delay. Sidorin grimly ordered his battered divisions forward; the German I Reserve Corps smashed the attacks and drove off the survivors, netting another 5,000 prisoners.[21] On 16 November the Germans pushed on over the River Bzura, and Rennenkampf decided that whatever Ruzsky might order about extending his front west to link up with Second Army, his priority was to prevent the Germans from driving on towards Warsaw. But Mackensen had no intention of attacking so far east; his desire had been to secure a line along the Bzura before turning south and southwest, into the rear of the Russian forces threatening Germany. He wrote home that everything was going as well as could be expected, both at the front and in his headquarters:

I am well, and things are going particularly well for me as army commander. West Prussia, Posen and Silesia no longer need to fear a Russian invasion. God was with us in these days of great decision.[22]

Early on 16 November, orders were issued temporarily abandoning the planned attack on Silesia and across the Warta towards Posen (now Poznań). The elements of Scheidemann's Second Army that had not yet been involved in the fighting between Łódź and the Vistula and were deployed to the west of the city – IV and I Corps – were ordered to fall back on Łódź itself. Fifth Army was to close up with Scheidemann's left flank, and was also to send its V Corps to Skierniewice, roughly midway between Łódź and Warsaw, to form an operational reserve. Even this redeployment was hindered; only a single division of V Corps was eventually dispatched northeast. It remains unclear who was involved in issuing these orders. Danilov implies that they emanated from Ruzsky, but in his account of the battle, Fiodr Novitsky, who was the chief of staff of I Corps, recorded that the withdrawal order came from Scheidemann.[23] He checked the veracity of the order with Second Army Headquarters, and was advised of the deep German penetration to the northeast, and that speed was of the essence. Despite roads choked with rear area units, I and IV Corps managed to withdraw some 30 miles (50km) in less than two days, and were immediately ordered to deploy northeast of Łódź. Contrary to Danilov's implication, it seems that Ruzsky was in the dark about the withdrawal of Scheidemann's Second Army to Łódź, as were Grand Duke Nikolai and *Stavka*. Nikolai sent an angry signal to Ruzsky, stating 'extreme irritation at some of your senior commanders' dispositions'. Ruzsky responded that the retreat was an error. 'Everything has followed from this blunder. The details are not worth going into. They are too depressing.'[24]

German wireless stations continued to intercept Russian communications, and by this stage of the war were able to decipher them as quickly as the Russians. On this occasion the general confusion amongst Russian forces gave a misleading picture. An initial intercepted message, presumably from Second Army, suggested that a withdrawal from Łódź was imminent, while a second message, from Grand Duke Nikolai, ordered the troops to remain in their positions. Convinced that the Russians were ripe for a serious defeat, Ludendorff urged Mackensen to move against Łódź from the, cutting off the city from the east, to isolate and destroy the troops that had gathered there; the capture of Strykow by XX Corps opened the way for such a drive. Meanwhile, still trying to make sense of what was happening, Ruzsky and the grand duke agreed to counter the German successes to date by launching concentric attacks, with Rennenkampf's First Army in the northeast, the battered V and VI Siberian Corps and II Corps in the east, and the forces concentrating around Łódź in the southwest.

The German thrust against Łódź was assigned to Scheffer's XXV Reserve Corps. One of its infantry brigades had been assigned elsewhere, and it was now reinforced byLitzmann's 3rd Guards Infantry Division. The group was to march on Brzeziny, about 12 miles (20km) due east of Łódź. For Litzmann, it was a welcome move, as his division was no longer part of the Guards Reserve Corps; he had not enjoyed the experience of working with Gallwitz as his corps commander. He had served as a young officer in the Guards in his youth, and as his men marched to the front, he felt proud of their attitude:

> Determined to take part in the decisive fighting, we force-marched an average of 50km (30 miles) a day and in doing so crossed the 'black earth' country, where the ground was sodden from the rain, guns and other vehicles sinking up to their axles and being laboriously set in motion again by the efforts of the men. From sunrise to sunset we marched on with the utmost exhausting efforts. But the morale of my solders was wonderful! They were advancing again! During these days, my magnificent troops endeared themselves to me forever.[25]

Such comments are almost completely absent from the memoirs of senior officers in the armies of Russia and Austria-Hungary, and say a great deal about the differences in military culture between the various nations on the Eastern Front.

At the same time as the German advance east of Łódź, Plehve ordered his XIX Corps to join V Corps in its march towards Skierniewice. In atrocious weather, the Russian troops moved with a speed that they had seldom shown in better conditions, covering about 40 miles (64km) in two days.

On 18 November Scheffer advanced in the face of only light resistance to Brzeziny. From here, with additional support from 6th Cavalry Division, he was ordered to push on southwards to Będków, while to his west XX and XVII Corps enveloped the defences of Łódź. It was a day of hard fighting around the outskirts of the city, as the Germans were surprised to encounter tougher resistance than they had expected. The Russian I Corps had actually been ordered to advance east from Łódź to Brzeziny, and had it done so, it is likely that XXV Reserve Corps would have had a much harder task taking the town. However, Dushkevich, the elderly corps commander, who had been wounded in the chest in the Russo-Japanese War and was frequently forced to take to his bed, deferred to the advice of Novitsky, his chief of staff, who reasoned that this would leave the entire corps exposed on its northern flank. Instead, the Russians remained in their positions northeast of Łódź.[26] Scheffer's troops, too, faced a hard battle. Elements of 3rd Guards Division seized Malczew, 2 miles (3.5km) southwest of Brzeziny, in heavy fighting, and then had to beat off three determined Russian counterattacks.[27] As the nights grew increasingly cold, Litzmann's men, already tired from their strenuous march to the battlefield, made the best of whatever shelter they could find and consoled themselves that while they had suffered casualties in Malczew, the Russians had lost far more men.[28] But the colder weather was not entirely without benefits. The terrain north of Brzeziny was relatively hilly, but as the troops pushed south, they entered flatter country, crisscrossed by numerous streams and separated by marshy meadowland. With frosts every night, these meadows froze, allowing better movement than would otherwise have been possible.

Rennenkampf's army might have been weakened by the losses it had taken, but it now received almost all of the reinforcements arriving via Warsaw. Despite this, and the constant urging of *Stavka*, Rennenkampf still made little attempt to advance against Mackensen's forces, repeatedly insisting that he had to defend the approaches to Warsaw. In the south, Ivanov also responded to urges for action by listing the difficulties he faced. The Austro-Hungarian defences around Krakow were almost insurmountable, he insisted, and the presence of substantial enemy forces along the Carpathians meant that his southern armies were unable to concentrate against Krakow as previously planned.[29] With Scheidemann's Second Army concentrated around Łódź, the only Russian force that appeared to be moving with serious aggressive intent was Plehve's Fifth Army, which intercepted the German troops advancing south to cut the Russian lines of communication running east from Łódź. After a short battle, Plehve was able to halt the march of the German XXV Reserve Corps, bringing to an end the German plan to complete their encirclement of the city. At the same time, elements of Plehve's army blocked attempts by the *Landwehr* formations southwest of Łódź from encircling the city from that direction.

Throughout the previous few days the Germans had controlled events, forcing the Russians to react to their moves. As the battle approached its intended climax at Łódź on 19 November, numerical reality began to assert itself. The Russian forces in Poland greatly outnumbered their German opponents, and even in the vicinity of Łódź, Mackensen's troops were attempting to encircle a force that was significantly larger than their own. Russian forces from Fifth Army attacked the German lines to the northwest of Łódź, driving them back. Elsewhere along the perimeter north of the city, German attempts to push back the Russians were almost universally unsuccessful in the face of determined resistance, though defensive fighting in this environment was not always straightforward:

Conditions were difficult for passive defence, mainly due to the weather. As is usually the case in Poland in mid-November, there were hard frosts in the morning, making defence difficult, because it was very hard to build trenches and earthworks with worn-out entrenching tools, and rivers and swamps were frozen, greatly facilitating German movement into any gap [in the line], and we were also deprived of natural cover.[30]

The most important development in this part of the battlefield was at the southern end of the sector held by General Scholtz's XX Corps, to the northeast of Łódź. In an attempt to turn the southern flank of the opposing Russian troops, 72nd Infantry Brigade edged further south, losing contact with the rest of Scholtz's corps. Although it was still in contact with XXV Reserve Corps further south, the infantry brigade was unable to communicate with its line of command, and the Russians moved troops into the gap.

To the east of Łódź, Litzmann's 3rd Guards Division turned west and marched through snow showers towards the city, but it was clear to the commanders on the ground that they were unlikely to make much more progress. Unfortunately, in his headquarters in Hohensalza, about 90 miles (145km) from the front, Mackensen was forced to rely on increasingly fragmented reports. Although he had intended to move to Lenczyca, he acted on advice that communications were likely to be even harder from there, given the degraded state of Polish infrastructure, and chose to remain where he was, particularly as the reality of the situation around Łódź began to become clearer. A radio message from Plehve to Scheidemann, intercepted by the Germans, advised that the southern tip of the German penetration to the east of Łódź would come under heavy attack on 21 November, and that Rennenkampf would also be taking the offensive.[31] But Mackensen remained determined to see the matter through. Despite the numerical superiority of the Russian forces facing him, he was confident that his troops had the better fighting ability. To this end, XX and XXV Reserve Corps were to outflank the Russian defences around Łódź and deal a decisive blow to the Russians.[32]

Litzmann's guardsmen found themselves involved in increasingly hard fighting; regardless of the hardness of the ground, the Russians continued to show their traditional strength in digging in:

The fighting at Bedon [about 6 miles (10km) due east of Łódź] was very tough. During the night, the Russians had dug in firmly in the village and particularly in the estate grounds and swept the attackers with accurate machine-gun fire.

The advance came to a halt, and the entire attack looked like it would fail. Then the commander of the *Lehr* Regiment, Oberst Freiherr von Humboldt, and his battalion commanders leaped into the most foremost battle line and stormed forward with the men. The badly wounded Oberst was later carried back. But by 9pm, the estate grounds and neighbouring buildings were occupied by the brigade, which captured over 1,000 prisoners and six machine-guns here.[33]

The balance of power in and around Łódź was shifting firmly in favour of the Russians, though for the moment, it still seemed possible – probable, even – that the Germans would succeed in capturing Łódź and thereby crushing Scheidemann's Second Army. German pressure around the city failed to make any significant progress on 20 November, and the gap in XX Corps' sector remained open. To make matters worse for Scholtz, Rennenkampf's First Army finally began to advance the following day. A force had been concentrated at Lowicz, under the command of General Vladimir Slyusarenko, with his 43rd Infantry Division from II Corps, Gennings' 6th Siberian Infantry Division, and three additional brigades.[34] This group now began to advance slowly towards Łódź from the northeast, attempting to close the 30-mile (50km) gap between First and Second Armies, and thus threatening the rear of XX Corps. Despite its numerical strength, the new group was weak in heavy artillery and almost completely lacking in normal corps-level communications, medical, and other support, greatly reducing its ability to function for any prolonged period.

Only the cavalry of the German 19th Dragoon Regiment opposed Slyusarenko's troops, but the inbred caution of the Russians hindered them as much as German resistance. Nevertheless, the threat to the German positions had to be covered, and this could only be done by weakening the forces facing Łódź itself. The threat was so great that Scholtz drew back his southern flank, leaving his corps facing southwest, south, and east in a great curve. Inevitably, this resulted in the gap between the mass of XX Corps and 72nd Infantry Brigade growing still larger. Scheffer's force continued to make attempts to penetrate the Łódź defences from the east and southeast, with 3rd Guards Division – now reinforced by 72nd Infantry Brigade – enjoying limited success, but the pressure elsewhere around the German salient prevented troops being redeployed to exploit the gains.

For Mackensen, difficulties in determining the exact state of the battlefield were now intensifying. Aerial reconnaissance was limited due to variable weather and the limited daylight hours, and often gave contradictory reports. For the moment, the intervention of Slyusarenko's Lowicz detachment from the northeast appeared to be contained. Scholtz reported that 'in view of the apparent absence of energetic leadership, the enemy advancing on and south of Strykow is not causing any concern'.[35] Indeed, Morgen's I Reserve Corps was meant to be advancing on Lowicz, which would have eliminated any threat from that direction, but despite reporting gains the previous day, Morgen was unable to reach the town. Towards the end of the day Mackensen wrote in his diary:

> The desired decision has not been achieved today, either. The resistance of our opponents is so tough, being that of a brave opponent fighting for his very existence, that nothing else can be expected. But a decision in our favour is coming.[36]

Perhaps in an attempt to force the issue, a German officer was sent across the front line under a flag of parley, bearing a note for the Russians that called upon them to surrender. Novitsky ordered the man to be treated as a prisoner, as strict protocols such as blindfolds had not been followed, though he recorded that the call for surrender was understandable:

> To be perfectly frank, I have to admit that the situation on the evening of 21 November was so tough and held so little promise of good fortune that many of us inwardly felt that the drastic German suggestion was not without good reason. But in order to maintain morale, we tried to keep the German proposal completely secret, even amongst those in high command...
>
> We felt an extraordinary sense of pressure, feeling that in the event of a disaster, the blame for the fate of the army would fall upon us. In such a situation we would have expected energetic support from the army command, but the situation was completely the opposite – we were unsettled, did not believe in our orders, received criticism for any minor and temporary failure, however unavoidable, and ultimately, fearing that we were hiding information, Vyalov, the chief operations officer of the army, was sent to keep an eye on us. I was personally very happy to have him as a guest, because he was a friendly individual, not displeased with our efforts, and being trusted by the army command, he could testify that we really were doing everything in our power.[37]

Danilov, the quartermaster-general of the Russian Army, was not convinced that the call for surrender was a genuine approach. Writing after the war, he speculated that the officer had merely stumbled into the Russian positions, and then portrayed himself as an emissary in an attempt to prevent himself being taken prisoner.[38]

On 22 November Morgen reported to Mackensen that his I Reserve Corps could do no more:

> I Reserve Corps remains in battle, which has proved difficult in view of great fatigue (10th day of battle) and heavy losses. As before, Lowicz remains our objective; complete certainty about reaching this objective cannot be assured.[39]

Urged on by both Rennenkampf and *Stavka*, Slyusarenko's 'Lowicz detachment' began to advance more aggressively. Organised in three columns, the group advanced on Bielawy in the north and Strykow to the south. 6th Siberian Infantry Division, the last element of the group to arrive, followed on as fast as it could. Scholtz had already dispatched elements of his XX Corps to reinforce the hard-pressed 19th Dragoon Regiment, and now sent an improvised brigade under the command of Generalmajor Reifer to Strykow. At the same time, Scheffer dispatched three squadrons from 9th Cavalry Division to Brzeziny, which came under heavy attack during the afternoon, primarily from Cossacks operating on the southern flank of the Lowicz detachment. The main field hospital for 3rd Guards Infantry Division was positioned in the town, replete with nearly 700 wounded soldiers. One of the wounded, Leutnant von Witzmann, gathered together a small group of men able to fight, and succeeded in holding off the leading elements of the Russian forces long enough for the field hospital to be evacuated towards the south. Together with whatever other troops he could scrape together, Witzmann covered the evacuation, even capturing two Russian officers and eighty men.[40]

The bulk of the Lowicz detachment was heavily committed advancing on Strykow and the area to the north, and Gennings' 6th Siberian Infantry Division was ordered to support the Cossacks at Brzeziny. Hindered by confusion about which roads the division's columns should take, and by bridges destroyed by the Germans, the division made slow progress, and arrived at its destination in darkness. The first attempt to take the town was easily beaten off by the small German force, primarily the cavalry that Scheffer had sent. At first light the Russians tried again, this time with artillery support. By midday the Germans had withdrawn. In their haste, they left behind some 600 Russian prisoners, as well as several of their own men.[41]

When Brzeziny fell to the Russians, XXV Reserve Corps was effectively cut off. An operation that had been launched with the intention of isolating a substantial Russian force in Łódź had changed into a campaign in which it was the Russians who had isolated a substantial German force. Mackensen had accepted the reports from the front that the Lowicz detachment was ineffectually led without question, partly as a result of his earlier experiences during the fighting in the Tannenberg and the Masurian Lakes battles, where such operations by the Russians had been singularly unsuccessful. But now, in mid-afternoon, Scholtz had to pull back his left flank even further to face the approaching Russians. Any lingering hope of executing the German plan to capture Łódź and thus destroy Second Army was extinguished. Indeed, if the Russians could destroy the isolated German forces east of Łódź, the campaign would end in disaster.

Mackensen sent orders by radio to XXV Reserve Corps, instructing Scheffer to break contact with the Russians during the coming night, with a view to attacking towards Brzeziny the following day. Richthofen's cavalry corps would protect the rear of Scheffer's force. The situation of XXV Reserve Corps and its attached forces was serious. Isolated from German units further north, the troops were short of ammunition and food, and the weather was poor, with frequent snow showers – at a time when the men of both armies had not been issued with winter clothing. Scheffer had about 3,000 wounded with him, as well as some 10,000 prisoners that his units had captured during their advance, and he had no intention of leaving any of his wounded or prisoners behind. Late on 22 November, the temperature fell to -10°C, as the troops made the best of their limited cold rations; at least the hard frost would ensure that the ground remained frozen. Just before dawn, mist developed across the battlefield, allowing XXV Reserve Corps to break contact with the Russians without being detected.

The Lowicz detachment pushed on westwards after taking Strykow, forcing the German XVII Corps to divert units from its positions northwest of Łódź to Biala, in order to protect its rear areas. In the circumstances, it was understandable that Hoffmann, serving as First General Staff Officer in Hindenburg's headquarters, contacted Mackensen by telephone and suggested that Ninth Army might wish to retreat to Lenczyca. Mackensen, though, was determined to stand his ground, at least until Scheffer succeeded in breaking out. Hindenburg then enquired whether it was actually possible for Ninth Army to hold its positions. Mackensen's reply was resolute and pointed:

> Army Command remains quite hopeful, and should be grateful if its view, based upon on-the-spot observations, were taken into account by the higher command. Army Command takes full responsibility. It would be deeply regrettable if a decision were to be imposed upon Army Command on the grounds of the current situation, which confounded the superhuman endeavours of the troops.[42]

At the time, Litzmann and Scheffer were critical of Mackensen for making decisions from a distant headquarters without up-to-date information from the front line; nevertheless, Mackensen was still closer to events than either Hindenburg or Ludendorff.

General Danilov – the officer in charge of logistics in Northwest Front, known as 'Danilov the Red' to distinguish him from Yuri Danilov, the quartermaster-general, known as 'Danilov the Black' – had ordered trains to be made available for the transport of over 20,000 German prisoners. The capitulation of Scheffer's forces was already regarded in some Russian circles as a fait accompli, and some of Hindenburg's concerns about the safety of the rest of Ninth Army were the result of the Germans intercepting Danilov's signal regarding the expected haul of prisoners. But even at a moment when they had gained the upper hand over their opponents, the Russian senior commanders failed to show sufficient determination and self-belief. The ever-cautious Ruzsky complained to *Stavka* about the losses suffered by Second and Fifth Armies around Łódź, the exhaustion of his men, and the news that further German formations were being sent from the distant Western Front – even though these formations would take several weeks to arrive. Although the German I Reserve Corps had not succeeded in reaching Lowicz, any German success here would cut the lines of communication of the forces pushing towards Łódź. Ruzsky therefore requested permission to withdraw the Lowicz detachment to Lowicz, effectively relinquishing the grip the Russians had on XXV Reserve Corps. When this request reached *Stavka*, Quartermaster-General Danilov was shocked:

When I approached the telegraph office, I heard the characteristic clicking of the Hughes apparatus; I will never be able to forget it. Already prepared for important and unexpected news, I cast an eye over the first paragraphs of the strip of paper and immediately I was struck by the profundity of the abyss that separated the few men gathered at each end of a cold, inert wire ... in front of me, the apparatus coldly tapped out the phrases of General Ruzsky: 'Attempts at an attack by VI Siberian Corps have failed... V Siberian Corps completely incapable of advancing ... losses have reached 70 per cent of effective strength... Attacks by fresh German forces against the left and rear of Plehve's army... German attacks from Piatek towards Lowicz'...

It was a retreat, with all its unwelcome consequences, for Second and Fifth Armies. General Ruzsky wanted to commence it on 24 November – 'otherwise it might be too late,' he reported.

Even today [writing in 1927], I am unable to comprehend completely the motives behind such a decision and I spent the rest of the following day trying to prevent the consequences. After contacting the quartermaster-general of Northwest Front by telegraph, I managed to discover that General Ruzsky was primarily preoccupied by the concept of a new encirclement, this time in the direction of Lowicz, which would be possible as a result of the new enemy forces that were rumoured to be coming from the Western Front. The general had completely lost confidence in his troops' ability to manoeuvre; he was particularly tormented by the lack of reliability in the group (V and VI Siberian Corps) that was operating around Lowicz ... and whose retreat would open the road to Warsaw...

I replied [to Northwest Front's quartermaster-general] that the best way of protecting the Lowicz area was probably to carry out an energetic attack with V and VI Siberian Corps, which according to all our calculations of the forces in this sector were at least twice as numerous as the enemy, if not more; that it was almost always the leaders who gave way, not the troops. Therefore, it was necessary to place at their head a strong-willed man and to take the offensive... In addition, the morale of Second Army seemed to have recovered and no longer seemed so low. General Scheidemann had telegraphed the Grand Duke: 'The spirit of the troops is good, they are fighting heroically. I have complete confidence in the success of this difficult operation, which has been bravely executed.[43]

The overestimate of the number of Germans in the encirclement didn't help. In reality Scheffer had perhaps as few as 11,000 combat troops with him, whereas the Russian estimates ranged from 20,000 to as high as 40,000.[44] When *Stavka* reacted to Ruzsky with outrage, Sukhomlinov intervened from Petrograd on behalf of his protégé, warning that failure to withdraw in a timely manner would run the risk of a repeat of the Battle of Mukden in 1905.[45] Plehve, whose troops were attempting to close in on the encircled Germans from the southwest, also objected to Ruzsky's plans, as did Rennenkampf, who ordered the dismissal of Slyusarenko, sending General Piotr Shuvalov to take command in his place. Ruzsky, however, remained determined to retreat, and overruled the appointment of Shuvalov as commander of the Lowicz detachment, sending General Vasiliev, one of his inner circle, to take command instead. A furious Rennenkampf drove to the headquarters of II Corps at Glowno, to deliver orders personally for a continuation of attacks. It is characteristic of the attitude of Russian senior officers of the day that this was regarded as an impetuous and irresponsible move – by contrast, German generals frequently visited their corps commanders. During this period of command confusion in the Lowicz detachment, the troops themselves barely moved at all. Some troops had reached the outskirts of Łódź, where in the absence of control by their own chain of command, they found themselves commandeered by Scheidemann's Second Army. Other elements of the detachment, primarily 6th Siberian Infantry Division, took up positions along the embankment of the railway to the south of Brzeziny. The line along the railway was not particularly well positioned, with the Russian artillery not able to support all the defenders, some areas too thinly manned, and not enough attention given to flank security.[46] Meanwhile, 43rd Infantry Division withdrew towards Lowicz, as Ruzsky had ordered.

Within the encirclement Scheffer had organised his forces into three columns. Litzmann's 3rd Guards Infantry Division was to form the left column, nearest Łódź, with 49th Reserve Division forming the central column, and 50th Reserve Division on the right, protecting the eastern flank. To the rear Richthofen's cavalry fought an aggressive rearguard action, possibly the most effective fighting carried out by German cavalry during the war to date. As they advanced north, the main columns first encountered Russian forces south of Brzeziny, where they ran into the vanguard of 6th Siberian Division. The Russians were operating in something of a vacuum; the division had no maps of the area, and had been reduced to asking locals for directions.[47] Scheffer's central column's vanguard became involved in an increasingly tough battle until reinforcements arrived, forcing the Russians to withdraw. When the strengthened vanguard attempted to pursue, it ran into a spirited counterattack by the Russian 17th Dragoon Regiment. General von Waenker, commander of 49th Reserve Division, personally rounded up what men he could, and drove off the Russian cavalry; when the fighting was over, he was amongst the dead.[48] Fighting continued through the day, with much of the German vanguard being overrun as it fell short of ammunition. As night fell, 6th Siberian Division withdrew and took up positions around Brzeziny.[49]

A short distance to the west, Litzmann's 3rd Guards Division set off on its march north a little later than the rest of Scheffer's corps. In the preceding days the division had divided into three segments, and Litzmann was anxious that the withdrawal order had not reached all sections, particularly the infantry brigade commanded by Generalmajor von Friedeburg, which was a little to the northwest. In addition, communication between the Guards and XXV Reserve Corps had been sporadic for a day, and now broke down completely. With his division's entire fighting strength reduced to perhaps 4,000 rifles, Litzmann waited until his division's rearguard had arrived, but the resultant delay led to a sudden Russian attack from the outskirts of Łódź. Artillery fire fell on the massed wagons of the division's rear area formations, and their riders streamed east across an open field to avoid the shellfire. After the Russians had been driven off, 3rd Guards Division began to move north. Unwittingly, this conformed with Scheffer's plans for it to form the western column of the German forces, and it entered the woodland near Gałków, repeatedly fighting its way through groups of Russian infantry:

> Then, we – my staff officers and me – rode into the wood. A half-platoon of infantry accompanied us; the division's military judge advocate was amongst them serving as a rifleman. High above our heads, Russian shells were bursting; below, on the ground, groaned severely wounded Siberians. Enemy stragglers constantly appeared, particularly from the denser parts of the wood. Suddenly, Oberleutnant Freiherr von Krane, who was riding next to me, pulled out his Mauser pistol from his holster with a loud cry of 'Leave them to me!' – in a thicket in front of us, his sharp eyes had spotted grey Siberian felt hats. They now crawled out, about a dozen Siberians, laid down their weapons, raised their hands and gave themselves up to the young officer.[50]

Unaware of the exact plans of the rest of XXV Reserve Corps, Litzmann decided to push on through the night, intending to reach Brzeziny before dawn. He had correctly calculated that the main line of retreat for XXV Reserve Corps would still be through this town, in accordance with the last communications he had received from Scheffer. Exhausted stragglers broke away from the division during the following evening and night, with men falling asleep in the snow whenever they stopped moving, but in the small hours of the morning, Litzmann's men reached Gałków:

> Nights of combat without sleep in the recent past, hunger, and the cutting cold had taken a heavy toll upon us all. Exhausted, we stumbled over the frozen ploughed fields, falling and pulling ourselves up again to press onwards. Neither our enthusiasm nor our confidence was diminished. We felt that we were succeeding.
>
> We reached and surrounded the village of Gałków; the sleeping Russians were hauled out of the houses and taken prisoner. Then we pressed on through the bitterly cold winter's night.[51]

Further south, Russian attempts to break through Richthofen's cavalry screen were easily beaten off. It seems that Plehve's formations feared that Scheffer might be concentrating for an attempt to escape encirclement by driving west, bypassing Łódź to the south. In the absence of clear instructions from above, Plehve's units spent much of the day screening against such a move. Neither Rennenkampf nor Mackensen received clear information about the events of the day, and nor did senior Russian commanders. Consequently, news of the fighting south of Brzeziny, which might have alerted the Russian Fifth Army to the fact that Scheffer was heading north, not west, was not passed on.

On 24 November Mackensen received reports of the situation, none of them encouraging. Scheffer sent a radio message advising that his men were surrounded, with an estimated two Russian divisions blocking their escape route via Brzeziny; ammunition and food were running out. Radio intercepts showed that Novikov's cavalry corps was about to strike at the rear of Scheffer's group, and that up to sixty trains had been prepared to haul away the expected prisoners. In an attempt to help the encircled troops, Mackensen ordered Morgen to dispatch elements of his I Reserve Corps towards Brzeziny. Aware that his men were exhausted from their constant fighting on the approaches to Lowicz, Morgen replied that he doubted such a move would be successful; in any case, his corps was now coming under attack along its entire front, and he had few troops to spare.

Before dawn Litzmann's division reached Brzeziny:

> The attack was to be overwhelming and sudden, against the western edge of the town. We set off with unloaded guns.
>
> A Russian outpost was subdued with bayonets, and we entered the town without a shot fired. The success reinvigorated us; we moved forwards through the darkened streets. Doors to right and left were kicked open, the grenadiers and fusiliers dragged the sleeping Russians out. Those who did not submit easily were silently subdued... But bitter fighting erupted in the market place. The Russians finally awoke and opened fire from doors and windows. They were overwhelmed, and the houses around the market place were swiftly stormed.[52]

Vasiliev, commander of the Russian Lowicz detachment, barely succeeded in escaping capture.[53] The line of march of 3rd Guards Division had taken it past the flank of the Russian forces that had held up Scheffer's central column, and these Russians, with additional troops from the east, launched a counterattack barely an hour later. When further columns of infantry were spotted approaching from the northwest, the troops of 3rd Guards Division, at the end of their strength and ammunition, must have thought that the end had come. To their surprise and joy, the columns were the troops of Friedeburg's missing brigade. The division, once more concentrated in one location, swiftly drove off the Russian counterattack.[54]

Meanwhile, the Russian Fifth Army belatedly became aware of the German withdrawal from its front, and informed higher commands. Given the command chaos in the Lowicz detachment (to which he had greatly contributed), it was perhaps understandable that this was the first concrete information that Ruzsky received about events on the battlefield. Immediately, he abandoned all of his cautious views of the previous day and ordered a general assault on the retreating Germans, telling his subordinates that the encircled enemy was scattering and trying to break out at multiple points. There was no evidence whatever to support such an assertion, and Rennenkampf remained concerned about the German threat to Lowicz. Consequently, despite his previous short-lived enthusiasm for an advance by the Lowicz detachment, he was now reluctant to follow Ruzsky's instructions to rush troops to link up with the troops at Brzeziny. Only Plehve appears to have had a good grasp of what was happening, but his troops were in the south, too far from Brzeziny to intervene.[55]

The confusion in command was widespread throughout the Russian formations involved in the fighting. A brief summary of the main events of the previous days shows how Ruzsky vacillated between extremes. On 22 November he had urged his subordinate formations to be ready for an attack on the Germans, but had not specified where the attack was to take place. The following evening he cancelled the planned attack, but within hours issued new orders, primarily for attacks north of Łódź. The same day, these orders were expanded to include reinforcing 6th Siberian Infantry Division at Brzeziny, only for this phase to be postponed within hours. Scheidemann, whose army had taken heavy losses in its defence of the Łódź perimeter, was happy to accept any reason not to attack, and only Plehve seems to have been determined to act – but as has already been described, the aggressive stance of Richthofen's cavalry persuaded many of his subordinates to ignore his urgings and to adopt defensive positions.[56]

In Brzeziny, Litzmann and his men could hear the sounds of fighting to the south. The forces of 49th Reserve Infantry Division, supported by elements of 3rd Guards Division, had advanced on the railway embankment near Gałków, which was now back in Russian hands. Gennings' 6th Siberian Infantry Division remained the only major Russian unit attempting to stop the German breakout; in vain, Vasiliev had ordered the rest of the forces assigned to him to concentrate in the area, but only a single regiment responded. It seems that the moves by

Mackensen to aid the breakout by directing elements of XX Corps and I Reserve Corps to attack the encircling Russians distracted many local commanders, who directed their troops into positions from where they could cover any new German advance from the north, rather than a breakout from within the encirclement. Whilst such covering moves were not without justification, some formations, such as the Russian 43rd Infantry Division, remained entirely stationary through the critical day for no apparent reason at all, ignoring Vasiliev's orders completely.[57] The troops of 6th Siberian Infantry Division blocking Scheffer's path amounted to barely the strength of a single regiment, and were almost leaderless. Gennings, the division commander, had suffered a complete nervous breakdown, and the only forceful commander in the field was General Zhelinski, commander of the division's 6th Artillery Brigade. Unfortunately for the Russians, the traditional rivalry between the different branches of the army meant that, as an artilleryman, his knowledge of infantry tactics and dispositions was minimal, and coordination of his guns with the infantry thus remained poor.[58]

Nevertheless, the individual Russian soldiers fought bravely. Heavy Russian fire rapidly brought the German attack to a halt, and further Russian troops approaching from the west threatened the flank of 49th Reserve Division. These troops, a battalion from 63rd Infantry Division, played no part in the fighting; having approached the battlefield, they halted, and then inexplicably withdrew back to the west.[59] Zhelinski's artillery inflicted heavy losses amongst the columns of horse-drawn vehicles in the rear of the German attack wave, and a large column of Russian prisoners of war, mistakenly identified as German troops by the Russian artillery, also came under shellfire, suffering many casualties. As the German attack faltered, two intrepid messengers on bicycles reached XXV Reserve Corps Headquarters to report that Litzmann had succeeded in capturing Brzeziny. The situation remained nevertheless serious, as Generalleutnant von Thiesenhausen, who had taken command of 49th Reserve Division after the death of its previous commander, recorded in a brief message that he sent to Scheffer:

> There is no doubt: if we don't get through today, we will all be left lying on this ground, or we will be en route for Siberia.[60]

A little to the east General Hans von der Goltz had ordered his 50th Reserve Infantry Division to push forward towards Brzeziny. Somewhat to his surprise he encountered only modest resistance. Hearing the sounds of intense fighting to his left, he ordered his men to turn to support 49th Reserve Infantry Division's stalled attack. As the Germans turned the flank of the Russian defences, Litzmann arrived to join Goltz, and the two men watched as 50th Reserve Infantry Division's artillery rapidly silenced the Russian guns before turning their fire on the Russian trenches. By midday the entire Russian position along the railway embankment was in German hands. An additional 800 prisoners and eight guns had been captured, and a small number of German guns that had been lost the previous day, when 49th Reserve Infantry Division's vanguard was overrun, were also retaken. Using the last of their ammunition, elements of 3rd Guards Division attacked towards the south, and 6th Siberian Infantry Division effectively ceased to exist. Vasiliev abandoned the battlefield aboard an armoured train, under German artillery fire, and Gennings broke down completely as his division disintegrated. Zhelinski, who had fled the battlefield and headed north, was taken prisoner by the Germans. Late in the afternoon the entire German force was united in Brzeziny. Continuing its excellent rearguard performance, Richthofen's cavalry arrived late in the day, successfully holding off the pursuing Russian cavalry commanded by Novikov.[61]

It was the end of the encirclement of Scheffer's command. The German XX Corps had exerted pressure from the north, and somehow I Reserve Corps had scraped together enough men to attack towards Strykow, in the rear of the Russian forces. Alexei Churin, the commander of II Corps, still hadn't recovered from the mauling his troops had suffered the previous week, and at the first sign of a German threat announced that he would not be able to hold Strykow, even calling on Gennings and the shattered remnants of 6th Siberian Infantry Division to come to his aid. Churin's chief of staff begged him to remain in his positions, pointing out in vain that a great prize was about to slip through the fingers of the Russian forces.

In Łódź, Novitsky, the chief of staff of I Corps, who was effectively running the unit, received sudden orders on 24 November to attack towards Brzeziny as soon as possible. Aware that such a move would open a gap between his troops and the neighbouring II Siberian Corps, Novitsky asked Scheidemann's headquarters for confirmation and instructions on how to protect his flanks. Failing to receive any reply, he kept his forces in their positions, where they were already coming under attack from the German XX Corps, part of the German attempt to help XXV Reserve Corps. Novitsky later learned that an increasingly exasperated Plehve had sent detailed suggestions to Scheidemann, pointing out precisely which troops could be released for a thrust towards Brzeziny or against XXV Reserve Corps. However, Second Army Headquarters ignored the message until the following day, by which time it was far too late. But while Scheidemann was definitely at fault, Novitsky's refusal to act on his own initiative also contributed to the overall Russian failure.[62]

In the face of a threat more imagined than real, Churin abandoned Strykow, allowing Scheffer to link up with XX Corps. In addition to their wounded, the triumphant men of XXV Reserve Corps brought with them over 12,000 Russian prisoners – many captured during the breakout – and sixty-four Russian guns. The 63-year-old General Sheffer had not slept for seventy-two hours, and had been present at almost every critical moment to inspire and lead his troops to their remarkable escape. Litzmann, too, was constantly in the front line with his riflemen, inspiring them to ignore their fatigue, hunger, and the bitter cold to fight their way out of the encirclement. Whatever doubts Gallwitz might have had about the wisdom of appointing a man in his mid-60s as a division commander were clearly disproved. Perhaps the only blemish was that the Germans had used their Russian captives to pull many of the rear area units' wagons, and the captured Russian guns.

On 25 November, after the Germans had successfully escaped, Scheidemann issued orders along the lines of Plehve's suggestions for an attack towards Brzeziny. Novitsky travelled to Łódź to meet the army commander, to point out that such an operation was now too late:

> When I entered his office, he was dressed ready to travel, and warned me that he had to go to Pabianice urgently to meet Plehve, and that I should be brief. I reported the situation, and fervently implored Scheidemann to abandon the attack on Brzeziny, because it would not end well; we would merely concentrate our forces for a strike at empty space. Scheidemann looked very depressed, and listened patiently and politely, but then said that although he believed everything that I had said, he could change nothing, because Plehve had committed himself to an attack. Scheidemann added that Plehve believed that there were two German princes – Joachim and Oscar (sons of the Kaiser) – with the German troops in Brzeziny, and that we had to capture them, come what may.[63]

Given that the two princes in question were 16 and 14 years old respectively, this assertion should have been seen as simply absurd to anyone who had any knowledge of the kaiser's family. Despite continuing pressure on his corps, Novitsky found it difficult to concentrate enough men for a meaningful attack. He received a stream of anxious telephone calls from Scheidemann's headquarters enquiring as to why the attack had not commenced, and when he remonstrated with Second Army's chief of staff that, instead of passing on impossible orders, the headquarters staff should make their superiors aware of the real situation, he was told that Plehve wanted the attack to be carried out at all costs – the German princes had to be captured.

When they finally advanced, the soldiers of I Corps encountered almost no resistance – Scheffer and his men had retreated to the north. Nevertheless, the Russian troops advanced at a slow pace, digging in whenever they halted. Novitsky tried to hurry them along, but Dushkevich, his corps commander, was apparently more concerned with finding warm quarters for the coming night. In any event, there was nothing to be done. The Germans were gone, and the battle was over.[64]

Reviewing the battle in 1930, Novitsky gave an assessment of the German performance at Łódź, in which the virtues he ascribed to his former enemies highlight corresponding weaknesses in the Russian Army:

> Especially in recent times, there has been a tendency to discredit the performance of the Germans and to try to prove that they were not as capable as we thought at the time … but I think that anyone who wishes to remain objective and impartial cannot ignore a sense of astonishment, I would even say admiration, when studying the actions of the Germans in the operation at Łódź. Personally, I find great credibility in the German accounts of how they not only extricated themselves with honour, but also showed great determination in battle, and did not leave any trophies for the enemy, but actually took with them all the spoils of war, and in contrast to us, showed great skill in leadership, and valour in both the fighting arms and the rear area units.
>
> When speaking about the virtues that can be attributed to them, first is the great moral courage of their leaders, who took responsibility without hesitation; secondly, the initiative and understanding of the overall situation at all levels, leading to great consistency in actions; and thirdly, a clear statement of objectives, and unswerving perseverance in their achievement.[65]

Litzmann had his own opinion of the factors that contributed to the victory of the encircled German troops:

> I have often asked myself who should be credited with the success of my 3rd Guards Infantry Division, and have come to the conclusion that, in addition to God's help, the wonderful attributes of my troops, their excellent training, and in particular their high moral strength, all contributed to the favourable outcome. An abiding love for the Fatherland, a strong sense of German honour, heroic self-sacrifice, iron discipline, the finest camaraderie and a tough, unshakable will to win, these

contributed to the moral strength that filled German soldiers of all ranks at that time. This created the spirit that swung victory our way despite the most severe conditions.[66]

Estimates of the casualties suffered by the two sides have been labelled as biased. In December 1914 the *New York Times* reported losses as amounting to 160,000 Germans and 120,000 Russians, but this report was strongly coloured in favour of the Russians.[67] It appears that the estimate included the Russian figure of expected German prisoners, and the Russian losses may have been understated. The primary German objective was to prevent an invasion of German territory, and was therefore a success. However, during the operation an opportunity arose to strike a killing blow against Scheidemann's Second Army, and in attempting to carry this out, XXV Reserve Corps found itself surrounded. The Russians claimed success in that they felt they had successfully headed off a German advance on Warsaw, but this had never been Mackensen's intention. The isolation of XXV Reserve Corps by the Lowicz detachment was not part of any clear plan – the rapidly assembled detachment attacked towards Łódź primarily to reduce pressure on Scheidemann's perimeter. Once the Russians had surrounded Scheffer's forces, they lacked the coordination and determination to overwhelm them. Only Plehve, it seems, had any clear idea of the importance of crushing the encircled Germans, but even his units were dilatory in their pursuit, allowing Richthofen's cavalry to hold them at arm's length.

The encirclement of XXV Reserve Corps was broken for several reasons: lack of coordination by First, Second, and Fifth Armies; the extraordinary muddle of command in the Lowicz detachment; and Ruzsky's oscillation between his deep-rooted caution and his almost impulsive issuing of orders for all-out attacks. The speed and decisiveness of Scheffer's response to the encirclement also played a huge part, and stands in stark contrast to the complete lack of coordinated leadership in the Russian Second Army during the closing phases of the Tannenberg fighting. Long before Novitsky grudgingly acknowledged the skills and virtues of the encircled Germans, the German high command had already done so. Mackensen, Scheffer, and Litzmann were all awarded the *Pour Le Mérite* for their roles in the fighting. The latter earned the nickname 'the Lion of Brzeziny' for his exploits.

Even before the end of the war, the battle had developed its own mythology. The Russians regarded it, with some justification, as the epitome of everything that was wrong with the tsar's armies. In a war dominated by the bloody stalemate in northern France and western Belgium, the Germans were anxious to celebrate any victory, and in parallel with the growth of the cult of Tannenberg, the story of Łódź changed rapidly from an extraordinary escape from disaster to one of a shining victory. But the most lasting impact of the battle was on the psyche of the two armies. During the American Civil War in the previous century, the outstanding performance of Robert E. Lee's Army of Northern Virginia in a series of battles left the Union generals with a deep-seated sense of awe, resulting in them repeatedly failing to exploit tactical and operational advantages. By the end of the Battle of Łódź, the Russian attitude towards the Germans, already partly established before the beginning of the war, was similarly one of profound awe and fear. From the German perspective, the Russians – already perceived to be inferior fighters after Tannenberg and the Masurian Lakes – were regarded with growing disdain.

CHAPTER 14

THE FIRST CHRISTMAS

As autumn turned to winter, all prospects of a decisive victory on the Western Front died in the mud and slaughter of Ypres. Despite stretching the British Expeditionary Force to the very limit, the Germans failed to achieve the elusive breakthrough that they had desperately needed if their pre-war strategy of winning a victory in the west before turning east in strength was to be achieved. Despite his conviction that, ultimately, the war could only be won in the west, Falkenhayn had to consider sending troops to the east, if only to prevent Russian numerical superiority bringing about a collapse of the position of the Central Powers. Even before the Battle of Łódź, several cavalry divisions, in addition to XXV Reserve Corps, had been transferred east; a steady stream of other formations now followed them. II Corps, XIII Corps, III Reserve Corps, and XXIV Reserve Corps all boarded trains for Poland, where they were fed into the line of battle. In addition, 1st Infantry Division was finally transferred from Eighth Army to Mackensen's command.

The casualties suffered by the Germans during the fighting around Łódź were heavy, as Litzmann recorded when he visited one of his regiments, reduced to only four weak companies on 25 November:

> The regiment commander Graf Schulenburg and five officers were standing on the main road. I asked him to assemble his officers so that I could thank them for their achievements during the past few days. But they were already 'assembled'; apart from these five and a very few officers who were with [Hauptmann] Delius or on other tasks, I was told that the rest were dead or wounded. I took this very hard.[1]

During the eventful days of the Battle of Łódź the German and Austro-Hungarian positions further south, defending Silesia and Posen, came under intermittent attack from the Russians, though without the force that had originally been intended. All the attacks were beaten off, though when the kaiser visited Woyrsch's *Landwehr* Corps, the activity in the front line was still of a sufficient intensity that it was not possible for Wilhelm to visit the troops in the trenches. For Woyrsch, it was a day of great honour. He assembled over 500 officers of his corps, representatives of every company and battalion, in his headquarters, where they lunched with the kaiser:

> At 1 p.m., tables were laid in the great hall of the castle, where His Majesty chatted with those closest to him in the most lively and affable manner. Here, the Supreme Military Commander was not Kaiser, but rather a comrade amongst comrades.[2]

Despite all his aspirations and expectations, Wilhelm was by this stage of the war marginalised from decision-making. Given his character, this was not surprising:

> [He was] talented, quick to understand, sometimes brilliant, with a predilection for the modern – technology, industry, science – but at the same time superficial, hasty, restless, uneasy, without any depth of gravity, without any will for hard work or determination to see things through, without any sense of sobriety, balance and boundaries, or even for reality and real problems, uncontrollable and barely capable of learning from experience, desperate for praise and success – as Bismarck said during his early life, he wanted every day to be his birthday – romantic, sentimental and theatrical, unsure and arrogant, with limitless exaggerated self-confidence and desire to show off, an immature cadet, who never took the tone of the officers' mess out of his voice, and brashly wanted to play the part of the Supreme Military Commander.[3]

Wilhelm had been reduced to little more than a figurehead, often pathetically grateful if any officers at Falkenhayn's headquarters spared him their attention and time. At the front line, though, he clearly remained popular, and on this occasion, took advantage of his visit to promote Woyrsch to the rank of Generaloberst.

Although his troops were not directly involved in the fighting around Łódź, Woyrsch did what he could to ease pressures on Mackensen. Aerial reconnaissance identified the presence of III Caucasian Corps in the northern part of the sector held by the *Landwehr* Corps, and when it seemed that this formation would move north to reinforce the Russians at Łódź, Woyrsch launched an energetic attack with 1st Guards Reserve Division, together with the Austro-Hungarian 27th Infantry Division, which had been subordinated to his command. The result was that the Russians were forced to leave III Caucasian Corps in its positions facing west. Böhm-Ermolli's Second Army was also ordered to attack, with its IV Corps directed to strike at the seam between the Russian Fourth and Fifth Armies. This was intended as a move to take advantage of the weakening of the Russian front, as Russian forces hurried north towards Łódź. At first, the commander of IV Corps, General Tersztyánszky, believed that he was facing a single infantry division and three cavalry divisions, but reconnaissance soon detected the presence of the Russian Grenadier Corps and XIX Corps. In light of this, Tersztyánszky requested that reinforcements were made available. Conrad refused, not least because he had no troops to spare. When the attack began, in early December, Böhm-Ermolli was relieved to find that resistance was not as tough as expected; his men, in combination with the German XXIV Reserve Corps, made initially good progress.[4]

After the disappointment of failing to capture Scheffer's troops east of Łódź, Grand Duke Nikolai summoned his front commanders to Siedlce for a conference on 29 November. Four months of operations had left Russia's armies in a poor state. Casualties had been crippling, and the consumption of ammunition and other supplies had far exceeded any forecasts or expectations. In particular there was a worrying shortage of replacement officers at all tactical levels; in common with armies throughout Europe, the Russians had discovered that the distinctive uniforms and weapons of officers inevitably attracted the attention of snipers. Whilst *Stavka* had grown accustomed to Ruzsky's doom-laden messages, the news from Southwest Front was scarcely better. Although his troops had driven the *k.u.k.* Army back to the Carpathians, reported Ivanov, his losses had been severe, with many regiments reduced to half their normal strength. The system by which depot battalions trained replacement drafts had failed to deliver the planned numbers of troops, let alone the numbers required to make good the heavy losses of infantrymen, and even if the troops had appeared, the shortage of rifles was causing huge difficulties. Indeed, the shortage of weaponry prevented several rifle brigades from being augmented to division strength.

Discussions then moved on to what was to be done next. Danilov was in favour of a further effort against East Prussia; he argued that a drive into the heart of Germany was only possible once the northern flank of the entire front was established along the lower Vistula. The Russians were aware that German troops such as 1st Infantry Division had been transferred from East Prussia to Mackensen's Ninth Army, and Danilov felt that the time was right for a two-

pronged attack on East Prussia, with one army retracing the route taken by
Samsonov's doomed effort in August, while a second thrust attempted to turn
the northern flank of the Masurian Lakes position. In other words, the two
attacks in August would be repeated, except this time they would occur
simultaneously. The only new feature was the creation of a third powerful force
centred on Soldau, which would thrust directly towards the lower Vistula to
protect the western flank of the operation.

Neither front commander was enthusiastic about such a plan. Ruzsky
repeated that his troops were too weak to consider any such assault, especially
with German reinforcements expected from the west. The conference broke up
without any definitive agreement on future operations, except that Grand Duke
Nikolai agreed to a withdrawal in Poland to a more defensible and shorter line,
allowing for troops to be freed up as reserves; these could then be committed to
whichever Front was chosen to mount the next offensive.[5]

One of the few concrete results of the conference was the dismissal of Pavel
Rennenkampf. His performance throughout the war to date had been the target
of much criticism, and Ruzsky argued strongly that the poor performance of
First Army had contributed greatly to the losses at Łódź. The reality was that
Rennenkampf had found his army deployed on both banks of the Vistula,
with inadequate bridges to connect the two parts. Then, he scraped together the
Lowicz detachment and sent it towards Łódź, only for Ruzsky to lose his nerve
and demand an immediate withdrawal. In many respects his dismissal was a
continuation of the feud between men like Ruzsky, from the Sukhomlinovite
camp, and their opponents, in whose numbers Baltic German descendants like
Rennenkampf featured strongly. In addition to poor performance and military
mismanagement, Rennenkampf was the subject of much innuendo that he had
used his post to enrich himself, though no such charges were ever proven.
Similarly, suggestions that he was less than entirely loyal to the tsar seem to be
based more upon his ancestry than any real evidence. His replacement in
First Army was Alexander Ivanovich Litvinov, who had commanded a corps
in Fifth Army.

Despite telling the conference that he felt further advances were unlikely to
be successful, Ivanov changed his tone the following day. He telegraphed *Stavka*
to inform them that he had discussed matters with the commander of Third
Army, Radko Dimitriev, and the two men had concluded that an assault
on Krakow was a distinct possibility. *Stavka* replied that, regardless of this, the
armies to the north – First, Second, and Fifth – would still be withdrawing
to their prepared positions; however, the southern flank of these armies would

still be centred on Piotrkow, which should allow Southwest Front to avoid any retreat. The pressure exerted on the southern flank of Fifth Army, where it joined Fourth Army, was of course the precise point that had come under attack by Böhm-Ermolli.

By a curious coincidence, there was a similar conference on the other side of the front line on 1 December, in the city of Posen. In addition to Hindenburg and Ludendorff, the kaiser and Falkenhayn, the new chief of the general staff, were present. Much like their Russian counterparts, the participants failed to come to any firm conclusions. Falkenhayn remained convinced that victory could only come in the west if France were defeated; the entire eastern war would become irrelevant. Ludendorff countered that it was only in the east that there was still sufficient room for manoeuvre, while in the west the war had degenerated into a bloody stalemate of frontal assaults. In any event, he argued, reinforcement of the east was vital to prevent the Austro-Hungarian Empire being knocked out of the war. But there was an additional dimension to the argument. In the heady days of the German advance across Belgium and France, thoughts had turned to the possible shape of post-war Europe, and in September, Kurt Riezler, an official working for Chancellor Bethmann-Hollweg, produced a document entitled – appropriately enough – the 'September Programme'. This outlined the creation of a German-dominated empire, stretching from newly acquired territories in the west – such as Luxembourg – to incorporate the Baltic region and even the Ukraine. Such a radical redrawing of the map to create what became known as *Mitteleuropa* would require a decisive victory over Russia, and Falkenhayn now suggested that Germany's war aims should be limited to defeating France, and then negotiating a cessation of hostilities in the east. Clearly, this would result in the abandonment of any attempt to create *Mitteleuropa*.[6]

Whilst the September Programme was never adopted as German policy, it is understandable that German leaders fighting on the Eastern Front were attracted to the plan. They had, after all, enjoyed considerable success at a tactical and operational level, even though the failures of the *k.u.k.* Army and the weakness of German forces in the East rarely resulted in any lasting advantages. In any case, Hindenburg and Ludendorff resented their theatre being reduced to little more than an untidy irrelevance to be settled by diplomats after the real war had been won elsewhere. Ultimately, the conference in Posen was as inconclusive as the Russian conference in Siedlce. Falkenhayn and the eastern commanders parted, deeply unimpressed by the arguments of the other side.[7]

The reinforcements received by the Germans were used to renew assaults all along the front, with little tactical gain. As was so often the case in the First

World War, initial gains were rapidly lost in a series of counterattacks. Typical of the fighting was an attempt by elements of 176th Infantry Regiment to clear a wood of Russian troops. A platoon primarily made up of replacement drafts, though with an experienced NCO, was assigned the task, as a lieutenant in the regiment later recorded:

> Whether it was prudent to assign such a task to troops unfamiliar with the local situation, I cannot say. In any case, Wiczoreck [the platoon NCO] did not hesitate for a moment from carrying out the orders with his 3 Platoon. In his zeal for battle he apparently set out on his mission in the darkness; I remained unsure of the fate of this platoon for days and had the gravest concerns about it. Nobody could give me a report where the platoon was, and it wasn't until later, when the positions had been taken, that the picture of the entire tragedy became clear. During their advance, Wiczoreck encountered the millstream from Antoniew; at that moment, he saw the Russian position before him and gave the order to attack it. The thin ice of the stream couldn't hold, as a result of which the platoon was stranded in the water. Wiczoreck ordered, 'Fire, boys, or we're all lost.' Then Russian machine gun fire began, and not a single man in the platoon was left alive. On 6 December, I laid Wizefeldwebel Wiczoreck and his 23 men to rest in a mass grave. The company paraded by the grave, and despite the hardness that the war had already put into our souls, in that moment there was nobody who did not shed bitter tears. Wiczoreck was one of those NCOs that the Prussian army had by the thousand, who loved his men and did everything he could for them in moments of danger and need, but who demanded all from them in return. Every task that was given to him was carried out without any regard for himself. I will never forget my dear Wiczoreck, with whom I had lived through every day of the first difficult months of the war.[8]

Given that there were no German survivors of this episode, the final words attributed to Wiczoreck are perhaps imagined by his company commander in this description. Nevertheless, the sense of loss felt by Wiczoreck's comrades would have felt familiar to tens of thousands across Europe, mourning their former companions. All armies were feeling the pain of their losses, both in terms of the unprecedented numbers, but also because casualties were heaviest amongst the core of well-trained officers and NCOs without whom it was almost impossible to rebuild the ranks.

Late on 5 December German wireless interception services passed a most welcome item of news to Hindenburg and Ludendorff: the Russians were preparing to evacuate Łódź. The news was relayed to the Austro-Hungarian line of command, and Böhm-Ermolli immediately ordered his men to attack, hoping that here, too, the Russians were weakening their front. To his disappointment, the attacks made almost no headway. However, matters were different further north. The 6th of December was Mackensen's sixty-fifth birthday, and he ordered his troops to move forward against Łódź. He wanted to avoid costly street fighting, and was relieved when messages arrived towards dusk that the city was in German hands. One of the first units into Łódź was a detachment from Karl Litzmann's 3rd Guards Infantry Division, which many Germans regarded as fitting, given the significant role played by both the general and his infantry during the fighting of the previous weeks. In later years, Litzmann's role in the battles was honoured by a different German regime: Łódź was renamed Litzmannstadt by the Nazis in April 1940, and in recognition of Litzmann's nickname of 'the Lion of Brzeziny', the town that he had captured after a night march in order to secure XXV Reserve Corps' line of retreat was renamed Löwenstadt. Both Łódź and Brzeziny reverted to their Polish names in 1945.

The Russian troops who pulled back from Łódź had no way of knowing that they were withdrawing from what would prove to be the high-water mark of the Russian Army's war. They would never again threaten the German heartland.

As reinforcements continued to arrive from the west, Ludendorff was keen to exploit what he saw as Russian weakness, and to pursue the retreating armies of Northwest Front with the intention of reaching Warsaw before the end of the year. Mackensen was less enthusiastic, having concluded – correctly – that the Russians were pulling back to a more defensible line, but Ludendorff's will prevailed. For the following ten days the troops arriving from the west, most of them replacement drafts for original personnel who had perished in the grinding frontal assaults in Flanders, found themselves committed to similar frontal assaults in northern Poland. Despite his protestations that only in the east was a war of manoeuvre possible, Ludendorff now discovered that Ruzsky's armies had pulled back to the line of the Bzura and Rawka rivers. Here they occupied well-constructed defences, and proceeded to force Mackensen to repeat the same mistakes that he had accused Falkenhayn of making in the west.

As part of their preparations for the defence of the line of the two rivers, the Russians evacuated most of the civilians from their villages. Whilst this may have saved their lives, they were left destitute, unable to take with them their few belongings or their livestock. The empty villages were then turned into miniature fortresses, linked to each other by communications trenches. Despite heavy artillery bombardments, the Germans found that it was almost impossible to suppress the Russian defenders, who subjected every attack to a withering fire. As one participant observed:

> Wherever their defenders were cleared away, new ones seemed to grow directly out of the ground.[9]

Near Skierniewice, wave after wave of German attacks left a branch of the River Rawka almost completely dammed with corpses. In contrast to the relative ease with which the German forces had succeeded in penetrating the Russian lines in previous attacks, there was almost no progress aside from localised successes. More in hope than expectation, Mackensen prepared two attack groups to thrust towards Warsaw in mid-December, but through a combination of poor weather, artillery ammunition shortages, and continued stubborn Russian defence, these too failed to break through.

A British observer with the Russians described some of the fighting:

> The battles of the Bzura – the plural is used advisedly, because they extended over a period of two months – can be in a way likened to the campaigning along the Yser. I first visited the actual scene of conflict on December 22, 1914. At that time the Germans were directing their main offensive against Sochaczew and Bolimow.
>
> At the latter point they achieved certain local successes. I read afterwards in American papers that the Germans claimed a tremendous victory, going so far as to grant the school children a holiday in honour of their success. It certainly did the school children no more harm than it did the Russians.
>
> In justice to the enemy, however, it must be admitted that they showed the sternest courage in face of most appalling conditions. Time and time again whole battalions would wade through the freezing waters of the Rawka to struggle out on the opposite bank, where the snow covered entrenchments poured forth immediate destruction on those who survived the passage of the river.
>
> Daylight fighting ceased very early in these operations, and most of the attacks were carried through at night. Of course, both sides kept up intermittent artillery and rifle fire during the day, but it was only under cover of darkness that troops could be formed for the notorious mass attacks. Often the Russians would allow large bodies of the Germans to reach their side of the river, only to close in on them from three sides and either annihilate or capture them.
>
> Throughout this period the Germans were unable to bring up the heavy artillery, owing to the awful state of the roads. Most of these heavy guns were not German, but Austrian. Finally, Von Morgen, who commanded at Bolimow,

managed to get up two of the famous 30.5 centimetre Austrian guns and commenced the bitter contest for the possession of Mogely farm.

At first the great shells disconcerted the Russians, but after a time they paid as little attention to them as they did to the smaller projectiles. The 30.5 centimetre shells would often make a crater eleven feet deep and forty paces in circumference. When they actually hit a trench, which fortunately was seldom, it ceased to exist, and the occupants disappeared, completely covered with earth, but after being dug out were often found but little hurt. Sometimes, however, they would suffer from concussion, which it often took two months to cure, although there would be no visible wound.

The Germans suffered severely from the cold. Forty prisoners captured in a counter-assault were brought into Guzow. A cart carrying two machine guns followed. But it was not the trophies of war but the men who interested me. Only about half had overcoats. And these were made of a thin, shoddy material that is about as much protection as paper against the Russian wind.[10]

After suffering heavy losses – the Russians claimed that the German casualties, including prisoners, exceeded 100,000 – for almost no gain, the Germans abandoned their assaults, bringing to an end what became known in some circles as the Second Battle of Warsaw. Much as had happened on the Western Front, both sides settled down to a period of trench warfare.

In southern Poland and Galicia the Russian pursuit of the retreating Austro-Hungarian forces was dilatory at best. Brusilov's Eighth Army pinned the Austro-Hungarian Third Army back against the Carpathians, and even succeeded in forcing several of the passes, opening the way for a possible invasion of Hungary. To Brusilov's north, Dimitriev's Third Army slowly closed in on his primary objective, Krakow. As he did so, his front commander, Ivanov, grew increasingly nervous about either flank. If Ruzsky retreated in central Poland, the northern flank of Ninth and Fourth Armies (to the north of Dimitriev) would be exposed. Similarly, with Brusilov's troops spread out along the length of the Carpathians, there were fears for the southern flank. His troops had penetrated into the mountain range towards Bartfeld (now Bardejov), driving a wedge between Joseph Ferdinand's Fourth Army and Boroević's Third Army. Although this prevented the two Austro-Hungarian armies from cooperating, it also proved a distraction. On its own this penetration was insufficient to exert much pressure upon the Austro-Hungarian Empire, but it diverted troops away from the far more important area to the south and in front of Krakow, where Dimitriev's advance had come to almost a complete halt.

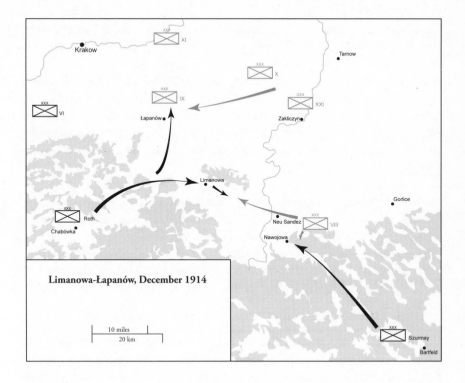

Limanowa-Łapanów, December 1914

10 miles
20 km

Conrad, too, was aware of the possibilities of turning the southern flank of Dimitriev's Third Army, and decided that this would be his next plan for an offensive. He had pressed Ludendorff to assign German troops to the sector, and in addition to his own men he had the German 47th Reserve Infantry Division at his disposal. This division, together with Fourth Army's XIV Corps, under the collective command of Feldmarschalleutnant Roth, was moved to threaten Dimitriev's southern flank at Chabówka. Progress in assembling the force was slow, as the only railway line available was a single track, of limited capability. Nevertheless, by early December the bulk of the strike force had assembled.

Boroević's Third Army, along the line of the Carpathians, was utterly exhausted, and Boroević advised his corps commanders that he intended to withdraw across the mountains to Kaschau (now Kosice), where supply depots had been established. Conrad only became aware of this as a result of a message from one of these corps commanders, and immediately enquired what was being planned. Boroević responded that he had only intended to retreat if absolutely necessary, and remained ready to counterattack as soon as the Russians showed signs of withdrawing. From Conrad's point of view, this was barely adequate. He wanted Third Army to maintain pressure on Brusilov's forces, to prevent them being moved west, and such pressure could only be exerted by mounting local attacks. Whilst Boroević grudgingly agreed not to withdraw as he had planned, he made it clear that his army lacked the power to intervene with any significant weight in any new attacks on the Russians. Nevertheless, he agreed to attack the Russian troops in Bartfeld as soon as he had assembled a suitable force. Conrad's response was uncompromising:

> Fourth Army's operations mean that it is absolutely essential that any move by the Russian Eighth Army towards the west and northwest is rendered impossible. In order to prevent an undetected concentration [of Russian forces] in front of Third Army, the enemy is to be pinned by maintaining close contact and any attempt to withdraw forces is to be met with an immediate attack. The concentration of strong forces on the western flank of Third Army [i.e. around Bartfeld] is fully approved.[11]

Further orders from Conrad called for an early attack towards Neu-Sandez, and a slightly exasperated Boroević asked for clarification: was he to attack Bartfeld first, then proceed towards Neu-Sandez, or was he to give up his plan to attack Bartfeld completely? Conrad could see the need for Boroević to secure his western flank by recapturing Bartfeld, but was also anxious to offer whatever help he could to Joseph Ferdinand's Fourth Army as soon as possible. Characteristically, he ordered Boroević to pursue both objectives at the same time. However, a final decision regarding the Bartfeld attack was postponed until 7 December. But the movement of the troops of Third Army in preparation for the attacks – particularly 38th *Honvéd* Infantry Division – suffered considerable delays, and Boroević advised *AOK* that the attack against Bartfeld could not possibly start until at least 8 December. Regardless of difficulties of movement, Conrad demanded an attack no later than that date. News was trickling through about the change of fortunes in the Serbian campaign, with Potiorek's troops facing major counterattacks that would eventually result in their complete rout, and fearful that any further Austro-Hungarian setbacks would sway opinion in Italy, Bulgaria, and Romania against the Dual Monarchy, Conrad was desperate to secure a victory.[12] *AOK* was not the only body to be concerned with high politics. It seems that some of the decisions being made at Third Army Headquarters were in response to political pressure; Hungarian Prime Minister Tisza had been in contact with Boroević, urging him to prevent further Russian penetrations into Hungarian territory, and to regard this as his main priority.[13]

On 3 December, with the German 47th Reserve Infantry Division still delayed in its journey to the assembly points around Chabówka, Roth's other troops began to advance, rapidly reaching Limanowa. From here Roth sent a small cavalry force probing along the road towards Neu-Sandez and turned his three infantry divisions – 13th Rifle Division in the west, 3rd Infantry Division in the centre, and 8th Infantry Division in the east – towards the north, threatening the southern flank of the Russian IX Corps. Belatedly, both IX Corps and XI Corps to its immediate north dispatched their reserves to the southern flank. Resistance to the Austro-Hungarian advance grew steadily throughout the following day.

Unknown to Roth and Conrad, other Russian troops were heading towards the critical area. Brusilov had dispatched VIII and XXIV Corps to Neu-Sandez, much as Conrad had feared would happen unless Boroević pinned down Brusilov's troops further south. The leading elements of the former formation were now in the town. Initial Austro-Hungarian estimates put the number of Russians in the town at only a few battalions, later escalating to at least a division. Roth was aware that an advance from the town by a strong Russian force would turn his flank, much as he was trying to do to Dimitriev, but Joseph Ferdinand overruled any diversion of troops to cover what seemed only a potential threat. The main effort was to be the drive towards the north.

This effort ground to a halt on 5 December in the face of stiffening resistance. Even the German 47th Reserve Infantry Division, finally assembled in the key area, made only limited progress; much like the Russians, the Austro-Hungarians had high estimations of the ability of German troops to prevail in combat where their own men failed. Finally, details began to emerge about the Russian troops in the area. A wireless intercept not only identified VIII Corps in Neu-Sandez, but also the approach of X and XXI Corps; originally, they had been deployed north of the Vistula, and were now making haste to cross to the south in order to support Dimitriev's southern flank. The threat from Neu-Sandez could no longer be ignored. Conrad ordered 45th Rifle Division, which had been serving as part of the Krakow garrison, to the area immediately east of Limanowa. In addition, the relatively weak 39th *Honvéd* Infantry Division was dispatched to the exposed flank, together with the command elements of VI Corps. But even as Roth redoubled his efforts, the Russians began to withdraw. It was increasingly clear to Dimitriev that his two corps facing Krakow were increasingly exposed, and they began to pull out towards the east. IX Corps continued to hold off

Roth, admittedly at considerable cost, while to its north XI Corps fell back in steady stages.

47th Reserve Infantry Division had been deployed on the eastern flank of Roth's drive towards the north, and a gap of about 9 miles (15km) opened up between the Germans and the Austro-Hungarian forces covering Neu-Sandez. The Russian VIII Corps now began to make its presence felt in this area. Despite radio intercepts revealing the presence of the Russian corps, the Austro-Hungarians were still unsure whether it was actually in the area. Their aerial reconnaissance, admittedly interrupted again and again by poor weather, had failed to spot sufficient troop movements to reveal the presence of such a large formation. As the Austro-Hungarian 10th Cavalry Division sent a steady stream of reports about the threat from Neu-Sandez, Roth asked for the transport of 45th Rifle Division to the area to be accelerated. Using the same inadequate railway that had been the cause of the delayed deployment of the German 47th Reserve Division, the Austro-Hungarian staff did their best to comply.

In an attempt to prevent the Russians from pulling back to safety, Roth shifted troops to his eastern flank; in this, he was aided by the steady shortening of the front line brought about by the Russian withdrawal. The emphasis of the battle changed sharply on 7 December as the Russian VIII Corps began to attack, with its 14th and 15th Infantry Divisions, from Neu-Sandez. Although the Russians outnumbered and outgunned the weak screen facing them, their attack rapidly ran out of momentum as the Austro-Hungarian forces pulled back a short distance into well-constructed positions that Roth had prudently prepared in the preceding days. One of the units in the path of the Russian 15th Infantry Division was a group of Polish volunteers, organised by Josef Piłsudski, who would play a central part in the struggle for Polish independence. Born into an impoverished family of Polish aristocrats, Piłsudski became hostile to Russian rule early in life, particularly the forcible 'Russification' of everyday activities, and was sent to Siberia for several years as a young man, returning to his homeland in 1892. He was arrested again for publishing anti-Russian literature, and after escaping custody (he feigned mental illness, and then absconded from the hospital to which he was taken), he founded an anti-Russian paramilitary organisation. This attracted the attention of the Austro-Hungarian Empire, and in 1906 Piłsudski received funding from Vienna for his activities; he augmented these funds by raids on Russian targets in Poland, including a train carrying taxation revenues.[14] At the beginning of the war, Piłsudski committed his forces to support the Austro-Hungarian cause, believing that Poland's best chance for independence lay in a victory of the Central Powers over Russia, followed by the defeat of the Central Powers by France and Britain. He had talks in secret with the Western Powers, assuring them that his men would never fight against them, only against the Russians. At the head of the group, which a few days later would formally be organised into the 1st Brigade of the Polish Legion, Piłsudski now took part in the fighting against the Russian VIII Corps outside Neu-Sandez.[15]

Fighting raged on through the next few days, from Łapanów in the north to Limanowa in the south, with very little movement of the front line. Casualties were – inevitably – heavy on both sides, with frontal assaults across frozen ground being followed by equally bloody counterattacks. Roth estimated that his men had taken some 10,000 prisoners since the beginning of his offensive, but the strength of his formations was also ebbing away. On 10 December, acting on aerial reconnaissance and radio intercepts that incorrectly suggested the Russians were withdrawing, the Austro-Hungarian 3rd Infantry Division launched a major attack on the Russian positions at dawn. Although there were initial successes, the Russians then counterattacked in strength, with most of X and XXI Corps. Despite support from the neighbouring 8th and 30th Infantry Divisions, and a thrust into the flank of the Russian forces by the German 47th Reserve Infantry Division, all of the gains of the morning were swiftly lost. A new line was established along the River Stradomka, about 5 miles (8km) north of Łapanów, almost exactly where the two armies had started the day. Further south, the arrival of Feldmarschalleutnant Arz and his VI Corps stabilised Roth's flank facing Neu-Sandez. Despite Brusilov's constant urging, the Russian VIII Corps made little progress in its attacks.

At the very southern end of the long Eastern Front, Boroević began his offensive on 7 December. Since its retreat, Third Army had done what it could to restore its battered formations, and even to improvise new ones. Some of these left much to be desired; 56th Infantry Division, operating at the eastern end of the army, had been rebuilt from the remnants of a variety of units and using *Landsturm*, and had almost no regular officers in its ranks. The men had been equipped with whatever weapons were to hand, resulting in at least three different rifles being used, and the division was deficient in almost every support service.[16] Both the Austro-Hungarian Third Army and the opposing Russian Eighth Army had pulled units out of their front lines and dispatched them towards Neu-Sandez. As a result, Boroević's assault troops found themselves opposed along much of the Carpathian front by little more than the two divisions of the Russian XII Corps. Part of the Russian line to the east was now the responsibility of Eleventh Army, which had to reduce the strength of the troops besieging Przemyśl in order to provide the necessary troops. The critical area, though, remained further west, and late on 8 December, with the attack on Bartfeld still delayed, *AOK* urged Boroević to make haste. Increasingly conscious that he lacked the resources to pursue the objectives of both Bartfeld and Neu-Sandez, Boroević placed the bulk of the forces gathered to attack Bartfeld under the command of Feldmarschalleutnant Szurmay, with orders to strike towards Neu-Sandez.

The Russian forces in Bartfeld had already begun to withdraw, rather than risk being isolated. Undisturbed by Russian activity, Szurmay marched towards Neu-Sandez, his leading elements coming within 12 miles (19km) of their objective by the end of 9 December. The indecision about whether to prioritise this advance over the recapture of Bartfeld had cost Szurmay about a day, in which the Russians had strengthened their defences south of Neu-Sandez. Conrad sent a message to Third Army, blaming Boroević and his subordinates for failing to tie down the Russians and giving them time and room to reposition their forces. This ignored the fact that Boroević had asked for prioritisation regarding Bartfeld and Neu-Sandez, but Conrad himself had ducked the decision. Boroević was aware that his army had been too exhausted and weakened after the fighting of the preceding weeks to have accomplished more, but chose to pass on the rebuke to his corps commanders, with an added exhortation to try to make amends in the coming days.[17]

On 10 December Szurmay pushed down the road towards Neu-Sandez with 38th *Honvéd* Infantry Division, which amounted to only eight under-strength battalions. The drive was halted by strong Russian defences, manned by 3rd Rifle Brigade and elements of 10th Cavalry Division and 13th Infantry Division, in Nawojowa, about 4 miles (7km) from the centre of Neu-Sandez. Attempts to outflank the Russian position were frustrated by a lack of suitable roads through the mountainous terrain. Similarly, troops that had been earmarked for the assault on Bartfeld hurried along the road towards Neu-Sandez, but despite forced marches in poor weather, they were unable to reinforce Szurmay's assault group on 10 December. However, the concentration of Russian forces around Neu-Sandez created gaps elsewhere. The Austro-Hungarian IX Corps, marching north from Bartfeld, encountered minimal resistance.

The steady accumulation of forces in Roth's group had now reached the impressive number of nine infantry and three cavalry divisions. The losses of the preceeding weeks, and of the heavy fighting in December, had reduced the strength of these to a fraction of their establishment, with most infantry divisions now able to muster barely 3,000 men. Despite their reduced combat strength, Roth's troops continued to defy attempts by the Russian VIII Corps to drive from Neu-Sandez to Limanowa. On 11 December Szurmay tried again to reach Neu-Sandez, but found the flank of his position threatened by a powerful counterattack carried out by 48th Infantry Division, part of the Russian XXIV Corps. As reinforcements arrived Szurmay dispatched them to secure the high ground on his left, immediately to the south of Neu-Sandez. Nevertheless, a combination of bad roads, bad weather, determined Russian resistance, and the short winter days ensured that the town remained in Russian hands. Further exhortations and criticism from *AOK* did little to improve the mood of the local commanders.[18]

With Boroević's army attacking all along its front, the pressure upon the Russian forces was relentless. XXIV Corps could not intervene in the fighting at Neu-Sandez if the Austro-Hungarian IX Corps was marching north from Bartfeld across its lines of communication, and the failure of VIII Corps to break through to Limanowa left the troops concentrated in Neu-Sandez in an increasingly precarious position. Accordingly, Ivanov decided that it was time to withdraw. VIII Corps was to pull back towards Zakliczyn, with XXIV Corps to its east and XII Corps continuing the line to the southeast. On 12 December Szurmay's exhausted men finally captured Neu-Sandez. Although Roth urged Arz to pursue the retreating Russian VIII Corps, the losses of the previous days, together with the poor weather, ensured that any such pursuit was feeble at best. With their own ranks badly depleted, and ammunition shortages becoming critical, the Russians were grateful for the pause in fighting as they pulled back to their new positions.

The Battle of Limanowa–Łapanów, as it became known, was regarded by the Austro-Hungarian forces as a great victory. The Russians were driven back from their positions threatening Krakow, and their penetration through the Carpathians was also eliminated. Roth was awarded the Knight's Cross to the Military Order of Maria Theresa, and the honorific 'von Limanowa-Łapanów' was added to his name. Conrad took great pride in the victory, coming as it did after so many catastrophes. Both at the time and in his memoirs, Ludendorff exaggerated the importance of the fighting around Łódź, claiming that the Germans had won a major victory as opposed to narrowly escaping from possible disaster. In a similar vein, Conrad and other Austro-Hungarian officers perhaps inflated the value of the December fighting. It was perhaps singularly inappropriate for Conrad to take personal credit, as his interventions during the conflict were either detrimental, such as the confusion over Bartfeld and Neu-Sandez, or ineffective, such as the constant urging for haste by Boroević's Third Army. In some respects it also suited the Russians to inflate the performance of their opponents. The reality was that despite Dimitriev's optimistic assertions that the capture of Krakow was still possible, such an advance was probably beyond the strength of his forces. In any event, the withdrawal of Ruzsky's armies in the north would have exposed the northern flank of Southwest Front to the full weight of German counterattacks, had Dimitriev succeeded in penetrating to and beyond Krakow. Consequently, attributing the outcome to the performance of the enemy helped avoid questions about whether Russian expectations had been over-optimistic. Unsurprisingly, given his own views and desire for a withdrawal to a more defensible position, Ruzsky – from his distant position at Northwest Front Headquarters – wrote to a Canadian politician the following year in glowing terms about the performance of the *k.u.k.* Army:

> The Battle of Limanowa–Łapanów was a strategic masterpiece, brilliantly conceived and executed with virtuosity, forcing us to abandon further operations against Krakow and preventing our crossing of the Carpathians. The Battle of Limanowa–Łapanów was the first major defeat that the Grand Duke's armies experienced in Galicia. The position of the Austrians during the great Carpathian battles was unenviable. We in Russia believed at the time in the total destruction of the Austro-Hungarian Army; the outcome of the Battle of Limanowa–Łapanów was all the more surprising for us, as the dashing Austrian attack came as a complete surprise for us and struck us at the most dangerous position of the entire front.[19]

All along the line, troops settled down to face the grim reality that this war would not be over by Christmas. Only in the Carpathian passes and foothills did the fighting continue at any intensity. To the east of the front line, the garrison of Przemyśl continued to hold out, mounting limited sorties to test the surrounding Russian ring. The Russians made no attempt to storm the city; after the futile attacks during the first siege, they had settled down to allow time and hunger to wear down the garrison. For the troops inside the fortress, Christmas provided little cheer. Josef Tomann was a doctor with the garrison, struggling to deal with men laid low by typhoid, influenza, and other infectious diseases that swept through the crowded fortress, and his reflections on Christmas Eve were typical not only of his fellow soldiers in the city, but also of hundreds of thousands of men in the front lines of Europe:

> It is Christmas Eve and I'm here, on my own in a hostile country. I cannot rest today, my weary mind is troubled by dreams and sweet visions, that fill the air like phantoms. When we were children we looked forward to Christmas Eve with

great excitement. It was a time we always spent with our dear mother, but she will be on her own today crying over her three sons away at war.

Else was born this year. It was only last summer that Mitzl and I talked about how lovely it would be to have our first Christmas together. But we couldn't decide where to spend it. The war has made that decision for us. What is it like this year at home, I wonder? Do the lights on the tree twinkle as brightly? Sister Victoria [a nurse in Przemyśl] showed me the Christmas tree, sprinkled with chalk and decorated with a few small candles. The poor chaps will be glad. I don't want to see or hear anything – I'll stay at home and try in vain to bury myself in a book. And yet twice I have felt hot tears on my cheeks. The war and its miseries have hardened me. Why am I so pathetic today? We cry every year, but this year we cry bitter tears.[20]

The following day a patrol sent out by the garrison found three Christmas trees in no-man's land, left there by a Russian patrol. A message was pinned to one of the trees, wishing the men of the garrison a happy Christmas and hoping that peace would come soon. As was the case in parts of the Western Front, the guns remained silent on Christmas Day.[21]

CHAPTER 15

DISAPPOINTMENTS AND ILLUSIONS

The armies of the Great Powers in Eastern Europe – Germany, Austria-Hungary, and Russia – entered the war with a mixture of fear and anticipation. None of them dreamed that the outcome would turn out to be so far from their expectations.

The Russians had feared the power of the German Army, and its speed of mobilisation, for many years. Although they had put in place many steps to improve their own performance in these respects – and had spent a lot of French money doing so – most senior officers in the Russian Army must have been aware that serious deficiencies remained. *Stavka* came under great pressure to move faster than it might have wished. Much of this pressure came from the French, who were desperate to see a major Russian incursion into Germany to divert troops from the west, but the Russian high command itself was also keen to strike against the Germans before they could defeat France and turn east. After all, with such a great part of Germany's military might tied up in France, there would surely be opportunities for Russia to make substantial gains in the east. Russian haste was not, therefore, an entirely altruistic matter.

Nevertheless, there was an expectation that once it took the field, the Russian Army would overwhelm its opponents, by sheer weight of numbers if all else failed. Eventually, Grand Duke Nikolai managed to get his steamroller moving, but after marching across Poland, which the Germans had ruthlessly devastated during their retreat, the Russian armies ground to a halt in the face of counterattacks and, more importantly, the restrictions imposed by reliance on railheads to keep supplies flowing. In some respects the Russians proved to be best suited to the realities of warfare in 1914. Their natural strengths in determined defence, the speed with which they could dig in and turn improvised positions into excellent field fortifications, as demonstrated during the fighting against the Germans in central Poland in December, and of course the ability of Russia to produce vast numbers of soldiers were all ideally suited to a war in which defensive firepower was supreme. Unfortunately for her armies, Russia's generals showed as little ability as those of other nations to learn these lessons quickly. The cult of the offensive, so widely promoted in the years before the war, ensured that tens of thousands of Russian soldiers perished in futile attacks.

The cult of the offensive was perhaps strongest in the armies of the Austro-Hungarian Empire. Conrad had written extensively on the subject, and his insistence on the importance of maintaining offensive operations so long as it was physically possible to do so cost the *k.u.k.* Army huge casualties. Despite the failures in Galicia, he constantly sought to launch attacks wherever he could. Even if he had noticed the enormous potential for defensive fighting with the technology to hand, it would have been almost impossible for him to embrace such a shift of policy. The consequence for his troops was terrible. By the end of the year, the Austro-Hungarian armies in Galicia and Poland had lost nearly 995,000 men dead, wounded, sick, or taken prisoner. A further 274,000 had been lost in the disastrous Serbian campaigns.[1] Although many of the wounded and sick would eventually return to the front, the army would never be the same again. The field army was reduced to a little more than 50 per cent of its establishment strength; 44 per cent of the peacetime officer strength was gone, and with it irreplaceable expertise.[2] As was the case in all armies of the era, losses of officers were proportionately heavier than of other ranks – in the case of the *k.u.k.* Army, the casualty rate amongst officers was twice as high.

Of the three Great Powers, Austria-Hungary perhaps had the least to gain from a war, other than the short-term unity that it brought to the empire. It is therefore particularly ironic that Conrad's desire to force a decision in the Balkans was a major factor in the decisions that plunged the entire continent into war.

Germany's plans and military preparations were to a large extent driven by fear of being caught between the French, who were determined to extract revenge for 1870–71, and the Russians. The constant gloomy forecasts of Russian rearmament, and the fear that Germany would be left helpless unless she were able to overcome one or other of her powerful enemies in the near future, played a major part in the thinking of Moltke the Younger. The greatest fear of all for Germany was that the country would find itself involved in a two-front war, hence the desire to deal a knockout blow to the French before turning east.

When this failed to happen, *OHL* found itself facing exactly the nightmare that it had wished to avoid at all costs. Moltke was unable to deal with the consequences of his failure, and it was left to Falkenhayn to try to find a way for Germany to continue the war.

Perhaps the only nation that could look back at the preceding months and regard its achievements as more than it could have expected was Serbia. Hugely outgunned by the *k.u.k.* Army, its forces had fought with immense determination and self-sacrifice to prevent Serbia from being overrun. Exhausted by their endeavours, thousands of Serbia's soldiers died during the winter from infectious diseases, particularly from a typhus epidemic that swept through the country. If Serbia could defy Austria-Hungary long enough, it was hoped, Russia would march to her aid. With her military resources drained after the bitter fighting against Potiorek's armies, Serbia could only look north and wonder how long it would be before Russian pressure elsewhere brought about a satisfactory end to the war.

All three Great Powers had expected a quick war, and none of them were prepared for prolonged hostilities. Armies throughout Europe struggled to cope with unprecedented casualties, and the equally unprecedented consumption of ammunition. It would take many months for their industrial heartlands to gear up for wartime production. In the meantime, the soldiers in the front line coped as well as they could, though the pressure on Russia to divert German troops away from the west remained strong, as Danilov later recalled:

> At about the same time [Christmas 1914], our military attaché in Paris, who had informed the French General Staff of the situation on our front and the decisions we had made, telegraphed General Joffre's response. The French supreme commander hoped that if the shortage of munitions prevented us from resuming the offensive in Poland, 'we would nevertheless be able to persevere in Galicia, where perhaps the nature of the terrain requires less artillery.'[3]

This was, at best, wishful thinking. The reality was that any fighting was hugely influenced by the weight of artillery that could be brought to bear, regardless of the terrain.

After five months of fighting, stresses were beginning to appear in some of the armies involved. Nationalist tensions in the Austro-Hungarian forces had never been far from the surface, and the loss of so many experienced officers, and their replacement by men who did not necessarily speak the language of their troops, did nothing to improve matters. Reports of defections by Slav formations, while limited, made alarming and depressing reading for the Austro-Hungarian hierarchy. The divide between front-line soldiers and officers on the one hand, and staff officers on the other, was a source of increasing resentment. Conrad almost never visited the front line in 1914 after the retreat from Lemberg, preferring to remain with *AOK* in Teschen (now Cieszyn), between Krakow and Vienna. In his headquarters in a school, he studied the maps and urged his generals to renew their attacks. Those who visited him there could see the strain of high command in his drawn features, and an involuntary muscular twitch by one eye; some knew that he continued to mourn the death of his son in battle, north of Lemberg.[4] To most of the men fighting for the Dual Monarchy he remained a distant, unknown figure. By Christmas, many of the troops in the front line had lost their first flush of patriotic fervour, and were already showing alarming signs of war-weariness. An awareness of this played a large part in Boroević's reluctance to commit his army to Conrad's counteroffensive in December. Nevertheless, given the political fragility of the Austro-Hungarian Empire, its armies showed remarkable durability, surviving the shattering defeat in Galicia in September, the setback in the Vistula valley in October, and the disaster in Serbia in December to continue the war into the depths of winter. It is particularly tragic that this durability was greatly undermined by the inability of senior figures to learn even the most elementary lessons from the events of the war to date. Whilst it is understandable that tactical and operational doctrine was deeply ingrained and would take months or even years to change, it seems astonishing that the Austro-Hungarian troops defending the Carpathians had still not received winter clothing, despite the clear evidence from the disastrous Serbian campaign that such clothing was essential.

The Russians had always prided themselves that their men were stoical and resilient in the face of hardship. Whilst this was probably true of much of the rank and file, some of the officer corps showed far less ability to endure hardship, as Alfred Knox recorded as early as November:

> An officer returning from sick leave said that Petrograd is full of convalescent officers, who are not sent back to their regiments quick enough, and very many of whom try to get away on 'side shows' such as automobile machine gun companies.[5]

Knox was also deeply unimpressed by the lack of initiative and cooperation shown by Russian commanders. During the fighting at Stallupönen the Russians considered the spontaneous close cooperation of neighbouring divisions from different corps as a remarkable achievement, as opposed to something that should simply have been expected. When 6th Siberian Infantry Division attempted to hold back Scheffer's columns at Brzeziny, Russian troops in Łódź showed little willingness to provide support without specific orders:

> Throughout most of the eight days [of the Battle of Łódź], 18th to 25th [November], the German and Russian Supreme and Army Commands must have been enveloped in a 'fog of war.' In such cases the side whose corps, division and regiment leaders have been trained in peace to cooperate selflessly has inestimable advantages. If placed in a similar position, no German corps commander would have hesitated, as the commander of I Corps hesitated on the evening of 23rd November, about sending help to the hard-pressed 6th Siberian Infantry Division.[6]

As was the case with Russian observations of the Germans, the opinions of the Germans about the Russians speak volumes about the areas in which the two armies differed:

> The Russian infantry has a great capability for marching. Frequently, prisoner interrogation revealed they had covered 60km [36 miles] a day on poor roads and with poor supplies. However, the Russian infantryman is less encumbered than the German. Like their capability for marching, the readiness of Russian infantry to establish field positions must be acknowledged. They are masters of the subject. The Russians are particularly skilled at defending woodland. Their marksmanship is generally bad.
>
> In one area however, the Russian infantry fails completely: in carrying out attacks. Clumsy by nature and poorly trained, the Russian is the opposite of a skilled rifleman. The attacks commence with great masses and almost immediately collapse with heavy losses after advancing only a few hundred metres. Of course, after learning of these deficiencies, and in order to avoid the fire of our superior numbers of guns, they undertake many night attacks; but these too fail in almost all cases as a result of the watchfulness and firepower of German infantry and artillery.
>
> In defence, the Russians are determined and endure the heaviest losses…
>
> The Russians lack the moral will for victory. Poorly led, they do their duty only through the threats of their superiors, rather than following the good example of others. Thousands of prisoners show no enthusiasm, or love for their country. Most are happy to be prisoners.[7]

The army that had perhaps held out the greatest hope for a quick victory, particularly in the west, was that of Germany, which now faced the worst possible outcome – a protracted two-front war. Despite this, of the three Great Powers caught up in the battles in Poland, the German Army perhaps finished the war in the best fettle. Although the southeast corner of East Prussia remained under Russian occupation, the soldiers of the divisions facing the Russians could claim that they had won every significant battle they had been asked to fight, including the crushing victory at Tannenberg and the less decisive but nevertheless impressive triumph at the Masurian Lakes, with the exception of the December drive into central Poland. Although Mackensen and Woyrsch had led their men across Poland and back (in the case of Woyrsch's troops, they had made the journey twice), the withdrawals did not affect morale, and the belief of the soldiers in their leadership remained strong. Both Mackensen and Litzmann repeatedly described the warm mutual trust between senior officers and their men, an ethos that seems to have been deeply established in the German Army. When Curt von Morgen received a letter from the Kaiser informing him that he had been awarded Germany's highest award, it was characteristic that the letter also addressed the role played by Morgen's troops:

> Your victorious advance in Poland and your brilliant successes against a numerically superior enemy have given me great pleasure, and have led me to award you the *Pour le Mérite*. Pass my royal thanks and acclamation to your brave and exemplary troops.[8]

It was almost always the case in the German Army that officers regarded their successes as being due to the efforts of their men. The simple measure of making the soldiers aware of this realisation did much to build morale and maintain high levels of trust.

The reservists who had been thrown into the early battles, and the poorly trained volunteers who fought at Łódź, had acquitted themselves outstandingly, showing a similar spirit and determination to the regular formations. Despite François' refusal to allow the veteran I Corps to be used in the Battle of Łódź, the performance of the reservists of XXV Reserve Corps was as good as any troops could have delivered. It is ironic that the insubordinate act that cost François his post probably had little impact on the campaign. Even the *Landwehr*, never intended for prolonged campaigns, had shown great determination and resolve. By contrast, the Austrian *Landwehr* and Hungarian *Honvéd* had proved to be far less resilient than regular formations. This was not merely a question of inferior levels of equipment – similar criticisms could have been levelled at the German reservists. Some of the relatively poor performance of Austro-Hungarian reserves was due to their formations having fewer regular officers and NCOs than their German counterparts, but some was perhaps simply a matter of expectation. Woyrsh and other German commanders who found themselves leading reservists into battle did all they could to praise their men and keep up their morale, in a manner that neither the Austro-Hungarian nor Russian commanders emulated. Morgen wrote that he regarded the greater distance from the front line required by duties as a corps commander to be an unwelcome necessity, but added:

> Despite this loss of personal contact with the troops, higher commanders must strive as far as is possible to keep their finger on the pulse of the troops, in order to remain aware of the mood of the junior commanders and troops.[9]

Morgen's Russian or Austro-Hungarian counterparts rarely, if ever, mentioned such sentiments. At this stage of the war, at least, the mutual trust between German officers and their men remained unbroken. Conrad might have written extensively about the need for field commanders to remain as close to the front line as possible, but once he was established at Teschen, he rarely visited even the headquarters of his forces in the field.

The performance of German troops was a source of great satisfaction to the German High Command, and this allowed for troop numbers to be reduced within formations, to allow new formations to be created:

> The moral and technical superiority of the German soldier over his opponents, that was daily becoming more evident, also offered a way out [of the problem of too few formations for a two-front war]. It turned out to be so great that it was possible to entertain the suggestion of the Director of the General War Department, Colonel von Wrisberg, to reduce by about 25 per cent the strength of the fighting units, the divisions, without doing any harm to their effectiveness, to correspond to that of the enemy units in their original strength. This created the possibility of forming new fighting units out of the surplus of the old formations that were already trained, equipped and provided with leaders. This plan was adopted with great success after the artillery, guns and other war material, which was needed to supplement the arrangement, could be supplied.[10]

The Russians entered the war with very low expectations of their reservist formations, and this attitude had resulted in these units receiving very low priority in terms of supplies, equipment, and good officers and NCOs. When they saw action, the reservist divisions often fought well, particularly in defensive actions. However, Russian generals did not hesitate to criticise them when their weaknesses were exposed, or blame them for setbacks where the blame lay elsewhere. There was to a very large extent a sense of inevitability about the performance of the Russian reservist divisions. Nobody expected much from them, and given how they had been neglected in the years before the war, it was no surprise to anyone when they failed to perform particularly well. The most lamentable part of the Russian Army was its logistic support. As has already been described, senior Russian commanders had no time for such trivialities, and consequently the problems of supplying a modern army had not even been discussed in any detail prior to the war. The reality of keeping so many men fed and armed, particularly after the Germans had devastated the infrastructure of Poland, would have taxed the best-organised services, and proved to be far beyond the capabilities of the Russian logistics officers.

In a similar manner, the system of training replacement drafts for the Russian Army proved to be completely inadequate. In conscious mimicry of the Western Powers, Russia had established a series of service battalions, which would be responsible for training these drafts prior to their dispatch to the front, but much like the logistic services, the service battalions had attracted little if any interest prior to the war. They became the homes of men who were unfit or otherwise unsuitable for front-line service. Whilst this may have been a convenient arrangement in peacetime, it was hopelessly inadequate when the fighting began, particularly as the demand for replacements was so great, and the influx of volunteers far larger than anticipated. Similar criticisms could be made of the service battalions of the Western Powers, which also often became comfortable posts for overweight or invalided officers and NCOs, but they also contained significant numbers of motivated, experienced training officers. It is striking, however, that all the armies fighting in late 1914 were alarmed and disappointed by the quality of training of replacement drafts. To an extent, this was a reflection of the widespread belief that the war would be a short one – as a result, there was little expectation that replacement drafts would have to make major contributions before it was over. On the Eastern Front physical fitness was a particularly important consideration, as the armies regularly marched distances that rapidly became unknown to the soldiers on the Western Front.

Some of the commanders who had expected to play a major role in the war had already disappeared by the first Christmas. The entire command of the Russian Northwest Front had changed. Zhilinski, widely regarded as a political appointee even before his dismissal, languished in Petrograd for several months before suddenly being appointed to the Russian military mission in Chantilly.

He remained in France until late 1916, when he was recalled to Russia, and ordered to retire a year later. After the October Revolution his movements are not known with any certainty. He may have joined White Russian forces, or he may have tried to leave Russia. In any event, he was captured by the Bolsheviks in 1918, and executed.

Zhilinski's two army commanders in Northwest Front had also left their posts by Christmas. Samsonov shot himself during the shattering defeat suffered by his army at Tannenberg, and Rennenkampf was dismissed after the Battle of Łódź. There is no question that Rennenkampf played a large part in the poor performance of Northwest Front in 1914. His initial invasion of East Prussia was dilatory and hesitant, and his insistence on leaving behind his reservist divisions reduced his army to a far lower strength than it should have had. After the Battle of Gumbinnen his lack of urgency in advancing into East Prussia contributed greatly to Samsonov's defeat at Tannenberg – any sort of major thrust by First Army would have forced Hindenburg and Ludendorff to divert troops to face him. When he was finally dismissed in December, there was, ironically, less justification for his removal than there might have been at the end of August. Ruzsky, who was greatly instrumental in his dismissal, was far more to blame for Russian failures at Łódź than his subordinate. However, the two men were from opposing camps in the continuing internal struggle within the Russian Army, and Ruzsky ensured that Rennenkampf shouldered the blame, rather than allowing any blame to be directed at Ruzsky himself.

After his dismissal, Rennenkampf waited in vain for a new post, but when one didn't appear, he resigned from the army in October 1915. After the February Revolution of 1917, old accusations that he had used his position for financial gain resurfaced, as did rumours about his alleged lack of loyalty to Russia on account of his Baltic German roots. Pierre Marquis de Laguiche, the French military attaché in Russia, has frequently been quoted as suggesting that Rennenkampf received bribes from the Germans for allowing the destruction of Samsonov's army, but there is little hard evidence that Laguiche actually made such allegations, or that they were true. Enquiries into the affair were stopped after the tsar accepted Rennenkampf's resignation in 1915, leading to further suggestions that the tsar had acted to protect a personal friend. There appeared to be sufficient grounds in early 1917 for him to be re-arrested, and he was confined to the Peter and Paul Fortress in Petrograd. In October, following the Revolution, he was released and travelled to Taganrog, on the coast of the Sea of Azov. Here he attempted to fade into anonymity, adopting the name Mandusakis and claiming to be Greek. However, in March 1918 he was recognised, and appeared before Vladimir Antonov-Ovseyenko, the Bolshevik commander in the Ukraine. Ovseyenko offered Rennenkampf a command in the Red Army; when Rennenkampf refused, Ovseyenko placed him under arrest, and had him executed almost immediately. There is nothing to suggest that Rennenkampf had been made aware of the probably fatal consequences of not cooperating.

Sergei Scheidemann, who had commanded the reformed Second Army during the Battle of Łódź, was also dismissed for his perceived failings. He disappeared from active service and did not hold high command again and died in 1922. His replacement was Vladimir Smirnov.

Senior German commanders, too, had been replaced. Prittwitz and Moltke did not see further military service, and both died before the end of the war. Hermann von François, who was dismissed from command for repeated insubordination, spent only a few weeks as a reserve officer, before he was appointed to command of the newly created XLI Reserve Corps on 24 December. This formation, made up largely of men who had volunteered for service since the outbreak of war, was sent to the Western Front, but François would return to the east the following year.

In the process of eliminating officers whose peacetime skills proved to be completely unsuitable for wartime service, all three armies also managed to find good leaders. In the Russian Army, Brusilov performed well on the extreme southern flank of Russian operations, where his army was left to fend for itself in the belief that the decisive theatre was in the central region. Plehve's swift march with his Fifth Army during the Battle of Łódź almost certainly prevented Scheidemann's army from being encircled and destroyed, and he was perhaps the only senior Russian commander in the entire battle who had a clear understanding of the overall situation. In the *k.u.k.* Army, Auffenberg had commanded his unit well, but was dismissed after the defeat at Rawa Ruska; he wrote at great length after the war about how he felt he had been treated unfairly. Viktor Dankl, whose First Army had a similar mix of fortunes, ended the year still in his post, and with his reputation actually enhanced. The Vienna press had made much of his victory at Kraśnik, and by Christmas he was something of a popular hero in an empire where such heroes were in very short supply. Eduard von Böhm-Ermolli had acquitted himself well, improvising in the face of often-chaotic conditions as his troops were laboriously moved from the Serbian front to Galicia. His family background was remarkable in this era. His father, Georg Böhm, was serving as a sergeant when he was awarded a field commission in 1849, and rose to the rank of major before he retired. Subsequently, he was raised to the rank of hereditary nobility, adding the maiden name of his wife, Maria Josepha Ermolli, to his own.

Eduard von Böhm-Ermolli must have been almost unique in the armies of the Great Powers to have risen from such lowly roots.

Opinions in Vienna regarding Conrad were varied. He had cast such a huge shadow over the development and training of the *k.u.k.* Army, and so many officers had imbibed his principles, that the disasters of 1914 did not have the effect that they might have done on his reputation. Even officers like Auffenberg felt that the defeats had been because Conrad's principles had not been applied as they should have been.[11] Many men who were critical of Conrad, such as Alfred Krauss, took the same line.[12] Amongst civilians there was less certainty regarding the judgement not only of Conrad, but also of other senior military figures. Josef Redlich, a Bohemian politician who was a close friend of Conrad, wrote in early October that there was deep mistrust in Vienna not only of Conrad, but of all the army's generals.[13]

Within the army many criticised Conrad for not issuing sufficiently detailed orders to lower commanders. In some respects the *k.u.k.* Army ended up with the worst of all possible worlds. Conrad had taught that the slavish adherence to dogmatic methods was to be avoided, and that officers were to use their initiative depending on the circumstances of the battlefield. But his personal influence and teaching had such a powerful effect that most officers did their utmost to implement the policies that he had taught, with no regard whatever for local circumstances. Orders were written almost in the manner of the examinations that many staff officers had undertaken, trying their best to win the approval of their venerated chief.[14]

The nation that had perhaps found the best pool of capable wartime leaders was Germany. Whilst François was temporarily going through a period of unpopularity with the high command, his reputation as a field commander was undiminished, and many of his contemporaries during the early campaigns – Mackensen, Below, and Woyrsch – had shown themselves to be determined, skilful commanders. If Germany was to survive and prosper in a two-front war, it would require all of their skills. In Hindenburg and Ludendorff, Germany had stumbled across one of those rare combinations of men where the whole greatly exceeds the sum of its parts. Neither of the two men would have been remotely as successful without the other, and the combination of the mercurial but sometimes-unstable Ludendorff with the far steadier Hindenburg would prove to be a priceless asset. The relationship between the two men was complex; perhaps Hindenburg summed it up best, in a passage that also says a great deal about the unapologetic philosophy of military professionalism in the German officer corps:

DISAPPOINTMENTS AND ILLUSIONS

It has been suggested that these relations [between the two men] find a parallel in those between Blücher and Gneisenau. I will venture no opinion as to how far such a comparison reveals a departure from true historical perspective. As I have already said, I had myself held the post of chief of staff for several years. As I knew from my own experience, the relations between the chief of staff and his general, who has the responsibility, are not theoretically laid down in the German Army. The way in which they work together and the degree to which their powers are complementary are much more a matter of personality. The boundaries of their respective powers are therefore not clearly demarcated. If the relations between the general and his chief of staff are what they ought to be, these boundaries are easily adjusted by soldierly and personal tact and the qualities of mind on both sides.

I myself have often characterised my relations with General Ludendorff as those of a happy marriage. In such a relationship how can a third party clearly distinguish the merits of the individuals? They are one in thought and action, and often what the one says is only the expression of the wishes and feelings of the other.

After I had learnt the worth of General Ludendorff, and that was soon, I realised that one of my principal tasks was, as far as possible, to give free scope to the intellectual powers, the almost superhuman capacity for work and untiring resolution of my chief of staff, and if necessary clear the way for him, the way in which our common desires and our common goal pointed...

I had to show General Ludendorff that loyalty of a brother warrior which we had learnt to find in German history from youth up ... and indeed his work and his determination, his whole great personality were truly worthy of such loyalty.[15]

It is a trait of human nature to discount the role that luck plays in success, and instead to assign the credit to oneself, and Ludendorff and Hoffmann were particularly prone to this. Whilst the victory at Tannenberg had been remarkable, Ludendorff ignored the way that actions by François in particular, contrary to the orders from Eighth Army Headquarters, had proved decisive in the German triumph. Hoffmann claimed credit for issuing the original orders that placed François' corps on the western flank of the Russian Second Army, but there is little to suggest that he intended this to be the prelude to a huge encirclement when he drafted the instructions. The rest of Ludendorff's performance on the Eastern Front in 1914 was far less impressive. Whilst he oversaw the savage mauling of Rennenkampf's army in September, his overreaction to the Russian counterattack diverted François at a critical moment, reducing the scope of the final victory considerably. The advance from the Silesian frontier to the gates of Warsaw might have helped bolster sagging Austro-Hungarian morale, but the outcome of the campaign was of no real benefit, and only incompetence by the Russians – and resolute local leadership by the Germans – prevented the Battle of Łódź ending in disaster. Ludendorff's final operation, the drive into central Poland with the newly arrived reinforcements from the West, was strategically pointless, and resulted in little more than increasing an already high casualty count.

Losses on all sides had been severe, far higher than anyone had anticipated. Despite the deaths of so many highly trained soldiers, the German Army emerged perhaps the least damaged, although even this early in the war, as already mentioned, commanders repeatedly noted the inadequate level of training of replacement drafts. Russian casualties had been appalling in numerical terms, but given the scale of Russian mobilisation, the tsar's forces had recovered remarkably quickly. However, even more so than in the German Army, the poor quality of the replacements meant that the fighting power of Russian forces was considerably diminished. But the impact of this was, perversely, perhaps less than in the German Army. Russian strength lay in dogged defence, and the ability to endure hardship, factors which made less use of experience and training than the German strengths of innovation and improvisation. The *k.u.k.* Army had lost its professional core, and was perhaps more severely damaged than any of the armies of the other Great Powers; after only a few months of war, many Germans were already looking at their ally as more of a burden than a support. Within a few months, it became increasingly commonplace for German officers to refer to their relationship with Austria-Hungary as being 'shackled to a corpse'.

As they reorganised their formations and considered the future, the commanders of all sides must have looked back on the preceding months, and considered what else they might have done to achieve the quick victory that they had all expected. Perhaps the Great Power that had the greatest reason to rue its missed opportunities was Russia. Zhilinski's inability to enforce close cooperation between his two armies in August had far-reaching consequences. Even if Prittwitz's army had escaped destruction at the hands of Rennenkampf and Samsonov, it could (and perhaps should) have been forced back to the line of the Vistula. Once they were established along the Vistula, the two Russian armies would have been difficult to dislodge, and the arrival of other Russian armies to their south later in the autumn would have put huge pressure on the Germans. But such close cooperation was a concept beyond the abilities of the Russian generals. Southwest Front showed greater singularity of purpose in its advance across Galicia, but rivalry between the two fronts ensured that the gains in the southern half of the Eastern Front were not used to maximum effect for the greater good.

Conrad's armies had perhaps the least prospect of winning a decisive victory in 1914. There were few, if any, clear-cut objectives within reach at the start of the war, and given Conrad's insistence on offensive operations, it was almost inevitable that the strength of the *k.u.k.* Army was dissipated by advances along divergent axes, none of which had any finite target that would allow forces to be concentrated elsewhere after the target had been reached. Driven by pressure to divert Russian strength away from Germany's vulnerable frontiers, Conrad urged his men forward to disaster, much as the Russians drove forward to disaster at Tannenberg in an attempt to divert German strength away from France. It was only in Serbia that an Austro-Hungarian campaign could have been conducted to achieve something approaching a strategic success, and Potiorek's insistence on invading Serbia by about the most difficult route imaginable – twice – doomed his forces to casualties that were both unnecessary and crippling. A strike into Serbia from the north could have placed Potiorek's armies in control of central Serbia at least six weeks earlier, with every prospect of finishing the campaign before the winter weather arrived.

For the Germans, there had never been any intention of winning a victory in the east before the conclusion of matters in the west. All German plans had been based upon the concept of holding the Russians as far to the east as possible until a French defeat allowed for troops to be transferred for a major counteroffensive. The dazzling victory at Tannenberg rapidly achieved almost mythical status, but senior German officers had studied almost precisely such operations in war games for many years. Nevertheless, Hindenburg, Ludendorff, and their subordinates – and indeed all German soldiers – had good reasons to be proud of their achievements. With the exception of the southeast part of East Prussia, they finished the year with German territory safe from Russian invasion. Some of the Eastern Front commanders looked back on their tactical triumphs and speculated whether more might have been achieved. Litzmann reflected on what might have been accomplished at Łódź:

> Hindenburg's great operational objective – the destruction of the Russian Army in the Vistula bend – was not achieved, as the forces required were missing. And yet, these forces could have been made available! If the German Army's Chief of General Staff at the time, Generalleutnant von Falkenhayn, had known what a rare opportunity had presented itself to strike a lethal blow against the Russians, if he had abandoned his assault in Flanders (at Ypres) and immediately assigned

the troops that would thus have been made free to Hindenburg, this would have doubled the number of divisions available to him for his operation. Mackensen would have been able to hold strong reserves behind both his flanks of his army, and with their help the encirclement of Łódź would have succeeded, despite all the enemy's attempts at counterattacks.[16]

Such sentiments can be regarded as being wise after the event – at the time, there were several moments when it seemed that a victory was imminent at Ypres, though it is interesting to speculate whether the impact of such a victory would have been greater than a victory at Łódź. It would have taken extraordinary courage to abandon the German plan to knock France out of the war before turning on Russia at such an early stage of the war, but by attempting to achieve victory both in the East and the West at the same moment, the Germans perhaps lost the opportunity to win on either battlefield.

Despite their clear successes, many in the German camp felt that they could have achieved even more. Max Hoffmann wrote extensively about his personal role in the war, and clearly felt that Hindenburg and Ludendorff shared credit that should have come to him. Much of his writing benefits hugely from hindsight, and it is not at all clear that he saw things as clearly at the time as he later portrayed. However, he does seem to have pushed for an earlier commitment of reinforcements to the east:

The greatness of the Russian defeat [at Łódź] could have been increased if at the same time as the outflanking movement ... was begun, an attack had been made towards Warsaw by several army corps from the direction of Mlawa, on the other side of the Vistula. At that time the command of the Russian Army would have sent all the stronger forces from the north bank of the Vistula to the south bank, to repulse the attack of Ninth Army. It had been possible for the *Landsturm* of Zastrow's corps, strengthened only by 2nd and 4th Cavalry Divisions, to penetrate as far as the line Ciechanow – Przasnysz. An advance of two or three strong army corps would have found it easy to reach Warsaw and the Great Warsaw Railway, which was the chief line of communication of the Russian Army. The results of such an operation are scarcely to be imagined. At that time the Chief of the Operations Staff, Colonel Tappen, while passing through the town stopped in Posen, and I saw him in his railway compartment, where I implored him, almost on my knees, to persuade the Commander-in-Chief in the east to put at our disposal, besides the promised reinforcements, at least two army corps for such an attack from Mlawa to Warsaw, but it was refused.[17]

The people who had suffered the most were those who had no national army serving their cause: the Poles. Most of Poland west of Warsaw had been turned into a battlefield, and large areas were deliberately devastated by the Germans during their retreat from the Vistula. Treated with disdain by Germans, Russians, and the Austro-Hungarians alike, the Poles could only endure through a cold winter in their shattered towns and villages, and hope for a better future.

Thoughts turned to the future in all camps. For the Germans, there would be difficult negotiations between Falkenhayn, who still believed that only in the west could the war be brought to a satisfactory conclusion, and Hindenburg and Ludendorff, who wished to repeat their successes of 1914 to knock Russia out of the war. In November Falkenhayn had told Chancellor Bethmann-Hollweg that he believed that the powers arrayed against Germany – Britain, France, and Russia – had to be separated. If they remained united, Germany would ultimately be brought to her knees. The solution he suggested was to negotiate a separate peace with Russia, based upon a further 'moderate victory' over the tsar's armies. He explicitly recognised that such a separate peace might not be in the interests of Austria-Hungary, and could even be seen as a betrayal of Germany's ally – after all, Germany had explicitly entered the war in support of Austria-Hungary after Russia mobilised. Once peace with Russia had been achieved, Falkenhayn argued, sufficient force could be brought to bear upon France to achieve a victory. This would leave Britain isolated, and if necessary, submarine warfare could be used to starve the British to agree terms. Bethmann-Hollweg accepted that Falkenhayn's suggestions regarding a separate peace with Russia had to be considered seriously, but doubted that this was likely to be achieved:

> Until now, I have seen no signs that Russia is ready for an accommodation. In my view, even another victory by Hindenburg would not suffice to make Russia acquiesce. To this end, either we or Austria would probably have to occupy most of Poland. We would probably need this leverage to force Russia to pay an indemnity, most of which would then fall to Austria. For its part, the Dual Monarchy would also doubtless claim a part of Serbia in addition to such an indemnity...
>
> If it were to be unsuccessful, the entire Triple Entente would interpret an initiative from us as a sign of weakness, and it would destroy any notions of peace in France.[18]

Despite Falkenhayn's best efforts, Bethmann-Hollweg accepted the assurances of the commanders in the east that a decisive military victory was possible, and chose not to follow the advice of the chief of the general staff. But all sides in the argument were tacitly united in their views about the kaiser. He was increasingly sidelined from all decision-making in Germany.

All through the winter Conrad sent a stream of reinforcements – a mixture of men brought back from the Serbian front and fresh drafts – to his divisions along the Carpathians, where bitter fighting continued unabated. Conrad's son Erwin, wounded in fighting near Przemyśl, spent Christmas with his father in Teschen, but then returned to front-line service; his departure must have deepened Conrad's sense of pessimism. The best that the Dual Monarchy could hope for, it seemed, was that Germany would send sufficient forces east to allow a decisive blow to be struck against Russia. Whether that would be sufficient to help heal Austria-Hungary's internal divisions was doubtful.

The Russians, too, prepared for the coming year. Despite their failures, they still had reasons for optimism. The Germans had proved to be frighteningly formidable opponents, but the tsar's generals felt they had the measure of the *k.u.k.* Army. Provided sufficient guns and ammunition could be gathered, there was still every prospect of defeating Austria-Hungary, and once that had been achieved, it would be inconceivable for Germany to continue the war alone. As Knox observed, however, Russian efforts continued to be hamstrung by bitter infighting between different factions, combined with what appeared to be deeply ingrained traits. Attempts to centralise decision-making and control resulted in paralysis, not least because different factions had differing views on who should take overall control, and frequently chose not to cooperate with central authorities of which they did not approve. The tendency of even senior commanders, that Danilov, too, had observed, to avoid revealing the true state of affairs for fear of attracting criticism, ensured that problems were frequently allowed to grow out of control. The shell shortage, experienced to a degree by all European powers in the first months of the war, was far worse in Russia, and was exacerbated by the refusal of senior officers to face reality:

> On 25 September General Joffre had enquired by telegram whether the resources of the British and Russian governments permitted of the indefinite continuance of the war at the then rate of expenditure of ammunition, and if they did not, up to what date did the supply suffice. The French ambassador in Petrograd passed on the question to the Russian government in an official letter. The Minister of War [Sukhomlinov] replied on 28 September that the question of the supply of ammunition in the Russian Army gave no cause for anxiety, and that the Ministry of War was taking all the necessary steps to provide everything

required. At the same time the French military attaché learned from an unofficial source that the output of factories in Russia then amounted to only 35,000 shells a month. Unfortunately, he had no means of ascertaining that the rate of expenditure at the front then averaged 45,000 a day, and he believed that the initial stock on mobilisation was more than twice as large as it really was.

If General Sukhomlinov and his staff had worried to appreciate the situation at the end of September, they must have known that the initial stock only provided shells for two more months of war, and they should then at once have taken adequate measures to cope with the difficulty by ordering them abroad.

It subsequently became known that the officials in Petrograd received ample warning. On 9 September the staff of the Southwest Front had telegraphed to the Artillery Department: 'It is essential to replace the almost exhausted supplies of shell.' On 26 October Ivanov had telegraphed: 'Supplies of ammunition are entirely exhausted. If not replenished, operations will have to be broken off and the troops retired under most difficult conditions.'

Over a year later I learned on unimpeachable authority that in the middle of October General Kuzmin Karavaev, an honourable old man, whose nerves had been shaken by his immense responsibilities as Chief of the Artillery Department, went to Sukhomlinov, weeping, and said that Russia would have to make peace owing to the shortage of artillery ammunition. The Minister of War told him to 'go to the devil and quiet himself.' How strange it is that orders were not then placed abroad![19]

This last statement is a little misleading, as it is likely that by the time Sukhomlinov could have placed any orders overseas, companies would already have had their order books full of demands from Britain and France. Nevertheless, the Russian solution to the problem was, to a large extent, simply to ignore it. Similarly, as the supply of rifles began to run out, there was the same mixture of denial and false assurance, followed by frantic attempts to procure weapons in Japan and elsewhere.[20]

The months since the fateful assassination in Sarajevo had left hundreds of thousands dead and maimed, on both the Eastern and Western Fronts. In the west all the armies involved were resigned to positional warfare, with no scope for the sort of manoeuvres that they had rehearsed in peacetime. There was growing awareness that this was a war in which success would be measured in yards, not miles. In the east there remained, it seemed, considerable scope for movement, not least because the vastness of the front precluded the troop density that was normal in the west. During the fighting at Ypres in late 1914, the Germans deployed Fourth and Sixth Armies and additional forces, a total of thirteen infantry corps, on a front of perhaps 10 miles (17km), and managed to advance just 4 miles (7km). With troops amounting to a fraction of this force, Hindenburg and Ludendorff repeatedly advanced tens of miles at a time. It was always possible to find a weaker area, where the defenders were more thinly spread. However, the fighting of 1914 had shown that, contrary to their expectations, the armies of Germany, Austria-Hungary, and Russia had been unable to land a decisive blow. The Germans were acutely aware of the restraint placed upon movement by the railway system – no army could operate more than about 72 miles (115km) from its railhead, a lesson that the Russians either ignored or did not regard as relevant. Soldiers had marched back and forth across Poland, devastating the countryside and leaving civilians to cope with the destruction as best they could, and tens of thousands of their comrades perished on the battlefields they crossed. But despite the casualties, and despite the great victories and defeats, the amount of land that had changed sides was modest. The Russians controlled most of Galicia and a small part of East Prussia; they had lost parts of western Poland to the Germans and the Austro-Hungarians. It remained to be seen whether 1915 would bring the Great Powers any closer to a conclusion.

APPENDIX: PLACE NAMES

The naming of towns and cities is complicated by the multitude of names used by the different nationalities over the years. Wherever possible, the name in use by the nation in possession of the location has been used in the text. This is a list of significant locations that have had their names changed since 1914.

Allenstein – Olsztyn (Poland)
Angerburg – Węgorzewo (Poland)
Arys – Orzysz (Poland)
Bartfeld – Bardejov (Slovakia)
Bialla – Biała Piska (Poland)
Bischofsburg – Biskupiec (Poland)
Breslau – Wrocław (Poland)
Brest-Litovsk – Brest (Belarus)
Brzeżany – Berezhany (Ukraine)
Chyrów – Kyriv (Ukraine)
Czernowitz – Chernivtsi (Ukraine)
Danzig – Gdańsk (Poland)
Deutsch Eylau – Iława (Poland)
Elbing – Elbląg (Poland)
Gilgenburg – Dąbrówno (Poland)
Graudenz – Grudziądz (Poland)
Gumbinnen – Gusev (Russian Federation)
Hohenstein – Olsztynek (Poland)
Insterburg – Chernyakhovsk (Russian Federation)
Ivangorod – Dęblin (Poland)
Johannisburg – Pisz (Poland)
Kaschau – Kosice (Slovakia)
Kattowitz – Katowice (Poland)
Königsberg – Kaliningrad (Russian Federation)
Kovno – Kaunas (Lithuania)

Kraupischken – Ulyanovo (Russian Federation)
Lemberg – L'viv (Ukraine)
Lötzen – Giżycko (Poland)
Lyck – Ełk (Poland)
Marienburg – Malbork (Poland)
Neidenburg – Nidzica (Poland)
Neu-Sandez – Nowy Sącz (Poland)
Nikolaiken – Mikołajki (Poland)
Nowo Aleksandrya – Pulawy (Poland)
Novogeorgievsk – Nowy Dwór Mazowiecki (Poland)
Noworadomsk – Radomsko (Poland)
Olita – Alytus (Lithuania)
Ortelsburg – Szczytno (Poland)
Osterode – Ostróda (Poland)
Passenheim – Pasym (Poland)
Port Arthur – Lüshun Port (China)
Posen – Poznań (Poland)
Pregel, River – Pregolya (Russian Federation)
Rastenburg – Kętrzyn (Poland)
Reval – Tallinn (Estonia)
Rudczanny – Ruciane-Nida (Poland)
Seeburg – Jeziorany (Poland)
Semêndria – Smederevo (Serbia)
Semlin – Zemun (Serbia)
Soldau – Działdowo (Poland)
Stallupönen – Nesterov (Russian Federation)
Stanislau – Ivano-Frankivsk (Ukraine)
Stary Sambor – Staryi Sambir (Ukraine)
Tarnopol – Ternopil (Ukraine)
Teschen – Cieszyn (Poland)
Thorn – Toruń (Poland)
Tollmingkehmen – Chistye Prudy (Russian Federation)
Usdau – Uzdowo (Poland)
Wartenburg – Barczewo (Poland)
Willenberg – Wielbark (Poland)
Wirballen – Virbalis (Lithuania)
Vilno, Vilna – Vilnius (Lithuania)

NOTES

INTRODUCTION

1. Gill, M., *Germany: A Modern History* (University of Michigan Press, Ann Arbor, 1970), pp. 128–29
2. McElwee, W., *The Art of War: Waterloo to Mons* (Indiana University Press, Bloomington, 1974), p. 46
3. Hughes, D. (ed.), trans. H. Bell and D. Hughes, *Moltke on the Art of War: Selected Writings* (Novato, Presidio Press, 1993), p. 124
4. Moltke, H. von, *Militärische Werke*, 14 vols. (E.S. Mittler & Sohn, Berlin, 1892–1912), vol. 2, pp. 33–40
5. Quoted in Horne, H., *The Price of Glory: Verdun 1916* (Penguin, Harmondsworth, 1962), p. 16
6. Hamilton, I., *A Staff Officer's Scrap Book during the Russo-Japanese War*, 2 vols. (Edward Arnold, London, 1908), vol. 1, p. 5
7. Quoted in Snyder, J., *The Ideology of the Offensive: Military Decision Making and the Disasters of 1914* (Cornell University Press, Ithaca, NY, 1984), p. 126
8. *Stenographische Berichte über die Verhandlungen des Reichstages 1890-1891* (Verlag der Buchdruckerei der Norddeutschen Allgemeinen Zeitung, Berlin) 114: pp. 76–77
9. Herwig, H., 'Germany and the Short-War Illusion: A New Interpretation?' *Journal of Military History* (Society for Military History, Lexington, 2002), vol. 66, 3: pp. 681–693

CHAPTER 1

1. Moltke, H. von, trans. C. F. McClumpha, C. S. L. Barter and M. Herms, *Essays, speeches, and memoirs of Field-Marshal Count Helmuth von Moltke*, 2 vols. (Harper & Bros., New York, 1893), vol. 2, p. 116
2. Freytag, G., quoted in Silverman, S., *A Happy Life: From Courtroom to Classroom* (iUniverse, Bloomington, 2009), p. 184

3. Known to be a talented linguist, Moltke was once described as being 'taciturn in seven languages'.

4. Rich, N. (ed.), *The Holstein Papers: The Memoirs, Diaries and Correspondence of Friedrich von Holstein 1887–1909*, 4 vols. (Cambridge University Press, Cambridge, 1957), vol. 2, p. 421

5. Schlieffen, A. von, *Cannae* (E. S. Mittler, Berlin, 1936), p. 285

6. Görlitz, W., *The German General Staff: Its History and Structure, 1657–1945* (Hollis & Carter, London, 1953), p. 129

7. See Zuber, T. *The Real German War Plan 1904–1914* (The History Press, Stroud, 2011), and Fromkin, D., *Europe's Last Summer: Why the World Went to War in 1914* (Heinemann, London, 2004)

8. Letter from Moltke to the Austrian chief of general staff Conrad von Hötzendorf, *Forschungsarbeit Gemeinsame Kriegsvorbereitung Deutschland und Österreich-Ungarn*, BA-MA, N46/38, p. 15

9. Mombauer, A., *Helmuth von Moltke and the Origins of the First World War* (Cambridge University Press, Cambridge, 2005), pp. 100–05

10. See communication from Moltke to the German chancellor Theobald von Bethmann-Hollweg, 9 March 1914, Bundesarchiv, R.43.F/107

11. See *l'état-major de l'armée* 2nd Bureau memorandum, May 1914, Le Service Historique de la Défense, Vincennes 7N 1535

12. Dorn Brose, E., *The Kaiser's Army: The Politics of Military Technology in Germany during the Machine Age, 1870–1918* (Oxford University Press, New York, 2001), pp. 18–19

13. Moltke, H. von, *Geschichte des Deutsch-französischen Krieges von 1870–71* (E.S. Mittler & Sohn, Berlin, 1895), p. 195

14. Schlichting, S. von, 'Über das Infanteriegefecht', in *Beiheft zum Militär-Wochenblatt* (Berlin, 1879), p. 45

15. Kessel, B. von, 'Zur Taktik der Infanterie von 1880', in *Beiheft zum Militär-Wochenblatt* (Berlin, 1880), p. 391

16. Report of the Saxon military plenipotentiary to the Saxon War Minister 22 May 1902, Sächsisches Hauptstaatsarchiv, Dresden

17. Zedlitz-Trütszchler, R., *Zwölf Jahre am Deutschen Kaiserhof* (Deutsche Verlags-Anstalt, Berlin, 1925), p. 83

18. Foerster, W., *Prinz Friedrich Karl von Preussen: Denkwürdigkeiten aus Seinem Leben*, 2 vols. (Deutsche Verlags-Anhalt, Stuttgart, 1910), vol. 2, p. 493

19. Kähler, O., *Die Preussische Reiterei von 1800 bis 1876 in Ihrer Inneren Entwickelung* (E.S. Mittler & Sohn, Berlin, 1879), p. 286

20. Report by Prince Friedrich Karl of Prussia, 31 January 1882, Records of the Bavarian War Ministry, Kriegsarchiv, Munich

21. Bernhardi, F. von, *Denkwürdigkeiten aus Meinem Leben* (E.S. Mittler & Sohn, Berlin, 1927), p. 113

22. Kleist, G. von, *Die Offizier-Patrouille im Rahmen der Strategischen Aufgabe der Kavallerie* (E.S. Mittler & Sohn, Berlin, 1891)
23. Quoted in Dorn Brose (2001), p. 27
24. Report of the Saxon military plenipotentiary to the Saxon War Minister 19 June 1888, Sächsisches Hauptstaatsarchiv, Dresden
25. Report of the Bavarian military plenipotentiary to the Bavarian War Minister 28 September 1893, Kriegsarchiv, Munich
26. See, for example, Stone, N., *The Eastern Front 1914–1917* (Hodder & Stoughton, London, 1975), p. 39

CHAPTER 2

1. Quoted in Jukes, G., *The Russo-Japanese War* (Osprey Publishing, Oxford, 2002), p. 21
2. For casualties, see Menning, B., *Bayonets before* Bullets: *The Imperial Russian Army, 1861–1914* (Indiana University Press, Bloomington, 2000), p. 194, also *Statisticheski Raport Russogo Gloinskogo Voinskogo Meditsinskogo Direktorata*, 1914
3. Ascher, A., *The Revolution of 1905: Russia in Disarray*, 2 vols. (Stanford University Press, 1994), vol. 2, pp. 157–58
4. Quoted in Tsouras, P. (ed.), *The Book of Military Quotations* (Zenith Press, St Paul, 2005), p. 51
5. Stone (1975), p. 17
6. Marshall, A., *The Russian General Staff and Asia, 1800–1917* (Routledge, London and New York, 2006), p. 102
7. Golovine, N., *The Russian Campaign of 1914: The Beginning of the War and Operations in East Prussia* (Command and General Staff School Press, Fort Leavenworth, 1933), p. 49
8. Walsh, E., *The Fall of the Russian Empire: The Story of the Last of the Romanovs and the Coming of the Bolshevik* (Wildside Press, Rockville, 2009), p. 98
9. Stone (1975), p. 27
10. Doumbadze, V., A. Knapp (ed.), *Russia's War Minister: The Life and Work of Adjutant-General Vladimir Alexandrovitsh Soukhomlinov* (Simpkin, Marshall Hamilton, Kent & Co., London, 1915), p. 38
11. ibid., pp. 63–64
12. Golovine (1933), p. 34
13. Paléologue, M., trans. F. Holt, *An Ambassador's Memoirs*, 3 vols. (George H. Doran Co., New York, 1923), vol. 1, p. 83
14. *GUGSh*, quoted in Hamilton, R. and H. Herwig (eds.), *War Planning 1914* (Cambridge University Press, Cambridge, 2009), p. 86
15. Daniloff, N., 'How Russia's Military Tried to Undermine Lenin's Separate Peace', *Foreign Service Journal* (June 1980), pp. 19–20

16. Brusilov, A., *Moi Vospominaniia* (Voenizdat, Moscow, 1967), p. 9

17. Kersnovsky, A., *Istoriia Russkoi Armii*, 4 vols. (Tsarskii Vestnik, Belgrade, 1935), vol. 3, p. 621

18. Zaionchkovsky, A., *Podgotovka Rossii k Imperialistichekoi Vione* (Gosvoenizdat, Moscow, 1926), p. 348

19. Now known as Kaunas, Lithuania

20. Barsukov, E., *Podgotovka Rossii k Mirovoj Vojne v Artillerijskom Otnosenii* (Gosvoenizdat, Moscow, 1926), pp. 56–57, 70

21. Polivanov, A., *Iz Dnevnikov i Vospominanii Po Dolzhnosti Voennogo Ministra i Ego Pomoshchika 1907–1916* (Vyshii Voennyi Redaktsionnyi Sovet, Moscow, 1924), p. 97

22. Zaionchkovsky (1926), pp. 146–49

23. Danilov, Y., *La Russie Dans la Guerre Mondiale* (Payot, Paris, 1927), pp. 69–70

24. ibid., p. 71

25. General Maurice Pellé, quoted in Snyder (1984), p. 175

26. Shatsillo, K., *Russki Imperializm i Razvitie Flota* (Nauka, Moscow, 1968), p. 100

27. Menning (2000), pp. 251–54

28. Irving Root, G., *Battles East: A History of the Eastern Front of the First World War* (PublishAmerica, Baltimore, 2007), p. 50

29. Stone (1975), p. 41

30. See Stevenson, D., 'War by Timetable? The Railway Race Before 1914', *Past and Present*, 162:1 (1999), pp. 176–80

31. Hamilton and Herwig (2009), p. 87

32. Danilov (1927), p. 55

33. See letter from De Verneuil to Pichon, 17 September 1913, in *Documents diplomatiques français, 1871–1914* (Imprimerie Nationale, Paris), 3rd series, VIII, doc.156

34. Stone (1975), p. 48

35. Danilov (1927), p. 54

36. Stone (1975), p. 29; Irving Root (2007), p. 56

37. Golovine (1933), p. 44; the emphasis is in the original

38. Stein, H., 'Der Offizier des Russischen Heeres im Zeitabschnitt Zwischen Reform und Revolution 1861–1905', *Forschungen zur Osteuropäischen Geschichte*, 13 (1967), p. 380

CHAPTER 3

1. Temperley, H., *England and the Near East: The Crimea* (Longmans, Greens and Co, London, 1936), p. 272

2. *New York Times*, 12 May 1860

3. Rothenberg, G., *The Army of Francis Joseph* (Purdue University Press, West Lafayette, 1998), p. 128

4. Stone, N., 'Army and Society in the Habsburg Monarchy 1900–1914', *Past and Present*, 33 (April 1966), p. 96

5. Stone (1975), p. 71

6. Rothenberg (1998), p. 85

7. Rauchensteiner, M., 'Zum Operativen Denken in Österreich 1814–1914: Der Vor-Weldkriegs-Zyklus', *Österreichische Militärische Zeitschrift*, 1 (1975), p. 51

8. See Waldstätten, J., *Technik des Angriffsweisen Gefechts der Infanterie* (Seidel & Sohn, Vienna, 1885)

9. Conrad, F., 'Mannschafts-Menage und Offiziers-Mittagstisch', *Organ der Militärwissenschaftlichen Vereine*, vol. 12 (1876), pp. 161–69

10. Urbanski von Ostrymiecz, A., *Conrad von Hötzendorf: Soldat und Mensch* (Ulrich Mosers Verlag, Graz, 1939), p. 60

11. Sondhaus, L., *Franz Conrad von Hötzendorf: Architect of the Apocalypse* (Humanities Press, Boston, 2000), p. 40

12. Conrad, F., *Zum Studium der Taktik* (L.W. Seidel & Sohn, Vienna, 1893 – 2nd edn.), p. 4

13. Conrad, F., *Die Gefechtsausbildung der Infanterie* (L.W. Seidel & Sohn, Vienna, 1900), p. 26

14. See Csicserics von Bacsány, M., *Die Schlacht: Studie Auf Grund Des Krieges in Ostasien 1904–05* (L.W. Seidel & Sohn, Vienna, 1908)

15. Quoted in Sondhaus (2000), p. 84

16. For an account of the Redl affair see Markus, G., *Der Fall Redl* (Amalthea, Vienna, 1984)

17. Clark, C., *The Sleepwalkers: How Europe Went to War in 1914* (Penguin, London, 2012), p. 116

18. Letter from Conrad to Gina Reininghaus, quoted in Sondhaus (2000), p. 132

19. Kriegsarchiv, Österreichisches Staatsarchiv, Vienna, B/1450: 357

20. *The Day* (New London, Connecticut, 8 August 1914)

21. May, A., *The Passing of the Habsburg Monarchy 1914–1918* (University of Pennsylvania Press, Philadelphia, 1996), p. 199

22. ibid.

23. *Stenographisches Protokoll 113, Sitzung des Nationalrats der Republik Österreich* (2 Sept 1925), p. 2,683

24. See Wank, S., 'Some Reflections on Conrad von Hötzendorf and his Memoirs Based on Old and New Sources', *Austrian History Yearbook*, I (1965), pp.74–88; Deák, I., *Beyond Nationalism: A Social and Political History of the Habsburg Officer Corps 1848–1918* (Oxford University Press, Oxford, 1990), p. 72

25. Stone, N., 'Die Mobilmachung der Österreich-Ungarischen Armee 1914', *Militärgeschichtliche Mitteilungen*, 2 (1974), pp. 75–76

CHAPTER 4

1. Jovanović, L., *The Murder of Sarajevo* (British Institute of International Affairs, London, 1925), p. 3

2. Kautsky, K., M. Montgelas, and W. Schücking (eds.), *Die Deutsche Dokumente zum Kriegsausbruch* (Deutsche Verlagsgesellschaft für Politik und Geschichte, Berlin, 1924), vol. I, pp. 10–11

3. Clark (2012), pp. 406–08

4. Redlich, J., F. Fellner and D. Corradini, *Schicksalsjahre Österreichs: Die Erinnerungen und Tagebücher Josef Redlichs*, 3 vols. (Boehlau, Vienna, 2011), vol. I, p. 219

5. Albertini, L., I. Massey (trans. and ed.), *The Origins of the War of 1914*, 3 vols. (Oxford University Press, London, 1952–57), vol. 1, pp. 131–32

6. Clark (2012), p. 414

7. Albertini (1952–57), pp. 145–46

8. Fischer, F., *Germany's Aims in the First World War* (Norton, New York, 1967), p. 52

9. Unpublished report by Friedrich Gempp, *Geheimer Nachrichtendienst und Spionageabwehr des Heeres* (Abteilung Militärarchiv, Bundesarchiv, Freiburg), vol. 2 (1922–24): Sec. 1, p. 3

10. Trumpener, U., 'War Premeditated? German Intelligence Operations in July 1914', *Conference Group for Central European History*, 6 (March 1976), p. 65

11. Williamson, S., *Austria-Hungary and the Origins of the First World War* (Macmillan, London, 1991), pp. 199–200

12. Turner, L., 'The Russian Mobilisation in 1914', *Journal of Contemporary History*, 3:1 (1968), p. 79

13. Conrad, F., *Aus Meiner Dienstzeit, 1906–1918*, 5 vols. (Rikola Verlag, Vienna 1921), vol. 4, p. 61

14. See, for example, Quester, G., *Deterrence before Hiroshima: The Influence of Airpower on Modern Strategy* (John Wiley, New York, 1966), p. 17; Taylor, A., *Illustrated History of the First World War* (Putnam, New York, 1964), pp. 14–15; Albertini (1952–57) (all three volumes)

15. See, for example, Craig, G., *The Politics of the Prussian Army 1640–1945* (Oxford University Press, New York, 1964), pp. 291–95; Albertini (1952–57), vol. 2, p. 540; ibid., vol. 3, pp. 13, 27, 31, 190, 232, and 248

16. For a recent and arguably the best analysis of the miscalculations of the Great Powers, see Clark (2012)

17. Fischer (1967), p. 60

18. Paléologue (1923), vol. I, p. 10

19. Musulin, A., *Das Haus am Ballplatz 1892–1918* (Verlag für Kulturpolitik, Vienna, 1924), p. 241

20. Trumpener (1976), p. 67

21. Fay, S., *The Origins of the World War*, 2 vols. (1928 – 2nd edn., Free Press, New York, 1967), vol. 2, p. 321

22. Tunstall, G., *Planning for War Against Russia and Serbia: Austro-Hungarian and German Military Strategies 1871–1914* (Social Science Monographs, Boulder, 1993), p. 145

23. Lieven, D., 'Russia Accepts a General War', in H. Herwig (ed.), *The Outbreak of World War I: Causes and Responsibilities* (5th edn. – D. C. Heath & Co., Lexington, 1991), p. 109

24. McDonald, D., *United Government and Foreign Policy in Russia 1900–1914* (Harvard University Press, Cambridge, Massachusetts, 1992), p. 181

25. Quoted in Clark (2012), p. 266

26. Buchanan, G., *My Mission to Russia and Other Diplomatic Memories* (Cassell, London, 1923), p. 195

27. Buchanan to Grey, 25 July 1914, in Gooch, G. and H. Temperley (eds.), *British Documents on the Origins of the War*, 11 vols. (HMSO, London, 1926–38), vol. 11, p. 125

28. Bethmann to Pourtalès, 26 July 1914, in Kautsky, K., M. Montgelas, and W. Schücking (eds.), *Outbreak of the World War: German Documents Collected by Karl Kautsky* (Oxford University Press, New York, 1924), p. 219

29. Albertini (1952–57), vol. 3, p. 42

30. Geiss, I., *July 1914: The Outbreak of the First World War, Selected Documents* (Batsford, London, 1967), p. 52

31. Turner (1968), pp. 72–73

32. Geiss (1967), pp. 130, 206

33. Paléologue (1923), vol. 1, p. 55

34. Clark (2012), p. 472

35. See, for example, Trachtenberg, M., 'The Meaning of Mobilization in 1914', *International Security*, 15:3 (1990), p. 130; Stone, N., 'Moltke and Conrad: Relations Between the Austro-Hungarian and German General Staffs, 1909–1914', in Kennedy, P. (ed.), *War Plans of the Great Powers 1880–1914* (Allen & Unwin, London, 1979), p. 228.

36. Albertini (1952–57), vol. 2, p. 560

37. ibid., vol. 2, p. 549

38. Kautsky, Montgelas, and Schücking (1924), p. 396

39. Hoetzsch, O. (ed.), *Die Internationalen Beziehungen im Zeitalter des Imperialismus* (Hobbing, Berlin, 1931–34), vol. 1 part 5, p. 224

40. Jones, D., 'Imperial Russian Forces at War' in Millet, A., W. Murray (ed.), *Military Effectiveness. Volume I: The First World War* (Cambridge University Press, 2010), pp. 249, 256

41. Dobrorolski, S., *Die Mobilmachung der Russischen Armee, 1914* (Deutsche Verlagsgesellschaft Für Politik und Geschichte, Berlin, 1922), pp. 17–19

42. Albertini (1952–57), vol. 3, pp. 172–76

43. Tunstall (1993), pp. 178–79

44. Zweig, S., *Die Welt von Gestern* (Bermann-Fischer, Stockholm, 1944)

45. Danilov (1927), pp. 155–56

46. ibid., pp. 156–57

47. ibid., p. 157

48. Golovine (1933), p. 77

49. Zweig (1944), chapter 12

50. Quoted in Englund, P., trans. W. Butt, *Schönheit und Schrecken: Eine Geschichte des Ersten Weltkriegs, erzählt in neunzehn Schicksalen* (Rowohlt, Berlin, 2011), pp.19–21

CHAPTER 5

1. Danilov (1927), pp. 148–50

2. ibid., p. 150

3. Danilov (1927), pp. 151–52

4. Stone (1975), p. 51

5. ibid., p. 52

6. Gröner, E., *German Warships, 1815–1945*, 3 vols. (Naval Institute Press, Annapolis, 1990), vol. 1, p. 107

7. Paléologue (1923), vol. 1, p. 55

8. Golovine (1933), p. 78

9. ibid., p. 84

10. Gurko, V., *War and Revolution in Russia 1914–1917* (Macmillan, New York, 1919), pp. 26–27

11. Richthofen, M., trans. T. Baker, *The Red Battle Flier* (McBride, New York, 1918), pp. 31–33

12. Golovine (1933), pp. 91–92

13. Showalter, D., *Tannenberg: Clash of Empires, 1914* (Potomac Books Inc., Dulles, 2004), p. 155

14. François, H., *Marneschlacht und Tannenberg* (A. Scherl, Berlin, 1920), p. 166

15. *Kriegsgeschichtliche Einzelschriften der Luftwaffe*, vol. 3: *Mobilmachung, Aufmarsch und erster Einsatz der deutschen Luftstreitkräfte im August 1914* (E.S. Mittler & Sohn, Berlin, 1939), pp. 88–89

16. François (1920), pp. 168–69

17. ibid., p. 170

18. Golovine (1933), p. 111

19. Showalter (2004), p. 163

20. François (1920), p. 171

21. ibid., p. 173

22. Golovine (1933), p. 112

23. François (1920), p. 174

24. Danilov (1927), p. 190

25. Bulöwius, A. and B. Hippler, *Das Infanterie-Regiment von Boyen (5 Ostpreussisches) Nr. 41 im Weltkriege 1914–1918* (Wilhelm Kolk, Berlin, 1929), pp. 14–15

26. Golovine (1933), p. 117

27. Savant, J., *L'Épopée Russe: Campagne de l'Armée Rennenkampf en Prusse-Orientale* (Calmann-Lévy, Paris, 1945), p. 80

28. Mackensen, A., *Briefe und Auszeichnungen des Generalfeldmarschalls aus Krieg und Frieden* (Bibliographisches Institut, Leipzig, 1938), p. 36

29. Golovine (1933), p. 127

30. Quoted in Golovine (1933), pp. 126–27

31. François (1920), p. 185

32. Mackensen (1938), pp. 36–37

33. ibid., p. 38

34. Zipfel, E., *Geschichte des Königlich Preussischen Husaren-Regiment Fürst Blücher von Wahlstätt (Pommersches) Nr. 5* (Sporn, Zeulenroda, 1930), p. 21

35. Preusser, W., *Das 9. Westpreussisches Infanterie-Regiment Nr. 176 Im Weltkrieg* (Verlag Tradition Kolk, Berlin, 1931), p. 15

36. Hesse, K., *Der Feldherr Psychologos* (E.S. Mittler & Sohn, Berlin, 1922), p. 41

37. Quoted in Mackensen (1938), p. 40

38. Golovine (1933), p. 138

39. Morgen, C., *Meiner Truppen Heldenkämpfe* (E.S. Mittler & Sohn, Berlin, 1920), p. 6

CHAPTER 6

1. Elze, W., *Tannenberg: Das Deutsche Heer von 1914, seine Grundzüge und deren Auswirkung im Sieg an der Ostfront* (Hirt, Breslau, 1928), p. 226

2. ibid., p. 242

3. Hoffman, M., trans. A. Charnot, *The War of Lost Opportunities* (K. Paul, French, Trubner & Co., London, 1924), pp. 29–30

4. Elze (1928), p. 368; see also Reichsarchiv, *Der Weltkrieg 1914 bis 1918*, 15 vols. (E.S. Mittler & Sohn, Berlin, 1925–30), vol. 2, p. 102

5. Mackensen (1938), pp. 41–42

6. Showalter (2004), pp. 190–99
7. Schulte, B., 'Neue Dokumente zu Kriegsausbruch und Kriegsverlauf 1914', *Militärgeschichtliche Mitteilungen*, 25 (1979), pp. 154–55
8. Elze (1928), pp. 245–46
9. François (1920), p. 192
10. ibid., p. 195; Elze (1928), p. 236
11. Elze (1928), p. 235
12. Waldersee, A., *Meine Erlebnisse zu Beginn des Krieges 1914*, Bundesarchiv-Militärarchiv, w-10/51032, p. 10
13. Morgen (1920), p. 6
14. ibid., p. 7
15. Nachlass Groener, Bundesarchiv-Militärarchiv Freiburg, NL46/38
16. Mackensen (1938), p. 42
17. One of the most oft-quoted accounts of the alleged physical fight between Rennenkampf and Samsonov is Hoffmann (1924), pp. 18–19
18. Elze (1928), pp. 112–13
19. François (1920), pp. 191–92
20. Ludendorff, E., *Meine Kriegserinnerungen 1914–1918* (E.S. Mittler & Sohn, Berlin, 1919), p. 32
21. Hindenburg, P., trans. F. Holt, *Out of my Life* (Cassell, London, 1920), p. 81
22. Ludendorff (1919), pp. 35–36
23. Hindenburg (1920), p. 83
24. Hoffmann (1924), pp. 33–34

CHAPTER 7

1. Hindenburg (1920), p. 88
2. Quoted in Golovine (1933), p. 179
3. 'Reasons for the Failure of General Samsonov's Second Army in East Prussia in August 1914', *Voenny Sbornik*, IV (1916), p. 156
4. Quoted in Golovine (1933), p. 183
5. ibid., pp.171–72
6. Knox, A., *With the Russian Army 1914–1917: Being Chiefly Extracts from the Diary of a Military Attaché*, 2 vols. (Hutchinson & Co., London, 1921), vol. 1, p. 52
7. See Knox (1921), p. 57, and Plickert, H., *Das 2. Ermländische Infanterie-Regiment Nr. 151 im Weltkriege* (Stalling, Oldenburg, 1929), pp. 27–29
8. Quoted in Golovine (1933), pp. 187–88
9. Showalter (2004), p. 221

10. Ludendorff (1919), p. 36
11. Letter written by Colonel Philippov, quoted in Golovine (1933), pp. 161–62
12. Quoted in Golovine (1933), p. 189
13. Showalter (2004), pp. 224–26
14. Quoted in Golovine (1933), p. 191
15. Knox (1921), p. 64
16. Hindenburg (1920), p. 92
17. François (1920), pp. 196–97
18. Ludendorff (1919), p. 40
19. François (1920), p. 202
20. Golovine (1933), pp. 199–200
21. ibid., p. 204
22. ibid., pp. 204–05
23. François (1920), p. 204
24. Reichsarchiv (1925–30), vol. 2, p. 141
25. François (1920), p. 206
26. Stephani, W., *Mit Hindenburg bei Tannenberg* (Eisenschmidt, Berlin, 1919), p. 20
27. Reichert, W., *Das Infanterie-Regiment Freiherr Hiller von Gaertringen (4. Posensches) Nr. 59 im Weltkriege 1914–1918* (Stein, Potsdam, 1930), vol. 1, pp. 47–48
28. Showalter (2004), p. 239
29. Golovine (1933), pp. 225–26
30. ibid., pp. 218–19
31. ibid., p. 219
32. ibid., pp. 231–32
33. Mackensen (1938), p. 46
34. ibid., pp. 47–49
35. Seydel, A. *Das Grenadier-Regiment König Friedrich I (4. Ostpreussisches) Nr. 5 im Weltkrieg* (Oldenbourg, Potsdam, 1926), pp. 48–50
36. Golovine (1933), p. 233
37. Hindenburg (1920), pp. 94–95
38. Elze (1928), pp. 132–33
39. Hindenburg (1920), p. 95
40. Knox (1921), p. 69
41. Vatsetis, J., *Deyatelnyosty v Vostochnom Prussiyi v Yuly, Avgoost, y Nachale Sentybry 1914* (Isdat Politisheskoi Literaturi, Moscow, 1923), p. 83
42. François (1920), pp. 210–11
43. ibid., pp. 211–12
44. ibid., p. 214
45. Ludendorff (1919), p. 41

46. Hoffmann (1924), p. 42
47. Schäfer, T., *Tannenberg* (Stalling, Oldenburg, 1927), pp. 90–91
48. Golovine (1933), pp. 219–20
49. ibid., pp. 220–21
50. Quoted in Golovine (1933), pp. 224–25
51. op. cit. 'Reasons for the Failure of Second Army', p. 168
52. Mackensen (1938), p. 51
53. Preusser (1931), p. 25
54. Quoted in Mackensen (1938), p. 51
55. Preusser (1931), p. 26
56. Golovine (1933) p. 253
57. ibid., p. 235
58. Mackensen (1938), p. 53
59. Quoted in Mackensen (1938), p. 403
60. François (1920), p. 215
61. Golovine (1933), p. 270
62. François (1920), pp. 216–17
63. For Martos' account, see Golovine (1933), p. 263. For the German account, see for example Schäfer (1927), pp. 124–25
64. Morgen (1920), p. 9
65. François (1920), p. 217
66. ibid., p. 218
67. François (1920), p. 219
68. Fuchs, R., 'Brief Outline of the Operations of the Army of the Narev', *Voenny Sbornik*, IV (1916), p. 131
69. Quoted in Mackensen (1938), p. 55
70. ibid., p. 56
71. Preusser (1931), p. 28
72. Ludendorff (1919), p. 43
73. Notz, F. and F. Scholtz, *General von Scholtz: Ein Deutsches Soldatenleben in Grosser Zeit* (Siegismund, Berlin, 1937), p. 44
74. Golovine (1933), pp. 293–95
75. François (1920), p. 224
76. Plickert (1929), p. 57
77. Golovine (1933), p. 294
78. Morgen (1920), p. 12
79. Golovine (1933), pp. 296–98
80. Golovine (1933), p. 300
81. Quoted in Golovine (1933), pp. 300–01

82. Preusser (1931), pp. 28–29
83. ibid., p. 32
84. Showalter (2004), pp. 315–17; Preusser (1931), pp. 32–33
85. François (1920), p. 229
86. Hubatsch, W., *Hindenburg und der Staat: Aus den Papieren des Generalfeldmarschalls und Reichspräsidenten von 1878 bis 1934* (Musterschmidt, Göttingen, 1966), p. 152
87. François (1920), pp. 237–38
88. Sweetman, J., *Tannenberg 1914* (Cassell, London, 2004), p. 158
89. Knox (1921), p. 85
90. Morgen (1920), p. 13

CHAPTER 8

1. Jeřábek, R., *Potiorek: General im Schatten von Sarajevo* (Styria, Graz, 1991), pp. 118–32
2. Stone (1975), pp. 77–78
3. *Österreich-Ungarns Letzter Krieg 1914–1918* (15 vols.), vol. 1: *Das Kriegsjahr 1914* (Verlag der Militärwissenschaftlichen Mitteilungen, Vienna, 1931), p. 91
4. Letter from Moltke to Conrad, 2 August 1914, quoted in *Österreich-Ungarns* vol. 1 (1931), p. 156
5. ibid., p. 162
6. For detailed accounts of the battle, see Slivinski, A. and F. Keller, *Konnyi Boi 10-1 Kavaleriiskoi Divisii Generala Grafa Kellera 8/21 Avgusta Goda u d. Iaroslavitse* (Belgrade, 1921); Hoen, M., *Die Letzte Reiterschlacht der Weltgeschichte* (Amalthea, Vienna, 1929)
7. *Österreich-Ungarns* vol. 1 (1931), p. 162
8. Auffenberg, M., *Aus Österreichs Höhe und Niedergang: Eine Lebensschilderung* (Drei Masken, Munich, 1921), p. 265
9. ibid., p. 287
10. Rothenberg (1988), p. 173
11. Golovine, N., 'The Great Battle in Galicia: A Study in Strategy', *Slavonic and East European Review*, 5 (1926–27), pp. 27–28
12. *Österreich-Ungarns* vol. 1 (1931), p. 174
13. ibid., p. 175
14. Golovine (1926–27), pp. 31–32
15. *Österreich-Ungarns* vol. 1 (1931), p. 176
16. Auffenberg (1921), p. 288
17. ibid., p. 295
18. ibid., p. 307
19. For a detailed account of the fighting in August, see *Österreich-Ungarns* vol. 1 (1931), pp. 178–241, and Golovine (1926–27), pp. 27–32

20. Woyrsch quoted in Clemenz, B., *Generalfeldmarschall von Woyrsch und Seine Schlesier* (C. Flemming, Berlin, 1919), p. 120
21. Freytag-Loringhoven, A., *Menschen und Dinge Wie Ich Sie In Meinem Leben Sah* (E.S. Mittler & Sohn, Berlin, 1923), p. 221
22. See, for example, Krauss, A., *Die Ursachen unserer Niederlage* (Lehmann, Munich, 1921), p. 134

CHAPTER 9

1. Hindenburg (1920), pp. 99–100
2. Ludendorff (1919), p. 47
3. Danilov (1927), p. 241
4. François (1920), p. 252
5. ibid., p. 254
6. Gurko (1919), p. 40
7. Morgen (1920), p. 16
8. François (1920), p. 256
9. Gurko (1919), pp. 53–54
10. Mackensen (1938), p. 61
11. Morgen (1920), p. 21
12. François (1920), pp. 263–64
13. Danilov (1927), pp. 240–41, Ludendorff (1919), p. 50
14. François (1920), pp. 269–70
15. Mackensen (1938), p. 65
16. Danilov (1927), p. 244
17. François (1920), pp. 273–74
18. Hindenburg (1920), p. 110
19. Halsey, F., *The Literary Digest History of the World War*, 10 vols. (Funk & Wagnalls, New York, 1920), vol. 7, p. 34
20. Pahalyuk, K., *Romanoyi v Spazheneyakh v Vostochnoe v Prussii 1914* (Reitar, Kaliningrad, 2009), pp. 180–91
21. Morgen (1920), pp. 25–30
22. K. Wiegand, quoted in Russell, T., *The World's Greatest War* (Walter, New York, 1919), pp. 221–26

CHAPTER 10

1. Danilov (1927), pp. 206–07
2. Johnson, C., 'Brusiloff, Hero of the Hour in Russia, Described by One Who

Knows Him Well', *New York Times*, 18 June 1916

3. The main source for Austro-Hungarian deployments and operations in this campaign is *Österreich-Ungarns* vol. 1 (1931), pp. 242–335

4. ibid., p. 168

5. ibid., p. 187

6. From the diary of Pál Kelemen, quoted in Englund (2011), p. 28

7. Pastor, L., *Generaloberst Viktor Dankl, der Sieger von Krasnik und Verteidiger Tirols* (Herder, Vienna, 1916), p. 16

8. Zichowitsch, J., *Strategicheskii Issledovanyi Mirosvon' Voinii 1914–1918* (Voenizdat, Moscow, 1922), p. 54

9. *Österreich-Ungarns* vol. 1 (1931), pp. 205–06

10. Conrad (1921), p. 394

11. Freytag-Loringhoven (1923), p. 229

12. Golovine (1926–27), p. 34

13. Conrad (1921), pp. 578–79

14. Stone (1975), p. 51

15. Quoted in Golovine (1926), p. 36

16. ibid., pp. 36–37

17. ibid., p. 37

18. Gold, H. (ed.), *History of the Jews of Bukowina*, 2 vols. (Olamenu, Tel Aviv, 1958–1962), pp. 67–70

19. Auffenberg (1921), p. 268

20. ibid., pp. 337–38

21. ibid., pp. 340–41

22. ibid., p. 344

23. *Österreich-Ungarns* vol. 1 (1931), p. 284

24. Letter from Conrad to Gina von Reininghaus, 10 October 1915, Kriegsarchiv B/1450: 357

25. Auffenberg (1921), p. 346

26. Danilov (1927), p. 226

27. Quoted in Russell, T., *America's War for Humanity: Pictorial History of the World War for Liberty* (Walter, New York, 1919) – 2004 Kessinger edition, p. 248

28. Quoted in Auffenberg (1921), p. 357

29. Brusilov's *A Soldier's Notebook* (1930), included in Neiberg, M. (ed.), *The World War 1 Reader: Primary and Secondary Sources* (NYU Press, New York, 2007), pp. 110–11

30. Palmer, S. and S. Wallis, *A War in Words* (Simon & Schuster, London, 2003), pp. 71–72

31. See *New York Times*, 29 November 1914

32. Korolkov, G., *Varshavsko-Ivangorodskaia Operatsiia* (Voenizdat, Moscow, 1923), p. 55
33. Auffenberg (1921), p. 388
34. ibid., p. 389
35. Kriegsarchiv, Vienna, M-KR 64
36. Kriegsarchiv, Vienna, M-KR 74
37. Auffenberg (1921), pp. 426–41
38. Conrad (1921), p. 804
39. See, for example, *Daily Chronicle*, London, 10 September 1914; *Hobart Mercury*, 14 September 1914

CHAPTER 11

1. Jeřábek (1991), pp. 82–86
2. Remak, J., *Sarajevo: The Story of a Political Murder* (Criterion, New York, 1959), pp. 132–34
3. Morsey, A., 'Konopischt und Sarajewo', *Berlin Monatshefte*, XII (1934), p. 492
4. See, for example, *Reichspost*, 7 July 1914
5. Rothenberg (1988), p. 182
6. Czernin von und zu Chudenitz, O., *In the World War* (Harper & Collins, New York, 1920), pp. 102–03
7. *Österreich-Ungarns* vol. 1 (1931), pp. 99–100
8. Much of the following narrative is derived from *Österreich-Ungarns* vol. 1 (1931), pp. 91–154
9. ibid., p. 105
10. Quoted in *Österreich-Ungarns* vol. 1 (1931), p. 106
11. Conrad (1921), p. 358
12. Serbian General Staff, *Veliki Rat Serbije Za Oslobodelje i Ujedljelje Serba, Hrvata i Slovenaca* (Štamlarska Padionica Milistarstva i Mornarice, Belgrade, 1925) (henceforth, *Veliki Rat*), vol. 1, p. 62
13. ibid., pp. 76–80
14. Telegram from Potiorek to Bolfras 21/08/14, Kriegsarchiv Vienna, MKSM-SR
15. Telegram from Potiorek to Bolfras 22/08/14, Kriegsarchiv Vienna, MKSM-SR
16. *Österreich-Ungarns* vol. 1 (1931), p. 148
17. Barby, H., *Avec l'Armée Serbe: de l'Ultimatum Autrichien à l'Invasion de la Serbie* (Albin Michel, Paris, 1918), p. 101
18. ibid., p. 102
19. Glenny, M., *The Balkans: Nationalism, War, and the Great Powers, 1804–1999* (Granta, London, 2000), p. 316

20. Barby (1918), pp. 86–88
21. For a detailed analysis of alleged atrocities in Belgium, see Zuckerman, L., *The Rape of Belgium: The Untold Story of World War I* (New York University Press, New York, 2004); Horne, J. and A. Kramer, *German Atrocities, 1914: A History of Denial* (Yale University Press, New Haven, 2001)
22. Barby (1918), p. 112
23. ibid., pp. 115–16
24. For further details of atrocities committed by Austro-Hungarian troops in Serbia, see Reiss, R., *Comment les Austro-Hongrois Ont Fait la Guerre en Serbie: Observations Direct d'un Neutre* (Colin, Paris, 1915)
25. Letter from Greig to Crackanthorpe, 25 November 1913, National Archives, Kew, FO 371/1748, 364
26. For an account of the fighting on the Serbian front from September onwards, see *Österreich-Ungarns* vol. 1 (1931), pp. 603–764
27. Krauss (1921), p. 146
28. Barby (1918), p. 227
29. *Veliki Rat*, vol. 3, p. 254
30. Telegram from Potiorek to Bolfras, 20/11/14, Kriegsarchiv Vienna, MKSM-SR
31. Popović, N., *Srbi u Prvom Svetskom Ratu, 1914–1918* (DMP, Belgrade, 1998), p. 42
32. *Veliki Rat*, vol. 5, p. 368
33. Telegrams from Potiorek to Bolfras, 02/12/14-08/12/14, Kriegsarchiv Vienna, MKSM-SR
34. Jeřábek (1991), p. 171
35. Telegram from Potiorek to Bolfras, 09/12/14, Kriegsarchiv Vienna, MKSM-SR
36. Telegram from Archduke Frederick to Military Chancellery, 13/12/14, Kriegsarchiv Vienna, MKSM-SR

CHAPTER 12

1. See, for example, Mombauer (2005), pp. 104–05
2. Meyer, T. (ed.), trans. H. Hermann-Davey, W. Forward and M. Askew, *Light for the New Millennium: Rudolf Steiner's Association with Helmuth and Eliza von Moltke – Letters, Documents and After-Death Communications* (Rudolf Steiner Press, London, 1997), p. 83
3. Ludendorff (1919), p. 58
4. ibid., pp. 58–59
5. Preusser (1931), p. 46
6. Mackensen (1938), pp. 70–71
7. Danilov (1927), p. 261

8.   ibid., p. 258
9.   Korolkov (1923), pp. 89–90
10. *Österreich-Ungarns* vol. 1 (1931), p. 356
11. Danilov (1927), pp. 268–69
12. For an account of Fifth Army's move and the difficulties it encountered, see Korolkov (1923), pp. 81–101
13. Englund (2011), pp. 49–50
14. Neiberg (2007), p. 121
15. *Österreich-Ungarns* vol. 1 (1931), pp. 389–93
16. Neiberg (2007), p. 113
17. Danilov (1927), p. 279
18. ibid., pp. 280–81
19. Mackensen (1938), p. 72
20. ibid., p. 75
21. ibid., p. 77
22. ibid., p. 78
23. G. Graf von Schwerin, quoted in Mackensen (1938), p.79
24. Reichsarchiv, (1925–30), vol. 5, p. 450
25. Neiberg (2007), p. 111
26. ibid., p. 111
27. ibid., p. 115
28. Korolkov (1923), pp. 87–93
29. *Österreich-Ungarns* vol. 1 (1931), p. 424
30. Schemfil, V., *Das k.u.k. 3 Regiment der Tiroler Kaiserjäger im Weltkrieg 1914–1918* (Teutsch, Bregenz, 1926), p. 64
31. Conrad (1921), p. 139
32. ibid., p. 123
33. Ludendorff (1919), p. 70
34. Quoted in *Österreich-Ungarns* vol. 1 (1931), p. 443
35. Litzmann, K., *Lebenserinnerungen* (Berlin: Eisenschmidt, Berlin, 1927) vol. I, p. 238
36. ibid., p. 240
37. ibid., pp. 244–245
38. Knox (1921), pp. 158–59
39. Preusser (1931), p. 56
40. Pastor (1916), p. 23
41. Ludendorff (1919), pp. 70–73
42. *Österreich-Ungarns* vol. 1 (1931), p. 471
43. Knox (1921), pp. 159–60
44. Ludendorff (1919), p. 74

45. Litzmann (1927), p. 249
46. *Österreich-Ungarns* vol. 1 (1931), p. 480
47. ibid., pp. 481–88
48. *Österreich-Ungarns* vol. 1 (1931), p. 490
49. Clemenz (1919), p. 142
50. Knox (1921), p. 170
51. Ludendorff (1919), p. 74
52. *Österreich-Ungarns* vol. 1 (1931), p. 505
53. Quoted in Englund (2011), pp. 55–56
54. *Österreich-Ungarns* vol. 1 (1931), pp. 506–07
55. Palmer and Wallis (2003), p. 72
56. Quoted in Stone (1975), p. 101

CHAPTER 13:

1. Möller, H., *Geschichte der Ritter des Ordens Pour Le Mérite im Weltkrieg*, 2 vols. (Bernhard & Graefe, Berlin, 1935), vol. 2, pp. 249–50
2. Ludendorff (1919), p. 77
3. ibid., p. 77
4. Siderov, A., 'Otnosheniya Rossi s Soyuznikami I Inostran. Postavshchikami', *Istorischeskiye Zapiski* (Institut Istorii SSSR, Moscow), 15 (1945), pp. 128–79
5. Manikovski, A., *Boyevoye Snabzhenie Russkoye Armii v Pervoy Mirovoy Voine* (Voenizdat, Moscow, 1930), vol. 3, pp. 66 and 88
6. Korolkov, G., *Russkaya Armiya v Velikoy Voyne: Lodzinskaya Operatsiya* (Voenizdat, Moscow, 1934), p. 16
7. For a detailed account of Sanders' activities in Turkey, Liman von Sanders, O., *Fünf Jahre Türkei* (Scherl, Berlin, 1920)
8. Voss, H., *Porträt Einer Hoffnung: Die Armenier* (Schiller, Bonn, 2005), p. 90
9. Danilov (1927), p. 295
10. Korolkov (1934), p. 5
11. Ludendorff (1919), p. 79
12. Korolkov (1934), p. 13
13. Mackensen (1938), p. 90
14. Korolkov (1934), p. 31
15. Danilov (1927), p. 298
16. Mackensen (1938), pp. 92–93
17. Preusser (1931), pp. 63–64
18. Ludendorff (1919), p. 82
19. Danilov (1927), pp. 300–01

20. Wulffen, K., *Die Schlacht Bei Lodz: Unter Benutzung amtlicher Quellen bearbeitet* (Stalling, Oldenburg, 1918), p. 26
21. Korolkov (1934), pp. 46–47
22. Mackensen (1938), p. 96
23. Danilov (1927), p. 302, and Novitsky, F., *Lodzinskaya Operatsiya v Noyabre 1914* (Voina I Revolutsiya, Moscow, 1930), p. 112
24. Both quotes are from Stone (1975), p. 105
25. Litzmann (1927), pp. 254–55
26. Novitsky (1930), p. 117
27. Wulffen (1918), p. 32
28. Litzmann (1927), p. 256
29. Danilov (1927), pp. 331–32
30. Novitsky (1930), p. 118
31. Mackensen (1938), p. 101
32. See, for example, Reichsarchiv, (1925–30), vol. 6, p. 127
33. Litzmann (1927), p. 262
34. Danilov (1927), p. 307
35. Mackensen (1938), p.105
36. ibid.
37. Novitsky (1930), pp. 120–21
38. Danilov (1927), p. 309
39. Mackensen (1938), p. 106
40. Wulffen (1918), pp. 53–54
41. Novikov, N., *Russkaya armiya v Velikoy voyne: 6-ya Sibirskaya diviziya v boyakh pod Lodz'yu s 18(5) po 24(11) noyabrya 1914* (Voenizdat, Moscow, 1925), pp. 16–18
42. Mackensen (1938), p. 109
43. Danilov (1927), pp. 312–13
44. Novikov (1925), p. 28
45. Korolkov (1934), p. 135
46. Novikov (1925), p. 29
47. Novitsky (1930), p. 122
48. Wulffen (1918), pp. 72–73
49. Korolkov (1934), pp. 138–39
50. Litzmann (1927), p. 285
51. ibid., p. 288; Wulffen (1918), pp. 79–81
52. Litzmann (1927), p. 289
53. Korolkov (1934), p. 145
54. Wulffen (1918), pp. 82–83
55. Korolkov (1934), p. 143

56. Novitsky (1930), pp. 121–22
57. Korolkov (1934), pp. 144–45
58. Novikov (1925), p. 36
59. ibid., p. 37
60. Wulffen (1918), p. 89
61. ibid., pp. 85–93
62. Novitsky (1930), p. 123
63. ibid., p. 124
64. ibid., p. 125
65. ibid., p. 126
66. Litzmann (1927), p. 298
67. *New York Times*, 18 December 1914

CHAPTER 14

1. Litzmann (1927), pp. 299–301
2. Clemenz (1919), p. 146
3. Nipperdey, T., *Deutsche Geschichte 1866–1918*, 2 vols. (Beck, Munich, 1990–92), vol. 2, p. 421
4. *Österreich-Ungarns* vol. 1 (1931), p. 769
5. Danilov (1927), pp. 317–32
6. The September Programme has controversially been claimed to be the true reason why Germany went to war, though it seems to have been drafted after the beginning of hostilities. See Fischer (1967) and Zuber (2011).
7. Hart, P., *The Great War* (Profile, London, 2013), p. 301
8. Preusser (1931), p. 70
9. ibid., p. 80
10. Quoted in Horne, C., *Source Records of the Great War* (National Alumni, New York, 1923), p. 81
11. *Österreich-Ungarns* vol. 1 (1931), p. 795
12. ibid., p. 797
13. Pitreich, A., 17 May 1929, Kriegsarchiv
14. Urbankowski, B., *Józef Piłsudski: Marzyciel i strategy*, 2 vols. (Widawnictwo, Warsaw, 1997), vol. 1, pp. 121–22
15. For English accounts of Piłsudski's life see Humphrey, G., *Piłsudski: Builder of Poland* (New York, Scott & More, 1936); Watt, R., *Bitter Glory: Poland and its Fate 1918–1939* (Simon & Schuster, London, 1979); and Reddaway, W., *Marshal Piłsudski* (Routledge, London, 1939)
16. *Österreich-Ungarns* vol. 1 (1931), p. 798

17. ibid., p. 803
18. For an account of the difficulties he faced, see Szurmay's account of the fighting written in December 1928, Kriegsarchiv, Vienna, KA FA NFA KK XXIV 3256
19. Quoted in Roth, J., *Die Schlacht von Limanowa-Lupanow 1914* (Kinderfreund, Vienna, 1928), p. 82
20. Palmer and Wallis (2003), p. 76
21. ibid., p. 77

CHAPTER 15

1. Brauner, J., E. Czegka, J. Diaków, F. Franek, R. Kiszling, E. Steinitz, and E. Wisshaupt, *Österreich-Ungarns Letzter Krieg 1914–1918 Vol. 2: 1915* (Verlag der Militärwissenschaftlichen Mitteilungen, Vienna, 1930) Part I table 3
2. ibid., Part I, p. 9
3. Danilov (1927), p. 336
4. Glause-Horstenau, E., *Feldmarschall Conrad von Hötzendorf* (1938), Kriegsarchiv Vienna, B/1450, 421: p. 5
5. Knox (1921), p. 193
6. ibid., p. 213
7. Morgen (1920), pp. 56–57
8. ibid., p. 45
9. ibid., p. 9
10. Falkenhayn, E. Von, *General Headquarters 1914-1916 and its Critical Decisions* (London, Hutchinson, 1919), pp. 43–44
11. Auffenberg (1921), pp. 173–74
12. Krauss, A., *Theorie und Praxis in der Kriegskunst* (Lehmann, Munich, 1936), pp. 28–34
13. Redlich, Fellner, and Corradini (2012), vol. 1, p. 279
14. Zehnder, R., 'Habsburg Preparations for Armageddon: Conrad von Hötzendorf and the Austro-Hungarian General Staff 1906–1914', PhD Thesis (Kansas State University, 1987), p. 75
15. Hindenburg (1920), pp. 84–85
16. Litzmann (1927), p. 257
17. Hoffmann (1924), p. 131
18. Gutsche, W., *Herrschaftsmethoden des Deutschen Imperialismus 1897/8 bis 1917* (Akademie-Verlag, Berlin, 1977), pp. 210–11
19. Knox (1921), p. 221
20. See, for example, Knox (1921), p. 222

BIBLIOGRAPHY

RESEARCH INSTITUTIONS

Bundesarchiv, Berlin
Abteilung Militärarchiv, Bundesarchiv, Freiburg
Kriegsarchiv, Staatsarchiv, Munich
Kriegsarchiv, Österreichisches Staatsarchiv, Vienna
Le Service Historique de la Défense, Vincennes
Sächsisches Hauptstaatsarchiv, Dresden

PRIMARY SOURCES

Communication from Moltke to the German chancellor Theobald von Bethmann-Hollweg, 9 March 1914, Bundesarchiv, R.43.F/107

Documents diplomatiques français, 1871–1914 (Imprimerie Nationale, Paris)

Forschungsarbeit Gemeinsame Kriegsvorbereitung Deutschland und Österreich-Ungarn, BA-MA, N46/38

Gempp, F. – unpublished report, *Geheimer Nachrichtendienst und Spionageabwehr des Heeres* (1922–24) Abteilung Militärarchiv, Bundesarchiv, Freiburg

Letter from Conrad to Gina von Reininghaus, 10 October 1915, Kriegsarchiv B/1450: 357

Nachlass Groener, Bundesarchiv–Militärarchiv Freiburg, NL46/38

Report by Prince Friedrich Karl of Prussia, 31 January 1882, Records of the Bavarian War Ministry, Kriegsarchiv, Munich

Report of the Bavarian military plenipotentiary to the Bavarian War Minister 28 September 1893, Kriegsarchiv, Munich

Report of the Saxon military plenipotentiary to the Saxon War Minister 19 June 1888, Sächsisches Hauptstaatsarchiv, Dresden

Report of the Saxon military plenipotentiary to the Saxon War Minister 22 May 1902, Sächsisches Hauptstaatsarchiv, Dresden

Statisticheski Raport Russogo Gloinskogo Voinskogo Meditsinskogo Direktorata, 1914

Stenographisches Protokoll 113, Sitzung des Nationalrats der Republik Österreich (2 Sept 1925), p. 2,683

Telegram from Archduke Frederick to Military Chancellery, 13/12/14, Kriegsarchiv Vienna, MKSM-SR

Telegrams from Potiorek to Bolfras, 20/11/14–09/12/14, Kriegsarchiv Vienna, MKSM-SR

Waldersee, A., *Meine Erlebnisse zu Beginn des Krieges 1914*, Bundesarchiv-Militärarchiv, w-10/51032, p. 10

SECONDARY SOURCES

Albertini, L., I. Massey (trans. and ed.), *The Origins of the War of 1914*, 3 vols. (Oxford University Press, London, 1952–57)

Ascher, A., *The Revolution of 1905: Russia in Disarray*, 2 vols. (Stanford University Press, 1988 and 1994)

Auffenberg, M., *Aus Österreichs Höhe und Niedergang: Eine Lebensschilderung* (Drei Masken, Munich, 1921)

Barby, H., *Avec l'Armée Serbe: De l'Ultimatum Autrichien à l'Invasion de la Serbie* (Albin Michel, Paris, 1918)

Barsukov, E., *Podgotovka Rossii k Mirovoj Vojne v Artillerijskom Otnosenii*, (Gosvoenizdat, Moscow, 1926)

Bernhardi, F. von, *Denkwürdigkeiten aus Meinem Leben* (E.S. Mittler & Sohn, Berlin, 1927)

Brusilov, A., *Moi Vospominaniia* (Voenizdat, Moscow, 1967)

Bulöwius, A. and B. Hippler, *Das Infanterie-Regiment von Boyen (5 Ostpreussisches) Nr. 41 im Weltkriege 1914–1918* (Wilhelm Kolk, Berlin, 1929)

Clemenz, B., *Generalfeldmarschall von Woyrsch und Seine Schlesier* (C. Flemming, Berlin, 1919)

Conrad, F., 'Mannschafts-Menage und Offiziers-Mittagstisch', *Organ der Militärwissenschaftlichen Vereine*, vol. 12 (1876)

——, *Zum Studium der Taktik* (L.W. Seidel & Sohn, Vienna, 1893 – 2nd edn.)

——, *Die Gefechtsausbildung der Infanterie* (L.W. Seidel & Sohn, Vienna, 1900)

——, *Aus Meiner Dienstzeit, 1906–1918*, 5 vols. (Rikola Verlag, Vienna 1921)

Craig, G., *The Politics of the Prussian Army 1640–1945* (Oxford University Press, New York, 1964)

Csicserics von Bacsány, M., *Die Schlacht: Studie Auf Grund Des Krieges in Ostasien 1904–05* (L.W. Seidel & Sohn, Vienna, 1908)

Czernin von und zu Chudenitz, O., *In the World War* (Harper & Collins, New York, 1920)

Daniloff, N., 'How Russia's Military Tried to Undermine Lenin's Separate Peace', *Foreign Service Journal* (June 1980)

Danilov, Y., *La Russie dans la Guerre Mondiale* (Payot, Paris, 1927)

Deák, I., *Beyond Nationalism: A Social and Political History of the Habsburg Officer Corps 1848–1918* (Oxford University Press, Oxford, 1990)

Dobrorolski, S., *Die Mobilmachung der Russischen Armee, 1914* (Deutsche Verlagsgesellschaft Für Politik und Geschichte, Berlin, 1922)

Dorn Brose, E., *The Kaiser's Army: The Politics of Military Technology in Germany during the Machine Age, 1870–1918* (Oxford University Press, New York, 2001)

Doumbadze, V., A. Knapp (ed.), *Russia's War Minister: The Life and Work of Adjutant-General Vladimir Alexandrovitsh Soukhomlinov* (Simpkin, Marshall Hamilton, Kent & Co., London, 1915)

Elze, W., *Tannenberg: Das Deutsche Heer von 1914, seine Grundzüge und deren Auswirkung im Sieg an der Ostfront* (Hirt, Breslau, 1928)

Englund, P., trans. W. Butt, *Schönheit und Schrecken: Eine Geschichte des Ersten Weltkriegs, erzählt in neunzehn Schicksalen* (Rowohlt, Berlin, 2011)

Fay, S., *The Origins of the World War*, 2 vols. (1928 – 2nd edn., Free Press, New York, 1967)

Fischer, F., *Germany's Aims in the First World War* (Norton, New York, 1967)

Foerster, W., *Prinz Friedrich Karl von Preussen: Denkwürdigkeiten aus Seinem Leben*, 2 vols. (Deutsche Verlags-Anhalt, Stuttgart, 1910)

François, H., *Marneschlacht und Tannenberg* (A. Scherl, Berlin, 1920)

Freytag-Loringhoven, A., *Menschen und Dinge Wie Ich Sie In Meinem Leben Sah* (E.S. Mittler & Sohn, Berlin, 1923)

Fromkin, D., *Europe's Last Summer: Why the World Went to War in 1914* (Heinemann, London, 2004)

Fuchs, R., 'Brief Outline of the Operations of the Army of the Narev', *Voenny Sbornik*, IV (1916)

Geiss, I., *July 1914: The Outbreak of the First World War, Selected Documents* (Batsford, London, 1967)

Gill, M., *Germany: A Modern History* (University of Michigan Press, Ann Arbor, 1970)

Glenny, M., *The Balkans: Nationalism, War, and the Great Powers, 1804–1999* (Granta, London, 2000)

Gold, H. (ed.), *History of the Jews of Bukowina*, 2 vols. (Olamenu, Tel Aviv, 1958–1962)

Golovine, N., 'The Great Battle in Galicia: A Study in Strategy', *Slavonic and East European Review*, 5 (1926–27)

——, *The Russian Campaign of 1914: The Beginning of the War and Operations in East Prussia* (Command and General Staff School Press, Fort Leavenworth, 1933)

Gooch, G. and H. Temperley (eds.), *British Documents on the Origins of the War*, 11 vols. (HMSO, London, 1926–38)

Görlitz, W., *The German General Staff: Its History and Structure, 1657–1945* (Hollis & Carter, London, 1953)

Gröner, E., *German Warships, 1815–1945*, 3 vols. (Naval Institute Press, Annapolis, 1990)

Gurko, V., *War and Revolution in Russia 1914–1917* (Macmillan, New York, 1919)

Gutsche, W., *Herrschaftsmethoden des Deutschen Imperialismus 1897/8 bis 1917* (Akademie-Verlag, Berlin, 1977)

Halsey, F., *The Literary Digest History of the World War*, 10 vols. (Funk & Wagnalls, New York, 1920)

Hamilton, I., *A Staff Officer's Scrap Book during the Russo-Japanese War*, 2 vols. (Edward Arnold, London, 1908)

Hamilton, R. and H. Herwig (eds.), *War Planning 1914* (Cambridge University Press, Cambridge, 2009)

Hart, P., *The Great War* (Profile, London, 2013)

Herwig, H. (ed.), *The Outbreak of World War I: Causes and Responsibilities* (5th edn. – D. C. Heath & Co., Lexington, 1991)

Hesse, K., *Der Feldherr Psychologos* (E.S. Mittler & Sohn, Berlin, 1922)

Hindenburg, P., trans. F. Holt, *Out of my Life* (Cassell, London, 1920)

Hoen, M., *Die Letzte Reiterschlacht der Weltgeschichte* (Amalthea, Vienna, 1929)

Hoetzsch, O. (ed.), *Die Internationalen Beziehungen im Zeitalter des Imperialismus* (Hobbing, Berlin, 1931–34)

Hoffmann, M., trans. A. Charnot, *The War of Lost Opportunities* (K. Paul, French, Trubner & Co., London, 1924)

Horne, H., *The Price of Glory: Verdun 1916* (Penguin, Harmondsworth, 1962)

Horne, J. and A. Kramer, *German Atrocities, 1914: A History of Denial* (Yale University Press, New Haven, 2001)

Hötzendorf, Conrad von – see Conrad, F.

Hubatsch, W., *Hindenburg und der Staat: Aus den Papieren des Generalfeldmarschalls und Reichspräsidenten von 1878 bis 1934* (Musterschmidt, Göttingen, 1966)

Hughes, D. (ed.), trans. H. Bell and D. Hughes, *Moltke on the Art of War: Selected Writings* (Novato, Presidio Press, 1993)

Humphrey, G., *Pilsudski: Builder of Poland* (New York, Scott & More, 1936)

Irving Root, G., *Battles East: A History of the Eastern Front of the First World War* (PublishAmerica, Baltimore, 2007)

Jeřábek, R., *Potiorek: General im Schatten von Sarajevo* (Styria, Graz, 1991)

Johnson, C., 'Brusiloff, Hero of the Hour in Russia, Described by One Who Knows Him Well', *New York Times*, 18 June 1916

Jovanović, L., *The Murder of Sarajevo* (British Institute of International Affairs, London, 1925)

Jukes, G., *The Russo-Japanese War* (Osprey Publishing, Oxford, 2002)

Kähler, O., *Die Preussische Reiterei von 1800 bis 1876 in Ihrer Inneren Entwickelung* (E.S. Mittler & Sohn, Berlin, 1879)

Kautsky, K., M. Montgelas, and W. Schücking (eds.), *Outbreak of the World War: German Documents Collected by Karl Kautsky* (Oxford University Press, New York, 1924)

Kennedy, P. (ed.), *War Plans of the Great Powers 1880–1914* (Allen & Unwin, London, 1979)

Kersnosvky, A., *Istoriia Russkoi Armii*, 4 vols., (Tsarskii Vestnik, Belgrade, 1935)

Kessel, B. von, 'Zur Taktik der Infanterie von 1880', *Beiheft zum Militär-Wochenblatt* (Berlin, 1880)

Kleist, G. von, *Die Offizier-Patrouille im Rahmen der Strategischen Aufgabe der Kavallerie* (E.S. Mittler & Sohn, Berlin 1891)

Knox, A., *With the Russian Army 1914–1917: Being Chiefly Extracts from the Diary of a Military Attaché*, 2 vols. (Hutchinson & Co., London, 1921)

Korolkov, G., *Varshavsko-Ivangorodskaia Operatsiia* (Voenizdat, Moscow, 1923)

——, *Russkaya Armiya v Velikoy Voyne: Lodzinskaya Operatsiya* (Voenizdat, Moscow, 1934)

Krauss, A., *Die Ursachen unserer Niederlage* (Lehmann, Munich, 1921)

——, *Theorie und Praxis in der Kriegskunst* (Lehmann, Munich, 1936)

Kriegsgeschichtliche Einzelschriften der Luftwaffe, vol. 3: *Mobilmachung, Aufmarsch und erster Einsatz der deutschen Luftstreitkräfte im August 1914* (E.S. Mittler & Sohn, Berlin, 1939)

Lieven, D., 'Russia Accepts a General War', in H. Herwig (ed.), *The Outbreak of World War I: Causes and Responsibilities* (5th edn. – D. C. Heath & Co., Lexington, 1991)

Liman von Sanders, O., *Fünf Jahre Türkei* (Scherl, Berlin, 1920)

Ludendorff, E., *Meine Kriegserinnerungen 1914–1918* (E.S. Mittler & Sohn, Berlin, 1919)

Mackensen, A., *Briefe und Auszeichnungen des Generalfeldmarschalls aus Krieg und Frieden* (Bibliographisches Institut, Leipzig, 1938)

Manikovski, A., *Boyevoye Snabzhenie Russkoye Armii v Pervoy Mirovoy Voine* (Voenizdat, Moscow, 1930), vol. 3

Markus, G., *Der Fall Redl* (Amalthea, Vienna, 1984)

Marshall, A., *The Russian General Staff and Asia, 1800–1917* (Routledge, London and New York, 2006)

McElwee, W., *The Art of War: Waterloo to Mons* (Indiana University Press, Bloomington, 1974)

Menning, B., *Bayonets before Bullets: The Imperial Russian Army, 1861–1914* (Indiana University Press, Bloomington, 2000)

Meyer, T. (ed.), trans. H. Hermann-Davey, W. Forward, and M. Askew, *Light for the New Millennium: Rudolf Steiner's Association with Helmuth and Eliza von Moltke – Letters, Documents and After-Death Communications* (Rudolf Steiner Press, London, 1997)

Möller, H., *Geschichte der Ritter des Ordens Pour Le Mérite im Weltkrieg*, 2 vols. (Bernhard & Graefe, Berlin, 1935), vol. 2

Moltke, H., *Militärische Werke*, 14 vols. (E.S. Mittler & Sohn, Berlin, 1892–1912)

——, trans. C. F. McClumpha, C. S. L. Barter, and M. Herms, *Essays, speeches, and memoirs of Field-Marshal Count Helmuth von Moltke*, 2 vols. (Harper & Bros., New York, 1893)

——, *Geschichte des Deutsch-französischen Krieges von 1870–71* (E.S. Mittler & Sohn, Berlin, 1895)

Mombauer, A., *Helmuth von Moltke and the Origins of the First World War* (Cambridge University Press, Cambridge, 2005)

Morgen, C., *Meiner Truppen Heldenkämpfe* (E.S. Mittler & Sohn, Berlin, 1920)

Morsey, A., 'Konopischt und Sarajewo', *Berlin Monatshefte*, XII (1934), p. 492

Neiberg, M. (ed.), *The World War 1 Reader: Primary and Secondary Sources* (NYU Press, New York, 2007)

Nipperdey, T., *Deutsche Geschichte 1866–1918*, 2 vols. (Beck, Munich, 1990–92)

Notz, F. and F. Scholtz, *General von Scholtz: Ein Deutsches Soldatenleben in Grosser Zeit* (Siegismund, Berlin, 1937)

Novikov, N., *Russkaya armiya v Velikoy voyne: 6-ya Sibirskaya diviziya v boyakh pod Lodz'yu s 18(5) po 24(11) noyabrya 1914* (Voenizdat, Moscow, 1925)

Novitsky, F., *Lodzinskaya Operatsiya v Noyabre 1914* (Voina I Revolutsiya, Moscow, 1930)

Österreich-Ungarns Letzter Krieg 1914–1918 (15 vols.), vol. 1: *Das Kriegsjahr 1914* (Verlag der Militärwissenschaftlichen Mitteilungen, Vienna, 1931)

Pahalyuk, K., *Romanoyi v Spazheneyakh v Vostochnoe v Prussii 1914* (Reitar, Kaliningrad, 2009)

Paléologue, M., trans. F. Holt, *An Ambassador's Memoirs*, 3 vols. (George H. Doran Co., New York, 1923)

Palmer, S. and S. Wallis, *A War in Words* (Simon & Schuster, London, 2003)

Pastor, L., *Generaloberst Viktor Dankl, der Sieger von Krasnik und Verteidiger Tirols* (Herder, Vienna, 1916)

Plickert, H., *Das 2. Ermländische Infanterie-Regiment Nr. 151 im Weltkriege* (Stalling, Oldenburg, 1929)

Polivanov, A., *Iz Dnevnikov i Vospominanii Po Dolzhnosti Voennogo Ministra i Ego Pomoshchika 1907–1916* (Vyshii Voennyi Redaktsionnyi Sovet, Moscow, 1924)

Popović, N., *Srbi u Prvom Svetskom Ratu, 1914–1918* (DMP, Belgrade, 1998)

Preusser, W., *Das 9. Westpreussisches Infanterie-Regiment Nr. 176 Im Weltkrieg* (Verlag Tradition Kolk, Berlin, 1931)

Quester, G., *Deterrence before Hiroshima: The Influence of Airpower on Modern Strategy* (John Wiley, New York, 1966)

Rauchensteiner, M., 'Zum Operativen Denken in Österreich 1814–1914: Der Vor-Weldkriegs-Zyklus', *Österreichische Militärische Zeitschrift*, 1 (1975)

'Reasons for the Failure of General Samsonov's Second Army in East Prussia in August 1914', *Voenny Sbornik*, IV (1916)

Reddaway, W., *Marshal Pilsudski* (Routledge, London, 1939)

Redlich, J., F. Fellner, and D. Corradini, *Schicksalsjahre Österreichs: Die Erinnerungen und Tagebücher Josef Redlichs,* 3 vols. (Boehlau, Vienna, 2011)

Reichert, W., *Das Infanterie-Regiment Freiherr Hiller von Gaertringen (4. Posensches) Nr. 59 im Weltkriege 1914–1918* (Stein, Potsdam, 1930)

Reichsarchiv, *Der Weltkrieg 1914 bis 1918*, 15 vols. (E.S. Mittler & Sohn, Berlin, 1925–30)

Reiss, R., *Comment les Austro-Hongrois Ont Fait la Guerre en Serbie: Observations Direct d'un Neutre* (Colin, Paris, 1915)

Remak, J., *Sarajevo: The Story of a Political Murder* (Criterion, New York, 1959)

Rich, N. (ed.), *The Holstein Papers: The Memoirs, Diaries and Correspondence of Friedrich von Holstein 1887–1909*, 4 vols. (Cambridge University Press, Cambridge, 1957)

Richthofen, M., trans. T. Baker, *The Red Battle Flier* (McBride, New York, 1918)

Roth, J., *Die Schlacht von Limanowa-Lupanow 1914* (Kinderfreund, Vienna, 1928)

Rothenberg, G., *The Army of Francis Joseph* (Purdue University Press, West Lafayette, 1976 – paperback edition 1998)

Russell, T., *The World's Greatest War* (Walter, New York, 1919)

——, *America's War for Humanity: Pictorial History of the World War for Liberty* (Walter, New York, 1919)

Savant, J., *L'Épopée Russe: Campagne de l'Armée Rennenkampf en Prusse-Orientale* (Calmann-Lévy, Paris, 1945)

Schäfer, T., *Tannenberg* (Stalling, Oldenburg, 1927)

Schemfil, V., *Das k.u.k. 3 Regiment der Tiroler Kaiserjäger im Weltkrieg 1914–1918* (Teutsch, Bregenz, 1926)

Schlichting, S. von, 'Über das Infanteriegefecht', in *Beiheft zum Militär-Wochenblatt* (Berlin, 1879)

Schlieffen, A., *Cannae* (E. S. Mittler, Berlin, 1936)

Schulte, B., 'Neue Dokumente zu Kriegsausbruch und Kriegsverlauf 1914', *Militärgeschichtliche Mitteilungen*, 25 (1979)

Serbian General Staff, *Veliki Rat Serbije Za Oslobodelje i Ujedljelje Serba, Hrvata i Slovenaca* (Štamlarska Padionica Milistarstva i Mornarice, Belgrade, 1925)

Seydel, A., *Das Grenadier-Regiment König Friedrich I (4. Ostpreussisches) Nr. 5 im Weltkrieg* (Oldenbourg, Potsdam, 1926)

Shatsillo, K., *Russki Imperializm i Razvitie Flota* (Nauka, Moscow, 1968)

Showalter, D., *Tannenberg: Clash of Empires, 1914* (Potomac Books Inc., Dulles, 2004)

Siderov, A., 'Otnosheniya Rossi s Soyuznikami I Inostran. Postavshchikami', *Istoricheskiye Zapiski* (Institut Istorii SSSR, Moscow), 15 (1945)

Silverman, S., *A Happy Life: From Courtroom to Classroom* (iUniverse, Bloomington, 2009)

Slivinski, A. and F. Keller, *Konnyi Boi 10-1 Kavaleriiskoi Divisii Generala Grafa Kellera 8/21 Avgusta Goda u d. Iaroslavitse* (Belgrade, 1921)

Snyder, J., *The Ideology of the Offensive: Military Decision Making and the Disasters of 1914* (Cornell University Press, Ithaca, NY, 1984)

Sondhaus, L., *Franz Conrad von Hötzendorf: Architect of the Apocalypse* (Humanities Press, Boston, 2000)

Stein, H., 'Der Offizier des Russischen Heeres im Zeitabschnitt Zwischen Reform und Revolution 1861–1905', *Forschungen zur Osteuropäischen Geschichte*, 13 (1967)

Stephani, W., *Mit Hindenburg bei Tannenberg* (Eisenschmidt, Berlin, 1919)

Stevenson, D., 'War by Timetable? The Railway Race Before 1914', *Past and Present*, 162:1 (1999)

Stone, N., 'Army and Society in the Habsburg Monarchy 1900–1914', *Past and Present*, 33 (April 1966)

——, 'Die Mobilmachung der Österreich-Ungarischen Armee 1914', *Militärgeschichtliche Mitteilungen*, 2 (1974)

——, *The Eastern Front 1914–1917* (Hodder & Stoughton, London, 1975)

——, 'Moltke and Conrad: Relations Between the Austro-Hungarian and German General Staffs, 1909–1914', in Kennedy, P. (ed.), *War Plans of the Great Powers 1880–1914* (Allen & Unwin, London, 1979)

Sweetman, J., *Tannenberg 1914* (Cassell, London, 2004)

Taylor, A., *Illustrated History of the First World War* (Putnam, New York, 1964)

Temperley, H., *England and the Near East: The Crimea* (Longmans, Greens and Co, London, 1936)

Trachtenberg, M., 'The Meaning of Mobilization in 1914', *International Security*, 15:3 (1990)

Trumpener, U., 'War Premeditated? German Intelligence Operations in July 1914', *Conference Group for Central European History*, 6 (March 1976)

Tsouras, P. (ed.), *The Book of Military Quotations* (Zenith Press, St Paul, 2005)

Tunstall, G., *Planning for War Against Russia and Serbia: Austro-Hungarian and German Military Strategies 1871–1914* (Social Science Monographs, Boulder, 1993)

Turner, L., 'The Russian Mobilisation in 1914', *Journal of Contemporary History*, 3:1 (1968)

Urbankowski, B., *Józef Piłsudski: Marzyciel i strateg*, 2 vols. (Widawnictwo, Warsaw, 1997)

Urbanski von Ostrymiecz, A., *Conrad von Hötzendorf: Soldat und Mensch* (Ulrich Mosers Verlag, Graz, 1939)

Vatsetis, J., *Deyatelnyosty v Vostochnom Prussiyi v Yuly, Avgoost, y Nachale Sentybry 1914* (Isdat Politisheskoi Literaturi, Moscow, 1923)

Voss, H., *Porträt Einer Hoffnung: Die Armenier* (Schiller, Bonn, 2005)

Waldstätten, J., *Technik des Angriffsweisen Gefechts der Infanterie* (Seidel & Sohn, Vienna, 1885)

Walsh, E. *The Fall of the Russian Empire: The Story of the Last of the Romanovs and the Coming of the Bolshevik* (Wildside Press, Rockville, 2009)

Wank, S., 'Some Reflections on Conrad von Hötzendorf and his Memoirs Based on Old and New Sources', *Austrian History Yearbook*, I (1965)

Watt, R., *Bitter Glory: Poland and its Fate 1918–1939* (Simon & Schuster, London, 1979)

Williamson, S., *Austria–Hungary and the Origins of the First World War* (Macmillan, London, 1991)

Wulffen, K., *Die Schlacht Bei Lodz: Unter Benutzung amtlicher Quellen bearbeitet* (Stalling, Oldenburg, 1918)

Zaionchkovsky, A., *Podgotovka Rossii k Imperialistichekoi Vione* (Gosvoenizdat, Moscow, 1926)

Zedlitz-Trütszchler, R., *Zwölf Jahre am Deutschen Kaiserhof* (Deutsche Verlags-Anstalt, Berlin, 1925)

Zehnder, R., 'Habsburg Preparations for Armageddon: Conrad von Hötzendorf and the Austro-Hungarian General Staff 1906–1914', PhD Thesis (Kansas State University, 1987)

Zichowitsch, J., *Strategicheskii Issledovanyi Mirosvon' Voinii 1914–1918* (Voenizdat, Moscow, 1922)

Zipfel, E., *Geschichte des Königlich Preussischen Husaren-Regiment Fürst Blücher von Wahlstätt (Pommersches) Nr. 5* (Sporn, Zeulenroda, 1930)

Zuber, T., *The Real German War Plan 1904–1914* (The History Press, Stroud, 2011)

Zuckerman, L., *The Rape of Belgium: The Untold Story of World War I* (New York University Press, New York, 2004)

Zweig, S., *Die Welt von Gestern* (Bermann-Fischer, Stockholm, 1944) – available in German at http://gutenberg.spiegel.de/buch/6858/1

INDEX